Mississippi Forests and Forestry

Mississippi Forests

and Forestry

James E. Fickle

MISSISSIPPI FORESTRY FOUNDATION, INCORPORATED
UNIVERSITY PRESS OF MISSISSIPPI / JACKSON

www.upress.state.ms.us

09 08 07 06 05 04 03 02 01 4 3 2 1
∞

Library of Congress Cataloging-in-Publication Data
Fickle, James E.
  Mississippi forests and forestry / James E. Fickle.
  p. cm.
  Includes bibliographical references and index.
  ISBN 1-57806-308-6 (cloth : alk. paper)
  1. Forests and forestry—Mississippi—History.
  I. Title.
SD144.M7 F53   2001
634.9'09762—dc21

                                00-035166

British Library Cataloging-in-Publication Data
available

To Arthur W. Nelson Jr. and the late
Richard C. Allen, pioneer foresters
who graciously shared their love and
knowledge of Mississippi's forests
and people. They lived much of this story.

Contents

Acknowledgments

Many people and institutions have contributed in various ways to the creation of this book. Dr. John L. Loos of Louisiana State University originally encouraged me to explore the subject of southern forest history. The late Dr. Robert Maxwell of Stephen F. Austin State University advised and assisted me along the way. Joseph R. Strickland of International Paper Company recruited me to look into the history of the pulp and paper industry in the South and the story of industrial forestry. I have talked with and learned much from a cadre of foresters who were among the pioneers who rebuilt the forests of the South and of Mississippi from their devastated condition early in the century to became again the marvelous treasures that they are today. Among those who generously shared their time and knowledge were John S. Tyler, Fred Gragg, Jeff D. Hughes Jr., Zebulon W. White, Robert M. Nonnemacher, and O. G. "Tracy" Tracewitz. Especially helpful were Art Nelson and the late Dick Allen, who became not only sources and mentors but also friends and colleagues who helped me to see things through the eyes of the professional forester. It was Art's dream to see the history of the rebirth of Mississippi's forests recorded and published for future generations, and he encouraged me to tackle this project. The Mississippi Forestry Foundation sponsored the effort, and I thank them, and especially Stephen M. Butler, for their support. Also, Steve Corbitt of the Mississippi Forestry Association has been extremely helpful in supplying information and encouragement as needed. Bill Colvin of the Mississippi Forestry Commission has also gone out of his way to supply information, encouragement, and valuable advice. The late Professor Laurence C. Walker of Stephen F. Austin State University shared his knowledge of the southern forests, as did Dr. Rodney Foil of Mississippi State University.

I have worked in many libraries and archives while researching this book and I would like to thank the staffs of the Southern Hardwoods Laboratory at Stoneville, Mississippi, the Mitchell Memorial Library of Mississippi State University, the Mississippi State Forestry Commission, the Special Collections Department of the Louisiana State University Library, the Land and Timber Division of International Paper Company in Dallas, the American Forest Council in Atlanta, the Mississippi Department of Archives and History, the Louisiana State Archives, the Denkmann Library of Augustana College, the University of Mississippi Archives, the Lauren Rogers Museum of Art Library in Laurel, the Minnesota Historical Society, the Forest History Society, the Department of Archives at Tulane University, the Louisiana State Library, the Louisiana Department of Agriculture and Forestry, the Center for Regional Studies of Southeastern Louisiana University, the McCane Library of the University of Southern Mississippi, and the McWherter Library of the University of Memphis. I owe special thanks to Cheryl P. Oakes and Michele A. Justice of the Forest History Society, Judy Belan of Augustana College, W. Stone Miller of the Louisiana State University Archives, Mattie Sink of the Mitchell Memorial

Map of Mississippi counties and selected towns. Courtesy U.S. Bureau of the Census. Modified by Edward Ashley Fickle.

Library Special Collections Department at Mississippi State University, Michael Hennen of the Mississippi Department of Archives and History, and Donna Smith and Sandra Hayes of the Lauren Rogers Museum of Art.

Mississippians too numerous to mention shared information, pictures, and stories with me. Special recognition should go to the late Jim Craig who led the early effort to preserve the history of Mississippi's forests in book form. Craig financed a project to interview many pioneers of Mississippi forest history and was instrumental in the establishment of the Forest History Committee of the Mississippi Forestry Association. My friends and colleagues Drs. Charles McNutt, Donald W. Ellis, and Michael G. Huffman of the University of Memphis read the manuscript and offered helpful suggestions. Cyndi Long and Ashley Fickle provided valuable assistance with the illustrations. My research was made possible by grants from the Forest History Society, the Mississippi Forestry Foundation, and the University of Memphis. I also benefited from a University of Memphis Faculty Development Leave and from the support and encouragement of history department Chairs F. Jack Hurley and Kenneth W. Goings. Presidents Pete Steen and Steve Anderson of the Forest History Society provided assistance and advice. Craig W. Gill and Anne Stascavage of the University Press of Mississippi were both helpful and professional. I especially appreciate Ellen D. Goldlust-Gingrich's editorial work to make this a better book. When I needed a break from the forests I usually found it at the "donut shop" with Don and Billy; with my tennis and golfing buddies, Dr. Waymon W. Bilbrey, Dennis R. Hays, and Wayne Gutch; with my cycling, boating, skiing, and hiking companion, Mike Huffman; and with my family. I would especially like to thank Jeanne, Valerie, Shan, Steve, Terri, Ashley, April, Rick, Cyndi, Kenny, Angie, Kelsey, Billy, Matthew, Bryce, Inalee, and Susie for creating a loving and lively atmosphere that makes both work and play interesting and enjoyable.

Introduction

This book tells the story of the forest in Mississippi, particularly, how humans and society have interacted with that resource over the centuries. This is an interesting story that is in some ways at odds with popular conventional wisdom. For example, some writers state, or at least imply, that the forests "discovered" by Europeans in the fifteenth century had existed in their current form virtually forever. In fact, they were products of evolutionary change over the millennia, and modern scientists can trace both their origins and development. Also, many people believe that the forests at the time of discovery, up to the age of colonization and pioneer settlement, were "virgin" or "primeval." If a virgin forest is one that has not been altered by human activity, then the forests of early Mississippi certainly were not virgin. They had been significantly altered over the centuries by both prehistoric man and the Native Americans of the historic era. These alterations had occurred as a result of clearing, the use of fire for hunting and other purposes, and other Indian practices. As a result, Mississippi's land was not covered by a vast, unbroken, and dense forest. Rather, there was a mosaic of dense forests, open forests, hardwood forests, pine forests, mixed forests, swamps, savannas, prairies, "old fields," and other types of land. And if Mississippi was a wilderness—and *wilderness* is ultimately a matter of personal definition—it was so only for the white explorers and pioneers. For the Native Americans, Mississippi's lands were home— familiar, comfortable, and useful. The Indians used the forest for hunting, for farming, for gathering, and for pleasure. There is no indication that the Indians were particularly careful stewards. They used the land, and when it wore out, they moved their villages, cleared more fields, and repeated the process. When the Europeans came in and offered bounties for furs, the Native Americans overhunted and depleted their animal resources. In other words, like later groups and ages, the Native Americans used the forest in accordance with their own needs, values, and perceptions.

Early white settlers in Mississippi were mostly farmers and planters, and while they used the forests for lumber to build their buildings and fences, these settlers essentially viewed the trees as impediments to be removed in the name of "progress" and "civilization" as they "conquered the wilderness." Much of their time was spent in clearing, and a great deal of wood and many valuable trees were wasted. However, at the time they did not view the process as waste, for the forests of the nation were "inexhaustible," and, of course, society puts a high value only on that which seems scarce. A few pioneer lumbermen existed in the antebellum era, but for the most part Mississippi's most heavily timbered regions were bypassed during that period.

In the late nineteenth century a variety of factors coalesced to create the bonanza period of lumbering in Mississippi, and by the early twentieth century the state was briefly the national leader in lumber production. These factors included growing national markets for lumber as the national population grew and the country industrialized and urbanized. Also, the older lumber-production centers in the Northeast and the Great Lakes states were petering out, and lumbering, which was a migratory industry, was looking for new forests to exploit. Finally, railroads were beginning to crisscross Mississippi, giving the lumbermen access to both its forests and regional and national markets. Some of the largest lumber-manufacturing operations in the nation during this period were in Mississippi.

One of the prevailing legends of this period is that these lumbermen were ruthless exploiters who "cut out and got out" with no thought to the denuded lands and impoverished people and communities they left behind. It is true that the lumbermen of this period often cut over an area and then moved on to new forests. But they did not do so because they were inherently evil but because of the social climate, technological and scientific knowledge, and financial structure of the times. Briefly, the social climate was reflected in tax laws that did not reward—and in fact penalized—those who attempted to keep lands in forests or to reforest. The lumberman who clear-cut his holdings and moved on was responding to that structure. Technologically, this was the age of railroad logging with the use of steam skidders. These machines were expensive and damaged the land, but they were efficient, and this age worshiped technology and efficiency. In the scientific realm, lumbermen and early foresters (and there were very few professional foresters in this period) were not very knowledgeable about the growing properties of trees and the possibilities for selective cutting and regeneration in the southern forests. This knowledge would come through the activities of a few farsighted pioneers and in a sense by accident and observation. Finally, the lumbermen's enormous financial investment in mills and logging equipment, coupled with the tax structure and the cost of credit, meant that to survive, they were almost forced to clear-cut and move on to new territory.

The result of this system was that by the late 1920s many of Mississippi's forests were cut over and abandoned. Disposing of cutover land became a major focus of its owners. However, more and more professional foresters were coming onto the scene, many in the employ of the U.S. Forest Service, and scientific knowledge about the southern forests was progressing rapidly. During the Great Depression of the 1930s, the age of scientific forestry dawned, as foresters preached selective cutting, planting, control of hogs who rooted up young growth, and, above all, fire prevention and control. Some lands were set aside as national forests, and, to the surprise of many, new forests began to appear miraculously on cutover lands across the state, bearing witness to the trees' regenerative powers. Private companies employed growing numbers of professional foresters, and the tree-farm movement encouraged enlightened practices on private, noncorporate holdings. Also, new scientific breakthroughs created a market for southern pulpwood in the paper plants that were springing up across the South.

Landowners, lumbermen, pulp and paper operators, and foresters in this period saw the forests primarily as an economic resource. They practiced a form of conservation, but it was use-oriented conservation designed to keep the forests turning out crops of sawlogs and pulpwood on a regular basis. *Good forestry practice* was defined as utilizing the forest in a manner that was consistent with the landowner's objectives, and any larger public interest was not much considered. Even the national forests were run in consistency with Gifford Pinchot's definition of conservation as "wise use." The signs greeting visitors to national forests often billed them as "Land of Many Uses." Other uses took a back seat to sawlog and pulpwood production. For the most part, these patterns were consistent with society's values. The United States worshiped economic progress, and forests were just another economic resource.

Although this movement came somewhat late to Mississippi, in the 1960s and 1970s a new term, *environmentalism*, came into the vocabulary. There developed a constituency of people

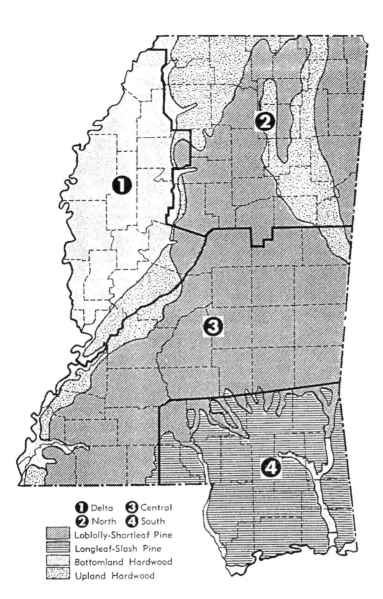

1 Delta 3 Central
2 North 4 South

⌀ Loblolly-Shortleaf Pine
≡ Longleaf-Slash Pine
Bottomland Hardwood
Upland Hardwood

Map of Mississippi forest types. Courtesy Mississippi Agricultural and Industrial Board, Jackson.

who looked at a forest and saw more than sawlogs and pulpwood. These people were interested in forest esthetics, wetlands, stream bed protection, wildlife, recreation, "wilderness experiences," and more. They particularly insisted that national lands be managed with respect for their values, and these environmentalists believed that even owners of private forestlands had a larger social obligation and that these owners could not simply manage their forests for their own economic benefit or in accordance with their own particular philosophies. Environmentalists be-

lieved that the owners were, in effect, trustees who owned the forest through the sufferance of society: with that sufferance came the obligation to manage the forest responsibly. This view and the views of individual owners or companies often clashed, although generally not to the extent in Mississippi that has been seen in other areas of the nation. However, there are and will be many issues to resolve. But all sides, whether they like to hear it or not, are operating in consistency with historical patterns. Human societies have always determined for themselves how their forests will be managed, and, in fact, their priorities have often changed over the years. There is no reason to believe that the future for Mississippi forests will depart significantly from this pattern.

This work is based on various kinds of sources, including original primary materials, government documents, newspapers, inter- views, and contemporary accounts. It also depends on various secondary works, which tell parts of the story of Mississippi's forests in other contexts. I seek to draw from all of these disparate sources to create a comprehensive account of the forests of Mississippi from the prehistoric era to the present.

Mississippi Forests and Forestry

1 Origins

Man and the Forest from Prehistory to Colonization

Mississippi is one of the most heavily forested states in the nation. From the piney woods region of the south to the cypress of the Mississippi River bottoms and the mixed hardwoods in the northeast, the Magnolia State is blanketed by a luxuriant cover of trees. By the late 1990s, 18.5 million acres of forest covered 62 percent of the state. In 1995 one in four manufacturing jobs in Mississippi was provided by the forest-products industry, and forestry-related employment accounted for 10 percent of all jobs. The forest industry's total impact on the Mississippi economy in 1995 was more than $11 billion. The forest's influence is felt in other ways as well. Roughly 12 million acres of Mississippi's forests are owned by more than 310,000 private, nonindustrial landowners. Government also has a presence. Mississippi has two wilderness areas totaling 5,500 acres and six national forest units that contain 1,140,215 acres and provide recreational opportunities as well as timber for industry. When one looks at a modern map of Mississippi's forests, the wooded environment in which so many Mississippians live, work, and play is dramatically evident.[1]

Despite the central importance of the forest in Mississippi, its history has been largely ignored or misrepresented. In a lavish 1982 picture book commissioned by the state Department of Economic Development, Natchez and the Trace, the Gulf Coast, and Oxford are well represented, but there is neither a word nor a picture devoted to the piney woods, Hattiesburg, or other centers of forest life. Library shelves are mostly bereft of works dealing with the forests of Mississippi, and some of what has been written is wrong. And the fact is, if the history of Mississippi's forests has been ignored and misrepresented, the treatment of their prehistory has been even worse. While scholars are increasingly knowledgeable about the physical environment in the Americas and Mississippi prior to human settlement, they have not been particularly successful in getting the word out to lay audiences. Similarly, popular knowledge of prehistoric societies, Native Americans, and the forest environment during early European contact and settlement are not generally up to the level of current scholarship.[2]

One of the enduring myths of American and Mississippi history is the idea that when Europeans first explored North America they were everywhere east of the Mississippi River confronted by a vast, unaltered, "virgin" forest. Henry Wadsworth Longfellow in *Evangeline* called it the "forest primeval," and a corollary of this theory is that the Native Americans encountered by the early Europeans were somehow mystically in touch with "nature," leaving almost no impact on the land and its forests. The image is that of an enormous unbroken forest of giant trees. Said a writer in 1933, the American wilderness encountered by the first Europeans consisted of "[e]ndless forests, black, untrodden, silent as the grave. . . . So thick set were the trees and so dense were the boughs and leafage that a savage might skulk from the Hudson to Lake Erie without once exposing himself to the glare of the sun."[3]

Even those who know better sometimes use dramatic and misleading statements to support their messages. Said a writer in a recent *New Yorker* article, "Ours was once a forested planet." The early European settlers "gazed upon these forests with a mixture of awe, fear, and greed." A Mississippi Forestry Association executive said essentially the same thing in 1963: "The original forest growth blanketed the entire state. . . . The white men who settled this vast area found . . . choice virgin forests." Distinguished southern historian Thomas D. Clark wrote of his boyhood in central Mississippi near the headwaters of the Pearl River, where "I was privileged to see the great monarchs that had stood for centuries. The line of virgin trees rolled off in a solid phalanx." Clark rhapsodically evokes memories of "the green eden of the primeval past." These views ignore the fact that even if the forests had not been altered by man, the effects of nature were not absent in the prehistoric period. For example, scholars believe that the average "virgin" pine lived no more than 150 to 200 years. Why? Because of the same forces that forest landowners deal with today—lightning, wind, ice, fungi, and beetles and other pests. As cultural geographer W. M. Denevan writes, "The myth persists that in 1492 the Americas were a sparsely populated wilderness, "a world of barely perceptible human disturbance." There is substantial evidence, however, that the Native American landscape of the early sixteenth century was a humanized landscape almost everywhere. Populations were large. Forest composition had been modified, grasslands had been created, wildlife disrupted, and erosion was severe in places. Earthworks, roads, fields, and settlements were ubiquitous."[4]

Why did these ideas become so firmly implanted in the national psyche? Some have argued that the image of what the distinguished historian John Bakeless described as the "great forests that swept across the United States, unbroken, from the Atlantic coast to the Great Plains" is a product of the nature-appreciation movement of the early nineteenth century. "Cultured" urban dwellers began to write and paint about the esthetic qualities of the American wilderness, and writers such as Ralph Waldo Emerson, Henry David Thoreau, and historian Francis Parkman added a critical perspective on the process of "conquering" nature and the continent. They were often quite willing to exaggerate and romanticize for dramatic effect. Similarly, for those who liked "progress" and "conquering nature," the victory was even greater if the foe was impressively formidable.[5]

J. Baird Callicott argues that because of the depopulation of North America resulting from the impact of European diseases on Native Americans, English colonists "could imagine that they had settled in a wilderness, not in a country once fully inhabited and significantly transformed by its indigenous peoples." Thus, said Callicott, "two allied myths established themselves in the Euro-American consciousness: one, that the whole of North America was a 'virgin' wilderness of continental proportions; the other, that North America's natural resources and especially its forests were inexhaustible." As William M. Denevan argues, "the Indian landscape of 1492 had largely vanished by the mid-eighteenth century, not through a European superimposition, but because of the demise of the native population. The landscape of 1750 was more 'pristine' (less humanized) than that of 1492." In addition, "The ignoble savage, nonagricultural and barely human, was invented to justify dispossession . . . and to prove that the Indian had no part in transforming America from Wilderness to Garden."[6]

Early European settlers and later writers and theorists who developed and perpetuated these myths operated first on the assumption that the forests Europeans encountered in the New World were virgin and second that they had not been significantly affected by Native American populations. Thus, the forests had developed essentially without human impact over many centuries.

There are also the implicit beliefs among later writers that the extent of the forests in that time must have been much greater than in our own and that they were far more physically imposing. Modern scholars have a significantly different view of the matter. As one writer puts it,

> The terms "virgin forest" and Longfellow's "forest primeval" conjure up an image of great and old trees standing undisturbed and changeless for centuries. Specifically, any disturbance by man is ruled out. They must be uncut and unharmed by man-set fires and the under-story must be ungrazed by domestic stock. In other words, we conceive of the virgin forest as being simply an unharmed old-growth forest. Such stands simply do not exist. . . . [F]orests of any age are in a constant state of change, arising from the growth and senescence of the trees themselves, from consequent changes in the micro-climate and edaphic site, from normal forest succession, and from regional climatic and geologic changes. Interferences with normal growth and development are common, and it is a meaningless semanticism to try to distinguish between "natural" disturbances and "artificial" disturbances caused by man. . . . Disturbances to tree development and growth are normal, instability of the forest is inevitable, and the changeless virgin forest is a myth.[7]

In fact, some writers seem to regard human involvement in the forest as almost an aberration. William Cronon in his seminal book, *Changes in the Land: Indians, Colonists, and the Ecology of New England,* describes the problem as follows:

> This brings us to the heart of the theoretical difficulties involved in doing ecological history. When one asks how much an ecosystem has been changed by human influence, the inevitable next question must be "changed in relation to what?" There is no simple answer to this. Before we can analyze the ways people alter their environments, we must first consider how those environments change in the absence of human activity, and that in turn requires us to reflect on what we mean by an ecological "community." Ecology as a biological science has had to deal with this problem from its outset. The first generation of academic ecolo-

> gists, led by Frederic Clements, defined the communities they studied literally as superorganisms which experienced birth, growth, maturity, and sometimes death much as individual plants and animals did. Under this model, the central dynamic of community change could be expressed in the concept of "succession." Depending on its region, a biotic community might begin as a pond, which was then gradually transformed by its own internal dynamics into a marsh, a meadow, a forest of pioneer trees, and finally to a forest of dominant trees. This last stage was assumed to be stable and was known as the "climax," a more or less permanent community which would reproduce itself indefinitely if left undisturbed. Its equilibrium state defined the mature forest "organism," so that all members of the community could be interpreted as functioning to maintain the stability of the whole. Here was an apparently objective point of reference; any actual community could be compared with the theoretical climax, and differences between them could then usually be attributed to "disturbance." Often the source of disturbance was human, implying that humanity was somehow outside of the ideal climax community. This functionalist emphasis on equilibrium and climax had important consequences, for it tended to remove ecological communities from history. If all ecological change was either self-equilibrating (moving toward climax) or nonexistent (remaining in the static condition of climax), then history was more or less absent except in the very long time frame of climatic change or Darwinian evolution. The result was a paradox. Ecologists trying to define climax and succession for a region . . . were faced with an environment massively altered by human beings, yet their research program demanded that they determine what the environment would have been like without a human presence. By peeling away the corrupting influences of man and woman, they could discover the original ideal community of the climax.[8]

Even in those situations where forests may in fact be unaffected by human impact, they are nonetheless constantly evolving. Their prehistoric origins and development are recorded in fossils found in various forms, including leaf fragments and other vegetative patterns. Modern paleobotanists use a large arsenal of tools in tracing forest origins and evolution, including tree-ring analysis of living and fossil materials, carbon 14 dating of fossil wood and other old organic material, the analysis of peat bogs, and pollen analysis. These techniques have been particularly useful in documenting changes in forests and trees over the past ten to thirty thousand years, the period since the last major glaciation of the northern hemisphere.[9]

The most important events in recent forest history are the periods of Pleistocene glaciation. At its highest point ice covered more than 30 percent of the earth's land surface, compared with approximately 10 percent today. The final stage of glaciation reached farthest into the continental United States about eleven thousand years ago and began to retreat shortly thereafter. Forests in the paths of advancing glaciers were slowly destroyed by climatic changes. Since many of those once denuded areas are wooded today, their forests have obviously developed since the Pleistocene ice retreated. Studies have clearly indicated that in northern glaciated areas there was a northward movement of spruce-dominated forests from eleven thousand to seven thousand years ago, followed by their return southward after the glaciers retreated. Similarly, there was an eastward movement of prairies, followed by their subsequent retreat, as well as significant changes in mixed conifer forests over the past eight thousand years.[10]

More controversial, however, is the question of what happened in areas like Mississippi that were south of the glaciation. Fossil spruce wood has been found in Louisiana, and fossil spruce pollen has been found in Florida and East Texas, supporting the idea that there was some modification of the forests. In the most distant past the southern forests consisted mostly of enormous club moss trees that occupied swamps. Over time "the forest evolved from club mosses and ferns to the first gymnosperms (relatives of modern pine trees) and finally to mixed forests of gymnosperms and angiosperms (broad-leaved deciduous species)." By 5000 B.P. in the coastal plains,

the oak and hickory forests were supplanted by southern pines. Following the retreat of the glaciers, tree species continued to evolve and migrate as a result of continuing climatic change. Evidence from lake fluctuations, tree rings, and other sources indicates that the first millennium of the Christian era was relatively warm, and that it was followed, from about 1300 to 1800, by a period of increasing cold. Tree species suited to cooler sites, such as beech and sugar maple, invaded areas occupied by trees that prefer drier and warmer areas, like oak and hickory. During the past two centuries the weather has warmed, and trees such as shortleaf and loblolly pine have done well in the south-central states, north of these trees' earlier range. One major scholar notes that there is "irrefutable evidence that vegetation has been in an almost constant state of instability and adjustment due to an almost constantly changing climate over the past ten thousand years."[11]

The evolutionary process that probably occurred in parts of Mississippi during the Holocene period of the last twelve thousand years is represented in the pollen and fossil record of a pond located northeast of Birmingham in St. Clair County, Alabama. There were major changes in the forests of the immediate and surrounding areas during three stages. In the early period, from 12,000 to 10,000 B.P., the forests were predominantly composed of broad-leafed deciduous trees, dominated by beech, with significant inclusion of hornbeam, oak, hickory, elm, and ash. Atlantic white cedar, a coastal species, also was found in the area, as were other trees that are today rare or absent in Alabama, including eastern white pine, hemlock, striped maple, and mountain maple. After 10,000 B.P. hickories and oaks became dominant, and then after 8,400 B.P. species found in the area today, including black gum, southern pine, red maple, buttonbush, and sweetgum, became established. While there are currently no similar published studies for Mississippi, it seems reasonable that areas of the same latitude, namely across north-central Mississippi, where stands of pine, oak, and gum exist today, would have a similar record of prehistoric forest development.[12]

In addition to the climatic change and glaciation that shaped the ancient forests, in the later prehistoric and modern historic ages the impact of humans must be considered. Most scholars agree that prehistoric people came from Asia, across a land bridge (Beringia) into Alaska, and then filtered down throughout the Western Hemisphere. There is no clear consensus on when this migration occurred: most estimates range from 17,000 to 30,000 B.P. However, one recent writer confidently, if not very precisely, says, "The human history of America—we should not have to argue any longer—began when Asian hunters first crossed the Bering land bridge, 15,000, perhaps, 25,000, possibly 50,000 years ago. . . . Twelve or fourteen thousand years ago these people began filtering into the southeastern regions of North America in search of big game and livelihood, and finding both, they stayed." Ongoing archaeological research and discoveries in the Americas continue to modify scholars' opinions concerning the processes and chronology of the peopling of the New World.[13]

In any case, there is a broad general consensus that humans had reached the southern United States by some ten to fifteen thousand years ago. These early residents, called Paleo-Indians by anthropologists, came into the region apparently in pursuit of both large Pleistocene animals such as mastodons and giant bison and smaller "contemporary" animals such as white-tailed deer. The Paleo-Indians were nomadic hunters, "best known for killing large, now extinct animals with stone-tipped spears or by stampeding them into various kinds of traps to their deaths." By about 8000 B.P., with the retreat of the glaciers and the warming of the climate, many of the large mammals became extinct, and, as noted above, the forest environment was changing as well. Forests that would be recognizable today were now in place, and the age of the Archaic Indians had arrived.[14]

The Archaic Indians hunted small animals with darts; collected wild plants; "gathered nuts,

berries, and shellfish; and became more sedentary." They made tools of stone, bone, and wood. Fire-cracked rocks and deeply burned areas that were probably hearths indicate that fire was part of their culture. By about five thousand years ago the Archaic Indians had begun some food cultivation, and as their population increased, they established increasingly sedentary seasonal camps concentrated in the river floodplains. Thus, in a small way, they were beginning to affect the forest environment.[15]

The Native American population increased slowly, if steadily, until about 900 B.P. This is roughly the beginning point of the Woodland period, the third phase of prehistoric development. The Woodland Indians were hunter-gatherers who also continued the development of rudimentary agriculture, planting sunflower, squash, maygrass, chenopodium, and gourds in patches cleared in the forests with the use of fire. These Indians made pottery and conducted trade over a wide geographical area reaching to the Rocky Mountains and the Great Lakes. The pottery made it possible to store food for year-round use. The Woodland Indians also built burial mounds, which are scattered around the South, including several sites in Arkansas, Tennessee, and Mississippi.[16]

Somewhere between 800 and 1000 A.D., the Woodland era gave way to the age of the Mississippian culture, the final phase of prehistoric Native American development. During this period the population grew, settlements became larger, and agriculture became more widespread as greater amounts of land were cleared. Influenced by the great civilizations of Mesoamerica, this was the golden age of the mound builders. Towns were constructed around ceremonial centers and were often surrounded by moats and palisades. Fire was a central part of the Mississippians' lives for hunting, land clearing, and ceremonial purposes. Large areas of the forest were cleared for mounds, buildings, ceremonial structures, and agriculture. Corn was introduced into the diet around 900 A.D., making its way north from Mexico, perhaps indirectly from the present-day southwest of the United

States. The Mississippians practiced intensive agriculture, growing corn, beans, and squash. They divided into what might be called political provinces or chiefdoms and competed with rival political units for the best lands, often resorting to organized warfare. The Mississippian culture reached its peak between about 1200 and 1600 A.D., with the highest development in northeast Arkansas, the Delta, and around Natchez. While its cultural patterns continued in Indian societies like the Natchez of Mississippi and Louisiana, by the time of early European contact in North America the Woodland culture was declining for various reasons.[17]

By the time of European contact with the New World, the Native Americans had moved well beyond primitive slash-and-burn agriculture. They lived in towns where they had small garden plots of about one hundred by two hundred feet. Their principal fields were located adjacent to the towns and were cleared by girdling large trees with knives and stone axes and then using fire and other implements to fell the trunks. The stumps either rotted or were destroyed by fire. When lightning did not do their work for them, the Native Americans deliberately burned the forests. Another factor to consider in assessing the Native Americans' impact on the land is that Indian villages moved periodically as the fertility of the soil declined, the local firewood supply was exhausted, or game became scarce or as other factors, including military considerations, dictated. This phenomenon explains, among other things, the Indian "old fields" described by early European settlers.[18]

James Adair, a colonial trader who lived among the Catawba, Cherokee, and Chickasaw, provides a good contemporary description of Indian agricultural practices during the eighteenth century:

The Indians formerly had stone axes, which in form commonly resembled a smith's chisel. . . . [B]y means of this simple and obvious invention, they deadened the trees by cuting through the bark, and burned them, when they either fell by decay, or became thoroughly dry. With these trees they always kept up their annual holy fire; and they reckon it unlawful, and productiv of many temporal evils, to extinguish even the culinary fire with water. . . . By the aforesaid difficult method of deadening the trees, and clearing the woods, the contented natives got convenient fields in process of time. And their tradition says they did not live straggling in the American woods . . . for they made houses with the branches and bark of trees, for the summer-season; and warm mud-walls, mixt with soft dry grass, against the bleak winter, according to their present plan of building. . . . Now, in the first clearing of their plantations, they only bark the large timber, cut down the saplings, and underwood, and burn them in heaps; as the suckers shoot up, they chop them off close by the stump, of which they make fires to deaden the roots, till in time they decay. Though to a stranger, this may seem to be a lazy method of clearing the wood-lands; yet it is the most expeditius method they could have pitched upon, under their circumstances, as a common hoe and a small hatchet are all their implements for clearing and planting.[19]

Adair also gave a good overview of the way Indian farming was organized:

Every dwelling-house has a small field pretty close to it: and, as soon as the spring of the year admits, there they plant a variety of large and small beans, peas, and the smalle sort of Indian corn, which usually ripens in two months, from the time it is planted; though it is called by the English, the six weeks corn. Around this small farm, they fasten stakes in the ground, and tie a couple of long split hiccory, or white oak-saplings, at proper distances to keep off the horses. . . . Their large fields lie quite open with regard to fencing, and they believe it to be agreeable to the best of their land here and there, as it suits their conveniency, without wasting their time in fence and childishly confining their improvements, as if the crop would eat itself. The women . . . tether the horses with tough young bark-ropes, and confine the swine in convenient penns, from the time their provisions are planted, till they are gathered in—the men improve this time, either in killing plenty of wild game, or coursing against the common enemy. . . . The chief part of the Indians begin to plant their out-fields, when the wild fruit is so ripe, as to draw off the birds from picking up the grain. This is their general rule, which is in the beginning of May, about the time the traders set off for the English settlements. . . . Corn is their chief produce and main dependance.[20]

In addition to agriculture, the Native Americans used fire for a variety of other purposes, including hunting. Charles Hudson describes the "fire surround" as "a communal hunting technique used in fall and early winter, when the leaves had fallen and were dry. A group of hunters—often as many as two or three hundred—would go into the woods and set the leaves on fire in a circle of up to five miles in circumference. This forced deer and other animals into a small area where they could be easily shot. In some cases deer were forced into a river and killed as they swam." Firing the forests also made travel easier and purged the burned area of pests such as snakes and insects. Fires fertilized the soil and were used to kill off large forest areas that could then be harvested for firewood and for ceremonial ritual cleansing and spectacle. Broadcast burning was also used for economic extortion and sometimes as part of military strategy.[21]

Hudson reports, "Some evidence suggests that [the Indians] intentionally burned portions of the woods in winter as a matter of course. . . . Not only did it reduce the threat of serious forest fires by reducing the accumulation of dead wood and litter on the forest floor, but it also laid down a bed of ashes, a soil nutrient, and it kept the forest open by clearing out underbrush, tree seedlings, and saplings. . . . This stimulated the growth of open meadows and plant life on which deer could browse, it probably made acorns and chestnuts easier to find and this in turn would have increased both the deer and turkey populations. . . . In view of this practice of regular light burning, it is not so difficult to explain why early Europeans in the Southeastern uplands reported seeing large park-like meadows with widely separated large trees and herds of deer and flocks of turkeys which seem to us to have been unnaturally large."[22]

The forests of North America and Mississippi were still evolving at the time of the early European explorations. But how extensively had the forests been affected by Native Americans' agricultural, hunting, and ceremonial practices? Some scientists report that current knowledge of their long-term impact is quite limited: "The effects of American Indians on native vegetation of the Southeast have been largely undetected by Quaternary paleoecologists." Nevertheless, reports another scholar, "Several ecologists have hypothesized that the primeval forests found by the white man upon his arrival had already been disturbed during many millennia by the activities of Indians." This idea has serious implications for earlier ecological theories:

In their original definitions of the climatic formation or "climax," ecologists visualized a uniform, mesophytic vegetation limited by climate alone; the effects of topographic diversity were assumed absent because the climax vegetation grew on a peneplain attained at the close of an erosion cycle. Further, the climax forest was considered self-perpetuating, i.e., to be composed of "tolerant" species, the seedlings of which can grow in the shade of the parent trees. Few ecologists now accept this definition in its entirety. Climate is not stable long enough to allow completion of vegetational succession occurring over many thousands of years, storms that disturb the vegetation are inherent in many climatic regimes, and the idea of an erosion cycle terminating in peneplanation . . . has itself been seriously challenged. Most ecologists applying the idea of "climatic climax" . . . use the concept loosely to embrace a vegetation with a great deal of local diversity growing on a diverse landscape. They use the term merely to indicate their conception of vegetation that would develop on upland soils in the course of several hundred years of stable climate, in the absence of human interference of any kind. Unfortunately, the word climax used in this way has many connotations and lacks any precise definition.[23]

Any conception that excludes human interference is problematical, for, as described above, Native Americans utilized both lightning and incendiary fires to accomplish various purposes, including land clearing, and in the process they deliberately altered their environment. "The Indian," says Stephen J. Pyne, "had little use for closed forests; their main attraction was as a potential source of fertilizer for swidden agriculture. . . . In the general absence of domesticated livestock, meat had to come from hunting, and through fire Indians maintained the reserves they required—the grassland or forest-grass ecotone (which maximized edge effects) that proved so productive of game."[24]

In areas where fire was "frequent and devastating, completely open ground was the result. The sparsely growing, parklike forest gave way to what were variously called plains, barrens, openings, deserts, prairies, or, particularly in the South, savannas, all individual patches of open grassland varying in size from a few acres to many thousands of square miles." The frequent burning had another permanent effect. As Michael Williams has observed, "It altered the composition of the forest. Repeated burning and clearing tend to reduce the number of species and to simplify the biological components of the forest. For example, the extensive, open loblolly (*Pinus taeda*), longleaf (*P. palustris*), and slash pine (*P. elliottii*) forests of the Southeast are thought to be a man-induced fire subclimax within the general deciduous region of the eastern woodlands."[25]

Also, says Williams, burning promoted "the permanent establishment of the pine by removing the vegetation and debris that surround and shade the slow-growing longleaf seedlings and by eliminating brown-spot needle disease." However, "the ecological response is yet more complicated, for although fire is essential for the perpetuation of the forest through the clearing of the accumulation of litter, it must occur in a proper ratio of winter fires to fire-free years; that is, there must be nonfire years properly spaced so that the seedlings can pass through their critical first and sixth to eighth years of growth without burning and being killed." In contrast, Williams argues, "the suppression of burning and the reduction in the incidence of widespread fire during the present century have led to the invasion of the southern pine forests by hardwoods, such as oak and hickory, to such an extent that in recent decades the pine forests have reached the late stages of their succession, have declined, and have become relatively stable hardwood communities." "Inferentially, therefore," Williams concludes, "contemporary trends in forest composition point to widespread Indian burning, which, on balance, must have favored the pinewoods and prevented the hardwoods from growing."[26]

The result of Native American burning was that "[t]aken in its broadest meanings to include plains, barrens, savannas, and wetlands, grasslands were probably the dominant cover type in North America at the time of European discovery. . . . [N]early all these grasslands were created by man, the product of deliberate, routine firing." Stephen J. Pyne, a leading student of fire ecology, writes that from the "vast corridor" of the "tall grass prairies east of the 100th meridian," which combined with the High Plains to form "the largest continuous grassland in the world," early humans "dispersed throughout America," and "anthropogenic fire extended the range of the grasslands north into Wisconsin, Michigan, and Minnesota, east through Illinois, Indiana, Ohio, and Kentucky, and south into central Alabama and Mississippi. . . . As these manufactured grasslands radiated outward," says Pyne, "their continuity broke down. . . . Individual 'barrens' appeared like skirmishers ahead of the main advance; these might be expanded in time and joined. Where heavier rainfall was encountered with the march eastward, bogs and bottoms prevented more or less complete conversions, leaving a mosaic of burned and unburned regions, of forest and grassland. . . . Under the natural regimes, fires came with summer thunderstorms. . . . After anthropogenic fire became dominant, the summer cycle was superseded by a pattern of spring and fall burning."[27]

To fully understand the extent of the changes brought to the land by prehistoric Native Americans, it is necessary to know about some other factors, including their population density and total population. These are difficult matters to pin down. For example, professional estimates of the Native American population in North America at the time of initial European contact range from 900,000 to nearly 10 million. These figures provide a range for population density of between two and twenty-one persons for every ten square kilometers. Over time in the twentieth century, scholarly opinions on this matter have fluctuated dramatically. For the Gulf States the classic figures were provided in 1910 by James Mooney in his article on population for the *Handbook of North American Indians*. Mooney estimated the Indian population at 114,400. Estimates for a new version of the *Handbook* being compiled by the Smithsonian Institution in the 1970s increased the estimate by 314 percent to 473,616. This remarkable increase was attributed by the scholar preparing the new *Handbook* edition to the "tendency of current scholars to view more favorably the liberal estimates that exist within the primary ethnohistorical literature." Consistent with this tendency, by the late 1980s anthropologists and historians generally agreed that the Native American population of North America at the time of "discovery" was between 3 and 5 million." Contemporary accounts seem to support the more liberal figures, with the highest estimates ranging up to 18 million. As Albert W. Crosby has observed, the chroniclers of Hernando de Soto "give us a clear impression of regions of dense population and many villages in the midst of vast cultivated fields of stratified societies . . . and scores of temples resting on truncated pyramids."[28]

Michael Williams accepts a somewhat higher population figure and concludes that "even if only a half of the estimated pre-conquest population of between 9.8 and 12.25 million for North America cleared and cultivated forest land, then between 19.8 and 24.50 million acres of forest would have been affected (and that would not have included abandoned clearings), which is approximately 10 percent of a total of 278.6 million acres of land in crops in the 31 easternmost states

today. . . . [T]he Indians were a potent, if not crucial, ecological factor in the distribution and composition of the forest."[29] On balance, the forests "discovered" by early Europeans were shaped both by nature and by significant human utilization and management. The fact that Native Americans had affected and were continuing to alter the forest environment was observed and reported by early European explorers and travelers.

There were several early contacts in the Southeast. The first that is documented is the expedition of Juan Ponce de Leon, who landed on the Florida coast in 1513. He returned in 1521 and on both occasions got a hostile reception from the Indians, which may indicate that they had earlier unpleasant contacts with Europeans. In 1521 a group led by a captain of Lucas Vazquez de Ayllon landed on the coast of South Carolina. One of the Native Americans they encountered, named by the Spaniards Francisco of Chicora, was taken to Spain. He was interviewed by the historian Peter Martyr (Pietro Martire d'Anghiera), who used him as a major source for the first major European description of North American Indians, the book *De Orbe Novo*. Another early Spanish expedition was the journey of Alonzo Alverez de Pineda, who sought a westward passage around Florida. Pineda, with four ships, made his way along the Gulf Coast and entered Mobile Bay in 1519. After sailing a short distance up the Mobile River, Pineda apparently spent about a month repairing his ships and trading with the local Native Americans before departing from the area.[30]

The early Spanish contacts were followed by the journey of the Italian mariner Giovanni da Verrazano, who sailed in the service of France in search of a southwest passage to the Pacific Ocean. Verrazano left France in 1524, after fifty days touched the American coast south of Cape Fear, and then sailed up to Cape Breton–Newfoundland. The Spanish activities continued as well, with an attempt by Lucas Vazquez de Ayllon to establish a colony with about five hundred settlers on the coast of South Carolina. This short-lived endeavor was thwarted by disease, and after only about six months some 150 survivors returned to the West Indies.

Two years later, in 1528, Panfilo de Narvaez landed with three to four hundred men near Tampa Bay and attempted to conquer the Indians of that area. The Spaniards left the Tampa Bay area and moved north into the territory of the Apalachee Indians, around present- day Tallahassee, explored that region, and under constant resistance from the Native Americans returned to the gulf, where the explorers constructed rafts and attempted to escape to Mexico. Most of the Spaniards died from various causes, including disease, starvation, Indian attacks, and accidents, but four survived and made their way along the coast back to Mexico. Most famous among the survivors were Cabeza de Vaca, who later returned as a trader, and Estevanico, a black man. There were probably other undocumented contacts as well, and they had a significant impact on the New World Indians.[31]

One result of these early contacts was a tradition of distrust between the Europeans and the Native Americans—not surprising, for the Europeans were exploitative, seeking to enrich themselves and to enslave and in other ways take advantage of the Indians. Also, the explorers and colonizers were condescending in their attitudes toward the Native Americans, regarding them as savages and failing to respect their cultures and achievements. The second result of the European expeditions was even worse. They brought to the New World diseases from Europe and Africa to which the Indians had no resistance. The extent of the impact of European diseases on the Native American populations has long been a lively topic of scholarly debate.

Various kinds of evidence are studied by scholars attempting to reconstruct the story, including ethnographies, census records, travelers' accounts, and examinations of burial sites as well as other sources. One of the leading students in this area, Crosby, concludes, "Something eliminated or drove off most of the population of . . . areas where heavy populations of people . . . had lived

two centuries before: along the Gulf Coast between Mobile Bay and Tampa Bay . . . and on the banks of the Mississippi above the mouth of the Red River. In eastern and southern Arkansas and northeastern Louisiana, where De Soto had found thirty towns and provinces, the French found only a handful of villages. Where De Soto had been able to stand on one temple mound and see several villages with their mounds and little else but fields of maize between, there was now wilderness." Crosby argues that the culprit was epidemic disease: "No other factor seems capable of having exterminated so many people over such a large part of North America." He argues as well that the process was under way prior to de Soto's expedition in the Southeast. Crosby theorizes that an epidemic in Mexico could have made its way around the Gulf Coast through the Indians of that area and then into the interior along waterways. He notes also that Spanish ships riding the Gulf Stream from Havana were sometimes driven by storms onto shoals along the Florida coast: survivors could have brought European diseases ashore with them. There were also early Europeans living in the area. On his expedition into the interior, de Soto employed as an interpreter one of the survivors of the Narvaez expedition who was living in Florida. And de Soto found European artifacts among the Native Americans he encountered on his journey.[32]

The Indians had virtually no immunity. In contrast, Europeans of the period "whose immediate ancestors were people who had survived the ravages of the Black Death, were likely among the most disease-resistant humans who ever lived but the disease organisms had survived, and . . . Europeans brought these foreign germs with them." As J. Leitch Wright Jr. has argued, "For centuries, and for all practical purposes apparently forever, the American Indians had been isolated. Suddenly they were exposed to such scourges as smallpox, measles, chicken pox, scarlet fever, typhus, influenza, and whooping cough from Europe and malaria, yellow fever, and dengue fever from Africa. Over the years Old World inhabitants had built up immunity to many

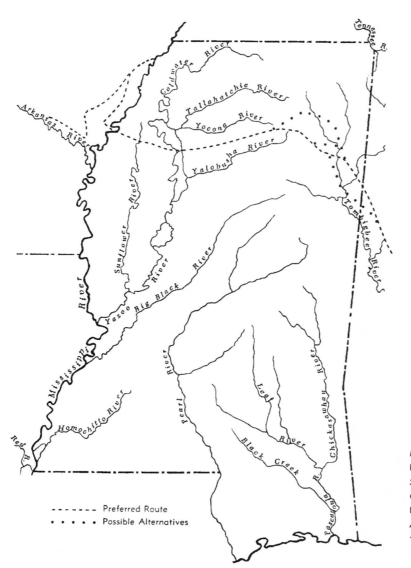

Map of de Soto expedition.
From *Report of the United
States de Soto Expedition
Commission,* found in John K.
Bettersworth, *Mississippi:
A History* (Austin, Tex.: Steck,
1959), 49.

- - - - - Preferred Route
• • • • • Possible Alternatives

of these maladies, and in time they became less virulent 'childhood diseases.' But in America, where there was no immunity, the diseases raged with all their pristine fury. Their effect can be compared to the Black Death (bubonic and pneumonic plague), which in the fourteenth century reduced Europe's populace by almost one-third. The difference in America was that the Indians suddenly had to confront not just one alien disease but a variety of microparasites coming simultaneously from both Europe and Africa." Some scholars estimate that between the time of the de Soto expedition and the arrival of the

French in the last part of the seventeenth century, the Native American population decreased by 80 percent. Where de Soto described numerous villages, the French found deserted forests.[33]

The most elaborate and best documented journey through the southeast and Mississippi during the early historic period was the expedition of Hernando de Soto from 1539 to 1542. In 1539 de Soto, the governor of Cuba, sailed from Havana to Tampa Bay, with nine ships; six hundred soldiers; about a hundred servants, slaves, and others; about two hundred horses; some mules; a herd of hogs; a pack of bloodhounds;

and a large supply of provisions. On July 15 de Soto set out on a search for gold that would take him through parts of Florida, Georgia, South Carolina, North Carolina, Tennessee, Alabama, Arkansas, Louisiana, and Mississippi.[34]

In late December 1540 de Soto moved into Mississippi, probably traveling along Indian trails, for "the territory through which he passed was not a trackless forest, but traversed by main trails and many cross trails, so one could travel throughout the county by following these trails." He apparently entered the present Mississippi region east of Columbus and traveled northwest across the northeastern part of Lowndes County, crossing the Tombigbee River near Aberdeen. He then moved westward into Chickasaw County. The expedition traveled on to the town of Chicasa, which may have been in Pontotoc County. It is difficult to determine the location of these settlements with certainty, for as John Walthall points out, "Indian towns were frequently moved to new locations for a variety of reasons, ranging from depletion of easily procured firewood, to decreasing yields on nearby fields, to flooding, and political turmoil."[35]

By this time the Spanish had encountered growing resistance from Native Americans and had suffered serious losses in several battles. After wintering, probably near Pontotoc, west of the Tombigbee River, in late April 1541, the expedition moved west. The lands they encountered included upland savannas and hardwoods along the valleys. Finally, in early May the Spaniards reached a village they called Quizquiz on the Mississippi River. After building barges and crossing the river, they moved into Arkansas, where for the first time they saw buffalo. After wintering in southern Arkansas, they moved south into Louisiana. After contracting a fever, de Soto became seriously ill, dying in May 1542. The expedition, now under the command of Luis de Moscoso de Alvarado, traveled west into arid country. With food becoming scarce, they returned to the Mississippi River to spend their final winter. In early July they set off down the river in seven small boats, and amidst periodic attacks and pursuit by Indians, they reached the Gulf Coast. On July 18 they departed for Mexico, with some three hundred survivors reaching the port of Panuco in September 1543.[36]

Several aspects of de Soto's expedition should interest students of Mississippi's forest history. First, the Spaniards' records indicate that they encountered fairly large populations of Native Americans on their journey through the interior. For example, the Spanish chroniclers report that de Soto was resisted by an army of ten thousand as he moved through Florida and that he was assaulted by some seven thousand warriors at Mabila, which is thought to be in present Clarke County, Alabama. Many of the towns described by the Spaniards had sizable populations. The de Soto expedition's experiences support the larger estimates of prehistoric Indian population cited earlier.[37]

The second important subject is the nature of the land the explorers traversed. As mentioned above, in northeastern Mississippi they encountered upland savannas and hardwoods along the valleys. Says Carl Ortwin Sauer, "The woodlands were far richer in diversity of flora than in any part of Europe. Except in wet lands they were open woods, not dense forests. The de Soto expedition, consisting of many people, a large horseherd, and many swine, passed through ten states without difficulty of movement, except occasionally swamp and high water. . . . Within the open woods there were treeless or nearly treeless upland tracts, called savannas by the Spanish. . . . Prairies and open woods in the humid east may be explained by long continued Indian practices of setting fires." According to Michael Williams, "The descriptions of the land en route were copious, the details of the alternating forest, savanna, fields, and burning and cultivating filling pages. . . . Everywhere the forest was open. . . . Fields were found alongside many of the rivers, particularly the . . . Tombigbee . . . and Mississippi, and all their tributaries."[38]

Another important result of the de Soto expedition was the introduction of wild hogs into the Southeast. The areas of Spain and Portugal from which many of de Soto's men came were also the homes of long-legged and long-snouted hogs that fed on mast. The Spanish took hogs of this type to the West Indies, and de Soto brought a herd on his expedition as a source of meat. In the course of the march many were lost or stolen by Indians. The de Soto Commission concluded that "swine were permanently introduced into the Southeast by the De Soto expedition. The Southeast was a prime ecologic niche for the Spanish range hog by abundance of diversity of food, lack of competition, and adoption into Indian culture. The agile, long-snouted razorback hog of the South is therefore attributed to Spanish ancestry, not to the heavy, short-legged breeds later brought by Dutch and English colonists." Of course, the legendary razorback became the scourge of foresters and land managers attempting to regenerate the forests of the South and of Mississippi in a later era.[39]

The last major Spanish colonizing expedition in the Southeast was an attempt by Tristan de Luna to establish a colony at Mobile. Luna created outposts on Pensacola Bay and Mobile Bay in 1559 and then explored the interior, moving the colony to a location a short distance up the Alabama River at the site of an abandoned Indian town. Because of inadequate provisions and internal dissension, the colony was abandoned in 1561, ending Spanish colonization efforts in the Gulf Coast area. There was also one final exploring expedition, the 1566 effort of Juan Pardo and Sergeant Boyano. They left South Carolina looking for a land passage to Mexico that would eliminate the sea voyage around the Florida peninsula. Facing Indian hostility, at one point from three thousand warriors on the upper Tennessee River, Pardo turned back after having reached no farther into the interior than northeastern Alabama. With this final retreat, the Native Americans of the interior region entered a period of more than a century without visits from Europeans.[40]

The Indians did not consider the lands they occupied to be wilderness. The lands consisted of swamps, savannas, meadows, cultivated fields, and various kinds of forests, many of which were strikingly open and easy to travel. Nature and time had shaped the Mississippi forests. But over the eons from prehistoric times to the Age of Discovery, the Indians had also altered their environment, including the "wilderness" later Europeans "discovered" and "conquered."

Spanish activities in the Southeast were among the early manifestations of the great race for discovery, riches, and empire among the European powers of the late fifteenth and sixteenth centuries. At the time the Spanish were exploring and attempting to colonize in the Southeast, their two greatest rivals for New World supremacy, England and France, were still preoccupied with internal matters and were not ready to mount challenges. In the century following the early Spanish endeavors, the balance of power in Europe and in the New World changed considerably. These changes brought adventurers from other nations to America and to Mississippi.

Significant developments also occurred within the Mississippi area. As a result of the diseases introduced by European explorers, the Indian population dramatically decreased. Also, the prehistoric Native American groups evolved into three main federations of tribes. The Chickasaw were centered in the northeast and across the northern part of the area; the Choctaw country was in the east central part of the region, south of the Chickasaw; and the Natchez, who did not survive long into the French period of control, had their strongholds along the Mississippi River in southwest Mississippi and in Louisiana.

In the seventeenth century the European powers struggled for supremacy in the New World. The English established agricultural colonies along the eastern seaboard from South Carolina to New England, while the French colonized Canada and moved into the interior regions in pursuit of the fur trade, a business that the English also coveted. The Spanish controlled Central and South America but also held Florida and explored in the Southwest. In their search for the fur trade and empire, the French moved up the St. Lawrence River, through the Great Lakes, and down the Mississippi Valley. In 1673 Louis Joliet and Father Jacques Marquette journeyed by canoe from Green Bay along the Fox and Wisconsin Rivers and down the Mississippi River as far as the mouth of the Arkansas. In 1682 the expedition of René-Robert Cavelier, Sieur de La Salle, reached the mouth of the Mississippi, where he claimed the interior country for France and christened it Louisiana.

In the late seventeenth century the French were concerned about potential English ambitions in the West. To secure their possessions, the French established fortresses, trading posts, and small settlements in the interior, including the Gulf Coast region. Sieur d'Iberville was dispatched to the mouth of the Mississippi to establish a colony, and in February 1699 he ascended the river for about ten days and returned to the gulf, convinced that the river was not suitable for navigation and the country was not attractive for settlement. He then sailed into Biloxi Bay and constructed Fort Maurepas near the present town of Ocean Springs, Mississippi's first permanent white settlement. Iberville sailed for France, leaving Sauvole in command, but in 1700 Iberville returned with instructions "to breed the buffalo at Biloxi, to seek for pearls, to examine the wild mulberry with a view to silk, timber for shipbuilding, and to seek for mines."[41] In 1702 the colonial capital of Louisiana was relocated to the Mobile River, although a few soldiers remained at Biloxi, which was a trading post.

In 1718 the French founded New Orleans, which grew to a size comparable with some of the English colonial cities along the Atlantic seaboard. In 1722 the Crescent City became the colonial capital. Farther up the Mississippi River, early French visitors, including La Salle, were struck by the hostility of the Natchez Indians, who by 1700 had 1,200 warriors and their families living at seven villages on the bluff and along two creeks in the vicinity of present-day Natchez. Jesuit missionaries who labored for eight years with the Natchez, following the establishment of the Louisiana Colony, gave up their work in despair.

Eventually in 1714 Governor Antoine de la Mothe Cadillac authorized Marc Antoine and Auguste de la Loire des Ursins to build a trading post under the bluff at Natchez. The objectives were to establish the fur trade in the interior, serve as a way station between Louisiana and the Illinois country, and counteract British influence among the Natchez, who were regularly visited by English traders and agents. After repeated difficulties with the Natchez and a 1716 Indian raid on the La Loire warehouse, Cadillac sent out a punitive expedition from Mobile. It was commanded by Sieur de Bienville, Iberville's younger brother and the former governor of the colony, who secured from the Indians a land grant on which the French (with Indian labor) constructed Fort Rosalie.

John Law's Company of the Indies acquired the proprietorship for Louisiana in 1717, and six years later Fort Rosalie became the headquarters of the Natchez district. The district encompassed a triangle extending from Fort St. Peter (constructed in 1719), near the mouth of the Yazoo River, to a line running eastward for forty miles along the 31st parallel from the Mississippi River. The population was concentrated in the country around Forts Rosalie and St. Peter, and the French officials encouraged tobacco production. However, by the 1720s the colony was also producing indigo, silk, rice, cotton, pitch, tar, and dressed lumber. There was an active fur trade and a great deal of commerce in horses. By 1729 the Natchez settlement had a population of more than 750, and nearly 6,300 arpents of land were cleared and in cultivation. (An arpent was a French unit of land measurement approximately equivalent to an acre.)

Amid growing tension between the French and the Indians, intermittent hostilities began in the early 1720s. Natchez Indians attacked Fort Rosalie in 1729, and the Yazoo Indians launched a similar campaign shortly thereafter against the small garrison at Fort St. Peter. For two years the French and their occasional allies the Choctaw pursued the Natchez, with little success, and by the early 1740s the Natchez were mostly absorbed into other tribes. However, the French Natchez settlement languished, and in 1751 a French traveler found the bluff "uninhabited" except for a few soldiers. From that time until the English took control in 1763, Natchez remained little more than a small military post.[42]

During the French period in Mississippi a number of travelers' accounts and government communications provide some idea of what the land was like. In 1708 Thomas Nairne, a member of the South Carolina Commons House of Assembly and the architect of that colony's Indian policy, along with Thomas Welch, a Carolina trader who dealt with the Chickasaw, traveled from Charles Town to the Mississippi River. Nairne hoped that the British would be able to use trade in furs and slaves to create a coalition of the interior tribes and use them against the French and Spanish in North America. In fact the British were actively involved in the affairs of the western Indians, and the situation was further clouded by the fact that in 1732 the English divided Carolina into two colonies and created the new colony of Georgia, which claimed lands extending all the way to the Pacific Coast, including, of course, a large section of what became southern Mississippi. A small area in the extreme north of Mississippi remained under South Carolina, even after the Georgia grant.[43]

In the course of his journey Nairne wrote numerous letters describing his experiences in the interior. In April 1708, Nairne reported, "The Chickasaws live in an Excellent hunting country, both for Larg dear, and other game." Traveling with the Chickasaws, Nairne reported hunting "Dear" and "Buffeloes," noting, "The tongues of these Creatures are extraordinary fine atasting like marrow, and that causes the death of many hundreds of them." He says that his greatest pleasure came from "fireing rings for in that we never missed 7 or 10 Dear." Nairne's is a fascinating description by a participant of how the Indians used fire rings for hunting:

Three or 4 hours after the ring is fired, of 4 or 5 miles circumferance, the hunters post themselves within as nigh the flame and smoak as they can endure. The fire on each side burns in toward the center and thither the Dear gather from all parts to avoid it, but striving to they fall into a Certain one from the Bullets of the hunters who drawing nigher together, as the circle grows less, find an esay pray of the impounded dear, tho seldom kill all for some who find a place where the Flame is less Violent, Jump out. This port is the more certain the longer the grownd has been unburned. If it has not for 2 or 3 years there are so many dry leaves grass and Trash, that few Creatures within escape, and the men are forced to go out betimes at some slack place to the leeward. In killing Buffeloes they Aim at the yearlings and heifers, being the tenderest and indeed no Beef exceeds them. After shooting 3 or 4 of these, no remonstrances can prevail with the savages to march farther that day.[44]

Nairne also describes another use of fire for hunting: "If then the savages of our Company were cloy'd with dear and Buffeloe, then they went a Bare hunting. This was the time of year in which these Creatures lye in their holes, for from the first of January to the middle of March they sleep and neither eat or Drink. The Indian way of hunting them dureing that time, is only looking in holes under the roots of fallen trees, or up such trees in the swamps, which have a hollow rotten place nigh the Top. In these Large holes the Bears make their nests and repose themselves dureing their sleeping season. The savages when they spy such a hole in a tree presently view it all round and see for the marks of the Bears Claws. . . . They either climb up some small tree that stands by together and prick him out with canes, or else fire. Thus I saw them take severall."[45]

Nairne also describes the region through which he traveled and remarks that after journeying most of the way through "a miserable barren stony uneven land," upon arriving near the Chickasaw country, "we had done with sand, stones and pines, the Country being pleasant open forests of oak chesnuts and hickerey so intermixt with savannas as if it were a made landscape. These savanas are not perfectly levell, like our's in Carolina, but full of gentle Ascents, which yet are not too steep for the plough, on the Top of these knowlls live the Chicasaws, their houses a Gunn or pistole shot asunder, with their improved ground peach and plum trees about them. The land from hence to the Chicasaws their country west to the great river and up it's Branches some hundred miles are all thus intermixt with savannas." Nairne also comments on the "old Feilds" which are covered "Over all" with "strawberrys inumerable and that good and Large."[46] In summation, Nairne paints a picture of a land that is a mosaic of forests and clearings, a land that has been cleared and cultivated by the Native Americans in places, and a land whose inhabitants commonly use fire.

Farther South, French officials in the late 1720s described the area from Bayou Manchac to the mouth of the Mississippi River as "a tongue of land which is bounded in front by the river and in the rear by Lakes Maurepas and Ponchartrain on one side and on the other by those of the Washas and Bayou Lafourche which comes down from the Bayagoulas. These lakes and the river are very low cypress swamps in which there is water three-fourths of the year. These lands will never be entirely cleared, so there will be timber for a long time." In the area of present-day southwestern Mississippi, "you have above Manchac, as you go up to the Tunicas, Natchez and above woods in abundance that are better than [those] in these regions because the land there is much higher. The oak prevails there much more than here."[47]

Colonial administrators in the late 1720s reported that there was only one sawmill operating along the Mississippi River, "constructed last year by an inhabitant who built it on his own account on his land, and it has not been in operation two months." Mills of this type were water powered, propelled by runoff from flooded areas, and "since the water is at almost the same level along the river these mills will turn at the most only four-months of the year." The administrators also reported plans to construct some mills to saw planks. The mills would each be powered by a horse, and "by their simplicity will cost little and

will be portable." There were also plans to produce stave wood, and the colonial officials reported that wood from upriver was better, with qualifications: "We agree that the timber from up the river must be of a much better quality than that from the lower river, but . . . this difference is only in the very distant countries both because of their elevation and because it is colder there. As for the difference of ten leagues above or ten leagues below New Orleans, it does not exist. The woods and the situation of the ground are the same there."[48]

French officials were evaluating the country, mostly with an eye to making the Louisiana colony profitable. They clearly found that the Native Americans had been reduced in numbers, with Bienville in a "Memoir on Louisiana," written around 1725–26, commenting, "Four leagues up the small river of the Yazoos . . . are three small Indian nations. . . . They formerly had more than five hundred men of whom there now remain only one hundred and twenty." Bienville described the terrain of this area as "a fine country of hills and groves intersected by a large number of small streams of very pure water." In addition to various agricultural products, Bienville believed that in the Natchez and lower Mississippi River area the colony could produce "all kinds of dressed timber," while "on the Mobile and Pascagoula Rivers and the shores of the sea, [the colony could turn out] masts, timber for shipbuilding, pitch and tar." However, he bemoaned the fact that the colony lacked workers for these enterprises.[49]

During this period the king of France encouraged his colonial administrators to "urge the settlers of Mobile to profit by the advantages that the pine forests offer them" by producing tar and pitch and to "make use of ship-building timber," arguing that "Commerce is in fact the most certain means for the increase of the colony and too great care can not be given to it." The king noted that the production of tar and pitch could become an "industry . . . of very great importance," telling his administrators to urge the colonists "to exploit ship building timber, timber for building houses and planks of spruce and cypress," because "it may contribute to the establishment of a coasting trade between the colony and the French islands." Early settlers discovered that the heartwood of dead pines was a rich source of pitch, used to waterproof the seams and sails of ships. To extract the pitch they cut and stacked the heartwood in earthen pits and boiled the pitch from the wood with slow-burning fires. The pitch then flowed into a barrel sunk in the ground outside of the circular pit. Tar was extracted from the pitch.[50]

Jean Baptiste Le Moyne, Sieur de Bienville, the governor of Louisiana, and Edme Gatien Salmon, the commissary general of Louisiana, wrote in 1733 to Jean Frederic Phelypeaux, Count de Maurepas, the minister of marine and colonies, that "several individuals of New Orleans" were prepared to ship to France two hundred barrels of tar "that they have had manufactured on the other side of Lake Ponchartrain where there are many pine forests." The colonial administrators reported the next year that "there are already three or four tarworks established on the other side of Lake Ponchartrain without counting those that people are preparing to build there. They expect to make at Mobile next year twelve to fifteen thousand barrels." They also noted the suspension of plans to obtain masts from the Mobile area and Dauphin Island, commenting, "Pines are so very numerous in this part of the government that there is no reason at all to fear that there would be a shortage of them; however, we have given orders that attention be given to the conservation of this timber."[51]

Another look at Mississippi in the French era is provided by Jean-Bernard Bossu, a French naval officer who, on two trips to the French colony, from 1751 to 1757 and from 1757 to 1762, traveled up the Mississippi Valley and into present-day Alabama. In his account of these journeys, Bossu describes some of the Native American groups he encountered, speculates on their origins, and describes the country, plants, and animals of the American interior. He comments on the plenitude and wide variety of fruit trees and "whole forests of nut trees. . . . There are trees in the forests which produce resin and tar, and gum similar to turpentine flows from others." He also notes, "There are a thousand species of curious, unknown animals, about whose existence the ancients never even dreamed." Of all of Louisiana's "curious and hitherto unknown animals," Bossu seems most struck by the fact that the "French settlers and the Indians make good use of the buffalo, a very large, strong animal. The meat is salted or smoked, and blankets are made of the hide. The bull is covered with very fine wool from which good mattresses are made, the suet is used for candles, and the sinews supply the Indians with string for their bows The horns are worked into spoons, with which the natives eat their corn meal mush, or into containers for their powder. The buffalo has a hump on its back like a camel, long hair on its head like a goat, and wool covering its body like a sheep. The Indian women spin this wool into yarn."[52]

The buffalo was a symbol of changes that occurred in the American interior between the time of the Spanish domination and the period of French control. The Native American population clearly had declined precipitously, probably, as mentioned above, as the result of diseases brought to the New World by Europeans and Africans. As one Frenchman put it, "Touching these savages, there is a thing that I cannot omit to remark to you, it is that it appears visibly that God wishes that they yield their place to new peoples." The process of change described by William Cronon for New England probably occurred in the Southeast as well:

As Indian villages vanished, the land on which they had lived began to change. Freed from the annual burnings and soon to be subject to an entirely different agricultural regime, the land's transformations were often so gradual as to be imperceptible. But a few changes were directly attributable to the depopulation caused by the epidemics. Fields which had still stood in grass when the Pilgrims arrived in 1620 were rapidly being reclaimed by forest by the time of the 1630 Puritan migrations to Massachusetts. . . . Some Indian fields were rapidly overgrown by the strawberries and raspberries in whose abundance colonists took so much delight, but these were an old-field phenomenon that would not reproduce themselves for long without the growing conditions Indians had created for them. When the Puritan migrations began, the animals that had relied on the Indians to maintain their edge habitats were still abundant beyond English belief, but in many areas the edges were beginning to return to forest. Declining animal populations would not be noticed for many years, but habitat conditions were already shifting to produce that effect.[53]

The buffalo represented the other side of the process. They had not been seen east of the Mississippi River by the de Soto expedition, yet by the time of the French they were present in great numbers. A reasonable assumption is that what ecologists call an econiche had opened, allowing the great beasts to expand their range from the Rockies to the gulf and even the Atlantic. Why? How? Crosby postulates that "[s]omething had kept these animals out of the expanses of parklike clearings in the forest that periodic Amerindian use of fire and hoe had created. That something declined or disappeared after 1540. That something was, in all likelihood, the Amerindians themselves, who naturally would have killed the buffalo for food and to protect their crops."[54]

Another change had occurred among the Indians of the interior. As rivalry in North America between the European nations heated up, the Native Americans became allies, enemies, and trading partners in various combinations. However, one fact remained consistent. The Indians were becoming involved in an economic world that threatened their old ways of life. In particular, the fur trade encouraged them to overhunt the game of the region to acquire the manufactured goods on which Native Americans were becoming dependent. While agriculture remained their major source of food, hunting for the fur trade became increasingly important in the Indian economy.[55]

In the early 1760s the major powers finally reached the end of the long period of warfare

that had been waged both on the Continent and in America off and on for the better part of a century. Near the end of the Seven Years' War (called by the British in America the French and Indian War), the French ceded Louisiana west of the Mississippi and the Isle de Orleans, which included New Orleans, to the Spanish. In 1763 France turned over to the British the area east of the Mississippi River to the Appalachians and from below Baton Rouge to the Great Lakes. The area of present-day south Mississippi became part of the British province of West Florida, with its capital at Pensacola. The northern provincial boundary was originally at the 31st parallel, but it was extended northward in 1764, running from the confluence of the Yazoo and Mississippi Rivers eastward to the Chattahoochee. Three years later the boundary was pushed a little farther north, to 32° 30', to protect whites who had settled on or wanted to claim some of the rich land in the vicinity. Under the Proclamation of 1763, the English colonies were restricted to the area east of the Appalachians, with the area westward to the Mississippi, with the exception of West Florida, reserved for the Indians.[56]

West Florida's economic future was brightened by the fact that the Spanish, controlling the land west of the Mississippi River, only sporadically enforced their trade laws. The British were notorious for ignoring them, and the Paris Treaty of 1763 gave the British free navigation of the Mississippi. The Choctaws, who had been allies of the French, assembled for meetings with British officials at Mobile, and eventually agreements were struck defining the Indians' boundaries and forbidding encroachment by English settlers on Indian lands. The Choctaws surrendered their claims to lands along the coast and lower Mobile and Tombigbee Rivers. The agreements about settlements on Indian lands were soon flagrantly disregarded. For example, a colonial official in 1771 complained of traders who "have made and do continue to make settlements or Plantations in the very midst of their [Chickasaw] Country, and that to such an Extent as to afford such a Number of Negroe Slaves as require (as I am informed) an Overseer or Driver."[57]

During the British period the timbered lands of south Mississippi were utilized to produce staves for use by sugar plantations, naval stores that were exported, and ships at Pascagoula. The British also viewed the region along the Mississippi River as an important area for agriculture and trade, especially the fur trade of the interior. However, problems with the Tunica Indians, concerns about the Creeks in the east, the relative isolation of the area from the British capital at Pensacola, and internal wrangling prevented the British from undertaking development in the west. As late as 1766 "the West Florida Assembly reported that the Natchez fort lay 'useless and neglected.'"[58]

Problems with the Indians were inevitable, for by this time "[s]tragglers of every description, even at that day bearing the name of 'Crackers,' were drifting down into the new country from Virginia, Carolina, and Georgia in large numbers, and many of these . . . were guilty of depredations and cruelties of the most horrible nature in their intercourse with the Indians through whose lands they passed . . . and wanton attacks by the white stragglers upon the native inhabitants." In 1771 the province passed a law to deal with "many Licentious Persons who come hither thro' the Indian Nations from the other Provinces and commit great abuses, and prevent them in future from building Houses and Huts on the Lands of the Indians" and another measure to punish "vagabonds and other idle and disorderly Persons, and to prevent persons hunting on the Indian Grounds." However honorable their intentions, British officials obviously were having difficulties in preventing whites from encroaching on Indian rights. Further complicating matters, the Spanish in this period continued to send emissaries into the interior to forge relationships with the Choctaws and other tribes.[59]

Settlers began to filter into the region along the Mississippi in this period. Governor Peter Chester reported to his superiors in 1770, "I have also received information that there is a large party consisting of a considerable number of families now on their way thro the back Country to the Mississippi, who it is Natural to Suppose will apply for Lands when they arrive. . . . [D]uring their Rout they subsist chiefly on Venison, Bufflo and game which they kill, so that when they first arrive on the Mississippi, they are . . . destitute of almost every thing." The governor sought permission to assist the settlers and promote the development of the Mississippi River region: "By the best information I can collect the Climate on the Banks of the Mississippi is healthy, the Lands exceeding fertile, and produce great Quantities of Timber fit for Ship Building, and making of different kinds of Lumber. No Soil is more proper for the Cultivation of Rice, Indigo, Hemp and Corn. . . . Corn Provisions and Lumber can be supplied to our Islands in the West Indies for their rum Sugar and Molasses." Governor Chester theorized that many of the earliest settlers of the region would be "persons out of the reach of Law, that have infested the back parts of the Carolinas, Virginia and Pennsylvania, for some years past," who might be "the only Persons we can expect that will first attempt to settle an uninhabited Country, surrounded on all sides by numerous Tribes of Savages."[60]

Governor Chester enclosed a letter and deposition from the settlers at Natchez. The writer of the letter claimed, "I have all furniture for erecting a Saw-Mill and Grist Mill which I intend to erect Imediately if encouraged by your Excellency and Council." The deposition was that of Daniel Huay, who had guided the party down the Ohio and Mississippi Rivers to Natchez from the junction of the Muskingham and Ohio. Huay claimed that the settlers possessed many tools and implements and seed, plus "three Saws for a Saw Mill with Cranks and Gudgeons and proper Materials for Erecting both a Saw and Grist Mill." He also claimed that the soil of the Natchez vicinity was "the best and richest Land in his opinion and judgment that he ever saw, and he believes will produce Indigo, Rice, Hemp, Corn &ca. most plentifully." The generous assessment of the Natchez area was not uncommon. Phillip

Pittman, an army surveyor, described the Natchez area as "the finest and most fertile part of West Florida . . . a most delightful country of great extent, the prospect of which is beautifully varied by a number of little hills and fine meadows."[61]

Descriptions of the Choctaw country, other parts of the interior, and the Natchez region in the early 1770s under the British are also found in long narrative travel journals that became part of the official record. Among these is a description by an Edward Mease, who journeyed from Pensacola into the interior in 1770. Mease traveled overland to Mobile and then sailed along the gulf past Dauphin Island, Cat Island, Horn Island, Ship Island, and the Chandeliers and Isle Breton before entering the Mississippi River channel. After traveling up to New Orleans, where Mease's party spent several days, the group sailed northeastward across Lake Ponchartrain, through the Rigolets, and thence to the mouth of the Pearl River. Traveling up the river, they found that the "Land here is not extraordinary high but seemingly fertile upon the Banks and back it is Pine Barren, the Trees of which are large & fit for Turpentine." They visited the home of Mr. Favre, who was the Indian interpreter at the Congress at Mobile in 1765 and who "makes a good deal of Tar, his Barrels . . . are shipped to the Bayou de St. Jean where they are sold to the Merchants of New Orleans." Mease reported that on the "Eastern side of this River as far as I went up the Land is extremely low & generally overflown as is likewise the Western side unless where a Bluff prevents it."[62]

After examining the lower Pearl River, Mease returned across Lake Ponchartrain to New Orleans. The party then started up the Mississippi River by canoe, and among other things, Mease saw "many Saw Mills." From Manchac (Fort Bute) the party traveled eastward to the mouth of the Amite River, went up that stream some distance, and then traveled back to the Mississippi. Two days from Natchez, Mease describes the land along the river as "Willowy in Front & Canes and Briars alternately. . . . The Main Land . . . cover'd with Gum Trees and Briars, Canes &ea." The

next day he noted, "The Land [is] always fine but bluffish & willowy alternately. . . . I walk'd into the Country. The Land in Front Canes for about 20 Yards, then Bulrush then tolerable clear Land with Tall Trees, such as Ash, Willow, Gum &ea and some Trees fit for Pot Ash." Along the river he found steep cliffs whose summit "is cover'd with Scrubby Pines."[63]

In Natchez Mease described the view from the deserted Fort Panmure (formerly Fort Rosalie) as "as noble and extensive a Prospect as can gratify the eye. Looking Eastward you see a Country Land not gradually rising into Hills but a fine undulating Country which even the celebrated Campania of Rome cannot exceed in Beauty. . . . To the S. East I saw several Smokes, where I conceive the Inhabitants mostly reside." On a trip into the countryside, Mease "met with a great deal of clear'd Land of an extreme rich Quality which had been lately planted. Met with several Old Fields, with broken Potsherds upon them (the Vestiges of their ancient Inhabitants) and remark'd the Trees to be of an extraordinary Magnitude, and mostly hard Wood such as Oaks, Wahoos [American elm] &ca." On another side trip, Mease found "Canes of an amazing Magnitude. The Soil equal to any I ever saw in my life. Found many Potsherds on the Old Fields which are remarkably well cleared." Traveling farther in the Natchez vicinity, Mease found "Old Fields, then level Land with some few Hills with Potsherds on them. The Trees which I mostly found in this Part were The Elm or Wahoo, Beech, various kinds of Oak, Linden, Black Walnut amazingly large, Hickory, Pecan which yields an oblong kind of Walnut & is much esteem'd, Holly, Yew, Juniper, Large Sassafras & very high, Gum, Ash, Maple or Sycamore, Locus, Magnolia, Plumb and Vines of a prodigious Magnitude." Mease reported "Beating through Canes which from their Size and Multitude made our way almost impracticable," after which "we came to St. Catherines Creek or a Branch of it which we cross'd with some difficulty."[64]

Continuing his explorations around Natchez, Mease describes the land of Lord Eglintown as "one of the finest Tracts I ever saw, a great Part is cleared, I mean so well that there are no Stumps or Roots to impede the Progress of the Plough. Upon some of the Eminences are Bosquets or Clumps of Pine Trees which seem to have been left expressly both as Shade for Cattle and the Adornment of the Country. The Old Fields as they are called (altho' there appear no signs of Inclosure) are cover'd with Strawberry Plants & various Flowers of the brightest Hues. . . . Wild Turkeys, Geese, Ducks, and all Aquatick Game is in conceivable abundance."[65]

Mease then set out in company with several other men for the Amite River. The party "proceeded over fine Land like the Natchez, then to Land mix'd with Pine, then to Pine Barren. The Country frequently much broken. . . . The Country all Pine Barren mix'd with small Oaks & Holly Trees. At Noon came to a Creek, the Land about which is level and full of Evergreens." They "Pass'd on through Pine Land" and crossed the Amite River. Then they "Pass'd on to where it is generally said there are the last Canes" and through country Mease described as "high Pine Barren with gravelly Hills," before they crossed the "Tangipao" (Tangipahoa), where the "Country still [is] Pine Barren with gravelly Hills and in the Bottoms tolerable good Land." The next day they "traveled through a Country still Pine Barren, but much more level" before reaching the "River of Pearl."[66]

Mease traveled up the Pearl, into Choctaw country, and then back down to Favre's residence, from whence he sailed back to Mobile. On the way up Mease found "the Land low & full of Oaks, then Pine Barren mixed with Oak, the Country not so hilly as formerly." After traveling through "low Oak Land with a few Pine Hills intervening alternately, We came to a most beautiful cleared Place, then to another." After more travel "over high Land cover'd with small Oaks, Pines, Elms &ca" they reached the Choctaw country.[67]

Mease's party encountered "a low Swampey Cane Break" and then traveled through "Hills & Vales." Then they came to "an Indian hunting Camp where we found many Peach Trees & some cleared Land." As their journey continued, Mease's group encountered "several Hills & Vallies" and then "pass'd through Oak Land mixed with Pines for about a League," until the end of the next day found them "at least five Days Journey from the Habitations on Mobile River." The following day they "came to a large Creek called 'Taliahatche,'" whose banks were "fertile." Then they "pass'd through a hilly Pine Barren Country, mixed with Oak, where we met with a great deal of Lime Stone & Rock." Next they "traveled . . . through a very fine Country, cover'd mostly with Oaks, mixed with Pines and Wahoos" into "a most charming Country, cover'd with Oaks, Beech, Wahoos, & a few Pines here & there." Then they crossed "some high Hills," followed by a swamp, and after passing through "a hilly Country cover'd with Oaks & Pines," they came to some "Natural Fields, the Grass of which having been burnt this Year made them look extremely pleasant." A trader told them they were five days from Mobile.[68]

Mease pressed on "through a hilly Country with here & there some beautiful Vallies, The Trees Oaks & Pines, Alternately, but generally mixed." He came to "Hills cover'd entirely with Oaks," and then "Proceeded through Pine Barrens mixed with small Oaks, sometimes Hilly & sometimes low swampy Land." On the following day Mease "proceeded through Pine Barrens for about a League." Then it was on through more pine barrens, cane breaks, swamps, bay galls, a "beautiful Meadow," and an area "cover'd with Pines and Scrubby Oaks." After finally moving through yet another "Pine Barren and Scrubby Oaks" and "Several fine Cane Breaks," Mease's party reached the residence of Simond Favre. Then it was on to Mobile by water, followed by a return to Pensacola.[69]

Even in this highly edited form Mease's narrative is repetitious but valuable. It provides a good detailed description of the land and forest over a considerable territory ranging across South Mississippi from Natchez to the Alabama border, up the Mississippi River from Louisiana to Natchez, and up the Pearl River into the southern Choctaw country. In the late eighteenth century, if Mease's description is accurate, this was an area of widespread pine barrens, large cane breaks, numerous Indian old fields and other "meadows," and extensive mixed hardwood and pine and hardwood forests. It had clearly felt the impact of Native American burning over the past decades.

More concise, but equally valuable, Bernard Romans's "Attempt Towards a Short Description of West Florida," was prepared for provincial officials in 1773. Noting that whatever he could say of the Mississippi River would be a "needless repetition," Romans begins his account with a description of the Pearl River, whose sources, he says, "encircle together with the branches of the Tombeckbe river, the whole Chactaw nation, and the sources of Pasca Oocoloo" (Pascagoula) River. "Its upper region," said Romans, "certainly yields to none in fertile grounds." He said that it is reputed to have along its course "equally good soil, as that which we see where it first springs," but notes that this description was based on "vague accounts from the hunters reports." Romans also reported that the Pearl "is known to be capable of admitting very considerable craft."[70]

Romans traced the Bouge Pasca Oocoloo "from its first original spring down to its confluence with the Bouge Aithee Tannee (vulgarly called Backatanne), which after receiving another not at all inconsiderable branch call Bougue Chitto, running between the Pasca Oocoloo and said Bouge Aithee Tannee . . . joins the Pasco Oocoloo below the Chactaw Nation about 170 miles directly north from said gulph." He said that none of these rivers or streams was "yielding to the first in fertility" and noted that the Choctaw Nation was called the "nation of bread" because of its "tilling of its fertile grounds" around the headwaters of the Bouge Pasca Oocoloo. Concerning navigability, which would be important both for farmers and for lumbermen, Romans said that it is better than in the Pearl, noting that a vessel built in Chicasahay, two hundred miles from the sea, was large enough to transport "600 bushels

of corn, besides a considerable quantity of Deer skins."[71]

Romans dismissed "the Iberville, Amite, Tungippoho and Chafuncto, all now beginning to be inhabited, & not without much reason, their fertility is much boasted of," although "they are of short course & never yet been explored." However, he eloquently assessed West Florida's forests: "In Timber no Country on earth can surpass it either in quantity, quality or variety. The quantity is such as makes it absolutely impossible to describe to an European who has not seen the like, and indeed it is beyond the conception of an inhabitant of any part of that quarter of the world; where such vast and continued forests and desarts are utterly unknown. . . . the live Oak, Juniper, Cedar & yellow pine are not to be equalled any where, and are a vast and inexhaustible mine for the building of those so necessary vehicles to Great Britain, Vizy., ships of all kinds whether for war or trade."[72]

An assessment of parts of the Mississippi region by a contemporary of Romans's provides an evaluation of a wider expanse of territory. James Adair, a Charleston, South Carolina-based trader among the Catawba, Cherokee, and Chickasaw from the mid-1730s until nearly 1770, published a history of the southern Indians in London in 1775.[73]

Adair offers a glowing assessment of the territory north and west of the Choctaw Nation to the Mississippi River: "The rest of the land is sandy pine barrens, till within forty miles of the Choktah contry, where the oak and the hiccory-trees first appear; from whence it is generally very fertile, for the extensive space of about six hundred miles toward the north, and in some places, two hundred and fifty, in others two hundred and sixty in breadth, from the Missisipi. This tract far exceeds the best land I ever saw besides in the extensive American world. . . . From the small rivers, which run throgh this valuable large tract, the far-extending ramifications are innumerable; each abounding with evergreen canes and reeds, which are as good to raise cattle in winter, and the best hay in the northern colonies. I need not mention the goodness of the summer-ranges; for, where the land is good, it always produces varius sorts of good timber, such as oak of different kinds; hiccory, wall-nut, and poplar trees." While noting that the area of West Florida close to the sea was "very low, sour, wet, and unhealthy," Adair observed that "it abounds with valuable timber for ship-building, which could not well be expended in the long space of many centuries." He goes on to report,

The land near the sea, is, in general, low and sandy . . . to a considerable extent from the sea-shore, when the lands appear fertile, level, and diversified with hills. Trees indicate the goodness or badness of land. Pine-trees grow on sandy, barren ground, which produces long coarse grass; the adjacent low lands abound with canes, reeds, or bary and laurel of various sorts, which are shaded with large expading trees— they compose an evergreen thicket, mostly impenetrable to the beams of the sun, where the horses, deer, and cattle, chiefly feed during the winter: and the panthers, bears, wolves, wild cats and foxes, resort there both for the sake of prey, and a cover from the hunters. Land of a loose black soil, such as those of the Missisippi, are covred with fine grass and herbage, and well shaded with large and high trees of hicory, ash, white, red, and blackoaks, great towering poplars, black walnut-trees, sassafras, and vines.[74]

Adair then turns to the lands of the Mississippi River region and provides this detailed description:

The low wet lands adjoining the river, chiefly yield cypress-trees, which are very large, and of a prodigious height. On the dry grounds is plenty of beach, maple, holly, the cotton-tree, with a prodigious variety of other sorts. But we must not omit the black mulberry-tree, which, likewise, is plenty. It is high, and, if it had proper air and sun-shine, the boughs would be very spreading. On the fruit, the bears and wild fowl feed during their season; and also swarms of paroquets, enough to defen one with their chattering, in the time of those joyful repasts. . . . On the hills, ther is plenty of chesnut-trees, and ches-nut-oaks. These yield the largest sort of acorns, but wet weather soon spoils them. In winter, the deer and bears fatten themselves on various kinds of nuts, which lie thick over the rich land, if the blossoms have not been blasted by the north-east winds. The wild turkeys live on the small red acorns, and grow so fat in March, that they cannt fly farther than three or four hundred yards; and not being able soon to take the wing again, we speedily run them down with our horses and hunting mastiffs. At many unfrequented places of the Missisippi, they are so tame as to be shot with a pistol. . . . There is plenty of wild parsley, on the banks of that river, the roots of which are as large as those of parsnips, and it is as good as the other sort. The Indians say, they have not seen it grow in any woods remote from their country. They have a large sort of plums, which their ancestors brought with them from South America, and which are now become plenty among our colonies, called Chikkash plums. . . . To the North West, the Missisippi lands are covered with filberts, which are as sweet, and thin-shelled, as the sealy bark hiccory-nuts. Hazel-nuts are very plenty, but the Indians seldom eat them. Black haws grow here in clusters, free from prickles: and pissimmons, of which they make very pleasant bread, barbicuing it in the woods. There is a sort of fine plums in a few places, large, and well-tasted; and, if transplanted, they would become better. The honey- locusts are pods about a span-long, and almost two inches broad, containing a row of large seed on one side, and a tough sweet substance the other. The tree is large, and full of long thorns; which forces the wild beasts to wait till they fall off, before they can gather that part of their harvest.—The trees grow in wet sour land, and are plenty, and the timber is very durable. Where there is no pitch-pine, the Indians use this, or the sassafras, for posts to their houses; as they last for generations, and the worms never take them. Chinquapins are very plenty, of the taste of chesnuts, but much less in size. There are several sorts of very wholesome and pleasant-tasted ground nuts, which few of our colonists know any thing of. In wet land, there is an aromatic red spice, and a sort of cinnamon, which the natives seldom use.[75]

Adair also observes, "As in Florida, so to a great distance from the shore of the gulph, the lands generally consist of burning sand, and uninhabitable, or wet ground, and very unhealthy. But a little beyond this dreary desert, are many level spots very fertile. . . . [T]he air is exceedingly pure in the high lands of this extensive tract. The soil is generally very rich." Adair also describes the territory between the Mississippi River and Alabama:

There is a number of extensive and fertile Savannas, or naturally clear land, between the Missisippi and the western branches of Mobille river. They begin about two hundred and fifty miles above the low lands of the coast, and are interspersed with the woods to a great distance, probably three hundred miles. The inland parts are unknown to any but the Indians and the English traders—the warlike Chikkasah were so dreadful to the French, that even their fleet of large trading boats avoided the eastern side of the Missisippi . . . for the space of two hundred leagues: so that, beyond what they barely saw from their boats, their accounts of the interior parts of this extensive country, are mere conjectures. The soil of the clear land, generally consists of loose rich mould to a considerable depth, and either a kind of chalk, or marl, underneath. We frequently find the grass with its seeded tops as high as our heads, when on horseback, and very likely it would bear mowing, three or four times in one season. As the Indians gather their wild hemp, in some of these open fertile lands, both it and our hemp would grow to admiration, with moderate tillage: and so would tobacco, indigo, cotton, and flax, in perfecction.[76]

The picture of Mississippi that emerges from official reports, travelers' descriptions, and other sources during the period of British control in the mid- to late eighteenth century is not surprising. In the lower areas near the gulf the land consisted of swamps, lowlands, and pine barrens. Moving northward through the Choctaw nation, the forest cover changed to mixed pines and hardwoods, while farther north in the Chickasaw territory, hardwood forests dominated. Everywhere, the signs of Indian occupation and agricultural techniques, especially burning, remained much in evidence. The woods were open, brush was minimal, and there were both savannas or open meadows and "old fields," which had once been cultivated by the Native Americans. Most observers agreed that much of the land was fertile and suitable for agriculture and that the forests offered economic potential as well. They were not, however, primeval or virgin forests: they had been significantly altered by human activity.

The American Revolution triggered an exodus of Loyalists from the Atlantic seaboard that more than doubled the population of the area from the mouth of the Yazoo to Manchac over the next four years. New settlements appeared at Bayou Pierre, Big Black River, and Walnut Hills. During the revolution the Spanish declared war on England and in 1779 captured Natchez, lost it to rebels, and took it again in 1781 in the wake of their capture of Pensacola. The Treaty of Paris ending the revolution established the southern boundary of the United States at the 31st parallel (the boundary between present-day Mississippi and Louisiana), although the Spanish controlled the land up to the mouth of the Yazoo River at 32° 26'. The treaty of the same period between Britain and Spain recognized Spanish control of West Florida without defining its northern border. The stage was set for territorial conflict between the new United States and Spain, as both countries claimed the area between the 31st parallel and the Yazoo. It was also significant that Britain and the United States recognized the rights of citizens of both countries to navigate the Mississippi River to its mouth. In fact, the Spanish controlled the lower river by possessing West Florida and Louisiana. Spain refused to recognize the British-American understanding and in 1784 closed the lower Mississippi to American navigation.[77]

The Spanish created the Natchez District, with borders similar to those under the British. But while Spanish and American officials disputed the territory, Georgia also claimed the region on the basis of its colonial charter. In 1789 the state sold lands in the northern part of the Natchez District. Later sales under questionable conditions led to considerable controversy and confusion regarding titles in what were sometimes called the Yazoo Lands, and in 1802 Georgia finally relinquished its western claims to the federal government. The Spanish reached an agreement with the Choctaws, who in 1790 allowed the Spaniards to build a fort near the 32° 30' line. The settlement was called Fort Nogales and was located at Walnut Hills near present-day Vicksburg. In 1795 under Pinckney's Treaty (the Treaty of San Lorenzo), the United States gained control of the east bank of the Mississippi River above the 31st parallel, plus free navigation of the Mississippi River and the right of deposit at New Orleans.[78]

In 1798 the Spanish government commissioned Sir William Dunbar to locate and survey the area along the 31st parallel. Leading a survey party down to the Mississippi River bank, Dunbar calculated that on the opposite bank "the height of the highest trees is 150 feet, 10.8 inches." Dunbar on August 28 observed that the boundary line had "now been carried . . . to the distance of about eighteen miles from the River Mississippi, including the whole of the cultivated lands." Dunbar, an enthusiastic amateur botanist, offered a detailed description of the plant and animal life of the area near the river: "We were infested with innumerable swarms of Gnats, and a variety of other Stinging and biting insects. . . . [T]he surface of the earth teemed with life . . . of the most disgusting forms and noxious kinds. . . . Serpents of the waters frequently entwined in clusters to the number of several hundreds, a vast variety of toads, frogs, including the bull-frog and the thundering Crocodile, all of hideous forms, with a multitude of others too tedious to mention. . . . [T]he face of the high country was covered with cane . . . growing so thick and strong, that it was impossible to penetrate through them but by the aid of edge tools." Dunbar also provided detailed descriptions of the trees in the Natchez District, starting with the cypress:

In passing through the portion of low grounds lying between the hills and the River bank I observed the following to be the most conspicuous productions of the Vegetable kingdom, Viz: The Cypress (Cupressus) both red and white, of which the former is the more valuable for strength and durability . . . its wood being impregnated with a considerable portion of Resin. . . . [T]he heart of the red wood when planted as a post or stake in the ground immediately after being cut down, is said to endure for three score year before it is impaired by putrefaction. This tree delights to grow in low grounds frequently overflown. . . . [T]he finest trees often ascend to the elevation of 130 or 140 feet. . . . The cypress timber is the most useful of any to the Inhabitants of this Country, being preferred before all others for house building, furnishing beams, scantling, planks and shingles of the best kind and rives advantageously into clap-boards, for the purpose of making handsome post and rail fencing, and inferior houses; the use, however, of this valuable timber is restricted to those who live within a moderate distance of the river swamps, being never found growing upon uplands. It is remarkable, that it is extremely difficult to rive this timber across the heart, but lifts into concentric boards with great facility.[79]

Dunbar then describes "A species of the White oak . . . found growing on ridges lying between lakes and ponds bordered by Cyprus": "The quality of this Oak is scarcely inferior to live Oak, its wood being of a very compact, solid grain, and extremely ponderous, it extends its boughs to a great distance on all sides and might furnish an inexhaustible store of curves or knees for ship-building. . . . [T]his species of Oak I have never found growing on high lands. . . . A species of the red oak, or rather black oak, growing on lands more elevated than the last has nothing remarkable in it, being found indifferently on high or low lands." Found "chiefly along the banks of the Mississippi and often where the depth of the inundation is very considerable" was the "Liarre, cotton tree or Water Poplar," which "appears to be the same with the Lombardy Poplar." Dunbar said, "Nature has wisely ordered that the growth of this tree from the seed is so extremely quick that from the end of one Inundation to the commencement of the next the young tree always surmounts the succeeding high water, and is the chief means used by nature to secure annually many thousands of acres of new formed lands of our American Nile, which otherwise might be washed away by succeeding floods. One of these trees growing single in the most favorable situation, has been known to arrive in the course of one season to the almost incredible hight of 30 feet. In other particulars this wood is of small value to our country, being soft and not durable . . . but [it] grows to so enormous a size that hunters, who fetch down wild-beef, &c., to the market of New Orleans, form rough boats of a single piece, which are sometimes 6 or 7 feet wide, but commonly from 4 to 5, joining 2 or 3 together."[80]

Dunbar also mentioned sycamores and willows as native to the river country, and like so many other travelers in the interior, he was impressed by the size of the "bamboo Cane [which] is found growing in all situations where the general rise of the innundation does not exceed 2 feet." Said Dunbar, "Those young canes which proceed from the Old Roots grow . . . in a manner surprisingly rapid, insomuch that in one month in an open new cleared field, they will reach the size and height of the old canes, which is from 15 to 35 feet according to the quality of the soil."[81]

Dunbar next discussed some of the animal denizens of the forest, including the panther, black bear, wolf, fox, "short-tailed Wild Cat" (Mink), and alligator. He then enumerated and described "the productions of the high land": "One of the Grandest and most admirable productions is the Magnolia Major. . . . It is one of the most perfect of ever greens . . . but I do not know that any discovery has been made of its utility in medicine or otherwise. Its wood becomes very hard and solid when worked up and preserved under cover, but little used, on account of the superiority of other timber equally common."[82]

The next tree described was "a noble tree called the Yellow Poplar, preserving its size and rotundity to a vast height without branches re-sembling a majestic pillar. . . . The tract along which we pass on the high ground furnishes a good variety of lofty and majestic trees. . . . The Acacia or Locust, the black Mulberry, Wild Cherry, the Black Walnut, the Sassafras are produced abundantly and are extremely serviceable to the Inhabitants for the value and durability of their Timber. The Wild Cherry when large enough to yield plank fit for furniture, rivals the mahogany in the diversity of its beautiful veins and the elegance of its polish." Dunbar also provided a long list of "vegetable productions of the high lands," some of which were marked to indicate that they were found in lowlands as well. This list included trees, vines, grasses, berries, and other plants or products. He also included a list of trees and plants cultivated by the inhabitants of the Mississippi Territory as well of the Spanish provinces. Dunbar's descriptions are valuable because of his acute eye, his comparisons to plants of other parts of the world, and his treatment of the breeding processes and growth cycles of some of the plants.[83]

Among the most famous travelers in Mississippi during the Spanish period was William Bartram, a botanist from Philadelphia, Pennsylvania. In 1791 Bartram traveled up the "Tombigbe," where he described a "swamp or low land" as "the richest I ever saw, or perhaps any where to be seen." He went on to say that the "Cypress, Ash, Platanus, Populus, Liqidambar, and others, are by far the tallest, straightest, and every way the most enormous that I have seen or heard of." "And as a proof of the extraordinary fertility of the soil," he declared, "the reeds or canes (Arundo gigantea) grow here thirty or forty feet high, and as thick as a man's arm, or three or four inches in diameter." He concluded, "I suppose one joint of some of them would contain above a quart of water; and these reeds serve very well for setting poles, or masts for barks and canoes." Bartram said that he passed by "the most delightful and fertile situations: observed frequently on bluffs of high land, deserted plantations, the houses always burnt down to the ground, and ancient Indian villages." Bartram also described the

Choctaw as "most ingenious and industrious hus-bandmen, having large plantations, or country farms, where they employ much of their time in agricultural improvements, after the manner of the white people; by which means their territories are more generally cultivated and better inhabited than any other Indian republic we know of."[84]

Another traveler into the interior in this period was Francis Baily, the twenty-one-year-old son of an English banker. Baily in the winter of 1796–97 traveled down the Ohio and Mississippi Rivers to New Orleans and returned via Indian trails. Baily entered what is today the state of Mississippi via the Mississippi River, stopping at the Chickasaw Bluffs (Memphis), providing interesting descriptions of the area's Indians. Traveling down the river, he was impressed by "the enormous poplar-trees which line the banks of this river. It is called the cotton-tree by the natives, from the quantity of downy substance (like cotton) which is scattered from its fruit-stalks at the time of a high wind. . . . They are of an amazing height, and of great thickness at the bottom, and cover the banks of this river, particularly at the lower parts of it, for a considerable distance." His comments on the Natchez area, where he declared "the land around is of an excellent quality," include a report on the value of property: "Land in the country is sold for about a dollar an acre: a five-acre lot close to the town sold for 150 dollars." "Dr Watrous (our fellow-passenger)," he reported, "bought a lot of 150 acres of uncleared land near the town for four-dollars per acre, and it was thought cheap."[85]

Writing in New Orleans, Baily said, "The trade of this place consists principally in the exportation of deer and bear skins, beaver furs, cotton, lumber, rice, and various other articles." He described the process of securing the lumber in interesting detail:

The article of lumber . . . is procured in the follow-ing manner:—The owners of the saw-mills in this neighbourhood send a number of men up the Missis-sippi at the proper season, to cut down timber on its banks. This timber, which is very fine and in very great

abundance, and which is had for the mere trouble of fetching it, is cut down before the floods descend, af-ter which time, and when the banks are overflowed, they go up and without any difficulty bring all their logs (which are now floating) to the river, where they form a raft of them, and let them drift down the stream to the saw-mill. At that place a number of men stand ready with ropes and hawsers to tow the raft to the shore, where it is cut up into planks, scantlings, &c. However, great care is necessary in conducting it down the river, as it is totally unmanageable when it gets into a strong current: and if suffered to come near the shore, the raft would inevitably be broken to pieces; or if it got within the suck of the Shuffle, it would undoubtedly be lost for ever.[86]

As Baily returned northward by land toward Natchez, he traveled through "200 miles; not above forty miles of which may be said to be in-habited." North of Lakes Ponchartrain and Mau-repas he saw "signs of persons having been there to make pitch, tar, turpentine, & from these trees; these articles they take to New Orleans, and turn to a good account." The area through which he traveled was "for the most part a light, sandy soil, and overgrown throughout its whole extent with large tall pines; very little of any other kind of wood being seen here, except on the immediate banks of the rivers. . . . These pines are of the species which is called by the inhabitants 'pitch pine,'" said Baily, "and [they] grow to an *enor-mous height and vast size*: they are bare of branches to near their tops; so that in traveling through them they appear like a grove of large masts." Baily described his party building fires against the "enormous trunks" using fuel from downed trees and "scattered limbs." He noted, "So exceedingly inflammable are these trees, that I have oftentimes laid a small fire at their roots when they have been standing in the ground, and in a few minutes this vast pine of wood has been enveloped in flames." Said Baily, "we have been sometimes frightened at the works of our own hands."[87] Native Americans and white pio-neers must have had similar experiences as they used fire in the forests of the interior.

Leaving Natchez in early July, on July 7 Baily reached Grindstone Ford, "about sixty miles from Natchez . . . the most northern frontier settlement in the district." Moving along trails across Mississippi from Natchez to the Pontotoc area, Baily said, "Our general course . . . seemed to be about east-north-east or north-east-by-north. The land . . . appeared to get gradually worse and worse as we proceeded from Natchez. Instead of that fine black mould immediately in the vicinity of the town, every day's journey exposed a more sandy and gravelly soil."[88]

Baily warned readers that "the general nature of the soil of the country is not to be taken from the particular parts through which we traveled as these paths are generally carried over the highest and consequently the worst, ground, in order to prevent swamps and other impediments arising from a low situation."[89]

In the course of the journey, Baily's group stopped at a Chickasaw settlement. Describing the habitation of an old man who fed them, Baily said, "This man's dwelling was situated upon an eminence from which he could behold the surrounding country for a great way. His fields consisted of corn planted irregularly through a kind of *natural meadow;* for they are too indolent to form a settlement where the country requires to be cleared." Baily said that in the winter the old man would range far afield, "traversing the continent with his family," hunting, and in the spring he would return and plant another crop of corn. However, if another "had arrived there before him, instead of contesting the point of right with him, he would go to another place unoccupied."[90]

Near an Indian settlement in the vicinity of present-day Pontotoc, Baily again addressed Native American agricultural practices: "we observed the remains of several Indian plantations, which appeared to have been cultivated for a few years, and then left a prey to time and nature. The few peach and apple trees which the owner had planted were overrun with weeds, and left to be enjoyed by the first possessor." Baily described the town as "in a large open prairie lying in a valley, the uncouth huts of the Indians, contrasted with the fertile corn-fields, presented a beautiful view." In the town between "these clusters of habitations the space was occupied by cornfields, which were fenced round with a rough kind of inclosure, formed partly of posts, and partly of light poles running from one post to another. Some of the houses . . . had gardens, which were fenced round much in the same manner as their fields, and in which they planted a few fruit-trees and some vegetables, such as pumpkins, squashes, &c." From the Pontotoc vicinity, the group moved northeastward toward the Tennessee River and out of the Mississippi region.[91]

The descriptions of travelers and surveyors in Mississippi during the Spanish era repeat a familiar story. Their descriptions are remarkably similar to those of the French and British periods. They tell of a southern region dominated by pine forests, with some lumbering and naval stores activities along the Mississippi River. The region around Natchez was fertile and covered with mixed forests. To the north and east the land remained forested but was of a lower quality. All across Mississippi the forest was broken by meadows and clearings that were created by Indian agricultural activities over the eons. The face of the land encountered by American pioneers as Mississippi became a U.S. territory and moved toward statehood was well established. In the next few years the outlines of the present state of Mississippi were filled in through actions of Congress, warfare, and the cession of Indian lands. Travelers continued to marvel at the future state's wooded resources, and pioneer farmers followed in the footsteps of their Indian predecessors, hacking and burning farms out of the forests and tilling the open lands. Pioneer lumbermen utilized the forests for lumber, naval stores, and other products.

2   Pioneers

Early Farmers Clear the Forests

On March 30, 1798, the Spanish flag came down and the United States took possession of Natchez. A little more than a week later, Congress created the Mississippi Territory. The territory included the Natchez District plus territory eastward to the Chattahoochee. The strip of territory along the Gulf Coast below the 31st parallel remained in Spanish West Florida and would not become part of the United States until 1812, when it was annexed in the wake of the West Florida Revolution of 1810. On the north the Mississippi Territory was bounded by a line running due east of the mouth of the Yazoo River. In 1804 the northern area up to the Tennessee line was added. When the state of Mississippi entered the union in 1817, the eastern half of Mississippi Territory became the Alabama Territory.[1]

The growth of the Mississippi Territory in the early nineteenth century was rapid as Native American lands were opened to settlement and pioneers poured in. The Treaty of Ft. Adams in 1801 established the right of whites to settle in the old Natchez District. Four years later the first Choctaw cession in the Treaty of Mount Dexter opened another section of present-day southern Mississippi. Near the end of the territorial period in 1816, the Chickasaws surrendered an area in the upper Tombigbee Valley along the Alabama border. In 1820 came the second Choctaw cession in the Treaty of Doak's Stand, which opened

land in central Mississippi and the lower Delta. This cession opened nearly 5.5 million acres of land to white settlement. Next came the Treaty of Dancing Rabbit Creek, the third Choctaw cession, which turned over all remaining Choctaw lands east of the Mississippi River to the United States. This cession opened to white settlement a large area running eastward from the middle Delta into north Mississippi. Finally, in 1832 an agreement was reached whereby the Chickasaws surrendered their titles east of the Mississippi River in the Treaty of Pontotoc, opening the northernmost section of Mississippi to white settlement. The state of Mississippi, with its present borders, was now totally open to white pioneers and settlers.[2]

As in the earlier periods of European contact, travelers during the territorial period and the years of early statehood were enormously impressed by Mississippi's lands and forests. In 1801, only three years after its creation, the first history of the Mississippi Territory appeared in print. The author, James Hall, was a Presbyterian missionary sent by his church to the new territory. Hall's view of the land between Nashville and the Tennessee River was unfavorable, until "you reach the low grounds of Tennessee river." His party crossed the river at Colbert's Ferry, near the mouth of Bear Creek, where he reported "a body of excellent low ground on both sides of the river." Hall then traveled about ninety miles to

31

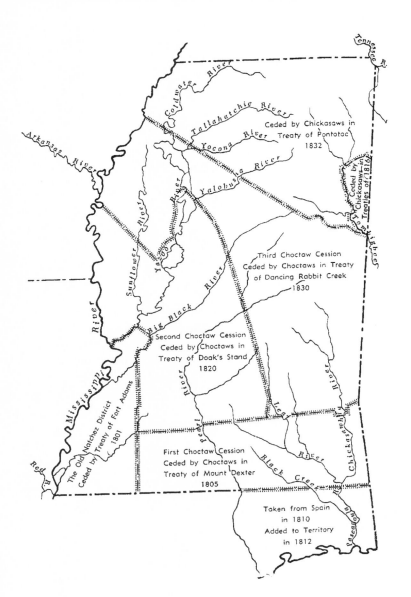

Map of Indian cessions, 1801–32. John K. Bettersworth, *Mississippi: A History* (Austin, Tex.: Steck, 1959), 176.

Labels within map:

Tennessee R.

Coldwater River

Tallahatchie River

Ceded by Chickasaws in Treaty of Pontotoc 1832

Yocona River

Ceded by Chickasaws in Treaties of 1816

Arkansas River

Yalobusha River

Yazoo River

Sunflower River

Third Choctaw Cession Ceded by Choctaws in Treaty of Dancing Rabbit Creek 1830

Big Black River

Mississippi River

Second Choctaw Cession Ceded by Choctaws in Treaty of Doak's Stand 1820

Pearl River

Leaf River

Chickasawhay River

The Old Natchez District Ceded by Treaty of Fort Adams 1801

First Choctaw Cession Ceded by Choctaws in Treaty of Mount Dexter 1805

Red R.

Black Creek

Pascagoula River

Taken from Spain in 1810 Added to Territory in 1812

the Chickasaw towns, through "great quantities of low grounds, abounding with excellent oak timber," and "some flats of good hickory land." Hall's narrative reflects the reduction in size of the Native American population and the tendency of Indian settlements to move frequently. Reaching the Chickasaws' "Big Town," he commented, "It was once the residence of the whole nation; but the strength of the soil being exhausted, the greater part of the inhabitants have moved out and settled in other villages." Even as Hall trav-

eled in Mississippi, whites were beginning to argue that the Native Americans were savages and should be displaced so that their lands could be "developed" and "civilized." Ironically, the missionary reported that among the Chickasaws, "husbandry, and consequently civilization, is making considerable progress . . . and also among the other southern tribes. . . . The culture of cotton is making considerable advances among them. Gins were erected or erecting last spring in all the three southern nations; and it is probable that in a few years the cotton trade will be considerable among them. . . . Some of the Chickasaws are men of considerable property, have number of slaves and farm largely, particularly the Colberts."[3]

Hall traveled for a time on a ridge between the Big Black River and the "Tom Bigbee" and Pearl Rivers. He reported "beautiful flats of hickory land" and "soil of the first quality." However, he noted, "The greatest inconveniency which attends that country is the scarcity of timber; scarcely any to be seen on the best land except short-bodied hickory and some black-jack," although "the low grounds which are of an inferior quality abound with good timber." "As the traveller approaches the territory," Hall reported, "the timber becomes heavier, the land more hilly and covered with cane."[4]

Hall's *History* provides an excellent contemporary survey of Mississippi's lands:

Along the Mississippi lies a body of land from fifteen to twenty miles wide, and extends to a greater distance up the water courses, scarcely any of which can be termed barren. The high ground is much broken with sharpe ridges and deep-narrow vallies; but the low grounds, of which there is a very large proportion, are very level; nor are they broken with ponds or marshes. When the flood has receded from the low grounds, except some of the flooded land, there is scarcely an acre of marshy or wet ground to be seen. . . . Proceeding up the watercourses, the high land becomes more level, though not so fertile but covered with groves of beautiful timber. . . . [T]he stream of the river . . . is almost universally lined with tall and dense groves of cyprus, cotton wood, sycamore, &c. . . . The greater part of the territory abounds with vast quantities of lofty timber, except where the cane is large. On the high ground, where the soil is thin, the greater part is red-oak. On the low ground those grow to an immense size. My curiosity led me to measure two of them, one of which was 22½, and the other 26 feet in circumference three feet from the ground. Upon the rich land, high as well as low, the timber is chiefly of the swamp kind, such as walnut, cherry-tree, mulberry, elm, ash, hackberry, iron wood &c. . . . Towards the lower end

of the territory, such is the size and quantity of cane, even on the highest hills, that, to those who never saw it, a description would appear incredible, and in many places almost to the entire exclusion of timber, except a few scattered trees of walnut, mulberry &c. which indicate the excessive strength of the soil.[5]

Hall also offered another bit of interesting information, reporting that he had counted the rings of trees growing on various old fields in the territory and "found, without exception, the age of the oldest between 60 and 73 years." Hall was kinder in his descriptions of Mississippi's lands than of its people, whom he said under the British and Spanish were "the dregs of the more northern parts of the continent." He noted that because of the confusion concerning land claims in the territory, no land office had been opened by the American government, thus impeding immigration.[6]

Hall's generally favorable assessment of the territory was endorsed by most early-nineteenth-century observers. Writing from Natchez in 1802, one citizen said, "I find this to be the garden of all America and will soon be a place of importance to the States. . . . No part of the United States possesses more Local advantages than this District. . . . The soil [is] fertile, the Climate genial and production precious." Of course, early settlers had to be optimistic to survive, and they were often prone to braggadocio and exaggeration. For example, one pioneer Mississippian boasted, "If the first settlers of Eden had seen the 'Mississippi Bottoms' they would have located there a heap quicker than in the other place." On the other side of the territory, a more realistic writer reported to President Thomas Jefferson in 1804, "The country on the west side of the Mobile and Timbigbie is generally a Pine-barren of great extent, and will not for a considerable length of time become otherwise useful, than as range for cattle. . . . As we ascend the River, the land on the west side becomes better, and when we arrive at the hillyert country, it is said to be universally good on both sides, and . . . will, when the Indian title is extinguished, admit a vast population."[7]

Dr. Rush Nutt provided another valuable contemporary view of Mississippi in the early territorial period. A physician from Virginia, Nutt in 1805 set out on horseback for a year-long tour which took him through the states of Virginia, Tennessee, Kentucky, Missouri, Louisiana, Texas, and Mississippi. Nutt went by flat boat from St. Louis to New Orleans, from whence on July 19 he journeyed across Lake Ponchartrain and then by river and land to Natchez. From Natchez he traveled on foot along the Natchez Trace and into the Chickasaw and Choctaw nations. After returning to Virginia, Nutt relocated to Natchez, which became his home.[8]

On the way to Natchez from New Orleans, Nutt observed "many large & valuable plantations, with excellent . . . cotton." The inhabitants of Natchez he described as "from the Carolinas & Virginia mostly." On August 1 he left the territorial capital at Washington, six miles from Natchez, and set out for the Chickasaw nation. For two days "the land remained hilly . . . & also clothed with the like growth after crossing the indian line . . . [then] the land became more even & clothed with a small growth of hickory & oak (this was thin so that in many places the country might be call'd a prairie) pine was very common & . . . some were small . . . while a few were very large." Nutt reported that in the Choctaw nation, "some of them [are] building log houses & cultivating the earth in corn, cotton, & other garden vegetables. Some houses I found deserted with their detached corn fields."[9]

Near the Tombigbee River in the Black Belt, Nutt said, "the lands are level & mostly open prairies or savannas, & of a deep black soil clear of grit, superior to the timbered lands adjacent. Those prairies extend up [the] Tombigbee forty miles, in which are to be seen vestiges of ancient buildings and fortifications." Nutt traveled farther down the Tombigbee to Line Creek (which he called the Noosacheea) in Clay County, which the doctor identified as the boundary between the Chickasaws and Choctaws. Far up the Noosacheea, in the vicinity of the Natchez Trace, Nutt said, "the lands are broken, soil barren, timber

pine, post & black oak, in some places black jack & hickory. [L]ittle of the land for 18 or 20 miles fit for cultivation." Nearby, in the same general area, Nutt found the lands considerably better, with some hardwood timber, notably blackjack, white oak, post oak, and black hickory, and numerous well-tended farms and orchards, some owned by whites with Indian families, some by half-breeds, and some by Native Americans. Much of this land was prairie. Nutt reported that many Indians had moved "for the convenience of the range, water & timber . . . & have turned their attention to farming, manufacturing & raising of stock," and he periodically mentioned the existence of "old fields." Traveling into the extreme northeastern part of Mississippi, Nutt said, "The land is poor, broken & clothed with blackjack & post oak; except on the creeks, where the land is good, timber lofty, & fit for cultivation." From a ridge "dividing the waters of Tennessee from those of Tombigbee" to Bear Creek, Nutt said there was "high broken pine land" and "thin soil," but on Bear Creek, near present-day Margerum, Alabama, he reported "some excellent land."[10]

Nutt next described the route from the Chickasaw nation to the Chickasaw Bluff (Memphis), a distance of 120 miles. The first twenty-five miles he characterized as "tolerable level & good farming land." Reaching a branch of the "Tallahatchee" (Tallahatchie), he said the area was "high broken pine land, very little fit for cultivation." He noted that the Indians used it "for the benefit of range, as they have horses, cattle & hogs." Moving on to the main channel of the Tallahatchee, Nutt traveled through "very high, stony, pine hills," where "little of the land would answer for farming." However, he also found in the area of present-day Holly Springs "some rich prairies" where "many families of Indians have settled & are making good improvements." He reported, "The country for many miles around . . . lays well for farming. Soil, fine dark & deep with a rich mould. [C]lothed with black walnut, cherry, sugartree, maple, mulberry, oak & hickory." The territory between this area and the Chickasaw

Bluff he described as "a high & beautiful country." Twelve miles from the bluff, "the grassy woods cease, the ground [is] then covered with peavine & rich herbage, the land level, timber mostly blackoak, poplar, elm, & some few sugartrees."[11]

Moving southward, Nutt said that from the Chickasaw Bluff to the Yazoo River, "all the country, or nearly so . . . overflows annually & renders it of no value." But "[o]n the east side of the Yazoo, the land is said to be of the first quality."[12] It is clear from Nutt's descriptions of central and north Mississippi that by the early territorial period the land remained heavily influenced by Native American usage—a mosaic of forests and savannas, some heavily timbered, mostly in hardwoods, with very active farming activities by the Chickasaws and Choctaws. The soil ranged from very poor to excellent.

Among the most interesting and significant aspects of Nutt's account are his observations on Mississippi's Native Americans. After the enormous Indian population losses following European contact and at a time when white pressure for settlement and land was on the immediate horizon, Nutt found signs of a Native American population resurgence. Describing Indian marital practices, he reported, "Their marriages are now fruitfull, since they have settled out on farms. . . . [T]he nation has for some years increased, the children appear healthy, not confined to the old towns where disease[s] became epidemical & fatal." This good news for the Indians may in fact have been an ominous sign for their future relationship with the white pioneers. Contradicting many whites, who characterized the Native Americans as itinerant hunters and savages, Nutt observed, "The Indians are falling off from their former customs & habits very fast, as they are fast mixing with the whites. There are a great many half breed among the Chickasaws & Chactaws. . . . They are done with the hunt. The men have laid down their gun & tomahawk & taken up the implements of husbandry. The women have exchanged their little hoes & skin aprons, for spining wheels, & home manufac-

tured cloth." Nutt argued, "The Indian game never grew scarce before the europians introduced a trade with them & encouraged a peltry & fur trade. They now made havock among the innocent animals of the earth merely for the skins, & the flesh wasted. From this time the game has been on the decline & now they are compell'd to resort to husbandry & raising live stock."[13]

Nutt left Mississippi in September, setting out from the Chickasaw nation for Nashville. He crossed "much good land clothed with hickory & oak. The soil fine & black with a red-clay foundation." Coming to "Bier-Creek," twelve miles from the Tennessee River, Nutt found "a large settlement of Indians on both sides of this creek" whose "large stock of cattle &c. & whose corn fields have the appearance of much labour being spent to make them." After crossing the Tennessee River at Colbert's Ferry, Nutt traveled on toward Nashville.[14]

One of the best-known travelers in Mississippi during the territorial period was Christian Schultz. In 1808 Schultz journeyed down the Mississippi River, leaving St. Louis in March and reaching Natchez in early April. Schultz provided a continuing commentary as he descended the river, characterizing planters in the vicinity of Walnut Hills (Vicksburg) as "in very easy circumstances. Their chief article of culture is cotton, which is of a far better quality than any I have seen on this river."[15]

Like some other travelers of the period, Schultz comments on the price of "Improved land round about Natchez," which he says "even considering its superior quality, is extravagantly high, bearing on an average the price of twenty dollars an acre, exclusive of the value of the mansion-house and improvements." However, Schultz noted, "The price of land along this river varies. . . . The lowest priced bank lands may be rated at two dollars an acre, and from above Natchez at not more than ten. . . . Swamp lands may be had in any quantities at six cents an acre, but they are in such situations as to be of no manner of use."[16]

Writing from New Orleans on April 28, 1808, Schultz reported, "Between Natchez and Point

Coupee there appear to be some large tracts of ground lying along the river, entirely unimproved: after passing these the whole country appears like a highly cultivated garden." He also described the timber along the Mississippi, pointing out, "There is little if any difference in the growth of timber on the lower part of the Ohio, and that part of the Mississippi which lies above the Arkansas River." Below the mouth of the Ohio, Schultz reported seeing "Hickories (variety,) hard maple, swamp maple, sugar maple, sycamore, black oak, red oak, white oak, chesnut oak, Spanish oak, live oak, pitch pine, yellow pine, peccan, red cedar, white cedar, cypress, juniper, willows (variety,) cotton wood, catalpa, sassafras, locust, honey locust, gum, persimmon, holly, pepperage, dogwood, elm, poplar, black ash, white ash, black walnut, beech, black birch, white birch, chesnut, cherry, plum, buckeye, sumach, pimento, chinquapin, tulip, cabbage or palmetto, and cucumber."[17]

Schultz, like some other travelers, also provided a dramatic description of the use of fire in cane brakes, which he describes as "altogether impassable, unless you occasionally fall upon some old bear or buffaloe tracks." "When a piece of this land is first attempted, they cut down about one hundred yards of the whole front of the piece intended to be cleared, which soon becomes dry as matches. They then wait for a favourable high wind, when the woods are generally dry, and set fire to the whole front, which creates such an astonishing large fire as effectually sweeps off two or three hundred acres at once. We very frequently heard these clearings at a distance of two miles, especially if it was a still evening; when the loud and frequent explosions strongly resembled an engagement with musketry between two hostile armies."[18] In 1808 Schultz sailed back to New York from New Orleans.

In the winter of 1807 Fortescue Cuming set out from Philadelphia, and over the next two years he traveled down the Ohio and Mississippi Rivers, through the Mississippi Territory, and into West Florida. His "sketches" of what he saw were printed in Pittsburgh in 1810. Cuming pro-

vides an interesting view of the country as he moves down the river, enumerating many of the settlements along the way. In late August 1808 he set out on horseback from Bruinsbury, near the mouth of Bayou Pierre and Port Gibson, seeking to visit "the most improved parts of the Mississippi territory." Among the striking features Cuming's narrative illustrates is the extent to which the country had been settled. Also, signs of earlier Native American habitation were present, as Cuming traveled through "some beautiful open woods" and, on crossing Cole's Creek, "an old deserted field, now an arid plain." Moving through Jefferson County, Cuming said that "the whole tract" from there to Natchez had soil that was "very light, and is soon washed off, and worn out, where it has been cultivated a few years." In the immediate vicinity of Natchez he found "a woody country, and a light soil."[19]

South of Natchez, in the Second Creek area, Cuming found the country impressive, noting, "The soil is much superior to that near Natchez, and the farms are generally the best improved in the territory." Cuming traveled through "pleasant open woods" and after being ferried across the Homochitto River, he found "the country hilly, but the road . . . pleasant, and the soil rich." Fort Adams he found depressing, for "there is nothing for the eye to rest on, not even a plantation to be seen, as they are all veiled by the surrounding forests, the gloom of which is heightened by the idea, that a principal portion of the vast tract in sight, is nothing but an unwholesome swamp, which will cost thousands of lives before it can ever be made habitable, or fit for cultivation." Near Pinckneyville, however, he found "alternate plains and gently sloping hills affording fine situations for plantations."[20]

Cuming also provides an overall description of the Mississippi Territory: "The soil is as various as the climate. The river bottoms generally, and some of the cane brake hills, not being exceeded for richness in the world, while some ridges and tracts of country after being cleared and cultivated for a few years, are so exhausted, as to become almost barren. . . . [T]he pine woods . . .

generally begin at from fifteen to twenty miles distance from the river." Cuming described the "face of the country," as "much diversified—a dead swampy but very rich level borders the Mississippi the whole length of the territory . . . from the Walnut Hills . . . with the exception of some ends of ridges, or bluffs as they are called, at the Walnut Hills, the Grand and Petit gulphs—Natchez and Baton Rouge." He reported that the "flat or bottom is in general about two miles broad, though in some places nine or ten." The lands between the streams that enter the Mississippi from the east, said Cuming, "are composed of chains of steep, high and broken hills, some cultivated, some covered with a thick cane brake, and forest trees of various descriptions, and others with beautiful open woods devoid of underwood. Some are evergreen with laurel and holly, and some, where the oak, walnut and poplar are the most predominant; being wholly brown in the winter, at which season others again are mixed, and at the fall of the leaf display a variety of colouring, green, brown, yellow and red."[21]

"On approaching the pine woods," according to Cuming, "the fertility of the soil ceases, but the climate becomes much more salubrious—that will however never draw inhabitants to it while a foot of cane brake land or river bottom remains to be settled." Cuming noted, "The pine woods form a barrier between the Choctaw nation and the inhabitants of the Mississippi territory." "The woods abound with bear and deer, which are sometimes killed and sold by the Indian and white hunters," said Cuming. This assessment is at odds with other observers, such as Nutt, who reported that game was becoming scarce.[22]

At a time when growing numbers of pioneer farmers were coming into the territory, Cuming reported that for cotton, the "river bottom lands generally yield from eighteen hundred to two thousand pounds to the acre, the uplands about a thousand." "Maize or Indian corn is produced on new land in the ratio of seventy or eighty bushels per acre," Cuming said, but "cotton so entirely engrosses the planters, that they are obliged to Kentucky for the principal supply of horses and pork and bacon," while "all the wheat flour used, comes down the Mississippi."[23]

By the 1820s legions of pioneer farmers were settling and bringing Mississippi's lands under cultivation. Whereas in earlier years of white exploration, travel, and settlement there was widespread recognition of the Native American impact on the land, many whites were now in denial, characterizing the Indians as savages who stood in the way of progress. The lands and forests were regarded as wilderness that needed to be conquered. Even though many of Mississippi's Indians had become farmers whose agricultural practices had much in common with those of pioneer whites, Native American removal from the state was justified as carrying out the natural progression of civilization.

Typifying some of these views was Gideon Lincecum, a pioneering physician and naturalist whose family relocated in 1818 from the Tuscaloosa area in Alabama to the "Tombecbee" River in Mississippi. Lincecum's father made a preliminary exploratory journey and reported that "there was not a house between Tuscaloosa and the Tombecbee, that the Choctaws were near the river on the opposite side, but that nowhere on the east side was to be found any signs that the country had ever been occupied. The forests were very densely timbered, and the bottom lands were covered with the heaviest kinds of cane. Altogether, he said, it was the wildest, least trodden and tomahawk marked country he had ever explored, and that the soil was rich enough." Lincecum remembered that his father's "description of the dark, heavy forests, the wide thick canebrakes and the clear, running river, full of fish put me into a perfect transport."[24]

On the trip from Tuscaloosa to the Tombigbee, "[w]e killed plenty of deer, turkeys, ducks, wild pigeons, and had the music of great gangs of wolves around our camp every night. The entire trip was delightful beyond comparison." During the journey, "[o]ur wagons, being the first that had ever traversed that unhacked forest, we, of course, had to make a sufficient road for them to pass. It fell my lot to go in advance and blaze the way, and by taking advantage of the open spaces amongst the trees, I saved a great deal of time. The woods having been burnt every year by the Indian hunters, there were but a few logs remaining, and we got along very nicely." Lincecum seemed unaware of the implicit contradiction between his description of the "unhacked forest" and the fact that the woods had been "burnt every year by the Indian hunters."[25]

The party settled near present-day Columbus, Mississippi, on the Tombigbee River. The family subsisted on "a superabundance of fish, fowl and venison, and occasionally a glorious fleece of bear meat." Lincecum gushed, "The quantity of game that was found in that dark forest and the canebrakes was a subject of wonder." Like most pioneer Mississippi farmers, Lincecum and his brother worked all day "clearing up ground to plant corn." In the early days he built a house and smokehouse and joined others in the area in clearing the forests and canebrakes to make fields.[26]

Lincecum became a trader with the Chickasaws and Choctaw and moved to the vicinity of Cotton Gin, eventually selecting a quarter section of public land in 1825. There he built a house among "clean, uncropped grass, in high dry open woods timbered with oak, hickory, chestnut and tall pines." His family remained in this location for eight years, and Lincecum occasionally got away by going hunting in "the canebrake and the dark, lonely forests." After moving to Columbus and practicing medicine for several years, Lincecum was again struck by wanderlust, and in 1848 he moved to Texas, where, after a five-year sojourn in Mexico, he died.[27] His comments on the fact that the forests had been altered, although he still termed them "dark, unhacked, and lonely," reflected the views of many white pioneers of that time.

An outside perspective in the same period was provided by Adam Hodgson, a Scottish clergyman who traveled in Mississippi shortly after Lincecum moved from Tuscaloosa to the Tombigbee. Hodgson repeated a common opinion of the time, noting that much of the land east of the Mississippi River and south of 35° was covered by pines and that "these pine lands are incapable of cultivation, and are destined to continue for ever in their native condition." Traveling in the Natchez area, Hodgson said that from the bluffs, "you look down . . . upon a dense forest, which stretches to the horizon. . . . Indeed, there is something in the vicinity of Natchez which perpetually reminds me of home. The thick clover, the scattered knolls with their wood-crowned summits . . . the magnificence of the foliage with which they are shaded, and the neat husbandry of the intervening plantations, give the whole country the appearance of an English park." Among the trees of the area he listed "gigantic plane and maple . . . a large proportion of the seventy or eighty different species of the American oak, the Sassafras, the Hiccory, the Pride of India, the Catalpa" and others.[28]

Hodgson traveled from Natchez to northeast Mississippi before moving into Alabama and crossing Bear Creek, which he termed "a beautiful romantic river," and then the Tennessee River just above Muscle Shoals. Through Mississippi, Hodgson traveled "some hundred miles in a deep forest, almost without seeing the tops of the thickly interlacing trees." Part of the trip was "through a forest of fine oaks; which, within ten or twelve miles of Yaloo Busha, was occasionally interspersed with small natural prairies, and assumed the appearance of an English park." Hodgson described Mississippi forests as "thick woods, in which for many days, our eyes had seldom been able to range beyond a narrow circle of a few hundred yards. . . . Not that we were tired of the wilderness . . . above all, the magnificent forest-trees which here attain their largest growth—all presented an unfailing succession of objects to interest and amuse us."[29]

Among the most interesting aspects of Hodgson's account are his comments on the rapidity with which farms were being cleared out of the forests. His description of a farm a few miles past Muscle Shoals, in northern Alabama, would undoubtedly fit the conditions in northeast Mississippi during the same period: "We took up our abode for the night . . . at a prosperous looking farm, which a year and a half since, was a wilderness. . . . Near the house he had one field, of one hundred acres in Indian corn, and another of one hundred in cotton; he cut down the first trees in January, 1819, and last year had a small crop of cotton and Indian corn. . . . I was surprised at the rapidity with which the new lands have been brought into cultivation. The fields are generally from eighty to one hundred and twenty acres in extent, cleared of a fair proportion of their timber, and the remainder girdled. The land is remarkably good, sometimes producing one hundred bushels of Indian corn per acre." Hodgson commented that "in passing through the northern part of Alabama, I was particularly struck with the rapidity with which it has been settled. It is little more than two years since these public lands were sold. At that time not a tree was felled; and now the road is skirted with beautiful fields of cotton and Indian corn, from 80 to 120 miles in extent."[30]

A young German duke, Paul Wilhelm of Wurttemberg, provided another foreign assessment of Mississippi during the early nineteenth century. Inspired by the expeditions of Meriwether Lewis and William Clark and Major Stephen H. Long, the duke came to America to see the lands, the flora and fauna, and the Native Americans, especially of the trans-Mississippi West. Paul Wilhelm arrived at New Orleans, spent two months in Cuba, and then in 1823 headed up the Mississippi from New Orleans toward the Ohio River and Louisville. He then went on to St. Louis and up the Missouri River. In April 1823 he traveled along Mississippi via the Mississippi River and offered several observations on the state. He accepted the growing perception that Mississippi's forests were virgin: "For more than one hundred English miles the state of Mississippi constitutes a flat, in part, swampy country. But further on the land rises, especially toward the northeast, forming attractive elevated areas, mostly covered by dense virgin forests and abounding in springs."[31]

In the vicinity of the Walnut Hills, the duke commented on the "abundance and variety adorning this primeval forest." Near the confluence of the St. Francis River with the Mississippi, he noted that his boat took on wood "at a little plantation situated beside a rectangular meadow." "Since a natural grass plain in this region of the Mississippi is a very rare phenomenon," he said, "I could not refrain from paying it a hurried visit." He reported that the meadow contrasted "markedly to the gigantic shapes of the woods in the nearby virgin forest" and that "this little patch of grassland . . . reminded me of a pasture in Germany." He speculated on its origin, noting, "I was not able to find any traces of uprooted trees on its surface, leading me to the conclusion that it does not owe its origin to an earlier clearing of the ground." According to Paul Wilhelm, "Any field well cleared of stumps and roots, if left uncultivated for only two or three years, develops trees several feet high because of the great fertility of the American soil. I was, however, not able to find the slightest vestige of young trees. Only a few ancient oaks proudly raised their magnificent foliage-covered limbs, revealing by their appearance the effect of an open location and the influence of light on vegetation."[32]

Judging from travelers' reports, emigrants' guides, the recollections of pioneer settlers, and other sources, by the 1820s several aspects of Mississippi's land and society seem obvious. The land was covered with a mosaic of heavy forests, open forests, canebrakes, savannas, swamps, meadows, prairies, hardwoods, pine, and mixed stands of trees. Much of the land had been altered by Indian use over long periods of time, but the Native American population was much reduced since the late prehistoric period. Many of the Indians were "civilized" and had taken up farming and planting. However, they were characterized by many whites as savages, either out of genuine conviction or because they occupied lands that the whites coveted. The story of the loss of tribal lands and eventual removal has been ably told elsewhere and needs not be repeated in detail here.[33]

The experiences of early white Mississippians moving into a region of modified forests were not unique. Pioneer settlers in the eastern forests also found that "[a]bandoned Indian fields and repeated firing of the forest by Indians to create new cornfields and keep up a supply of herbs and browse attractive to deer had inadvertently created ecological conditions favorable to the entry of white farmers. It has been claimed that it would have taken a generation of settlers to produce the extent of clearings which they found ready-made."[34]

Most of the white pioneers who came into Mississippi during this period were farmers, many from other states. The actual percentage of forested land is difficult to determine, but judging from the anecdotal accounts in travelers' writings and government documents, it was probably not much higher than today, if as high. The storied regenerative powers of the forests, as mentioned by Duke Paul Wilhelm, should be considered, for Native American villages moved frequently and cleared lands became old fields, which in a remarkably short period of time could be reclaimed by the forests. And as the Indian population declined, the prevalence of burning, which kept the forests open and meadows cleared, decreased. Some scholars believe that the forests of that time closely resembled those of today (with the notable absence then of tree plantations). For example, Stephen Spurr says, "In most cases, comparisons of the present forest with early descriptions show that the forests of the two eras do not differ substantially."[35]

Whatever the actual extent of the forests and whether or not they were virgin, many white settlers of this period saw the trees as impediments. And many of these pioneers viewed the forests as "virgin," "primeval," or "wilderness." In fact, the concept of wilderness is ultimately defined by society and by the individual. As Roderick Nash has observed, "The New World was also wilderness at the time of discovery because Europeans *considered* it such."[36] The white farmers and planters followed in Native Americans' footsteps by spending much of their time removing trees and burning the land for farming, as they "conquered" the "wilderness" and created a largely agricultural society. Those who saw other potential benefits in the forest and utilized it economically during this period were not in the mainstream of Mississippi society.

Emigrant guides and sourcebooks, sometimes of questionable accuracy, were available for those considering migration to the Mississippi Valley in this period. One of the best known is Timothy Flint's *A Condensed Geography and History of the Western States or the Mississippi Valley*, published in 1828. Flint, a New England schoolteacher who lived in the Southwest during the early 1820s, calculated Mississippi's land area at 28 million acres and described its character. He mentioned the hills and bluffs along the Mississippi River and singled out Pine Ridge for special attention, coming within a mile of the river and constituting "a high belt of pine land, like an island in the midst of surrounding rich land, timbered with hard woods." In the northern areas of the state, inhabited by "the Cherokees, and Chactaws," said Flint, "the land rises into regular and pleasant undulations. The soil is deep, black, and rich" and included "hills covered with high cane brake." The country of the Chickasaw, "north-west of the Yazoo River," Flint reported, was "charmingly variegated with swells, and valleys of great fertility."[37]

Flint extensively described Mississippi's waterways, a critical matter to farmers in an age of primitive overland transportation. The Yazoo River, he noted, ran through "a high, pleasant and salubrious country, chiefly however claimed and inhabited by Indians" for 150 miles from its mouth. The Big Black River, Flint reported, was excellently situated: "The soil is fine. The situation is eligible." Traveling along the Mississippi River, Flint said that much of the land was subject to regular inundation, and "[a]t present, in descending the river, the traveller looks in vain, along this very extended front, for the palpable evidences of the opulence, for which this state is so deservedly celebrated." However, he noted, once the river was contained by levees, "an immense body of the most fertile soil will be redeemed from inundation; and the state will gain as much in salubrity, as in opulence."[38]

Flint estimated the number of Choctaws in Mississippi at twenty thousand and the Chickasaws at four thousand: they were "in a semi-savage state, and exhibit the interesting spectacle of a people, intermediate between the hunter's and the civilized state." Noting the influence of missionaries, Flint rejoiced that "the sweet and cultivated strains of church music, resound in these ancient forests, instead of the war and death song of the savages."[39]

Flint reported that most Mississippians were engaged in agriculture and said that while a wide range of products could be grown, "[c]otton is the grand staple, and grows in perfection in all parts of the state. It is, perhaps, too exclusively the object of thought, attention, and cultivation. . . . [O]ne would suppose, that it was here considered, as almost the only article of much importance in the creation." The countryside near Natchez, Flint said, "is waving, rich and beautiful; the eminences presenting open woods covered with grape vines, and here and there neat country houses."[40]

H. S. Tanner's *View of the Valley of the Mississippi; or, The Emigrant's and Traveller's Guide to the West,* published in 1832, provides similar information for emigrants. Tanner listed the area of Mississippi as encompassing 47,680 square miles, or 30,515,200 acres. The valley of the lower Mississippi, he said, has "immense prairies, or savannas, where the eye sees nothing, in the summer season, but . . . a vast ocean of waving wild grass, flowers of various hues, and of six or eight feet in height. There are, however, large forests of trees of extraordinary size, particularly along the margins of the rivers." He discussed a long list of different tree species and said, "No country on earth is covered with a greater variety of useful trees, shrubs, and vines"; the "pine forests of the south can furnish millions of masts, spars, &c. &c. for our ships."[41]

Beyond the bluffs along the Mississippi River, said Tanner, was a "high, beautiful, and fertile table land, gently undulating and productive," which had a width of ten to forty miles. "Beyond this fertile belt of land," he reported, "there

stretches from south to north, and reaches eastward to the Alabama line, an extensive district of country, of various soils, but possessing much that is alluvial and fertile, contrasted with much that is light and covered with pine." Tanner said that "[a]s a whole, Mississippi possesses a great quantity of excellent lands" and further reported that "[i]n its natural state, in which almost the entire state still is, it was covered with a vast forest of oak, hickory, magnolia, sweet gum, ash, maple, yellow poplar, cypress in the swampy alluvial Mississippi bottoms, pine, holley, &c. &c. with a great variety of underwood, grape vines, pawpaw, spice wood &c."[42]

Like Flint, Tanner observed that Mississippi was suitable for the cultivation of various agricultural products. He reported that some diversity in crops previously existed, but for the past thirty years cotton had "prevailed" and "absorbs almost the whole attention of those who live on farms or plantations which possess a soil suitable for its production." Tanner predicted an influx of settlers into Mississippi in the near future: "There are 21,211,465 acres of public land now for sale in this state. There are also 6,529,280 acres, to which the Indian title had not been unconditionally extinguished on the 2d of April, 1832, but which will be, in the course of a year or two, it is expected. . . . It will be perceived from this statement that a very small portion of the land in this state is owned by individuals; and as the Choctaws and Chickasaws are expected to remove during this summer and next, we may expect that this state will soon become settled by emigrants from the Atlantic and other portions of our country, especially from the southern part of it."[43] In other words, taking Tanner's assessment in toto, Mississippi had a plethora of excellent land with good potential for agriculture, much of it was forested, and most of it was not yet in private hands. The opening of more land as a result of Indian removal was expected to trigger a land boom.

As early settlers moved into Mississippi, they were drawn first to areas that had good transportation and fertile soil. Thus Natchez and its environs were settled early, while the piney woods of south Mississippi languished, for the prevailing belief was that the soil in those areas was inferior. Conversely, luxuriant hardwoods indicated, the settlers believed, a richness of soil. Therefore, areas along waterways in north Mississippi attracted settlers. Prairies, savannas, and old fields were often desirable because they did not require the backbreaking labor of clearing that the forests necessitated. Timber was needed for houses, farm buildings, and fences, so land with both open areas and woods was desirable, and as Michael Williams has pointed out, "the contrast between forest and prairie was not stark everywhere. In between the extremes, and in a wide zone partaking of the characteristics of both environments, running north-south roughly through the center of the country, the settler could have timber as well as grass on his land."[44]

Agricultural settlement came late in Mississippi. The French emphasized the fur trade, and the settlement of a few hundred farmers and their families around Fort Rosalie (Natchez) in the early eighteenth century came to naught, for they were killed or driven away by an Indian uprising.[45] After the British took over in 1763, they encouraged agriculture by land grants to veterans and friends of the crown. In 1770 the first permanent settlers entered. Two years later, the lieutenant governor wrote that three hundred people, from Virginia and the Carolinas, were living on the Mississippi, with three or four hundred more families expected in the near future. In 1777, to satisfy the demand for more land, the Superintendent of Indian Affairs purchased from the Choctaws a one-hundred-mile strip of land along the Mississippi River from Loftus Heights to the mouth of the Yazoo River.

Nonetheless, relatively few immigrants settled in the Natchez District during the British period. However, Edward Mease, after traveling through the area around St. Catherine's Creek, reported to the Earl of Hillsborough in 1771 that some farmers and planters, "mostly from Maryland and Carolina," were settling; furthermore, "I met with a great deal of clear'd Land of an extreme

rich Quality which had been lately planted." Also, during the American Revolution there was an influx of American loyalists into the colony.[46]

During the American Revolution the Spanish took possession of the Natchez District, but under their control the population of the area remained predominantly English or American, although small. A 1785 census showed only 1,550 people living in the district, but during the years from 1787 to 1792 the white population of the district rose from 1,926 to 4,300, and the black population tripled. At the time of the area's formal transfer from Spain to the United States in 1798, the Natchez District's non-Native American population probably numbered around five thousand.[47]

In a great historical coincidence, the year of the Treaty of San Lorenzo (1795) also saw Eli Whitney's perfection of the cotton gin. Daniel Clark Sr., a planter from Wilkinson County, designed a machine based on Whitney's invention and in violation of his patent the same year. By September Clark's machine was in operation on his Sligo Plantation near Fort Adams, and it attracted great interest throughout the area. Mississippi farmers and planters produced a variety of crops, including indigo, tobacco, corn, and cotton, but they struggled economically. The cotton gin reduced the cost of processing cotton to such a degree that it dominated commercial agriculture in Mississippi almost immediately after the introduction of Clark's pirated machine, which made cotton a commercially viable staple crop.[48]

American control in Mississippi brought a new system for claiming and purchasing land. At the time of transfer, landowners held their property through various kinds of arrangements: French, Spanish, and British grants; Indian titles; and squatter rights. The United States tried to recognize all legitimate claims. The state of Georgia also had sold lands in Mississippi, but those transactions were canceled because of irregularities, and Georgia's lands were turned over to the federal government in 1802. The decision made at that time was that Mississippi and Alabama would be administered and eventually brought into the Union on the same terms as the states of the old Northwest Territory, with the exception of the prohibition of slavery. As a result, the system of rectangular survey would be used, with all land divided into townships of thirty-six square miles and sections of one square mile, or 640 acres. Each section would be further divided into quarter sections. No one could settle on the land until it had been surveyed and sold to the highest bidder, with a minimum price of two dollars an acre, reduced in 1820 to $1.25 an acre. If the land did not attract a bid at auction, it could later be sold at the minimum price. The rights of the Native Americans were to be recognized and protected.[49]

Sales were conducted at offices located in the general vicinity of the lands, which were staffed by a register and a receiver. The first land office in Mississippi was established in 1803 at Washington in Adams County. Before sales, prospective purchasers would acquire a map of the lands to be sold and would then go into the field—in a process called land hunting or land-looking—and mark on their plats the best lands or those on which they wished to bid. As the process became more sophisticated, surveyors who knew the country sometimes led their clients to the best land. The sales lasted for two to three weeks, and the schedules were staggered so that purchasers could travel from one location to the next. The sales sometimes attracted several hundred would-be purchasers. Mary J. Welsh, a pioneer who moved into Kemper County in the early 1830s, remembered the land sales as "a time of great excitement and anxiety to all, old and young."[50]

The land was sold by range and township, with the auctioneer going through the sections from one to thirty-six. The sales attracted people who stayed in tents and merchants who sold their wares at booths. Lucky buyers often provided whiskey to the crowd. Despite government policies and warnings, squatters moved onto the best public lands in large numbers before they were sold, and white pioneers often intruded on Indian property. The practice of squatting on public land was so common that Mississippi's territorial legis-

lature in 1816 provided representation to counties that did not have a single legitimate settler, thereby enabling a few men in an area to elect a member to the legislature. When offenders were apprehended and tried, local juries would not convict them. Judge Harry Toulmin of the Mississippi Territory got to the root of the problem in an 1816 letter to President James Madison: "How can a jury be found in Monroe county to convict a man of intrusion,—where every man is an intruder?"[51]

When the land on which squatters resided and farmed came onto the market, the settlers tried to claim it on the basis of "improvements" or at least to buy it as cheaply as possible. Part of their concern was based on the fact that speculators tried to buy up improved land at government sales. The squatters claimed that they had served as a buffer between civilization and the Native Americans and sought from the government a special preemption that would guarantee them the right to purchase at the minimum price. In 1803 Congress passed a special preemption act for land south of Tennessee that allowed settlers who had lived on their claims by October 1795 the right to purchase up to 640 acres at the minimum price of two dollars per acre. After 1820 the price was lowered to $1.25, and in 1830 another act allowed all settlers living on the public domain to buy up to 160 acres at $1.25 an acre. However, this legislation protected only settlers who were on the land by 1829.[52]

There were also difficulties with consortiums of speculators and squatters combining to purchase blocks of land for speculation and to eliminate competition. At Cochuma, Mississippi, in 1833, a company of speculators from Tennessee, Alabama, and Mississippi subscribed between one hundred and one thousand dollars each to purchase land and chose four commissioners to do the bidding. The speculators then auctioned off the lands and split the profits. Settlers were to have the lands on which they lived, up to eighty acres, at the minimum price if they would not bid at the government auction. Most of the prospective bidders at the government auction either were bought off this way or were members of the syndicate. At the Cochuma sale the speculators bought three-fourths of the land sold, most at the minimum price, and then held their own auction and resold their purchases. At Columbus the following year, speculators auctioned off from the steps of the courthouse lands that they had purchased in the government sale that had concluded the same evening. The participants in the speculators' syndicate netted $465 profit for each thousand dollars invested. In some cases corrupt government land office officials became involved with the syndicates, and in 1835 a congressional investigating committee found that some of the nation's worst abuses were in Mississippi. The volume of sales was phenomenal. In 1832 prospective farmers and land speculators purchased about a quarter of a million acres from the federal government. This amount increased to more than a million acres the next year and to nearly three million acres in 1835.[53]

As pioneers moved into Mississippi, they heeded the advice of travelers and emigrants' guides and other descriptions of the state's resources. The settlers moved beyond the Natchez area, which remained a prime and growing agricultural region, and filtered into other parts of the state: "Even before the War of 1812 rumors of wealth and opportunity in the Tennessee River Valley in Mississippi Territory gave it the name 'Happy Valley.'" Mississippi was known as the "Garden of America." Most pioneers heeded the conventional wisdom by largely avoiding the piney woods of the south. However, most areas they settled contained forests and trees, and an important part of the pioneer farmer's early years was consumed by clearing the trees and preparing land for cultivation. In fact, says one authority, "What European man did was to clear and keep clear much more of the forest than had ever been disturbed before." This pattern continued during much of the antebellum period.[54]

The two earliest regions of the Mississippi Territory with significant concentrations of settlement were the Natchez District, which at the turn of the century had about six thousand residents,

including slaves, and about eight hundred settlers along the Tombigbee and Mobile Rivers in what is now Alabama. There were also a few settlers north of Natchez near the Walnut Hills and along the Big Black River. Most were Anglo-Americans, and they came from several areas, including the trans-Appalachian area, the south Atlantic and middle Atlantic regions, and New England. By 1800 the Natchez District still had only 7,600 inhabitants, of whom 39 percent were slaves. A decade later, the Mississippi Territory's population was 40,352, of whom 12,850 were free whites, 240 free blacks, and 17,088 slaves. The population was concentrated in the counties around Natchez, but there were more than 1,200 people in Wayne County on the southeastern Alabama border, nearly five thousand in Madison County, nearly three thousand in Washington County (Greenville), and more than 1,100 in Warren County (Walnut Hills, Vicksburg). By 1811 five new counties north and south of Adams County and extending eastward to the Alabama line had been created, and Pickering County had been divided into Jefferson and Claiborne Counties.[55]

Like their Native American predecessors, the white farmers and planters of antebellum Mississippi cleared the lands and used them until the topsoil washed away or until they wore out. These settlers were constantly on the move to new lands, where they repeated the process. Those planters who anticipated the need to relocate and had the resources assigned their slaves to the clearing of new areas while the old ones were still in use. When the old lands were no longer profitable, they were allowed to revert to brush, weeds, and eventually forests. Planters and their slaves thus devoted much of their time to clearing new land. There were two methods of removing the timber. The first was to simply chop down the trees; the second was to girdle them. Girdling involved hacking around them deeply enough to cut off the flow of sap. While both methods were used, girdling was more common.[56]

A good example is Log Hall Plantation in Hinds County, near the town of Edwards. The

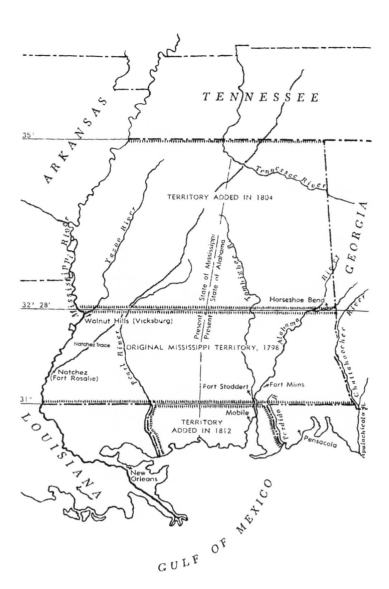

Map of Mississippi territorial growth, 1804–12, and the Natchez Trace. John K. Bettersworth, *Mississippi: A History* (Austin, Tex.: Steck, 1959), 84. Modified by Edward Ashley Fickle.

owner, Dr. Martin W. Phillips, settled at Log Hall in the 1830s and had what one writer called "an ideal plantation." Phillips's diary from 1840 to 1863 is replete with references to land clearing: for example, the entries for January–February 1840 alone contain nine separate references to removing timber.[57]

Phillips's diary ends in April 1863, when he fled from advancing Union armies, never to return. There are many gaps, particularly in the later period. During the diary's twenty-three-year span, there are more than 150 daily references to work by slaves clearing lands, opening new lands, rolling logs, burning logs, girdling trees, hauling lumber, clearing brush, mauling timbers, and other work related to clearing the forest, processing wood, and opening new fields for farming. In 1840 Phillips planned to plant 204 acres in cotton, corn, oats, potatoes, and grapes and to work the land with thirteen slaves, including men, women, and children. By 1853 Log Hall Plantation had nearly 370 acres under cultivation and

Pioneer farmers girdling and burning trees. *Journal of Forest History* 24 (January 1980): 14.

more than thirty slaves. The following year more than 450 acres were devoted to crops, with cotton, corn, and oats remaining the principal products. It should also be remembered that as new lands came into production, old ones wore out and were abandoned. By the time of the Civil War the plantation had more than five hundred acres under cultivation. Log Hall's records reflect Mississippi planters' extreme preoccupation with clearing the forests for farming.

Others moved and cleared new land simply because they disliked crowding or preferred fron-

tier conditions. From 1808 to 1820 the Ramsay family moved nine times before settling in southeast Mississippi. One European tried and failed to dissuade a man who was considering a move to Mississippi in 1832 without any knowledge of the area; the emigrant stated, "I have no elbow room. I cannot move about without seeing the nose of my neighbor sticking out between the trees." Lincecum, like most pioneer Mississippi farmers, worked all day with his family "clearing up ground to plant corn." He also joined others in the frontier Columbus area in "cutting down and clearing the maiden forest to make fields to plant corn in. I cut down six acres of the canebrake that jammed itself almost down to the place where I built my house," after which he burned the cane.[58]

Farther south along the Alabama border in Kemper County, settlers near the Noxubee River cleared land and produced crops, which they shipped via the river to nearby Gainesville, Alabama, and then down to Mobile. Welsh, who moved with her family from Alabama to Kemper County in 1833, remembered farmers' preoccupation with clearing land: "Most of the land in our immediate section was heavily timbered with a dense undergrowth. . . . New land was cleared every year for many years, the useless timber and brush being burned. At night these burning logheaps and piles of brush, which were dotted thickly here and there over the ridges, gave to the natural scenery an added beauty, peculiar to a new country." Not all of the land in this area was "heavily timbered," for the author also remembered that a "ride on horseback through the deep, green woods or the tall grass of the prairie was delicious pleasure." Also, the region was dotted with "spaces of open land, an acre or less in extent," which had been the homesites of Choctaw Indians who had been "removed" from the area.[59]

On the northern border of Carroll County, Ferdinand Lawrence Steele settled in the 1830s on a farm of 170 acres about five miles from Grenada, where the "land is beautifully rolling thinly sprinkled with large . . . trees without a particle of underwood." The area had just been opened for white settlement in the middle 1830s, and much of early farmers' effort was consumed by land clearing, which was sometimes a community project. Equipment was borrowed, and logrolling in particular brought neighbors together: "We rolled logs Mr Pinkney Beck sent us 2 hands. Mr Wm Beck helped us. So also did Mr Bernard & Mr Bell. We had a great many logs to roll, but we finished rolling."[60]

Settlement began in the upper Tombigbee region when the federal government began to survey and sell lands in the area between 1816 and 1821. Many early settlers came from Tennessee and Alabama, and they took up residence in scattered locations, with a concentration around Cotton Gin Port on the Tombigbee River and a bigger settlement at Columbus, which by 1820 was a growing village. By that year the region had a population of 2,721, of which 522, or 19 percent, were slaves. A decade later, Monroe County had 2,918 whites and 943 slaves, while neighboring Lowndes had 2,109 and 1,064.[61]

In central Mississippi, Yazoo County was created by the legislature in 1823 and originally included the present counties of Yazoo, Madison, Holmes, Issaquena, and parts of Warren and Washington. The area was marked by Indian old fields and some "prairies of several miles in length and of one or two miles in width on which not a tree or shrub grew." Many of the woods were open: "It was the custom of the Choctaws every fall or winter in order to prevent the forest from becoming too dense to destroy the undergrowth by setting fire to and burning off the woods." As in other parts of the state, land clearing was the settlers' first priority. For example, "In the latter part of 1825 and in 1826, Richardson Bowman entered a large body of land and the table lands of Big Black river. . . . In the two subsequent years, he cleared and fenced his farm."[62]

Southern farmers' tendency to wear out their land and clear new areas was also seen in Leflore County, which was opened to white settlement in 1833. Some settlers entered because "the exhaustion of fertility in the older parts of the state, especially in the hill region of Claiborne, Warren, and Adams counties, caused farmers and plantation owners to move their families and slaves to new and more profitable lands." Once there, the "stumps and logs must be removed from the ground before [they] could cultivate it."[63]

Pioneer Mississippi farmers and planters obviously devoted a great deal of their time, money, and energy to clearing land for cultivation. Since much of the land on which they settled was forested, they removed a large amount of the state's forest cover. In the early period there is no way of knowing the impact in actual acres or percentages. Reliance on diaries, journals, travelers' observations, and so forth gives the impression of a society furiously girdling, burning, and hacking away at the trees.

In 1850 the federal census began to distinguish between "improved" and "unimproved" land, but it must be remembered that in Mississippi there were many prairies, savannas, old fields, and so on, so it cannot simply be assumed that improved land is synonymous with cleared land. Prairie or open land that was broken to the plow was also considered improved However, Williams argues that in the eastern United States generally, only a small amount of improved land came from natural clearings or abandoned Indian old fields. One expert calculates that in Mississippi 4.4 million acres of land were cleared before 1850 and that another 1.6 million acres were cleared between 1850 and 1859. The 1850 U.S. Census reported 3,444,358 acres of improved land on farms in Mississippi and 7,046,061 acres of unimproved land. To put these figures in perspective, Mississippi has roughly 29.8 million acres of land, of which 18.5 million acres are today covered by forests. Thus, the clearing by antebellum farmers and planters amounted to more than 32 percent of today's forests. Furthermore, the census shows a total of 10,490,419 acres in farms, which leaves more than 19 million acres unclaimed or not devoted to farm use.[64]

In 1830 Mississippi's population consisted of 70,443 whites, 519 free blacks, and 65,559 slaves. By the eve of the Civil War, the state's population had risen dramatically to 791,000, including 354,000 whites and 437,000 blacks, virtually all of them slaves. Some 21,000 people were classified as urban and 771,000 as rural.[65] Most of these Mississippians were farmers, planters, and agricultural slaves, and their impact on the forests was not limited to removing the timber to cultivate the land. They also used and sometimes sold forest products. The antebellum period was an age of wood—not simply wood for houses, fences, and buildings but also for such other uses as charcoal and potash and as a major source of energy.

During the 1850s, an estimated 878.5 million cords of wood were used for fuel. In the early period it was burned mostly in fireplaces, and later wood-burning stoves were used. Despite the fact that it was more energy efficient than wood, coal accounted for less than 10 percent of the nation's energy consumption in 1850. By 1860 coal had risen to just over 16 percent, with the rest of the market served by wood. During the 1850s, some 50 million acres of land were cleared nationally, producing 75 million cords of wood for fuel. Land clearing probably supplied the bulk of the fuel wood, and some additional supplies came from recutting woodlots. Selling cordwood was a profitable sideline for many pioneer farmers and planters.[66]

In Mississippi there was an additional drain on the forest coming from the demand for wood by steamboats on the Mississippi River. Flint said in 1828 that along the river, the land was "inundated by swamps, very thinly inhabited, except by wood cutters for the steam boats." Four years later, an emigrants' guide reported that along the river in Mississippi, "A large portion of its bank . . . is for a very considerable width an inundated swamp, covered with cypress, and inhabited only at intervals, by those who cut wood for the passing steam boats." The 1840 census reported that in the river counties from the Delta to the Wisconsin border, 503,458 cords of wood were sold in 1839. Some of this wood was supplied by farmers in the river regions who pursued this trade during the off-season from their farms.[67]

During the antebellum period, wood was the primary fuel for steamboats, which grew larger and more powerful and consumed ever bigger quantities of fuel. During the period from 1820 to 1860 the number of cords required by an average steamboat to make a round-trip voyage between Louisville and New Orleans rose from 483 to 529. Coal was cheaper than wood. It was estimated that ten to twelve bushels of coal, at seven cents per bushel, would supply as much power as ten

Steamboat wooding by night, color lithograph by Henry Lewis, 1854–58. *Journal of Forest History* 21 (July 1977): 130.

to twelve cords of wood, at a range of from $1.25 to $6.00 per cord. However, wood remained the fuel of choice because of its ready availability. A passenger on the steamboat *Philadelphia* in 1820 reported that the vessel burned 128 cubic feet, or one cord per hour, amounting when they were "pushing hard" to thirty cords per day. A standard cord was four feet high, four feet wide, and eight feet long, and because of limited fuel storage capacity most steamboats required several wooding stops per day.[68]

Most of the wood was supplied by itinerant workers, often called woodhawks. Some worked only in winter when other jobs were scarce; others labored year-round. As mentioned above, some farmers supplied cordwood to the boats while their lands were being cleared, but in remote locations, woodhawks were more common. They often squatted on land and stole wood from the forests, whether private or public. The woodhawks sometimes had lethal battles with competitors who attempted to settle in the same area. One traveler on the lower Mississippi River in the late antebellum period reported that planters who were clearing their lands operated wood stations, which they often left unattended. The steamboat captains would take on wood and leave money or payment in kind, such as corn or pork. Planters occasionally left notes at the woodpiles, telling their customers what form of payment they preferred.[69]

In the course of clearing land; burning or selling wood for heat; providing cordwood for steamboats; and constructing homes, buildings, and fences, like the Native Americans before them, pioneer Mississippi farmers, planters, and slaves had a significant impact on the forest environment.

3   Pioneers

Early Lumbermen Log the Forests

Farmers not only cleared the forests but also used their wood for fuel, homes, fences, furniture, tools, and other purposes. But these uses were almost taken for granted: the main emphasis was on clearing the land and making it "productive." Other pioneers looked beyond the trees and saw the forests' larger economic benefits. Although minuscule in comparison with the giant industry that developed later in the century, harvesting the products of the forests, the lumber and naval stores, became the focus and the work of Mississippians who labored in the woods in relative obscurity during the antebellum period. Their lives were not as glamorous as those of the planters of Natchez, the Delta, or Columbus, but these early lumbermen were pioneers in an industry that in some ways eventually dwarfed the planters in long-run contributions to Mississippi. In fact, even by 1860 lumbering was the state's largest industry.[1]

Constructing the early history of the lumber industry is difficult. Many of the participants were small farmers who did not leave written records. Those who specialized in logging and lumbering in the early days were usually illiterate, so again they did not leave correspondence or other written evidence of their activities. Even as small companies emerged, the record keeping was sporadic, and boiler explosions and fires in sawmills were common: any records that existed often

perished. Such was also the case for some of the larger operations that came later. Cutting timber and processing lumber in the South were omnipresent. So travelers' accounts, newspapers, and other sources were not likely to mention such a mundane activity, unless there was an accident or some spectacular reason to notice what was considered a rather humdrum business. In Mississippi during the antebellum era cotton was clearly king, and it got the lion's share of the attention.[2]

Lumbering and naval stores industries developed along the Mississippi Gulf Coast during the French colonial period. The French colonists erected small sawmills and converted tall longleaf and slash pines into masts and spars for ships. By the 1720s the colony was also producing pitch, tar, and dressed lumber. There were also plans to produce stave wood, and colonial officials reported that wood from upriver was superior, with qualifications: "We agree that the timber from up the river must be of a much better quality than that from the lower river, but . . . this difference is only in the very distant countries both because of their elevation as because it is colder there. As for the difference of ten leagues above or ten leagues below New Orleans, it does not exist. The woods and the situation of the ground are the same there."[3]

French officials were determined to make Louisiana profitable. In addition to various agricultural products, Governor Jean Baptiste Le

Moyne, Sieur de Bienville, believed that in the Natchez and lower Mississippi River area the colony could produce "all kinds of dressed timber," while "on the Mobile and Pascagoula Rivers and the shores of the sea, masts, timber for shipbuilding, pitch and tar." However, he complained that the colony lacked sufficient workers for these enterprises. The king of France encouraged his colonial administrators to "urge the settlers of Mobile to profit by the advantages that the pine forests offer them" by producing tar and pitch and to "make use of ship-building timber," arguing, "Commerce is in fact the most certain means for the increase of the colony and too great care can not be given to it." The king noted that the production of tar and pitch could become an "industry . . . of very great importance" and advised his officials to urge the colonists "to exploit ship building timber, timber for building houses and planks of spruce and cypress," because "it may contribute to the establishment of a coasting trade between the colony and the French islands."[4]

Bienville and Edme Gatien Salmon, the commissary general of Louisiana, wrote in 1733 to Jean Frederic Phelypeaux, Count de Maurepas, the minister of marine and colonies, that "several individuals of New Orleans" were prepared to ship to France two hundred barrels of tar "that they have had manufactured on the other side of Lake Ponchartrain where there are many pine forests." Bienville and Salmon reported the next year that "there are already three or four tar-works established on the other side of Lake Ponchartrain without counting those that people are preparing to build there. They expect to make at Mobile next year twelve to fifteen thousand barrels." Bienville and Salmon also noted the suspension of plans to obtain masts from the Mobile area and Dauphine Island, commenting, "Pines are so very numerous in this part of the government that there is no reason at all to fear that there would be a shortage of them; however, we have given orders that attention be given to the conservation of this timber."[5]

The French efforts eventually paid off. New Orleans became the shipping and trading center for lumber as well as a major consumer of the products from regional mills. Under the French there was an active trade in lumber between Louisiana and the French West Indies, although that with the mother country was inconsequential. In the last year of French rule roughly sixty-two thousand dollars in lumber and naval stores, about one-fourth of the colony's exports, were shipped from New Orleans.[6]

The Spanish took control of Louisiana near the end of the Seven Years' War and crippled the lumber business by limiting the colony's trade to Spanish possessions and its shipping to Spanish-owned and -manned vessels. Since New Orleans was the major market and shipping point for lumber and naval stores from the Mississippi area (which had become part of the British province of West Florida in the same period), this policy had serious implications. However, this problem was relieved somewhat by lax Spanish enforcement of these trade restrictions and by the British willingness to ignore them. Plus, as mentioned earlier, the Paris Treaty of 1763 gave the British free navigation of the Mississippi River. Under lenient Spanish administration, the lumber trade and naval stores business revived, and new sawmills appeared along the lower Mississippi River and the Gulf Coast. Under the Spanish the chief exports of the Natchez region included furs, tobacco, and lumber.[7]

During the British period, the timbered lands of south Mississippi were utilized to produce staves for use by sugar plantations; naval stores, which were exported; and timbers for shipbuilding at Pascagoula. The English colonists also constructed new sawmills along the Gulf Coast. In the 1770s several travelers and observers described the forests and their fledgling lumbering and naval stores activities (see chap. 1 for the accounts of Edward Mease, James Adair, Bernard Romans, Sir William Dunbar, and Francis Baily). Thomas Hutchins also reported in his 1784 book that settlers on the north shore of the lake were engaged in the production of pitch, tar, and turpentine.[8]

During the early-national period, especially after the United States acquired Louisiana in 1803, New Orleans became the marketing and export center for vast quantities of goods that came down the nation's interior river system. The Appalachian mountain chain separated the interior from the East Coast, and until the later construction of the Erie Canal and the National Road, westerners had little choice other than to rely on the Mississippi and its tributaries as their links to the outside world. Lumber and timber were rafted down the rivers to New Orleans. Some of the lumber was exported, but most was marketed and consumed locally to supply the construction needs of the Crescent City, which enjoyed tremendous growth in the antebellum period.[9]

New Orleans became a great lumber market, with boats arriving from cities as far north as the upper Ohio. Lumber was also imported from Gulf Coast ports such as Pensacola. Occasional shipments of lumber were sent to England and to various places in the West Indies. However, relatively little lumber was exported from New Orleans in comparison to cities such as Pensacola, Mobile, and Savannah. The consumption of lumber by the construction industry in New Orleans acted as an important stimulus for the development of the lumber industry along the lower Mississippi and the Mississippi Gulf Coast.[10]

Water mills dominated lumber production in the lower Mississippi Valley until the introduction of steam power in the early nineteenth century. During a trip down the Mississippi River in 1808, Christian Schultz reported, "There are no mill seats in this lower country. . . . After descending as low as the island of New-Orleans, you find a considerable number of saw-mills, which are built a small distance from the banks of the river, from which a canal is cut large enough to admit a sufficient supply of water for about four or five months in the year. . . . After the water has fallen below the level of the wheel they remain dry for the remainder of the year." Schultz also observed, "These mills are always situated near the borders of the swamps, and the water which has served to supply them, passes off through the lakes in the rear."[11]

The surviving records of lumbering operations in Mississippi during the American territorial period are fragmentary. A traveler who passed through Natchez in the summer of 1790 remembered, "Boards were scarce, and I do not remember of seeing any saw or grist-mills in the country." However, naval stores activities were frequently cited. A continuing problem was theft of cypress from along the low-lying Mississippi River areas. According to John Eisterhold, "Irresponsible people who poached timber from public and private lands were a much more serious concern of area lumbermen than fire."[12]

During the summer of 1811 one citizen complained to the governor of the territory, "I am at this moment, informed, by my neighbor . . . that, for some time past, a large party of men principally from the other side of the Mississippi, have been engaged in committing depredations on the lands of the U States adjacent to the bed of the Old River near the Mouth of Homochito." These men, he said, "have now 15, or 16, large Rafts of public timber ready to float out with the current, which will take place on the fall of the Waters of the Innundation." He concluded that if the United States did not take action, it would sustain a "considerable loss," for the lands' value resided in the cypress, "which so large a party would soon cut off." Warned that their activities were illegal, the axe men stated their determination to resist all authority, including that of the United States, and float their rafts.[13]

In July 1811 a government surveyor reported from his office in Washington, Adams County, "These Cypress swamps are covered with Water during the Annual innundations of the Mississippi. . . . Yet the Cypress Timber is so very valuable that the lands covered by those swamps will sell at .2 dollars P Acre and in some instances for much more. Similar depredations to that complained of, are every year committed. I have reason to believe that there are temporary sawmills constructed near the banks of the River, to cut up the cypress on the public land—

In the great swamp or low lands of the Mississippi, the cypress swamps are not numerous particularly near the Mississippi where they are considered as very valuable. This timber where ere it can be procured is made use of for buildings, and fences, in consequence of its great durability—When the timber of these swamps is once destroyed, the land not only becomes useless, but, offensive."[14]

Three years later another spokesman confirmed that "much of the public lands lay on the river, and is only Valuable for the timber, much of which is cut and rafted down the river by marauders,—those lands would all sell if offered before destroyed—the timber Off; it will not be worth any thing." Identification of the thieves was relatively easy, but convincing witnesses to testify against them was another matter.[15]

Timber thievery declined when mills began to send their own logging and rafting crews into the swamps, but piracy of log rafts themselves along the Mississippi River remained a problem. Writing of Yazoo County in the 1820s and 1830s, one student says, "Cypress was then very abundant in the Delta, it was not considered trespass to cut and carry the logs away from Government land or even from the land of private individuals."[16]

The cypress swamps along the Mississippi River provided raw material not only for thieves but also for Mississippi's first significant commercial logging and lumbering activities. Lumbering did not become commercially important until the introduction of steam engines and the growth of markets. The first steam sawmill in New Orleans was owned by James McKeever and Louis Valcourt, who in 1802 imported an engine manufactured by Oliver Evans of Philadelphia to power a boat to run between New Orleans and Natchez. Before the boat could be tested, it broke from its moorings and was swept into a swamp, so McKeever and Valcourt salvaged the engine and used it to power a sawmill. The mill was destroyed by fire in 1806, but its success inspired others to apply steam power to the manufacture of lumber.[17]

By the early nineteenth century the desirability of longleaf and slash pine and of cypress for various uses was known in England and other areas of Europe. The French government purchased pine for spars and square timbers for their navy, and markets developed in Cuba, Mexico, and Texas. However, New Orleans was the major market for Mississippi lumbermen. Cypress logs and lumber from the southern Mississippi River region were rafted down the river to be marketed in the Crescent City.[18]

By 1832 H. S. Tanner reported, "The cypress is a very valuable species of timber. Thousands of trunks of this tree are every year floated down to New-Orleans and other places, to be sawed at the Steam Saw Mills, or to be used for other purposes. Below 31° . . . the live oak . . . is found; valuable for ship timber. . . . The pine forests of the south can furnish millions of masts, spars, &c. for our ships." Tanner also reported that in Mississippi, "The cypress and swamp gum, are large in the swampy lands. Vast quantities of cypress are floated down to New Orleans from this state. They are cut when the waters are high, by the negroes in canoes, who cut them above their cone-like buttresses."[19]

Arguably the most famous antebellum Mississippi logging and lumbering firm originated at Natchez in the 1820s. Andrew Brown was a Scotsman who migrated to the United States early in the decade. Trained as an architect, Brown found employment in the building trade in both Pittsburgh and Natchez. By the late 1820s Brown had acquired his own construction firm in Natchez. In 1828 he purchased a steam-powered mill at Natchez-under-the-hill, constructed by Peter Little in 1825. Here Brown began to produce lumber for his own use.[20]

The Scotsman gradually developed his firm from a relatively small one-saw operation into a sophisticated manufacturing establishment of large capacity utilizing the latest equipment. During the prosperous 1830s the enterprise grew without experiencing significant marketing problems. During this period Brown focused his attention on sources of raw material and moved from reliance on transient log rafts and casual purchases to systematic contracts with professional loggers and the acquisition of cypress-bearing lands.[21]

Following the collapse of cotton prices in 1839, Brown combated the ensuing depression by canvassing markets along the Mississippi River between Natchez and New Orleans, utilizing various methods to dispose of his lumber. As success came in these endeavors, Brown again worked on systematizing his activities. In 1844 he opened a wholesale and retail lumber yard in the thriving market of New Orleans.[22]

By the late 1840s Brown's was the largest such enterprise in Mississippi, and he was operating two sawmills beneath the bluff. The smaller mill employed ten workers and produced more than 1.1 million feet of boards and sawed lumber, worth $19,800 in a year. *DeBow's Review* described the larger mill: "The engine of Andrew Brown's splendid mill is in action fourteen hours each day, and its various operations employ from forty to fifty hands, producing a daily average of 15,000 feet of all kinds of lumber, or four million, five hundred thousand feet in a year. The lumber turned out at this mill is of such value that its average price is twenty-five dollars per thousand, amounting by actual sales, during the year 1847, to *fifty-six thousand dollars,* with an increase of stock on hand of half a million feet of sawed lumber. One half of the above sum, or $28,000, was a clear profit over and above all expenses—a sum larger than that produced by any two of the best Plantations in the State." The culminating step in the expansion of Brown's interests came in 1852, when he constructed a New Orleans woodworking factory to produce various finished products for the construction industry. Thus, by the eve of the Civil War, the Brown firm had developed into a vertically integrated operation encompassing activities from logging in the cypress brakes of the Yazoo River through the production and sale of lumber and finished wood products.[23]

Brown's firm survived the Civil War and, following the conflict, received a contract to supply lumber for the U.S. Army. The firm was succeeded by the R. F. Learned Company of Natchez, which was the oldest continuously operated sawmill on the lower Mississippi River when it closed in the 1980s. In addition to its longevity, the Brown firm is remembered today for the amazing survival of virtually all of the company's records from 1829 until 1865 in the face of the frequent fires and boiler explosions in southern sawmills as well as the rigors of the Civil War. These records provide the foundation for John Hebron Moore's classic history of the firm. The Brown firm offers possibly the best inside look at a successful and growing antebellum Mississippi lumber-manufacturing firm.

Another aspect of Brown's firm makes it historically significant. Brown preferred to utilize slave laborers rather than free whites in his operations, and he allowed those with ability to rise to positions of unusual responsibility. In fact, black workers were preferred over whites in many antebellum sawmills. For a time Brown was the leading Natchez slaveholder, but during the 1830s and 1840s Brown secured more slaves from outside owners than he owned himself. One particularly able slave, Simon Gray, became a flatboat captain and foreman. He received a regular salary, commanded mixed crews of whites and black slaves, handled large sums of company money, bought and sold materials for the firm, lived with his family in a privately owned residence, was allowed to own and bear arms, traveled virtually without restriction between Natchez and New Orleans, and was permitted to conduct private business operations concurrently with his activities for Brown. Another slave, James Matthews, also supervised both blacks and whites as a master of the firm's rafts and flatboats. On occasion the Brown firm even purchased salvaged materials from Matthews. However, in slow periods Matthews was sometimes hired out to steamboat captains. While Brown used punishment, including whippings, to discipline his slaves, he preferred positive incentives, especially monetary bonuses, to stimulate their performance. While one can question whether Brown's treatment of slaves was representative, Gray's situation and, more generally, the experiences of Brown's slaves provide a window into the use and treatment of slaves in southern industrial settings. The situation at Natchez was not unique. Slaves were used extensively in the mills of the Gulf Coast and other areas as well.[24]

While Brown prospered in Natchez, the development of logging and lumbering in other parts of the state was sporadic. Lumbering's growth came late in some localities. One student of Yazoo County says that as late as the 1820s, "Saw mills, planks, shingles and window glass were then unknown in that section of country." One of the first sawmills in this area was a small operation, built by Stephen Howard, just below Manchester on the Yazoo River in the early 1830s. Another mill was that of Calvin Taylor, who in 1826 moved from New Hampshire to Yazoo County, where he operated a plantation and sawmill. By the 1850s at least one New Orleans lumberyard owner purchased lumber from a large mill on the Yazoo River.[25]

In nearby Leflore County lumbering in the antebellum period was usually a seasonal industry carried on by farmers in connection with clearing the land. Their timber was often sold to Vicksburg or New Orleans sawmills, whose logging operations extended far up the Sunflower and Quiver Rivers and into the Yazoo Valley. In the 1830s in Kemper County, the "only mill within reach was on Running Water creek about twenty miles away, more or less, according to the season and the state of the roads. Sawed lumber was costly and could be used only in building the family room." In the same period, Greenwood Leflore built a sawmill at Point Leflore, where the Tallahatchie and Yalobusha Rivers form the Yazoo.[26]

Besides the Natchez region, the only major lumbering areas in Mississippi during the antebellum period were in the piney woods along the Gulf Coast. While there was some production of both hardwood and pine lumber in other areas of the state, it was mostly manufactured for local consumption. In fact, lumber or other wood products do not show up in the 1810 U.S. census figures for the Mississippi Territory, and the 1823

Digest of Accounts of Manufacturing Establishments also does not include figures for the Magnolia State.[27] Not until the 1840s did lumbering become significant in Mississippi's overall picture, and even then lumbering's impact was in scattered areas across the state.

In the 1840 census thirty-three of Mississippi's fifty-six counties did not show any lumber production. Of course, some of these counties probably had small mills, but they did not produce enough lumber to appear in official statistics. Only nine counties produced naval stores (tar, pitch, turpentine, and resin). Sales of wood by the cord were restricted to twenty-six counties, with the larger producers (of more than three thousand cords) generally restricted to counties where the wood was sold as fuel for steamboats. The exceptions were Amite County, which was close enough to the Mississippi River to supply that market, and Hancock County, which met a similar demand for boats along the gulf. The leading counties in lumber production, all with a value of at least eight thousand dollars, were, in order, Coahoma ($45,399), Hancock ($29,498), Jefferson ($25,370), Madison ($14,700), Lawrence ($12,550), Lowndes ($11,000), Pontotoc ($9,235), Lafayette ($8,939), Tunica ($8,195), and Adams ($8,000). These counties are scattered around the state, with two in the northern Delta on the Mississippi River, two in the south on the river, two in the north-central region, one on the gulf, one in the piney woods of south Mississippi, one in the center of the state, and one in the northeast, on the Alabama border. Most of the leading counties are on navigable water, including the Mississippi, Pearl, Big Black, and Tombigbee Rivers. By far the leading lumber-producing counties were Coahoma in the northern Delta, Hancock on the gulf, and Jefferson, a southern Mississippi River county. In 1840 several of the piney woods counties of south Mississippi do not show up as lumber producers.[28]

The longleaf pine belt in Mississippi extends from the Alabama border in the east to the Bluff Hills in the west, and north for about 150 miles from the Gulf Coast. Within the area between the

Pearl and Pascagoula Rivers, in the early nineteenth century more than 75 percent of the forests were pure longleaf. Other species, including shortleaf, loblolly, slash, and bottom, plus such merchantable hardwoods as cypress, white oak, gum, hickory, poplar, magnolia, ash, and beech, were also found in the area. Most of the pure longleaf forest lay between the Pearl River and the Alabama border. An 1881 map of the Mississippi forests shows the following counties with a substantial amount of longleaf: Hinds, Rankin, Smith, Jasper, Wayne, Franklin, and Amite. Counties totally forested with longleaf included Hancock, Harrison, Jackson, Greene, Perry, Marion, Pike, Lincoln, Copiah, Lawrence, Covington, and Jones. An area of mixed longleaf and hardwood forests covered parts of Jasper, Smith, Rankin, Scott, Newton, and Wayne; all of Clarke; and most of Lauderdale, extending northward into Kemper. Loggers had worked in south Mississippi and along the Gulf Coast since the French colonial period, and Hancock and Lawrence Counties were among the state's leading producers in 1840. However, prior to this time production had been confined largely to areas along waterways and was primarily for local use.[29]

Early travelers often described the beauty and parklike appearance of the longleaf forests. However, because of its extensive cover of pine trees, south Mississippi was regarded as an area of poor soil for farming. Most early settlers chose to avoid the region, choosing to clear farms in areas that were suitable for cotton culture. In 1808 Fortescue Cuming described the piney woods region as having a healthier climate than the Mississippi River counties but also as having poor soil, and he predicted that the area would "never draw inhabitants to it while a foot of cane brake land or river bottom" remained to be settled in other sections. More than 90 percent of the longleaf pine counties were considered unsuitable for either cotton or corn production, and they were settled by hunters and cattlemen, or, more properly, herders, who scattered across the region. Most settled in bottomlands adjacent to streams and in a few scattered upland areas, ranging from a few

acres to several sections in size and covered with hardwoods where the soil was more fertile. They raised small crops for their families and earned their cash income largely by grazing cattle on the open range. However, by the 1840s this pastoral economy was threatened by a growing population, overgrazing, and the destruction of the piney woods by fire.[30]

By the late antebellum period population growth was placing greater demands on the land. This was an area of open range. The gradual disappearance of cane and reed was ominous for the cattle drovers: during the winter, when the grass of the pine forests was coarse and inedible, the cattle depended on the cane and reed for survival. Also, for perhaps the first time, contemporaries commented on fire's devastating impact on the area. However, these observers were mourning the loss of pasture rather than forests. Eugene Hilgard noted in 1860 that "those who heretofore have relied on the range, during all but a few weeks in winter, for the support of their cattle, will soon be compelled, as many are now, to raise feed for them on their poor soil, which, at present, will but just furnish comfortably the prime necessities of life for the population itself. The beautiful park-like slopes of the Pine Hills are being converted into a smoking desert of pine trunks, on whose blackened soil the cattle seek more vainly every year the few scattered, sickly blades of grass whose roots the fire has not killed."[31]

The most important visitors of this period included J. F. H. Claiborne, who in 1841–42 published a series of sketches in the *Natchez Free Trader and Gazette*, of which he was the junior editor. Traveling east from Natchez across the counties of south Mississippi, Claiborne commented extensively on Jones County's longleaf pine forests, which he said were "thinly settled and adapted chiefly to grazing." More than two-thirds of the land belonged to the government, he reported, and "will not be entered for years to come at the present prices." Much of the land "is covered exclusively with the long leaf pine; not broken, but rolling like the waves in the middle of the great ocean." Claiborne also noted, "Thousands of cattle are grazed here for market." Describing the lives of the area's settlers, he stated that "many of the men spend days in the woods herding cattle or deer stalking." In Greene County Claiborne found that "[m]any of the people here are herdsmen, owning large droves of cattle, surplus increase of which are annually driven to Mobile." The area's settlers, he observed, also earned money in the fall and winter by killing deer, which they sold in Mobile: "Since the disappearance of the Indians, game has multiplied wonderfully."[32]

While conceding the ability of the pine forests to support "immense herds of cattle," Claiborne offered a prophetic and eventually famous assessment of the south Mississippi piney woods country's future:

The great source of wealth in this country must ultimately be—for it is now scarcely thought of—the lumber trade. The whole east is thickly planted with an almost unvaried forest of yellow pine. Finer, straighter, loftier trees the world does not produce. For twenty miles at a stretch in places you may ride through these ancient woods and see them as they have stood for countless years, untouched by the hand of man and only scratched by the lightning or the flying tempest. The growth of giant pines is unbroken on the route we pursued for an hundred miles or more, save where rivers or large water courses intervene, and then we find in the extensive swamps that bound them on each side a heavy growth of white oak, chestnut and evergreens. The former is particularly large, shooting up frequently a smooth and limbless sixty feet, and of proportionate circumference. The time must arrive when this vast forest will become a source of value. The smoke of the steam mill will rise from a thousand hills. Rafts and lumber boats will sweep down the Pearl, the Leaf and Chickasawhay, and a railroad will transport millions of feet to the city of Mississippi to be shipped in vessels, built there of our own oak, to the West Indies, Texas and South America, countries that furnish the best lumber market in the world, and to which we are so much more accessible than the hardy mariners of New England, that now monopolize the

trade. A rail-road to the gulf could be constructed at little expense. . . . [T]he heart of yellow pine and white oak growing on the whole line would furnish the finest materials. . . . *The opinion that East Mississippi is poor and barren, and* therefore destitute of resources, is erroneous.[33]

Claiborne mentioned deserted houses and decaying towns in several locations but seemed most struck by Wayne County, where he witnessed "all along memorials of the former wealth and prosperity of this county. Comfortable homesteads, once, now unoccupied; large plantations abandoned; venerable oaks still casting their paternal arms over mansions now deserted," and "wornout and deserted fields." The town of Winchester, he said, "is literally tumbling to pieces, and one finds only the skeleton of the flourishing Winchester which existed twenty years ago." The reason for the decline, Claiborne argued, was the Choctaw treaty of 1830, which "threw open such an immense extent of productive territory in the center of our State" and "drew off her population by the hundreds." Wayne and Lawrence Counties, he said, sent the largest numbers of emigrants to the new counties in the center of the state. B. L. C. Wailes said that in 1852 there were only two houses remaining that were fit for habitation in the formerly bustling town of Columbia in Marion County. L. A. Besancon said of Perry County in 1838, "The population . . . is small in proportion to the square miles; when this part of the county was brought in to market it was settled with astonishing rapidity, and in a very short time became very populous; a few years, however, served to convince its inhabitants of the uncertainty of their prospects; and the . . . opening of a new purchase . . . from the Choctaw nation of Indians, caused the tide of immigration to flow as rapidly from the county as it had previously done towards it."[34]

The sixteen Mississippi pine counties in 1860 were, except for the Yazoo-Mississippi Delta, the most thinly settled region in the state. Immigration had been fairly heavy prior to 1820, but between 1830 and 1840 Greene, Wayne, and Perry

Counties declined in population, while others grew very slowly. Even those piney woods counties that did not lose population stagnated. In the period from 1820 to 1850 Perry County's population grew by 569 people, Green by 787, and Wayne by only 368. In other counties of the region the growth was also extremely slow. Farming at its best was risky and hazardous, and on the hills large-scale cultivation was impossible. Large numbers of farmers looking for better land moved northward following the removal of Native Americans from middle and north Mississippi.[35]

Several factors helped make Claiborne's vision of a lumber empire into reality. The piney woods of south Mississippi attracted growing attention from lumbermen in the 1840s as a result of reports from visitors who marveled at the region's rich pine forests and of the increasing awareness of the attractive qualities of pine, especially longleaf. Southern pine had long been known for its strength, beauty, toughness, resistance to decay, and suitability for ship construction and as a source of naval stores. By the 1840s its desirability for railway ties, spars, shingles, piling, and railroad car construction was also becoming known. Markets for lumber were growing in the South and in other parts of the nation as well.[36]

The growth of lumber markets mirrored the expansion of the American economy. Wood was a central part of the story, even though the use of coal and iron was on the rise. From the early nineteenth century until the Civil War, America evolved from a rural agricultural society into a nation that was predominantly urban and industrial. The South and Mississippi remained overwhelmingly rural, but Dixie's forests facilitated the changes in other sections.

In 1836 James Hall said, "Well may ours be called a *wooden country,* not merely from the extent of its forests, but because in common use wood has been substituted for a number of most necessary and common articles—such as stone, iron, and even leather." As Michael Williams has observed, Hall "was thinking not only of houses, fences, furniture, and fuel but also of wooden

roads, bridges, locks, nails, hinges, and machinery, all of which had not yet been replaced by iron." Wood was employed for all sorts of mundane uses. Packing containers constituted a major market. Sugar was shipped in large-bellied hogsheads and triggered a business in gathering and riving staves. Tobacco also was shipped in hogsheads, and flour, cornmeal, whiskey, lard, lard oil, pork, pickled beef, tar, and pitch were transported in barrels. There was a thriving business in common and pipe staves and wine pipes. In 1839 some 84 percent of houses were constructed of wood.[37]

The first half of the nineteenth century was a period of technological innovation as well as demographic change. People were moving across the continent and from farms toward cities. From 1810 to 1860 the United States population grew from 7.2 to 31 million, an enormous increase in the domestic market. The American economy was poised at what some have called the "take-off period," a time when the confluence of various forces propelled the nation into an era of sustained economic growth.[38]

Among the symbols of the American economy in this period was the steam engine, associated in the public mind with the advent of an age of coal and iron and steam. But in fact, wood, not iron and coal, supported and fueled these developments. Steam engines were rare in the United States until the 1820s, and as late as 1838 there were only 1,616 known and another 238 estimated in the country. The leading states were Pennsylvania, Massachusetts, and Louisiana. Most steam engines were used for manufacturing, including applications in Louisiana sugar mills. By 1830 there were only 337 steam locomotives in the country, and there were only 243 steamboats by 1834. The latter number grew to seven hundred steamboats, plus another hundred estimated, by the latter part of the decade.[39]

Like steamboats, most locomotives were fueled by wood before the Civil War. Wood was cheaper and more convenient for railroad use, and by 1860 there were some four thousand locomotives, of which all but about 350 to 400 were fired with wood. By that time there were thirty thousand miles of track in the United States, and railroads in some parts of the country converted to coal as their wood supplies were depleted. However, in the South, where trains were light and pine abundant, wood continued to be burned into at least the 1880s. By 1870 approximately 10 million cords of wood were consumed for motive power annually, although household wood consumption continued to dominate the market.[40]

The national lumber harvest grew from less than a half million board feet in 1801 to 1.6 million in 1839 and 8 billion by 1859. The national center of production shifted from the Northeast to the Great Lakes states.[41] While the South had not yet moved into a position of national leadership, the growth of the lumber industry gradually altered the traditional patterns of the south Mississippi piney woods.

The first steam sawmill along the Gulf Coast may have been erected at Pascagoula in 1835, but it only operated for a brief period. Later in the 1830s several more steam sawmills were constructed at the junctions of waterways and Mississippi Sound. By 1840 there were ten sawmills in Hancock County, including the area that became Harrison County in 1843. Jackson County had two mills, and Lawrence had ten. Most of these mills were on navigable water. In the antebellum period most of the raw material that fed the mills was rafted down rivers and streams from the logging sites, some of which were far in the backcountry. The finished products were also shipped out by water.[42]

In the 1840s the lumber industry became significant in the Gulf Coast counties. One industry pioneer was Asa Hursey, a native of Maine who moved to Pearlington, near the Gulf Coast, in the early 1840s. Formerly a partner in a Canadian sawmill, by the latter part of the decade Hursey had formed a partnership in a water mill, bought out his partner, and converted the mill to steam power. He shipped most of his lumber in rafts down the Pearl River and then on schooners to New Orleans, where he sold his products. Hursey

used both free and slave labor in his expanding operations, marketing his products both locally and regionally. Hursey's firm survived the Civil War, and he remained active until his death in the late 1880s. Among Hursey's models was W. H. Brown, a pioneer Hancock County lumberman who owned a steam sawmill.[43]

Another early area lumberman was W. J. Poitevent, who came from South Carolina to settle in Gainesville, on the Pearl River, in 1832. By the mid-1840s Poitevent was wealthy, with enterprises that included sawmilling, shipping, and a mercantile operation. He built schooners and by 1860 had sawmills at both Gainesville and Pearlington. Poitevent owned large timbered properties in both Mississippi and Louisiana. Following the Civil War, in partnership with Joseph Favre, he owned the largest sawmill on the Gulf Coast.[44]

Among Poitevent's associates was D. R. Wingate, a fellow South Carolinian who came to the Pearl River area in 1824. By the mid-1840s he operated a sawmill in partnership with Poitevent, and after the partnership was dissolved later in the decade he joined W. W. Carre, Carre's brother, and Henry Weston in a new venture. In 1856 Wingate sold out to his partners and moved on to Texas, where he built a large mill at Sabine Pass.[45]

Weston was a Maine native who was trained by his father in the lumbering business. He arrived in Mississippi in the 1840s. Weston had migrated to Wisconsin at the age of eighteen and worked running logs on the Eau Claire River and as a sawyer at a steam sawmill. He moved to New Orleans in 1846 and secured a position as a sawyer, claiming to produce "double what anyone else in the territory is sawing." After a short stay in the Crescent City, he moved to Pearlington to take over the management of a small steam sawmill. He earned fifty cents for every thousand board feet of lumber produced and ten cents for each thousand laths. Weston earned $550 in his first six months managing the mill. However, in 1851 the mill closed and Weston was forced to return to New Orleans as a sawyer.

Times were hard, and Weston reported that only four of the forty sawmills on the south side of Lake Ponchartrain were operating. Weston soon returned to Pearlington to enter the partnership with Wingate and the Carres.[46]

The partnership suffered some of the common disasters of the early lumber industry, including a fire that destroyed the mill. The partners rebuilt, constructing a new sash mill with a daily capacity of nine thousand board feet. Using a labor force consisting mostly of slaves, the partners bought high-quality pine and cypress logs and turned out lumber at a handsome profit in the 1850s. Weston noted that he made money like smoke. The partners established the foundations for a prosperous postwar business and for the Weston family firm, which became a major lumber manufacturer in south Mississippi.[47]

Other mills of the Pearl River area produced lumber and squared timbers for both domestic and foreign markets. Important producers included D. R. Walker and John Toulme, whose mill, valued at nine thousand dollars, sawed 1.2 million board feet between May 31, 1849, and June 1, 1850. W. M. Brown employed eleven men and two women and grossed $11,200 at his operation in Shieldsborough. Hursey and his partner, a man named Henderson, sawed about 700,000 board feet. During the following decade sawmilling along the Pearl River continued to expand, with Wailes reporting in 1852 that there were eight mills at Pearlington and two more under construction. There were seven mills near the Bay of St. Louis, which shipped collectively one million board feet of lumber. Lumber and timber from the area were shipped around the world.[48]

Lumbering developed somewhat more slowly on the Pascagoula River. One of the earliest mills was owned by Sark and Dameron and was built in the early 1830s. It was a combination sawmill and gristmill, and its products were marketed locally. One of the earliest, if short-lived, steam mills was that of Tetar, erected at West Pascagoula in 1835. John Beardslee and John Bradford built what may have been the first mill in Moss Point in 1836, near the confluence of the

Escatawpa and East Pascagoula Rivers. The mill was well situated to receive logs from upriver and to ship out lumber via schooners in the Gulf. The mill was purchased by David Files, who in turn sold out to Walter Denny and Sons in 1853 and then built another mill.[49]

Three men from Massachusetts, J. M. and J. P. Arnold and W. M. Sheldon, began to manufacture lumber with a muley mill at Moss Point in 1847. In 1849 the men were joined in their partnership by William Griffin, who had formerly been involved in rafting timber and logs down Black Creek and the Pascagoula River to the Gulf. Griffin also had large holdings in cattle, land, and slaves. Griffin came to Moss Point in 1850 or 1852 from Perry County, and after one of the Arnolds was killed in a boiler explosion, Griffin became the mill manager while the other partners handled marketing. One of the most significant technological changes in the mill was converting from the muley saw to a gang saw, which remained in use until 1905. The firm expanded vertically, operating lumberyards in Boston, schooners to carry goods to market, and a brick kiln. On the eve of the Civil War, the northern partners sold out to Griffin, who was well positioned for further expansion.[50]

In 1845 D. A. Vermillion built a small mill at the mouth of the East Pascagoula River. Malcolm McRae later purchased the mill and operated it until 1860. McRae owned a farm and slaves on Red Creek, a tributary of the Pascagoula, and he used the slaves to log and haul timber by land and raft to his mills. In 1850 McRae's mills were sawing 700,000 board feet of lumber. A much larger mill in the Moss Point–Pascagoula area was that of John S. Dees, which sawed 2,000,000 board feet of lumber between May 31, 1849, and June 1, 1850. The Dees mill was water powered and employed twenty-five workers, including five women, at its site on Jackson Creek, a few miles up the Escatawpa River. A mill owned by William Deggs at Moss Point cut 500,000 board feet during the same period.[51]

During the 1850s the number of mills in the Pascagoula vicinity grew, and they became larger, primarily because of the adoption of the circular saw, which was much faster and therefore increased a mill's capacity. The circular saw was first adopted in the Pascagoula area by Thomas and Rufus Rhodes and by Garland Goode and Dees. Goode's mills above Franklin Creek on the Escatawpa River used both circular saws and a double gang saw and cut about twenty-five thousand board feet per day. Goode also added a planing mill to his operations, which he organized under a departmental system that resembled the structure of large operations at the end of the century. Most of his labor force consisted of slaves, with the department managers the only hired workers. Goode's superior organization and the efficiency of his operations allowed him to prosper during the late antebellum period.[52]

Another successful operator on the Escatawpa River was Walter Denny, who erected a circular sawmill in 1853 and, using slave labor, manufactured lumber, which he shipped to New Orleans in his own vessels for marketing. Other manufacturers in the Pascagoula area included the partners Plummer and Williams. In the 1850s the Bayou Bernard Lumber Company operated ten steam sawmills in the vicinity of Biloxi. The company was actually a producers' association that fixed prices and sold lumber directly to New Orleans consumers. The association was short-lived, a victim of competition in the New Orleans market from other lumbering centers such as Mobile and Pensacola and of the good times resulting from rising prices and growing foreign markets. In fact, much of the Gulf Coast mills' production went on consignment to wholesalers or commission salesmen in New Orleans, and in some cases Crescent City merchants sold the lumber for whatever the market would bring.[53]

The Bayou Bernard Lumber Company's Mississippi operations were part of another pioneering Gulf Coast lumbering community. Nollie Hickman says that the Bayou Bernard area "was known in the 1850's as the principal center of lumbering within a hundred mile radius of New Orleans. In volume of production, number of mills, capital invested, and related industries, the district was further advanced than other sections of Mississippi prior to 1860." The area's big attractions were the longleaf and slash pines bordering the banks of the streams, and logs could be cheaply and easily transported by water. Most mills were built in close proximity to one another on protected water that provided both storage ponds for logs and berths for lumber schooners. Some early manufacturers existed in the 1830s, but the real development began in the late 1840s.[54]

In 1844 a French immigrant named Fernando Gautier ran a sawmill on Tchoutacabouffa Bayou, and two years later Calvin Taylor started a lumber business that lasted for almost half a century. In the late 1840s many lumbermen came to the area, including Henry Leinhard and Jacob Salmen from Switzerland and several from New England. Among those who became important manufacturers were Taylor and his partner, Samuel Fowler; the firm of Hand Brothers and Prother; H. Bingham; S. S. Henry; and a South Carolinian named Nimwood McQuire.[55]

Taylor's career mirrors the growth of the area's lumber industry. As mentioned earlier, Taylor came to Yazoo County from New Hampshire in 1826. There he operated a plantation and sawmill. Twenty years later Taylor and Gordon Davis purchased a sawmill on Bayou Bernard. The operation suffered in the early period due to their foreman's inability to handle the machinery and manage the mill's slave labor force. Difficulties with labor were endemic in the industry during the antebellum period.[56]

There was usually a shortage of competent, white sawyers in Louisiana and Mississippi. Workers were sometimes discovered by mill owners through personal advertisements in New Orleans newspapers. To protect against hiring incompetents, employers often required references. Many Louisiana and Mississippi lumbermen were hired for temporary jobs as woodchoppers. They worked for a salary or on a piecework basis, in both cases with room and board provided. The crews included various combinations of whites, free blacks, and slaves. Sawmill owners considered slaves excellent lumber mill workers, for the workday was long, from sunup to sundown, and required a great deal of strength and physical endurance under hot and humid conditions. Much of the work did not require a great deal of training and could be closely supervised in the mill setting. Some employers excluded blacks, but others preferred blacks because they were easier to control and less likely to quit. Slaves and free blacks were also sometimes employed as sawyers and engineers, and it was not unusual for a black to be head sawyer.[57]

Despite their disappointments, Davis and Taylor continued to pour capital into their operation and to upgrade their facilities and labor force. However, they struggled and even sold lumber at below the manufacturing cost. By 1848 the mills were operating efficiently, but Davis died during the year, and Samuel Fowler came in as a part owner. Finally, with lumber prices in decline, Taylor sold his mill interests in about 1852 and moved to New Orleans, where he became an agent of the short-lived Bayou Bernard Lumber Company. With that company's collapse, he returned to Mississippi City and became a partner with Gordon Myers in another mill, which operated until the Civil War. The partners purchased a planing mill, which gave them a competitive advantage over many of their neighbors, and during the late 1850s the firm prospered. With his increased capital, Taylor purchased timber lands, additional equipment, and more slaves. After acquiring five slaves, a saw, and a planing mill belonging to Fowler at public sale, the firm of Taylor and Myers became the largest lumber producer in the Harrison County region. By 1860 the firm had two sawmills and a planing mill and generated a gross income of forty-eight thousand dollars.[58]

Even while acquiring considerable timberland and rafting their own logs to their mills, Taylor and Myers secured much of their raw material from independent log men. These men employed their own labor forces and sold their logs to the mills on contract, often receiving cash and merchandise advances from their customers. An example of this kind of operator was Goodman Hester, who lived on Tuxechaena Creek and sold

logs to Taylor and Myers in the late 1850s. Hester cut logs on Taylor and Myers's property, on his own land, and on the public domain. Another such operator was Alexander Scarbrough, who lived near the creek and occasionally sold logs to Taylor from 1847 until 1860. In 1847 Scarbrough marketed logs to Taylor for three dollars per thousand board feet and later to Taylor and Myers for thirty cents per log. Other log men included Jacob Stronger and Hiram Williams, who in 1859–60 rafted logs to Taylor's mills for 73.5 cents each.[59]

At Delisle, where the Wolf River empties into the Bay of St. Louis, other firms were established by Thomas Gorray, G. L. Thomas, Leonard Staples, John Huddleston, W. J. White, and others. In 1850 the mills of this area produced about 17 million board feet of lumber. However, at that time salable sawmill timber had to be eighteen inches wide at the shortest end and clear of knots, requirements that meant that the mills utilized only superior timber. Consequently, by the early 1850s the Bayou Bernard mills faced a timber shortage. They had cut much of the land near their mills, the streams on which they were located were short, and it was considered uneconomical to haul timber for more than three miles to a stream for transport to the mill. The mill owners worked toward building a railroad to resolve the problem, and in 1852 several owners secured a state charter for that purpose.[60]

The Bayou Bernard lumbermen upgraded their facilities with the introduction of circular saws and planing mills. The area continued to attract new producers, including J. T. Liddle, Marvin Holcombe, James Fewell, L. T. Burr, W. J. Blackman, and L. M. Taylor. Some equipment came from the immediate vicinity, for Bayou Bernard was the home of the L. N. Bradford foundry and its competitor, S. B. Hand. Both produced boilers and steam engines for the lumber operators.[61]

Lumbering along the Gulf Coast prospered in the 1850s. By the latter part of the decade shipments of lumber, squared timbers, and spars to Europe and the West Indies were growing, and mills along the coast were sending cargo all over the world, including twenty-eight thousand dollars worth of lumber, sawed timber, and deals (pine boards cut to standard dimensions) to England and Australia during the latter half of April 1857. There was also an extensive coastwise trade with Texas and Mexico, and J. F. H. Claiborne reported, "Mississippi pine is now sent on almost every steamer that leaves New Orleans for St. Louis." By 1858 pitch pine from Ship Island was encroaching on the domain of producers around Savannah.[62]

Mills in the backcountry developed later and on a smaller scale, especially in areas where there were no railroads. New Orleans was the major outside market and merchandising center, but most of the lumber and timber that arrived in New Orleans prior to the Civil War came by water. While some was shipped by rail, it was not until after the war that the railroads rose to dominance. Wailes reported in 1852 that in low, flat, interior regions where there were no natural streams, some loggers cut ditches that were miles in length and deep enough to float a single line of logs. When rain filled the ditches, the logs were pushed to their destinations. Many of these interior operations were water-powered combination mills that manufactured lumber but also ground grain and ginned cotton. Some also cleaned rice. Since these mills lacked access to navigable water, most products were sold locally. In 1852 there were fifteen water mills in Pike County and nine in Covington County. Copiah and Rankin Counties also had mills, with one in Rankin producing nine thousand dollars worth of products in 1850. U.S. Census statistics for 1850 reflect the relatively small scale of the Mississippi industry. The state was credited with 259 establishments, capitalized at $711,130. There were 1,079 workers, turning out products valued at $913,197. Mississippi ranked nineteenth of thirty-six states and territories in number of establishments, and twenty-second in value of production.[63]

The situation changed somewhat for the interior counties when railroads were built in some areas during the late antebellum period. The Mobile and Ohio on the eastern border of the long-leaf belt and the New Orleans, Jackson, and Great Northern in the western section built lines into the piney woods between 1852 and 1857. Steam sawmills were erected along the lines since the mills could now reach outside markets. Establishments in Clarke County began to produce significant amounts of lumber and squared timbers, some of which were shipped overseas through Mobile. In the West, Copiah and Pike Counties also benefited from the railroads. Copiah had eleven steam-powered mills by 1860, whereas in 1850 there had been only water-powered operations. Similarly, in 1855 W. W. Vaught built a steam-powered circular saw mill, which may have been the first in Pike County. An important firm established in Pike County in 1859 was that of J. J. and Robert Emmett White. The White firm maintained an important presence in the lumber industry for more than half a century.[64]

By the time of the Civil War, lumbering was the leading industry in Mississippi, but the Magnolia State lagged far behind the national leaders. The state had 228 saw and planing mills in operation, producing approximately $1.8 million worth of lumber. A minimum of 1,413 people were employed in the mills, with total wages of $431,844 paid to them in 1860.[65] Most of the state's acreage of forested lands had not been touched by the loggers' axes and saws. A great deal of land had been cleared by farmers and planters, but vast tracts of woods and trees remained. Much of Mississippi's lumber was produced for local consumption, and, while the state's forest products were shipped around the world, New Orleans was far and away the leading outside market. Technology evolved during the period from primitive pit saws and water-powered mills to sophisticated steam-powered circular sawmills, often operated in conjunction with planing mills. Most of the mills and logging operations were located along streams or the coast so that the logs could easily be rafted to the mills and the lumber transported to markets. By the late antebellum period some logs and lumber moved by rail, but water transportation remained dominant. The industry was concentrated in two areas: in the lower Mississippi River and Yazoo River region, and along the Gulf Coast. The labor force consisted of a mixture of whites and blacks, with slaves extensively utilized for the heavy work. While some mill owners were prospering and growing, the size of individual firms was generally rather small.

The late nineteenth and early twentieth century brought unprecedented growth to Mississippi's forest-products industries. National and international markets expanded, the lumber industry exhausted its raw materials in other parts of the country, and railroads connected vast new timbered areas with the outside world. Loggers and lumbermen descended on the Magnolia State in droves, and no merchantable timber was safe from the axe and saw. Big money and large firms came into Mississippi, and in the early twentieth century the state became the nation's leading lumber producer. The euphoria was brief. Within a short period of time the lumber industry cut over the state, and most of the lumber firms departed for untouched forests in other parts of the country. For years afterward Mississippians struggled with their legacy of cutover lands and abandoned people and communities.

4   The Bonanza Era

Mississippi Lumbering's Rise to National Prominence

Early in the twentieth century an enormous outpouring of timber from Mississippi's forests made the Magnolia State the national leader in lumbering. Development of the lumbering industry in the late nineteenth and early twentieth centuries differed in several respects from that of earlier periods: in ownership and control of timberlands and mills, in technology, in marketing, in transportation, and in philosophy. Various forces and trends coalesced in the post-Civil War period to propel Mississippi into a lofty position among lumber-producing states. And just as suddenly as it had happened, it was over. Mississippi's forests today are products of the ways in which Mississippians dealt with the legacy of denuded, cutover land that the lumber companies left as many departed the state for greener climes in the early twentieth century.

Economics, technology, and the state of forestry knowledge combined to spawn the devastating procedures that leveled Mississippi's forests and left them without any apparent prospects for regeneration. The economics of lumbering were determined by the ownership and cost of standing timber; fixed costs in mills, logging railroads, and the other machinery of sawmilling; the price of credit; markets; and government policies, including most importantly the public land laws and the tax structures. The large lumber mills and the logging equipment and timber holdings that fed them represented enormous fixed costs. Lumbermen believed that they needed to cut over their lands quickly and convert the trees into dollars to justify their investments. The cost of credit was high in what was considered an unpredictable business. Lumber manufacturers needed quick profits to service and liquidate their debts.

Little was known in the late nineteenth and early twentieth centuries about the enormous regenerative powers of the forests, especially southern pine. Lumbermen believed that they could profitably cut their forests only once and that, because of the time involved and tax policies, they could not afford to manage forests with an eye toward reforestation. Open range, which allowed hogs to roam freely through the countryside, was an enormous problem, for hogs were notorious for rooting at and killing young seedlings. Fire was also a major concern. Burning the woods was traditional in the rural South, and whether caused by nature, custom, or malicious incendiarism, fire was a significant threat to owners of timbered lands.

Finally, the woods technology of the period was a culprit. Again, the emphasis lay on getting the wood out of the forests quickly and turning an immediate profit. Thus, selective cutting was almost unheard of. The prevailing methods were to clear-cut the forest, with no thought of regeneration, or to "high grade," taking only the best timber and leaving inferior trees behind. This was the "golden" age of railroad logging, with the use of steam skidders to pull logs through the forests to railroad spurs, where they were loaded on trains for transport to mills. As the logs were dragged across the ground, they destroyed everything in their paths, including the young seedlings that represented forest renewal. There has never been a more short-sighted or destructive method of logging.

Among the factors that made the development of large-scale lumber manufacturing possible in the United States, and in Mississippi, was the evolution of lumbering from a primitive, low-technology industry into a highly mechanized and sophisticated activity. In the early years of the industry in Mississippi, lumber was produced by whipsawing, or, as it was sometimes called, pit sawing. The logs were sawed by hand, with one man in a pit and the other standing above on a platform. The next phase was the development of water-driven sash saws. A sash saw was a straight saw running in a sash or frame. The wooden rectangular frame moved up and down with the saw, which cut only on the down stroke. Power was provided by a crank or shaft that was attached to a waterwheel, and the log was pushed into the saw by a mechanical feeder. The sash saw was in turn replaced by the muley saw. A muley saw resembled a sash saw but eliminated or lightened the frame. Some muley saws ran in guides, and the stroke was faster. Another production boost came from the introduction of the gang saw, in which two or more saws were installed in the frame. Some mills also used the so-called peckerwood saw, which consisted of "an iron bar six to eight inches wide and about seven feet long, swung at the center with teeth on each end. It literally chewed its way through the log."[1]

During the days of water-powered sawmilling, a typical operation had a millpond or storage area for logs. From the pond workers used chains to drag the logs up an incline onto the log deck. They were then placed on a carriage and moved toward the saw. After each cut the log was manually repositioned on the carriage . The early mills produced lumber that was rough and uneven,

with a maximum output of five hundred to two thousand board feet per day. As late as 1870 the U.S. Census reported that Mississippi still had forty-eight water-powered mills. In fact, by 1909, with the expansion of the lumber industry, the number of water-powered lumbering establishments in the state had more than quadrupled.[2]

The major technological changes that ushered in the modern era of sawmilling included the introduction of steam engines, circular saws, and band saws. Circular saws were patented and used in English shipbuilding yards by the 1770s but did not appear in the United States until 1814, when a New York lumberman invented a crude hand-forged blade, which he installed in his mill. Other northeasterners improved and used the design in the 1820s, and in 1846 a Californian designed a blade with removable teeth that made repairs easier. Powered by steam, the circular blade could eventually cut up to eighty thousand board feet per day.

There was early resistance to circular saws. Workers feared that these saws were dangerous since they ran at high speeds. Also, circular saws had a wide cutting grove that took a quarter to a half inch of the board at each cut. Michael Williams calculates that a circular saw with a bite of five-sixteenths of an inch produced 312 feet of sawdust for every thousand feet of one-inch boards produced. Robert S. Maxwell and Robert D. Baker report that some critics of this period described the circular saws as "sawdust-making machines that produced some lumber as a by-product." There were constant efforts to make the circular saws thinner, faster, and more dependable, but by the 1880s many mills used them only for cutting rough timber and replaced them with band saws for other applications.[3]

The band saw was probably invented in France during the early nineteenth century. It was used in Baltimore by 1819 and in New York by about 1860. Jacob R. Hoffman of Ft. Wayne, Indiana, is credited with introducing it into the modern lumber industry in the late 1860s, and both he and the Disston Saw Company experimented with various improvements. The big breakthrough was a Disston exhibition at the Philadelphia Centennial Exposition in 1876 that featured an enormous band saw.[4]

One of the technological pioneers of the Mississippi lumber industry was Rufus F. Learned, the stepson of Andrew Brown. Learned took over the Brown firm after the Civil War, and in 1876 he visited the centennial exposition. The Disston exhibit inspired him to use a band saw to manufacture lumber, and in 1884 he installed a custom-designed six-inch band saw in his mill. Learned increased the size of the saw to ten inches and developed a system for tensioning the edges of the saws. The Eastman-Gardiner Lumber Company of Laurel also claimed to be among the first mills in Mississippi to introduce the band saw.[5]

Steam power came slowly to lumbering. The first steam engine was supposedly used in sawmilling in 1811 at New Orleans. There were other applications in scattered locations, but as late as 1838 only 208 steam engines were installed in American sawmills, with another sixty-five in planing mills, mostly in Massachusetts. Steam engines offered greater reliability and speed than water power but were costly. Their widespread adoption came with the expansion of markets and the arrival of larger and more adequately capitalized firms following the Civil War. Even then their victory was slow and incomplete. As late as 1870 there were 16,562 waterwheels producing 327,000 horsepower in lumber mills, compared with 11,204 steam engines turning out 314,000 horsepower. In Mississippi by 1870 there were 192 steam engines producing 5,666 horsepower employed by sawmills. In the south Mississippi piney woods, the adoption of the turbine in the last quarter of the nineteenth century enabled many mills to continue operating with water power well into the early twentieth century.[6]

The improvement of saws and introduction of steam power were not the only changes that came to the sawmill. Edgers to square boards were invented in 1825, and mechanized carriages to carry the logs past the saw in 1850. The plan-

ing machine was invented in 1828, and by 1850 there were a variety of planers that produced many specialized products. There were machines to make shingles, to cut lathe, and for mortising as well as for other purposes. Steam-powered machinery began to replace manual labor in moving the logs from the pond, through the mill, and toward shipment.[7]

Large, steam-powered band-saw mills generally had two or three levels. A jackladder, a long trough with a continuously running hooked chain at the bottom, ran at a downward slope from the mill to the log pond. The logs were maneuvered into the trough, snagged by the hooks, and pulled up into the mill, where a circular cutoff saw broke them down into specific lengths. They were then moved out of the trough by a mechanical log kicker and rolled down a slight incline to a holding point on the log deck parallel to the carriage. Some larger mills had two carriages, one on either side of the trough. The carriage grabbed the log as it rolled off the deck and held it in place as it moved past the head rig. The head rig was the second saw that cut the log after it entered the mill, and it could be either a circular saw or a band saw. After the log passed the saw, it was repositioned for the next trip. All of this work was done manually in the early period and later was done mechanically with hydraulically powered machines controlled by an operator at a control board. One of the first Mississippi firms to acquire a modern band-saw mill was the Butterfield Lumber Company at Norfield in the late nineteenth century.[8]

The carriage traveled on railroad tracks parallel to the saw blade, pushed by a long piston rod called the shotgun feed. The sawyer rode the carriage and decided how the log would be cut. He was assisted by two block setters, who repositioned and clamped the log into place after each pass. Other than the sawyer, who was highly paid, the most important workers in the mill were the saw filers, who sharpened and inspected the blades. The saws were usually pulled twice daily for sharpening, cleaning, and inspection. This process was essential, for clean, sharp blades cut

Saw filer. Courtesy Mississippi Forestry Commission, Jackson.

faster and cooler, and friction generated by dull blades could and did cause fires. Furthermore, the material and human damage caused by a broken blade could be devastating.[9]

The furnaces and steam engines were housed on the first floor and were connected to the saws on the upper floors by pulleys and drive belts. Post-1850 mills with circular saws could produce twenty-five to twenty-seven thousand board feet of lumber daily, or about 9 million board feet in a year. A mill with a band saw could produce fifty to seventy-five thousand feet daily, and a larger mill with two band saws and two carriages could turn out 100,000 or more feet daily. By the late nineteenth century fifty thousand board feet daily was considered the threshold of commercial or industrial production. Most mills large enough to employ railroad logging were one- or two-band-saw operations. By 1900 there were 211 large mills in the South that produced more than 10 million board feet annually, and by 1919 this

number had grown to 352. In Mississippi there were twenty-five such mills in 1900 and sixty-four in 1919. Along with Louisiana and Texas, the Magnolia State led the nation in the percentage of production coming from large mills.[10]

The first phase of the mill turned out squared timbers called cants, boards, and beams. Some of the beams became railroad ties, ships' keels, and trestle posts. Others were run through gang saws, or resaws, often consisting of several parallel blades, and emerged as low-quality boards used to build containers and other common articles. The larger boards traveled on gravity-powered rollers and conveyors toward edgers (small circular saws) and trimmers that determined their final shape and size. All along the process decisions were made concerning the optimal conversion of the logs, cants, beams, and boards into merchantable products, but in the bonanza period of the industry there was incredible waste. An estimated 40 to 60 percent of the original tree was not converted into merchantable lumber. After the lumber was dried, it was processed by planing machines with revolving knives, which gave it its final appearance. Edgings were cut into smaller products such as shingles or laths, and the remains were chipped to make fuel, which was blown into the furnace to provide power.[11]

In 1920 the Long-Bell Lumber Company of Kansas City, one of the largest southern pine lumber manufacturers, with holdings in Texas, Louisiana, and Mississippi, including a mill at Quitman, provided an excellent description of the manufacturing process in a state-of-the-art mill at the height of the bonanza era:

When train loads of logs hauled from the woods reach the mill, possibly twenty miles or more distant, they are automatically dumped into the mill pond. This pond is common to all Southern pine sawmill plants, for the reason that logs can be handled, sorted and stored in water more economically than in any other way, and are there preserved against decay and injury from wood destroying insects while awaiting their final journey to the saws. The logs make their entrance in the mill over an inclined chute equipped with an endless spiked chain conveyor. The logs are floated into place until one end is brought into contact with the conveyor, when they are caught by the chain spikes and lifted from the water and up the chute. As they enter upon the "log deck" inside the mill they pass under the inspection of a scaler and deck-saw man, skilled in judging the size and quality of the logs and their fitness for conversion into certain forms of lumber. If a log chances to be of very large size, free from imperfections and dense in its structural fibre, the deck-sawyer may permit it to pass on its way, to be squared and dressed into a great timber suitable for use in heavy construction. If it might better serve some other purpose, the deck-sawyer halts the progress of the log, and with the pressure of a lever a giant circular saw descends, cutting the log in two with the speed and seeming ease of a knife cleaving new cheese. From the log deck the log or each of its sections is "kicked" by steam-driven steel arms onto a skidway, down which it rolls to a resting place in front of the band-saw carriage. The band-saw, the carriage and all of the "rig" pertaining thereto are highly important parts of sawmill equipment, under the control of the most important and highly skilled workman in the mill—the sawyer. A good sawyer not only must know the anatomy of a tree and be able to judge it at a glance, but he must be extremely sensitive to the amount of force at his command, represented in the complex mass of powerful, steam-driven machinery he controls, and be able to divide his attention into three or four channels at the same time and all the time he is on duty. He directs and regulates the speed of the log carriage, using both hands and feet in applying and cutting off steam power; manipulates the log on the carriage as it travels to and from the saw; determines the size of every cut made from the log, and meanwhile is constantly "sizing-up" and classifying the log as cut after cut is removed—all simultaneously. A crew of three to six men ride on the log carriage and manipulate the "setting" device and the "dogs" which hold the log in place while it is being sawed. These workmen take their orders from the sawyer, receiving them in the form of signals made with the fingers, since the incessant roar of ponderous machinery moving at top speed makes speech inaudible. The log carriage moves to and from the band saw at such a rate that makes riding upon it seem precarious work, requiring close attention to the business at hand, and at each trip a slab or plank is ripped from the log. The slabs, or outer cuts of the log, fall upon running rolls and are hurried to a machine called a slasher, which cuts them into four foot lengths for lath stock. Planks or boards cut from the log pass over conveyors to the edger, a machine which, at the direction of the operator, may merely trim the bark edges from the planks or may rip them into various combinations of widths. From the rear table of the edger the boards drop to conveyors which carry them to the trimmer, where they have faulty ends removed and cut out. This accomplished, the resulting product is finished rough green lumber, and the first important step in the manufacture of logs into building material is completed.[12]

Technological change also came to the woods. In the late 1880s in south Mississippi, crosscut saws replaced axes for felling trees. Early saws

Crosby Lumber Company mill at Crosby, 1939. Courtesy Forest History Society, Durham, North Carolina.

were not successful because the kerf choked and clogged them. The resin from southern pine logs formed a layer of gum on the saw teeth that prevented them from cutting. Improvements included cutters that removed sawdust and the discovery that sprinkling kerosene on the teeth and sides of the saw removed the gum and made it possible to cut southern pine. The crosscut tripled the productivity of labor and lowered logging costs.[13]

The logging crew consisted of two men: the fallers or timber cutters, who cut down or felled the tree; and the buckers, who removed the limbs and cut the tree into log lengths, or bucked it. The timber cutters used axes, crosscut saws, and wedges and usually carried a bottle containing coal oil or kerosene to lubricate the saw and remove resin from it. Once the tree was felled and bucked, the log had to be taken to the mill. In the early days of water-driven mills, the logs were usually dragged to streams and floated individually or as rafts.[14]

As the steam engine became more prevalent and mills were located away from water, the logs were delivered to the mills by teams of horses, mules, or oxen that pulled carts or wagons. The common wisdom was that the maximum feasible distance for dragging logs by oxen to water was three miles. In the late nineteenth century the bummer cart, which was a self-loading skidder that had probably been developed in Michigan, was introduced in the southern forests. Before 1900 in south Mississippi the logs were pulled through the woods to a stream by four yokes of oxen dragging a caralog or boomer, which consisted of two enormous wheels connected to an axle. The axle supported a perpendicular long boom. To lift its cargo, one end of the boom was fastened to the logs with chains and tongs, and when the other end was lowered for attachment to the ox yoke, the boom lifted the front end of its load. The wheels were originally somewhat small and narrow, but Usan Vaughan, a slave from Pearlington, Mississippi, improved the design by widening the tread and increasing the size of the wheels to more than seven feet in diameter, thereby making the device more practical for Mississippi. The caralogs could carry three small logs or two large ones and were locally produced by piney woods blacksmiths.[15]

After the turn of the century caralogs were replaced by eight-wheeled wagons, developed by John Lindsay of Laurel, that doubled their predecessors' carrying capacities. Excellent for hauling logs over wet, muddy terrain, the Lindsey wagons had four-wheel independently-sprung trucks that allowed the vehicle to move over rough ground while keeping the load relatively level. Oxen loaded the logs onto the wagons, pulling the logs up skids. By 1904 there were supposedly five thousand of these wagons in the South. Built in Laurel, by 1929 they cost between $200 and $245.[16]

Transporting the logs with oxen power was expensive and slow. The cost was twenty cents per ton mile, or one dollar per hundred pounds per hundred miles. Thus, because of the need for both speed and economy, by the time of the bonanza era, many big mills used railroad logging. A steam skidder dragged the logs to a yarding point or skidway, where they were loaded onto railroad cars and transported by a tram or logging railroad to the mill.[17]

Lumbermen and speculators purchased large blocks of timber and systematized their cutting. Until the late nineteenth century most southern lumbermen lacked the financial resources to own large tracts of timber to feed their mills. Lumbermen found it more economical and convenient to contract with individual timber owners and loggers. The cutting of individual trees was replaced by the organized harvesting of large areas by the big companies. In the late nineteenth century timber holdings often became more valuable than the manufacturing operations. While lumber prices fluctuated, the price of timber almost never fell. In fact, the value of timberlands rose twentyfold to fiftyfold in the period from 1860 to 1900. By 1913 there were an estimated 2.8 billion board feet of timber standing in the United States, of which 2.2 billion were privately owned. Nearly 80 percent of that total in the Lake States, the Pacific Northwest, and the southern pine region was owned by 1,802 of the largest landholders. The new technologies and philosophies in the woods and the mills made it possible for Mississippi lumbermen to serve growing national markets by the late nineteenth and early twentieth century.[18]

The bonanza era truly could be called the age of railroad logging: from the woods to the mill to the customer, the railroad was an indispensable element of most large-scale lumbering operations. Goods and services in early Mississippi moved mostly by boat, and the state's earliest railroads were built to give interior regions access to navigable water, especially along the Mississippi River. In the early nineteenth century several relatively short railroads were constructed for precisely that purpose, stretching from port towns such as Natchez, Port Gibson, Vicksburg, and Grand-Gulf into the lands of the interior cotton planters. A line from St. Francisville, Louisiana, to the nearby interior town of Woodville, Mississippi, served the same purpose. These short lines ran east and west and fed the interests of the river towns. The early railroads were relatively primitive. As late as the Civil War, some lines still had wooden rails with a thin strip of iron on top, rather than modern T-shaped iron rails.[19]

During the 1830s railroad promotion raged in Mississippi. The state chartered at least twenty-four companies to build lines, but by the end of the decade only about eighty-three miles of track had been completed. The interior regions lobbied for the creation of a railroad running north and south through the middle of the state, connecting the area with New Orleans. Supporters sought to escape the control of the merchants and brokers in the river towns and to free themselves from the often difficult task of transporting their cotton to the river over dirt roads, which were often muddy and nearly impassable. In fact, many planters believed that freighting distances of greater than ten miles were uneconomical. They were thus essentially chained to the proximity of navigable water.[20]

Big Wheels and mules in a Mississippi forest. Courtesy Forest History Society, Durham, North Carolina.

Advertising brochure for the Lindsey log wagon. Courtesy Lauren Rogers Museum of Art, Laurel, Mississippi.

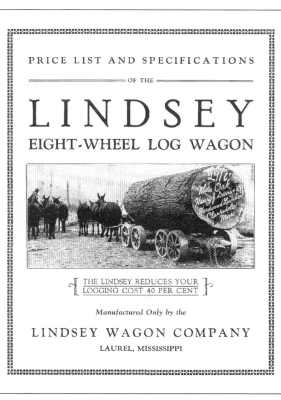

PRICE LIST AND SPECIFICATIONS
OF THE

LINDSEY
EIGHT-WHEEL LOG WAGON

THE LINDSEY REDUCES YOUR
LOGGING COST 40 PER CENT

Manufactured Only by the

LINDSEY WAGON COMPANY
LAUREL, MISSISSIPPI

Logging crew. Courtesy Lauren Rogers Museum of Art, Laurel, Mississippi.

In 1833 the Ponchartrain Railroad, connecting New Orleans to the lake, became the first steam railroad in the Mississippi Valley. Also, after complicated economic and political maneuvering, a line from Vicksburg to Jackson was tied in to another road running eastward from the capital. It then linked up with the north-south-running Mobile and Ohio at Meridian in 1861. This was the first Mississippi railroad built largely through forested country. An extension of the line to Selma, Alabama, was completed the following year.[21]

The first long north-south line was the New Orleans, Jackson, and Great Northern Railroad, stretching from the Crescent City to a link with the Canton and Jackson in 1858. From there it ran northward and connected with the Mississippi Central, which stretched from Canton to a junction with the Memphis and Charleston at La-Grange, Tennessee, about forty miles east of Memphis. With the absorption of these lines, the New Orleans, Jackson, and Great Northern forged a connection with the Mobile and Ohio at Jackson, Tennessee, thus providing a linkage with the northwestern railroad network. Through a series of reorganizations, transfers of control, and name changes, in the late nineteenth century this line became the famous Illinois Central.[22]

Second came the Mobile and Ohio Railroad, which operated under charters granted in 1847 by Alabama, Mississippi, Tennessee, and Kentucky. It was built with private funding, local and state public assistance, and a federal land grant of alternate sections along the route in Alabama and Mississippi. In 1861 the line north from Mobile reached one running south from Columbus, Kentucky, completing the main line. The railroad had a significant impact in promoting agricultural development and boosting land prices.[23]

These connections with the northwestern railroad network transformed the lumber industry. As the northern pine forests were cut over, southern pine moved in to capture their markets in the late nineteenth century. Southern pine producers west of the Mississippi River sold their products primarily in the northern plains and prairie states west of the river, while the mills east of the river, including those in Mississippi, marketed most heavily in the states of the old Northwest. As the lumber industry grew in Mississippi during this period, many companies located along the trunk-line railroads and then extended logging spurs into the woods to feed their mills. Many of Mississippi's railroads were short-line operations that originated in this way. These railroad logging operations were confined primarily to the large mills and companies, for the cost of construction was high. For example, in the Great Lakes states in this period, construction of a logging railroad ran between $1,900 and $7,600 per mile. Also, linkages into the main lines were troublesome, for they used various gauges that usually differed from the trunk-line roads. In the 1890s many converted to standard-gauge rails and equipment.[24]

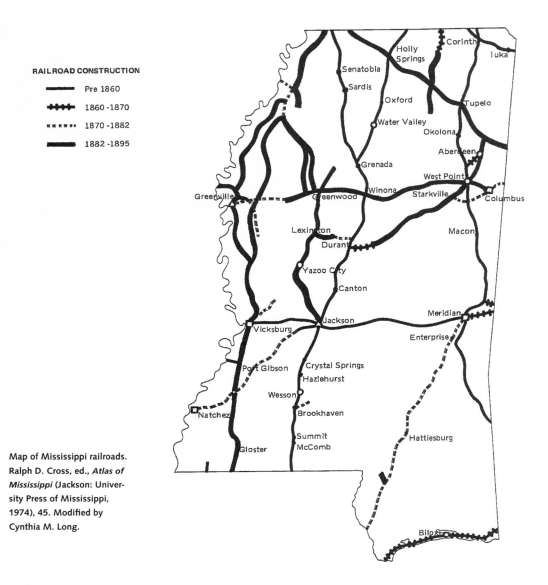

RAILROAD CONSTRUCTION

Pre 1860

1860-1870

1870-1882

1882-1895

Map of Mississippi railroads.
Ralph D. Cross, ed., *Atlas of
Mississippi* (Jackson: University Press of Mississippi,
1974), 45. Modified by
Cynthia M. Long.

Six trunk-line railroads eventually operated in Mississippi. In addition to the Mobile and Ohio (which became the Gulf, Mobile, and Ohio) and the Illinois Central (New Orleans, Jackson, and Great Northern), there were the Gulf and Ship Island (running from Gulfport to Jackson with branches extending to Laurel and Columbia); the Mobile, Jackson, and Kansas City; the New Orleans and Northeastern (later the Southern); and a new New Orleans and Great Northern, which ran along a different route than the Illi-

nois Central. By 1873 the Mississippi and Tennessee Railroad from Grenada to Memphis had become part of the Illinois Central system. It was eventually purchased by the Illinois Central. Also, in the 1880s the Yazoo and Mississippi Valley Railroad built a network of rails in the Delta and Natchez areas, and those too were absorbed by the Illinois Central system. Thus, through construction, alliances, and purchases, the Illinois Central constructed a trunk-line system with branches running from Chicago to

New Orleans. The Great Southern Lumber Company of Bogalusa, Louisiana, built the New Orleans and Great Northern, using the tracks of the New Orleans and Northeastern from the Crescent City to Slidell, Louisiana, and then building a line from that point to Rio, Louisiana, where it split, with one branch reaching to Tylertown, Mississippi, and the main line through Bogalusa to Jackson.[25]

A plethora of mills, large and small, sprang up along the railroads, and by 1880 Mississippi had 295 lumbering establishments capitalized at more than $900,00 and producing 168,747,000 board feet of lumber. While the large mills eventually dominated, in the late nineteenth century operations producing between five thousand and fifteen thousand board feet produced a considerable percentage of Mississippi's lumber. They often got their timber from smaller tracts that the large companies found inferior or difficult to reach. Many smaller operators specialized in producing lumber to build railroad cars, a relatively simple product. The small operations came and went with the vagaries of the economy and the supply of available timber.[26]

The Gulf and Ship Island demonstrates the impact of the railroad in stimulating the proliferation of lumbering operations. Over its three hundred miles of track there were between fifty and sixty mills, and in 1902 the seventy-four-mile section from Hattiesburg to Gulfport averaged one sawmill and one turpentine distillery every three miles. In 1901 mills located on the road cut 300 million board feet of lumber, and between January and October 1902 27,879 carloads of lumber were transported over the road, a figure that was exceeded during the same period the following year. The importance of the road became even greater in 1902 with the completion of a channel from Gulfport to deep water, facilitating the lumber export trade. By 1906 the total daily output of mills on the Gulf and Ship Island was estimated at 4.5 million board feet, and in 1907 about one-tenth of all yellow pine lumber produced in the South—about 800 million board feet—was carried by the Gulf and Ship Island Railroad.[27]

On the Mobile, Jackson, and Kansas City, the section between Newton and Shipman had forty-five mills. By 1905, this figure had risen to sixty mills producing 1.5 million board feet daily. The New Orleans and Northeastern Railroad by 1900 had mills producing 300 million board feet along its line. While the Mobile and Ohio did not have large production along its tracks, it was a major carrier, consistently transporting more than twenty thousand carloads of lumber to its northern terminus at St. Louis in the early years of the twentieth century. By 1902–3, Mississippi railroads carried an average of 12,300 carloads of lumber per month, roughly 147,600 per year. Of this 118,000 cars, carrying 1.5 billion board feet, served the domestic market, while the remaining cars moved products for the export trade. By 1891–92 the main-line roads hauled more than half of Mississippi's lumber toward northern markets.[28]

In the 1880s Mississippi's railroad mileage more than doubled from 1,127 to 2,366 miles, and by 1910 it totaled 4,223 miles. The railroads were both carriers and consumers of timber. Railroad builders purchased large quantities of bridging materials, and construction of each mile of track required approximately 2,500 to 3,000 wooden ties, an important early market for hardwoods. Ties delivered to the railroads by independent contractors sold for about a dollar, and some of these operators also cut fuelwood for cotton gins, railroads, and steamboats. Some eventually became independent contractors for the early pulp and paper industry. The untreated ties lasted only between five and twelve years, but treatment with preservatives such as creosote greatly extended their life. In 1875 the Louisville and Nashville Railroad built the first wood- treatment plant in Mississippi, at Pascagoula. Much of the growth in mileage was a direct product of the booming lumber industry. In fact, a good deal of the mileage represented unincorporated short-line logging railroads.

In 1900 eleven Mississippi lumber companies operated logging lines and tramways ranging from five to twenty miles in length. Many logging roads were shoddily constructed, but others were built more substantially than some of the trunk lines. Many of the unincorporated logging roads were later incorporated so that they could collect revenue payments from the trunk lines for freight that originated in their territory and moved over their tracks and onto the main lines. These lines were known in the industry as tap lines. Incorporation eliminated the stigma of the payments being considered illegal rebates under the terms of the Interstate Commerce Act of 1887 and the Elkins Act of 1903. Most such railroads began to haul other kinds of freight and passengers, in addition to timber and lumber, and thus became true common carriers.[29]

A good example is the Fernwood, Columbia, and Gulf, which ran through the south Mississippi counties of Pike, Walthall, and Marion, connecting the towns of Columbia and Fernwood. The railroad had connections in the west with the Illinois Central and in the east with the New Orleans and Great Northern, and with the New Orleans and North Eastern via a junction with the Gulf and Ship Island. There was also a spur that ran southeast toward the Pearl River. The road originated with the expansion of a lumbering business started by John Fletcher Enochs and his son, Isaac Columbus Enochs, near Crystal Springs in Copiah County in the early 1870s. Despite a boiler explosion and a later fire, Isaac expanded the operations to tap the developing markets of the old Northwest, purchasing timberlands and constructing a mill between Magnolia and McComb in Pike County on the main line of the Illinois Central.

After the timber near the mill was cut, in 1881 Enochs built a crude tramway into the forests, over which mules pulled log wagons, and two years later he installed wooden pole rails and utilized a steam locomotive with wide grooved wheels to run on the primitive tracks. He later laid steel rails and extended the logging line farther east into Pike County. Spurs running north and south were built into the forests at several locations.

In the mid-1880s Enochs brought two of his brothers into the operation, which now included lumber and planing mills, timber holdings, and a

retail yard in Jackson. In 1884 the lumber operation was incorporated in Pike County, with a capitalization of $100,000, as the Fernwood Lumber Company. They built the company town of Fernwood and operated a mill with a capacity of 30 million board feet, drawing on timber from seventy-one thousand acres between the Bogue Chitto and Pearl Rivers. The company continued to expand and in the 1890s acquired properties in the Florida parishes of southeastern Louisiana, including the Banner Lumber Company and the Pearl River Lumber Company.

The Enochs brothers originally shipped most of their products to Jackson, where they marketed through their own retail operations. After the turn of the century, they increasingly consigned much of their output to the region north of the Ohio River. The brothers also became involved in one of the largest lumber operations in the South when they assisted Frank H. and Charles W. Goodyear in the acquisition of timberlands in southwest Mississippi and Louisiana. In 1905 the Goodyears founded the Great Southern Lumber Company of Bogalusa, Louisiana. The Enochs traded the Pearl River Lumber Company and timberlands in Louisiana for stock in the Great Southern, of which Isaac Enochs became a director. The Enochs story is a good example of the symbiotic relationship between Mississippi's lumber industry and railroads in the late nineteenth and early twentieth centuries.[30]

Other examples of Mississippi logging railroads were the Natchez, Columbia, and Mobile, a twenty-five-mile road owned by the Butterfield Lumber Company, and the Mississippi Central, which was owned by the J. J. Newman Lumber Company and had twenty-six mills along its route even before completion of the line in 1906. The J. J. White Company had the Fernwood and Gulf Railroad, which ran thirty-three miles west from McComb, and the W. Denny Lumber Company built the Chickashaway and Jackson Railroad, which became the Pascagoula and Northern. Brookhaven was the site of Hamilton, Hoskins, and Company, which built the Meridian, Brookhaven, and Natchez Railroad. Four miles south of Brookhaven was Hartman, the

Gilchrist-Fordney Lumber Company train in the woods. Courtesy Lauren Rogers Museum of Art, Laurel, Mississippi.

Crew laying tracks. Courtesy Lauren Rogers Museum of Art, Laurel, Mississippi.

home of the Hartman Lumber Company, which operated several dummy lines. The Keystone Lumber and Improvement Company constructed facilities at various sites in the vicinity of Bogue Chitto as well as various railroad logging spurs. In north Mississippi's delta, the Carrier Lumber and Manufacturing Company's Sardis and Delta Railroad, with about thirty miles of standard-gauge track, ran between the mill site at Sardis and the woods operations near Bobo Lake (later renamed Lake Carrier).[31]

By 1905 all of the large interior mills and many middle-sized operations turning out twenty-five to sixty thousand board feet daily transported their timber over logging roads or dummy lines on trains that were often pulled by shay locomotives. The logging roads were expensive to build, at a thousand dollars or more per mile, but once up and running these roads cut the cost of hauling logs by oxen by three-fourths. However, the roads were economical only if a company had a large supply of timberlands. Most of the lines extended an average of six spurs per square mile into the woods, and the spurs were moved to new locations when the timber was cut over. Although the tracks were often rather primitive, the cost of constructing the spurs varied, with one firm in 1911 spending sixty cents per thousand board feet of timber carried and three firms in 1915 spending between 27 cents and 48.4 cents. Lumbermen calculated railroad logging required land that would yield timber for at least twenty years. For the railroad to pay its expenses, at least one million board feet of timber per mile of railroad built had to be cut annually. Doing so required clear-cutting and utilizing even the small timber for poles and pulpwood. To supply a mill cutting 100,000 board feet, a company needed between forty and fifty flatcars and from one to three locomotives or shays.[32]

While the railroad was the vehicle that Mississippi lumbering rode to its peak, even in the age of the iron road a good deal of timber and lumber continued to move by water. Numerous streams ran through the piney woods, and the trees were easy to float. Most were between 150

and 200 years old and thus contained a large percentage of heartwood, which contributed to their buoyancy. There were few picturesque log drives on the northern model. Most logs were rafted, although there were drives on sections of the faster-flowing rivers such as the Pascagoula, its tributaries above the junction with the Red and Black Rivers, and the Pearl. The logs fed the mills of the Gulf Coast, particularly at Moss Point. One observer noted, "So thick were the moving rafts, that they were seldom out of eye-sight of one another from the junction of the Leaf and Chickasawhay to Moss Point." A rafts-man remembered that "the reflection of the fire-light [of raft fires] on the water made the river appear in flames." At Moss Point a huge boom reached from the middle of the river to hold the logs for five miles up the eastern bank. Between 1890 and about 1910 up to half a million logs were floated down the Pascagoula annually. In 1891–92, 163 million board feet were shipped down the Pascagoula and Pearl, 48.9 percent of all lumber shipped in Mississippi; 170 million board feet, or 51 percent, traveled on the state's railroads. However, by 1910 most of the timber near the rivers had been cut over, and soon only sunken logs, or "deadheads," headed by water toward the mills.[33]

The only other area of Mississippi where the movement of logs by water remained important after the advent of the railroad was in the cypress swamps of the Yazoo River region. In this area the trees were girdled to drain off the sap and make them more buoyant. They were then felled from boats and towed or poled out by men standing in the water (swampers). At the end of the 1880s William Baptist of New Orleans perfected a steam-powered pull-boat system to skid cypress logs out of the swamps. In the early twentieth century the Anderson-Tully Company transported logs primarily by water and had a sizable fleet of steamboats, barges, and towboats that serviced the company's hardwood and veneer mills at Memphis and Vicksburg.[34]

Mississippi's booming lumber industry captured its markets from the declining producers of white pine. By the time of the Civil War, the Great Lakes States (Michigan, Wisconsin, and Minnesota) surpassed the Northeast (Maine, Pennsylvania, and New York) in lumber production. The Great Lakes producers' era of supremacy occupied a window in the late nineteenth century as the country moved west, with most of its lumber needs met by northern white pine.[35]

The window closed quickly as the lake states' enormous lumbering operations rapidly exhausted their timber supplies. In 1869 those states provided more than 28 percent of the nation's lumber, and the percentage rose steadily to a peak of 36.7 percent in 1889. But the decline was precipitous. By 1899 the Great Lakes supplied only 24.8 percent of national production, a number that fell to 13.1 percent in 1909, 7.8 percent in 1919, and 4.3 percent by 1929. Many northern lumbermen began to invest in and migrate to the enormous timbered regions of the South, a trend that began as early as the 1870s.[36]

Still, the perception remained that the Northeast and the lake states were the true lumbering centers. For example, the massive *History of the Lumber Industry of America* (1906–7), written by James Elliott Defebaugh, the editor of the influential trade journal *American Lumberman,* barely mentions the South, with the justification that "while the southern pines were and are famous in the export trade, they supplied at home, until within a generation, hardly more than a local requirement." Defebaugh emphasizes the central importance of white pine and in fact says that his book is "devoted very largely to the history of the white pine industry."[37]

The vacuum created by the decline of the lake states and northern white pine was quickly filled by southern producers, especially of southern or yellow pine. Early production figures are somewhat unreliable, because not until 1904 did the U.S. Forest Service and the Bureau of the Census begin to cooperate in the compilation of yearly statistics. Between 1880 and 1920 southern lumber production rose dramatically from 1.6 billion board feet to 15.4 billion board feet, with the peak in 1912. By the turn of the century, the South led the nation. In 1919 the South produced 37 percent of all U.S. lumber, and early in the century the South and the south Atlantic seaboard produced almost as much lumber as all other sections of the nation combined. By 1919

Log boat on the Pearl River at Carthage, Mississippi, ca. 1853. Courtesy Mississippi Forestry Commission, Jackson.

lumber and timber represented 60.4 percent of Mississippi's manufacturing industries, turpentine and resin were responsible for 4.2 percent, and planing-mill products contributed 2.4 percent. Mississippi produced 168,747,000 board feet of lumber in 1880, 1,208,739,000 board feet by 1900, and 2,380,303,000 board feet by 1919. Ironically, the heyday of the southern producers was equally short-lived, and by the 1930s they too were in a state of free fall as the industry's focus shifted to the Pacific Northwest.[38]

As the lake states were deforested, necessity forced both lumbermen and consumers to begin looking at southern pine from a different perspective. Northern white pine had traditionally been the softwood of choice. The prevailing wisdom was that tall, fast-growing trees from a warm climate were not as strong as slower-growing species from colder regions. There were also objections to the high resin content of southern or yellow pine and a belief that it warped excessively and split easily. However, in the late nineteenth century, southern pine, especially longleaf, moved from regional popularity to national and even international prominence.

The first post–Civil War markets that opened up were in the South, where lumber was needed to repair plantations, farms, and cities which had been damaged by Union forces or neglected during the conflict. Southern pine also invaded northern markets, becoming especially popular in bridge and house construction because of its strength and resistance to decay. Among the key marketing centers was St. Louis, which was soon relegated to secondary status by Chicago. In Chicago, Thomas K. Edwards, the lumber agent of the Illinois Central Railroad, and a few merchants who specialized in southern pine sales worked diligently to gain acceptance for yellow pine. In 1875 only about 2 million feet of lumber was delivered in Chicago by the Illinois Central, but by 1910 the shipments had risen to well over 500 million feet. Most of the deliveries were of southern pine. By 1929 the leading out-of-state markets for Mississippi lumber were Illinois, Ohio, Indiana, Tennessee, and Kentucky.[39]

Forest products were widely used in industry and as fuel in the late nineteenth and early twentieth centuries. It has been estimated that total consumption for fuel, lumber, pulp, veneer, poles, and other purposes totaled 3.76 billion cubic feet annually in 1859, nearly doubled in the next twenty years, and almost doubled again to reach 13.38 billion cubic feet in 1907. Southern lumber producers were major beneficiaries of this heavy and increasing usage. The U.S. Bureau of Corporations estimated in 1913 that as much as one-third of southern pine was sold directly to such large consumers as railroads, producers of railroad equipment, and "those engaged in the construction of buildings, bridges, and other structures requiring material in large quantities." The remainder was sold to wholesalers, brokers, and retailers. Most of the lumber sold to retailers came directly from manufacturers, and many of the manufacturers were themselves retailers, often through subsidiary corporations. Some lumber producers owned as many as one hundred retail yards. Those possessing a large number of yards were called line-yard companies. In some cases, the retail yards conspired to control prices in their city or area.[40]

There were several marketing approaches in the southern pine industry. Some manufacturers had their own sales organization and traveling salesmen. Other companies sold their entire output to wholesalers or marketed through commission salesmen. Some companies that owned several mills formed marketing corporations with large sales staffs to handle their entire output. Lumbermen in some cases contracted to sell their entire output to wholesalers. Sometimes lumbermen were financed by wholesalers. There were a few attempts to form sales companies to handle the products of a large number of independent mills, but none came to fruition.[41]

The establishment of lumber trade associations resulted from many manufacturers' desire for both uniform prices and manufacturing quality or grading standards throughout the industry. The earliest efforts to establish grading rules were undertaken by seventy-five mill operators meeting in Texarkana in 1886, by North Carolina producers in 1888, and by the Georgia Sawmill Association in 1889. Both the Southern Lumber Manufacturers' Association and its successors, the Yellow Pine Manufacturers' Association and the Southern Pine Association, adopted grading rules. The associations maintained staffs of lumber inspectors, and members were authorized to grade mark their lumber, indicating that it met a certain standard. The grades for export lumber were local, with both Mobile and Pensacola having their own rules. In 1897 the Gulf Coast Lumbermen's Association adopted a standardized system, which was in turn endorsed by the Southern Pine Association. In 1924, as a result of efforts by the U.S. Department of Commerce, the American Lumber Standards were adopted as the basis for grading rules for all associations. Grade marking, certifying manufacturing standards, became a valuable marketing tool.[42]

With a new appreciation of the marketing possibilities plus an infusion of capital from northern lumbermen and speculators, southern lumbering grew dramatically. As early as 1870 the Mississippi lumber industry surpassed prewar production levels. Ten years later there were 295 sawmills in Mississippi with a total investment of just under $1 million. In the next decade the capitalization had risen to $3,092,684 and the number of mills to 338. These figures grew to 608 mills with a capitalization of $10.8 million by 1899, and the state was producing more than 1 billion board feet of lumber annually. The capital continued to pour in, and new mills went up along the state's ever-lengthening railroad lines. By 1909 total investment reached $39,455,000, mills numbered 1,647, and the total value of output was $42,793,000. Mississippi moved from eighth among lumber producing states in 1904 to fifth in 1906, fourth in 1907, and third from 1908 through 1915. Most of the production was longleaf pine. In 1905, 1,107,191,000 board feet, of a total state production of 1,299,390,000, was longleaf pine. The following year only 500,000,000 board feet of a total cut of 1,840,250,000 represented species other than

longleaf. In 1909 some 82 percent of the state's lumber production was longleaf pine.[43]

In assessing the growth of markets and of the Mississippi lumber industry, it is important to note that the southern pineries were two thousand miles closer to the major lumber consuming areas in the northern and eastern states than were the forests of the Pacific Northwest. And, of course, Mississippi's lumbermen now had the rail connections to serve those markets. Mississippi was also closer to foreign markets in Western Europe, Africa, and the eastern cities of South America via the ports of the South Atlantic and the gulf than was the Pacific slope.[44]

By 1902–3 Mississippi lumbermen sold a large quantity of lumber in the domestic market, most in the North, and eighteen thousand cars carried lumber to be shipped overseas. A large part of the superior grades went to foreign markets. For example, Laurel's Eastman-Gardiner Lumber Company sent lumber north by railroad and south to be shipped out through Gulfport or Mobile to foreign markets. Eastman-Gardiner had its own vessels to take the lumber overseas, and "only the best trees and the most valuable section of these trees were transported abroad." In the late 1800s square timbers, ship masts, planks, and other timber products were moving through Mississippi ports to markets in Europe, Australia, the West Indies, and Latin America. Southern pine was going to Germany, where it was used for the manufacture of window casings, wagons, freight cars, and other outdoor applications. By 1911 Gulfport became the world's leading port for the export of pine lumber.[45]

The most profitable operations combined ownership of timbered lands, or stumpage, and the manufacture of lumber. Thus, the first stage in the rise of the southern lumber boom was a race to purchase and control forested lands. This process involved both economics and politics. On the eve of the Civil War, the five southern public-land states—Alabama, Arkansas, Florida, Louisiana, and Mississippi—had 47 million acres of federally owned land, about one-third of their total land area, most of it covered with heavy stands of cypress and yellow pine. Considered largely unsuitable for agricultural settlement, portions of this land had been open for entry for many years at $1.25 per acre. With the adoption of the Graduation Act in 1854, its price dropped to as little as 12.25 cents an acre, depending upon the length of time it had been on the market.[46]

After the Civil War, administration of the South's public lands became involved with the politics of Reconstruction. Radical Republican leaders hoped to reserve the lands for Union loyalists and former slaves. The Southern Homestead Act of 1866 ended cash sales in the five southern states, reserved public lands for homesteaders, limited grants to eighty acres, and excluded ex-Confederates from the homesteading process. By the end of Reconstruction there was a growing demand to open southern timberlands for entry without restrictions. Southerners claimed that most public lands were unfit for cultivation and of little use to the freedmen. Limited land sales had not contributed much to the federal treasury or the development of the southern economy. Furthermore, the lands were being illegally stripped of their timber by lumber interests that had developed after the Civil War.[47]

There was strong opposition to repeal of the Southern Homestead Act, with many opponents motivated by a desire to prevent concentrated ownership of the timberlands. However, many southerners continued to view the forests as both inexhaustible and of limited value. In fact, to some extent they were viewed as impediments to progress. As Thomas D. Clark has noted, "Pinebelt backwoodsmen regarded a good forest as one lying in log and brush heaps ready for the application of the torch." Conversely, lumbermen in both the North and South could not wait to get their hands on these forests. As late as 1880, when the South had 5,573 sawmills, most were small and located on or near waterways. The industry had scarcely penetrated the vast forests of the interior.

In 1876 the Southern Homestead Act was repealed, eliminating all restrictions on public land transactions in the southern states and legalizing private sales. There was no limit on the size of purchases, and the lands were to go on sale as soon as possible. They were offered to the highest bidder at public auction, and, if unsold, could be purchased later at a minimum price of $1.25 per acre. The minimum price became standard for timberlands, and the law opened the door for large-scale purchases and speculation. Over the next twelve years, vast amounts of valuable timberlands were gobbled up by speculators at bargain-basement prices.[48]

During the late 1870s and 1880s timber speculators and lumbermen acquired enormous tracts of southern forests. The speculation was most feverish in Louisiana and Mississippi, with some landholders and lumber manufacturers operating in both states. While both native southerners and northerners were involved, the Yankees became dominant. Northern financiers, speculators, and lumbermen sent "timber cruisers" into the South to examine the public lands. The emissaries returned with glowing reports of huge stands of "virgin" timber that could be easily logged and purchased for next to nothing from the federal and state governments. One of the cruisers, James D. Lacey, worked as an agent for the Goodyears, among others, and traveled the counties of southern Mississippi and the Florida parishes of Louisiana on a mule as he "located several million acres for Northern lumbermen" and worked for himself as a land speculator. Lacey told a committee of the U.S. House of Representatives, "In 1880 when I first went South . . . we estimated what the value of Government land was. It was nearly all vacant then; and it was timberland. In 1889 it was offered at $1.25 per acre. We located several million acres for northern lumber companies. We estimated those lands would cut about 6,000 feet per acre, as they were then cutting timber. They were not going above the first limbs, the balance was left in the woods and burned up."[49]

Michael Williams calculates that at these prices, timber was being purchased at about five to ten cents per one thousand board feet, while average quality lumber was selling for five to ten dollars per one thousand board feet. To promote its own business, the Illinois Central Railroad ran a series of special trains into the southern piney woods for would-be purchasers, and the *American Lumberman* in 1902 reported that individual lumbermen were investing $100,000 or more in the South. Far from being viewed as carpetbaggers, Yankee lumbermen were strongly encouraged by local citizens to bring capital into the South. One Tennessean said, "As for these investments of Northern capital, the South is glad to have it come. We welcome the skilled lumberman with the noisy mill." Mississippi's state legislature passed an act in 1882 that exempted new industries from taxation for ten years after starting operations. And the northerners brought more than capital. Many of them had managerial experience with large lumber operations in the Northeast and Great Lakes, which brought a new level of sophistication to the southern forests.[50]

Estimates of the amount of timber available varied widely. Figures for the volume of southern pine available ranged from an estimate of 237,141,500,000 board feet in the 1880 census to 300,000,000,000 board feet in the 1900 census, 187,250,000,000 estimated by Robert A. Long in 1903, and 300,000,000,000 estimated by the *American Lumberman* magazine in 1905. In any case, a 1907 U.S. Forest Service study predicted, "Whether we accept the lowest or the highest estimate of stumpage, it is evident that within ten to fifteen years there will be a most serious shortage of yellow pine."[51]

The costs of purchasing large tracts of timber were high, despite the low prices. And if the purchaser's objective was to manufacture lumber rather than merely to speculate in timber, the cost of constructing a mill, a railroad, and logging machinery drove the investment even higher. While men of enormous wealth were among those who purchased southern timberlands, even the wealthy had to find financing and operate in a manner that did not ignore the bottom line. Among the pioneers in developing the methodology for financing southern lumbering operations

was Kansas City's powerful Robert A. Long, head of the Long-Bell Lumber Company, which had large operations in Mississippi and Louisiana and later in the Pacific Northwest.

In 1905 Long was involved in one of the first purchases of timberlands on credit through the issuance of timber bonds. Timber bonds, issued with the timberlands as collateral, allowed the lumber companies to fund their indebtedness and stretch the payments out over a period of years at a reasonable rate of interest. Most of the paper was issued as serial bonds, with maturities at regular periods during the life of the issue, and semiannual interest payments. The borrower was obligated to deposit a certain amount with a trustee for each thousand feet of timber harvested, with the money going into a sinking fund to pay the serial accounts as they became due.

The Royal Trust Company of Chicago made Long's pioneering loan. After initial reluctance and a trip to examine the tract, trust company officials provided a $560,000 first mortgage at 6 percent interest. The bond issue was a first lien on 42,390 acres of longleaf timber in Calcasieu Parish, Louisiana, which was appraised as containing 508,680,000 feet. The value was appraised at twenty-five dollars an acre, or a total of $1,059,780. The bond issue also covered the sawmill, logging railroad, and equipment, with a cash cost of $330,000. The Chicago firm soon followed this loan with additional bond issues for another Louisiana company and an operation in Texas, both guaranteed by Long-Bell. The bank officer remembered, "From that time the issues on Southern timber were brought out in considerable volume." Long-Bell later acquired the Mississippi Lumber Company mill at Quitman, which was at one time the largest on the Mobile and Ohio Railroad.[52]

Among those who purchased southern timberlands were northern lumbering families who sent younger sons, nephews, sons-in-law, friends, and associates into the South to manage their interests. Some of these men settled permanently in the region and became fiercely loyal to the South. An example is the Gardiner family of

Laurel, Mississippi's Eastman-Gardiner firm. The founder of the company, Stimson Gardiner, was born in New York and moved to Pennsylvania and then Iowa. His sons, George and Silas, came south from Clinton, Iowa, to inspect timber resources in 1890 because of the exhaustion of white pine. With their brother-in-law, George Eastman, they purchased sixteen thousand acres of land around Laurel from John Kemper for four dollars an acre. Kemper, who had built a mill to provide timber for the construction of the New Orleans and Northeastern Railroad, was amused by the Yankee purchasers' "gullibility." After initial purchases in Jones County, the Gardiners continued to acquire timberlands, and by 1903 they had about 180,000 acres mostly in Jones, Jasper, and Smith Counties.

The Eastman-Gardiner firm became one of Mississippi's largest, and by the early twentieth century its capital investment, not including timberland, was between $600,000 and $700,000. The company eventually owned nearly all the yellow pine between Laurel and the Strong River, which was sixty-five miles distant, and from ten to fifteen miles on each side of the Gulf and Ship Island Railroad. Eastman-Gardiner operated both pine and hardwood mills. Another "crafty" southerner who sold a tract of timber for far less than its actual value told his "victim," "Now you have made your bargain—live with it." Mississippi's Alcorn Agricultural and Mechanical College sold 23,040 acres for eighty-five thousand dollars, or about $3.69 per acre, to five companies, including the J. J. Newman Lumber Company of Hattiesburg and Delos A. Blodgett of Grand Rapids, Michigan.[53]

Other northerners hesitated because Civil War emotions had not totally subsided. Frederick Weyerhaeuser, for example, originally resisted investment in the South. He "kept a lingering memory of Civil War antagonisms," and "the idea that some members of his family would have to live in the South was repugnant to him." He was also concerned about the climate and prejudiced against yellow pine. However, he made two scouting expeditions into the South, and during an 1894 excursion to look at southern timber and mills, Weyerhaeuser was converted. Traveling with a group of lumbermen and friends on two special cars of the Illinois Central Railroad, he was wined and dined by Memphis businessmen and charmed by an old Confederate general in Vicksburg. Weyerhaeuser told E. W. Durant of Stillwater, Minnesota, who arranged the trip, "I think I would better take back my ideas of this southern lumber and the people."[54]

In 1902 the Denkmann Lumber Company, originally based in the Midwest and part of the Weyerhaeuser empire, acquired five mill properties in Mississippi and the Natalbany Lumber Company near Hammond, Louisiana. The Denkmann operation was described as "one of the largest in the South and in the nation." In 1908 the Denkmanns purchased the Butterfield Lumber Company, which had been incorporated in 1900 and was located in the town of Norfield in Lincoln County. The primary assets acquired with the Butterfield purchase were a sawmill at Norfield, 450 million board feet of stumpage, and the Natchez, Columbia, and Mobile Railroad. The company's other Mississippi mills in this period were at Ellisville, Ora, Brookhaven, and Mish. While the total extent of its landholdings is unknown, the company was one of the largest operations in Mississippi and the South, producing both lumber and naval stores.[55]

Among the other large purchasers in Mississippi was Delos A. Blodgett of Grand Rapids, Michigan, who cut out in that area and bought 126,238 acres of pineland in the Magnolia State and more than half a million acres in Louisiana. Blodgett, who had built the largest mill in Michigan in the 1870s, increased his holdings to 721,000 acres with the purchase of state lands in 1906, mostly in Jackson, Wayne, Greene, Perry, Marion,, and Pearl River Counties. Blodgett assumed mythical proportions among the children of Marion County, who visualized him as "some mysterious person worth millions and millions of dollars . . . the richest man in the world . . . the head man in this giant business that was sweeping the South." Blodgett later resold much of this land to other lumbermen for between thirty and forty dollars an acre. Among the land transferred was a tract in Pearl River County acquired by prominent Mississippi lumberman L. O. Crosby from John Blodgett. The Brackenridge brothers of Oscoda, Michigan, bought and resold 700,000 acres of southern pine and cypress in Mississippi and Louisiana. In 1883 a British syndicate purchased 1.3 million acres in the Yazoo delta.[56]

Some of the large sales were made by railroads and by the original speculative purchasers. The railroads realized how valuable timber speculation and the freight from lumber operations could be. In 1905 James J. Hill of the Great Northern remarked that one acre of timber was more valuable to a railroad than forty acres of agricultural land. As the acquisition and exploitation of southern timber accelerated, it became common for large lumber interests to acquire stumpage from several sources. As the competition became heated, prices and tempers rose. In a single decade around the turn of the century, the price of some southern pine acreage rose from $1.25 to $60.00 an acre. In the period from 1880 to 1888, among purchasers of five thousand or more acres of federal land in Mississippi, thirty-two were northerners, buying a total of 889,259 acres, and eleven were southerners, purchasing 134,270 acres. The northerners represented 86.8% of all purchasers. Michael Williams speculates that many of the purchases by southerners were made possible by northern capital.[57]

Southern lumbermen and their spokesmen belatedly realized that they were being shut out of the timber supply. Much of the southern forest acreage was held by northern and foreign speculators. Some of the timber was being shipped north to feed mills in that section. Lumbermen were keenly aware of the critical importance of an adequate timber supply. A large mill cutting 30 million board feet annually required roughly twenty thousand acres of uncut forest for a ten-year run, and most mill owners hoped to operate mills for fifteen to twenty years. The *Southern Lumberman,* a major trade journal that had encouraged northern investments in southern tim-

berlands, reversed its position, lamenting that southern lumbermen had "stood by and looked complacently on, not seeming to realize the fact that the material for their future business was quietly but surely slipping away from them."

While an 1884 survey predicted that Mississippi's pine forests would last for 150 years, the local agent consulted by the authors noted that two-thirds of the timber in Copiah, Hinds, Madison, Rankin, and Yazoo Counties was already gone and that in the area around Meridian the forests were all cleared within a range of five to eight miles of the railroads. The study also noted that with railroad logging, more than two hundred square miles were being cut yearly in Mississippi, and another 150 square miles were destroyed by turpentining. Said the Mississippi correspondent, "English and Northern capitalists are fast purchasing our magnificent pine forests. The avarice of capitalists and the great number of saw-mill men, if not in some way checked, will ere long destroy the grand pine forests of this section."

These concerns, plus the failure of large land speculators to enrich Dixie, led to a reconsideration of public land policies. Led by southern legislators, antimonopolists, and conservationists, a movement to shut down large-scale timber sales in Alabama, Arkansas, and Mississippi worked its way through the Senate. In the interim, sales and homestead entries jumped from 200,000 acres in 1886 to 883,000 acres in 1887 and to 1.224 million acres in 1888. The next three years brought the end of cash sales and baronial purchases of huge blocks of public land. Nevertheless, a timber cruiser active in Mississippi remembered that large amounts of federal land still came under the control of lumbermen and investors, "mainly through bogus homestead entries."[58]

Mississippi also had state-owned public lands in the pine country as well as the swamplands. After permitting unrestricted sales, in 1877 the state limited individual acquisitions to 240 acres within a twelve-month period. However, false entries were rampant, as both individuals and corporations violated the law. The Phillips Marshall Company, predecessor of the Delta Pine Land Company, bought more than 100,000 acres of pine forests in the 1880s, and Calvin Griffin purchased state lands using the names of his employees, oxen, and the deceased.[59]

While the bonanza period of southern timber buying brought many enormous purchases by very large companies and investors, the lumber industry was characterized by the presence of producers of various sizes. Although there was some cooperation between companies through industry associations, an effective lumber trust was beyond the far-flung and highly volatile industry's grasp. Nevertheless, in the late nineteenth and early twentieth centuries, large-scale producers dominated in Mississippi, as in other parts of the South. Much of the timber was controlled by large investors and by a few manufacturing companies that survived until the old-growth timber was cut over. Much of the lumber production came from the large operations, although there were regional variations within the state. By 1903, two-thirds of Mississippi's longleaf forests were owned by nonoperators, and half of that number by six people. Seven mill owners possessed the other half. Dr. Charles S. Sargent's 1884 report on the forests of North America said that in Mississippi, the "principal centers of lumber manufacture are at the mouth of the Pascagoula river, in Jackson county, at Mississippi City, in Harrison county, along the lower Pearl river, upon the line of the Chicago, St. Louis, and New Orleans railroad in Lincoln county, and in the northeastern counties, where are located many small railroad mills, manufacturing in the aggregate a large amount of yellow-pine lumber (*Pinus mitis*)."[60]

On the Gulf Coast in the 1880s much of the production was shipped in the form of boards, scantlings, and other building materials to Cuba, the Windward Islands, Mexico, and Brazil, with some shipbuilding materials going to Germany, France, Spain, and the Low Countries. The eleven sawmills at Moss Point drew their raw material from the Pascagoula River and its tributaries. The Gulf Coast was past its peak by 1915, and the only large operation was the L. N. Dantzler Lumber Company, with two mills at Moss Point as well as facilities elsewhere. By 1913 the Dantzler operations were valued at $3,372,691.40, and the company owned between 400,000 and 500,000 acres of land. Most of its production was marketed overseas, with much of it transported to Latin America in the firm's own schooners. Medium-sized operations at the mouth of the Pascagoula River, with an annual production of 15 to 40 million board feet, included Hunter-Benn, Wyatt Griffin, J. Bounds, and Will Farnsworth. Near the mouth of the Pearl River were the medium-sized operations of H. Weston at Logtown and Poitevent and Favre at Pearlington. In 1913 Poitevent and Favre moved to Mandeville, Louisiana, on the northern shore of Lake Pontchartrain. The Ingram-Day Lumber Company had a large mill at Lyman, just north of Gulfport.[61]

West of the Pearl River much of the timber was cut before the turn of the century. Thus, during the peak years of the bonanza era, the mills of the west were smaller than those east of the river, where enormous areas of untouched forest remained. In the early twentieth century the west had only four reasonably large operations. One of these was the Pearl River Lumber Company, which produced more than 40 million board feet annually. This firm was a creation of A. E. Moreton, who earlier was a partner in the firm of Moreton and Helms Lumber Company of Brookhaven, formed in 1879. This firm was among the first to ship lumber to Chicago, and it was sold to E. H. Easterling and F. A. May in 1899. Moreton and his son, S. F. Moreton, along with other associates then organized the Pearl River Lumber Company. They acquired 150,000 acres of longleaf pine timberland along the Pearl River in Copiah, Lincoln, Lawrence, and Simpson Counties and built a three band-saw mill. Control of the company was acquired in 1903 by W. T. Joyce and then by the Goodyear interests in 1905. The Goodyears operated the Brookhaven plant until their giant mill at Bogalusa, Louisiana, was completed. At that point the Brookhaven mill closed and the timber was diverted to Bogalusa.

S. F. Moreton later participated in the organization of the Central Lumber Company at Brookhaven and of the Homochitto Lumber Company, with 125,000 acres of timberland in Amite and Franklin Counties as well as of a large sawmill at Bude, a town the company built on the Mississippi Central Railroad.[62]

One of Mississippi's most storied lumbering careers and families originated not far from Brookhaven at Bogue Chitto. L. O. Crosby, a son of a local farm family, became partners with J. W. Welch in a small sawmill two miles west of Bogue Chitto in 1905. According to Crosby, who told his story to lumber-trade journalist James Boyd, having "some experience in the woods, having sawed and hauled logs in Louisiana in 1892," as well as other similar work for the Moreton-Helm Lumber Company in Mississippi, his job was to "secure the timber, see that the logs were properly cut, get them into the mill, check the wagons as they went out with the lumber, secure the orders, and see to the loading of the cars." Welch did the manufacturing, and the partnership prospered. However, Crosby soon left to look for greener pastures in the wholesaling business.

Operating from an office in the local bank at Bogue Chitto, Crosby "went early and late. Often I would get in as late as 10 or 11 o'clock at night . . . enter the orders, and invoice them getting through anywhere from 12 to 1:30. I would rise early in the morning and start out again." Working with financing from the Bogue Chitto bank, Crosby's business again prospered, and in 1907 he opened an office at Brookhaven and began selling to the International Harvester Company. By 1913 he had built a band mill at Canton and formed a partnership with two other men at Red Lick. In 1916 he got an option on the Blodgett holdings in Pearl River County and exercised it in 1917, buying out the R. J. Williams mill at Picayune, which operated as the Rosa Lumber Company. In 1918 Crosby built the Goodyear mill in partnership with Lamont Rowlands and the C. A. Goodyear interests, but over the next several years Crosby bought out both the Goodyears and Rowlands. By this time

he was one of Mississippi's most prominent lumbermen.[63]

Another interesting operator in the Brookhaven area was John Bernard Nalty, who moved back and forth between Mississippi and the Florida parishes of Louisiana from the late nineteenth century until about 1930. Among his operations were the East Union Mills south of Brookhaven, which cut out in 1895, and a sawmill at Hyde, Louisiana, that cut out in 1903. Nalty also had a planing mill at Brookhaven as well as several additional sawmills, including the Hammond Lumber Company at Hammond, Louisiana, and he became, according to Boyd, the "largest producer of yellow pine piling. . . . He furnished over 65 per cent of the piling used in the Panama Canal, some of which were 132 feet long."[64]

Turning out between 15 and 40 million board feet annually were J. J. White at McComb (who also claimed to have shipped one of the first carloads of southern pine to Chicago in 1882), the Enochs brothers at Fernwood, and the Butterfield Lumber Company at Norfield. John J. White was the son of a lumberman who operated a water-powered mill in the 1830s. In 1859 J. J. White formed a partnership with his brother at Summit, Mississippi, and furnished timber for Confederate gunboats. After the Civil War he resumed operation of the mill and in 1873 moved to McComb, where the shops of the Illinois Central Railroad were located. White was reputed to be the first to build a logging railroad utilizing a steam locomotive in Mississippi. The sawmill operations were later moved to Columbia.[65]

The Butterfield firm originated during the 1880s in Chicago as Butterfield and Norwood, a lumberyard specializing in southern pine. The firm had a large order, and when several small manufacturers in Mississippi tried to furnish lumber that was not up to specifications, Butterfield bought a mill near Brookhaven to fulfill the contract. After three years the mill was moved to Norfield. By 1907 the Butterfield operation had an annual capacity of 30 million board feet and controlled between forty-five thousand and fifty thousand acres of longleaf in Lincoln, Lawrence, Marion, and Pike Counties. As mentioned earlier, the Denkmann interests, a branch of the extended Weyerhaeuser family, acquired the Butterfield operations in 1915.[66]

Another example of Weyerhaeuser involvement in Mississippi was the Hines Lumber Company. The company was founded by Edward Hines, a Chicago wholesaler and retailer who began to acquire timberlands and sawmills to assure a supply of lumber for his sales operations. Frederick Weyerhaeuser was a major stockholder in the Hines Lumber Company. The Hines properties originated with the Camp and Hinton Lumber Company, which began operations at Lumberton shortly after completion of the New Orleans and Northeastern Railroad. The Hinton Brothers' firm also operated in Lumberton. In 1905 Hines purchased 150,000 acres, estimated to have 2 billion feet of stumpage, and the sites of both the Camp and Hinton and Hinton Brothers mills. Hines eventually acquired between 240,000 and 300,000 acres of timberlands, sawmills, railroads, and a turpentine distillery in the area east of the Pearl River. He built a large mill at Lumberton and operated others at Orvisburg and Kiln.[67]

Other medium and large firms predominated east of the Pearl River. Hattiesburg and Laurel became Mississippi lumbering centers. By 1893 the Hattiesburg area had fifty-nine mills with daily production of 1 million board feet, and by 1915 Laurel was the largest lumber-producing city in Mississippi, with a daily output of 750,000 board feet. Hattiesburg was an important site for buyers of southern pine and in the early twentieth century was home to about seventy-five resident buyers. Meridian had the offices of many lumber manufacturers, wholesalers, and buyers for northern firms.[68]

Nollie Hickman lists at least twenty-three medium-sized firms east of the Pearl River, most with between twenty thousand and one hundred thousand acres of timberlands and all with annual production between 15 million and 40 million board feet. There were also eleven large firms, including the J. J. Newman Lumber Company at Hattiesburg; Edward Hines, with mills at several locations; the Finkbine Lumber Company, with mills at D'Lo and Wiggins; and Eastman-Gardiner at Laurel. Also at Laurel were the Marathon and Wausau (later Wausau-Southern) companies, owned by W. H. Bissell and associates, and Gilchrist-Fordney. The F. C. Denkmann Lumber Company, with several mills in Mississippi and Louisiana, was one of the largest producers in the state and the South. Other large producers included the Chicago Lumber and Coal Company, with a mill at Lumberton, and the Mississippi Lumber Company, which had a mill at Quitman. Most of these companies had large timber holdings, although some did not.[69]

The Gilchrist-Fordney Company was organized in 1907 and purchased the mill and timberlands of the Kingston Lumber Company, a New Hampshire corporation, which had succeeded the earlier Kemper-Lewin Company. By the late 1920s Gilchrist-Fordney had a mill with 140,000 feet of daily capacity as well as a tract of longleaf timber. Wausau-Southern was formed by the Bissell family and C. C. Yawkey, longtime Wisconsin lumbermen who also formed the Marathon Lumber Company.[70]

A famous firm north of Meridian was the Sumter Lumber Company operation at Electric Mills. The owners were from Aurora, Illinois, and had other mills in Mississippi, Arkansas, and Alabama plus retail yards in Illinois. The company took its name from Sumter County, Alabama, where it operated the Pioneer Lumber Company mill at Elrod as well as the facility at Electric Mills. That name originated in the fact that the Sumter mill was supposedly the first in the South to be powered by electricity.[71]

Prominent Mississippi lumberman Tom De-Weese remembered that Electric Mills was "the largest lumber mill in the south and the most beautiful, soft, softwood timber you ever saw, and the first all electric mill in the south . . . a model for the entire United States, including the West Coast, of being all electric. Everything they operated was run with electric motor. They gen-

Gilchrist-Fordney mill at Laurel. Courtesy Lauren Rogers Museum of Art, Laurel, Mississippi.

erated their own electricity. . . . [B]ack in those days, everybody else was using steam engines and belts. . . . But Electric Mills was famous for its modern machinery and beautiful timber . . . and mill town. They had a beautiful mill town there. Well kept, good houses for the employees to live in, doctors, hospitals . . . baseball teams that traveled over the countryside for entertainment. It was just a model community, and it cut out in 1939. . . . [T]hey quit, and the timber later was bought by . . . Flintkote in Meridian and Kemper County and north of Lauderdale County and a little bit in South Winston County. . . . [L]ater Weyerhaeuser Company . . . bought that same timberland from Flintkote."[72]

North of Newton was the Adams-Newell Lumber Company, which succeeded the New Deemer Manufacturing Company of Deemer, founded in 1908 by Congressman Elias Deemer from Pennsylvania. Deemer bought timberland for $12.50 an acre from a speculator who had purchased it earlier from Adam Bond and J. D.

King for $4.85 an acre. Bond and King had paid fifty cents an acre for forty thousand acres at a tax sale in 1900. These transactions illustrate the pattern of timberland speculation that was rampant in Mississippi.

Other historically important operations in this area included those of A. DeWeese, who built a mill near Philadelphia in 1905; the Henderson and Molpus Lumber Company, which constructed a plant at Philadelphia in 1912; and J. R. Buckwalter, who erected a sawmill at Union in 1915. Also in 1915 N. C. Schriever built a plant at Louisville, using mules to pull his logging trains. The D. L. Fair Lumber Company was established in Louisville in 1917. Ab DeWeese's son, Tom, later remembered, "Out of all these many large sawmills all over the central and southern parts of Mississippi . . . less than 5 percent of them . . . were owned by native Mississippians, operating right where they were born and raised. The rest of these large operations were northern people with capital who came south from all across the northern tier of states

. . . and bought up this timberland and built these so-called large sawmills."[73]

The J. J. Newman Company became the largest lumber manufacturer in the interior of Mississippi by the early twentieth century. The primary owner, Fenwick Peck, was a native of Pennsylvania who came to Mississippi in 1896. Peck had lumber interests in other parts of the country, including Pennsylvania and New Mexico, and controlled the Mississippi Central Railroad. At their peak the J. J. Newman mills at Hattiesburg and Sumrall produced 200 million board feet annually, and the company owned 400,000 acres of timberland. Peck helped to organize other companies as well, including the Homochitto Lumber Company at Bude, and by 1905 his operations' total investment in Mississippi was valued at $26 million.[74]

Columbus housed several companies that purchased the output of small mills and owned small operations. The lumber was collected at concentration yards and remanufactured for specialty markets. The Columbus area mirrored the history of sawmilling in Mississippi, with the earliest mill, a whipsaw operation, dating back to 1822. This mill was succeeded by the first circular-saw mill in 1855, water-powered operations along the Tombigbee River, and a sash-saw mill that was burned by Union troops during the Civil War. The peak of sawmilling activity in Columbus occurred between 1909 and 1920.[75]

Along the Gulf and Ship Island Railroad between Gulfport and Jackson there were nine companies that were called the "Si Pine" group of sawmills and that jointly marketed "Si Pine," high-quality longleaf pine lumber. The companies included the Kola Lumber Company of Kola, the J. J. White Lumber Company of Columbia, the F. V. B. Price and Company operation at Pine Bur, and the W. C. Wood Lumber Company of Collins. Others were the Ingram-Day Lumber Company of Lyman, the Ship Island Lumber Company of Sanford, the Bond Lumber Company (a Dantzler property) of Bond, the Bond Lumber Company of Columbia, and the Gulledge Lumber Company of Mendenhall. By the late 1920s the largest mill on the Gulf and Ship Island was that of the Batson and Hatten Lumber Company at Lyman, the successor to the Ingram-Day Lumber Company, which was organized in 1906 by lumbermen from Wisconsin, Iowa, and Minnesota. They bought a mill and logging equipment from the Gulf Coast Lumber Company and operated until 1924, when they cut out. Batson and Hatten bought the mill to manufacture from their own timber tract.[76]

The six-hundred-square-mile shortleaf pine area in northeast Mississippi had a number of small railroad mills that collectively turned out a fairly large amount of lumber. There were several sawmills in the 1880s, all with an annual capacity of less than 3 million board feet, at Glendale, Burnsville, and near Iuka. There were also portable sawmills whose products were hauled in wagons to the Mobile and Ohio and Memphis and Charleston railroads. The major shipping points in the area were Burnsville in Tishomingo County and Corinth in Alcorn County. Much of the raw material came from second-growth forests on exhausted agricultural land.[77]

While most Mississippi lumber producers specialized in pine, there were hardwood operations as well. As mentioned earlier, the Anderson-Tully Company began cutting cypress and hardwoods along the Mississippi and Yazoo Rivers in the late nineteenth century and manufactured boxes, hardwoods, and veneers at mills in Memphis and Vicksburg. In Leflore County, large nonresident speculators with no intention of manufacturing lumber purchased both pine forests and hardwoods and cypress in the Yazoo Delta. Lumbermen from Michigan, Wisconsin, Iowa, and Illinois traveled to Mississippi to personally inspect the lands, and one firm bought 5 to 6 million acres of Delta land and 150,000 acres of pine forests. At one point, about half of the county was owned by timber companies, and the Delta and Pine Land Company, headquartered in England, had more than 50 percent of those lands. Despite selling off large holdings, the company still had more than fifty thousand acres in Leflore County in 1900. In 1891 one mill near Berclair manufactured 1 million feet of quartered oak for the European market. Natchez's R. F. Learned and Son Company, which originated in 1828 as the Andrew Brown firm, continued to be a major hardwood producer, cutting not only cypress but also cottonwood, willow, oak, and red gum from lands along the Mississippi River.[78]

In 1898 Cassius and Bob Carrier cruised the area along the Coldwater River. They found hardwoods that they estimated would produce fifteen to twenty thousand board feet per acre. The swampy areas and bayous had cypress. The Carriers acquired forty thousand acres of timberland between the Tallahatchie and Coldwater Rivers in southwestern Panola and northeastern Quitman Counties. The Carrier Lumber and Manufacturing Company built a mill on the Illinois Central Railroad at Sardis and a logging road, the Sardis and Delta, to connect the mill and the woods. The Carriers logged hardwood timber and manufactured lumber from the area between the Tallahatchie and Coldwater from 1901 to 1929.[79]

Another northern firm that invested in Mississippi hardwoods was Nickey Brothers. Operating originally in northern Indiana, in 1898 the company moved its operations to Princeton in southern Indiana. After about ten years there, the brothers had accumulated a considerable amount of capital. As Samuel Nickey Sr. recounted the story, "We . . . had this half million dollars, when we said, 'Let's go South and see what we can find.' So we went down to Memphis. The first place we contacted was along the Illinois Central Railroad, the Y. and V. There was a tract of timber of about 8,000 acres, at Pritchard about 34 miles south of Memphis. Got off at Robinsonville and got some mules and rode across through the woods. We stayed about two weeks in this timber, this 8,000 acres, came back to Memphis and bought it, the whole 8,000 acres, for $5.13 an acre. . . . After we bought that, we waited 30 or 60 days, and came down here and bought 3,000 more acres at Marks, Mississippi, spending about $100,000." The Nickey firm manufactured hardwood lumber at its mill in Memphis, and in the early 1930s Nickey even experimented with the manufacture of plywood. By the 1950s the company was making plywood, practicing selective cutting on its own lands, and providing timber-management assistance to small landowners from whom the company purchased timber.[80]

By the late nineteenth century the southern lumber industry was dominated by yellow pine producers. The industry featured large concentrated landholdings dominated by northern interests but sprinkled with southerners. Southern lumbering was characterized by highly competitive producers who scrapped heatedly over timber acquisitions and sales. They were divided into regions, with the most significant boundary the Mississippi River. Finally, the industry was led by men who were caught up in ruthless competition that seemed to many of them unnecessary and wasteful. This perception spawned the development of trade associations, including the Mississippi Lumbermen's Association, the Mississippi Pine Association, the Yellow Pine Manufacturers' Association, the Southern Pine Association, and the Southern Hardwood Manufacturers' Association.[81]

In the early twentieth century southern lumbering led the nation, and Mississippi rose to third place among lumber-producing states by 1908. But there were clouds on the horizon. The activities of lumber trade associations; large, concentrated timber holdings; and the specter of monopoly attracted the attention of reformers and resulted in an investigation by the U.S. Bureau of Corporations. The printed study that resulted provides an excellent view into the dynamics of Mississippi's lumber industry during the peak years of the early twentieth century. Who controlled the timber, how large were the mills, and how were estimates of timber holdings and stumpage derived? Other questions were largely beyond the investigation's purview, but they too were extremely important to Mississippians: what logging and harvesting methods did the big companies use, and what was the impact of their timber- and mill-management policies on Mississippi's forests and people? The legacy of those methods and policies would linger into the middle of the twentieth century.

5 "Like Locusts through a Field of Wheat"

The Devastation of Mississippi's Forests and Their People

The control of huge areas of southern forests by a few Northern investors and companies by the late 1880s contributed to national fears of a lumber trust. There was growing trepidation about the rise of monopolies and trusts that would threaten traditional American practices and values. The southern pine industry was frequently charged with monopolistic practices and price fixing, partially as a result of the activities—real or perceived—of its trade associations. These concerns led the U.S. Bureau of Corporations to investigate the entire lumber industry, issuing a report in 1913–14. The report quoted prominent lumberman Edward Hines of Chicago, president of the National Lumber Manufacturers' Association and a major Mississippi southern pine manufacturer. Hines told the members of the Yellow Pine Manufacturers' Association (the predecessor of the Southern Pine Association) in 1910, "[Y]ou have practically got this situation in your own hands. I think it is up to you, gentlemen, to, in a measure, regulate the lumber prices from Kansas City to the Atlantic coast absolutely." The Bureau of Corporations report said that Hines's statement meant "that they can raise the price of lumber, and so increase their gains from their timber holdings, by restricting lumber production."[1]

The Bureau of Corporations report included an excellent overview of the lumber industry and of the condition of Mississippi's forests at the height of the bonanza era. Unlike Bureau of the Census reports, which reflected the timber reported by sawmills, the Bureau of Corporations study attempted the first serious census of the total amount of standing timber in the Pacific Northwest, the lake states, and the southern pine region. These areas contained about four-fifths of the privately owned timber in the United States.[2]

The study provided an excellent description of the methods timber cruisers used to determine the volume and value of timber on a piece of land:

The measurement or "scaling" of logs . . . is not a mathematically accurate determination of their volume, but an approximate determination of the quantity of lumber they are likely to yield. For this purpose, lumbermen commonly use a measure called a log scale or scale stick. This is a flat stick, a quarter of an inch or more in thickness and about an inch and a quarter broad. The edges are often graduated in inches. On the faces are usually six graduations, three on one and three on the other, for six lengths of logs. These graduations run lengthwise of the stick, and show the contents in board feet, at each diameter, for logs of each length. The length of a given log is first determined, usually by the eye; the stick is then laid across the small end, and the contents in board feet are read off. The reading is supposed to give the contents of a straight, sound log; and if a log is crooked or unsound, the scaler makes a deduction according to his judgment. The measuring sticks are graduated according to tables, called log scales or log rules, which give the supposed product of logs of different diameters and lengths. Many such tables have been constructed; some from diagrams, some by mathematical formulae, some by measurement of logs sawed and their product, and some by combinations of these methods. The Woodsman's Handbook, published as Bulletin 36 of the Forest Service, gives 44 different rules. The differences among them are astonishingly wide. For a 16-foot log, 24 inches in diameter, the computed contents range from 268 board feet to 500: for a 12-foot log, 6 inches in diameter, from 3 board feet to 20. For a log 12 feet long and 6 inches in diameter, most rules give values ranging from 12 feet to 20. Yet the Doyle rule, which gives only 3 feet, is more widely used than any other. It is far more inaccurate for small logs than for large, yet in great areas of the country it is used for small logs only. There is another rule of long and wide acceptance, the Scribner, which gives smaller values than the Doyle for the larger diameters and much larger values for the smaller diameters. A combination of the two has been made, by taking the smaller value for each size of logs with very few exceptions. This combination, called the Doyle-and-Scribner rule, is the scale chiefly used in many parts of the Eastern, Southern, and Middle-western States.[3]

The study noted that the actual counting and measuring of trees was prohibitively expensive: "Even if the trees are counted, the average diameter is usually estimated by the eye, and the supposed normal content of the tree of this diameter is multiplied by the number of trees. This normal content is based on the estimator's experience or on volume tables. Even the counting of trees is not only slow and expensive, but difficult. It is hard to be sure of getting them all and counting none twice." The study described the timber cruiser's common methodology:

Oftener no attempt is made to count every tree, but sample plots, perhaps of an acre each, are laid off by pacing or with a surveyor's chain, and the trees on them are counted. The result is taken as the average

stand on the larger area which the samples represent. Far the commonest method of estimating, however, is simply to look the forest over, without any counting or measuring. The examination may be made with less or greater care. The cruiser may tramp back and forth on parallel paths only a few rods apart, or he may make only one trip through a strip a mile wide. He may tramp all day without making a note, and set down at night his estimate of the area he has covered and of the whole amount of timber he has passed through. By long experience, men learn to form judgments, by these rough methods, which, on an average, approximate fairly the scale of the logs. The general tendency is to estimate below the truth, because the estimator desires to be "safe"; that is, not to have his estimate subsequently proved too large by other cruisers or by the results at the mill. To overestimate reflects on the cruiser. The owner will not complain if the cut shows more timber than the estimate, but he will be displeased—especially if he bought on the estimate—if the cut shows less.[4]

Estimates of the amount of stumpage were done in each decade from the 1880s to the 1930s. The estimates varied, in part because logging standards changed over time. In the early period, lumbermen generally cut only the largest diameter trees and left high stumps. Over time the trend was to cut anything that could be made into lumber and leave the stumps as low as possible. Furthermore, because of variation in methods of measurement, it was difficult, if not impossible, to equate estimates from different surveys.[5]

Bureau of Corporations Commissioner Herbert Knox Smith argued that ownership of timber, more than size or ownership of mills, was the key to control in the lumber industry. In 1911 he noted, "Only 40 years ago at least three-fourths of the timber now standing was (it is estimated) publicly owned. Now about four-fifths of it is privately owned." Said Smith, "Whatever power over prices may arise from combinations in manufacture and distribution (as distinguished from timber owning), such power is insignificant and transitory compared to the control of the standing timber itself or a dominating part thereof." The commissioner estimated the value of standing timber in the United States (excluding the value of the land) at $6 billion.[6]

Smith argued that the southern pine region had a high concentration of ownership in the more valuable species. Sixty-seven holders owned 39 percent of the longleaf pine, 29 percent of the cypress, 19 percent of the shortleaf and loblolly pine, and 11 percent of the hardwoods. Considering the effect of the situation, Smith concluded, "Such concentration in standing timber, if permitted to continue and increase, makes probable a final central control of the whole lumber industry. A few strong interests, ultimately holding the bulk of the timber, can set the price of timber and its products." He also argued that some of the largest holders were cutting little of their own timber (probably in the Pacific Northwest), planning to profit from the nation's diminishing timber supply while "protesting against conservation and the national forest system because of the 'tying up' of natural resources."[7]

The Bureau of Corporations report concluded that there were 2.826 billion board feet of standing timber in the United States, of which 2.197 billion were privately owned. The southern pine region possessed 634 billion feet. Since the land had been owned by the government, said the report, the value had increased "practically everywhere . . . manyfold—sixfold, tenfold, twentyfold, thirtyfold, and in some cases fiftyfold." In Mississippi a tract that had sold for $10,000 in 1897 sold for $124,000 in 1907. The price per acre increased from five dollars in 1900 to thirty dollars in 1907.[8]

The average price of southern pine stumpage rose from $1.12 per thousand feet in 1899 to $3.16 in 1907. The price in Mississippi for longleaf in 1899 ranged from two dollars to five dollars per thousand feet. Cypress brought the same amount. In some areas of southeastern Mississippi, the price of longleaf stumpage was said to have increased from five- to twenty-five-fold in ten years. A 6,240 acre tract of hardwood in Yazoo County was purchased in 1897 for $1.50 an acre, or less than $10,000. Ten years later a $100,000 offer for the same tract was refused.[9]

The Bureau of Corporations study concluded, "The interest on the present value of a supply of standing timber for such a period as twenty or thirty years would be prohibitive, of course, were it not for the rapidly rising value of the standing timber itself." The study repeated "the common saying, heard even among those who have made fortunes in the lumber industry, that there is no profit in the sawmill, that the profit is in the timber."[10]

In the southern pine region there were 232.3 billion feet of longleaf, 152.1 billion feet of shortleaf and loblolly, 40.4 billion feet of cypress, and 209.2 billion feet of hardwoods, which were considered the least valuable. The Bureau of Corporations study reported that "a large part of the hardwood in the Southern Pine Region is as yet of very low value. Till late years gum was worthless, and even mixed stands of other hardwoods were often considered only an encumbrance on the agricultural lands of the lower Mississippi." Even though the rise in lumber prices had increased the value of gum and other hardwoods, "little effort has yet been made to determine the amount of it, and the quantity of the more valuable hardwoods is much less known than that of pine." The study went on to say that the average value of hardwoods was low, "because of the high proportion of inferior timber, especially the great quantity of gum. . . . Within the last half dozen years land has been leased for terms of years in the Yazoo-Mississippi delta, under contracts which required no payment from the lessees, but only that they should clear the land of timber. . . . Since the year 1900 many thousand acres of virgin hardwood have been deadened and burnt in . . . Mississippi."[11]

Mississippi had 95.3 billion feet of privately owned timber. Of the hardwoods, 33 percent were oak, 25 percent gum, 4 percent hickory, 3 percent ash, and 35 percent miscellaneous. Hard-

Table 1. Mississippi Timber Holders, 1913

	Size of Holding (in billions of board feet)	Amount of Timber Controlled (in billions of board feet)	Total Acreage Controlled*
Group 1	> 25	--	--
Group 2	13–25	--	--
Group 3	5–13	6.5	579,000
Group 4	3.5–5	4.3	259,000
Group 5	2–3.5	7.9	619,000
Group 6	1–2	7.7	797,000
Group 7	.5–1	4.6	501,000
Group 8	.25–.5	7.2	908,000
Group 9	.125–.250	5.5	573,000
Group 10	.060–.125	4.1	483,000
Total		47.8	4,719,000
	< .060	47.5	7,344,000

*Includes outright land ownership and timber rights

Source: U.S. Department of Commerce and Labor, Bureau of Corporations, *The Lumber Industry,* pt. 1, *Standing Timber* (Washington, D.C.: U.S. Government Printing Office, 1913), 23, 107, 163.

woods constituted 32.5 percent of Mississippi's timber, and the 1.9 billion board feet of cypress made up 2 percent. Sixty-two billion board feet, or 65.5 percent of Mississippi's timber, was yellow or southern pine, including 47.6 billion board feet (50 percent) longleaf and 14.8 billion board feet (15.5 percent) shortleaf.[12]

The leading longleaf counties were Forrest, Perry, Greene, George, Jackson, Harrison, Pearl River, and Hancock. The greatest stands of hardwoods and cypress were in Tunica, Coahoma, Quitman, Bolivar, Sunflower, Tallahatchie (Delta section), Leflore, Holmes (Delta section), Yazoo (Delta section), Washington, Sharkey, and Issaquena Counties. The study concluded that the public and private forests of the nation had about a fifty-five-year supply of timber at the current

rate of consumption and that natural regrowth in the cutover areas was "only a small part of the annual cut."[13]

The bureau's investigation divided timber holders into size categories, with group 1 consisting of holders of more than 25 billion feet— the Southern Pacific Railroad, the Weyerhaeuser Timber Company, and the Northern Pacific Railway Company. (The Weyerhaeuser holdings in the report did not include lands controlled by individuals or companies of the extended family.) The degree of concentration was greatest among the largest holders. Because of the South's lack of large railroad land grants, the higher price of southern timber, the scattered nature of most timber tracts in the area, and the fact that southern stands had lower timber den-

Table 2. Mississippi Sawmills, 1909

Size (in millions of board feet)	Number	Production (in millions of board feet)
> 50	3	190.546
25–50	8	256.355
15–25	20	362.660
10–15	26	303.734
5–10	54	377.563
2.5–5	97	329.200
1–2.5	271	403.314
.5–1	234	160.233
.05–.5	914	185.040
< .05	134	4.024
Total	1,761	2,572.669

Source: U.S. Department of Commerce and Labor, Bureau of Corporations, *The Lumber Industry,* pt. 1, *Standing Timber* (Washington, D.C.: U.S. Government Printing Office, 1913), 278–79.

sity than those in the West, the southern pine region had a lower degree of concentration than the West, and the region had no holders of more than 13 billion feet. Even so, sixty-seven holders, each with more than a billion feet, owned 39 percent of the longleaf, 19 percent of the shortleaf and loblolly, 29 percent of the cypress, and 11 percent of the hardwood. Many of the southern holders owned timber rights rather than possessing the land outright. Ordinarily, they had a set period of time in which to harvest the timber. The study found that most large lumber manufacturers were also large owners of timber, but large timber owners were not necessarily manufacturers.[14]

Table 1 summarizes the study's findings regarding Mississippi's timber holders. Owners of more than 500 million feet controlled more than one-third of all Mississippi's standing timber. The two group 7 holders had 17.7 percent of the longleaf, and ten holders with between 1 and 5

billion feet controlled 24.8 percent of the total timber, 41.2 percent of the longleaf, 11.5 percent of the shortleaf and loblolly, and 5.8 percent of the hardwoods.[15]

With regard to the size and economics of sawmills, the Bureau of Corporations simply restated the conventional wisdom among lumbermen. There was a limit on the optimal size of a sawmill, for a mill that was too big would exhaust its timber supply in a short period of time. The costs of transporting timber were high, so it made sense to locate mills close to the raw materials. Small mills, unless close to cheap water transportation, had to move from tract to tract. It was impossible for them to work profitably far from a railroad. For large mills, "a low cost can be reached only by having a fairly compact tract of timber and building logging railroads through it." The study concluded that it did not pay to build a large mill unless it was to cut a tract of timber that the company already controlled. And

Table 3. Mississippi Lumber Production by Species, 1909

Species	Production (in board feet)
Yellow Pine	2,114,706,000
Red Gum	120,731,000
Cottonwood	46,222,000
Cypress	41,666,000
Yellow Poplar	25,833,000
Hickory	21,967,000
Tupelo	6,146,000
Elm	6,090,000
Chestnut	1,692,000
Maple	770,000
Beech	680,000
Basswood	591,000
Sycamore	379,000
Birch	85,000
Cedar	55,000
Walnut	33,000
Ash	15,017
Cherry	5,000
Others	1,493,000
Total	2,280,669,630

Source: U.S. Department of Commerce and Labor, Bureau of Corporations, *The Lumber Industry*, pt. 1, *Standing Timber* (Washington, D.C.: U.S. Government Printing Office, 1913), 79–80, 82, 88–92.
Note: These figures include all mills reporting lumber, lath, or shingles and are therefore greater than the figures reported in table 2.

life of at least 15 or 20 years, within which the cost of mill and logging outfit, less the removal value, may be written off." The life of the mill could be extended by buying up small tracts of timber in the area, and "[s]ometimes the cost of shipping logs even so far as 50 or 75 miles may be less than the loss involved in moving or abandoning the mill."[16]

The study concluded, "If there were any great gain in concentrating the manufacture of lumber, the cost of transporting the logs even longer distances might be overcome. But there is no such gain. To enlarge a mill beyond a capacity of 20 or 25 million feet a year is to duplicate mechanical units, with small or doubtful advantage in manufacture, and with certain disadvantage in the cost of transporting logs. It is a matter of dispute among lumbermen whether a mill of 20 million feet capacity, under the usual conditions of transportation in the southern pine territory, is not more economical than a larger one. The conditions of the industry tend to keep the bulk of the production in plants of moderate size, say under 25,000,000 feet a year. If a single interest wishes to cut a large amount of timber, it is apt to build two or half a dozen mills, rather than one of extraordinary size."[17]

In fact, after the turn of the twentieth century the middle-sized mills turned out most Mississippi lumber production. In 1902 the *American Lumberman* noted that several lumbermen were investing $100,000 or more in south Mississippi, and by 1907 twenty mills produced more than 20 million board feet annually in the state. Table 2 shows Mississippi's 1909 sawmill production.[18]

By 1909 yellow or southern pine was by far the leading lumber species produced in the United States. Of a total cut of 44,509,761,000 feet, southern pine contributed 16,277,185,000 feet, or 36.6 percent. Its closest rival was Douglas fir, with 10.9 percent. Mississippi's lumber cut in 1909 totaled 2,572,669,000 feet, or 5.8 percent of the national total. Table 3 shows Mis-

the report said, "The size of the mill is fixed with regard to the quantity of timber available, and is usually made small enough to give a probable sissippi's lumber production by species of tree. These figures represented 3.4 percent of the state's stand of pine, 2.2 percent of the cypress, and 1.3 percent of the hardwoods.[19]

The Bureau of Corporations report unknowingly addressed an important aspect of the lumber industry that had a profound impact on Mississippi. The study noted that "mills large enough to operate to the best advantage in the virgin forest under present conditions can not be moved without a loss of the greater part of the investment; consequently, these mills as a rule have logs delivered at one place until the exhaustion of the available timber ends their usefulness." According to the report, "To work most economically, a mill, in many localities, should have a logging railroad; but a mill of very moderate size will justify such a road."[20] This statement reflected the early-twentieth-century lumber industry's orthodox view. Optimal performance and profits could best be achieved through the use of railroad logging. Railroad logging usually meant clear-cutting and the use of steam-powered skidders, which virtually destroyed any prospects for natural reseeding of the cutover lands, which constituted the crux of the problem.

As early as 1903, a little more than two decades before Mississippi reached the apex of its lumber production, one Mississippi writer, citing a U.S. Forest Service publication, commented on the "wanton waste of raw materials" in the state and reproduced the following description: "Inasmuch as cutting has been unusually severe and wasteful, and since fire almost invariably follows lumbering, more than half of the long leaf pine land of the State has been converted into a blackened and barren waste. This means that over the larger part of the area there is little or no reproduction of the timber which, when once gone, will not be replaced by a new growth, which should be now coming on."[21]

Industry growth and new technology brought a far more destructive method of logging than had been used in earlier times. Logging contractor Horace Butters of Ludington, Michigan, developed what some consider the first steam-

powered log-skidding machine in 1883. He used a steam engine built by the Lidgerwood Manufacturing Company of Brooklyn and worked with two of the company's engineers, Spencer Miller and J. Harris Dickenson, in improving his machine. While Butter's skidder was not especially popular in the lake states, it was used extensively in the cypress swamps of the South. Butters himself acquired timber holdings in North Carolina's Green Swamp. William Baptist of New Orleans made further improvements, developing the pullboat system for swamp logging. In 1891 or 1892, the Ruddock Cypress Company of Louisiana and the Louisiana Cypress Company replaced the pull-boat system with a railroad with a car-mounted steam skidder, introducing railroad swamp logging. Mississippi also had small portable mills mounted on barges or rafts that sawed timber in the swamps or river bottoms where the larger companies found it uneconomical to operate.[22]

In 1908 Asa S. Williams, forest engineer for the Lidgerwood Manufacturing Company, published an instructive article entitled "Logging by Steam" in *Forestry Quarterly*. He described the southern piney woods as an area where "there are broadly speaking no physical difficulties; the ground is flat, railroad or log wagon can go anywhere, there are no rocks or cliffs, little mud, generally no underbrush. Common logging is cheap, easy and efficient. . . . *Then why the skidder?* Because it is inanimate, does not die, eats nothing when it does not work, is unaffected by the weather, disease or insects, is constant and tireless, and gets cheap logs: in other words, there is money in it."[23]

Following the early developmental work by Butters, Lidgerwood, and Baptist, several types of skidders and loaders became standard in the southern piney woods. First was a semiportable snaker originally developed for use in the pine forests of Georgia. It was simple and inexpensive and was popular among small operators. The machine consisted of a one-, two-, or three-drum engine mounted on a flatcar. The flatcar was run off on a side track at each setting, and skidding lines with tongs were attached to a spar tree.

Mules or horses were used to return the lines to the log to be skidded. The logs were rolled up on inclined skids for loading onto cars. The principal disadvantage of this type of rig was the amount of time and trouble it took to set up at each new location.[24]

In the mid-1890s W. A. Fletcher of Beaumont, Texas, improved on the semiportable snaker by developing the portable pine logger. This machine consisted of separate Lidgerwood skidding and loading engines mounted on a long platform. Loading and skidding booms were raised overhead to handle the lines. Again, the lines were returned to the logs by horses or mules. The machine remained on the tracks during skidding operations and was raised by a system of engine-operated levers to allow the empty cars to pass underneath. To move to a new setting, the portable pine logger was lowered to a flatcar and pulled by a locomotive. A further refinement was the Baptist type, built by Woodward, Wight, and Company of New Orleans. This machine was built on the Fletcher design, but the operation of the booms was simplified, and the steam-powered loading boom was allowed to swing, for greater flexibility. The Baptist type could be raised by pulling it by locomotive up a slightly inclined auxiliary track that allowed the empty cars to pass underneath. The Dequede was a further refinement; it could be raised into position by screw jacks to allow empties to pass underneath.[25]

The Lidgerwood Manufacturing Company acquired the patents for all of these portable machines and further developed its own design for the Lidgerwood portable logger and loader. This machine remained on the track when in operation but was raised by four hydraulic, steam-operated jacks to allow the passage underneath of empty log cars. There were refinements in the arrangements of the booms, and the system used for the skidding lines eliminated rehandling. The machines came in several sizes, with two, three, or four skidding lines, and the price was six to ten thousand dollars.

Steam skidder. Courtesy Special Collections, Mitchell Memorial Library, Mississippi State University, Starkville.

The Lidgerwood machine had an average daily hauling capacity of twenty to thirty-five thousand feet for each skidding line, which translated to a cost of fifty to ninety cents per thousand feet in timber averaging five thousand feet or more to the acre. The daily cost of operating a three-line machine, with a daily capacity of seventy-five to one hundred thousand feet, was roughly fifty dollars.

The practical limit for snaking logs with this machine was one thousand feet, which was considered the maximum distance that a single horse or mule could return a line. While two animals were sometimes used for longer distances, doing so was awkward, slow, and expensive. The Lidgerwood became "the standard, almost the only large capacity machine used to-day in the Long Leaf Pine belt, and for original investment and operating cost [it] is by far the cheapest means of logging, be it compared with oxen, horses, mules, or other machinery." Another variation on these machines was built by the Russell Wheel and Foundry Company.[26]

The Lidgerwood Manufacturing Company and the Clyde Iron Works built double-ended snakers, which snaked at both ends but did not load. Pond snakers were often used in pulling logs across ponds or sloughs in the pine woods, and cableway skidders (also known as overhead, suspended, swamp, cypress, Lidgerwood, or high-ball skidders) were commonly used in logging southern cypress swamps.[27]

Once the logs were skidded or snaked to the railroad, several types of loaders placed the logs on the log cars. Goodyear of Pennsylvania is credited with producing the first machine to quickly and cheaply load logs, the Barnhart loader. Loaders that passed from car to car as each succeeding car was loaded included the Barnhart and the Marion, the American, and the Rapid. The Barnhart had a portable track that was laid on the car tops as the loader pulled itself from car to car by a wire rope attached to the end of the train. Loaders that remained stationary on ties or rails and allowed the empty cars to pass through or under them were the Decker, the

McGiffert, and the Parker. There were also several types of American loader, which were self-contained on their own cars and had no provision for the passage of empty cars. The loaders cost from $3,500 to $6,500 and could load anywhere from 30,000 to 150,000 feet daily, depending on the logs and conditions. A day's operation cost about twelve dollars, or about twelve cents per thousand board feet. Wilson pointed out that the steam loader "will load logs in swamp, water, rocks, brush and other conditions where neither horse, ox, mule or man could. As with other logging machinery it is not effected by flies, heat or rain, and has no running expense on holidays or shut-downs."[28]

Beyond the matters of cost already mentioned, the use of steam skidders and loaders was justified on the grounds that they were labor saving and that the work was not hard. Also, they did not require many skilled workers, since the men were merely required to "work levers, a signal, then tong or dog logs, ride a mule or look on, things that even a negro does not object seriously to doing." The machines would also save the cost of purchasing and maintaining animals. Williams argued that the "average logging horse or mule costs about two hundred and fifteen dollars, five hundred dollars a pair are commonly paid, so that the operator in the pine woods for instance can sell his stock and for half the value secure a machine that will do the same amount of work. It costs fifty or sixty cents a day to feed per head, so that Sundays, holidays, or other shutdowns are expensive luxuries. . . . [T]he idle machine has no expense."[29]

Other factors that the lumbermen and timber owners considered were taxation and indebtedness. Timberland was taxed on an assessed value or an annual ad valorem basis. If even a few trees remained on an acre of land after the timber was harvested, it was classified as timberland for tax purposes, and timberland was usually taxed at a higher rate than agricultural acreage. As stumpage prices rose, so did taxes. The assessment of the Blodgett properties in Pearl River County rose from $808,000 to $1,334,665 in a year, increasing their tax by almost $16,000. Also, many lumber operations were financed by timber bonds with a fixed schedule of timber liquidation. The companies borrowed money to purchase timber, often in excess of their needs, and then bonded the timber to finance mill construction. The harvesting of timber poured money into a sinking fund for bond redemption, and in many cases debt and tax obligations forced the cutting and dumping of timber on glutted markets. A 1917 U.S. Forest Service study by William B. Greeley concluded that both the instability of the lumber business and the sorry state of forest conservation were largely based on these economic conditions.[30]

In 1920 the Long-Bell Lumber Company published a promotional booklet that captured the feel of steam logging:

Hard upon the heels of the log cutters comes the skidding and loading crew. . . . [T]he most economical and most efficient operation is to assemble and load the logs by machinery. . . . Long steel skidder cables with "grabs" like ice-tongs attached are hauled from the skidder to the fallen logs by stout horses, ridden by boys; or by the most modern method, the cables are steam-hauled on trolleys by what is known as the "rehaul." The grab is attached to a fallen log by a "grab-setter," a signal is passed to the operator known as the "drum puller" on the skidder, and as the steam power is applied a drum or winch reels in the cable and the log races to the side of the skidder. There the logs are seized by a cable from a loading boom, hoisted into the air, and deposited on log cars set to receive them. As each car is loaded to capacity it is pulled forward to make way for an empty car, the operation being repeated until a train load of logs is made up. Prosy description can give little idea of the spectacular and strenuous activity of logging forces at work in the woods. Horses and men rushing to and fro, seemingly in constant and imminent peril from falling trees; giant logs, with skidder cables attached, plunging though the undergrowth on their way to the skidder, there to be tossed into the air and whirled dexterously into place on the log cars; the "boom-boom" of falling trees, the roar of steam exhausts, engines puffing,

workmen shouting warnings and instructions—all contribute to a medley that makes the forest seethe with motion and resound with a confusion of noises.[31]

The large mills using railroad logging had ravenous appetites. One student estimates that the Great Southern Lumber Company of Bogalusa, Louisiana, arguably the largest mill, cut over between forty and one hundred acres a day as it logged in Mississippi and Louisiana. As the lumber companies began to cut out and desert the forest regions, out of frustration, anger, need, or greed local communities tried to get as much in taxation out of the timber and mill owners as they could. Some landowners simply abandoned the cutover lands rather than attempt reforestation and pay taxes. The Hines Lumber Company, on the other hand, attempted to allow its lands to regenerate by leaving seed trees. However, on learning that his 241,000 acres of cutover lands were to be taxed as timberlands, Edward Hines instructed his loggers to cut everything in sight and leave not a stick of wood standing. Mississippi lumberman J. R. Weston remembered that Hines "ordered his woods crews to go back over the cut over land and cut every pine tree over 2 inches in diameter and I understand his woods crews followed those instructions until he ceased operations in 1930 in Hancock, Pearl River, and Lamar Counties."[32]

N. Floyd McGowin, a prominent lumberman from Alabama, recalled "a statement Mr. Edward Hines made at a meeting of Southern Pine operators held in the early '20s. He said he was running his Mississippi mills two shifts; that the State of Mississippi held a first mortgage on all of his properties there and he was cutting out and getting out of Mississippi as fast as he could." Hines's story was not unique. Visiting Laurel in the mid-1930s, McGowin met with officials of Eastman-Gardiner, Gilchrist-Fordney, Marathon, and Wausau-Southern. "They, too, were plagued by the tax policy of the State of Mississippi," McGowin recalled. "Mr. Phil Rogers, general manager of Eastman-Gardiner, told me they would give their land to anyone who would assume the back taxes, which he considered more than the value of the land." Lumber industry journalist James Boyd reported in 1931, "One Mississippi lumber company that had a capital of $1,200,000 has paid in taxes during 20 years an amount of money greater than its capital stock." A land agent and forester who was active during part of the bonanza era blamed what happened in part on "the disposition of local taxing officials of those days, or at least a percentage of such officials, and but for them many of these former sawmills might have been operating."[33]

Boyd saw a direct correlation between taxation and lumber-company operating policies: "It has been discovered by investigations made in all of the states that cut-over lands have been assessed at higher values than any other class of real estate. The tax burden has been given as the cause of so many lumber companies operating day and night, in order to save something in taxes, by not having the timber to be assessed. There have been two theories of handling a lumber manufacturing business. One is that by running day and night and saving the amount that would have to be paid for taxes and other overhead, the profit would be larger than by following the second plan, which was to prolong the cut as long as possible with a hope that higher prices after the others had finished would bring a higher profit than to cut out at the earliest possible moment."[34]

Most observers and writers have attributed much of the devastation wrought on cutover lands in the South to clear-cutting and the use of steam skidders. However, those who ran the industry in the bonanza era either did not or chose not to see their negative impact on Mississippi's forests and people. These lumbermen thought they had good reasons for their actions. They received support and even encouragement for their practices from very respectable quarters. As Michael Williams puts it, "Undoubtedly, clear-cutting was a response to high stumpage prices, timber scarcity, lack of capital or access to long-term credit, and also just plain greed, but the conception of the forest as a completely exploitable

resource in which nothing was to be wasted did herald a new attitude." It should also be noted that the lumbermen of the "cut out and get out" era were harvesting large, old-growth timber. They overestimated the amount of time it would take to grow new trees to merchantable size.

Clear-cutting was the most efficient method of harvesting timber, and the U.S. Forest Service's 1918 handbook endorsed clear-cutting. A prominent southern pine lumberman told the annual meeting of the National Lumber Manufacturers' Association in 1912, "The theory is constantly advanced that only large trees should be cut and the smaller ones, which are supposed to be immature, should be left to mature, but this is not true, not only for the reason that they will deaden but for the further reason that they are frequently over-ripe and should be manufactured." His remarks were published in the association's official report under the title "Selective Cutting Impracticable." Consequently, large holders of timberland pursued policies of "cut out and get out" lumbering, clear-cutting, moving their logging spurs frequently, and leaving the land bare—and their consciences untroubled.[35]

In his *Forestry Quarterly* article, Asa Williams promoted steam skidders and loaders from a conservationist standpoint, arguing that steam skidders always pulled logs over the shortest direct distance from the stump to the loading point. Thus, he said, "a smaller amount of young growth need be removed than in skidding with animals which follows the meandering and therefore longer road of least resistance or otherwise best passage." In steam skidding with wire ropes or cables, he said, the "skidding road is very narrow, being little wider than the width of the largest log to be skidded. With carts, sleds, or jumpers a wide way must be swamped or trodden and much young growth is destroyed or damaged."[36]

Conversely, a lifelong resident of Neshoba County remembered that "wherever they logged by pulling it in with those skidders and cables and stuff, they completely tore up everything that was left, just about. There wasn't anything left, and at that particular time, they didn't cut the small trees like they do today. Their trees were 18 inches on up to 4 foot. Large trees. But they didn't fool with little trees. They were too unhandy to handle, I guess, but wherever they logged back then . . . they just tore it completely up. . . . They'd carry the train out, and then they'd load up, and they'd carry it back to the mill. That was over here at Deemer."[37]

In any case, some lumbermen and their supporters argued that harvesting timber was simply part of a natural process in the forests. Writing for the 1890 census, Dr. Charles Mohr said, "Many people have thought that the trees that made lumber for the present generation were growing at the time of the discovery of America by Columbus, but that is not so. It is rare that a virgin tree is found that is older than 200 years. The predecessor of the forest of the present day has passed on like the human beings that lived in that period. Some of them were blown down, some succumbed to the ravages of disease and fire. The pines that have been so useful to the present generations started as seedlings in early colonial days. They, too, would have died, if the lumbermen had not saved them to a more useful career." Long after the era of clear-cutting and steam skidding was over, apologists for the lumbermen still existed: one land agent and forester termed these lumbermen "trailblazers." He argued that society, as well as the mill and timber owners, were responsible for what happened, and he urged critics not to be "too hard on these former sinning lumbermen." Describing the use of railroad logging and steam skidders and loaders during the bonanza period, a U.S. Forest Service publication of the late 1980s said, "New logging methods were needed to reduce costs and step-up production."[38]

Despite these claims and arguments, most nonindustry observers found clear-cutting and steam skidding to be extremely destructive. Jack Holman, a Mississippi State University forester, said, "Steam-powered skidders with long cables dragged the logs from the stump to the rail siding. This process tore at, broke off, and often dug

up young trees in the path of these logs. This type of operation left the land bare with stumps as the only reminder of what was once there . . . beautiful stands of trees. The bare soil began to erode and small rivulets grew into gullies." One contemporary observer remembered, "Loggers were chewing up the pine forests like locusts cutting a swath through a field of wheat." Said the *Hattiesburg American*, "The giant virgin pines were being felled like matches. . . . What trees they didn't cut were ripped and torn by the high-powered skidders. And the tree tops and litter left in the loggers' wake dried out and [fueled] raging wildfires that consumed any remaining seedlings and saplings."[39]

Some companies simply abandoned their cut-over land and left; others struggled with largely unsuccessful attempts to sell it to farmers as cropland. Only a few attempted to introduce selective cutting and reforestation to continue operating. An Alabama lumberman remembered, "At no time before 1935 did the management of the company ever believe they would be able to operate longer than eight or ten years." The secretary of a large sawmill company in the 1920s said that "about 90 percent of such manufacturing projects are temporary establishments. . . . [A] sawmill operation can last only as long as it has a timber supply. When this supply of raw material is exhausted there is little left to a sawmill operation that can be classified as much better than junk. In view of those conditions . . . it is always a foregone conclusion when starting a sawmill operation that there is only a limited number of years during which it can be operated."[40]

Most lumbermen also considered their cutover lands virtually worthless. Former Crown Zellerbach forester Jeff Hughes remembered, "A lot of 'em wanted to move on out to the West Coast where the big money and the big trees were, and they were glad to get rid of the land. . . . In the early days the tax rates on cutover pinelands were exorbitant. . . . My grandfather used to gamble with deeds to lands he'd cut the timber off of. . . . Somebody'd raise the ante five bucks, and [if] he didn't have five bucks to cover it, he'd throw a deed for forty acres of cutover land on the table. . . . I've had some reliable witnesses tell me of watchin' that scene. . . . So land wasn't worth very much." Consulting forester Zebulon W. White recalled his boss saying, "When you buy timber, be careful they don't slip the land in with it." Said White, "that's how much land was worth in those days." As the mills shut down and the land was abandoned, the railroads that had helped build the industry were discarded as well. They were left with nothing to transport, and between 1920 and 1932 more railroads were abandoned because of the depletion of natural resources than for any other reason.[41]

The large timber owners and mill operators had already made their money out of timberlands that were now nearly worthless denuded acres of land. But what of the people and communities left behind as the lumbermen abandoned the cutover areas of Mississippi and moved their operations out to the West Coast?

Life in the woods, the mills, the lumber camps, and the company towns of Mississippi was hard, even before the industry's dying days. The advent of the big mills and companies brought specialization and impersonality to the employer-employee relationship. This problem was aggravated by the fact that many of the owners lived elsewhere and had no personal relationships with their employees.[42] And beyond the impersonality, hard work, long hours, and dangers of logging and sawmilling, the lumber industry imposed industrial values and expectations on a labor force composed largely of people from rural backgrounds and culture—blacks, whites, sharecroppers, tenant farmers, yeomen. What they had in common was their poverty and their appreciation of the opportunity to earn a cash income in the woods and the mills. And what divided them, as always in the South of this period, were the misconceptions, prejudices, and conflicts of race. While some of the work in the woods and sawmills was done without much consideration of race, life in the logging camps and sawmill towns was structured according to the prevailing standards and rules of racial segregation.

On occasion Mississippi lumber workers rose above their transcendent racism and joined together, black and white, to confront their common problems. However, even those efforts often foundered on the shoals of race. It was symbolic that the workers' labor unions were often segregated. To deal effectively with their complaints and conditions, lumber workers desperately needed to pull together, for the lumber companies clearly tried to make sure that they hired no employees with union sympathies.

Wages in the Mississippi lumber industry were low, and the hours of labor were long. While the wage scales varied from region to region, in the 1880s the average wage for a fourteen-hour day in the mills along the Gulf Coast was one dollar, with unskilled workers probably earning even less. By 1889 common laborers received twenty dollars a month, and skilled workers about $2.50 per day. In some companies the workers were occasionally paid in company scrip rather than cash. While some outside merchants would accept scrip at a discount, it could often be used only at the company-owned commissaries, again at a discount. In the Hattiesburg area in 1913, scrip could be exchanged for cash at a 10 percent discount. When some lumber operators were short of cash, they did not pay their workers at all, simply providing food and clothing.

Sometimes the workday was even longer than fourteen hours, stretching from before sunup until after sundown. In the 1890s, most mills operated at least twelve hours a day and some ran as long as fifteen. If the mill shut down, the time was later made up by lengthening the workday. In many cases, workers labored thirteen hours a day to earn a half day off on Saturday. In most mills the eleven-hour day was standard by 1912. One former resident of a sawmill town remembered, "Most mills . . . operated on an eleven-hour day from six in the morning to six in the evening, with an hour off at noon. Whistles blew at these hours, preceded by a short quarter-hour blast. On Saturdays the workmen quit earlier." J. Roland Weston said that in the lower Pearl River Valley, the "men left their homes at 4:40 or

Eastman-Gardiner Company logging crew. Courtesy Lauren Rogers Museum of Art, Laurel, Mississippi.

5:00 in the morning for the forest." In 1912 the Mississippi legislature established the ten-hour day in manufacturing, exempting loggers and timber haulers. The law was passed with the support of some Mississippi lumbermen, who believed that it was humane and that workers would produce as much in ten hours as in twelve. In fact, Philip S. Gardiner's company voluntarily reduced the workday to ten hours as early as 1906.[43]

The labor forces in the woods and the mills were integrated although living and social arrangements were not. In the mills, the sawyers, filers, carriage men, and others were skilled workers. They were well paid, and they came from both races, although most were white. Most of the manual laborers who moved the lumber around in the mills, yards, and finishing facilities were black, and they were poorly paid. The clerks, secretaries, and other office personnel were almost exclusively white, as were the sales staffs and other white-collar workers. Both blacks and whites labored on the woods crews, and

most workers on the logging railroads were black. The woods workers were poorly paid and worked long hours under unpleasant conditions, and in dangerous circumstances.

During much of the late nineteenth and early twentieth centuries, a shortage of laborers existed in the Mississippi lumber industry. As lumbering grew, so did its workforce. The state had 16,421 sawmill workers in 1899, a number that grew to 24,415 by 1904 and 37,178 by 1909. Some mills were forced to shut down in 1904–5 because of a labor shortage. There was a brief labor surplus during the Panic of 1907 and ensuing depression, bringing racial conflict to some firms as whites tried to forcibly prevent blacks from holding scarce jobs.

The shortages returned with the production demands for World War I. Companies recruited workers from Mississippi's agricultural population, black and white, and brought in workers, especially experienced, skilled operatives from the North, who occupied the key positions. Mississippi lumberman I. C. Enochs observed that department heads and skilled workers were usually imported, as was the case when the Finkbine Lumber Company built its large mill at Wiggins in 1902. When Eastman-Gardiner moved to Laurel, the company brought workers from Wisconsin and Iowa and used local blacks for unskilled jobs. However, after a few years of operation, more of the key employees came from the local population. At another Finkbine mill, at Ten Mile, the important position of saw filer was occupied by a native of the Mobile, Alabama, area.[44]

Some companies attempted to attract foreign laborers, including Italians, Germans, and Scandinavians, but these efforts met with little success. Camp and Hinton employed a large number of Italians and found them only partially satisfactory. The Finkbine Lumber Company employed a few Danish workers, but they soon left. Irish, Swedes, Norwegians, and Germans had reputations as reliable workers with ambition, but thirty Germans employed by one firm left before the end of their first day because of the lack of beer. A former resident of a south Mississippi sawmill town remembered that "Dantzler sometimes brought in skilled labor from other states but ordinarily used natives as unskilled laborers, both black and white."[45]

In north Mississippi's hardwood industry, "sawmill operators found labor scarce until after the cotton crop had been harvested." Manufacturers advertised in local newspapers for loggers and log teams. They believed that blacks preferred work in the cotton fields over the sawmills because it was easier and they were fed. Some companies imported Mexicans but found them of little value in the woods. The Carrier Lumber Company used itinerants, although they were not dependable.[46]

Many employers had a condescending, paternalistic attitude toward their workers, especially the blacks. J. J. White said that he had utilized both slaves and free blacks and that they became progressively worse. The more they were paid, the less they worked, and they were inefficient and undependable. He said they would work only half of the time, because as wages in the industry increased they could eke out an existence working part time. When paid for two or three days, many common laborers would simply take the rest of the week off. The Camp and Hinton Lumber Company of Lumberton employed as many as six hundred African-Americans, and a company official complained that they were "more no-account and trifling every day." The treasurer of the Finkbine Lumber Company, with a large mill at Wiggins, said that the black worker was "unstable and unreliable as a laborer." The editor of the *Pascagoula Chronicle Star*, who came from a lumbering background, wrote in 1893 of a New Jersey firm that came to the area "expecting to teach our 'tar heels' how to saw lumber and make money, and to elevate the colored man." The editor reported that the company "lost all their money and admitted they did not know how to saw hard pine. Yet, they succeeded in elevating at least a few colored men as they exploded the boiler of their mill and blowed to eternity several negroes." A logging superintendent damned black workers with faint praise, saying that they were better than Mexicans or white Americans and that they would stay and work if they were given plenty of food, a place to shoot craps, a place to preach, and a decent place to live. A large group of lumbermen, meeting in Hattiesburg, said that black workers were undependable, shiftless, and worsened by high wages. To keep blacks on the job, the state legislature enacted a stringent vagrancy law in 1904, but it backfired, prompting hundreds of potential workers to leave the state to escape its penalties.[47]

Even some who praised black workers did so in a condescending and racist manner. A *Southern Lumberman* editorial in 1898 argued that southern blacks were unexcelled in heavy work requiring strength, noting that a log-turning device used in sawmills was called the "steam nigger." Two German foresters who toured the southern pineries in 1906 said that only African-Americans were fully acclimated to the subtropical climate and the swamp fevers. Walter Barber, a mill superintendent and business manager for the L. N. Dantzler Lumber Company, said that sometimes in dealing with black workers it was necessary to use rough treatment. Another observer in 1895 said that lumbermen preferred blacks over whites because blacks were stronger and had greater endurance. S. S. Henry, a native southerner, said that blacks were the best sawmill workers in the world. They did twice as much work as whites and expected only three meals daily and regular weekly wages. Barber said that many illiterate blacks could perform complicated mental calculations that required speed and exceptional skill. They were also, he said, reliable and dependable.[48]

Promoting the replacement of men with steam skidders and loaders, Asa Williams said, "The labor difficulty is common to many of our industries, but its perti[n]ent features have been intensified in the woods. The man of energy and ability goes to the cities. The hardy woodsman of the north and west, that went in with the frost and stayed till the drive, is extinct; he had training and skill of a lifetime and intuition drawn from his fathers. Who has replaced him?" Williams, of course, had the answer: "Drunks that must keep away from some of the cities, foreigners of many kinds, and not to be forgotten in the South, the negro. They must all be bossed, pushed, told, and shown, petted, coaxed and paid without stint, and then they will not work. In other words, woods labor is both expensive and inefficient."[49]

During World War I, with the labor shortages exacerbated by both military and civilian industrial manpower mobilization, some manufacturers used private labor agencies and the U.S. Department of Labor's Employment Service Bureau to secure workers. One manufacturer's representative in St. Louis described the Employment Service Bureau's procedures in terms that clearly reflected the racism of the time:

I have learned that the U.S. Department of Labor Employment Service Bureau has shipped niggers to the South in considerable numbers. . . . For 40 or more niggers the department sees that a special train for them is put on a regular passenger train, and this car goes with them straight through to destination. You would pay the railroad fare and expense of the trip, same to be deducted from the nigger's wages. . . . It is necessary for an escort to come and make the trip with the gang. . . . If you want 70 or 80 niggers, they will furnish two cars. . . . I told these people you would not want a lot of niggers that had labor union ideas in their heads and asked them where most of them came from. They stated a large majority of them had been shipped up here from the South and their work had given out or else they had not caught on and were dissatisfied in the North. . . . The department furnishes these niggers with a form of pledge or contract as to what they can expect and an obligation that they will go to the destination named and work when they get there. There is really nothing that will absolutely bind the nigger of course, but they bluff him a little and try to make him think he is bound. . . . A very important feature to these niggers is the board they will have to pay or what it will cost them to live. I was told the niggers were pretty well scared up by papers published by those of their own race, stating they would be mistreated in the South; that a lot of niggers had been lynched in Mississippi, Alabama, and Louisiana—and some of them consequently did not want to go South. Whoever you send should of course be experienced in handling niggers, and if he is I believe with the assistance of this bureau he could pick up a good bunch. . . . The Bienville Lumber Co. at Forest, Miss. got two shipments of niggers in this way and the Hall & Lincoln Lumber Co. at Morton, Miss., a neighbor, also got a shipment.[50]

Labor troubles occasionally arose in the industry, especially among the mills along the Gulf Coast. In the late 1880s workers in the area joined the Knights of Labor and demanded a twelve-hour day. Both blacks and whites joined the union but had separate meetings, and each group had its own leader. Unable to achieve their goal peacefully, workers in the Moss Point–Pascagoula area struck. After a few days, the operators gave in. The victory gave a boost to union organization efforts. In 1889 three hundred workers struck seeking a ten-hour day, weekly wage payments, and union recognition. The union attempted to support its members by providing food rations, but after about a month, during which only seventy-five of six hundred men were working, the strike was defeated with the use of strikebreakers.

The Knights of Labor won another conflict in Handsboro in 1888, a strike for shorter working hours and union recognition. The same issues continued to fester among workers along the Gulf Coast, and about a decade later the Knights of Labor struck again for shorter hours, weekly payment of wages, and union recognition. Five hundred workers, mostly blacks, struck the Denny, Dantzler, and Bounds mills in April 1900. The conflict got ugly, with racial conflict, a court injunction against the union, and the formation of an extralegal organization called the Committee of Public Safety that forced some union leaders to leave town. Eight union members accused of firing on workers were convicted and sentenced to ten years in the penitentiary.[51]

Racial animosity was partially responsible for the failure of workers in the interior regions to form effective unions. Although most of the better, safest, and well-paying jobs went to whites, competition for the same positions contributed to the rise of the White Cap movement in southern Mississippi during the 1890s. The White Cap members were determined to keep blacks out of the mills and on the farm, by coercion if necessary, and fulminated against industrialists, foreigners, Jews, minority groups, and businessmen. In December 1893, the White Caps burned the engine house of the Norwood-Butterfield Lumber Company at Brookhaven. The company had suffered earlier losses from the activities of the same group. Foreign workers on Gregory Luce's logging crew in Jackson County were threatened by the White Cappers.[52]

Early in the twentieth century southern pine lumbermen organized an employers' association, the Southern Lumber Operators' Association, to deal exclusively with labor matters, thus protecting the image of their trade associations, the Yellow Pine Manufacturers' Association and later the Southern Pine Association. During the 1920s the operators' association worked diligently to combat the Great Migration of blacks from the South toward northern cities, so-called radicalism, and attempts at unionization. A 1923 survey revealed that Southern Pine Association subscribers considered the exodus of black labor in Mississippi, as in several other southern states, severe. An important part of the operators' association's work was gathering and disseminating information about southern pine workers and their activities among the association's members. During 1921, for example, the operators' association conducted 485 investigations into "strikes, intimidation of negro labor, sabotage, arson and the activities of the I.W.W. and I.U.T. Organizers. These required the services of thirty-eight (38) trained operatives."[53]

The operators' association informed members of conditions in the industry generally as well as at their own plants. For example, a November 1923 report to members said, "Reports on Mississippi situation is that while Labor is satisfied with treatment and living conditions and there is no indication of organization, there is an undercurrent of discontent, especially amongst Negroes with wide-spread talk of Northern movement in the Spring." A May 1923 report said, "Special investigations have been made within the past 30 days on calls from Texas, Louisiana, Mississippi, Tennessee, and North Carolina on account of reported attempts to organize, sabotage, arson and to locate cause of unrest amongst the Negro labor. . . . A careful analysis of reports from all sources indicate that the most serious problem confronting your industry is the movement of Negro labor. . . . This movement has been brought about through propaganda appearing in Negro papers and magazines and other papers published in the North and circulated freely throughout the South as well as through Labor Recruiters representing Northern and Southern industrial plants." In June the operators' association sent out a report showing the average monthly labor turnover based on member responses to an inquiry. In Mississippi, nineteen mills reported white turnover of 10.2 percent, eighteen mills reported black turnover of 16.1 percent, eight mills reported no labor turnover, and thirteen mills reported no black migration.[54]

Not all workers' movement resulted from the blandishments of other industries' recruiters. Loggers and sawmill workers often tended to be drifters, moving from one job to another and staying only for a few months or a year or two. Lumber companies sent recruiters into their competitors' camps in efforts to lure away workers and advertised in newspapers for woods and mill laborers. Workers tried to avoid areas that had a reputation for malaria infestation.[55]

By the mid-1920s, some lumbermen realized that they were losing workers and that some African-Americans might be susceptible to union organizers' appeals not because of "radical agitators" and other "troublemakers" but because the South was not a paradise for black workers. Several Southern Pine Association subscribers reported that "persecutions, brow-beating and bulldozing by petit officers, who profit by arrests, is the cause of much dissatisfaction among negro labor in various localities." Association subscribers' common suggestions for improving the blacks' lot included "providing of better housing and living conditions for the colored labor, increased school facilities, fair wages and protection for the negroes against unscrupulous officers of the law." There was good reason for the lumbermen to be concerned about the treatment of black workers, for a sizable percentage of the industry's labor force was African American. By the late 1930s, for example, the Crosby Lumber Company's logging crews consisted of whites and blacks who "worked side by side. The ratio of negroes to whites was about four to one." Conversely, many lumbermen looked down on their African American workers, and, as one put it, "The sawmill Negro is rather shiftless and is not inclined to stay long in one location and consequently there is little incentive on the part of the operator or owner to carry on welfare work in any extensive manner."[56]

Many lumbermen's prevailing attitude was reflected in one Mississippian's recollection of a walkout at his north Mississippi mill. As James W. Silver tells the story, "One morning his superintendent, called Memphis, asked for a new Negro crew. Unfortunately, a colored worker had gotten hold of some 'mean' whiskey and had 'cussed' a white foreman. When the other Negroes came to work next day, they found their erstwhile co-worker swinging from a limb. They walked out. Forty years later the narrator of this incident smiled and said proudly, 'You know, we got a new crew down there on the afternoon train and only lost one day's work.'" According to Silver, "Mississippi timbermen were prudently pleased with their surroundings and reasonably content with their work during the early twentieth century." He notes that no attempts were made to organize the Carrier Lumber Company's workers either in the woods or in the Sardis plant , but possibly goes too far in asserting that "it is doubtful whether the thought of unions ever entered their minds." Nollie Hickman attributes the relative infrequency of union activity to the fact that the "native white, strongly individualistic, was not prepared to accept the discipline and co-operation demanded by a successful labor union. Moreover, the presence of the Negro as a competitor for the unskilled and often for the skilled jobs created a division of labor into ranks often bitterly hostile to each other. The white mill workers were more apt to oppose the Negroes than their employers."[57]

Labor in the sawmills was extremely demanding and, depending on the job, required intelligence, quick-thinking, agility, strength, and the ability to withstand brutal heat and humidity amid the deafening screams of high-speed saws. The noise level was so high that sawyers communicated with block setters through hand signals. Some of the work was extremely dangerous. The log carriage, which moved the logs to the head saw at great speed, sometimes split into sharp, pointed pieces, endangering the workers who operated the carriage blocks. The band saw blades sometimes fractured, sending sharp steel projectiles throughout the space in the vicinity of the head rig. Carriage gears broke, and the carriage would run out of control and crash, throwing its operators into the air and into great danger. One longtime industry observer remembered that a "man with five fingers had trouble getting a job in some planing mills. The foreman figured that unless he had lost a finger or two he lacked experience." [58]

Kenneth L. Smith's book on sawmilling in Arkansas describes other job-related dangers of the lumber industry: "An injured finger . . . wasn't really getting hurt; worse things happened. . . . A sawyer . . . decided to ride the log carriage, lost his balance, and was thrown into the band saw. A laborer . . . was feeding slabs into the hog (the fuel grinder) when a snag on a slab caught his overalls and jerked him in head-first. . . . Workers were also hurt or killed by tumbling logs, falling trees, runaway trains and trucks, whirling saws and pulleys. While most lumber companies gave at least lip service to safety . . . [i]t was hard to get either workers or supervisors to pay attention, even though logging and sawmilling were filled with dangers." A former resident of a Mississippi sawmill town remembered that "accidents did occur. Once the bursting boiler of a logging locomotive killed an engineer named Steinwinder. . . . At another time a busting steam pipe at the mill injured A. E. Duncan, who recovered sufficiently to be able to work for awhile afterward. Then there was the case of H. Gilmore, whose arm caught in the planing mill roller. Eventually this accident left him paralyzed." [59]

Work in the woods was also physically demanding and dangerous. Before the age of railroad logging, trees were leveled by loggers who wielded double-bitted axes that were sharpened to a razor's edge. Later, loggers utilized crosscut saws. After the trees were felled, they were bucked and cut into proper lengths. As one industry source described the process,

The log cutters work in pairs, a right-handed and a left-handed man in each pair. The implements with which they work are a cross-cut saw, an axe, an assortment of thin wooden wedges, and a bottle of kerosene with which to "oil" the saw. The trees are first "notched" on the side toward which they are to fall, that the tree may not split as it starts to descend. That done, the saw is started into the tree on the opposite side. If the tree settles in its position and "pinches" the saw, the wedges are introduced to relieve the pressure, and the sawing continues until the tree is severed and crashes to the ground. The giant trunks, comparatively free of limbs, produce a peculiar and far-reaching sound as they strike the earth—a resonant and sonorous "boom," like the muffled report of a cannon shot far away. When a large gang of loggers is cutting down trees the incessant "boom-boom" of the falling trunks, reverberating through the forest aisles, is more suggestive of a distant battle than of the progress of a peaceful industry. The log cutters trim the branches from the fallen trunks with the axe, and saw off the small tops. Frequently, the long main trunk is sawed into two or more lengths, according to requirements for the class of material being manufactured at the mill.

One contemporary writer, perhaps momentarily overwhelmed by the theories of Frederick Winslow Taylor, suggested that through the implementation of time-and-motion studies and other principles of "scientific management," the logging crews could become even more productive.

The logs were then snaked by horses, mules, or oxen to the spur track, where they were loaded aboard the log cars. Eventually, steam-powered skidders and loaders replaced the animals and some of the humans in these last phases of woods work. The workers were fellers (also called fallers, cutters, or flatheads), buckers, members of train crews, and drivers of the animals. Sometimes those who drove mules were called "skinners" or "mule skinners," those who worked with oxen were "punchers," "bull punchers," or "bull whackers." The woods foreman was sometimes called the "Bull," or the "Bull of the Woods." With the advent of power equipment, working with the tongs, grabs, and chains was both physically demanding and dangerous. Representative was the experience of a

Logs on Lindsey log wagon pulled by oxen. Courtesy Mississippi Forestry Commission, Jackson.

skidder foreman with the J. J. Newman Lumber Company at Sumrall during World War I: "I had a drum man who was not good and he got his line tangled up in the skidder. I got up on there to help him untangle that and got in the gear wheel and cut my foot off." At the time of the accident he was twenty-two years old. The loading crews sometimes included a boy who was stationed in a tall tree to direct the work of the skidder operator with hand signals.[60]

Former residents of the Cohay I and Cohay II logging camps, operated by the Eastman-Gardiner Lumber Company, remembered them as places where serious injury and death were constant companions. Ben Hurst of Clinton recalled one month in which there were forty injuries and two deaths, and Dorsey Hurst of St. Louis remembered, "When the dummy trains were bringing in the dead and injured, the engineer keep tooting the whistle so all in camp knew something was wrong." All of the camp inhabitants would gather anxiously at the station to determine the victims' identities. Ben Hurst

remembered the skidders as the biggest threat: "Those long chains, with knife-sharp points on them to hook the logs would sometimes snap under a big load. When they did the chain would swing wild and free, with enormous power. If it hit a man, it could—and did—snap his head off. Or an arm or leg." The Hursts also remembered that when oxen were used for hauling, some logs could get loose and crush the men driving the animals or working behind them. Ben remembered a workman who was brought into the camp doctor with a mashed foot, and "we kids looked through the window. I saw the doctor cut his foot off." The felled trees sometimes crashed down on the workers below, and on occasion a limb from a falling tree could instantly impale and kill a man who was two hundred feet or more from the base where the cut was made. Falling limbs sometimes caused injuries or death. Workers called them widow makers.[61]

Asa Williams downplayed the necessary level of skill and the physical rigors, arguing that the work was "not of the hardest physical kind nor need it be." In fact, the skills required for many of the jobs were considerable and were usually acquired by observing or doing the work. Some skills required a combination of common sense and instinct. For example, one ox driver who was active in the early twentieth century around Laurel remembers "straightening out" a recalcitrant member of his team:

One of my boss men . . . had an old yoke of male steers. And one of them—ole Nig— . . . would turn around there every time you'd get in a tight and that would turn that yoke. I knew I was getting in them bigger timbers and that morning I went to my yard out there and got me a strand of wire. . . . I tied ole Nig's tail to that tongue chain down there but not—I gave him plenty of room to move without hurting his tail and he fooled around there when I called on him to pull that log—these old red oak logs—he pulled around there and he squealed. I said, uh huh, you fool. He thought he was going to turn that yoke. I hollered at him to get straight there. And I had done fixed my figure eight

knot in the end of my Jump Foot and I begin to feed that to him in them hocks right there in that front foot. After a while he commenced bellowing—oh, he went to bellowing—he'd get down on his knees and I'd holler, Get Up, Nig. He'd get up and when he did, I'd punch him again in the same place. I'd tell him to get up with the rest of them—You'd better get up there, Nig. Boy, he'd hit that yoke and we'd come out of there with that log. The Boss Man would come around there—he'd say, "Mr. Wade, I ain't mad about nothing—I want you to know that." I said, "Yeah?" He said, "What did you do to ole Nig that had him a bellowing down there?" He said, "I've whipped that ox with cant hooks and limbs and things, and he never has bellowed. That's the first time I've ever heard him bellow." I said, "You'd have bellowed, too, if you'd have been getting what Nig's been getting." He said, "I knowed he was in trouble when I heard that bellow." From then on Nig knowed to move when I called on him, then.

Ben and Dorsey Hurst remembered that two men could notch all the way around a big pine tree

Skidding logs with oxen. Courtesy Mississippi Forestry Commission, Jackson.

Eastman-Gardiner Company logging camp in Jones County, Mississippi, ca. 1925. Courtesy Forest History Society, Durham, North Carolina.

and then saw through it in about twenty minutes.[62]

Woods and mill workers' living conditions varied tremendously. Some lumber workers were also small farmers who labored in the woods or mills but lived and grew crops on their own small patches of ground. Many woods workers lived in isolated small camps or settlements that were often temporary in nature. With the advent of railroad logging, the size of the woods operations increased. As the timber close to the main-line railroads was cut over, the work sites became more and more remote. The logging crews lived deep in the woods for extended periods. In 1905 Mississippi had 527 logging camps housing 8,185 workers. By 1913 about two-thirds of the mills maintained logging camps. About half of these camps had portable houses, while in the other half the workers lived in railroad camp cars. The living conditions were spartan: as an official of one sawmill company put it, "a sawmill operation

having only a short life cannot very well construct expensive dwellings for its employees, or expand too much in the way of recreational work."[63]

In Eastman-Gardiner's logging camps, "[h]ousing was sometimes provided by converting railroad cars into homes, department stores, and drug stores. . . . Other camps were temporary structures which required little or no effort or expense to build. These were low, flat buildings." A retired lumberman remembered the Eastman-Gardiner facilities as "the best camps anywhere." In an effort to attract desirable workers, Eastman-Gardiner's Wisner camp, home to about eight hundred people, provided schools, churches, recreational facilities, and a YMCA.[64]

In north Mississippi the most permanent logging camp of the Carrier Lumber and Manufacturing Company was constructed in 1910 and abandoned in the mid-1920s. The camp was twenty miles from Sardis on Bobo Lake (later renamed Lake Carrier) and was accessible only by railroad. The camp had electric lights, running water from artesian wells, separate hotels for blacks and whites, segregated schools for both races, churches, a post office, a commissary, a hospital, an icehouse, and juke joints. Workers could stay in the white hotel for fifty cents a day, which included room and board plus a packed lunch. There were also company-owned cottages for both black and white families, and the workers paid a dollar a month for a doctor. The major complaints were broken bones and malarial chills and fever, which took a heavy toll on the logging crews and for which massive doses of quinine were prescribed.[65]

To keep the men satisfied and entertained and to prevent them from heading off to Memphis for long weekends, the company allowed a wide-open town, possibly with the paid approval of local officials. There were pool rooms and honky-tonks for both races. The blacks' hangout had music, poker, dice, and whiskey, while the whites' drinking and gambling were conducted at the white hotel. Professional gamblers were not allowed. A bootlegger supplied both groups, and hookers from Memphis came in on payday weekends. The pleasures of the Lake Carrier camp attracted visitors from nearby areas, who participated in the weekend revels.[66]

The camp had little racial trouble. Most conflicts occurred within the races and, as Silver puts it, "Negroes assumed what was considered their proper place—and that was that." However, although a camaraderie existed among those who worked in the woods, black and white, a "colored straw boss would lose his influence (and his job) once he got the reputation of being 'a white man's nigger.'"[67]

In south Mississippi, an Albany, New York, newspaper called Eastman-Gardiner's Cohay camp "one of the finest of its kind." The camp was reached via a logging railroad and contained 137 white and 96 black families, for a total of about one thousand people. The men worked ten-hour days for daily wages ranging from $1.75 to $7.75. They lived in modular portable homes of from two to five rooms, with the aver-

age size of a room being eighteen feet long and nearly seven feet high. All houses were painted red. There was no charge for rent until after 1910, when the price became $1.50 monthly per room. When the time came to move to the next logging location, the rooms of the houses were separated and individually lifted by steam loaders onto railroad cars. The camp facilities included a general store, drugstore, post office, company business office, and separate schools for the 100 black and 175 white children. The center of social and religious life was the YMCA hall.[68]

The small mill towns were, like the logging camps and most other Mississippi institutions, segregated. Some mill communities were company towns, but others were not. In the company towns, the company owned everything: houses, stores or a commissary, medical facilities, churches, and schools. Residents of the mill towns often looked back fondly on the experience, although their remembrances may reflect a tendency to edit out the bad and remember only the good. But the facilities in the company-owned communities probably exceeded those of many towns on the outside. For example, one resident of a south Mississippi company town remembered that the "mill provided certain fringe benefits. We enjoyed running water for the house and electric lights until ten o'clock at night. In the event of a new baby the lights stayed on for the doctor."[69] But the company towns were isolated. The isolation did not begin to break down until the advent of the automobile and improved roads provided easier access to the outside world.

One typical sawmill town in south Mississippi, with a medium-sized mill producing eighty thousand board feet, was surrounded by trees and split by the Gulf and Ship Island Railroad. On one side of the tracks were homes for officials and workers and a boardinghouse. One building served as school, church, and meeting place for the Odd Fellows Lodge. Across the railroad tracks was a commissary, which also housed the post office and ticket office. The commissary porch was a prime spot for loafing and socializing among

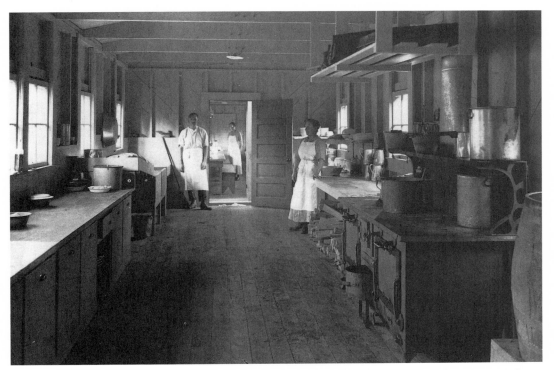

Logging camp kitchen of Sumter Lumber Company, Electric Mills, Mississippi. Courtesy Forest History Society, Durham, North Carolina.

the men. The sawmill buildings spread along the tracks beyond the commissary, and behind them were the black quarters and a black restaurant patronized by both races.[70]

While life and work in the sawmill towns and logging camps was hard, the most woebegone of the workers were those who labored in the turpentine and naval-stores industries. The turpentine industry came late to Mississippi. In 1860 the state had only one turpentine still, and by 1880 there were eleven. As late as 1884 Charles Sargent reported that Mississippi's pine forests had suffered "but little damage from the manufacture of naval stores." However, he reported, "Turpentine orchards . . . have been recently established in the vicinity of the coast, near the mouth of the Pascagoula river, and at other points in the coast counties." There were twenty-four stills in 1890 and 145 by 1900. The industry migrated to Mississippi because of timber exhaustion in the Carolinas and the construction of railroads. The

operators brought to Mississippi hundreds of black laborers who had been naval-stores workers for generations. One employer, Joseph Simpson, came to Wiggins in 1900 accompanied by one hundred black workers. Other companies began operating along the Gulf and Ship Island Railroad.[71]

Many lumber companies in the longleaf belt also conducted naval-stores businesses. After the trees were worked for three years, they were felled for timber, with almost all of the labor provided by black workers. Naval stores were also extracted from the rosins that saturated the pine stumps. In the early years lumber manufacturers believed that the turpentine face on a tree would weaken the timber. While this theory was disproven by pioneering forester Bernhard Eduard Fernow in 1893, the early "chop box" method of collecting gum wasted a lot of material, especially where the faces had been burned. Around the turn of the century W. W. Ashe and Charles

Holmes Herty developed more conservative methods that employed shallow chipping. A cup and gutter replaced the chop box. A system utilizing metal cups and gutters became popular after about 1910. To protect the faces from fire, the turpentine operators raked a strip around each tree and control-burned the area.[72]

Turpentine workers developed special skills, depending on their ambition and talents. They usually did not receive wages but earned money for chipping trees, dipping gum, and boxing trees on a piecework basis. Chippers, who cut the streaks on the trees, were expected to chip from seven to nine thousand faces per week and ordinarily worked from Tuesday through Friday. Both women and children worked as dippers, and they were paid for each barrel they filled with gum. The workers seldom were paid cash but instead received credit at the commissary and were encouraged to go into debt, thus chaining them to the company. When and if they were paid, they received company scrip called brozines that was

honored at the commissary. Sometimes they received cash at Christmas.

The boss or manager of the operation wielded godlike power. He hired and fired, extended or denied credit at the company commissary, and even enforced criminal law and administered or withheld punishment. Recruitment of labor was a special problem, and each operator was alert to preventing others from pirating his workers. Turpentine workers were nomadic, seldom staying in the same place for more than three years, and sometimes an unscrupulous turpentiner would send some of his men into another camp to lure laborers away. On occasion recruiters paid with their lives for this practice.

Naval-stores employees resided in isolated camps provided by their employers. The commissary furnished groceries, work clothes, and other supplies. The workers lived in one-room huts, with rudimentary, company-owned furnishings. The huts were crowded into rows along narrow streets. A water pump usually supplied the entire

Moving day at Eastman-Gardiner Lumber Company camp at Wisner, Mississippi. Courtesy Lauren Rogers Museum of Art, Laurel, Mississippi.

Pine trees cut for turpentine production. Courtesy Mississippi Forestry Commission, Jackson.

village. The turpentiners' lives represented repression and mistreatment even beyond what happened to blacks in sawmilling and logging.[73]

By the end of the 1920s the bonanza era of lumbering in Mississippi was over. In 1929 the state led the nation in lumber production, but only because the output in other southern states, such as Louisiana and Texas, had fallen off earlier and even more precipitously. And the large lumber-producing states of the Pacific Northwest had not yet reached their peaks. Mississippi's production reached its apex in 1925, with an output of 2,562,120,000 board feet.[74] Most of the large companies either were out of business or had exhausted their timber supplies in the Magnolia State and moved on to the Pacific Northwest.

The disappearance of the pine forests changed the economic lives of the timber and mill owners. But the industry's decline had its greatest impact on the Mississippians left behind. An important part of the story of Mississippi lumbering's bonanza era is how it affected these people of the forests, those who worked in the woods and in the mills and who lived in the towns and small logging settlements. And the effects extended beyond those directly employed by the industry. Local and regional merchants, governments,

schools, and other industries were also affected. In 1915 John E. Rhodes, secretary-manager of the Southern Pine Association, estimated that more than 65 percent of Mississippi's people depended in some way on the lumber industry. The big mills both attracted and generated capital that went into other Mississippi enterprises. For example, both Eastman-Gardiner and J. J. White built cotton mills. The Finkbine Lumber Company had the world's largest pickle plant, and the Dantzler Lumber Company was a major force in the establishment of a paper mill at Moss Point.[75]

Some mill towns simply disappeared, while others, such as Hattiesburg, Laurel, and Meridian, were fortuitously located and survived as significant communities long after the mill whistles were silenced. Some lumber towns became permanent communities, including Collins, Lucedale, Lumberton, Moss Point, and Wiggins. Many towns simply disappeared, like the towns mentioned in south Mississippi writer James Street's description of the piney woods route traveled by railroad engineer Jimmie Jackson:

De voodoo lan's railroading hero was Jimmie Jackson. He used to bring "Old 42" out of New Orleans for Meridian. He left the Louisiana station exactly at

The Devastation of Forests and Their People 117

8 P.M., crossed the seven-mile bridge over Lake Ponchartrain and started the ghost run through Mississippi. He passed a chain of dead towns, wholly deserted villages, which once were bustling little places in the "voodoo lan" until men stole the cypress from the swamp and the pine from the ridges and left the people with only mud and mortgages. Red Top, Wilco, Nortac, Pytonah, Orvisburg, Hillsdale, and Richburg, all were thriving mill centers a few years ago. Now they are stark and bare, their buildings still intact, their plants cold and forlorn, their streets a wallow for hogs. But Jimmie, remembering in his old age the days of his youth when he picked up hundreds of cars of lumber along the route, always blew a salute to the towns' memories as he made the ghost run through the "voodoo lan."[76]

Mississippians mourned the passing of these towns, the forests, and a way of life. Native son William Faulkner utilized the theme of the lumber industry's impact on the forest and on people in his writings. In *Light in August* he wrote of a doomed sawmill town, "All the men in the village worked in the mill or for it. It was cutting pine. It had been there seven years and in seven years more it would destroy all the timber within its reach Then some of the machinery and most of the men who ran it and existed because of and for it would be loaded onto freight cars and moved away. But some of the machinery would be left, since new pieces could always be bought on the installment plan—gaunt, staring, motionless wheels rising from mounds of brick rubble and gutted boilers lifting their rusting and unsmoking stacks with an air stubborn, baffled and bemused upon a stumppocked scene of profound and peaceful desolation, unplowed, untilled, gutting slowly into red and choked ravines beneath the long quiet rains of autumn and the galloping fury of vernal equinoxes." In "The Bear" Faulkner described Ike McCaslin's reaction to the logging of the forest as he saw the "new planing mill already half completed which would cover two or three acres and what looked like miles and miles of stacked steel rails red with the light bright rust of newness and of piled crossties sharp with

creosote, and wire corrals and feeding-troughs for two hundred mules at least and the tents for the men who drove them." McCaslin rides a logging train into the forest's "wall of wilderness" for the last time: "From the cupola he watched the train's head complete the first and only curve in the entire line's length and vanish into the wilderness, dragging its length of train behind it so that it resembled a small dingy harmless snake vanishing into weeds, drawing him with it too until soon it ran once more at its maximum clattering speed between the twin walls of unaxed wilderness as of old. It had been harmless then. . . . But it was different now. . . . [I]t was as though the train . . . had brought with it into the doomed wilderness even before the actual axe the shadow and portent of the new mill not even finished yet and the rails and the ties which were not even laid."[77]

Other Mississippians, less celebrated than Faulkner, also remembered and mourned what once had been. Returning to her girlhood home, Annie Louise D'Olive found that "Ten Mile no longer has a roadside sign to designate its location on Highway 49. . . . The mill company, when shutting down, dismantled all buildings, but I found where our house stood. I climbed the hill and looked across the railroad to the overgrown mill site where lay a pile of rusty machinery, souvenir of the once bustling center of the town's economy. The town is gone, but the name persists."[78]

Some Mississippians, like this writer in 1940, were consumed by guilt, recriminations, and sadness:

We thought this supply of the most magnificent timber the world ever saw was inexhaustible, and we cut and slashed with a carelessly prodigal hand. Not only the lumbermen destroyed with axe, saw and fire, but the land owner and squatter deadened and destroyed literally thousands of acres of virgin timber to get lands for cultivation. It was a common sight to see plows running on lands where the entire growth of timber still remained, stretching its naked, dead limbs to the sky until eventually falling from decay; then, being carelessly bucked up and burned. Log

Rollings were an event all over Mississippi, when a farmer called in his neighbors to help him roll logs into piles for burning. And the lumberman was not solely to blame for the fires; then as now, many people burned over the woods every year seeking early pasturage, destroying all young growth and damaging standing timber to an almost incalculable extent. So much for the past. Today, driving through miles and miles of cut-over lands where once stood this beautiful forest; past old saw mill sites and ghost towns that once bloomed with life and action, now dead, almost obliterated, and forgotten, by all except a few old timbers, brings to me a feeling of inexpressible sadness, and the thoughts of what might have been.[79]

Towns were gone, and huge expanses of the Mississippi forests had been leveled. But it was not just that they had been cut over and abandoned, it was the way they had been cut over and the condition in which they were left as the lumbermen fled to repeat the process elsewhere. Most survivors believed that Mississippi's former forest lands were virtually worthless and useless, that the state's green legacy had been destroyed in an orgy of greed. And worst of all, while Mississippians were left with devastated lands, the beneficiaries were corporations owned by people in other parts of the nation and the world.

Yet a closer look revealed that, amazingly, some of those denuded lands showed signs of rebirth. Fortunately for Mississippi, some people possessed the knowledge, vision, and determination to restore forests to lands now covered with scruffy growth, ashes and charred timbers from fires, and ravines carved out on bare soil by Mississippi's torrential rains. A new age of scientific forestry was dawning in the South and in Mississippi, and none too soon.

Other changes on the horizon would drastically change the management of Mississippi's forests. Even as a few pioneering companies and foresters were beginning to realize the regenerative potential of the timberlands, a new industry with different timber needs, a different capital structure, and a different woodlands philosophy was beginning to invade Dixie. As pioneering forester Inman F. Eldredge saw it, "The biggest single thing that has stimulated the South has been the coming of the pulp and paper industry."[80] The evolution of the southern lumber industry into the forest-products industry, the rise of "scientific forestry," and the rebirth of Mississippi's forests were on the horizon.

6 "Scientific Forestry": Developments in the South and in Mississippi

In the early-twentieth-century southern lumber industry, timberland was acquired at relatively low prices, large mills were constructed, and the operations were based on getting a rapid cut to pay interest, dividends, and taxes and to depreciate the plant on the theory that everything—plant, railroad rolling stock, equipment, town, and so on—would be liquidated when the last tree was cut. The prevailing attitude was summed up in 1919 by the general sales agent of the powerful Kirby Lumber Company, which operated in Texas and Louisiana. "As a lumberman," said he, "my interest in forestry is nil. . . . When the lumberman of today saws the trees he owns and scraps his plant, his capital will enable him to become the banker, the ranchman, or the manufacturer of some other commodity."[1]

Most lumbermen were not convinced that forest management made sense economically. J. B. White, one of the most influential leaders of the southern pine industry, delivered an address to the American Forestry Association in 1912 at Biltmore, the cradle of American forestry. But after paying homage to Vanderbilt, Pinchot, Schenck, and others associated with the Biltmore efforts, White concluded, "Conservation of natural resources comes only when it is discovered where and how it will pay to conserve. Until then there is no inducement to save and develop, for the effort would result in loss." The lumberman's standard cry was that forestry was not practical,

while, as an editorialist in *American Forestry* magazine pointed out, "the claim is continually made by individual lumbermen and lumber journals that their business is conducted at a loss, that the only money made in it is by speculation in timberlands. If that is true lumbermen as a whole are a most unpractical class." The editorial pointed out that the days of logging and lumbering the virgin forests were nearing their end. "The lumbermen of the future will be foresters," it said, "The difficulty now is that lumbering is still in the hands of men of the old idea . . . seeking large and quick returns. . . . But the great and quick profits of the old days of lumbering accessible virgin forests are gone. . . . It is necessary for [lumbermen] to readjust their view and to recognize forests as a resource in the perpetuation and permanent productiveness of which the whole people have an interest that must dominate any private interest."[2]

Most lumbermen of the time did not have that sort of vision, and pioneering southern forester Inman F. Eldredge recalled that "by 1920 the lumber business, insofar as it was measured by big mills, was declining. Mill after mill was closed up, tore up their steel, junked their mills, blew the locomotive whistles for the last time, and moved out. Some men went to the Coast and some just simply liquidated and bought yachts and polo ponies." Many of the southerners left behind probably shared the feelings of those famous fictional Georgians Scarlett O'Hara and Will Benteen, who bemoaned the incursion of pine seedlings into their agricultural fields. Fortunately, in real life there were farsighted pioneers who recognized that the South's economic salvation might lie in the growth of those seedlings.[3]

Some lumber companies, timberland owners, and railroads that served the formerly timbered areas attempted to promote agricultural settlement on the cutover lands. But most of these efforts were tragically unsuccessful, as poor farmers struggled in vain to scratch out a living on land that was better suited for growing trees. Some lumbermen knew this fact and callously promoted the sale of lands that simply were not suited for agriculture. Others were honestly ignorant. C. B. Sweet, an official of the Long-Bell Lumber Company, which owned lands in Texas, Louisiana, and Mississippi and a mill at Quitman, brashly promoted his company's experimental farm in southwestern Louisiana as "one of the best of friends, not only to owners of cut-over timberland and the communities to which they are adjacent, but to thousands of people who are destined to found happy and prosperous homes on land until recently looked upon as unproductive, and valueless."[4]

In 1920 the company announced, "Extensive tracts of the Long-Bell cut-over lands are now open to purchase by farmers and stockmen on easy terms, and at prices that are ridiculously low as compared to present-day land prices in the older and more densely populated agricultural communities of the North and Middle West." Long-Bell claimed, "With the natural advantages of climate, unfailing water supply, abundant rainfall, good soil and the proximity of markets and transportation facilities already established, this region is destined quickly to develop into one of the great agricultural and stock producing sections of the country." Long-Bell eventually sold a sizable amount of land through a subsidiary but was plagued with a very high percentage or repossessions and left a legacy of tax delinquencies and defaults in Louisiana. In south Mississippi the H. Weston Lumber Company also considered alternative uses of its lands, including experimental farming operations that were abandoned as unprofitable after several years. The company also experimented unsuccessfully with cattle, including Brahmas imported from India in the late 1910s or early 1920s.[5]

In 1917 the Southern Pine Association sponsored a cutover land conference in New Orleans that promoted the conversion of the denuded timberlands to farms, although it gave lip service to forestry. The Southern Pine Association and many landowners, railroads, and others also cooperated with the Southern Settlement and Development Organization, which was organized in 1912. This group expected most of its funding to come from lumber interests and railroads and tried to promote immigration and agricultural settlement in the South. Affiliated landowner and community development associations were organized at the state and local levels, and the Southern Pine Association announced that the Mississippi organization would be a prototype for similar groups in other southern pine states.

The cutover land conference had a positive impact on forest regeneration. Partially as a result of the conference, the Great Southern Lumber Company of Bogalusa, Louisiana, hired three patrolmen and a professional forester, J. K. Johnson. The company decided to reforest 175,000 acres and established its own nursery to grow pine seedlings. In 1922, a year after its establishment, the Southern Forest Experiment Station put a substation in Bogalusa, and in 1924 the station's tree-planting research was located in Bogalusa to tie in with the Great Southern's planting program. This work resulted in the publication of Philip C. Wakeley's *Artificial Reforestation in the Southern Pine Region*, which became the primary manual for pine planting across the South. Wakeley's work was undoubtedly influenced by his observation of the early planting efforts of F. O. "Red" Bateman, the chief ranger of the Great Southern Lumber Company.

It soon became evident to anyone who was willing or able to see that agricultural settlement was not the solution to the cutover land problem.

As historian Vernon Jensen put it, "the encouragement of people . . . to settle on the cut-over lands heaped tragedy on tragedy." The proponents of agricultural settlement on cutover lands ignored what the lands themselves could have told them. Such advocates refused to learn from history, for similar attempts had been glaringly unsuccessful in the lake states. By the mid-1920s *American Forests and Forest Life* railed against the agricultural schemes in an editorial entitled "Good Forests or Bad Farms?" The quick fix of agricultural development had peaked, and southerners left with hundreds of thousands of acres of denuded land were forced to look elsewhere for solutions.[6]

By the late 1920s a few companies struggled to introduce more responsible woods practices and to maintain businesses in Mississippi, but most of the big operations, especially those owned by out-of-state and international investors and companies, were gone. They simply squeezed everything they could get out of the state's forests, tried to sell the lands to farmers or defaulted on their tax payments, and then moved to the West to repeat the process.

Tax laws that penalized those who tried to cut the forests selectively and allow them to naturally reseed also bore partial blame for the state of Mississippi's land. And the tax laws were supported by a public and enacted by politicians whose purpose was to get everything possible out of the big companies before they left the state. The fact that there was little or no organized fire control in a region where natural fires and incendiarism were endemic was part of the problem. So too was the system of open range, which allowed hogs to roam the woods, where they were notorious for rooting up and destroying young seedlings. But above all, the situation was exacerbated by the remarkable lack of knowledge about the forest growth cycle, especially of southern pines.

Most lumbermen and citizens simply did not know how rapidly the forests could regenerate under proper conditions. And most did not even know what the proper conditions were. The "virgin" forests of the "cut out and get" out era consisted of many trees that were two hundred years old, and thus lumbermen were at least subconsciously misled into thinking that producing trees

Great Southern Lumber Company planting crew, 1925. Courtesy Louisiana State University Archives, Baton Rouge.

of merchantable size was an extremely long-term proposition. Forestry as a profession was in the early stages of infancy, and Mississippi did not even have a forestry school. It would not have a forestry degree-granting program until the 1954 establishment of Mississippi State College's School of Forestry. Mississippi did not have a state forestry commission until 1926, and it was grossly underfunded for years; the Mississippi Forestry Association was not formed until 1938.

The Magnolia State's pioneering forestry work was done largely by foresters who came in from other areas, and even the native-born were trained elsewhere. In the 1930s foresters employed by the U.S. Forest Service, by enlightened pioneering lumber companies, and by the newly emerging pulp and paper industry did the groundbreaking work that brought the state's forests back from the ashes and laid the foundations for the greening of Mississippi.

The forestry profession arrived relatively late on the American scene. The United States had no professionally trained foresters until the late nineteenth century. Even then, the only professional foresters in this country were either European immigrants or Americans who had been trained in Europe. While these early foresters did not espouse any single approach to forest management, they were heavily influenced by the examples and experiences of European, particularly German, forestry.[7]

Modern German forestry was born in the latter half of the eighteenth century as a new approach to forest management based on "forest mathematics" replaced the older concept of a forest as a wide expanse of trees, animals, and sanctuary. Now the forest was viewed as an area composed of timber or wood that could be measured. Foresters could calculate the volume of wood, the rate of growth, and the ideal rate of harvest. They were developing the philosophy of what would later be called sustained-yield forestry. Forest science and professional foresters became the foundations of modern forest management. One of the first vehicles for establishing the German forestry philosophy in the United

States was the establishment of the Biltmore Forest School in North Carolina on the property of George Vanderbilt in the area of today's Pisgah National Forest. Over fifteen years of existence, the Biltmore School graduated 350 trained foresters.[8]

Pioneering southern forester Inman F. "Cap" Eldredge, who attended the Biltmore Forest School, vividly remembered the German style communicated to his students by Biltmore founder Dr. Carl Alwyn Schenck. "We were all required to have horses. Schenck himself said it was based on the master schools that were prevalent in Germany, in which a master took a number of young men with him in his daily rounds where they could ride at his heels, watch him, hear him lecture, and pick up forestry in that manner. . . . He wore a uniform from one of the German forest services he'd been in before he came over here."[9]

Schenck was one of a number of pioneers who helped to create a concern about resource management and an interest in the profession of forestry at the national level. Among the other influential national figures were George Perkins Marsh, Gifford Pinchot, and Bernhard Fernow. They were not all trained as foresters, and they did not share a single philosophy of resource or forest management. Yet each in his own way contributed to the birth of forestry as a profession in the United States.

Probably most significant among the nonprofessionals was Marsh, a Vermont lawyer, editor, farmer, businessman, congressman, and diplomat who had interests ranging from Scandinavian languages to the lumber business. After years of observation and study both in his native New England and abroad, during which he had witnessed the devastation of forests and despoliation of the land under the impact of human "development," Marsh in 1864 published *Man and Nature; or, Physical Geography as Modified by Human Action.* In this famous work Marsh discussed the relationships between human society, water, soil, and vegetative cover. He pointed out the wide-ranging ramifications of indiscriminate clearing of the woods and stimulated a good deal of interest within the scientific community and among concerned and thoughtful laymen. Marsh's work helped to create the climate that gave birth to the concepts of scientific resource management. As Thomas R. Cox put it, Marsh's work "signaled a turning point in American attitudes toward forestlands [and] marked the beginning of an accelerating campaign for the husbanding of the nation's forests."[10]

Another major figure was Pinchot, who was both the white knight and the bête noire of American forestry at the turn of the century. One of the earliest professional foresters, Pinchot was educated at Yale, the French Forest School at Nancy (where he spent only six months), and in the Sihlwald in Zurich. After managing Phelps, Dodge, and Company's Pennsylvania lands, Pinchot was hired to supervise the huge area of mountainous lands in western North Carolina that constituted George Washington Vanderbilt's Biltmore estate. Pinchot moved to Washington in 1898 to head the Forestry Division of the Department of Agriculture. Along with President Theodore Roosevelt, Pinchot became a hero of the Progressive conservation movement and a significant figure in attempting to implement scientific and technical principles in resource management, part of what historian Samuel P. Hays termed the "gospel of efficiency." Because of his charisma, the Pennsylvanian helped to capture the public's interest and focus it on natural-resource issues. Pinchot recruited young, able, enthusiastic men to staff the Forest Service and certainly had a great deal of influence in shaping the public image of foresters or rangers. Unlike John Muir, who favored preservation of natural resources and lands by closing them off from development, Pinchot advocated multiple use; regarded conservation as "wise use"; and wanted to bring rational, efficient, scientific management to the nation's forests.[11]

However, Pinchot distrusted big business, and his attacks on the lumber industry alienated him not only from many lumbermen but also from his colleague, Schenck, who regarded Pinchot's views and rhetoric as unwise and counterproductive. Nonetheless, Pinchot played an important role in raising the consciousness of the country (and the forest-products industry) with regard to the profession of forestry, the importance of the nation's forest resources, and differing strategies of forest management. He is also considered a major figure in elevating the practice of forestry to the status of a profession by, among other things, serving as a driving force behind the founding of the Society of American Foresters, helping to endow the Yale School of Forestry, and providing employment for most of the nation's young foresters in the U.S. Forest Service.[12]

One of Pinchot's great adversaries was Schenck, who followed Pinchot as manager of the forests on Vanderbilt's Biltmore estate. Among the pioneers of the U.S. forestry profession, Schenck probably came closest to sharing the outlook and philosophy of the modern industrial forester. Schenck believed in the management of forests for use, and as former International Paper (IP) forester and woodlands administrator Fred Gragg put it, Schenck would have endorsed the use-oriented philosophy of today's industrial forester because "Colonel Schenck was a pretty smart German. . . . What he couldn't abide was waste."[13]

The man who is considered the first technical forester to reside and practice in this country permanently was Dr. Bernhard Eduard Fernow, a Prussian who was trained in the German forest service and came to the United States in 1876. Fernow became manager of the Cooper-Hewitt and Company timberlands in Pennsylvania. In 1882 Fernow was a founder and the early secretary of the American Forestry Congress. He served as chief of the Division of Forestry in the U.S. Department of Agriculture from 1886 to 1898, leaving to become professor of forestry at Cornell University. Fernow prepared the first federal-reserve law, which provided the foundation for the creation of the federal forest preserves. In 1891 Congress passed the Forest Reserve Act, which permitted the president to establish forest reserves from the public domain, and by 1897 some 40 million acres had been set aside as forest reserves. However, these reserves were not managed forests in the European tradition.[14] Nonetheless, the acquisition of public forestlands created a need for foresters and stimulated the growth of the forestry profession. Most early foresters were publicly employed.

While a few early foresters were employed in the South, the innate conservatism and prevailing "cut out and get out" philosophy of the lumber industry, plus the lack of silvicultural knowledge and regressive tax structure, slowed the acceptance of forest management. In 1907 one forester reported that opportunities for foresters with lumber companies in the southern pine region were "beginning to develop," but he warned that "as yet the duties required of a man holding such a position . . . are indefinite in character and but slightly understood." Eldredge remembered the "communications gap" between the lumbermen and early foresters:

None of the men who taught [forestry] at that time, or practiced, had any experience in utilization. . . . You produced the timber and cared for it, and then you turned it over to the roughnecks to cut it up and ship it around. There wasn't any science or art to it; it was just a process—running a sawmill or driving oxen and pulling logs. . . . [T]he people who did manufacture lumber knew nothing about forestry and didn't give a tinker's damn for the concept. The two lines of thought were as different as night and day. There wasn't any kinship; the people who were in lumbering thought forestry was next door to bird watching. . . . [T]hey had no use for forestry, no real use. It just didn't fit into the picture. Foresters did not grow virgin timber, and that's what they were cutting. It's quite understandable. It wasn't entirely ignorance. As a matter of fact, fifty years ago forestry had no part in the lumber industry. Only if you were looking forward to a crop fifty years hence could you see where forestry might come in.

A. E. Wackerman, division forester for the Southern Pine Association, noted in 1935 that in his own case, "it was with some misgivings, personally, that I undertook . . . to make personal calls on as many southern pine operators as we could contact, because of the old prejudice that existed between lumbermen and foresters in years gone by. It is not so long ago that all foresters were considered impractical theorists by lumbermen and that lumbermen were viewed by many foresters as inhuman woods butchers." However, as Wackerman pointed out, a number of figures were shaping the development of southern forestry even though many lumbermen paid little attention. These pioneers included Charles Mohr, Schenck, Charles Holmes Herty, Austin Cary, Eldredge, and Walter J. Damtoft.[15]

These people were not all professionally trained. Some of them moved back and forth between the public and private sectors and thus helped to bridge the gap between public and industrial foresters. They did not all advocate precisely the same methodology, but they were imbued with a sense of mission, a feeling that they were doing something positive and important. And at least, whatever their prescriptions, they were doing something to manage the forests—the key difference between good forestry and bad. Doing nothing except stripping the land bare and making no effort to regenerate was the dominant approach among the old lumber companies. The enlightened pioneers among the lumber companies, or the pulp and paper companies that came later, could be described as practicing good forestry, whatever their specific approach, because at least they were trying to do something.

Controversy and disagreement about philosophy, prescriptions, and methodology have been endemic among those in the forestry profession from its earliest years in this country. Eldredge remembers of Schenck that "in technical matters—what should be done—he differed from all of the other leading foresters. . . . [T]he good Doctor didn't think that they were right more than half of the time, and he was very outspoken about it. He used to say in class that this was one of the peculiarities of foresters—they always fight each other; they never believe in each other's carryings-on."[16]

There was no simple or single textbook definition of good forestry, and it was implicit in this fact that the important thing in these formative years was to try. In such attempts, the companies with forestry programs were discovering and accumulating the knowledge that would give greater definition to forest practice as the forest-products industry evolved. A major figure in the accumulation of that knowledge was Charles T. Mohr.

Mohr was a native of Esslington, Wurttemberg, who arrived in the United States in 1848. He drifted into the South and settled in Mobile in 1857 to pursue his botanical interests. Living in the heavily forested Gulf Coast, area he became enamored of the piney woods, and by 1880 he had become a well-known and respected botanist. In 1884 he published part of his huge report on southern pines under the title *The Timber Pines of the Southern United States*, and three years later he produced a far more complete survey that was published in the Department of Agriculture's revised *Bulletin 13*. Mohr's work became one of the basic sources in the literature pertaining to southern forestry. By 1890 Mohr was generally recognized as the best-informed authority in the nation concerning the South's timber resources.

One of Mohr's signal contributions was the preparation of the southern forest estimate that appeared as part of the tenth census report of 1880. By this time, according to Thomas D. Clark, Mohr had "perhaps . . . the soundest overview of regional forest resources of any southerner." Much of the census text applied to the South and was based on the Mohr report, which included a detailed description of Mississippi's forests at that time. Mohr's work was far more specific than earlier efforts in estimating the overall inventory of timber in the South, and it was particularly good with regard to the volume of southern pine.[17] Mohr helped to establish the informational base on which later forest policies would be constructed.

Charles Holmes Herty, like Mohr, was not a forester. Dr. Herty was a chemist, and as Eldredge remembers, Herty's "main contribution was to find that southern pine was a fine source of paper pulp . . . and his broadcasting as he did with the utmost energy the fact that good kraft paper could be made out of southern pine." Henry Clepper, former executive secretary of the Society of American Foresters, said that Herty's "demonstration and promotion of newsprint manufactured from the southern pines dramatized the economic possibilities of forestry for profit." Retired forester Clinton H. Coulter described Herty as "a high-class, almost inspirational, promoter" who "did a lot of good to get industry down to the South." Noting that Herty should not "be credited with all the work of converting southern pine to pulp because that was done by the Forest Products Laboratory at Madison[, Wisconsin,] and others," Coulter nonetheless argued that Herty "talked to people. . . . [H]e talked to anybody he could get an audience with on the growing power of southern pine and how much they could make for the South. . . . I knew him and thought a lot of him for his pioneer promotional work."[18]

Cary was a forester, and he came South in 1917 as a logging engineer for the U.S. Forest Service. Cary was struck by the backwardness of southern forest practices, and he hoped to promote sound forestry among the South's large and small landowners. He tirelessly toured southern lumber operations and convinced the lumbermen to experiment on small plots to prove the efficacy of improved forest practices. Eldredge remembered that Cary "did a tremendously fine job in getting interest started. He didn't convince anybody to the extent that the day after he left they went out and did something, but he was a persistent old New England Yankee and he'd come back talking all the time. They liked him and enjoyed him. . . . He generated a lot of interest that grew little by little and men commenced to do something . . . but the thing that made it all blossom was that the price of land and timber went up under the impact of the pulp development. Then it became economically possible and profitable to hold land for successive crops of timber."[19]

Elwood L. Demmon recalled that Cary "could do better than almost anybody in interesting lumbermen in forestry. He really had a knack for taking businessmen out into the woods and showing them how trees grew and instilling in them the fundamentals of forestry. He always carried an axe with him and did not hesitate to cut down a tree just to illustrate its growth rate by counting the annual rings. Observations such as this made a deep impression on many of these old-time lumbermen, and they had great respect for old Dr. Cary." Demmon concluded,

I would say that of all the foresters who have worked in the South, he probably had more influence with the lumbermen, selling them forestry, than any other technical forester. Dr. Cary was a technical forester, and he was also a very practical man and knew how to speak the language of the lumberman. . . . Dr. Cary did a lot of good in getting forestry started in the South. . . . He would barge right in to a lumberman's office. He wouldn't spend time with any of the underlings; he'd just go to the general manager or company president and tell him that he ought to be interested in the future of his timberlands. He would take these men right out into the woods and cut down a tree or two and show them how rapidly these trees were growing and that forestry was not such a long-time proposition as they might have thought. Many a hard-headed lumberman became interested in forestry by just such tactics. . . . Dr. Cary would get them right out in the woods and show them on the ground. He spoke their language.[20]

Frank Heyward, former general manager of the Southern Pulpwood Conservation Association, summed up Cary's contribution: "Austin Cary dedicated the last 19 years of his life to awakening southern wood-using industries to the possibilities of timber growing. He was successful to a remarkable degree, and his accomplishments in the fields of fire protection and forest management comprise the greatest contribution by any single person to southern forestry."[21]

In some ways Schenck was the most impor-tant of the pioneers who shaped the background of industrial forestry, not only because of his charisma and the number of students he trained at Biltmore but also because of the philosophy of forest management he espoused. While a lot of professional foresters—Pinchot, for example—favored a multiple-use concept rather than simply locking up resources in the name of preservation, many of them had at best an ambivalent attitude toward the businessmen and companies who owned large tracts of timberland. These foresters were not at all sure that the private sector could be trusted to manage its lands responsibly.

Schenck had a totally different attitude. "His concept of forestry included not only the cultivation, raising and protection of timber, of trees, but their utilization, their processing as well. He thought . . . that sawmilling and the manufacturing of lumber are just as much a part of forestry as the growing and producing of the trees. That was the main way he differed . . . from all of the other foresters of his time in this country." One of the expressions he used frequently was, "The best forestry is the forestry that pays most." "In other words, not silviculture for silviculture's sake, not forest management just because it's a process, but forestry that pays most is the best forestry."[22]

One of Schenck's Biltmore students, Eldredge, became a legend in his own right. Following graduation from the Biltmore Forest School, Eldredge worked for the Forest Service. He left in 1926 to join the Superior Pine Products Company in Georgia, managing its forests for six years before returning to public service to direct the Forest Survey of the South. As Heyward describes it, "The forest survey was more than a gigantic timber cruise. Equally as important as total volume of wood by individual species was information on industrial use, mortality, and net growth. For the first time each state knew the ratio of growth to drain. The survey removed any guessing as to highly important conditions of supply, use, and mortality. Industry for the first time had factual data pertaining to the timber resource."[23]

Demmon remembered Eldredge as "the forerunner of technical foresters in the South . . . one of the foremost industrial foresters in the South. . . . [W]hen the Forest Survey got under way in the South in 1930 while I was director of the Southern Forest Experiment Station, we looked over the field very carefully for a man to head up the survey. There was no one who had a better background of southern experience than Cap Eldredge."

Demmon continued,

I think that Cap Eldredge personified the Forest Service to many people and was, through the friendships he established in industry, largely responsible for the excellent relations that grew up between the Forest Service and forest industry in the South. . . . Cap was one of the few southerners who had gone into forestry. Most of us who worked in the South came from other parts of the country. . . . [M]ost of the state foresters and other technical foresters in the South were educated in the North. . . . [F]orestry education got under way rather slowly in the South, and the southern schools did not graduate many foresters until along in the thirties, so it was an advantage to have someone whom southerners could consider as one of their own boys. Cap Eldredge spoke their own language, knew their customs and way of life, and he was also a technical forester with a national reputation. . . . What Cap said meant a lot more to southern people generally than what some of the rest of us would say. They listened to Cap with respect, and he appeared on the program at many of the forestry meetings down here. Whenever industry representatives became interested in the South, one of the first men they'd get in touch with was Cap Eldredge."[24]

Damtoft, a Yale graduate who was employed by the Champion Paper and Fibre Company in 1920, was the first industrial forester hired in the South. In 1959 Elwood R. Maunder of the Forest History Society conducted an interview with Reuben B. Robertson, who spent more than half a century in Champion's management, serving as both president and chairman of the board. Maunder asked Robertson about Champion's de-

velopment of an industrial forestry program following World War I and its employment of Damtoft. Robertson explained, "It was primarily the thought of safeguarding our capital expenditures here. We knew that when you spend several million dollars on a plant, you can't afford to write it off in a short period for lack of raw material." Damtoft established one of the South's first seedling nurseries and implemented programs in public education, landowner assistance, fire control, replanting, and selective cutting in the region and on Champion's 100,000 acres. Ironically, some of the land that Damtoft was protecting and regenerating was lost to the company, for 90,000 acres of Champion land were included in the new Great Smoky Mountains National Park in the early 1930s.[25]

These pioneers helped to stimulate concern about the state of America's forests. The formation and activities of a number of organizations also reflected this growing interest. In the 1870s the American Association for the Advancement of Science lobbied Congress and state legislatures for legislation to promote forest preservation and timber cultivation, and in 1875 lumbermen and scientists organized the American Forestry Association for the same purposes. A year later Dr. Franklin B. Hough was appointed as a special agent in the U.S. Department of Agriculture to study the nation's timber supply and usage and to consider possible measures for forest renewal and preservation. Hough and his successors during the next decade and a half were aware of the principles of forest science in Europe but did not know if they could be applied to resources in this country. In 1878 Hough produced the first volume of his comprehensive *Report upon Forestry*, which was the first major attempt to describe the condition and extent of the forests in the United States.[26]

The work of these forestry pioneers contributed to the passage of federal legislation that helped to create the public agencies that provided jobs and facilitated the development of the forestry profession. Congress passed the Weeks Act in 1911, providing matching funds for any state that set up an acceptable system of protection against wildfires. The legislation also authorized the acquisition of land for national forests in watersheds along navigable streams. The law marked the beginning of extensive cooperation among private industry, the states, and the federal government to protect forests from fire and other threats. The law triggered a spurt of state activity, and some states established or strengthened their forestry departments.[27]

Many southern states were slow to establish forestry agencies (Mississippi did not do so until 1928), and in response to a U.S. Senate request, the Forest Service compiled the 1920 Capper Report, which described continuing forest depletion and the need for fire control and forest management. The report contributed to the 1924 congressional approval of the Clarke-McNary Act, which ended years of debate among those favoring various approaches to forest and conservation policy. It authorized increased funding for cooperative federal-state fire protection programs. The law added to the programs of the Weeks law, including the acquisition of lands for national forests outside the watersheds of navigable streams. The law also provided assistance for tree planting on private land as well as increased funding for farmers to undertake forest management. It also authorized a comprehensive study of forest taxation. The Clarke-McNary Act emphasized cooperation among the federal, state, and private sectors rather than confiscation or coercion to improve conditions on private forestlands. The hope was that cooperative action would solve the problems of fire and taxation and enable private owners to profitably retain their forestlands as continuing producing units.[28]

Despite the spate of federal and state activity, the first efforts to manage a forest and practice forestry originated in the private sector in 1892, when Vanderbilt hired Pinchot to supervise the lands of the Biltmore estate. The Biltmore holdings eventually grew to about 125,000 acres, and Pinchot managed the forest in much the same way as a modern industrial forester would approach it. Schenck, Pinchot's successor, opened the Biltmore Forest School in 1898 to provide practical forestry training. The school represented one of the first steps toward the development of professional forestry education in the United States. Biltmore was joined by the New York State College of Forestry at Cornell University in 1898 (the first four-year undergraduate course in an academic setting) and the Yale University's graduate school of professional forestry two years later. Clepper argues that while in 1897 "there were a few technical foresters in the United States—Fernow, Pinchot, Schenck, and Graves—who had received technical training . . . there were none who could be described as professional foresters, because they lacked the kind of education in forestry that is available today."[29]

Virtually all of the early professional foresters were employed by public agencies, primarily the U.S. Forest Service, which evolved out of the old Division of Forestry in the Department of Agriculture. Private forestry developed slowly, and its origins are sometimes traced to the northeastern United States, where pulp and paper companies were becoming concerned about an adequate timber supply to serve their expensive plants. One of the pioneers was Finch, Pruyn and Company, which implemented forest management plans on its New York holdings in 1904.[30]

By the post-World War I era, when the number of industrial forestry positions was growing, eighteen colleges and universities offered forestry training. But fewer than 1 percent of the some two thousand graduate foresters trained from 1900 to 1920 were privately employed as foresters. In 1933 the Copeland Report estimated that 146 technically trained foresters were employed by seventy-nine U.S. companies. A year later a survey of Society of American Foresters members revealed that only about 11 percent were privately employed. By 1937 a similar survey showed that private owners, who by then controlled 75 percent of the country's forests, employed less than 10 percent of its professional foresters. However, the employment of industrial foresters rose markedly in the post-World War II period, and another Society of American Foresters study showed that the number of industrially employed foresters increased from 4,400 in 1951 to 6,050 in 1961.[31] Much of this growth occurred in the South.

The people hired in the 1930s and 1940s were among the pioneers in the development of southern forestry. As late as the 1930s the number of people trained and employed as professional foresters by private industry in the South was minuscule. Eldredge remembers that on graduation from the Biltmore Forest School in 1905, "there were very few openings in forestry. If you couldn't get into the Forest Service, you were stymied. The chances in industry were very few at that time." Richard Allen, a native Mississippian trained in forestry at the University of Georgia, said that when he went to work for the DeWeese Lumber Company of Philadelphia, Mississippi, "I was probably the first forester that they ever had in that part of Mississippi, and there just wasn't any forestry going on. Just about that period of time is when forestry got born."[32]

Allen also recalled that when Art Nelson went to work for Flintkote in Meridian, "I was still the only [forester] that was operatin' in that part of the world. . . . And I thought it was great that this land was sold to a company that had a forester. And Art moved in and married a girl and they had . . . their first or second honeymoon . . . in a tent out on that Flintkote land. Typical of Art Nelson. Save a little money, plus get that girl off to himself." Nelson went to work for Flintkote in 1940, handling the forestry and timber procurement for a new wood fiber insulation board mill. Nelson later recalled that he was immediately impressed by the "incredibly fast timber growth" and the fact that "if nature was given just half a chance—a little fire protection—saving some seed trees—the forest would start on its way back." IP forester Buff Reaves was the first professional forester in Leake County., Mississippi. "I think Mr. Buff was Mr. Forester of Leake County, really," said Allen, "because there weren't any technical foresters there until IP moved in."[33]

Another early professional forester—and a native Mississippian—was J. R. Weston, who earned a forestry degree from the University of Washington in 1921 and became "as far as I know, the first native Mississippian to acquire a Forestry degree." Said Weston, "When I first graduated from forestry there was only one other Forestry graduate in Mississippi." Weston returned to Mississippi to work for the family-owned H. Weston Lumber Company. Also among the pioneering Mississippi foresters was James W. Craig, a native of Panola County, who earned a bachelor's of science degree in forestry from Purdue University in 1936 and a master's degree from the New York State College of Forestry at Syracuse in 1938. Craig served as chief of fire control for the Mississippi Forestry Commission after World War II, became a consulting forester, and established a major forestry supply house in 1948. He also claimed to be, along with two other men, one of the first consulting foresters in the state. In 1952 Craig became the Mississippi state forester, serving until 1955, when he returned to his consulting business and forestry supply operation.[34]

One of the legendary early Mississippi foresters was not formally trained. P. N. "Posey" Howell was a native of Alabama and lived in Howison, Mississippi. For many years he was an employee of the L. N. Dantzler Lumber Company. By the early 1930s Howell had been employed by the Dantzlers for more than forty years and was serving as their land manager. Using wild stock, Howell planted one of the earliest pine plantations in Mississippi, and he was also famous for convincing company officials to leave seed trees. He called these trees "Mother Trees" and marked them with two-by-three-inch tags that read "This is a Mother Tree. DO NOT CUT" or a similar message. Ray Conarro of the Forest Service later remembered, "Usually these trees were spike top or so crooked that very little lumber could be cut from them."[35]

The stories about Howell are the stuff of legend. In the early years he traveled five counties on horseback selling the gospel of forestry and fire prevention. He followed a razorback hog for eight hours to learn that it uprooted more than five hundred longleaf saplings and prepared a placard showing that the hog destroyed more seedlings in a day than a man could plant in a week. J. E. Bryan, who began working for Dantzler in 1945, was assigned to work with Howell because "he had all this information in his head. And he was one of the worst drivers in south Mississippi. He drove on the wrong side of the road and everything else, and Mr. Dantzler was convinced that Mr. Howell was going to run into a tree or somebody one of these days and all this knowledge would be gone. So he wanted me to devise some method of getting this information from Mr. Howell and putting it down on paper." Howell also toured the South with a U.S. Senate reforestation committee and argued that the best solution to the cutover land problem was reforestation, not conversion to agricultural use. He served on the first Mississippi Forestry Commission.[36]

These men and others like them shared a sense of mission about their work. They believed deeply in the need to manage the nation's forests, public and private, responsibly to perpetuate the country's timber supply. Arthur W. Nelson Jr. remembered that as he was finishing forestry school at the University of Idaho in the 1930s, "I was . . . told by a number of people that if you really wanted to accomplish something in your lifetime in forestry, the place to head for was the South. At that time Yale Forestry School had an outstanding southern program in which they operated on the lands of the Crossett Lumber Company . . . and the Urania Lumber Company. . . . My interest in coming South prompted me then to apply to Yale." As Demmon put it, "Most of us went into forestry because we liked the work and we liked to be doing something that would benefit the country."[37]

All of these professionals did not share a single approach to implementing responsible policies on the timberlands they managed. In fact, R. D. Forbes, director of the U.S. Forest Service Experiment Station at New Orleans, emphasized this fact in a speech before the Southern Pine Association annual meeting in 1921: "One point cannot be overemphasized at the outset. If you insist that we put down in black and white requirements which will apply to all operations of the Southern Pine belt . . . you must expect that the best land for timber growing will be penalized on account of the poorest land. Forestry is not, and never will be, something which can be intelligently applied from a swivel chair in an office. The only place to practice forestry is in the woods. Conditions on one type of soil may be most unfavorable to reforestation, while conditions on another soil may be extremely favorable. If you ask us to name measures which will secure the natural reforestation of the entire pine region, which includes bad conditions as well as good, you must not complain if those measures are more than is really necessary to secure natural reforestation under the best conditions." Forbes went on to summarize the requirements for keeping southern pinelands "reasonably productive" as follows: "1. That four seed trees of longleaf pine, or two seed trees of any other kind of pine, be left standing and uninjured on each acre of land cut over. . . . 2. That all tops and slash left in logging be removed to a distance of 20 feet from the seed trees, unless twice the prescribed number of seed trees is left per acre, in which case the slash may be left untouched; the slash to be burned the first winter, or carefully protected by patrol and fire lines for five years. 3. That the cutover lands, when once reseeded, be rigidly protected from fires at all seasons of the year for 3 years in the case of longleaf pine, and for 10 years in the case of other pines, after which less careful protection will be sufficient. 4. That wherever razor back hogs are sufficiently numerous to keep longleaf pine seedlings from reforesting the land the hogs be excluded, unless the land will reforest to other kinds of pine." Part of Forbes's prescription had long been accepted. As early as 1880 in his "Report on the Forests of North America" for the tenth census, Professor Charles S. Sargent of Harvard College had noted that "fire and browsing animals inflict greater permanent injury upon the forests of the country than the ax, recklessly and wastefully as it is generally used against them."[38]

The activities of the Yale Forestry School and of a few pioneering lumber companies inspired foresters and other lumbermen across the South to believe that there might be a profitable future in regeneration and selective cutting of their timberlands. The later arrival of pulp and paper companies on the scene made the potential even more attractive. These people were conservationists by some definitions, but they were definitely not preservationists or environmentalists in the modern sense. They sought simply to work toward a continuing supply of timber as an economic resource, not for recreational use or for scenic or biological preservation. Their efforts eventually contributed to acceptance of the multiple-use concept, but other uses were always subordinate to sustaining the forests as suppliers of timber. Companies that practiced conservation did so because they believed it would pay.[39]

Several southern lumbermen and firms stand out as pioneers in the realization that their timberlands might be held and regenerated profitably. First was Henry Hardtner of the Urania Lumber Company in north-central Louisiana. Hardtner's was not a big operation by the standards of the industry giants, but his hands-on approach, close to the lands and the mill, produced significant long-term dividends for the South. Hardtner reacted strongly against the efforts of many lumber companies to unload their land for agricultural usage once it had been cut over. Hardtner derided the Southern Pine Association's 1917 cutover land conference as "a big scheme to try to sell land that was not worth while for agriculture at all," and he later charged that the entire plan was "just a skin game to fool people in the north and west, to think that they could make a whole lot of money out of poor lands." Hardtner was absolutely correct in his negative assessment of the suitability of cutover lands for agricultural use. A 1920 description of farming on cutover lands is typical: "Anyone who has ever seen the cut over pine land, where the people are

trying to farm ought to realize the sadness of this situation. I don't know which is the sadder, the devastation of pine lands, or the people who are trying to live on them. Year after year these people go on . . . and try to farm on this land. It is so poor that it will scarcely grow peanuts, but still they go on there."[40]

At the time Hardtner first became interested in the regeneration of his lands, virtually no scientific information was available regarding the reproductive abilities of southern pine, so as he later recalled, "At first I had to pioneer every step in my investigation of the reproduction of long-leaf pine. I thought it would take 60 to 100 years to grow a merchantable crop. No one could tell me what was possible, no yield tables . . . were then available. I had to work out the problem for myself." The fact was that the "virgin" forest that had been harvested by the lumbermen of the "cut out and get out" era was not a typical forest. Thomas C. Clark observed, "The fact that ring counts made on stumps in this area revealed excessively long life spans did not necessarily indicate that it took so much time to produce a marketable tree." Or, as Nelson later noted, the trees harvested by the cut-out-and-get-out lumbermen "consisted of 200–300 hundred-year-old survivors in a wild and uncared-for forest. This gave rise to the idea that no one could wait that long for another crop of trees to mature."[41]

Hardtner implemented three policies to restore his lands. First, he tried to control fires and hogs; second, he enforced a diameter limit on the trees to be harvested; and third, he insisted that seed trees be left on each acre logged. Hardtner was regarded as a foolish visionary by many of his more "practical" contemporaries. He later recalled ironically that "you didn't hear any of them talking about putting timber back on the land did you?" Nonetheless Hardtner had faith in what he was doing, with the best evidence provided by the fact that he was purchasing additional cutover lands as early as 1904 and 1905. Hardtner's program was not based on romanticism; he believed that there was a sound economic basis for his reforestation efforts. He also was instrumental in the establishment of the Louisiana Forestry Commission, and his timberlands became the sites for annual summer camps and experimentation by the Yale University School of Forestry. Hardtner did a great deal to provide the informational foundations on which others would later build.[42]

One of the first products of Hardtner's influence occurred in May 1920. He invited officials of the Great Southern Lumber Company of Bogalusa, Louisiana, to visit Urania to get a firsthand look at what he was doing. Colonel W. L. Sullivan, general manager of the Great Southern, had already traveled to Norway and been influenced by the forest management he saw there. He was obviously impressed by what he observed in Urania as well, for on the trip back to Bogalusa he announced to members of the New Orleans press that his company was planning to implement a comprehensive reforestation and conservation program. Whether it was the Norwegian experience or the trip to Urania or both that made the difference is a matter for speculation. In any case, Cary was brought in for consultation. The incident represented a good conversion effort for Hardtner, who in the words of Wakeley, a Southern Forest Experiment Station and Great Southern Lumber Company forester, "had an old rattletrap mill and . . . [a] town, [that] was nothing to look at."[43]

Back in Bogalusa, F. O. "Red" Bateman, chief ranger for Great Southern, designed a dibble and planted some twenty thousand acres of longleaf seedlings. Working with primitive tools and both planting and direct seeding, Great Southern also began implementing hog and fire protection. Great Southern produced what may have been the first commercial hand-planted forest in the South. At first the company went out and dug up wild plants for its plantations, but it then established a nursery to provide seedlings. The company's seedlings suffered from fires, and many of the planted trees died, but the effort continued, and as Cary remarked, if the Great Southern plantations survived, "forestry was fool proof in the South." Great Southern also owned several hundred thousand acres of timberland in Mississippi.[44]

Another pioneering firm in the implementation of a sustained-yield program was the Crossett Lumber Company in Arkansas. The Crossett story is legendary within the southern forest-products industry. As former Mississippi state forester Allen remembered,

Crossett was one of the largest mills in the country. And they were fixin' to shut that big plant down. And so the board members came down to Crossett, Arkansas, to see the last logs bein' sawed and to decide what to do. . . . [T]his director they said, walked up on the green chain where the logs were bein' pulled up to the saws, and he saw a log comin' up there about 14 inches in diameter. The rings were pretty far apart. And right ahead of it had been a log that was just real dense. . . . And he stopped it, and he said, "I wanta' know where this log came from and where this came from." And he counted the rings and this one here was 28 years old . . . this one over here was 60 sumpin years old. And he said, "What's goin on here?" . . . They . . . found some more logs like that on the yard and they said that logger that's bringin' these in, came from, and they gave the location. . . . [T]hey went out there and they had had a cyclone through that site some 25 years before then. And there was plenty of seed sources, it had blown these trees down and opened up the forest and it reseeded into this young growth, and so this 25 year old cruiser said, "All we've gotta do is reseed it. You don't just go in and cut it, and burn it, and get out and let it go back for taxes. And that's when Crossett became what it is today.[45]

In Mississippi the H. Weston Lumber Company struggled to survive and preserve its timberlands. The Westons were a lumbering family, with J. R. Weston noting, "my father and all of my uncles, except one, on both sides of the family followed the lumbering business until the end of their days. It was equally true of my grandfathers and on the Weston side of the family, on back to Joseph Weston who was the first settler and who had the first sawmill in Skowhegan, Maine in

1770." The Westons had a deep commitment to lumbering and to Mississippi, unlike some of the speculators and operators who came in briefly to seize the opportunity of the moment. Weston also admired Hardtner's forestry efforts at Urania.[46]

The H. Weston Lumber Company implemented railroad logging with the use of steam skidders in 1901, but "after a few years discard[ed] all except one on account of the damage they did to non-commercial trees. . . . From about 1905 onward our company never used skidders except in branches or swamps when animals such as oxen or mules could not go. This resulted in the leaving of many vigorous trees 12 and 14 inches or under." The Westons adopted other practices that became canons of responsible industrial forestry in the South. For example, Weston remembered that his uncle, Horatio S. Weston), who was president of the company, "impressed upon me the need of good public relations. . . . [I] still appears to me that one of the major keystones to Forestry and good forest practice today is good Public Relations." J. R. Weston also remembered a Sunday in 1920 when, dressed in his churchgoing clothes, he helped some farmers extinguish a fire on company land: he thought it was "the first instance of a timber owner or for that matter any one suppressing a fire in Mississippi with the motive of protecting growing timber."[47]

The company's efforts were reinforced by the results of a field survey or cruise of some 81,360 acres of its lands undertaken in 1923 by the New York City forest engineering firm of Vitale and Rotherty. The survey sought to "ascertain in as far as possible the status of the land in regard to the raising of a future crop of pine timber and to estimate the cordage of pulpwood that might be taken out of the hardwood swamps on the holdings." The survey determined that about three-quarters of the land was pineland and that a "very small percentage of this land, only about one percent of the whole area examined, will need artificial aid in reproducing itself if the necessary protection from fire and hogs is afforded in

the area." Vitale and Rotherty basically recommended the implementation of a program of sustained-yield management, leaving seed trees and providing fire and hog protection.[48]

The H. Weston Lumber Company's efforts to regenerate its lands by leaving seed trees were threatened by the fact that Mississippi had open-range laws until 1926. Farmers frequently burned the land to improve the pasturage for their cattle, and the "company went so far as to hire men on horseback to ride over the company's lands during fire seasons to prevent arson. Dad often recalled the incident of one of the range riders being shot in the leg while trying to perform his duties." When J. R. Weston returned to Mississippi from college in 1921, his uncle "[i]mmediately began to assist me in carrying out what I had learned. . . . We formed a fire fighting crew. We purchased the largest plows available and used mules from our farm and from the logging teams to plow fire lines about 100 feet each side of our logging railroad. Since we had about 60 miles of rail this was quite a job. We also started marking seed trees. We got a number of signs made. They were painted white [with] messages upon them such as 'Do unto others as you would want them to do unto you, Don't burn the woods,' 'You would not burn a man's house, Why burn his trees?' etc. . . . To the best of my knowledge the efforts mentioned above, fire lines, signs, seed tree selection, were the first efforts made by an individual or corporation to practice Forestry in Mississippi." At about the same time that Weston returned to Mississippi, *American Forestry* magazine reported that the "Tatum Lumber Company of Jackson and the Batson-McGhee Company of Millard, both in Mississippi, have been cutting conservatively for several years and attempting fire protection on their lands." The H. Weston Lumber Company's commitment to reforestation was strong. In 1933 the board of directors, all members of the Weston family, authorized president Harold B. Weston to mortgage "any and all property of this Company to the United States Government" to borrow $200,000 from the

A. DeWeese Lumber Company mill at Philadelphia, Mississippi. Courtesy author.

government to continue "reforesting the lands of this Company."[49]

Another lumber firm that struggled to survive the shrinking of the forests and the Great Depression was the DeWeese Lumber Company of Philadelphia. The company's founder, Ab De-Weese, started a small mill in 1894 as a young man. When the railroad was built through Philadelphia, he located a small rough mill on the line and added a planing mill. In 1910 he built a complete saw and planing mill about a mile south of Philadelphia. DeWeese's son, Tom, who succeeded him as the company president, remembered, "There were large companies that came down here from the north. Nearly all of them cut out in the 20's, and a few left over went out in the 30's, early 30's. And they even moved. . . . They went back north where they came from, or some of them went out west and started a lumber business, but my father's business stayed here all the way through and survived the depression . . . by the hardest. It was very tough, but the bigger companies, they didn't go broke necessarily. They cut out the timber holdings. . . . And after the early 30's there were hardly any of them left."[50]

The DeWeese company and its workers struggled to survive the depression. Tom DeWeese remembered that the company paid workers seventy-five cents for ten hours work in the early 1930s, and "the irony of it was he couldn't afford to do that. He was doing that so they could buy groceries out of the commissary and live on it, hand to mouth. And of course, some of them didn't live on it, and every year they'd have to charge off their debts. To make it worse, they didn't work full time. He just had half a crew." It was amazing that the DeWeese firm survived, for according to Tom DeWeese, "I can remember distinctly in 1929 when my daddy cut out, and he talked about it. He mentioned it ever once in awhile that the timber was all gone." In fact, said DeWeese, "My daddy, essentially, went broke during the depression, but he managed to struggle through. Of course, he had a good name and a good reputation. . . . My daddy was just losing money hand over fist, but he kept operating giving his employees something to do, and most of them shut down for 2, 3, 4, or 5 years. Then they started back up, some of them."[51]

The Crosby Lumber Company was also an

early practitioner of forestry. In 1940 Crosby owned more than 100,000 acres of land in south Mississippi, and its mill at Crosby was cutting nearly 60 million board feet of lumber annually. The company purchased about half of its logs, some forty-five cars daily. On the lands of its timber suppliers, Crosby attempted "to educate the owner to the value of the further growth from the residual stand." The company "cut to a diameter limit of as high as 16 inches, urges the owner to protect the cutover land from fire, and to think of the woods as a crop." Still, the company noted that despite Crosby's efforts, "one or more sawmills in the vicinity make a living acting as scavengers on the cutover lands left by the Crosby Company." On its own lands Crosby utilized selective cutting, and by the early 1940s all company land was under the program, leaving the mill "enough logs to keep it going for five or six years more." The plan was to "keep protecting the cutover lands in the hope that after a low period of ten or fifteen years, sawlog cutting can be resumed." The company employed "two or three foresters, one of whom is a L.S.U. man and the other who maintains one of the towers is an ex-CCC enrollee." To make sure that the logging crews carried out selective cutting, Crosby's marking crews slapped two dashes of paint on the trees chosen to be cut, one five feet above the ground and another at ground level. As the "LSU man" recalled, "The purpose of the double mark [was] (1) to make it (the high mark) readily visible to the tree cutters and (2) provide evidence (the low mark) that only painted trees had been cut." During the depression Crosby also began to experiment with growing tung trees and producing tung oil, which became a sizable industry in south Mississippi.[52]

These firms led by example, and it is significant that while there were common themes in their approach to managing the forest, there were also variations. All of the companies were concerned about the prevention of wildfire, uncontrolled burning of the woods. All adopted the technique of cutting to a diameter limit. Both Hardtner at Urania and Sullivan at Bogalusa were cognizant of the damage that grazing could bring to their forests and tried to keep hogs out of their timberlands. However, they used different methods of regeneration. Hardtner left seed trees and depended largely on natural reseeding. The original situation at Crossett and with the Westons was much the same. At Bogalusa the Great Southern undertook the South's first large-scale planting effort. All of these firms provided early examples of enlightened forest practices, but each operated in its own way in a manner that was best suited to its economic situation, site characteristics, and company objectives.

There was another wasteful aspect of the lumber industry's operations that reached beyond harmful logging practices. During Mississippi's bonanza era the mills disposed of huge quantities of slabs, edgings, and other "waste" wood in "wigwam" burners. Even after the pulp and paper mills began to come in, this material was wasted, for it contained too much bark for their needs. William H. Mason, an expert on wood derivatives and former associate of Thomas A. Edison, observed lumber-mill operations in Laurel, Mississippi, and was appalled by the waste at a time when the South's timber supply was disappearing.

Mason was married to a woman whose family had investments in the mills of Laurel, and on April 22, 1924, he wired her uncle, Walter Alexander, in Wausau, Wisconsin: "HAVE NEW METHOD FOR DISPOSING OF SAW MILL WASTE FROM ANY WOOD AT A PROFIT WANT TO MEET YOU AND EVEREST AND POSSIBLY OTHERS TO GET YOUR ADVICE ON THIS PROPOSITION WIRE WHEN IT WILL BE CONVENIENT FOR YOU TO SEE ME IN WAUSAU." Mason actually wanted money, and he got it from the Wausau Group, Wisconsin lumbermen and speculative investors who, following a demonstration (which may have been rigged) in Laurel, where they had lumber investments, underwrote a small insulation board facility and Mason's research, which would be conducted at one of its paper-mill laboratories.

Mason had been experimenting with exploding wood chips into a soft, fluffy material. His method was to heat a closed vessel loaded with chips, and when the temperature and pressure reached a certain point, he opened an orifice, which caused the chips to explode into fiber. But what could be done with it? The money from the Wausau group and luck led to a breakthrough development. Mason was experimenting with using a letter press to compress the material from exploded chips into an insulation board. One day Mason went to lunch, forgetting to release the press, and when he returned he found that the material in the press had been converted into a tough, thin sheet because the heat and pressure had been applied for an unusual length of time. Mason pounded, soaked, and cut his "invention" and found that it was tough and durable. But again, did it have any real value?

The Wausau group secured patents and expanded the original project to include both insulation board and hardboard manufacture, and Mason became general manager of the world's first hardboard plant, producing Masonite. Most importantly, Mason got a product patent on hardboard, which meant that other hardboard producers would be prohibited from marketing their products if they had physical characteristics similar to Masonite. Later, in 1928, the Celotex Company, a pioneering insulation board producer, unsuccessfully attempted to break the patent. In addition to Mason and the members of the Wausau group, some outsiders became in-

Press and blowtorch used by William Mason while inventing Masonite. Courtesy Lauren Rogers Museum of Art, Laurel, Mississippi.

vestors, including the Eastman-Gardiner Lumber Company of Laurel and some of its officers, including Charles Green. The company changed its name to Masonite Corporation in 1928 and became a major employer in Laurel and an important force in the building materials industry.

However, the early days were not easy. Manufacturing and quality-control problems plagued the enterprise, and the second year the outside investors bailed out of the endeavor. During the Great Depression several of the original investors had to personally guarantee bank loans to keep the company operating. However, as Masonite prospered over the years the original shareholders were bountifully rewarded. For every free share of common stock issued to the original preferred stockholders in 1925, by 1975 there were, as a result of splits and value enhancement, 370 shares worth roughly $9,250.

One of the important developments of the depression era was the negotiation between Masonite and Celotex, which were both struggling, of a complicated agreement whereby Masonite produced hardboard, which Celotex sold under its own label as an agent. Other manufacturers, including Johns Manville, Armstrong Cork, National Gypsum, Flintkote, Insulite, Wood Conversion Company (a Weyerhaeuser subsidiary), Certain-teed, Dant and Russell, and Hawaiian Cane Company, were among the licensed agents selling privately labeled Masonite. These arrangements persisted, with some court-ordered modifications, until the early 1960s, when the original patents expired. By the 1970s some fifteen companies in the United States manufactured hardboard. Because of extreme competition and the oversupply of the original commodity boards, Masonite eventually shifted its focus to the production of processed products with various textures, patterns, colors, grains, and laminates. By 1975 the Laurel plant had been expanded and modernized to produce roughly 2 billion square feet annually on seven production lines and had become the largest hardboard producer in the world, with the complex employing 1,750 workers.

Masonite's use of sawmill waste to produce hardboard and other products was so striking that it was emulated by both lumber and pulp and paper companies. However, the company eventually was forced to begin using pulpwood as a raw material, and in 1937 consulting forester William L. Hall was employed to create an organization to purchase and reforest cutover lands so that Masonite could grow part of its own raw material. Events came full circle. By the late 1960s there was a shortage of sawmill waste to feed Masonite's plants, so the company began to acquire its own mills to assure supplies. Among these acquisitions was Mississippi's Hood Industries, which by 1970 had eight lumber operations and was the largest producer east of the Mississippi River. Masonite also attempted to promote its timber supply by distributing millions of seedlings to farmers. Masonite began to accumulate timberlands in 1935 and by 1975 owned some 381,000 acres in the Laurel area, many of which were planted with genetically improved stock.[53]

Mason's breakthrough was one in a series of technological innovations and discoveries than transformed the southern forest-products industries over time. The development of wood-preservation chemicals created a market for southern railroad cross ties, timbers, poles, pilings, and posts. Researchers at the Southern Forest Experiment Station in New Orleans discovered practical methods of controlling the fungus that produced blue-stain discoloration in southern pine lumber in the late 1930s. The Forest Products Laboratory at Madison, Wisconsin, conducted research on laminated beams and timbers that led to the manufacture of these products by southern pine mills.[54]

There was less sophisticated change as well, especially in the woods. The technology of logging changed significantly during the 1930s and 1940s. Prior to the 1940s, Tom DeWeese remembered, loggers used "crosscut saws, about 6 feet long that the two men leaned over in back breaking labor of the very worse kind you've ever heard of." Then, in the early 1940s loggers began to use power chainsaws. Also, in the 1930s, transporting the logs to the mill by railroad or tramways began to give way to trucks: "Just small T-model Ford trucks . . . it was a good many years before there was any real, sure enough, big trucks developed, and the roads improved enough to where the big trucks could be used," said DeWeese, "And that's been quite an evolution in itself, the whole idea of the trucking of logs. They must be hauling tonnage now probably five (5) times as heavy, more than that really, than they were hauling in those days with these big trucks and improved roads."[55]

An old-timer from Neshoba County who had worked in mills, owned mills, and dealt in timber remembered the crosscut saw as "old gappy, we called it. You know, a cross cut saw . . . anywhere from 6 to 10 foot long. . . . Sometimes take a half a day to cut one of them big trees." The triumph of the chainsaw was not instantaneous. In 1945 a Southern Pine Association survey of seventy-three mills in ten states found that twenty-four mills used power saws, fifteen had discontinued using them, and thirty-four had not tried them. Four Mississippi mills utilized the power saws, and five did not.[56]

Another change was the method of loading logs onto trucks to be transported to the mills. One lumberman who operated along the Mississippi-Alabama border remembered that in the 1950s his brother "was using mules to load his trucks" but that the mechanical "logger's dream" was coming into use and "everybody had to have" one. He noted, "About the 50's. . . . That was what they graduated to from mules and horses. Kind of graduated from them into that." The 1950s also brought changes for workers involved in girdling hardwoods as part of programs of "timber stand improvement." Until 1954, girdling was done by laboriously ringing trees with an ax, but then a tree-girdling machine called the Little Beaver was introduced. The machine had a small gasoline engine carried on a backpack frame by the worker. The engine transmitted power to a cutter head via a flexible shaft.[57]

By the mid-1930s only eleven sawmills in Mississippi had a capacity of eighty thousand board feet per ten-hour day. These mills were cutting mostly the 12 percent of old-growth timber remaining in the state. However, there were also another 1,680 sawmills, only twenty-one of which had a daily capacity of twenty thousand or more board feet, and they were operating primarily on second-growth timber of sawlog size and smaller. The Mississippi Forestry Commission and U.S. Forest Service believed that this timber should be allowed to grow larger. The small mills, often called peckerwood, groundhog, or pepper box mills, were making inferior lumber, paid low wages and almost nothing or nothing in taxes, and moved about frequently, attacking the mostly immature timber. The Forestry Commission and Forest Service deemed them among "the most important factors contributing to depletion of the timber resources of the State." However, this second-growth timber constituted more than 75 percent of Mississippi's supply and was the raw material base that would attract another industry to Mississippi's forests.[58]

Just as the concept of sustained yield was beginning to catch hold among a few lumber firms and as Mason was developing a use for sawmill waste, a competing market for timber was developing in Mississippi. This new inhabitant of the piney woods, the pulp and paper industry, invested a far greater amount of money in its productive facilities than did the lumber firms and from the outset planned to locate only in areas that could provide long-term, if not permanent, supplies of timber to feed the mills. It would have seemed a perfect complement to the lumber industry if not for one key difference—the pulp and paper mills used timber cut to a much smaller diameter limit, and thus the lumbermen of the early days viewed the pulpers as a threat, taking the young timber off the land of independent timberland owners before the forests could produce merchantable sawlogs.

The appearance of pulp and paper mills in the South was an important juncture on a long road that stretched back in time over centuries and in distance to Europe and the Far East. The origins of papermaking have become ritualized as part of the industry's folklore. The Chinese began to manufacture paper from cellulose fibers about two thousand years ago. The process was introduced into western Europe in the twelfth century by Muslims, and by the middle of the fifteenth century paper had replaced vellum as the continent's common writing material. The paper was made by hand, a sheet at a time, and rags provided the principal raw material. The first power-driven machine used in paper manufacture was a rag macerator introduced in Holland in the eighteenth century. However, the modern era of paper manufacture began some fifty years later when a machine to make paper in continuous sheets was perfected. The first effort to produce paper by machine was made in 1799 in France, but it was not until 1803 in England that the first workable machine went into operation. The introduction of this machine, named for the Fourdrinier brothers of England, who perfected it, made the mass production of paper possible.

The first Fourdrinier machine was installed in the United States in 1827. However, the industry still had a major problem, for while markets were growing, the raw material supply was limited. After a long period of experimentation with various raw materials, in 1840 German papermakers developed the groundwood process whereby wood was fiberized with mechanical grinders. In 1852 the English government issued a patent for the production of pulp by boiling wood in caustic alkali, the basis of the modern soda process. An American discovered the sulfite process in 1867, and the sulfate process was discovered accidentally in 1844 by a German who was seeking a cheaper substitute for sulfite. This process produced a new kind of long fiber pulp, and as a result of further refinement in the Scandinavian countries the sulfate process and the paper it produced came to be known as kraft, the Swedish and German word for strong.

Concurrent with the refinement of the technology and machinery to mass-produce paper came the explosion of the U.S. paper market.

Compulsory-education laws, a rising literacy rate, mass-circulation newspapers, and other factors brought forth new machines to meet these demands: the Linotype machine and rotary press, newspaper cutting and folding machines, machines to produce paper bags, a machine to fill handmade cartons, and other developments too numerous to mention.[59]

The South had no paper mills until the early twentieth century. The pulp and paper industry was confined to the northeastern part of the United States, but as that region was cut over and much of the land cleared for agriculture, papermakers turned south to find a larger source of raw material. The U.S. Forest Service's first forest survey in the South in the early 1930s reported that the "second forest" could produce large quantities of pulpwood. Papermakers were also attracted by the South's cheap labor, its abundance of power and water, and its proximity to markets. Interestingly, in the early period paper-mill operators did not consider growing trees specifically for pulp production, for as one of them observed, yellow pine "was too valuable to be worked directly into paper and it is only the waste of the logging and milling operations that the papermaker can hope to touch."[60]

One of the earliest efforts to manufacture paper from southern pine was an unsuccessful attempt by the firm of Smith and Thomas at Pensacola, Florida, in 1903. However, this failure eventually yielded positive results, for the first successful pine pulp paper mill in the South, the Yellow Pine Paper Mill, was constructed at Orange, Texas, in 1909, using machinery that had originally been part of the Pensacola operation. Utilizing yellow pine waste materials obtained from local lumber yards, the mill originally used the soda and then the sulfite processes. It was converted to the sulfate process in 1911, and after six years of experimentation it produced an excellent grade of kraft paper from pine. According to one historian of the pulp and paper industry, the Orange mill demonstrated two important facts: first, that it was not feasible to manufacture paper from pine using the soda process, and second, that sawmill waste could not provide an adequate and dependable wood supply. It would be necessary to harvest trees specifically to feed wood pulp mills.[61]

The first mill to successfully manufacture sulfate pulp from southern pine was the Roanoke Rapids Manufacturing Company of North Carolina, which was built in 1906 and switched to the sulfate process three years later. The company's resident engineer recorded the breakthrough in his diary: "Feb. 26, Friday: Cooked and blew both digesters. Everything held! A great success! From Southern pine, the first Kraft pulp blown in America."[62]

Another early operation was a mill built at Braithwaite, Louisiana, in 1898 by English interests to produce paper from bagasse, the cane residue from sugar making. The Braithwaite mill was converted to the kraft wood process in 1916 but was destroyed a decade later. A third early mill was constructed near Moss Point, Mississippi, by English interests in 1913. The mill site was selected in 1908 by the International Process Company (which had no connection with IP) because of the area's abundant water supply and the availability of wood waste from local sawmills. The Southern Paper Company was organized in 1911, construction on the mill began in 1912, and it was completed in 1913. The original capacity was twenty-five tons per day. A bleach plant was installed in 1934. The Moss Point mill became IP's property in 1928.

Finally, in 1916, an unsuccessful paperboard plant at Bogalusa, Louisiana, was converted into a sulfate paper mill. It was later owned by the Gaylord Container Division of the Crown Zellerbach Corporation. By 1930 there were fifteen major kraft mills in the South, and the region produced more than half of the nation's sulfate pulp. By the mid-1980s there were 108 kraft mills, and the South was producing about 70 percent of the nation's pulp.

The potential of the early southern paper mills was limited, because sulfate pine pulp was considered good only for wrapping paper. It was extremely difficult to bleach, and high rosin content

offered more difficulties. However, research by industry scientists and the Forest Products Laboratory solved that problem, and by the early 1930s IP's Panama City, Florida, mill accomplished the first successful production of bleached kraft paperboard on Fourdrinier machines. This development established the technological foundation for the industry's spread across the South.[63]

During the same period Herty and others were working on the problems associated with manufacturing newsprint from southern pine. Their efforts culminated in the construction of the Southland Mill at Lufkin, Texas, in 1939–40, ushering in the newsprint component of the southern pulp and paper industry. The Champion Paper and Fibre Company "pioneered in perfecting a chemical process for producing fine white paper from southern pine," thus creating another market for southern pine pulpwood. While the South was especially known for the production of containerboard and a variety of brown papers, research, such as that by Champion, enabled southern mills to produce a wider variety of bleached pulps used in printing papers.[64]

Another important industry development was the introduction of the Andersson barker and Soderhamn chipper from Scandinavia into the southern paper industry in the mid-1950s. Until that time, the use of slabs from lumber mills was uneconomical because of the high cost of debarking and chipping machinery. Both IP and the St. Regis Paper Company played important roles in introducing the equipment by working out arrangements with lumber firms to install and pay for the machinery. Both groups benefited. The pulp and paper mills got reasonably priced chips, and the lumber firms acquired another market. IP also pioneered in the development of mechanical wood yards where pulpwood producers or dealers could deliver pulpwood by truck to railroad sidings or barge landings and IP installed machinery that would unload the truck and load the barges or railroad cars. The first railroad facility was installed in 1951 at Bucatunna, Mississippi, to service IP's Mobile mill. Other companies,

Flintkote wood fiber insulation board plant at Meridian, Mississippi, 1941. Courtesy Art Nelson.

mills, and wood dealers emulated IP's system. By the 1960s more than 90 percent of IP's wood came through mechanized wood yards.[65]

Among the later paper-industry breakthroughs was research at the Forest Products Laboratory that led to the development of a semichemical process and a high-yield soda process that made the pulping of hardwoods more efficient. The hardwood pulp was used in the manufacture of such products as the corrugating medium of containerboard, printing papers, and rayon. By the mid-1980s hardwoods constituted some 31 percent of the round pulpwood harvested in the South.[66]

The Great Depression of the 1930s interrupted the growth of the pulp and paper industry. In fact, during the first half of the decade nearly 40 percent of the nation's paper mills went into bankruptcy. However, the kraft paper revolution helped to trigger a comeback, and southern production increased by more than 200 percent dur-

ing the period from 1936 to 1940. With the exception of the 1937–38 recession, the industry recovered and grew rapidly during the late 1930s. During a two-and-a-half-year period beginning in August 1936, twelve new sulfate mills were constructed in the South, and a number of other plants were enlarged. Altogether, from 1936 to 1940 fourteen new mills were built, and many older ones were expanded. During the decade more than $80 million was invested in the southern pulp and paper industry.[67]

By 1942 there were fifty pulp and paper mills in the South. Nonetheless, the pulp and paper industry's movement into the region was slow, partially because of the high initial cost of a new mill, ranging from $4 to $12 million, partially because of bankers' reluctance to finance southern mill operations, and partially because of the "birth control" provision of the industry's code of industrial self-regulation under the National Recovery Administration, which restricted the construction of new facilities.[68] The slowness may also have reflected the industry's lack of knowledge concerning the extent of southern timber resources.

Eldredge remembered that when he took over direction of the Forest Survey in the South for the U.S. Forest Service in 1932,

> I wasn't at all impressed with the pulpwood setup. . . . [T]here were a few mills in the South, but they were of no significance—just isolated operations. . . . So I went over to see a man named Allen in Georgia who had a pulp mill and was promoting another. After I had explained what we were doing, and what figures we could put out, and what degree of accuracy we could probably achieve, I said, "What do you want out of this?" He said "Above all we want to know the volume of this timber expressed in cords as well as thousand board feet. I know you probably know that there's an awful lot of wood for pulpwood here in the South. If that can be made known to the pulp industry, it's going to have an immediate reaction." Well, I did just that. . . . [W]e greatly expanded our treatment, got advice from several different pulp people on just how they wanted it—by species, by sizes, by location geographically, by stands per acre (whether it's practical to operate or not). So we got all that into it and that's what brought the pulp industry south within the next few years. . . . It was something that they could visualize and evaluate. A statement that so many billion feet of saw timber was there couldn't help much, but if you said that there were actually so many acres of timber with so many million cords of pine and of oak and of cypress, and that a certain percentage of it is below eight inches, and a certain percentage of it is eight inches to twelve inches, and a certain percentage is twelve to fourteen, then they've got the picture right off the bat.[69]

The pioneering firms already in the South contributed to the process. As Eldredge remembered, "Everybody was skeptical to start with, everybody. Nobody had ever thought that big. You can understand that . . . the sawmill man, no matter how big he is thinks only of the timber that's available to him within transporting distance of his plant. He doesn't give a rap what's . . . sixty miles away, so he's not a big thinker in that line. He thinks small. . . . But the pulp people are big thinkers. They have to be. When you put $30 to $40 million, or even $50 or $60 million in a plant that requires 2,000 cords of wood every day of the 365, you've got to think in great big terms." Among the pioneering companies who saw the potential Eldredge listed IP, Mead Corporation, Gaylord Container, National Container, Scott Paper, St. Regis, and several others he did not specify.[70]

The wood supply was critical. Former Champion Paper and Fibre Company president and chairman Reuben B. Robertson pointed out in a 1961 interview, "Most pulp and paper mills today—well, they all call for the expenditure of a lot of capital—thirty, forty, sixty million dollars—and very often it has to be financed. When you get with the Wall Street banker he wants to know what the chances of survival are for a company investing that much money. How permanent is the raw material supply? So in order to properly finance many of these new jobs, they have to spend money on forests and they have to see that those forests are operated on a management plan, a sustained yield basis."[71]

When the pulp and paper industry built its southern operations, a major part of the process was land acquisition to assure adequate pulpwood supplies. Timberlands were purchased from lumber companies, land companies, and other private owners, and substantial areas were leased to supplement supplies produced on company lands and acquired on the open market. The total timberland in forestry-industry ownership (including lands leased or under management contracts) increased from 33.4 million acres in 1952 to 42.3 million acres in 1985, about 23 percent of all southern timberland. About 4 million acres were under lease.[72]

Some feared that the pulp and paper industry would follow in the footsteps of the lumber industry, cutting over the lands and then moving on to other climes. F. A. Silcox, head of the U.S. Forest Service, warned that building "new pulp and paper plants upon the thousands of lumber and other forest industries already established there means that, without some form of intelligent forest management, certain southern forest areas may be left in an unproductive condition for generations." He also argued that pulp mills engaged in indiscriminate cutting and would not leave enough sawtimber for the lumber industry. In 1947 the governor of Mississippi summoned representatives of sixteen pulp and woodboard mills drawing wood from the state to meet with the Mississippi Forestry Commission and discuss efforts to get them to observe the requirements of Mississippi's Timber Cutting Practice Act. Among the companies represented were IP, Gaylord Container Corporation, Gulf States, Brown, Advance, Masonite, Flintkote, U.S. Gypsum, Johns Manville, and several others. The companies agreed to cooperate and pushed for the implementation of Southern Pulpwood Conservation Association cutting standards but also urged the commission to provide better fire protection, which the state officials were forced to admit was "very ineffectively handled."[73]

Demmon, the director of the Southern Forest Experiment Station, also questioned "the ability of the forests of the South to support these additional plants, and the desirability of producing pulpwood at the expense of other forest products." The Southern Forest Experiment Station's survey of southern forests from 1935 to 1940 found that in some areas of the South the wood-using industries were consuming timber faster than it was being replaced. Southern economic promoters howled loudly at Demmon's heresy. As an editorial entitled "He's Hollering Too Soon" in Mississippi's *Jackson News* put it, "Demmon, director of the southern forestry experiment station at New Orleans—a queer place for a forestry station—must be a very cautious sort of person. He is afflicting the press with a long winded article, in which he gives warning against a too rapid development of the paper and pulp industry in the South. Inasmuch as the South has only a few paper and pulp mills but an almost unlimited supply of slash and loblolly pine, Mr. Demmon is barking up the wrong tree, so to speak. . . . Mr. Demmon

is worrying quite too much about the possibilities of young timber in the South being quickly depleted by paper manufacturers. Mississippi is soon to have a $2,000,000 paper mill, and the project will be consummated in spite of any and all chronic objectors who call themselves conservationists."[74]

However, a map under the title "Region within Mississippi That the Development of the Pulp and Paper Industry Is Possible" prepared by the Mississippi State Planning Commission and crediting the "Southern Experiment Station" as its source, put only the southern half of the state within that category. Still, on a more rational level it was recognized at the time that the South could have both its forests and the new mills of the pulp and paper industry. The key was intelligent and responsible forest management. For example, the American Institute for Economic Research concluded in a 1938 report that even though the growth of the pulp and paper industry would increase the pressure on the southern forests, it would still be a positive development if the pulp mills used proper forest management and coordinated "their cutting of wood with requirements of existing industries."[75]

The Southern Forest Experiment Station published reports of its surveys of the southern forests between 1935 and 1940 and noted that in some areas of the South there was room for expansion of the paper industry. It pointed out that southern Mississippi was among those areas in which the paper industry could expand if reasonable forest management was practiced. Also, the industry would make the forests more efficient from a commodity standpoint. Trees that were not of potential sawtimber quality could be used by the pulpers, as could the tops of sawtimber trees, which were formerly wasted. Pulp and paper company officials carefully studied the Forest Service surveys and sent personnel into the South to evaluate and acquire mill sites and timberlands. Most pulp and paper industry leaders believed in acquiring or leasing as much forestland as they could afford, and few operated without company-controlled lands.[76]

While it was obvious that shortsighted or impractical pulp and paper operators could threaten the timber supply, the real problem rested largely with timberland owners who did not provide proper land management and with lumber operations that were anxious to quickly liquidate the timber on their lands and make a quick buck as they cut out and got out. In response to this situation and to Southern Forest Experiment Station reports of negative growth and drain statistics in some areas of the South between 1935 and 1940, leaders of the pulp and paper industry formed the Southern Pulpwood Conservation Association (SPCA) in 1939. The association sought to develop specific rules regarding pulpwood cutting and forest management and to undertake public education to promote forest conservation. It also established pilot forests to demonstrate good forestry practices and assisted individual landowners in obtaining technical assistance from conservation foresters on matters such as timber harvesting and reforestation.

Five years after the SPCA's establishment, its president recalled that at the beginning public foresters were skeptical of the industry's willingness to do anything other than make "fine gestures by the adoption of lofty statements of policy," but he said this skepticism simply increased the organizers' determination. However in 1943 the SPCA general manager conceded, "In spite of our educational efforts there is still much clear cutting for pulpwood." In 1948 longtime consulting forester E. A. Sterling, who worked a great deal for Johns Manville, observed of paper-company executives, "One of the fallacies is the quick and remarkable results they expect from the conservation programs under way. SPCA and the others spout publicity that looks grand, and they are making progress, but percentage-wise the surface is not scratched." Nonetheless, by 1953 the SPCA employed 126 conservation foresters, and their work was supported by the major firms in the pulp and paper industry, although some firms refused to join. In 1968 the SPCA merged with the southern office of the American Forest Institute and was re-named the Southern Forest Institute. In the 1980s it became part of the American Forest Council, which later became the American Forest and Paper Association.[77]

Most pulp and paper companies also hired one or more conservation foresters who worked with private landowners to promote better harvesting practices and forestry activities such as fire prevention, tree planting, and thinning. The foresters held cutting demonstrations and forestry field days across the South and presented slide and motion-picture shows to civic clubs. The companies distributed rules of forest practice and erected forestry billboards. The companies also supported the hiring of assistant county agents to promote good forestry. Fire prevention was a major theme of all of this activity, as were responsible cutting practices and leaving seed trees on harvested lands. Programs were implemented to monitor the implementation of responsible forestry practices on private land.

The industry also tried to implant its messages in young people's minds through various avenues. One of the most famous activities of IP's conservation foresters was the distribution of comic books featuring a young man named Jackie Davis who learned various lessons about forests and forest management. Readers could also sign up as "junior fire-fighting wardens." This effort was especially timely, for in 1939 the first president of the SPCA said that in his opinion "until the South demonstrates its ability to keep the fires out of the growing crops of timber . . . very few more pulp and paper mills will come South." Longtime consulting forester Zebulon W. White later noted that while the Civilian Conservation Corps did valuable work in the South, the SPCA "really was one of the first ones that insisted that the pulp companies with their large holdings practice acceptable forestry. The big planting programs, the big seed tree programs—all of that started really when they got together."[78]

Hostility between early lumbermen and pulpers was palpable. Former Weyerhaeuser vice president Dick Allen remembered taking forester

A. K. Dexter to a meeting of the Mississippi Lumbermen's Club because "he didn't want to go by himself. . . . He figured he needed plenty of protection because . . . he was a pulp representative, see, with International Paper Company." As Allen recalled, "The lumbermen . . . thought that the pulp people were gonna ruin this country. There would be no sawlogs left. They were goin' in and cut all the small timber, and there would be no sawtimber left, and they were up in arms." However, Allen tried to explain to the lumbermen that "actually the pulp business in the South could be the salvation of land ownership and growin' timber and buyin' sawlogs if it was used properly. And that was to get rid of the culls, insect damage, tops, defective timber, and thinned and let the good stuff go on to sawlogs." Allen concluded, "I guess I got my story over because after dinner . . . everybody was jolly and shakin' hands and havin' a drink, and from then on K got along fine with those lumbermen."[79]

Dexter's trepidation was understandable, for in the early period pulpwood loggers "acquired a reputation as shifty, disreputable gypsies, more inclined toward timber theft than honest dealing. . . . The careless men pursuing this marginal enterprise were hardly Chamber of Commerce material." However, their unsavory reputation started to improve as the increasing demand for pulpwood brought "higher caliber men to the business." Still, there was legitimate concern that the pulp mills, utilizing smaller logs than the sawmills, could represent a threat to the timber supply, a concept that pulpwood spokesmen labored tirelessly to rebut.[80]

It took a couple of decades before some lumbermen fully realized that the pulp and paper companies could actually complement the lumber industry's efforts to bring the southern timberlands back into profitable production. Conversely, lumber firms looking to get out of the business now had a new market for their timberland holdings. Demmon said that "there's a competitive field for trees of around eight to twelve to fourteen inches, which both the industries are interested in to an extent, but if they have any siz-

able stands of timber that will make good saw logs, practically all of the pulp mills sell them for saw timber or exchange them for pulpwood stumpage. Some of the sawmill people carry on an active program of thinning their smaller size timber where it's necessary and it goes into pulpwood, so they're largely working out their differences." Also, as early as 1948 the SPCA and Southern Pine Association were exploring the implementation of a joint pulpwood and sawmill industry program of improved harvesting. Spokesmen for both industries believed that logging operations simultaneously serving both industries represented the most responsible utilization of timber resources.[81]

In 1948 Vertrees Young, executive vice president of the Gaylord Container Company in Bogalusa, Louisiana, personified this effort at reconciliation when he addressed a New Orleans meeting of the Southern Pine Association. Young told the assembled lumber producers, "Inasmuch as both industries derive their raw materials from the same source, a common point of interest is immediately evident. Whether it is in future to be a conflict of interest or a community of interest depends principally upon how we conduct our respective operations. In the past our two industries have been looked upon as open and avowed competitors for raw materials. Actually, each if properly managed can do much to support and compliment the other to their mutual benefit." Young went on to cite an example of cooperation between the two industries: "International Paper Company in the past ten years has sold 753,000,000 Bf. of saw logs, about half of its pine, from its pulpwood lands and in turn has received 1,627,000 cords of pulpwood. In 1947 it cut 150,000 cords of pulpwood from tops behind logging operations. Other mills, ours included, are also getting sizable volumes from tops. This is wood that is otherwise wasted, and which, if left in the woods, adds materially to the fire hazard."[82]

Just as there were differences in objectives and methodology among lumber companies, there were contrasts between the forest practices of the lumber companies on one hand and the pulp and paper firms on the other. With the exception of a few pioneering firms, most lumber companies in the 1930s and 1940s made little or no effort to manage their lands on a long-term basis. The pulp and paper companies, conversely, generally implemented forest-management programs upon settling in the South. The lumber firms and pulp and paper companies operated differently largely because of the two industries' vastly divergent capital structures. As A. M. Dantzler of Mississippi's Dantzler Lumber Company explained, "we didn't have millions tied up in paper mills like they do." A history of IP's woodlands noted, "A paper mill . . . had a multimillion-dollar investment in site, power, water sources, buildings, machines and equipment. It was fixed, and once established, the complex was permanent and for all practical purposes, immovable."[83]

Still, there were legitimate concerns about the pulp and paper companies' impact on southern forests during the 1930s. The expansion of the industry during the Great Depression led to serious overcutting in the South, especially on private lands. Desperate for cash, timberland owners near pulp mills were clear-cutting their timber or allowing others to clear-cut it for sale to the mills. In its survey of southern forests between 1935 and 1940, the Southern Forest Experiment Station found that in some areas competition among the pulp and paper industry and other wood-using industries produced a negative balance of growth against drain. And a mill's timber requirements were considerable. In the late 1930s the U.S. Forest Service and Mississippi Agricultural Extension Service estimated the demands of a sulfate or kraft mill at from 270 to 1,100 cords of pulpwood per day (fifteen to sixty-one railroad carloads) or from 72,000 to 352,000 cords of wood per a 320-day year. Some feared that the pulp mills were following in the footsteps of the cut-out-and-get-out lumbering firms. The difference, of course, was in the scale of the pulp and paper companies' investment in plants and equipment, which made them much less likely to

migrate. Their best economic option was to stay and regenerate the forests in the areas where they operated. However, some foresters and consultants working for the pulp mills also feared overcutting or at least too much competition for the same timber. In 1948 a consultant for Johns Manville reported, "Our regional and local investigations during the past six months have stopped at least one 500 ton pulp mill and perhaps put the brakes on new machines in two existing mills. But the executive heads are still production-minded and expansion will continue."[84]

Demmon argued that "rapid progress in forestry did not come about until the pulp mills expanded so greatly in the thirties." As Demmon recalled, "I would say that the coming of the pulp and paper industry to the South was the boost that the South needed to promote a real forestry program because it offered an outlet for much wood that otherwise was valueless. In the late twenties and early thirties when the pulp mills first came in, pulpwood could be had for twenty-five to fifty cents a cord stumpage. Then as more pulp mills were established and competition for wood increased, the price of pulpwood stumpage rose until now it is often five dollars or more per cord. That means that the timberland owner . . . can now afford to invest money in his forest where before he couldn't. In the early days it was difficult to prove the financial advantages of practicing forestry when the market might not be available for twenty, thirty, or forty years in the future, and very few people are interested in what may happen that far ahead. . . . Here is where the pulp and paper industry has been a great boon to the South." Nelson said that the "pulp and paper industry provided a cash market for small trees and was thus a major factor in making private forestry feasible in the South . . . by providing a cash return in a relatively few years and allowing the profitable thinning or removal of trees which would otherwise interfere with the growing of larger trees for sawlogs, poles, etc." Damtoft also argued that "in the South the consciousness of the real value of timber came with the expansion of the pulp and paper industry." In the early 1950s Lyle F. Watts, chief of the U.S. Forest Service, said, "It was a great day for forestry in the South when paper from southern pine was made practical. That development brought a demand for small-sized trees that made intensive forestry possible, the dream of practicing foresters."[85]

Three different wood-supply systems developed in the industry: the company-crew system, the direct-purchase system, and the dealer system. As Warren Flick describes them, "In a company crew system, a wood manufacturing company hires woods workers, buys logging equipment, and directs its workers to cut, sort, and perhaps transport timber to its mill, though the transporting may be contracted to independent truckers, railroads, or barges. . . . In a direct purchase system, a manufacturing company contracts with producers, who are independent wood harvesting contractors, to cut and deliver the timber to a railroad yard, a barge loading point, or directly to a wood using mill. The company assigns producers to its own timberland or to timber it has purchased from other landowners. . . . Finally, in a dealer system, a manufacturing company contracts with wood dealers to supply wood to its mill. Dealers are middlemen who buy timber from landowners, arrange for producers to cut it, and coordinate its delivery to a railroad yard, barge loading point, or directly to a mill."[86]

Despite the concerns about overcutting mentioned earlier, during the 1930s and 1940s the southern pulp and paper industry's implementation of forestry programs was impressive. St. Regis moved South during the 1940s and probably would have done so sooner if not for financial problems. George J. Kneeland, chief executive officer during the 1970s, said, "Our delay was purely a matter of money." St. Regis entered the South with the purchase of the stock of the Florida Pulp and Paper Company of Pensacola in 1946 and continued to build its holdings. Forest-management practices were already in place on much of the acreage acquired, and St. Regis con-

tinued them. By the 1950s the company was operating comprehensive forestry programs in the South.[87]

During the early 1940s the Flintkote Company began to purchase cutover lands in eastern Mississippi to serve as a pulpwood reserve for its plant in Meridian. The Flintkote Forest eventually comprised some ninety thousand acres. Flintkote employed three graduate foresters plus two experienced woodsmen to administer the lands and to direct the work of fourteen laborers who worked year round on the forest. By 1946 pulp and paper companies employed 265 foresters in the South, and much of their effort was directed toward education and assistance programs for the small timberland owners from whom they purchased much of their wood supply. Reflecting the dramatic growth of the industry and its commitment to industrial forestry, by 1953 pulp and paper companies in the South employed 753 foresters.[88]

By the late 1950s IP owned and leased more than 4 million acres of timberland in the South and employed 235 foresters. During the 1930s IP foresters were primarily involved in fire control and timber cruising, but a movement toward actual forest management began in 1937 under the direction of Joseph E. McCaffrey. By 1969 IP employed 330 foresters in the nine states of its Southern Kraft Division, with most of them supervising management and harvesting operations on IP lands.[89]

In the 1930s Union Bag and Paper Corporation (later the Union Camp Corporation until its acquisition by IP) built a mill at Savannah, Georgia, and announced that it was adopting a "constructive forest policy" and would promote good management on its own lands and on those of its neighbors.[90] These and other pulp and paper companies that moved into the South during the next two decades generally planned to operate on a permanent basis and thus created a need for trained industrial foresters who could manage the land and help to make that dream a reality.

World War II interrupted the growth of the pulp and paper industry, but at the end of the conflict the industry began to take off again, and five new mills were constructed between 1947 and 1950. By 1950 the South led the nation in wood-pulp production, turning out 50 percent of the country's supply. IP modernized its mill at Moss Point and began to build a new rayon pulp mill at Natchez. This mill produced rayon pulp from hardwoods by use of the sulfate process and was the first of its kind in the world. In the late 1940s the Johns Manville Corporation purchased a large tract of land from the Central Lumber Company in southwest Mississippi and built an insulating board plant at Natchez.[91]

The industry's expansion was financed in part by the postwar prosperity of the southern pulp and paper manufacturers. Sales and net profits after taxes increased, and retained earnings jumped sharply as the industry operated at an average of 93 percent of capacity during the period. By 1950 the South turned out 90 percent of the nation's sulfate production. From 1945 to 1950 southern paper and board production increased 67 percent, while the national increase was 40 percent. By 1950 the total investment in the southern pulp and paper industry was more than $1.2 billion. The prospects for continued growth were good, but only if an adequate timber supply was maintained.[92]

The rapid movement of the industry into the South was not without controversy. Some resented the industry's rapid rise, and in 1952 the SPCA board discussed "reported rumblings of dissatisfaction over acquisition of forest lands by the pulp and paper industry in the South." The acquisition of vast timberland holdings triggered concerns and criticisms both within and outside of the corporate world. As a longtime forestry consultant for Johns Manville put it in 1948, "Prices on timberland may be dropping, and the world going to hell, but some of the big pulp and paper companies are still aggressive in their land buying." He noted, "The big pulp companies are scared and busy buying. . . . I happen to know that in recent weeks IP has made offers on two properties at a total cost of over 10 million dollars." During the period Crosby Lumber and

Manufacturing Company purchased 135,000 acres in Wilkinson, Amite, Jefferson, and Copiah Counties; the Gaylord Container Corporation bought thirty-five thousand acres in Lawrence, Pike, Marion, and Walthall Counties; and Masonite was looking at 7,200 acres in Lawrence and Simpson Counties. IP bought 11,047 acres in Mississippi during 1946, bringing its total in the state to 203,000 acres (including the Denkmann-leased lands).[93]

Johns Manville, with a mill at Natchez, faced competition for wood from mills in both Louisiana and Mississippi. Johns Manville executives came to believe that the "mistakes of the past ten years have been mainly in not buying more timberlands at what seemed to be high sale prices." They concluded that "an aggressive, sustained acquisition program is essential, if a more critical future situation is to be avoided." At the time the company owned forty thousand acres of timberland but believed that this amount was "not enough to safeguard the future or provide for expansion." Thus, the company planned to purchase an additional 110,000 acres, which it thought would produce an annual growth of half a cord per acre and support its annual mill requirements of seventy-five thousand cords. One factor driving the Johns Manville program was concern about IP building facilities in Natchez and competing for wood.[94]

Intense competition was a fact of life in the industry as the large companies bought land to gain an inroad into a territory, to feed their own mills, or to keep others out. The companies did not attempt to acquire enough land to totally supply their own needs, but most hoped to eventually get a maximum of about 50 percent of their timber from company-owned lands. In 1948 the Gaylord Container Corporation bought forty-eight thousand acres in Lincoln, Copiah, Lawrence, and Simpson Counties, and as Johns Manville officials speculated, "It may be that they just happened to find desirable properties at these locations, or it may be a deliberate effort to establish themselves in this territory and forestall J-M and other competitive mills." These officials also observed that IP owned more than 200,000 acres in Mississippi and was "adding steadily" to its holdings, and that "[n]ew mill projects now depend on prior control of strategic timberlands properties." Crown Zellerbach, they said "stresses strongly the investment values of their . . . timberlands as effective protection against the long-range trend of inflation."[95]

The pulp and paper companies' rapid acquisition of large landholdings triggered a reaction. Some newspapers condemned the companies for being responsible for losses in rural populations, for the reduction of areas available for public hunting and fishing, and for the reduction of game populations due to programs of eradicating cull hardwoods. In the 1950s the Mississippi legislature considered legislation to impose a "graduated privilege tax" of five cents per acre for landholdings of five thousand acres and fifty cents per acre for holdings of fifty thousand acres. The legislature also debated restricting the size of corporate ownerships to a maximum of twenty thousand acres and increasing the ad valorem taxes. The SPCA undertook a public-relations campaign to defend the companies' activities.[96]

By 1984 softwood timber harvests on company owned lands totaled 1.8 billion cubic feet, 2.5 times the production in 1952. Hardwood production was up 1.7 times from the 1952 total, to 534 million cubic feet. Other private owners in 1984 supplied 2.9 billion cubic feet of softwood roundwood and 1.8 billion cubic feet of hardwood roundwood, nearly 60 percent of the softwood and 70 percent of the hardwood roundwood supplies. The leading pulpwood-producing counties in Mississippi by the mid-1970s were Clarke, Attala, and Copiah.[97]

One of the critical points with regard to the timber supply was the fact that a large percentage of the wood came from noncompany land. Eldredge recalled that in the early days of the southern pulp and paper industry, private timberland owners supplied more than 75 percent of the pulpwood for the mills. The large companies originally were "saving their own for the simple reason that . . . they had to build up what we foresters call 'growing stock.' They bought land that had been cut over, . . . and they had to build up timber growth. . . . [O]n the whole some of them take as much as 80 percent of their cut outside because the land they've bought and are managing is not over 10 or 15 percent of the territory they draw from." Thus, said Eldredge, "The pulp companies without exception are very conscious of the fact that they will always be dependent on this outside supply. As a consequence . . . the Southern Pulpwood Conservation Association is working with pulp mills to build up better forest practices on these small noncompany lands."[98]

The large companies often provided financing for their pulpwood suppliers. In 1948 a Johns Manville internal report noted, "Both International Paper Company and Gaylord Container Corporation have been liberal with their pulpwood dealers in the matter of financing timber purchases." "Trusted International dealers," according to the report, "can obtain a check for timber purchases by telephoning the wood procurement office at the mill in emergencies. Such loans apparently are often carried on open account with the dealer." The Johns Manville report recommended a similar system for the company to cover cases where "it would be more desirable to finance a contractor than to purchase timber ourselves," such as acreages where "you have over half the timber value in sawlog trees which the pulpwood buyer would have to resell." The large companies also financed the sale of trucks to their pulpwood contractors, who passed them on under the same terms to the producers who logged for them. A 1946 Johns Manville memorandum noted that the pulpwood dealers were "almost completely equipped" with trucks under these arrangements.[99]

In 1948 Johns Manville consulting forester E. A. Sterling observed, "The industry has failed to prevent destructive cutting by most of its own pulpwood dealers and producers . . . and has been production-minded without making adequate provision for its future wood supply."

Johns Manville itself was struggling with these problems. Describing the situation regarding small private landownings and contract cutters in the vicinity of Sontag, Mississippi, a company memorandum reported "total disregard for the State Forest Harvesting Act." It noted that "no effort is being made to enforce the present laws in the Sontag vicinity" and that "[t]his destructive cutting with repeated annual burns has created a situation which is one of desolation." The typical pulpwood operator, according to the memorandum, was a "one-truck man the truck being in poor repair and an old model." Former Champion Paper and Fibre Company president and chairman Reuben B. Robertson noted one technique his company used in promoting better forest practices among its suppliers: "Many years ago, in our contracts with the small farmer, we put in a clause that we could cancel the contract if he was not handling his wood lot in accordance with sustained yield principles. We seldom had to do it, but we provided field men to help in marking the trees for cutting."[100]

By the late 1950s the U.S. Forest Service reported that 81 percent of all industry lands in the South were being cut in a manner that would leave them in a high state of productivity. For the pulp and paper industry, the figure was even higher, with 96 percent of its lands being cut in such a way. However, as an IP official reported, "the rating of lands owned by farmers and other small landowners is poor. In fact, only 34% of the private non-industrial holdings in the South were rated as obtaining maximum use of their forest lands."[101]

Thus by the late 1940s the pulp and paper industry had moved into the South in a big way. It owned and leased large tracts of land, much of it cutover timberland that had once belonged to lumber companies, but the industry obtained much of its wood needs from small, private timberland owners. The large companies in the industry were cognizant of the need for proper management of their own lands to protect their enormous investments in productive facilities. The companies also realized that it was critical to promote enlightened management practices on the timberlands of the small owners from whom they obtained so much of their wood. Thus, they began to employ experts to help them define, develop, and implement responsible forest policies on their lands and to provide assistance and examples of good management for their neighbors. The evolution of their attitudes and policies regarding timberland management is part and parcel of the story of the rise of industrial forestry and the restoration of forests in the South.

Conversely, while a few lumber manufacturers were struggling to continue in operation and to implement fire control, selective cutting, and reforestation on their lands, many big companies and timber owners had abandoned their cutover lands or were looking desperately for a way to unload them and eliminate their tax obligations. Their situation was a major factor in opening the door for the federal government to become a major Mississippi timberland owner. The 1924 passage of the Clarke-McNary Act enabled the federal government to purchase land for the purposes of growing timber and providing watershed protection, and the U.S. Forest Service began surveys to choose possible sites for National Forest Purchase Units. Among the units established was one on the Homochitto in Mississippi, but while some land was examined and title searches undertaken, no lands were purchased due to lack of funding.

Franklin Delano Roosevelt's election to the presidency brought a new emphasis on expanding the national forests in the eastern United States, and more land studies were done in Mississippi. Mississippi Senator Pat Harrison, chairman of the Senate Finance Committee, was instrumental in the eventual designation of $50 million for land purchases. Ray M. Conarro was appointed forest supervisor of the Homochitto Purchase Unit and eventually forest supervisor of the national forests in Mississippi, in which position he served from August 1933 through June 1940. Conarro had the task of locating, surveying, and purchasing the lands that would constitute the original Mississippi national forests.

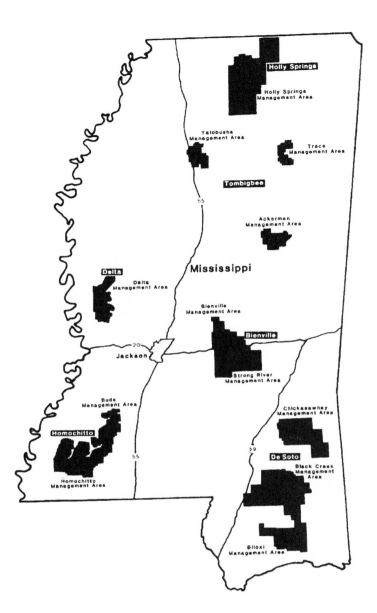

Map of Mississippi national forests. Courtesy U.S. Forest Service. Modified by Edward Ashley Fickle.

These lands would eventually house five national forests, including the Bienville, Delta, De Soto, Homochitto, and Holly Springs. The Tombigbee National Forest was added later. Most of the acreage was devastated cutover pineland, although the Delta purchase unit was in low-lying hardwood areas, and the Holly Springs unit in north Mississippi was made up almost entirely of worn-out farmland. Except for the Holly Springs unit, the bulk of the land was purchased from large

lumber companies and timberland owners who were delighted to turn it over to the government, although they sometimes tried to secure exorbitant prices in the process. Conarro arrived in Brookhaven on July 31, 1933, and immediately went to work.[102]

C. E. Beaumont, a longtime Forest Service employee, conducted the land surveys in Mississippi. He recommended purchases in what were then called the Biloxi, Chickasawhay, Leaf River, and

Holly Springs units. By June 30, 1934, more than 600,000 acres had been approved for purchase. Conarro described it as "the largest area ever purchased, or under purchase agreement, by any one Forest in such a short period of time." In 1926 the Mississippi legislature passed an enabling act that required that all land purchases for national forests must be approved by the State Forestry Commission, which was created the same year. The commission further stipulated that county boards of supervisors had to agree on the amount of land that they would authorize for purchase in their jurisdictions. Most county boards were happy to have the national forests, except in cases where they saw agricultural potential in the lands. The counties realized that proper management and fire protection under the auspices of the Forest Service was to their advantage, for 25 percent of the revenues from timber harvests would revert to the counties from which the timber was cut, with the money used for public schools and roads. The Mississippi Forestry Commission did everything it could to facilitate the land purchases.[103]

Surveys concentrated on areas where large owners held most of the land. Among those first identified were the Quitman unit in Clarke, Lauderdale, Newton, and Jasper Counties, where the Long-Bell Lumber Company was a major landowner; the DeKalb unit in Kemper and Neshoba Counties, where the Sumpter Lumber Company was the principal landowner; and the Bienville unit in Scott, Newton, Smith, and Jasper Counties. Conarro was authorized to recommend one of the three for purchase, and he designated the Bienville unit based on the "ground survey of each . . . all phases of land acquisition, timber growing quality, stream protection and wildlife potential." The large landowners included the Adams-Edgar Lumber Company, Bienville Lumber Company, Eastman-Gardiner Lumber Company, and Marathon Lumber Company, which collectively owned approximately 112,693 acres. The unit included 328,820 acres, and by June 30, 1934, more than 120,000 acres were under option. In 1938 there was a big addition of land in

Scott, Madison, Rankin, and Leake Counties, where the principal owner was the Pearl River Lumber Company. Alton B. Farris Sr., an employee of the Adams-Edgar Lumber Company, later remembered that the fifty-seven thousand acres that Adams-Edgar sold to the government went for $2.65 per acre, including mineral rights. The company, he said, sold the land because it "simply could not pay the taxes."[104]

The Biloxi purchase unit included 409,600 acres in Harrison, Stone, and Jackson Counties. The Wilbe Lumber Company, the Newton Naval Stores Company, the Batson and Hatton Lumber Company, and the Dantzler Company were the major landowners, with Dantzler owning 90,500 acres inside the unit and about 125,000 acres outside. By June 1935, 126,061 acres had been approved for purchase. An attempt was made to add more land from the Hines Lumber Company's holdings in Harrison County, but the effort failed because the company wanted more for the land than the government was willing to pay.

Some of the most interesting activities with regard to the purchase involved the Dantzler Lumber Company and its longtime land manager, Posey Howell. When Conarro arrived in the purchase area for negotiations, he found that the Forest Service's Beaumont, who was in charge of examining the Dantzler land, was using one of the company's field offices as his headquarters and leaving his examination maps and appraisal data on a desk where company officials could view them. Conarro "required Beaumont to move to Gulfport the same day. However, the Dantzlers knew enough appraisal data to make it impossible for me to negotiate with them except at the top valuation." The last strange twist came at 10:30 P.M. on the night of December 31, 1933, when Howell and one of the Dantzlers arrived on Conarro's doorstep and tried to turn over the deed for ninety thousand acres of the purchase to avoid 1934 taxes.[105]

The Chickasawhay purchase unit included 192,000 acres in Jones, Perry, Greene, and Wayne Counties. The principal landowners were the Robinson Land and Lumber Company, the

Kalmia Realty and Insurance Company, Bently and Pope, John W. Blodgett, and the Alabama Land and Development Company, a subsidiary of the Gulf, Mobile, and Ohio Railroad. These five owners held more than 100,000 acres. Conarro reported, "I had never viewed an area so large with so much devastation. Nearly 100% of the area I saw that day had been burned over in recent months." The state forestry commission reported that much of the land was stocked with small timber but that it was rapidly being destroyed by fire. By June 30, 1935, 134,000 acres were under purchase agreements.[106]

The son-in-law of one of the owners of the Kalmia Realty and Insurance Company was also the cashier of a family-controlled bank that held a mortgage on the land being sold to the government. When the cashier signed the purchase option for the bank, he handed it to Conarro, saying, "Here is the option, sucker." Conarro had the last laugh, for several years later the Texas Company paid the government more than $700,000 for the drilling rights on one of the sections acquired from Kalmia. Conarro noted that "This $700,000 was about 29 times more than the Government paid for the total Kalmia tract." After the drilling rights were sold, the bank and the Kalmia company unsuccessfully sued to contest their land sale, claiming that they had been defrauded by the government.[107]

The Leaf River purchase unit originally included land in Forrest, Perry, Greene, and George Counties. Later additions in Lamar, Forrest, and Marion Counties increased the total land area to 624,000 acres, the largest unit in Mississippi. The major landowners included the J. J. Newman Lumber Company, the Batson and Hatton Lumber Company, the Perry Land Company, Ralph L. Jackson, and Robert Newton. By the end of 1935 some 203,766 acres were approved for purchase. According to Conarro, "Some of the lands had recovered from the early logging, but it was noted that sheep and hog grazing on the open range had caused considerable damage to young longleaf seedlings." This area became the De Soto National Forest, and a later U.S. Forest Ser-

vice publication said that at the time of purchase "more than half the acreage was classified as 'less than 10-percent stocked.'"[108]

The Delta purchase unit originated in the U.S. Forest Service regional forester's desire for a bottomland hardwood demonstration forest to promote hardwood management. The unit was located in the drainage areas of the Big and Little Sunflower Rivers, and the large owners included Houston Brothers, the Frank Houston Estate, the Belgrade Lumber Company, the W. W. Cary Lumber Company, the McLean Hardwood Lumber Company, the Gamill Investment Company, B. L. Mallory, and George McSawyn. A large block of the land had been owned by the Singer Sewing Machine Company, and much of it still contained old-growth timber. By 1940 the purchase unit boundary included 220,238 acres.[109]

The Holly Springs purchase unit was approved in considerable part because of the influence of Congressman Wall Doxey. Unlike the other units, the land parcels in the Holly Springs unit were small, usually less than one hundred acres. Most were abandoned and eroded farmlands. Much of the acreage had been farmed in the antebellum period but was abandoned around the time of the Civil War because of labor shortages and erosion. The purchase area was 320,000 acres, of which 110,000 had been acquired by 1940. Civilian Conservation Corps crews planted shortleaf pine in the eroded sections.[110]

The Homochitto purchase unit was approved by the National Forest Reserve Commission in 1930, and by 1936 a purchase area of 373,460 acres was authorized. The large landowners were the Homochitto Lumber Company, Central Lumber Company, Southern Forest Land Company, Gloster Lumber Company, and the Foster Creek Lumber Company. The conditions of these companies were typical of the situations of many lumber operators suffering from declining timber supplies and the economic pressure of the depression. The Homochitto, Central, and Gloster lumber companies were all operating in 1933 and continued to run for several more years. The Homochitto Lumber Company released its land as it was cut over. The Forest Service came up with a plan that enabled the Central Lumber Company to continue operating until 1944. The Foster Creek Lumber Company had more than sixty thousand acres of merchantable timber but was deeply in debt and could not raise capital to continue operations. The company was forced to shut down in 1929 due to the depression. The Forest Service decided not to purchase its land, and in 1935 it was acquired by L. O. Crosby, along with the town of Stephenson, which became Crosby. Conarro described the lands of the Homochitto purchase unit as "in a much better condition than those lands in other purchase units" because of "the logging dates, the richness of the soil, and the timber types." Even so, a later Forest Service publication described the Homochitto as "comprised of areas that were culled over, leaving only the defective material and inferior species."[111]

In 1960 federal land-utilization projects were discontinued, and the land was eventually given to the Forest Service. A new national forest of sixty-five thousand acres, the Tombigbee, was established in northeast Mississippi, and some lands were added to the Holly Springs National Forest, bringing its total to 143,000 acres. There were ultimately six national forests in Mississippi with a total of more than 1 million acres: the Bienville National Forest, with 175,000 acres in east-central Mississippi; the De Soto National Forest, with more than 500,000 acres in southeast Mississippi; the Holly Springs National Forest, with more than 143,000 acres in north-central Mississippi; the Homochitto National Forest, with more than 189,000 acres in southwest Mississippi; the Tombigbee National Forest, with sixty-five thousand acres in northeast Mississippi; and the Delta purchase unit, with nearly fifty-nine thousand acres in Sharkey County. Ironically, in the late 1940s, after the national forestlands had begun to recover under U.S. Forest Service stewardship, some large landowners who had sold their lands to the federal government for low prices recruited Mississippi politicians, including the former state attorney general, to attempt to

circumvent the Weeks Act so that the companies could regain their land. John Squires, the new supervisor of the Mississippi national forests, worked with the Mississippi Forestry Association, Governor Fielding Wright, and the state legislature to defuse these efforts.[112]

At the time of their purchases, most of the lands acquired by the Forest Service in Mississippi were cutover tracts in poor condition. The lands acquired for southern national forests in general were characterized as "the lands nobody wanted." Thus, the Forest Service's job was to restore the lands through planting, fire protection, and protection of young seedlings. Conarro even found time to write a children's book based on the Little Red Riding Hood story to promote awareness of the dangers of forest fires. With the exception of a few tracts, the sale of timber to the forest-products industry was far in the future, but it was in fact a major part of the Forest Service's approach to land management, which was based on sustained-yield and multiple-use principles. As a 1982 U.S. Forest Service publication pointed out, "Foresters in the 1890's and early 1900's envisioned that the United States Forest Reserves, then being created, would provide a continuous supply of timber for the needs of local industry, under federal control. Their vision has been realized in the National Forests, as the Reserves were renamed in 1907. Under the Forest Service's sustained-yield principles, these forests today furnish raw materials for one-third of the lumber and one-half of the plywood manufactured in the United States each year." In 1944 the U.S. forest supervisor, Hugh S. Redding, saw another purpose: "Our National Forest land," he said, "should be to a woodland owner the same as a farm demonstration of cultivated crops is to the farmer. . . . It is the aim of the administration of the National Forest to set such a good example that the private owners throughout the state will see the economic benefits from good forest practices so clearly that they will want to carry these practices out themselves."[113]

During the 1930s, as public foresters were struggling to reestablish forests on cutover lands in Mississippi, the plight of lumber companies that held large blocks of timber and were victims of the Great Depression caused the Forest Service to curtail timber sales in other parts of the country. However, timber produced on the national forests eventually again became an important source of raw material for the forest-products industry. The largest production areas have been in the West. While the South lags far behind the West in timber sales from national forests, the volume is still considerable, with roughly 1.349 billion board feet of timber harvested in southern national forests in 1985.[114]

Forest-products-industry leaders traditionally assumed that growing and providing timber for industry was the national forests' proper role. In 1955 an industry spokesman argued, "The rule of any governmental agency should be that of service to the citizens of the legal subdivision represented and to the industrial segments important to the fields with which it is concerned. The outstanding accomplishment of the Forest Service during the past fifty years has been in this service function. Through this function important benefits have accrued to the forest industries." While acknowledging the Forest Service's contributions in education, training and employing foresters,

cooperative fire-control programs, research, and other endeavors, the writer emphasized timber sales. And in making recommendations for the future, he argued, "Of primary importance is the development of access road systems and timber sale activities to the maximum of the allowable cut of each national forest." He urged the Forest Service to educate "conservation groups [that] interpret the word as 'preservation,' rather than 'wise use' [and] advocate forest practices that no sound, trained forester would accept as practical." Said the spokesman, "The Forest Service has a responsibility to help correct these misunderstandings."[115] The ideological foundations for some of the battles of the future had been established.

The new national forests brought in public foresters who labored to restore Mississippi's lands and forests. The state government, industry associations, railroads, civic groups, the Civilian Conservation Corps, and industrial foresters working for lumber and pulp and paper companies were also deeply involved in the resurrection endeavors. The cutover lands of the 1930s and 1940s presented formidable challenges, as all of these groups labored to revive Mississippi's forested heritage.

7 Transformations

Restoring Mississippi's Forests

In the 1930s and 1940s Mississippi's cutover lands presented formidable problems for the crusaders who attempted to restore their former splendor. Different groups and individuals, public and private, with a variety of philosophies and priorities, worked toward goals that sometimes intersected, sometimes did not. In the course of their efforts, foresters developed tools and techniques that are still used today in forest management. The collective result of all of these efforts was a remarkable greening of Mississippi and the revitalization of the forest heritage that Mississippians cherish today.

Among those who played important roles were industrial foresters working for the pulp and paper industry and for some lumbering firms. By 1940 the southern forest industries employed about 220 trained foresters. This number had risen to 750 by 1953 and to more than 2,200 by 1976. International Paper Company (IP) alone employed more than five hundred foresters between 1940 and 1970. There were also forestry technicians, researchers, and other professionals who were concerned with the restoration and health of the forests. The industrial foresters worked on company-owned and -leased lands and provided professional management advice and services to nonindustrial private landowners, often in return for the right of first refusal to purchase the client's timber when it was harvested.[1]

Their public-sector counterparts at the federal level were the foresters laboring to build Mississippi's national forests and the famous brigades of the Civilian Conservation Corps (CCC) who performed valuable work during the 1930s. Citizens' groups were also important, such as the Mississippi Federation of Women's Clubs, which played a critical role in the establishment of the Mississippi Forestry Commission (MFC). The commission, in turn, employed public foresters who preached the gospel of good forest management to private landowners and played an important role in the battles against fire. The American Forestry Association was an important force, sending its famous "Dixie Crusaders" into the Magnolia State to join the campaign against fire. The Southern Pulpwood Conservation Association, formed by members of that industry in 1939, labored tirelessly to bring about better forest practices on private land, especially small holdings. The Mississippi Forestry Association (MFA), formed in 1938, became an important participant, especially by sponsoring the Tree Farms program for small landowners as Mississippi became the nation's leading tree-farm state.

One should not forget the politicians. After twenty years of lobbying by citizens and organizations interested in forestry, in 1940 the state legislature passed the Timber Severance Tax Law. The state's ad valorem tax on standing timber was repealed, and timber was now taxed at the time of harvest. This change was important: "No longer did the taxes on standing timber eat up the value of the timber growing there. It was now possible for the landowner to grow timber at a profit." An in-house history of the MFC claimed, "This Legislation has been credited by many as the most important single factor in making possible a continuous production of timber in Mississippi." Two-thirds of the revenue from the severance tax was returned annually to the counties from which the timber was harvested. In 1944 the legislature passed the Forest Harvesting Act, which established minimum standards for the leaving of seed trees of the predominant species on forests that were harvested.[2]

At the federal level, the 1943 Revenue Act and Section 631 of the Internal Revenue Code allowed income from timber sales or use by owners to be treated as capital gains, with lower rates than those applied to ordinary income. When Congress in 1969 revised the Internal Revenue Code to increase taxes on capital gains by 40 percent, foresters considered it a disincentive for those who were growing trees. A 1980 amendment to the code allowed taxpayers to amortize over eight years the first ten thousand dollars spent for reforestation and provided a tax credit equal to 10 percent of the first ten thousand dollars of such costs. The 1986 Federal Tax Reform Act changed the capital gains tax rate to equal the rate on ordinary income but retained the amortization and tax credit for reforestation and the expensing of annual management costs. While there is limited data on the impact of state and federal tax laws on timber supplies, most Mississippi foresters and landowners agree that the adoption of Mississippi's severance tax was the breakthrough that made reforestation, forest management, and sustained-yield forestry economically feasible.[3]

Railroads also contributed to the revival of Mississippi's forests. Their interest was not surprising, for forest products constituted a considerable part of their business. In the 1940s forest products accounted for one-third of the tonnage leaving Mississippi on the Illinois Central and by 1945 35 percent of all railroad-car loadings in the

state. Forest car loadings represented nearly one-third of the traffic of the Gulf, Mobile, and Ohio, and 44 percent of the car loadings on the New Orleans and North Eastern. In the early 1920s the New Orleans and Great Northern Railroad arranged for a series of "forestry schools" in towns along its line. These schools emphasized natural reforestation and the control of razorback hogs, pine bark beetles, and fire.

In 1945 the Illinois Central established a forestry department, with one employee assigned to Louisiana and another to Mississippi. By 1954 the railroad employed four foresters and claimed to have the nation's largest railroad-forestry department. The Illinois Central sought to promote improved forest management and to reduce the prevalence of fires. Illinois Central agricultural agents staged tree-planting demonstrations, utilizing the famous "Illinois Central Tree Planter," and the foresters conducted short courses for farmers and provided field demonstrations of timber estimating and marking, fire prevention, and planting. The Illinois Central also started sponsoring short courses in forestry for high school students in 1946, and within a decade eight thousand boys in Louisiana and Mississippi had attended.

The Gulf, Mobile, and Ohio Railroad in 1950 enlarged its agricultural department to include forestry. The railroad placed great emphasis on sponsoring forestry improvement contests among Future Farmers of America and 4-H members as well as other forestry activities. The railroads thus joined the civic groups, politicians, private and public foresters, concerned citizens, professional associations, and others who labored valiantly during the 1930s and 1940s to restore Mississippi's forested heritage.[4]

The entry of a few professional foresters into the ranks of the lumber and pulp and paper industries has been outlined earlier, as have the early activities of U.S. Forest Service foresters. The primary public agency dealing with Mississippi's forests at the state level was the MFC. But during the era of cut-out-and-get-out lumbering and the struggles of early foresters to deal with

Mississippi's denuded lands, the state forestry commission was noticeably absent from the battlefields. And for a good reason—not until the mid-1920s did Mississippi even have a state forestry commission, and it was subsequently chronically underfunded: as late as 1945 the commission estimated the taxes paid by "forests and related economic activity" in Mississippi at $6 million, while the state appropriated only $108,000 in "direct state expenditures for forestry." Federal matching funds and county contributions amounted to $103,000, but the commission still concluded that this sum did "not meet the State's responsibility for the protection of its forest resource."

The effort to create a state forestry commission originated with public-minded citizens' groups. Possibly the most important was the Mississippi Federation of Women's Clubs, which had organized a Conservation Department in 1914. Its state chairwoman of conservation, Mrs. G. H. Reeves of Jackson, successfully spearheaded an effort to secure the services of a U.S. Forest Service spokeswoman, who toured Mississippi and spoke to women's clubs, schools, and other groups advocating the creation of a state forestry program. Her expenses were paid by the Forest Service and by the Mississippi Development Board. The state legislature created the MFC with an act passed on March 6, 1926. The law established a commission consisting of three ex-officio members, including the governor, commissioner of agriculture, and state land commissioner, plus six representatives chosen from the citizenry. Among the first commission members were Mrs. Reeves and legendary forester P. N. "Posey" Howell.[5]

The law provided for the appointment of a state forester and emphasized the development of programs for fire prevention and reforestation. The first state forester was Roy L. Hogue, a native of Michigan with a master's degree in forestry from the University of Michigan. As a result of a shortage of funds, the commission did not organize a fire-control force during the early period but put its efforts into information and education.

Hogue was appointed at a salary of only three hundred dollars per month.[6] In addition to several other employees, the forestry commission joined the extension director in appointing an extension forester whose job was to work with county agents, high schools, and farmers to promote fire prevention and forestry programs across the state. The MFC and extension director hired as extension forester H. C. Mitchell, who was trained at the University of Michigan. In the same period fire protection was implemented in some Mississippi counties.

By 1929 a number of large landowners agreed to pay four cents per acre on 400,000 acres for fire protection. Among these landholders were the Gloster Lumber Company, Southeastern Paper Company, Great Southern Lumber Company, Finkbine Lumber Company, Sumpter Lumber Company, and L. N. Dantzler Lumber Company. With these contributions, Mississippi could receive its full allocation of matching funds from the federal government under the Clarke-McNary Act. The funds would be used to build a fire-control organization, but full-scale fire-control efforts were not possible until 1932, when the state legislature enacted a law permitting counties to levy taxes for fire protection.[7]

In the mid-1920s the commission inaugurated a program of tree planting, and in 1930 the first nursery in the state was established in cooperation with the U.S. Forest Service. In 1939 another state nursery was constructed in conjunction with the CCC at Mt. Olive, and by 1945 this nursery distributed more than 2.7 million seedlings to state landowners. In 1946 the commission established another nursery at Winona, which began production in 1948. By 1950 the two nurseries were producing 24 million seedlings annually. The MFC eventually acquired yet another nursery, the Waynesboro Nursery, in 1956. The capacity of this facility was 50 million seedlings per year, and by 1959 seedling production in the state nurseries reached 105 million.

In the late 1960s a program to produce nursery seedlings from superior stock was initiated. The program included both the collection of seed from high-quality trees and the establishment of a superior seed orchard on Kurtz State Forest (Mississippi's only state forest). The ultimate goal was to establish 325 acres of superior tree-seed orchards. In 1974 the MFC purchased 480 acres from Crown Zellerbach in Lamar County, near Lumberton, to be utilized for the establishment of tree-seed orchards and related genetic projects. The commission also employed a tree-improvement forester, who was assigned to the Kurtz and Baxterville seed orchards. In 1980 the first superior seed was collected from the Kurtz orchard.[8]

By the mid-1930s the commission was supervising management practices, including planting, thinning, pruning, and selective cutting on forests belonging to the University of Mississippi in the southeastern part of the state as well as cutover lands adjacent to roads in the Delta. A later commission history proclaimed this effort "the beginning of real forest management in the Delta." Over the years the MFC implemented programs to promote forestry on private lands and to assist landowners in various forestry-related activities. However, the commission had a hard-and-fast rule that its foresters would not compete with foresters engaged in private practice. The American Forestry Association assisted the commission's work during the 1920s and 1930s, providing money that, combined with state funding, paid for a forest-education program in cooperation with the commission. The educational messages emphasized fire protection and timber growing. The commission did valuable work over the years in helping to restore Mississippi's forests, although its claim in a 1976 publication that the reasons for this regeneration "lies largely in the history of the Forestry Commission and its achievements" is overstated and ignores the contributions of other public agencies, private organizations, forest-products companies, and individual landowners.[9]

The most glamorous conservation organization of the Great Depression era was the CCC. The longtime executive secretary of the Society of American Foresters and managing editor of the *Journal of Forestry* termed the creation of the CCC "the single event which was to do more than any other to dramatize and publicize forest conservation." He said that federal and state conservation programs were advanced from twenty-five to forty years as a result of the corps' work.

As the Forest Service acquired land for national forests, the young men of the CCC went to work. CCC camps were created in various parts of Mississippi in 1933. At its peak, the corps had 311 forestry camps in the South, with 125 on national forests and 186 under state foresters. Many of the corpsmen worked under the direction of professional foresters who were hired to supervise reclamation projects. CCC workers installed towers and telephones for fire fighting as well as training personnel. They also planted trees from seedlings grown at the U.S. Forest Service Nursery and at the state nursery, which they established at Stone-Harrison Junior College at Perkinston. A new national nursery was established on the De Soto National Forest, and it produced 20 million trees in 1937, including longleaf, slash, loblolly, and shortleaf pine. The CCC workers also built roads, bridges, and recreation areas.

The type and volume of the work is demonstrated by the performance of Company 4441 at Camp F-24, near Richton and Piave in southeast Mississippi. Work began on clearing land and constructing buildings in the summer of 1935, and within two years the company had planted 6,397,108 pine trees, built twenty-six miles of road, and constructed forty-five miles of hog-proof barbed-wire fence. It also built seven creosote bridges, maintained fifty miles of fire lanes, and put up ten miles of permanent telephone lines.

By the time the CCC programs were terminated in 1942, the corps had undertaken timber-stand improvement on 1,629,218 acres in the southern national forests. Corpsmen had planted and seeded on 273,806 acres and seeded and sodded on 909,704 square yards of gullies, with additional treatment of 412,069 square yards of gullies. They had built 11,225 miles of truck trails (seventy miles in Mississippi); 1,968 vehicle bridges; 103 foot/horse bridges; 197 lookout

Grading and counting seedlings at the Mt. Olive Nursery. Courtesy Mississippi Forestry Commission, Jackson.

towers (fourteen in Mississippi); sixty-four look-out houses; thirty-six shelters; 238 barns; sixty-six cabins; 146 dwellings; 496 equipment or storage supply houses; 205 latrines; 571 miscellaneous buildings; 1,497 sewage and water disposal systems; 6,169 signs, markers, and monuments; and 6,028 miles of telephone lines (395 miles in Mississippi). In Mississippi the CCC had collected 6,381 bushels of pine cones for seed and had planted 1,098 acres of trees. The corps obviously contributed enormously to the revitalization of Mississippi's national forests. Neshoba County's Edgar Pope remembered that the CCC workers "would set out trees. . . . That's the reason we've got timber here now. Started back there, and people seen that they would grow. You could reforest." The young corpsmen, despite their impressive accomplishments, did not spend all of their time working. As Marie King, who lived near a CCC camp, remembered, "I'll say one thing—they married some of our 'old maids' in the community!"[10]

Another New Deal agency concerned with re-

forestation and responsible forest management was the Tennessee Valley Authority, created in 1933. In addition to focusing on flood control, navigation, and power generation, the TVA promoted reforestation, fire control, and soil conservation on the denuded lands and worn-out farms in its region. Part of its concern was with eliminating soil erosion and siltation of its reservoirs. The agency hired a forestry staff, established two seedling nurseries, set up demonstration projects, and cooperated actively with federal and state agencies. Its lakes provided recreation, and some of its lands ultimately became state parks, such as J. P. Coleman State Park in northeast Mississippi, near Iuka.[11]

Another group of public foresters and scientists that played a critical role in the resurgence of Mississippi's forests operated out of a modest research facility at Stoneville, in the Delta. As early as 1927 the forestry commission authorized state forester Hogue to hire a man to work in cooperation with the state of Louisiana and the Southern Forest Experiment Station to investigate growth on Mississippi's hardwood forests. No such data were available, and the research conducted by the man Hogue hired, John A. Putnam, is believed to be the first growth studies of southern hardwoods to be conducted anywhere.

The Southern Hardwoods Laboratory was a product of the cooperation of the U.S. Forest Service, the Delta Council of Mississippi, the Mississippi Agricultural Experiment Station, and the Southern Forest Experiment Station. Putnam became its leader and started work with four foresters. Twelve scientists eventually served on the staff, studying the management, protection, and use of southern hardwoods, with major emphases in four areas: diseases, insects, product utilization, and timber management. Much of the work focused on demonstration forests at varying sites to show landowners that depleted stands could be restored to health and profitability. Putnam had completed three and a half years toward a forestry degree at the University of Michigan and had then gone to Gould, Arkansas, to manage a hardwood lumber company. Putnam became known as "Mr. Hardwoods," and forester E. C. Burkhardt of Vicksburg credited Putnam with an "evangelistic spirit," as he became "what could be called 'hardwood forester at large,' sharing his vast store of knowledge with industries and agencies across the South." Joseph Sidney McKnight became Mr. Hardwoods' understudy in 1942 and eventually his successor.

The laboratory originated in 1936 when the Mississippi legislature designated a tract of land at Stoneville for research in cottonwood planting and improvement cutting. It consisted of some 2,600 acres of tax-delinquent forestland in the Yazoo-Mississippi Delta that were turned over to the state Agricultural Experiment Station. The land was later named the Delta Experimental Forest. The researchers quickly became quite interested in cottonwood, the fastest-growing tree in North America, and used it to help reclaim abandoned, submarginal agricultural land, a process that became one of the project's continuing foci. The problem these pio-

neers faced was reflected in the title of a 1939 Southern Forest Experiment Station report, "What Are We Going to Do with Our Hardwoods?" The author, Cap Eldredge, expressed surprise on learning that "in both area and volume there is more hardwood timber in the lower South than there is pine." He argued that scientific research to make southern hardwoods suitable for pulping represented their best use for the future. In 1951 the laboratory published a guide to management of natural hardwood stands; it was revised and reissued in 1960 as *Management and Inventory of Southern Hardwoods* and became the standard work on the subject.[12]

The laboratory's staff and supporters sometimes felt that they were an endangered minority in a land dominated by southern pine. They may have been a little paranoid as they struggled to convince the world of hardwood's value and that it, not pine, should be planted and maintained in certain settings, especially in highlands and along stream bottoms. According to the laboratory's director, "hardwoods cover more than 40 million acres of river bottoms, swamps, creek courses, and loess hills in the South. There are at least 70 commercially important species, and they supply 40 percent of the raw material required by the southern forest industry to make lumber, veneer, dimension stock, specialties, cooperage, and . . . lumber for furniture, flooring, and boxes takes the major portion of the hardwood production." He also argued that "[i]n the South, the hardwood forest is indisputedly the best habitat and food source for deer and squirrel. The swamps, sloughs, lakes, and streams in and near hardwood stands teem with fish and attract and sustain waterfowl." He also warned that the "[f]ertile, deep soil and nearby sources of water create the conditions that make possible the lush growth of southern hardwood forests. These same conditions create a demand for use of the sites for farmland, reservoirs, waterways, wildlife preserves, and, in a few cases, pine tree production. Thus the hardwood forest must grow at its maximum and yield its full multiple benefits if it is to compete successfully with the numerous other land uses on an economic basis."[13]

The same interest in forestry and forest management that animated the creators of the Southern Hardwoods Laboratory and the MFC also inspired the citizens from all over Mississippi who organized the MFA in 1938. Among the participants were landowners, forest-products companies, businessmen, banks, and other citizens and organizations interested in the sensible management and use of the state's forests, soil, water, and wildlife resources. Henry T. Crosby of Greenville, who later served on the forestry commission, was MFA's first president, and Howard Suttle was the first field director.

The first executive secretary was Frank B. Pittman. Born in Wayne County, Pittman graduated from Mississippi A&M and worked as a county agent and farm manager. He was then elected to the state senate from Pearl River County and served the MFA from 1940 until 1958. As a state senator, Pittman was secretary of a joint committee to study forestry conditions in the state. The committee held hearings throughout Mississippi and developed proposals for legislation to address the problems. The committee recommended twelve bills in 1940, and most were enacted, in part through Pittman's efforts. Also, as the MFA's leader, Pittman was instrumental in the passage of the timber severance-tax laws, the establishment of the forestry school at Mississippi State University, and the sponsorship of the Boys' Conservation School, held in state parks during the summer, as well as the Mississippi tree farm program.

The MFA was also involved in the successful effort to introduce a forestry textbook, the *Mississippi Forest Reader,* into the public-school system for use in the seventh grade and the 1945 implementation of a public-relations campaign called "Keep Mississippi's Forests Green." The MFA became known as an organization that bridged the gaps between various public and private interests, including private landowners, the forest-products industries, state government agencies, and Mississippi's national forests.[14]

Professional foresters and land managers during the 1930s and 1940s confronted a wide range of problems. The severity and extent of these problems varied from property to property and from site to site. Thus, the prescription for one property or site could differ considerably from that for another. Also, the objectives of a particular landowner affected both long-range and short-range planning and decision making. Industrial foresters knew and accepted the idea that economics would usually be the final determinant of their actions. Long-range plans would sometimes be altered by short-run economic considerations. Industrial foresters realized full well that to separate problems and issues into "forestry" problems and "business" problems was artificial. Virtually every decision an industrial forester made was a forestry decision as well as a business decision, and it was sometimes a social decision, too. Looming large was always the matter of owner objectives. An industrial forester or land manager who ignored that dimension of his situation was soon unemployed. As Austin Cary put it in 1899, "Should the forestry practiced lead to loss, the business goes down and the forester's position and opportunity go with it."[15]

Some general patterns were evident across the South as these pioneer foresters viewed their terrain. First, most were dealing with cutover lands that had been left in pretty sad shape by lumber companies or other owners who had lacked the time, money, knowledge, or inclination to manage them responsibly with an eye toward regeneration. How to replenish and restore these lands was a major early consideration, and numerous factors would affect the prescriptions.

Second, the fire problem was endemic in the South. A product of culture, neglect, and poverty, wildfire and incendiary fires constantly threatened southern timberland owners and managers. It made little sense to put a lot of effort and money into managing timberland if it was likely to be destroyed by fire. Getting fire under control was a necessity and a major problem.

Third was the task of establishing and maintaining boundary lines, a critical problem on privately owned or leased lands. In many cases the old lumber companies had done a very poor job of determining and maintaining their boundary lines, and neighboring farmers were more than happy to encroach on the lands of their larger neighbors, farming some of these lands, grazing cattle and hogs on them, burning them, and sometimes legally claiming them through the doctrine of adverse possession. Clarifying boundary lines was a major priority of the early industrial foresters and land managers.

Early private land managers' concerns included taxation. It was not feasible to put a lot of money into managing lands and producing a crop of timber if excessive taxation endangered the opportunity for profit. Part of early industrial foresters' and land managers' jobs was to deal with neighbors, government representatives, and politicians and to attempt to create an atmosphere of goodwill in which the industry and company would be treated fairly.

Early industrial foresters were also affected by the prevailing lack of silvicultural knowledge. While the work of people like Mohr, Herty, Eldredge, Hardtner, and others had provided a foundation, much remained to be learned. The foresters of the 1930s, 1940s, and 1950s were developing the information and knowledge that gave their counterparts of the 1990s a greater arsenal of information on which to base decisions.

There was also the problem of community relations. The forest-products industry drew much of its wood supply from small, neighboring landowners. Thus, it made good business sense to promote improved forest practices on these lands so that they would become more productive and so that the company would have the opportunity to purchase their timber. Also, fire and boundary problems were affected by relationships with the local community, in addition to government relations and taxation.

As noted earlier, the industrial foresters of the 1930s and 1940s often found themselves dealing with properties that had been left in deplorable condition. The Capper Report of the early 1920s indicated that one-fourth of the land cut over by

the lumber industry had been left totally barren. Much of the land that had been converted into farms had long since been abandoned. The first director of the Southern Forest Experiment Station wrote a dramatic essay that described the "ghostly desolation" of thousands of square miles of land that had once been covered by magnificent virgin forests.[16]

The implications of this situation were far-reaching, for "not only were the best trees cut, the worst were left to reproduce. Destruction did not stop with the forest. The relationship between forests and soil, rivers, and wildlife amplified the losses, implying disruption of the linked systems which constituted the natural regimen of the landscape." One overly dramatic description of the land said, "Cool, green shadows of the virgin forest were only memories, and no longer did the resinous breezes sing through the tufted tree crowns. Instead the refuse of logging lay bleaching in the sun on millions of acres. Except for stumps and an occasional 'mule tail' pine the bared land was reminiscent of the western plains. Scrawny cattle picked at the coarse grass and razorback hogs rooted out the remaining seedlings. Buzzards circled overhead and frequently feasted on the carcass of a cow that had succumbed to the twin hazards of ticks and starvation."[17]

Industrial foresters who worked with the land in that period left descriptions that are only slightly less graphic. Arthur W. Nelson Jr. remembered that when he went to work for the Flintkote Company in Mississippi during the early 1940s, the company's properties consisted largely of "abandoned, submarginal land." Dick Allen joined the DeWeese Lumber Company of Philadelphia, Mississippi, in 1946 and said that at that time, "there had never been any selective cutting or forestry work done in that country. . . . It was just ridiculous. Everything was clear-cut."[18]

Despite these gloomy descriptions, some factors obviously attracted pulp and paper companies to acquire lands that seemed so thoroughly exploited and unattractive. First, they were cheap. Large amounts of land were virtually abandoned because their owners could not afford to pay taxes. Second, the companies needed the land. The industry's resource base in the Northeast was declining, and the companies needed new sources of supply. Third, the southern cutover lands were not quite what they seemed on the surface. The potential was there for profitable regeneration and on a fairly short-term basis.

Two factors brought industrial foresters and paper companies to this realization. First was the 1932 Forest Survey of the U.S. Forest Service conducted in the South under Eldredge's direction. This effort was the biggest timber cruise in the world, and it revealed some startling informa-tion—the pines were reviving. The survey re-vealed that far more timber remained in the South than anyone had previously imagined, and the report included precisely the kind of informa-tion about volume, mortality, and net growth that industry needed. For the mid-South as a whole, the survey revealed that about 80 percent of forestland was stocked with various degrees of second growth, while about 5 percent was un-stocked, and 15 percent contained uncut or par-tially cut stands of old growth.[19]

Second was the evidence on the land itself. While it was true that some of the loggers had left no seed trees at all, much of the cutover land

Cutover land reseeding naturally from seed trees in Harrison County, Mississippi, 1937. Cour-tesy Mississippi Forestry Commission, Jackson.

had not been cleared in a literal sense but had been "high-graded." As Allen remembered, "Clear-cut in those days are cuts to a diameter limit. . . . [Y]ou cut the big timber first. . . . So there was still plenty of seed left on the ground when you were through." Nelson said, "In many instances, the abandoned fields had seeded up directly in pine seedlings, giving rise to what is known as an 'old field' stand."[20]

What could the new stewards of the land do? According to IP executive Fred Gragg, "Management consisted mostly of trying to establish fire protection. The only method of regenerating was to try to protect enough seed trees to acquire reestablishment of the stand by natural reproduction." Where the young pines were already coming back, the companies tried to remove the overstory of older pines or hardwoods that was retarding the growth of young seedlings. Describing this kind of activity, Nelson noted, "Almost everything that we did, we copied from other earlier paper company efforts in the South, to take similar properties and get them into shape." Looking at the situation from an optimistic perspective, a 1938 editorialist in the *Journal of Forestry* argued, "There now appears to be a general awakening in the lumber industry to the fact that timber is a crop. No longer do progressive lumbermen regard timber merely as a God-given resource to be exploited with no consideration for the future." The editorial noted that "the most rapid advance in industrial forestry is being made in the South" and cited especially the adoption of harvesting standards by the pulp and paper industry. The success of these industry efforts would depend in part on the companies' ability to generate support, or at least to negate harassment, from their neighbors.[21]

Given the large percentage of southern timberland that was privately owned and the forest-products industry's heavy dependence on those lands for part of its wood supply, cultivating and maintaining good relationships with neighboring landowners was a very important part of the industrial forester's job. It would have been at the very least counterproductive to operate in the manner of pioneering forester Dr. Carl Alwyn Schenck, who in Eldredge's words, "being a German and fresh from Germany . . . couldn't understand the independence of the backwoodsman . . . who did things for which they would have had their heads cut off in Germany or, at least, be put in prison. . . . But here they'd be taken to court and the juries would turn them loose. It takes years to know how to handle the backwoods people, and it is never easy."[22]

While there were many dimensions to the relationship between forest-products companies and their neighbors, there were three areas in particular where the goodwill of the backwoods people of the South was critically important— wood supply, government relations, and fire protection. On the wood-supply front, Nelson noted that "when you worked with your neighbors . . . you'd find out who else would have some timber to sell."[23] It stands to reason that good relationships meant more timber for the company.

Jeff Hughes, longtime Crown Zellerbach forester and manager, emphasized the importance of community relations in shaping the governmental climate, noting, "You're at the mercy of public opinion. . . . They can increase taxes. . . . They can complain about your forest-management practices. . . . We operate at the mercy of the public. . . . There're laws that can be passed . . . logging restrictions, restrictions on the use of the public roads. . . . They can and do lobby legislatures and they do call their legislator . . . and they do vote—and they can seriously affect your ability to do business." Allen also emphasized the importance of community relations as it affects the political process: "A large company always has critics. And the local people around that ownership each sometimes have five or six members in their family that vote, and when legislation comes up that's detrimental to forestry, they'd think about, maybe those big companies were the only ones that profit from that, and if you have been workin' with them as neighbors, and helpin' 'em fight their fires, and helpin' them with their forestry problems, then you receive support with legislation for forestry and taxation." And some

Mississippians and politicians were bothered by the size of the large companies landholdings.[24]

The third area of community relations, fire prevention and control, was in some ways most critical. Without controlling wildfire, there was little point in attempting to regenerate and manage timberlands. IP forester and manager John Tyler, who worked around Canton, addressed the situation directly: "You have to get along with your neighbors. There is no other way out of it. . . . If they know who you are, and are on speakin' terms with you, they are not gonna burn you." And good community relations were important in fire control as well as prevention. As Allen emphasized, "We found that if we helped that neighbor, that neighbor helped us. . . . If fire got on his land and we stopped it, then he would say, 'Well, those people must be all right. They're helping their neighbor.' And he would help us keep fire off of our land. Many times, many times at night I would get calls—not many phones out in the country then—but I'd get a call, somebody would ride a horse several miles to get to a phone and let me know that a fire had started back in the woods. And I would go out and of course, we always made a point of thankin' 'em."[25]

Hughes summed up the situation when he said that "all good forest managers have to recognize that their success in managing a forest property really depends upon the good will . . . of [their] neighbors." "I use a different term for it," said former IP forester and manager Bob Nonnemacher, who worked for a time in Mississippi. "I call it statesmanship of the industry. . . . Ultimately it would benefit the industry by having more timber available throughout the South."[26]

Community relations was most immediately important in the area of fire prevention and control because of the historical traditions of southern incendiarism and wildfire and because of the tremendous threat that fire posed for timberland owners. Jonathan Daniels described the problem in 1957:

Fire is people. Nowhere is that so true as in the South, which has more than four-fifths of all the forest fires in the nation, and four-fifths, too, of all the area burned over year after year. The more tragic fact is that the South has 90 per cent of all the incendiary fires in the United States. It means faceless people making time bombs of cigarettes and matches, candles and cans which can be left in the woods to start the blaze after they have slipped away. It means the deliberate burning off of somebody else's land to open the woods to the quick growth of "sorry grass for sorry cattle." . . . Perhaps such action can be explained by the statement that it is a heritage from the frontier, when the forest could be regarded as open range for scrub cattle. In the sly setting of such fires, the arsonists themselves know they are not acting like pioneers. Certainly, no such claim can be made by hunters who deliberately set fires to provide a feeding and gathering place for wild turkey. There are grudge fires. Some grudges are of recent origin—some undoubtedly stem from ancient grudges going back through old Southern days when clusters of the landless squatted sullenly beside the great plantations. Also, apparently there are pastoral pyromaniacs who just like to see the forest in blaze and the exhausted wardens and foresters working desperately with small tools and great mechanized fire-fighting equipment to put it out. There was one case of a school bus driver who, for no reason he could afterward give, stopped his bus three times and, while the children watched, started three fires in the woods. There are the less deliberate, but no less dangerous, people who burn over their own lands every year in an ancient fatuous folkway which holds that such burning not only clears the brush but also gets rid of the snakes and eliminates the boll weevil. Actually, such burning bakes the soil and destroys the humus. . . . Yet, clear and present as is the danger of fire, the number of woods fires in the South has been hardly more remarkable than the reluctance of prosecutors and juries, even judges, to punish those caught most red-handed with the burning brand in their hands or squatting furtively over delayed-action fire-fuses which they intended to leave behind.[27]

Companies faced daunting difficulties in trying to protect their lands. In 1940 the Crosby Lumber Company owned more than 100,000 acres of land, which it tried to protect despite considerable obstacles. As a company statement put it, "Although the Crosby Company recognizes that fire protection is essential, it receives no cooperation from the State. Accordingly, the company has its own crews available for fire fighting, pays all bills in connection therewith, and employs two or three foresters. . . . To encourage and maintain the best possible local cooperation . . . the company, is sponsoring the Homochitto Fire Protection Contest among the school districts of the county. The children of each school strive to secure the best record with regard to fires, and prizes are contributed by the Crosby Lumber Company. In addition, the company makes available to each of the schools a subscription to *American Forests*." However, hope turned to disillusionment. L. O. Crosby Jr. later remembered, "One of the biggest problems I had was when I went into the reforesting in a big way we had so much trouble with the open range and cattle and sheep people burning the woods. . . . Some of them just became firebugs. One March, let's see, it must have been about 1950, some of the men came in one night smutty, black from the fires. They had fought forest fires all day long. We had better than 50,000 acres burned in one day there, going from the Hancock County line up. . . . In one day. They were burning as fast as they could try to fight down there. I just for a while, gave up on forestry. I said 'If that is going to be the way it is, there is no use to go into it. It is just [useless].'"[28]

The attitudes that forest managers and companies faced among those who were burning off the woods were primitive and rooted in deep-seated cultural and psychological conditions. These views were expressed very simply and directly, as in the case of a southern backwoodsman who stated, "Woods burnin' 's right. We allus done it. Our pappies burned th' woods an' their pappies afore 'em. It was right fer them an' it's right fer us." Philip C. Wakeley, who spent forty years in research at the Southern Forest Experiment Station, remembered, "Fire crews had to be doubled every Christmas Day, on which it was an old southern custom to shoot off fire-

crackers. Families too poor to afford holiday firecrackers for their children used to pack picnic baskets, go out and start fires in the company's woods, and watch them burn while they ate lunch." Thomas C. Croker Jr., another longtime forester with the Southern Forest Experiment Station, reported that in areas where the CCC was involved in fire prevention and suppression, some old-timers "set fires out of spite so the boys would have to work on Sundays and holidays. Sometimes the boys caught these old codgers in the act, and their supervisors had trouble keeping the crews from inflicting severe bodily harm to the firebugs."[29]

Why did they do it? In the late 1930s U.S. Forest Service psychologist John Shea conducted interviews with hundreds of rural southerners and concluded that they burned the woods because of psychological necessity: "With the closing in of the agrarian environment, it has become predominantly a recreational and emotional impulse. . . . [T]he light and sound and odor of burning woods provide excitement for a people who dwell in an environment of low stimulation and who naturally crave excitement. . . . Their explanations that woods fires kill off snakes, boll weevil and serve other economic ends are something more than mere ignorance. They are the defensive beliefs of a disadvantaged culture group."[30]

The subject continued to fascinate foresters, rural sociologists, psychologists, and other observers of southern society over the following decades. One writer in 1964 attributed the problem to "human careless or 'cussedness'" and concluded, somewhat simplistically, "all we need to do is teach people not to start them." A 1975 study noted that "it appears that fire-setting is more a matter of culture than of socio-demographic characteristics." A 1979 report concluded, "Most active woods-burners are young, white males whose activities are supported by their peers. An older but less active group have probably retired from active participation but act as patriarchs of the burning community. A small group whose actions are generally disapproved by the community and who are suspected of other illegal acts complete the major categories of wood-burners."[31]

Retired Crown Zellerbach forester Hughes came to many of the same conclusions, although without the psychiatric overtones: "We could spend all evening . . . talking about the reasons why people burn the woods. . . . I think the people that grew up, especially in the range area, believin' that the woods should be burned for the benefit of cattle, they believed that it kept the snakes down, they believed it eliminated mosquitoes and the ticks to some extent. It made it . . . easier to see game, to hunt, and all of those things entered into it. I think some of them just have a desire to see fire in the woods." Historian Thomas D. Clark blamed "ignorance and malevolence on the part of far too many people." "Burning of Southern woods at annual intervals reflected meanness, ignorance, and folklore."[32]

Certain areas were hot spots where the incidence of incendiary fires was unusually high. Of seventy-nine Mississippi counties that had fire protection by the early 1970s, twenty-three had very high fire rates. Another fourteen had rates classified as high. Most of the major fire problem was in the southern third of the state, with a block of eighteen of the southernmost counties in the very high category. Another three counties in this category—Alcorn, Lee, and Tishomingo—are in the extreme northeastern part of Mississippi.[33]

Coburn L. Weston of the Weston Lumber Company described the fire problem in a 1973 interview, noting, "I recall one old gentleman near Picayune up there said that as long as they made matches he would burn the woods, and I think he did every year—a certain time of year, late fall, he would get out and burn thousands of acres of land. . . . [T]hey would burn it and you couldn't stop them." Horatio S. Weston, Coburn's uncle, was one of the pioneers in Mississippi fire protection. At the time the MFC was created to bring forest management and fire protection to the state, Weston provided a dramatic demonstration of his enthusiasm and support. He shut down his two sawmills and put his employees to work clearing fire lanes, putting up fences to keep out

hogs, and erecting the state's first fire tower. He also erected telephone lines from the tower to various parts of the county and joined with two other landowners to create crews to assist all forest owners in fighting forest fires.[34]

The losses from fires were staggering. This development was nothing new, for the South traditionally dominated national fire statistics, both in terms of frequency and acreage burned. Nine of every ten forest acres burned in the nation were in the South. Mississippi suffered more devastation from wildfire than any other state. An American Forestry Association survey covering the period from 1917 to 1927 revealed that fires burned roughly one-third of the South's entire pine area. It was estimated that more than 98 percent of these fires were caused by humans. Between 1917 and 1926, 80 percent of all reported forest fires occurred in the South.[35]

It was with good reason that industrial foresters in the 1930s and 1940s regarded fire prevention and control as their first priority. In a 1941 Society of American Foresters meeting, P. M. Garrison, chief forester of the Gaylord Container Corporation, argued that "fire constitutes 90 percent of the South's forestry problem! This statement is so generally accepted by all southern foresters, regardless of field of employment, that it is no longer possible to generate an argument on the subject." The belief that fire prevention and suppression were the keys to the restoration of the southern forests was the conventional wisdom among foresters and federal and state policy makers. Congress addressed the problem by passing legislation that provided federal matching funds for state fire protection, but federal funds were inadequate and state cooperation sporadic and underfunded. In 1916 the American Forestry Association, Society of American Foresters, and various conservation groups organized a Southern Forestry Congress that promoted forest protection. Several subsequent congresses met through 1930. The Association of State Foresters, founded in 1920, eventually took the lead in promoting southern forest protection. In 1950 the American Forestry Association sponsored a highly publicized conference that concentrated heavily on fire legislation and law enforcement, spurring state actions against arsonists.[36]

The origins of organized fire control in the South date back to the early part of the century, when a few lumber companies, notably Crossett and Urania, attempted to protect their lands. The Weeks Act of 1911 initiated a program of federal-state cooperation in fire protection. Some areas had cooperative fire-control associations, and some states created forestry agencies, but they were not at all effective until the 1924 passage of the Clarke-McNary Act, which expanded the provisions of the Weeks Act and brought the U.S. Forest Service into the South as a large forest landowner and cooperator. The CCC during the Great Depression helped to create a large organizational apparatus and facilitated the acquisition of fire-control equipment. When the CCC was disbanded, public agencies and private companies moved toward mechanization to replace the labor-intensive system that the federal agency had provided.[37]

The American Forestry Association in 1927 undertook one of the most ambitious efforts to eliminate the fire problem through public education. The campaign was conceptualized and inspired by Ovid Butler, the association's executive secretary. With $260,000 in funds from state forestry agencies, citizens' organizations, and private individuals, in 1928 the association promulgated a three-year program that targeted Florida, Georgia, South Carolina, and Mississippi. This Southern Forestry Educational Project featured a team of young, southern-born, southern-educated foresters called the Dixie Crusaders.

The crusaders traveled in fleets of International trucks festooned with antifire slogans, giving talks and showing movies on fire prevention at schools, at churches, and before civic groups in even the most rural areas. The crusaders also visited sawmills and turpentine camps. By the end of

"Dixie Crusaders" truck in Bay St. Louis, Mississippi, 1929. Courtesy Louisiana Department of Agriculture and Forestry, Baton Rouge.

1931 every rural school in the four states had been visited at least once. The staff members wrote, produced, and acted in their own movies when they found the existing ones boring and ineffective. One of their productions, "Burnin' Bill," was especially popular with their audiences.

The project leader was W. C. McCormick, and Erle Kauffman, who later became the editor of *American Forests* magazine, was the force behind the movies. The Dixie Crusaders made their presentations before an estimated 3 million adults and children, traveled 300,000 miles, and distributed an estimated 2 million posters, leaflets, and bulletins. During thirty-three months on the road, the Dixie Crusaders presented 7,371 shows and lectures and 259 exhibits at fairs. They enjoyed the cooperation of the U.S. Forest Service and the state forestry associations and agencies. One forester who helped to present the shows estimated that 90 percent of those who attended not only believed in annual woods burning but also participated in it.

Mississippi State Forester Fred Merrill considered the project a success in combating the fire problem. Howell argued that the project's value "has been such as to revolutionize our people in their regard for forest protection and reforestation." I. J. Turner, the principal of Flora Rosenwald School at Flora, reflected "the sentiment of 500 colored citizens" in observing that "much good will follow[s] the service. . . . Our children now talk of carefulness about fire." Mississippi state senator Willie David Womack Jr. of Belzoni in Humphreys County remembered in 1954, "I have been interested in forestry ever since that young feller drove a truck up to our schoolhouse and spent an afternoon showing us motion pictures and talking about pine trees. I've never forgotten what he said."[38]

The origins of Mississippi's organized state fire-protection system date back to the early 1930s, following an earlier system of "protective units," but it was underfinanced and not very effective. The MFC also promoted fire prevention through meetings with community groups, movies, forestry field days, and other activities,

with the first program introduced in Simpson County.[39]

Full-scale fire-control efforts were not possible until 1932, when the state legislature passed a law permitting counties to levy taxes for fire protection. The counties could request countywide fire protection from the MFC and reimburse the commission with revenues from a two-cents-per-acre tax on forest and uncultivated land. During World War II, the federal government provided special emergency funds under the Clarke-McNary Act for fire protection, and Mississippi used the money to greatly expand its system. The Mississippi Forestry and Chemurgic Association also emphasized fire prevention, as in the poem, "De Woods of Pine," by Warren Nicke, published in its *Forest Facts* magazine in 1942:

> An old darkey singin' in de woods of pine,
> A-workin de trees fer turpentine;
> "My luck, hit grows with de piney wood
> An' while pines grow my luck stays good—
> Food in de kitchen and times ain't hard,
> When a man works out in God's front yard.". . .
>
> When you hear de big, ole pine trees moan
> Dere's a fire in de woods dat makes dem groan.
> De little fire kills de li'l baby trees
> De grass and de birds, but no ticks or fleas;
> De big fires kill de big trees too—
> We gotta stop fires, whatever we do!!!
>
> *Chorus*
> Pay-day's comin' while de pine trees grow,
> Hit's de surest thing dat a man can know.
> When de old piney wood ain' heah no more
> De wolf am a-comin' right in de door.[40]

In the early years, fire-fighting equipment was primitive: hand rakes, fire flaps, backpack pumps, and even pine tops were the standard tools. Lookouts were stationed in tall trees that functioned as fire towers, and permanent firebreaks did not become common until later. Spotters telephoned to crews standing by, who would then race in their Model Ts to the fire. Chronically short of funds, the Mississippi Forest Service improvised and developed cut-rate equipment, such as homemade fire finders to be used in the state's towers. As the Louisiana state forester later remembered, "The basic concept of fire fighting in the South from the beginning of the effort was a direct attack on the small fire with a fire rake and a fire flap, the latter consisting of a piece of heavy belting securely fastened to a hoe handle. The flap was the more widely used of the two for many years because it was light and easily transported on muleback."[41]

Nelson remembered that one old-timer told him, "You will never be able to keep fire out of these woods." "The State forestry crews . . . were very poorly manned, very poorly financed in the very early days," he recalled. Looking back on his experiences with Flintkote, Nelson recalled, "In the very early days we used the backpack pump and we carried spare water around in old milk cans. The prevention of woods fires was rather new in that area and we had quite a lot of fires to attend to. . . . [T]he Mississippi Forestry Association had towers around, but they were very poorly financed and they had only one primitive fire crew per district again which only had hand tools. . . . The only communication that was between the towers were telephones. We were equipped with a folding pole, with two copper clips on it and a portable telephone and we could stop anywhere along the road where the forestry telephone was and put this pole up and hook it on the wires and talk to the tower men to find out what was going on with the various fires. We did not get two-way radios until 1946."[42]

Much of the equipment that became standard for firefighters by 1940 was developed by the U.S. Forest Service, including the fire rake, flap, backpack pump, backfiring torch, portable pumps, and tractor-powered fire line plows. The Panama Pump Company of Hattiesburg developed a truck-mounted pump with a fifty-gallon tank that could fight fire directly, refill backpack pumps, and be refilled from a creek through a suction hose. By 1940 the standard method of detection in Mississippi counties that had fire protection was one-hundred-foot steel lookout towers. The towers were connected by open-wire magneto telephone lines. The fire location was determined by triangulation from two or more towers. Fire crews were stationed at the towers during fire seasons and dispatched from those points. Once the crews left the towers there was no way to contact them until two-way FM mobile radios became available at the end of World War II and enabled communication from tower to crew, from crew to crew, and between towers or crews and the newly utilized fire-patrol airplanes.[43]

In 1934 the total area burned in Mississippi was less than 5 million acres for the first time since the forestry commission's creation in 1926. By mid-1935 thirteen counties had state fire protection covering 3 million acres of land. Fire-protection efforts were also bolstered by the CCC, which built fire towers, installed telephones, and trained fire-fighting personnel. Jack Hollingsworth, a forester employed by the U.S. Forest Service as a foreman and project superintendent with the CCC in Mississippi, remembered that "without the CCC boys I don't know what we would have done. . . . The Forest Service would take them and train them in this fire fighting before they ever went on a fire, so they were well trained and without them . . . [t]he whole National Forests would have just burned off every Spring."[44]

The disbanding of the CCC in 1942 as well as the loss of fire-fighting personnel to the military hurt fire-protection efforts. State funding remained meager. By 1940 the fire-protection appropriation for the biennium was just forty-five thousand dollars, and only twenty-one counties were under organized fire protection. In 1943 Mississippi state forestry appropriations totaled $11,267, while the neighboring states of Alabama and Louisiana appropriated $103,873 and $129,759, respectively. As late as 1936 the commission's total fire-control equipment consisted of 264 flaps, 240 rakes, 252 pumps, six lookout towers, one fire truck, one pickup truck, and one automobile.

From 1934 through 1937 Mississippi ranked first among eleven southern states in lumber pro-

Early fire tower. Courtesy
Mississippi Forestry
Commission, Jackson.

Art Nelson with early two-
way radio experimental
set. Courtesy Art Nelson.

duction but last in state appropriations for forestry programs. The results were predictable. In 1944 75 percent of all fires reported and 96 percent of all acreage burned in Mississippi were on unprotected lands. In 1947 an official of the Gaylord Container Corporation in Bogalusa, Louisiana, flew to Jackson and back and reported, "The State of Mississippi has damned near burned clean—not meaning all the timber has been destroyed but an unbelievable quantity of young growth has been destroyed and damaged in the last two years." He noted that on the morning flight to Jackson he saw no fires, but on the way back in the afternoon he "counted twenty-eight fires burning merrily within a radius of perhaps fifteen miles over a 14,000 acre tract we own in Simpson County." The official commented that the MFC admitted that "both fire prevention and fire suppression were very ineffectively handled in Mississippi."[45]

The forestry commission obviously was poorly equipped to deal with the fire problem, particularly in the areas of Mississippi where the incidence of fire was unusually high. Tyler remembered that in 1945 "there was very little

fire-control activity other than what the state was offering. And they had an inadequate number of . . . tractors and plows . . . to handle the situation." Tyler describes the way IP foresters stepped into the breach: "we built equipment depots . . . five different ones . . . and we had at least one mechanized unit, which was a tractor, plow, and a truck, at each one of those with radios. We had a base radio in our office . . . and we had radios tied in with the state fire towers. We did not use at that time any aerial activity, but we had our radio system set up. . . . I built . . . a little station right at the base of the fire tower where we put in our own radio setup and crossed radios with the state there." "We had a very good fire-control system," Tyler concluded. Gragg later noted that "the typical industry fire crew helps to suppress more fires occurring off of its lands than it does fires that occur on its lands."[46]

The 1946 annual report of the forestry department for Mississippi's Dantzler Lumber Company observed, "No planting was done during the year. While there are many areas within the company holdings where planting will be necessary, it is felt that the fire problem must be overcome be-

Fighting a fire with pine tops. Courtesy Louisiana Department of Agriculture and Forestry, Baton Rouge.

fore planting on a large scale will be economically feasible." In 1948 some 82 percent of all forest fires in the United States occurred in the South. As pioneering forester Zeb White later remembered, "If you traveled in Mississippi in the late 30's and early 40's it seemed as though the state was burned from one end to the other." This impression was accurate, for the tree tops and heavy brush left by cut-out-and-get-out lumbering fed wildfires that consumed more than half the state's timbered and cutover lands annually. Some fires were so big and hard to fight that they took on a character all their own. A large March 1954 fire in Issaquena and Sharkey Counties was so fierce that firefighters named it Big Red.[47]

One of the problems was the inability of the MFC and the Forest Service to work together effectively during the 1940s. As former state forester Jim Craig told John Squires, supervisor of the state's national forests, "there was prior to our getting together almost an antagonism between the two agencies." Squires replied that the schism "had just grown from the problems, the great problems that existed around each unit. . . . [T]he real cooperation I think began to accomplish results after Jim Craig and myself got to know one another and knew what we were trying to do in the State." According to Squires, part of the problem was that the previous state forester, Albert Leggett, was not a graduate forester and was thus jealous of Squires and the U.S. Forest Service programs.[48]

As pulp and paper companies moved into Mississippi, they had at least two important considerations as they looked at the fire situation. First was the threat to existing timber on the lands they had inherited from the lumber companies and other owners. If they were to manage it and profit from the land, it obviously had to be protected, which sometimes seemed an impossible task. Nelson recalled that when Flintkote bought the Sumter Lumber Company properties, they "had regenerated very well with young pine seedlings, although there was a terrific amount of post oak overstory that had grown up over the years, and many of the local people thought that

the post oak was going to take over the lands and they told us that there were two things they did not think we would ever be able to do; and one was to control the fires and the other one was to get pine back on the lands because the original folklore was that it couldn't be done." Of course, hardwood stands were also vulnerable to the ravages of wildfire. Also, as new crops of trees were established, many companies undertook programs of "timber stand improvement," which usually consisted of girdling or poisoning scrub hardwoods to promote the "release," or growth, of pines. This procedure angered squirrel hunters, who objected to the perceived loss of acorns and consequently ignited "spite" fires in protest. According to legend, at one such site they left a sign that said, "You've got the money, We've got the time. You girdle the hardwoods, And we'll burn the pine."[49]

The second consideration related to lands that were not well stocked. There was obviously no point in putting a lot of money into regeneration if such efforts were frequently destroyed by fire. Also, these considerations would affect the methodology of regeneration. The costs of natural regeneration through the use of seed trees, site preparation and direct seeding, and planting differed considerably. Even though prescribed burning had become an accepted, although controversial, silvicultural treatment by this time, fire at the wrong time during the growth cycle could be disastrous. The amount of money a company was willing to put into a site was affected by the land's value, its productivity, its location, and, of course, by its vulnerability to fire. As a 1948 Johns Manville report noted, "The first requirement in timber growing is control of forest fires."

The tentative outline for Johns Manville's forestry program estimated (probably optimistically) that by spending six thousand dollars annually, the company could hold the burn rate to 1 percent of its lands. The company purchased two Dodge Power Wagons for fire fighting and recruited local men to assist its forester in the effort. After determining that U.S. Forest Service towers could not detect fires on all of the company's lands, Johns Manville obtained assistance from the Crosby Lumber Company, which operated a fire-patrol airplane in the Amite–Wilkinson County area, and chartered its own aircraft in Natchez. Early air patrollers dropped notes to the fire crews, but by 1949 the company was using radio equipment.[50]

Johns Manville's chief forester said in 1951 that "Mississippi's fire record is bad" and noted that he considered an acceptable annual burn as 1 percent of total acreage. He noted that 1,135 of Johns-Manville's 53,000 acres under fire protection had burned during the previous year, while the Crosby Lumber Company had burns on 2.37 percent, or 3,296 of its 139,263 protected acres. Johns Manville was spending 7.8 cents per acre and Crosby 9 cents per acre for protection. Johns Manville had personnel in radio-equipped vehicles with hand tools as well as bulldozers and fire plows. The company had a radio network with two fixed stations and nine mobile units, including one unit in a contracted surveillance airplane. The company was planning to increase its investments in both men and equipment. By the end of 1953 fire losses on company lands were within "acceptable limits."[51]

By 1954 the entire area of the Yazoo–Little Tallahatchie Flood Control Project had organized fire protection under the MFC, but the project's leaders believed that "the degree of protection the poorly financed commission could offer was not sufficient to ensure survival for the millions of pine seedlings planted each year." The Yazoo-Tallahatchie project foresters utilized U.S. Forest Service personnel and equipment to deal with fires that the state operation could not handle. The project also provided matching funds to the commission to upgrade its equipment. The forestry commission obviously could not provide adequate protection for the land, and if it was to be regenerated, others had to step into the breech.

From the 1940s on much of that role was assumed by private companies. Private timber protective organizations made up mostly of large forest owners took the lead. As early as 1927 be-

tween 350,000 and 560,000 acres in the Pascagoula area were protected (with the help of supplementary funds from the U.S. Forest Service), as were more than 100,000 acres of potential forest land in Hancock County by 1929. Two protective units, the Big Scooba and the East Mississippi, were established in central Mississippi in 1932, with a total of about 175,000 acres.[52]

The effort reached out in two directions—fire prevention and fire suppression. Dick Allen, then of the DeWeese Lumber Company, remembered private fire-control efforts in Mississippi: "they entered into an agreement with a Central Fire Control Association. . . . IP furnished most of the money and most of the personnel, and at any time that we had fires on our land, our cooperative lands, IP helped us put 'em out, and we in turn helped them put 'em out." Allen remembered that fire protection went from "nothing to good in . . . 5 to 6 years time."[53]

The improvement in fire protection and prevention became a point of pride and even a valuable asset for land owners and forest managers. In 1963 James M. Vardaman, acting as the agent for sale of the E. L. Bruce Company timberlands in the vicinity of Bruce, boasted, "The Company fire control record is phenomenal. In the past 7½ years only 201 acres of the property has been burned by wild fire. The total loss for the last full year was less than 6 acres. . . . This record is a good indication of the Company's relations with its neighbors."[54]

Private foresters' efforts provided some lasting images and memories. Allen recalled fondly the early fire-fighting exploits of IP forester Buff Reaves, of Leake County:

Mr. Buff . . . hated woods fires. . . . And one night I went on this fire line . . . this was after midnight and you could tell where the glow was, you could tell where the fire line was. And I stopped and we walked in to try to get at one end of it, and I could hear flop, flop, flop. You could hear pine tops hittin' the ground. That's all we had to fight fire with then. And Mr. Buff was comin' from one end and Mr. Adcock was comin' from the other . . . fightin' that fire, and they had fought so long that night that it was hard for them to straighten their backs. You had to help 'em to straighten up. . . . I knew Mr. Buff Reaves and thought a lot of him. . . . I guess that he developed the first tower that there was in Leake County as far as I can remember. He prided himself in pickin' out four or five high hills and then findin' the highest tree on those four or five hills and then takin' some two-by-fours and nailin' them on the trunk of those trees, makin' him a ladder. Cut the top of the tree out so that the limbs, where he could see, and that was his tower. I've been up two or three of 'em with him, and it's kind of treacherous there. Those two-by-fours don't hold too well, and they kind of shake. . . . But old Buff, as old as he was, up those towers he would go, and hours didn't mean a thing in the world to him, or holidays and anything. He hated fire. And at the same time he did a wonderful job, I think, with all the neighbors of IP's lands, preachin' good forest management to 'em.[55]

The use of airplanes for fire-protection work dated back to the post–World War I era in some national forests of the West but came slowly to the South. The Texas Forest Service began utilizing planes in 1943, and by 1954 several other states joined in. The MFC experimented with an airplane just after World War II, but a belly land-ing and unsuccessful attempt to take off over some trees damaged the commission's only plane beyond repair and ended the aerial experimentation for more than a decade. The state later contracted with private operators for air patrol, and by 1952 twelve planes were flying.[56]

The Crosby Lumber Company, the L. N. Dantzler Lumber Company, and IP's Tyler were Mississippi pioneers in the use of airplanes for fire detection and dispatch of fire-suppression crews. Tyler remembered, "In the summer of '49 . . . we found that the Crosby Lumber and Manufacturing Company . . . had purchased an airplane and they were using it in their fire-control activities. . . . I kept lookin' for used planes that were in the money we felt we had available in Central Fire Control Association. Found one . . . up in Cleveland. . . . I went up and looked at it, . . . gave 'em a check, and took off. And we brought it back to Mississippi, and we . . . got a radio system. . . . We put a radio in the plane, and we had our . . . contacts, with our own fire crews, and our own fire towers, and we started operating. Your idea of . . . aerial fire organization is probably some guy running around looking at smokes and all this, but it's not exactly that. We refined it. The whole fire organization was controlled by the

Early Mississippi Forestry Commission airplane. Courtesy Mississippi Forestry Commission, Jackson.

plane. The plane dispatched the fire crews, did everything, and we really became effective. It was costly for the time; now, it seems like peanuts."[57]

Tyler purchased a Bellanca Cruisair Senior, which cruised at 140 to 145 miles per hour. The area patrolled was about seventy miles long and thirty-five miles wide, encompassing about 1.6 million acres. The air patrols supplemented a ground system owned by the Central Fire Control Association that consisted of four fire towers with radios, about fifteen radio-controlled mobile units, and eight tractors and plows to go with those units. The plane was flown daily if there was fire danger and intermittently when the danger was relatively low. Tyler argued that coupled with the towers, the airplane surveillance made fire detection and suppression more efficient and in fact anticipated that three of the four towers could possibly be eliminated through the use of the aircraft. During the spring of 1950 nearly half of the acreage lost resulted from nighttime fires set by people who were frightened by the airplane's daytime patrolling.[58]

In late 1952 the worst fire season in the history of the MFC occurred. During the year 10,521 fires burned more than 354,644 acres of protected land. That fall the smoke was so thick in southwest Mississippi that Crosby Lumber Company pilot John Pruett, who was flying from dawn to dark, reported that the only way he could detect a fire was to look straight down. The previous year the forestry commission installed a loudspeaker in a patrol plane that was used over Lincoln County. The pilot spotted a man on the ground who was making no attempt to control the fire he was burning and instructed him over the loudspeaker to extinguish the fire. The man quickly complied and later told a fire crew, "When they start speaking from above, it's time to obey."[59]

Tyler claimed that states using aircraft had been able to cut their fire losses between 20 and 33 percent. He said that the Central Fire Control Association had steadily reduced the acreage per fire lost during the period air surveillance had

been in operation. Tyler pointed out in early 1955 that for IP's Canton Division in 1954, "exactly 84.5 per cent of our fires were of an incendiary origin. Areas not under the aircraft fire control operations of the Central Fire Association had an average fire size of 19.36 acres. Those covered had an average of 3.83 acres per fire." Tyler concluded, "It is very evident that an aerial fire control operation is worthwhile. Apparently, the fire control problem narrows down to a matter of the land owner's decision as to how much he wishes to spend for fire control and how much of a fire loss he is willing to suffer annually." By 1955 Tyler reported, "In our Carthage and Brandon Districts we have one fire unit for every 20,000 acres under protection. . . . All of these units are crawler tractors. . . . And all of them are equipped with hydraulically operated plows. We are stressing extreme mobility of equipment and use only tractors and plows which can plow lines very rapidly. The fire control groups are able to concentrate and/or disperse tractor truck units quickly. The airplane, of course, greatly increases the effectiveness of each unit."[60]

Tyler believed that being a forester made his work in the air more effective. He publicized his views in a *Journal of Forestry* article that strongly recommended using forester-pilots for airplane fire patrol. Tyler's work attracted a good deal of interest around the country, and in 1955 he was asked to address the annual Louisiana State University Forestry Symposium. Professor A. B. Crow of the LSU School of Forestry told Tyler, "Word about your association of private owners has got around and we should like to hear about it."[61]

During the period from 1941 to 1962 state fire-protection efforts gradually improved. Albert Leggett became state forester in 1941, and under Leggett, funding for the agency increased dramatically from $200,000 in 1942 to more than $500,000 by 1950. The area under state fire protection increased from 5.5 million to more than 12 million acres, and, because of improved equipment and training, the size of fires was cut in half. By this time state fire crews were equipped with jeep-plow units. These vehicles, with their rear-mounted plows, added speed to the firefighters' arsenal. By 1951 fifty-two of the state's eighty-two counties were receiving state fire protection. Enthusiasm for the fire crusade was undoubtedly stimulated by the 1956 Southern Forest Fire Prevention Conference in New Orleans, sponsored by the American Forestry Association and several other national and regional organizations.

During Jim Craig's tenure as state forester from 1952 until 1955, the forestry commission acquired new fire units with trucks and light crawler tractors. By 1961 the jeeps acquired after World War II had been replaced with trucks and tractors, and the commission owned 128 light crawler tractor plow units, sixty-five medium tractor units, and two heavy tractor units. All district headquarters had an emergency truck and tractor unit. By 1960 seventy-four counties were receiving state fire protection, and the commission was again experimenting with its own aircraft, both airplanes and helicopters. At the end of 1962 only six Mississippi counties remained without state fire protection, and sixteen contract airplanes were used for fire patrol. Still, the state had a long way to go in controlling fire. In 1963 nearly 2 percent of the forested area was damaged by fire, and Mississippi had more human-caused fires per year than any other state. From 1953 through 1963 more that half of Mississippi's forest fires were incendiary in origin.

The commission continued to upgrade its fire-fighting equipment throughout the 1960s, and in the early 1970s it began a three-year program of replacing all fire-fighting equipment. By the latter part of the decade the MFC maintained 170 fire towers. In its fiftieth anniversary year, 1976, the MFC was in a self-congratulatory mood, noting that the state now had fewer than five thousand fires a year with an average size of ten to twelve acres. A commission employee cited a "veteran fire fighter" who bragged that "the fire might not be dead out but we've sure cut down the flame. Five thousand fires a year ain't hardly enough to make Smokey Bear growl."

However, Smokey needed to remain alert, for the value of money spent for fire protection was easily demonstrated. In 1979 fire damage was down across the South, except in Mississippi. Mississippi was the only southern state to significantly reduce funds for fire protection that year and was the only state to suffer more fire damage than in the previous annum. On a more positive note, in 1974 rural volunteer fire departments in Mississippi began getting 50 percent cost-share assistance under the Rural Development Act of 1972. The program was administered by the state forestry commission. By 1982 more than two hundred rural fire departments were receiving the assistance.[62]

The best way to deal with wildfire is to eliminate it before it ignites. The MFC directed much of its educational work toward fire prevention and in 1945 joined forces with the Mississippi State Textbook Rating and Purchasing Board to publish a textbook, *Elementary Forestry for Mississippi,* that was widely distributed among children and used in the state's public schools. In a chapter entitled "Enemies of the Forest," humans were identified as "the greatest enemy of the forest." The textbook identified the transgressions: "Clearing lands for agriculture, destructive methods of logging, the destruction of young trees by grazing cattle and hogs, and 'burning off' the woods. . . . But the greatest enemy is man's carelessness with fire which destroys more of the woods in Mississippi each year than all other enemies combined."[63]

In 1965 the MFC inaugurated the Fire Prevention Contractor Program. The program was aimed at hot spot areas with a history of incendiarism. Local residents were hired and trained to visit others in the community and preach fire prevention. In some communities the number of fires was reduced as much as 30 percent a year over a six-year period. Because of its success the program was enlarged in Mississippi and copied by other states. Some fire-prevention efforts were less formal. In 1952 a forester for the Crosby Lumber Company informed his counterpart at Johns Manville "of what goes on insofar as fire occurrence on or adjacent to your land." He described a fire that Crosby crews had fought for

Modern fire tower. Courtesy Mississippi Forestry Commission, Jackson.

Mississippi Forestry Commission jeep with fire plow. Courtesy Mississippi Forestry Commission, Jackson.

two days and reported, "My foreman says a ne-gro by name of Eugene Butler set this fire. It might be a good idea for you to let Grady or one of the boys visit him and scare him up a little."[64]

Some pulp and paper companies regarded hunting lease programs as part of their fire-prevention efforts. Hughes considered this technique effective: "One of the things that helped us is leasing some of our land to hunting clubs and giving them . . . the responsibility of helping to eliminate the fire." Both the paper and the lumber companies also found that one of the most effective ways to "defuse" woods burners was to hire them to look out for fires or to give them other low-paying jobs. J. E. Bryan of the L. N. Dantzler Lumber Company remembered that "it was cheaper to pay those fellows than it was to try to put those fires out that they were setting. I can't say they didn't set some other fires, but they didn't set any inside the fenced areas that we were paying them to look after for us."[65]

Industrial foresters did not do it alone, but they contributed significantly to the fire-prevention and -suppression efforts that changed the face of the South over the course of two or three decades. Those who were active during that period are the most perceptive witnesses. Allen looked back with satisfaction on the changes that better fire control brought to Mississippi: "In Brooklyn, Mississippi, that's where I was raised, . . . you could see as far as your eye could see, there was nothin', not one tree standin'. But there were a lot of fires goin' on. Everywhere you'd look there was fires. . . . I got a quarter a day for leadin' cars as a boy down Highway 49 south of Brooklyn into a little town called Epps. . . . The smoke was so thick along Leaf River that the cars couldn't see where to go. So I would get . . . a quarter to go ahead of that car and get him through that smoke. And then there'd be another car at the other end and I'd bring him back and get a quarter for that. . . . And today, that particular part of the country . . . depend[s] entirely on the forest economy. And it's because that they brought those forests back from nothing to something."[66]

Reflecting on the changes industrial forestry brought to the South, Gragg observed,

One of the things that I remember very clearly was both driving and flying across the South from the mid-1930s until now. The thing I remember first is how . . . I never could get out of sight of a forest fire in the 30's . . . particularly if I was flyin'. . . . But during my career I realized that I was seeing less and less fires. And the other thing that I remember very clearly is how red the rivers were from the Atlantic Coast to the Texas plains in the '30s and '40s. . . . The rivers were red because . . . the farms, the hill farms, were worn out and eroding into the rivers and now those hill farms have trees on 'em and the erosion is reduced. It hasn't stopped, but it's reduced. . . . I remember also in south Mississippi and southwest Louisiana, that there were so few trees left after the logging and after the fires that you could really, truly stand on the ground and see the curvature of the earth in a great distance away. It was that bare. And now, of course, those south Mississippi and southwest Louisiana [lands] are both well-timbered.[67]

O. G. Tracewitz recalled, "They used to say you could see a cow on stumplands a mile away. . . . There were no trees in between. Nothing but a sea of stumps. And flying over the land in the '40s . . . the fires were burning all over. Especially at night you could see them all over the horizon. . . . There was very little good growing young timber of merchantable size in the South." Confirming this testimony, the U.S. Forest Service in its late-1980s study, *The South's Fourth Forest,* stated, "it can be fairly said that fire protection is the most widespread and most effective timber management activity practiced in the South. It made possible the natural regeneration of much of the South's second and third forests."[68]

While fire control was obviously the top priority for foresters by the early 1950s, the Timber Resource Review reported that disease damage to southern timber exceeded that from fire, insects, weather, animals, or other causes. Both hardwoods and softwoods were affected. Research on these problems dated back to the early 1900s, and by the late 1920s pathologists at the Appalachian Forest Experiment Station at Asheville, North Carolina, and at the Southern Forest Experiment Station at New Orleans were involved in disease research. Among the diseases they studied were fusiform rust, little leaf, brown spot, red heart, and several other kinds of rust. By the mid-1950s the chief of the Division of Forest Disease Research of the Southeastern Forest Experiment Station reported that while knowledge about the causes and control of most southern tree diseases had been developed, "the control measures available for some of our forest diseases such as brown spot and fusiform rust are imperfect or too expensive."[69]

The research of Yale professor H. H. Chapman during the 1920s and of others later established that brown spot needle disease among longleaf pine could best be controlled by prescribed burning at the proper moment of the seedling stage. However, over the next three decades the incidence of fusiform rust actually increased in the South, particularly in pine plantations. As in so many other areas of forest practice, there were differences of opinion regarding the managerial and silvicultural treatment of the problem. Some said that the best way to control the problem was through the careful selection of seed from resistant trees.[70]

The major insect threat to southern pine operations comes from the pine beetle, which tends to cause major epidemics on a five- to ten-year cyclical basis. In 1947 Congress passed the Forest Pest Control Act, which offered federal financial and technical assistance to states for the control of insect and disease infestations. The insect program was administered by the Bureau of Entomology and Plant Quarantine and the disease program by the Bureau of Plant Industry, Soils, and Agricultural Engineering. The programs were transferred to the Forest Service in 1954. The last major outbreak of pine beetles in 1983 damaged some 26 million acres of southern timberland and wrought losses of about $500 million. While there are various preventive, treatment, and salvage approaches in dealing with beetle attacks, "no pine stand is totally immune to southern pine beetle infestation." In industrial forestry operations, the treatment of insects, fungi, or other organisms—"forest pests"—

depends on "determination of whether [the] costs of proposed actions are likely to be less than the value of the resource being destroyed."[71]

The MFC was deeply involved in efforts to control pests and disease. In 1952 Mississippi's forests were struck by a southern pine beetle infestation, which the commission monitored in part by aerial surveillance. Wilkinson, Amite, Franklin, and Adams Counties were the most heavily infected. While large landowners and the U.S. Forest Service were fighting the insects, small landowners were doing little, and many seemed unconcerned. Thus, the commission began a program of control that lasted into the early 1960s and dramatically decreased the infestations. The state efforts were assisted by nature, for many of the beetles were consumed by woodpeckers. In the 1970s the commission established an Insect and Disease Department and utilized aerial surveys to keep abreast of insect and disease infestations.[72]

A manual for small southern pine timberland owners, published in the late 1980s, says, "Establishment of clearly marked boundary lines is a top-priority job." The early industrial foresters of the South agreed. In fact, many of them found boundary establishment and maintenance to be nearly on a par with fire prevention and control among their concerns. There was plenty of work for the boundary crews to do. Nelson said that many of the old lumber companies who were cutting out in the 1930s and 1940s encouraged encroachment on their lands: "A lot of the lumber companies had the idea that when they got the timber cut off that they could turn around and sell it, and . . . if they couldn't sell it they would let somebody use it for a while so that maybe he'd buy it. So you found all kinds of patches, pastures, you'd see a fence that would be over on your land and nobody would ever have said anything about it. . . . They encouraged encroachment."[73]

Encroachment on the land, simply using it, was a problem, particularly if the encroacher used it for grazing, which could be destructive, or if he burned his garden or cultivated ground, thus creating a fire danger. It was also entirely possible that the encroacher might eventually try to claim the land legally through the doctrine of adverse possession. Hughes noted, "It is a very difficult problem incorporating and maintaining the boundary lines and securing the boundary lines so that you don't get some sort of encroachment. . . . The problems go back to some bad surveying work which was done [by the] General Land Office. . . . They sent government surveyors down that laid out the townships and the sections and they made errors. The equipment was crude. . . . Every reading they made was subject to an error . . . and as a result of that these sections that looked so pretty on the map—it's just not like that when you get out in the woods. . . . You just can't retrace those old GLO land lines and have them come out exactly correct. Now, not much was done about that situation out in the forestland. . . . [I]f your deed called for so many acres, more or less, that was exactly what it meant, more or less. You got what you could get. You maintained your lines."[74]

Remembering his early days with Flintkote in Mississippi, Nelson noted, "A lot of times the boundary lines were nonexistent and when we would run them out, we would find evidences of trespass or . . . enclosing of land that didn't belong to them. So there was quite a lot of title corrective work that had to be done." Dealing with these problems could create ill will if not handled diplomatically. Nelson said that his crews generally tried to reestablish or locate the old lines rather than run new ones, because "you make a lot of enemies if you go in and try to run new lines when the community has established where the old line is."[75]

Many companies were not particularly concerned about trespass because of its relatively insignificant economic importance. A 1958 study by the American Pulpwood Association indicated, "Most companies regard timber trespass as being so negligible as to present no great problem." It concluded, "Court action is seldom used by companies to recover losses." The companies responding to a study questionnaire indicated that they relied largely on boundary maintenance and community relations to deal with trespass.[76]

Sometimes the difficulty did not really center on boundary location. Allen remembered,

A fella named Mike Sullivan . . . was a big World War I veteran. And he had single-handedly killed thousands of Germans and hand grenades had been thrown at him and . . . he told us about his medals. And he was also an avid moonshiner. . . . And we were runnin' a land line. The company had never even run their land lines. And people would go in there and steal timber. And they'd say, "Well, I thought I was on grampa" or somethin. So we were establishin' these lines. And I'd been told about Mike Sullivan. Never had met him. So we went down through the woods runnin' a line, and . . . I heard this fellow behind us say "What are you doing up here?" I turned around and he had a .45 strapped on his side. And he wasn't a big man, but you could tell he was tough. You know, he was ruddy faced, and you could tell he stayed in shape. And so I said "We're runnin' some lines up here. Who are you, sir?" He said, "I'm Mike Sullivan." I said, "Oh yeah, I've heard about you, Mike." Told him who I was. He says, "Now let me ask you a question." "Yes, sir." He said, "When y'all are runnin' this line and you got that instrument up there," he said, "Do you look where that instrument goin' or do you look around as you walk?" And I knew what he was gettin' at, so I said, "Let me tell you, fella, all we are interested in is right straight ahead down that line. There may be a highway over here, or there may be a house, but we are not interested in that. All we are interested in is a straight line." He said, "Keep it that way, boy." So he went along with us a little while, and we did pass his still. It was back on the company [land], of course, and that's the first time I ever saw whiskey up in a tree. Apparently he'd used quite a few of those pine trees to keep his whiskey in.[77]

Nelson and the Flintkote Company were not as fortunate. Allen said,

Where you got in trouble was you findin' the still, and then the revenuers happened to come in there within the next month or so, and then they immediately said you told 'em. And then you gonna get burned out. That's what happened in Art's [Nelson] 1,700-acre fire. . . . It was nothin' in the world but the crews ran across this still back in there, and it just happened that the revenuers came in there within fifteen, twenty days after that, and within two or three days after the revenuers came by the woods burned up. . . . Well, everybody back in those days, a little drink . . . a toddy was a medicine, you know? They'd mix a little sugar with it and take a little sip of it at night before they went to bed. There were very few people, even Baptists, back in that country that didn't occasionally take a swig. . . . But you know, one thing I never thought of until we sat down here is that one of the good forest practices of the past was a place to have stills on the land!

Or, as Jonathan Daniels put it, "in the woods foresters and moonshiners have both learned that the safety of men, trees, and stills is inseparable. Not seeing too much can sometimes be the best practice for foresters."[78]

Neighbors' goodwill or resentment could be reflected in another area as well. The pulp and paper companies were large corporations, and they were purchasing enormous blocks of land in the South. As Gragg remembered, "the companies were being criticized by some quarters for buying up a lot of land, and there was a tendency to try to limit that by specialized kind of taxes. In other words, there were a lot of people who thought because you owned a hundred thousand acres of land you ought to be penalized—you ought to pay a higher tax rate."[79] An unfavorable tax structure or other discriminatory legislation or regulations could endanger a company's ability to operate.

L. O. Crosby Jr. of Mississippi's Crosby Lumber Company said that his firm became involved in efforts at reforestation only when the tax structure in Mississippi changed: "My father . . . didn't go into reforesting during his time to much extent, because during that time the tax on timber land was so terrific that you couldn't afford to hold timber, you would have to cut it and let it go. . . . The taxes made this almost impossible to

hold. However, [with the] severance taxes in lieu of the ad valorem on the land. . . . When you cut the tree, you paid the tax. . . . [Y]ou could do it." One resident of Whynot, in eastern Mississippi, remembered that "it wasn't economically feasible to own timber land because you had to pay taxes on the timber before you sold it. . . . [P]eople . . . actually . . . hired people to cut the timber down and let it rot to keep from paying taxes on it because they couldn't sell it."[80]

The leaders of the communities into which the pulp and paper companies were moving in the 1930s, 1940s, and 1950s generally welcomed enthusiastically their new neighbors' investments and payrolls. But the companies and their foresters were well aware that disgruntled neighbors could influence local and state government officials. Governmental attitudes could change, and large companies could become easy targets for opportunistic public officials. Public and government relations thus were important concerns of the early industrial foresters. Pulp and paper industry spokesmen argued that it needed favorable tax laws and minimal governmental regulation if it was to thrive and expand in the South.

Even though pioneering lumbermen such as Henry Hardtner and foresters such as Austin Cary and Inman Eldredge had been accumulating knowledge about the characteristics of southern pine since the early part of the century, foresters were still working with a relatively limited arsenal of silvicultural knowledge during the 1930s and 1940s. They were handicapped by the inadequacy of scientific information and by the lack of equipment. They disagreed about the proper approaches, and they sometimes made mistakes. They learned and contributed to the knowledge of those who came later, who would also disagree about the particulars of their art and profession.

The disagreements continue down to the present and will probably extend into the future. As former IP forester and executive O. G. Tracewitz saw it, "You could . . . have . . . differences of opinion because of . . . the newness of the profession and various procedures and practices were not proven. . . . We can talk about genetics and we can talk about thinning, we can talk about precommercial thinning, but we never know the results because it takes a full generation. And we can draw empirical things, but we are never sure, so we try a lot of things which may fail. And reflecting now, perhaps we tried too much and tried to push the technology too high because some of the basic forestry procedures are hard to beat. Cut it when it's too thick, harvest it when it's too old, and plant it when there's nothing there."[81]

Regeneration of cutover lands was a major concern and source of disagreement among foresters. Some early efforts were done by planting, but that method was limited by the intensive labor involved and by the shortage of seedlings. "Some old fields were being replanted by hand, but most of the effort to establish new stands of timber was by natural regeneration," according to Gragg. "Reestablishment of the stand by natural reproduction. . . . In the middle '30s . . . that's about the only practical method that was available." Gragg also remembered, "In the early days of forestry in the South, we planted, probably through ignorance, slash on a lot of sites that we now know should have been planted in loblolly. . . . We thought we were doing the right thing at the time, but as it turns out, loblolly would have done a lot better on . . . a lot of those sites than slash. One of the reasons I say that is that we planted the slash in a lot of places out of its range and the ice storms did a lot more damage to the slash than they would have to the loblolly." In fact, what may have been Mississippi's oldest pine plantation, the Sam Byrd Plantation consisting of 11.75 acres of slash pine, was planted in Jackson County in 1926.[82]

From that time until the present there has been honest disagreement about the choice of particular species for specific sites, and scientists are continuing to conduct studies and discover new information in this area. In any case, most companies of the early period relied largely on natural regeneration, and from the mid-1930s through the early 1940s private industry lagged far behind the public agencies in planting. The authors of a standard 1956 forestry textbook described the methods of natural reforestation and planting, concluding that "both methods are used in good forest management." However, they went on to say that natural reforestation "should be employed when and wherever possible." The state legislature seemed to agree, for in 1944 it passed the Forest Harvesting Act, requiring the leaving of seed trees in all commercial cutting operations.[83]

While Hardtner, Great Southern, and Crossett had pioneered in attempts to plant and regenerate their lands, their ideas took hold only slowly across the South. Much of the reforesting of the South took place through natural reseeding, whose success depended on the improvement of fire protection. The U.S. Department of Agriculture through various programs under the Clarke-McNary Act (1924), the Agricultural Conservation Program starting in the 1930s, the Soil Bank Program of the 1950s, and the Forestry Incentives Program inaugurated in 1974 promoted planting on farms. By the mid-1980s the federal government paid as much as 65 percent of planting and timber-stand improvement costs on farms. Also in 1985 the Food Security Act established the Conservation Reserve Program to subsidize farmers who would plant grass or trees on erodible cropland. Farmers owned 22 percent of the South's timberland, and in earlier years the percentage had been much higher.

Only a few thousand acres annually were planted or seeded prior to the 1930s. CCC efforts bolstered planting in the late 1930s, but there was a hiatus during World War II. In 1954 Mississippi planted trees on more than sixty-five thousand acres; only Georgia and Florida planted more. Planting increased during the 1950s, peaking in 1959 at 1.7 million acres. It then slightly declined until starting to rise again during the 1970s, spurred by state and federal cost-sharing and management-assistance programs plus the 1985 reforestation tax credit. Planting since World War II has been concentrated on the lands of large forest-products companies and other big owners. By 1985 some 60 percent of the areas planted or seeded in the South belonged to large corporate owners, with 35 percent in the hands of other private owners, and 5 percent in national forests and on other public lands. Mississippi also implemented a cost-sharing incentive program to promote forestry on private lands. The planting and seeding efforts were facilitated by the development of new techniques and technologies, including most basically the inexpensive tree-planting machine.[84]

Various people tried to develop mechanical tree planters. Faced with a labor shortage and lots of seedlings to plant during World War II, Earl Porter, manager of woodlands in IP's southern operations, invented a machine that planted 375,000 seedlings the first year it was used near Panama City, Florida. Porter's design was based on tobacco and tomato planters he had seen, and the prototype was built by the Montegue Machine Company in Valdosta, Georgia, based on a picture supplied by Porter.[85]

The Illinois Central Railroad also perfected a mechanical planter. Noting that "[h]undreds of miles of railroads now constituting our southern lines were built primarily to move logs from the woods to the sawmills, planing mills, wood turning plants and later the paper mills and other processing plants," of the region, in its 1951 centennial report, the Illinois Central said that to stimulate the manufacture of paper and pulp board, the railroad had "encouraged and assisted in the reforestation of cutover lands to perpetuate the supply of pulpwood." Reflecting the importance of these businesses to the railroad in Mississippi, in 1953 the Illinois Central distributed an illustrated booklet at a presentation before the Mississippi Agricultural and Industrial Board in Jackson. The pamphlet emphasized the railroad's agricultural, passenger, and forestry activities in the state.[86]

The Illinois Central in 1948 enlarged its agricultural department with the appointment of three forestry agents, including John Guthrie, who had just finished forestry school at Purdue University. Guthrie remembered a jury-rigged mechanical tree planter that had been assembled from old farm machinery at Purdue by forestry professor Daniel DenUyl. The machine was borrowed in 1948 and demonstrated in several south Mississippi counties, but it did not perform well in the heavy clay soils of the central part of the state. Guthrie and William W. May, another railroad forester, began modifying and field testing the machine in conjunction with the Illinois Central's shops at McComb, and in 1949 the machine was demonstrated before a number of distinguished audiences of public and private foresters and officials, using pine seedlings from the MFC.

Pulled by a small tractor, the machine could plant one thousand seedlings per hour. However, Illinois Central officials thought the machine could be further improved, and it was refined in the railroad's shops at McComb, where two additional machines were constructed. Illinois Central forestry agents began a systematic program of planting seedlings for small farmers, and by 1959 railroad officials calculated that the agents had staged 1,440 demonstrations of the machines before forty-eight thousand people. The Illinois Central also allowed others to copy their machines and made the machines available for use. With the university's agreement, the Purdue Tree Planter became known as the Illinois Central Tree Planter.

The railroad tirelessly promoted the machine with field demonstrations during the next decade, including appearances in sixty-four of Mississippi's eighty-two counties. Blueprints of the machine were provided at no cost to individuals, schools, clubs, government agencies, and other interested parties both in the United States and abroad, and within a few years several manufacturers were turning out machines with the same basic design. By the end of the 1950s the railroad calculated that its machines had planted more than 10.5 million trees on twelve thousand acres of land, and in the same year the first pulpwood from machine-planted forests began to move over the Illinois Central's rails.

The machine's great advantages were in labor time and costs. One person could barely plant

John Guthrie seated on Illinois Central tree planter, 1949. Courtesy John Guthrie.

one thousand trees in a full day by hand, while the machine could plant one thousand in an hour. Also, the tree planter cost only three hundred dollars, and, as Nelson recalled in a 1976 lecture, "banks and soil conservation districts purchased a number to loan to those who wanted to use them. They were so popular you had to stand in line to apply for one." The great increase in planting ability also spawned a demand for increased nursery seedling production and the use of refrigerated storage for seedlings. May later said, "I got awfully tired of the 'thing' [tree planter] before we finally put it on the shelf. It became a byword on the I.C. I doubt that I will or have done anything for forestry to equal the work done on and with it, and not too many other foresters have either."[87]

There were various early efforts to regenerate Mississippi's forests through planting. Howell of the Dantzler Lumber Company and IP planted some 7,300 acres in slash pines between 1926 and 1937. There were scattered accounts of other individuals planting trees on their lands in the 1920s. In 1930, in cooperation with the U.S. Forest Service, the first state nursery was established at what later became Perkinston Junior College. In 1941 nurseryman Allen managed to buy some choice land for the state, finagled financing from the Masonite Corporation, and helped to convince CCC officials to locate a camp nearby and provide badly needed labor for another early nursery at Mt. Olive. The Soil Bank Act of 1956 later provided funding for the expansion of state nurseries. In 1957 and 1958 soil bank funds went directly to the states to upgrade, expand, and build new nurseries as well as drying facilities for cones and for the extraction and processing of seed. Permanent cold storage facilities for seed were also constructed. A number of forest-products companies also built nurseries and supplied seedlings for their own lands and for co-operators.[88]

In privately owned forests, regeneration, like other silvicultural issues, was affected by site characteristics, the economic climate, and, above all, company objectives. Gragg noted that economic factors weighed heavily in decisions regarding regeneration techniques: "All of those things, planting, direct seeding . . . the use of seed trees . . . have to be examined in the light of the economics . . . that prevail at a given time. And obviously [if] land was worth two or three dollars an acre at one point in time and if you let land take two or three years to regenerate that was the cheapest way to do it, but when land had to be bought at forty or fifty dollars an acre then you could no longer afford to leave that land idle for four or five years while it regenerated naturally. Then you had to think in terms of site preparation, planting, or direct seeding or something to shorten the cycle so as to reduce the amount of cost involved."

In response to a question about whether various companies could approach regeneration through different methodologies and still all be operating under the umbrella of "good forestry," Gragg replied, "Absolutely. Depends on . . . the site, depends on how long you can afford to let it go." As Professor John W. Johnson of the New York State University College of Forestry put it in 1971, "There is no single 'best' technique of regenerating pine stands. Natural or artificial measures may be used. . . . [T]he objective is prompt and complete stocking with the most desirable species at costs in line with expected returns."[89]

Much of Mississippi's terrain is relatively flat, making a high degree of mechanization possible and allowing intensive forestry practices such as frequent thinnings and site preparation for planting economically feasible. Industrial forest owners in particular have utilized the latest knowledge to increase the forests' productivity, employing various types of regeneration and site preparation on their lands: natural regeneration from seed trees, direct seeding, and planting.[90]

During the early period there was heavy re-liance on natural regeneration because of the site characteristics, economics, and the shortage of an adequate supply of seedlings. A typical situation was described in the IP Woodlands Department's annual report for 1946: "Present indications are that for the next year or two, it is going to be difficult to obtain the required supply of seedlings. The nursery stock available for the next planting season is extremely short. . . . [W]e do not expect to be able to obtain more than 260,000 seedlings during the next season. Practically all of the pine seedlings used in the South are produced by the various State forest agencies." However, by 1948 the company managed more than 2 million acres of southern forests and was planting 3 million seedlings annually despite the shortage of nursery stock.[91]

By the mid-1950s some exciting developments had taken place in forest genetics research. For example, IP was embarking on a research program to develop new strains of trees with superior characteristics in the areas of growth, resistance to disease, and wood quality. In 1955 IP foresters discovered a twenty-year-old pine tree with a crown seventy two feet high and a diameter of 15.2 inches. This tree, at Kilsock Bay near IP's Georgetown, South Carolina, mill, was promptly designated "No. 1." It was the father of IP's family of "supertrees."[92]

Forest genetics had practical results. For example, in addition to the selectively bred, genetically improved cottonwood seedlings it planted on its Fitler Managed Forest near Vicksburg, between the 1920s and 1973, Crown Zellerbach had planted more than 325,000 acres with pine seedlings and had directly reseeded another forty thousand acres in Louisiana and Mississippi. The bulk of the reforestation stock consisted of nursery-raised, genetically improved bare-root seedlings.[93]

In the early days, thinning and harvest rotation were not major issues among industrial foresters, for the age of large pine plantations was still on the horizon. However, many companies did implement programs of timber-stand improvement. As Nelson described the procedure on the Flintkote Forest in Mississippi, "The main idea . . . was to do everything . . . that needed to be done to put the timberlands in optimum growing condition. This meant for the first time, harvesting pine saw logs where they were ready to come out, or where they were an overstory on a good bunch of pine seedlings. . . . We had thousands of acres where the pine was already established but it was being shaded out by these cull hardwoods. . . . Almost everything that we did, we copied from other earlier paper company efforts in the South, to take similar properties and get them into shape."[94]

As thinning became standard procedure among the paper companies, there was usually no consensus, even within a particular organization, about an absolute standard. Various philosophies and differing views existed among industrial foresters. Hughes recalled, "We always had some folks that said, 'We'd be better off just to grow it twenty-eight years and cut it without ever thinnin' it.' On the other hand, there were those who'd say, 'No, let's grow it for forty years and give it two good thinnin's and grow a good stand of sawlogs and not just pulpwood.' And we fought that battle back and forth and we really never did get a decisive solution to it."[95]

The industry's harvesting practices were attracting increasing public attention by the latter part of the 1930s. While the pulp and paper companies were attempting to improve the quality of their own timberlands, small owners willingly stripped their lands bare as the market for pulpwood and the price of forest land rose. As Frank Heyward, who served as manager of the Southern Pulpwood Conservation Association and later as director of public relations for Gaylord Container Corporation, described it, "For the most part, little or no thought was given to forestry practices when cutting pulpwood. The main idea was to satisfy the gargantuan appetite of the big mills which ran 24 hours a day seven days a week. As a result many privately owned timber tracts were stripped as thoroughly of their second growth pines as had been the original virgin forests by steam skidders. There was an immedi-

ate outcry from the public, the press, and public foresters. Was the South again to see its forests reduced to waste stumpland?" Concerned about "waste, inefficiency and wanton destruction of the forest lands in the harvesting of forest products and the utilization of forest lands," based on the recognition "that only a small proportion of the privately owned forest lands in the State of Mississippi is now managed in accordance with sound forestry practices," Mississippi in 1944 enacted a timber-harvesting act that required the leaving of seed trees on harvested lands and set diameter limits for cutting.[96]

Even when timberlands were being managed responsibly, it was sometimes difficult for the public to know. Clear-cuts are in some situations necessary and desirable, but they are always ugly, and the ugliness and apparent devastation stick in the mind. As the director of the Southern Forest Experiment Station in New Orleans once put it, "Unfortunately for professional foresters and for many others who are managing their lands, the public does not distinguish between an exploitative cut and a planned harvest at the time the trees are being felled. After further management steps take place and perhaps several years elapse, the stand begins to reflect the effort, but by then people remember only the negative impression of the logging job. They have not kept track of the management activity, nor do they put a single tract in the perspective of a total forest landscape."[97]

While public opinion and perceptions are important, industrial foresters operated with the knowledge that their ultimate actions were determined by landowners. Rules and standards could be established, but in the final analysis there was one primary rule—the owner's objectives prevailed. There are various ways to express this common truth. Allen argued that it is not possible to ignore the importance of owner objectives:

Good forest management or good forest practice or good forestry . . . was mainly based on keep the dad-blamed fire out, let it reseed, and cut the biggest timber, and keep out trespass, and buy as much land as you can. . . . A lot of the good forest management in that day and time was just leavin' some seed trees and keepin' the fire out, lettin' it grow back as it can. . . . Companies that probably had a forestry program of long range . . . many times would have to forgo that [in the] short range because of storms or bad winters. . . . There have been a lot of changes in the way you look at forest management, but I think it still boils down to whatever that owner has that forest asset for. . . . That's bein' done today for example, in Mississippi. We've had probably the longest rainy season that we have had in many, many years . . . and in the wrong time of year, when it usually was dry and they could get into the swamps and get timber out. So the mills have started already cutting, and have been for the last three months, timber that was on the hills that they'd like to save and grow some, but they had to cut it because you can't shut those mills down, they've got to keep going.[98]

As the industrial foresters who joined the ranks of the pulp and paper companies and lumber-manufacturing firms in the South discovered, a myriad of problems confronted them, as did a plethora of methods to deal with those problems, as the foresters attempted to practice economically sound forestry. However, their situation was simplified somewhat by the fact that their performance was ultimately judged only by the landowner, and the ultimate criterion was profit. If the forester produced and protected forests that provided a continuous supply of raw materials for the pulp and paper mills and sawmills at a reasonable cost, he had done his job. In this period few questions were raised about the forester or the landowner's greater responsibility to the public or to society in general.

Public foresters operated within a different arena. They could set an absolute standard, a single standard of forest practice, and cling tenaciously to it. The ultimate responsibility of the foresters who were employed by public agencies such as the U.S. Forest Service was to the general public that owned the public lands. However, from the 1930s through the 1960s, Forest Service foresters, like their private-sector colleagues, also managed the forests from a largely economic perspective. The national forests became major sources of raw materials for private industry.

U.S. Forest Service foresters became important figures in Mississippi during the 1930s and 1940s. Some were employed by the Southern Forest Experiment Station in New Orleans, which did research and extension work among landowners across the South, including Mississippi. Others were involved in the process of putting together and revitalizing the lands of Mississippi's nascent national forest system. Still others were busy with the groundbreaking work of the Southern Hardwood Research Center at Stoneville.

Starting in the 1960s and intensifying until the present, some segments of the public began to expect more from the public forests than that they be managed as nurseries for the forest-products industry. The growing popularity of outdoor recreation spawned a demand for recreational opportunities and facilities in national forests. The romanticization of "wilderness" created pressures for the setting aside of wilderness areas on the public lands and the feeling that public forests should be managed with an eye to aesthetic values as well as economic purposes. Timber sales from U.S. national forests and clear-cuts, public or private, became highly controversial. Growing public concerns about aesthetics, wildlife, habitat, and endangered species created increasing pressures on private forest landowners as well. As the public became more interested in the nation's forests, private and public, and demanded that "multiple use" should be taken literally and include more than narrow economic uses, the roles of the forest, the landowner, and the forester, private or public, became more complicated.

As public foresters struggled to restore the newly acquired public lands of Mississippi, the forest-products industry's foresters were working with similar problems and lands. The pulp and paper industry presented unique challenges, for it invested large amounts of capital in its plants and thus needed to insure an adequate wood supply to protect these investments over a long period of time. Many paper companies put together large holdings of fee and leased lands, which they attempted to manage so that they would be continually productive into the distant future.

However, the pulp and paper companies also depended on small private landowners for a substantial portion of their timber requirements, so it was in their interest to promote goodwill and enlightened forest practices among their neighbors. As industrial foresters attempted to implement enlightened forestry practices on their own lands and those of their neighbors, three continuing threads ran through their activities.

First, was the realization that forestry is both an art and a science and that there are various ways to approach a particular issue or situation, all under the umbrella of responsible or enlightened forestry practice. Second, industrial foresters believed that in determining the uses and policies for any privately owned property, the ultimate criterion in determining policy is the owner's objective. Third, both objectives and forestry techniques change and evolve over time. It is difficult, if not unreasonable, to evaluate the performance of a company or its foresters outside of the time frame and context when decisions are made. The ultimate standard to be upheld is good faith and an attempt to perform within the parameters of acceptable practice at any given point in time.

Beyond protecting what was growing, forest-products companies tried to stimulate greater production. IP's "conservation foresters" were again instrumental in the promotion of responsible forest practices on the lands of small owners. Among other activities, IP distributed a great deal of literature among children and in schools promoting forestry and conservation. A number of companies also provided seedlings for small landowners and youth organizations. Nelson believed that this sort of program was quite effective during his career with Flintkote: "We found that giving away free seedlings to landowners was a good way to engender interest in forestry because anybody who takes the trouble to set out some trees had quite a lot of muscle work on

his own account. He is also gonna be careful not to let fires get out that would burn up the results of his efforts."[99]

The situation on small private landholdings frustrated many corporate industrial foresters. For example, as early as 1948 an internal report at Johns Manville's Natchez pulp mill reported, "It is unfortunately true . . . that the educational effort by private and public agencies has not been satisfactory with the great majority of small private owners." It concluded that Johns Manville should continue its conservation policy but that "it cannot be expected for the present to result in any marked increase in local wood production from private lands."[100]

Among the important private landowners groups' in the South is the Forest Farmers Association, formed in 1941 to give small landowners a greater voice in public forestry policy. The association supported private conservation efforts and attempted to develop better markets and timber prices for its members. It advocated increases in research money for the Forest Service and universities and increased governmental provision of forestry education, fire protection, and technical assistance for landowners. The organization was also a prime mover, along the with the Southern Pine Association, Southern Hardwood Lumber Manufacturers' Association, and the American Plywood Association, in the 1966 formation of the Southern Forest Resource Analysis project that produced 1969's *The South's Third Forest* report. This study, spearheaded by Philip Wheeler, recently retired from the Southern Forest Experiment Station, and Zebulon White, then professor of industrial forestry at Yale, analyzed the current situation of the southern forests and recommended policies for the future. In 1969 the Southern Forest Resource Council was created to implement the report's recommendations, including the promotion of various cooperative efforts by southern state governments to maintain and properly manage their forests.[101]

Another program that the forest-products industry promoted to stimulate farm forestry and timber production by small owners was the tree-farm movement. The program originated in the state of Washington in 1940 when the Weyerhaeuser Timber Company designated one of its reforestation projects the Clemons Tree Farm, and the concept spread across the nation and into the South. The movement was conceived as an attempt to prevent fire losses through the application of fire-prevention techniques and capturing the public's imagination and support. The effort sparked great interest, and less than six months after the Clemons Tree Farm was dedicated in June 1941, the National Lumber Manufacturers' Association started a national campaign among timberland owners under the title American Tree Farms System.

Coordination was assumed by the American Forest Products Industries Association (a National Lumber Manufacturers' Association subsidiary now known as the American Forest Institute) in 1942. During its infancy the program appealed mostly to large timberland owners, and 5 million acres were certified as tree farms in 1942, nearly 7.5 million in 1943, and more than 17 million by 1949. After three years, tree farms in the South averaged ten thousand acres. In the early period there were charges that much of the acreage certified belonged to lumbering operations that simply courted the favorable publicity and met minimal standards. The inspection and requirements for certification were stiffened in response to this situation and made to appear less industry controlled. Greater emphasis was also placed on enrolling smaller landowners. Critics also charged that the program was an industry effort to avoid government regulation of cutting and other practices on their lands. The industry's concern was well founded, for the 1941 *Report of the Chief of the Forest Service* said that the only alternative to regulation of private lands was public ownership and management of more land.

The tree-farm movement reached Mississippi in 1943 and was originally sponsored by the Southern Pine Association. Sponsorship of the program was soon assumed by the Mississippi Forestry and Chemurgic Association. In the spring of 1945 Mississippi had only forty-six tree farms,

with total holdings of 58,586 acres. However, by 1955 the Magnolia State led the nation in the number of private forest landowners using progressive forestry practices and recognized as Certified American Tree Farmers. Mississippi has subsequently remained the perennial national leader. By August 1966 Mississippi had 3,535 tree farms with a total of 3,279,468 acres. Some large companies put their own lands into the system. Critics charged that tree-farm boosters claimed too much, including the "initial discovery that trees grow and can be treated as a crop," but the program undeniably boosted the implementation of good forestry practices on many of America's forests, large and small.[102]

The early development of Mississippi's tree-farms system reflects the fact that there is no single or simple definition of good forestry practice. Nelson operated a tree farm in Mississippi at the time the system was organized, and he participated in the discussions to determine what good forestry practice was and what would be required to qualify an operation for tree-farm status. Said Nelson, "I remember that after much discussion, the idea of any set of numbers was discarded, and instead the concept of the proven practice of forestry by any one of a number of methods would be accepted for eligibility to participate in the TREE FARM program. The only two practices that were absolutely dis-qualifying were clear cutting and the absence of any attempt to control wildfires. . . . As the TREE FARM inspection reports began flowing into Jackson, they revealed a wide variety of treatments and programs to restore timber productivity for the particular property under consideration."[103]

The tree-farms program was a means for the lumber and paper companies to assure themselves of an adequate timber supply from small, private landholdings. One timberland owner from Meridian remembered, "There was a company up here in Philadelphia, DeWeese Lumber Company. They had sold out to Weyerhaeuser. . . . They had come over in this area. And they started tree farming, and it was one way they had of getting the timber and lumber. Getting people that had small tracts of timber lands like I did to get interested in their tree farming program, and they would look after our timber lands, and then we sold them our timber. So they had a steady supply that way." Tom DeWeese and Allen had introduced the "tree farm family" concept to the company long before the Weyerhaeuser takeover and were sometimes credited with introducing the idea to Mississippi.[104]

Mother Nature played a major role in the rebirth of Mississippi's forests. One of the first signs of encouragement for the future occurred on cutover lands, many of which had ostensibly been clear-cut, on which new trees began to appear and even to reach merchantable size in the 1930s and 1940s. Mississippi's "second forest" had begun to mature. And small, portable, peckerwood mills started to harvest that timber. A resident of Whynot, in eastern Mississippi, recalled that "there were little sawmills scattered throughout the countryside, and people would move those sawmills from one place to the other. This was in the 40's and the 50's and on up to the 60's." Although production lagged far behind Mississippi's peak in the mid-1920s, by 1940 the state was again producing more than 1 billion board feet of lumber.[105]

Dick Allen with DeWeese Lumber Company tree farm sign. Courtesy Forest History Society, Durham, North Carolina.

Helen Phillips, a Meridian resident who worked with her father in the lumber business in the 1930s, remembered that at a time when "the bigger companies felt like the timber was all gone . . . my father had a vision back then in 30 that we still had timber around here." Cicero Sellers, a resident of Clarke County who had a small sawmill in the 1940s, said, "The timber was cut out pretty well. Big mill here in Quitman, Longville Lumber Company, they cut out pretty well, and they let their land go back to the county as much as they could. And later on timber began to come back. It wasn't all as cut out as we thought it was because there were patches, tracts of timber that hadn't been cut. . . . [S]ince then there have been thousands and millions of trees have been planted. And we planted several hundred acres, and we have cut that timber a couple of times since then, and this is 1991, and that was in the 40's you might say."[106]

Another old-timer, Raymond Gressett, remembered that trees survived not because of a conscious conservation policy but because there was such an abundance of large timber and because the small trees had little value: "They did leave more stuff then than they do now. . . . They had so much of that old big stuff. They didn't have to fool with nothing. So, they left everything from about 30 inches down." Alfred Frazier, a resident of Kemper County who worked for the Molpus Lumber Company of Philadelphia in 1940 and 1941, remembered that in that period the lumbermen did not clear-cut "like they do now. . . . They just took the best stuff. You know, mature stuff," leaving the smaller trees.[107]

Edgar Pope also remembered high grading and noted that "clear cutting didn't come along until just a few years ago. . . . Back there . . . they made a deed. . . . [T]he timber buyer would come along and say, what'll you take for that piece of timber. . . . [T]hey'd specify certain size stumps. Say, 12 inches up or 8 inches, or whatever they agreed on. So high from the ground. Well, they got to where they'd get up an argument about cutting the stumps. . . . And they got to where . . . they'd say, at the ground. That meant low as you could cut it. . . . If you cut it down like that, in them bare spots, you had to leave so many trees. Seed trees they called them."[108]

By the late 1950s the public and private foresters of Mississippi, with the help of Mother Nature, had overseen a remarkable recovery of Mississippi's forests. Foresters were implementing significant programs in planting, harvesting, pest control, and timber-stand improvement. The national forests, despite heavy overuse and the abandonment of most reconstructive efforts during World War II, were moving toward the point where they could truly be managed for multiple uses. Despite concerns about harvests that exceeded growth, according to U.S. Forest Service timber surveys, and about underproduction from privately owned noncorporate lands, the private forests could amply support both a burgeoning pulp and paper industry and the recovering lumber industry. Forest-products companies were actively promoting improved forest-management practices among private, nonindustrial forest owners. The tree-farms movement was creating new forests on private land, and public-private cooperation was drastically reducing the fire risk in Mississippi's forests. The foundations for Mississippi's forests of the future had been established.[109]

8   The Greening of Mississippi

From Recovery to the Present

By the late 1980s it had become fashionable in forestry circles to describe the young forests that were being planted and nurtured at that time as the South's "fourth forest." In that theoretical framework the first forest was, as the U.S. Forest Service described it, the "forest that existed in the South before the first clearing or harvest." The second forest was the "forest that became established in the South following the harvest of the region's original forests of virgin timber . . . the source of the bulk of the wood used by the forest industries from the 1930's through the 1960's." The third forest was defined as the "forest that became established in the South in the period from the 1930's through the 1960s . . . the source of the bulk of the wood used by the forest industries from the 1970's through 2000." And the fourth forest would be the "forest that will exist in the decades beyond 2000, after the harvest or clearing of the third forest—the one that now exists in the South." In the late 1960s the Southern Pine Association, Forest Farmers Association, Southern Hardwood Lumber Manufacturers' Association, and American Plywood Association commissioned the Southern Forest Resource Analysis, which in 1969 produced a report entitled *The South's Third Forest* and recommended intensified management to increase timber production in the nation's third forest 2.3 times by 2000.[1]

Industrial and government foresters, trade associations, citizens'-action groups, and state private and public organizations such as the Mississippi Forestry Association and the Mississippi Forestry Commission helped to create and restore the second and third forests. By the 1950s Mississippi's forests were beginning to benefit from policies and practices that would combine to return them to more than a semblance of their former magnitude. The resurgence of the forests brought growth and change to the forest-products industries. For lumbering, the growth was jump-started by the World War II demand for lumber to construct military facilities in Mississippi, across the nation, and around the world. The need to produce lumber and pulpwood was so great that loggers and manufacturers resorted to the use of prisoners of war to supplement their depleted labor forces. Edgar Pope of Neshoba County was sawmilling at the time, and he remembered "that was when they were building Camp Shelby, and they were using a lot of lumber down there. . . . There was about two years there that every plank I cut went direct to Camp Shelby."[2]

The wartime thirst for lumber was followed by even greater demand in the postwar period, as Americans quickly undertook construction projects that had been postponed during the conflict. The demand for lumber was so great that concerns about quality virtually disappeared, opening the door for small mills with low standards to control much of Mississippi's market. Most of Mississippi's lumber mills in this period were small operations sawing logs from scattered and depleted timber stands. The demands of World War II and postwar markets strained Mississippi's timber supply, and a 1946–48 resurvey of the state's forests by the Southern Forest Experiment Station indicated a "deteriorating forest resource." H. H. Crosby argued that the drain as a result of portable sawmills was not noticeable until after 1941, but that by 1947 Amite County had been "almost completely stripped of timber." Johns Manville forester John W. Thompson observed "rapid depletion during and since the war for both pulpwood and small sawmill timber" in Franklin County. There was some doubt about the forests' ability to satisfy the raw material needs of Mississippi's forest-products industries. However, while housing starts in the United States by 1959 were 53 percent above the 1946 level, over that period of time Mississippi producers lost much of their market to Douglas-fir manufacturers from the West. Cost advantages, quality differences, consumer preferences, stumpage prices, and freight rates worked to the westerners' advantage, and many mills disappeared as the production of both hardwoods and softwoods declined.

The markets for Mississippi pine lumber changed after World War II, and so did the means of transportation. In 1930 51 percent of Mississippi's production went to Missouri, Kentucky, Iowa, Illinois, and Ohio. By 1959 those states bought only 13 percent of Mississippi's pine lumber. The volume dropped from 562 million board feet to 57 million. These markets were lost to nonwood substitutes, such as bricks, and to western producers of Douglas fir. By the early 1950s the western mills could produce and ship lumber to the area more cheaply than could their Mississippi competitors, largely because of low stumpage prices.

Consumer preferences were also important. Even in Mississippi, many builders preferred Douglas fir over southern pine, partly because southern pine producers converted their higher-grade timber into more expensive specialty products and produced two-by-fours and other construction material from less desirable logs. The growth of cities and industrial expansion along the Gulf Coast and in neighboring states partially offset the loss of the northern markets.

There was also a shift from shipment by rail to truck transportation as a result of high rail rates, the fact that trucks had more flexibility and could deliver directly to customers and construction sites, and a developing symbiotic relationship with Mississippi's growing chicken industry. Trucks carried lumber to the Midwest and returned with corn and other grain for the chicken producers. By 1959 Mississippi consumed nearly half of its own lumber production and shipped 36 percent into adjoining states. By 1961 western lumber was dominant in all markets outside of the southern pine-producing states.[3]

Western lumber replaced southern pine for use as structural timbers, in home exteriors, and for interior molding, cabinets, and trim. Softwood plywood took the markets for subfloors, roof decking, and wall sheathing in domestic construction. Insulation and hardboard were substituted for lumber; while aluminum was used for millwork in windows and doors and exterior siding and brick, stone, and glass were used for exteriors. Concrete slabs replaced crawl-space foundations, and steel and aluminum were utilized for structural materials. From 1946 to 1959, southern pine shipments fell by 25 percent. Also, the small lumber producers faced a shortage of stumpage. The new consciousness of forest management plus the pulpwood market persuaded some landowners to hold their timber off the market while improving their timber stands. Large pulp and paper companies were buying timberlands and putting them under management. Thus, the available lumber stumpage often came from small and scattered stands of relatively small, low-quality trees.[4]

A notable change in the Mississippi pine lumber industry after World War II was the shift from small to large mills. In 1946 there were 978 mills in the state, and by 1959 there were only 117.

Sixty percent of this change resulted from the disappearance of small mills producing less than 500,000 board feet annually. By 1959 more than half of Mississippi's mills were medium sized, and the average operation produced more than 2 million board feet annually, compared with less than 1 million board feet in 1946. Many small mills dropped out, and a lot of the survivors increased their production during the period. The disappearance of the small, peckerwood mills also brought a decline in the importance of the concentration yards that had been their principal markets.[5]

By 1959 the southern pine lumber industry in Mississippi, including sawmills, sawmill-planers, and concentration yards, employed 3,747 workers, including loggers. Seventy-two percent were employed by firms producing more than 3 million board feet annually. More than half the workers, 56 percent, were employed at sawmill-planers, 24 per cent at sawmills, and 20 percent at concentration yards. The workers were poorly paid, with 94 percent making less than $1.50 an hour as late as 1962. Sawmill production workers in 1962 earned $1.22 an hour, from one to two cents per hour lower than in other states of the Southeast, and from 1949 to 1957 they were paid, on average, twenty-six cents per hour less than the average for all manufacturing production workers in Mississippi. The high percentage of unskilled workers in the mills largely explains these figures. The total number of sawmill workers decreased, as did the number of mills, especially the small operations.[6]

However, after 1960 the southern lumber market improved, and by the mid-1970s, the South's forest industries produced a quarter of the nation's softwood lumber and half of its hardwood. The South also produced 29 percent of the nation's softwood plywood, 40 percent of its hardwood plywood, 60 percent of pulpwood, 62 percent of paperboard, 56 percent of newsprint, and 60 percent of treated wood. The South's output of pulpwood grew fourfold from 1946 to 1972, and its pulping capacity grew from sixteen thousand tons per day in 1946 to eighty-eight

thousand tons per day in 1972. By 1972 the South also produced 48 percent of the nation's particleboard, 57 percent of its hardboard, and 52 percent of its insulation board. Mississippi had five hardwood plywood plants with a capacity of 123 million square feet. By 1971 Mississippi had twenty-one thousand workers employed in the lumber and wood-products industry and fifteen thousand in paper and allied products. By 1968 forest-based industries furnished 28 percent of all manufacturing employment and 26 percent of all manufacturing payrolls. Also by 1968 value added in timber-based economic activities in the state was more than 500 million dollars, and timber-based manufacturing plants made up 36 percent of all manufacturing facilities. In 1972 Mississippi lumber reentered the world market, as a large shipment of southern pine moved through Gulfport toward Germany. In the same period the W. E. Parks Lumber Company signed a contract to cut and mill southern pine lumber for use in Japanese bowling alleys. In 1981 the Mississippi Cooperative Extension Service declared forestry the number-one crop in Mississippi, surpassing cotton and soybeans for the first time.[7]

There were some ironic stories behind the statistics. For example, the Edward Hines Lumber Company of Chicago was one of the largest Mississippi sawmill operators during the early-twentieth-century bonanza era of cut-out-and-get-out logging and lumbering. Hines was among those most anxious to get out, as he deliberately denuded his lands to avoid taxation and fled to the lush forests of the Pacific Northwest. In 1968 the Hines company returned to Mississippi and took over the property of the Hardy Graves Lumber Company in Hazlehurst. The Hines company's president said that the decision to come back to Mississippi was based in part on "recognition of the excellent conservation programs in effect in the state." The company's products were marketed through its own building-supply centers. In the 1980s a deteriorating economy, including a depressed home-building industry that saw housing starts drop to their lowest point since 1946, found the Hines company in deep trouble. In

1981 its southern mills had substantial financial losses, and the company decided to sell them. By 1983 two of the three mills were gone, and Hines was moving toward getting out of the manufacturing end of the lumber business entirely. The Hines Lumber Company saga in Mississippi had come full circle.[8]

There were also happier personal stories that reflected the larger patterns in society. Among these was the saga of Warren A. Hood, whose rise to economic power was made possible by the return of Mississippi's forests. Born in 1916 and raised on a farm in Copiah County, Hood left the family farm at age twenty-one to labor in a nearby sawmill. By the late 1930s he was working with a cousin who operated a sawmill near Crystal Springs. In 1939 Warren obtained financial assistance from a friend and purchased his cousin's peckerwood mill for nine hundred dollars. In 1944 Hood bought a planing mill at Hermanville in Claiborne County and established the Hermanville Lumber Company. A plant and then a wholesale lumber office in Jackson soon followed under the name Hood Manufacturing Company. By the 1950s Hood owned several mills that prospered during the post-World War II housing boom, and he had become a director of the Mississippi Forestry Association and a founder of the Mississippi Pine Manufacturers' Association. By the end of the decade the Hood Manufacturing Company moved from Jackson to Wiggins and became the Wiggins Lumber Company.[9]

In 1960 Hood combined a number of companies into a larger conglomerate called Mississippi Industries (changed to Hood Industries in 1969). Hood Industries advertised itself as "the largest lumber operation east of the Mississippi River." In the 1960s Hood also entered the paper business with the construction of a corrugated-box factory in Houston, Mississippi, followed by other paper operations in Clinton, Yazoo City, and Memphis, Tennessee. In 1966 Hood acquired the Crosby Lumber and Manufacturing Company from the St. Regis Paper Company. With the acquisition of Crosby, the total output of mills controlled by

Hood exceeded 110 million feet per year, making his conglomerate the largest producer of southern pine. In 1970 Hood Industries merged with Masonite Corporation, and Hood became one of that company's largest stockholders. He then moved on to a highly successful banking career.[10]

Hood's love for Mississippi was dramatically demonstrated in 1969 and 1970. On August 17, 1969, Hurricane Camille struck the Gulf Coast and brought timber damage to 1.9 million acres in fifteen counties. By the time the storm moved north and east and left the United States, the chief of the National Hurricane Center had termed it the greatest storm ever to hit the nation. Estimates placed Mississippi's timber damage at 285 million cubic feet, including sawlogs, poles, and pulpwood. The value of the hurricane-damaged timber was estimated at about $50 million. Governor John Bell Williams appointed a Forest Salvage Council, headed by Hood, and in the next several months it coordinated the harvest of some 77 million cubic feet of damaged timber. Working with both small landowners and the large forest-products companies, the council attempted to enable small owners to continue sales at the same levels and prices as before the storm. The companies, despite their own large supplies of storm-damaged timber, were persuaded to buy from the small producers at prestorm prices. Fleets of trucks from within and outside Mississippi hauled the damaged timber to mills before it could deteriorate. Praising Mississippi's efforts, the chief of the U.S. Forest Service wrote to the Mississippi state forester, "Even with almost unsurmountable obstacles, it was possible to harvest in less than seven months 800,000 cords of pulpwood and about 86 million board feet of sawtimber from the damaged timber stands. . . . [T]he timber losses to thousands of forest landowners were substantially reduced." The Forest Service and the Mississippi Forestry Commission performed yeoman service in the salvage effort, and under Hood's guidance Camille's devastating impact was somewhat lessened.[11]

Hood's story parallels the evolution of the

modern Mississippi forest-products industry. Starting in peckerwood sawmills that cut the remnants and scrubby regrowth left behind by the big mills of the bonanza era, Hood's operations grew along with the second forest until he had put together one of the region's largest multimill operations. He moved beyond lumber manufacturing and began to acquire pulp and paper operations as well. Then, like many other companies, he diversified and brought in companies in related fields. Finally, he joined forces with Masonite, a prime example of the technological innovation that brought change and revival to the forest-products industry. Hood consciously decided to remain in Mississippi and help to build the economy and provide jobs for his state. Early in his career, he seriously considered moving to the West Coast, as many others had done, but his allegiance to Mississippi was too strong. That strength of commitment, combined with loyalty to friends and family in both high places and the ordinary walks of life, energy, vision, and a willingness to allow the people he employed to do their jobs without interference were the keys to Hood's success. His story is a shining example of what the recovery of Mississippi's forests made possible.

There are other cases as well. Richard A. Allen was another Mississippi native and loyalist who helped to rebuild Mississippi's forests and then benefited personally and professionally from what he had wrought. A native of Brooklyn, in south Mississippi, Allen attended the University of Tennessee and earned a forestry degree from the University of Georgia in 1938. He then worked for the U.S. Forest Service as a nursery specialist, joined the Mississippi Forestry Commission as nursery and planting manager, and worked with the Mississippi Cooperative Extension Service as an extension forester. In 1946 Allen joined the A. DeWeese Lumber Company in Philadelphia as chief forester and later became general manager. When DeWeese was acquired by Weyerhaeuser, Allen served as vice president and general manager of Weyerhaeuser operations in Indonesia and then returned to Missis-

sippi as the company's vice president of Mississippi-Alabama operations. After retiring back to Philadelphia, Allen became a consulting forester. In 1980, however, he was called to become state forester at a time when the Mississippi Forestry Commission was in disarray. Allen capped his career by reinvigorating the agency and its personnel in just over two years of service from the spring of 1980 through the summer of 1982, when he again retired. Allen was one of the pioneers who helped to restore the forests that made his own distinguished career possible.[12]

Others who helped to rebuild Mississippi's forests were outsiders who came to the state and never wanted to leave. For example, Arthur W. Nelson Jr. came to Mississippi to join in a great crusade that has been the central experience of his life. An Illinois native who was deeply impressed by the natural reforestation of land in Minnesota's Chippewa National Forest, where he attended summer camp as a young man, Nelson decided to make growing trees his life's work and earned an undergraduate forestry degree at the University of Idaho. One of Nelson's professors told him, "If you really want to do something in your lifetime, go South." Nelson enrolled at the preeminent school for southern forestry at that time, Yale University, earning a master of forestry degree from the Yale Forest School. At Yale Professor Herman H. Chapman, who had worked with the Urania and Crossett Lumber Companies, led Nelson to temporary jobs in Louisiana and Arkansas, including a stint as a forester and timber cruiser for Crossett. In 1940 Nelson went to work for the Flintkote Company as chief forester; he subsequently joined the Champion Paper and Fibre Company as a special resources consultant in Texas. Nelson rose to become general manager of timber in Champion's Timber and Chemical and Woodlands Division in 1958, and in 1966 he was promoted to vice president for woodlands. In 1969 he became vice president for natural resources and in 1973 he became vice president for industry affairs for Champion International Corporation's timberlands operations. After assignments in Texas and Ohio, Nelson retired to

Meridian, where he consulted and managed his tree farm. He has been a frequent contributor to professional journals and has remained active in foresters' and forest industry organizations. Like Allen, Nelson's career helped to shape and benefited from the resurrection of the southern forests.[13]

Another northerner who came to Mississippi to stay was John Guthrie. Born in Florida but reared in northern Indiana, Guthrie earned a forestry degree from Purdue University. At Purdue he was involved in efforts to develop a mechanical tree-planting machine, and following graduation he moved to Mississippi as a forester with the Illinois Central Railroad, which developed one of the great railroad forestry departments. Guthrie was employed to promote better forestry on the Gulfport Branch (the Gulf and Ship Island Railroad) and participated in the development of the Illinois Central Tree Planter, which became a major vehicle for Mississippi's reforestation. Guthrie stayed in Mississippi to become a leading consulting forester and a pillar of the forestry community, serving as the first chairman of the board of registration as the state adopted a program of professional certification for practicing foresters.[14]

Another Purdue graduate, James W. Craig, was a native of Panola County. He earned his forestry degree in 1936 and then went on to the New York State College of Forestry at Syracuse, where he received a master's degree in 1938. Following World War II Craig returned to Mississippi and served as chief of fire control for the state forestry commission before establishing his own business as a consulting forester in 1948. He claimed to be one of the first three professional foresters in Mississippi to "offer forestry services for hire." Craig returned to public service as the successful state forester from 1952 through 1955. Craig also founded a Jackson company, Forestry Suppliers, which became one of the largest forestry supply houses in the nation. Craig's career also reflects the rebirth of Mississippi's forests.[15]

The return of the forests is one of the great stories of postwar Mississippi history. And in some ways today's forests are superior to the late, lamented, mythologized "virgin" forests of yesteryear. As Jonathan Daniels wrote at the end of the 1950s, "The forest of 1957 is not the wilderness of Daniel Boone or even Audubon. Not many pine woods now rise to make easy the picture of a brown, needle-carpeted cathedral nave of tall trunk and green crown. Actually, however, the virgin wilderness was less productive than the managed forests of today. The virgin forest of the United States averaged only about 18 cords of mature trees per acre, while a managed forest can produce in one lifetime nearly three times this amount. Also, the Southern forest is, of course, not merely the pine or all the pines, longleaf and loblolly, shortleaf and slash. It includes the oaks and gums, ashes and maples, sycamores, hackberries, hickories and cottonwoods, bays and magnolias."[16]

By 1958 the Forest Survey of Mississippi, part of a national forest inventory conducted by the Forest Service, reported encouraging news from the Magnolia State. By that time the state's forest area was increasing and had reached 17.2 million acres, some 57 percent of the total land area. The expansion of hardwood forests at the expense of pine had been reversed, and the stocking of forestlands had improved. The growth of softwood was increasing and exceeded the volume of harvests, while the opposite was true for hardwoods. Lumber production had declined slightly since the end of World War II, and the survey estimated that about one thousand commercial sawmills were operating in the state, down by roughly half since 1946. About seventy large mills produced two-fifths of the output from softwood sawlogs and more than half of the hardwood. Conversely, pulpwood production had risen dramatically and accounted for a third of Mississippi's annual roundwood output. The rise of hardwood pulpwood was the most dramatic, and roughly one of every three cords of pulpwood produced in the South came from Mississippi. The paper industry had also increased its use of wood residues, including sawmill slabs and edgings and veneer cores and trimmings.[17]

In the postwar period, Mississippi's forest-products firms grew significantly. Some of the old lumber companies sold out to pulp and paper firms, such as Crosby to St. Regis and L. N. Dantzler to International Paper. Others moved in to construct new facilities in the Magnolia State. In 1951, Georgia-Pacific Plywood and Lumber Company (later Georgia-Pacific Corporation) constructed a hardwood and cypress mill at Greenwood with an annual capacity of 16 million board feet. The company also constructed a southern pine plywood plant at Louisville, Mississippi. By 1963 Georgia-Pacific was the world's largest manufacturer of softwood and hardwood plywood. In 1982 the company, which had moved its headquarters from Georgia to the Pacific Northwest in the 1950s, returned to Atlanta. The move reflected the fact that by the early 1980s the Sunbelt states accounted for more than 70 percent of the nation's housing starts.[18]

In 1950 International Paper Company (IP) opened a pioneering new mill at Natchez that utilized the hardwoods of the river bottoms to produce pulp by the sulfate process. The mill consumed 700,000 cords of hardwood yearly to produce pulp that was used in the manufacture of rayon cloth and tire cord, plastic, cellophane, and other products. The Natchez mill was the first in North America to produce rayon pulp from hardwoods by the sulfate process. The mill created a new market for hardwoods, especially gum. By the early 1990s the mill had been reworked to reduce odor emissions by more than 80 percent and spent more than $30 million annually on wood purchases alone.[19]

The return of the southern forests was remarkable, for by the end of World War II the demands of the lumber firms and the pulp and paper mills for timber to support the war effort had taken a heavy toll. A U.S. Forest Service survey showed that good cutting practices had been followed on only 2 percent of private forests of less than five thousand acres during the war and had simply been abandoned on vast acreages of forestland during the conflict. Fortunately, the pulp and paper companies, some lumber firms, government foresters, and others labored mightily to bring the forests back. Through their efforts from 1935 to 1960, the standing tree volumes increased from 120 to 131 billion cubic feet and growth increased 35 percent, while during the same period 147 billion cubic feet were harvested. These successes and the growth of the second forest inspired many paper firms to build or expand manufacturing facilities. By the early 1960s some sixty paper mills were scattered across the South from Texas to Virginia. Among the companies that constructed large plants were Halifax, Champion, IP, St. Regis, Mead, Crown Zellerbach, Container Corporation, Rayonier, West Virginia, Brown, Scott, Buckeye, Union Camp, and Bowater.[20]

Mississippi was in the mainstream of this growth. In the period from 1963 to 1967 alone forty-six new plants and thirty expansions in the wood-using industries were recorded, including four plywood mills and three new pulpwood mills. In fact, by the early 1980s timber was the leading source of income in Mississippi, ranking ahead of both cotton and soybeans, and the forest industry accounted for 20 percent of the state's manufacturing employment. Companies were continuing to build, buy, sell, and trade facilities and assets. On the Mississippi River, in 1967 IP opened a new containerboard mill at Vicksburg that featured what was at that time the world's largest paper machine. In 1979 Weyerhaeuser doubled production at its Bruce plant and announced plans for a huge new pulp and paper complex at Columbus. Georgia-Pacific announced a new hardwood sawmill in southwest Mississippi, and IP dedicated a research facility at Natchez. The following year a partnership of landowners, newspaper publishers, and the Canadian newsprint manufacturing company Kruger announced plans for a $200 million newsprint plant in Grenada County, and Georgia-Pacific began operation of a new hardwood mill at Centerville. Great Northern Nekoosa Corporation and a Finnish firm released plans for a $540

FROM PULP TO PAPER

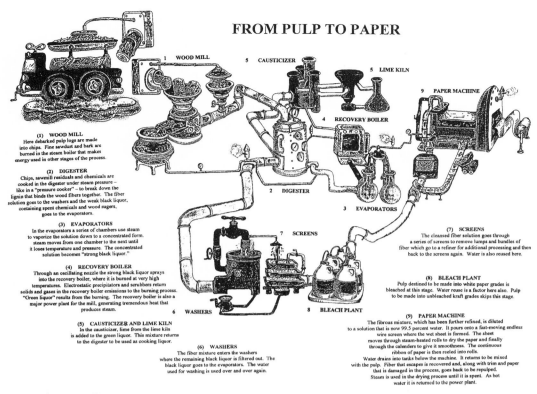

(1) WOOD MILL
Here debarked pulp logs are made into chips. Fine sawdust and bark are burned in the steam boiler that makes energy used in other stages of the process.

(2) DIGESTER
Chips, sawmill residuals and chemicals are cooked in the digester under steam pressure – like in a "pressure cooker" – to break down the lignin that binds the wood fibers together. The fiber solution goes to the washers and the weak black liquor, containing spent chemicals and wood sugers, goes to the evaporators.

(3) EVAPORATORS
In the evaporators a series of chambers use steam to vaporize the solution down to a concentrated form. The steam moves from one chamber to the next until it loses temperature and pressure. The concentrated solution becomes "strong black liquor."

(4) RECOVERY BOILER
Through an oscillating nozzle the strong black liquor sprays into the recovery boiler, where it is burned at very high temperatures. Electrostatic precipitators and scrubbers return solids and gases in the recovery boiler emissions to the burning process. "Green liquor" results from the burning. The recovery boiler is also a major power plant for the mill, generating tremendous heat that produces steam.

(5) CAUSTICIZER AND LIME KILN
In the causticizer, lime from the lime kiln is added to the green liquor. This mixture returns to the digester to be used as cooking liquor.

(6) WASHERS
The fiber mixture enters the washers where the remaining black liquor is filtered out. The black liquor goes to the evaporators. The water used for washing is used over and over again.

(7) SCREENS
The cleansed fiber solution goes through a series of screens to remove lumps and bundles of fiber which go to a refiner for additional processing and then back to the screens again. Water is also reused here.

(8) BLEACH PLANT
Pulp destined to be made into white paper grades is bleached at this stage. Water reuse is a factor here also. Pulp to be made into unbleached kraft grades skips this stage.

(9) PAPER MACHINE
The fibrous mixture, which has been further refined, is diluted to a solution that is now 99.5 percent water. It pours onto a fast-moving endless wire screen where the wet sheet is formed. The sheet moves through steam-heated rolls to dry the paper and finally through the calenders to give it smoothness. The continuous ribbon of paper is then reeled into rolls. Water drains into tanks below the machine. It returns to be mixed with the pulp. Fiber that escapes is recovered and, along with trim and paper that is damaged in the process, goes back to be repulped. Steam is used in the drying process until it is spent. As hot water it is returned to the power plant.

Diagram of a paper mill. *Crown Zellerbach Resource* 2 (summer 1973): 12–13. Modified by Cynthia M. Long.

million kraft pulp mill on the Leaf River at New Augusta in 1982. In 1983 alone Georgia-Pacific and Louisiana Pacific had plans to build strand board, wafer board, and lumber operations near Grenada, and IP opened a new concentration yard near Hardy. Crown Zellerbach announced a solid wood-conversion facility near McComb. Several large operations were planned for the McComb and Beaumont areas in south Mississippi as well.[21]

In 1968 the St. Regis Paper Company constructed, at a cost of roughly $100 million, a kraft paperboard facility called the Ferguson Mill near Monticello. It was described as "one of the largest manufacturing operations ever undertaken by a paper company anywhere in the world." The mill was built primarily to serve foreign markets and was ballyhooed by the company as a "Great New Kraft Mill." It would have two paper machines fed by two digesters, each

standing taller than a twenty-story building, and would utilize state-of-the-art computerized control and monitoring systems.[22]

The Ferguson Mill became an extremely important component of St. Regis's manufacturing: "its immense production supported all of the company's kraft operations." The mill was supported by the purchase of 152,000 acres of timberland, mostly in Mississippi, increasing the company's holdings in Mississippi and Louisiana to 350,000 acres. This supply was supplemented by a system that by 1966 was expected to furnish more than 800,000 cords of pulpwood annually. As one source describes it, "The Ferguson Mill was considered the axis for twenty-two concentration yards at outlying points in the supply territory. Contractors would deliver wood to the satellite-concentration yard and it would then be shipped to the mill. About one-half of the logs were debarked and chipped at plants set up in the forest, and the remainder were processed at the mill." The study concluded that the Ferguson Mill "profoundly affected many company operations" by making "possible a more extensive geographic distribution of the bag, kraft specialty paper, and container products. The company's smaller kraft mills, no longer burdened with the production responsibility assumed by Monticello, were freed to produce the specialized grades in which they best competed." Another major investment came in the late 1960s with the expenditure of $5 million for pollution-reduction equipment at the Monticello mill.[23]

In 1986 the Mississippi Chemical Corporation announced plans to construct a newsprint mill at Grenada, and in 1983 ground was broken for a Louisiana Pacific complex at Elliott, with a chipping mill going into operation first, to be followed by a wafer board plant. Georgia-Pacific began construction on an oriented strand board plant south of Grenada at Elliott in 1984. In north Mississippi by the late 1980s Weyerhaeuser continued to operate a large sawmill with chipping head rigs, and the Memphis Hardwood Flooring Company had large mills at Bruce and Potts Camp. The furniture industry of the area was beginning to rival North Carolina's production.[24]

In 1984 St. Regis sold the Monticello linerboard and kraft paper mill, as well as its Mississippi timberlands and cutting contracts, to Georgia-Pacific for $342.5 million. Champion's announcement of its acquisition of St. Regis soon followed. Champion was formed by the merger in 1967 of U.S. Plywood and Champion Papers. The paper company started in the 1890s at Hamilton, Ohio, near Cincinnati, and in 1905 it moved into the South with the acquisition of timberlands and construction of a mill in western North Carolina. The plywood company was originally oriented toward the West Coast, but in 1969 U.S. Plywood opened a $7 million particleboard plant at Oxford that used both pine and hardwood and was the largest of its kind in the world at that time. By the early 1980s Champion was producing particleboard at additional Mississippi facilities.[25]

The Crown Zellerbach Corporation, which originated in the pulp and paper industry of northern California and the Pacific Northwest in the 1870s, did not undertake a major effort away from its West Coast and Canadian bases until the 1950s. It then merged with Gaylord Container Corporation, whose origins were in the old Great Southern Lumber Company of Bogalusa, Louisiana, with extensive timber holdings in that state as well as in Mississippi. By the late 1980s Union Camp, whose southern facilities were concentrated in the Atlantic seaboard states and Alabama, operated a container plant in northeastern Mississippi.[26]

By 1980 Mississippi pulp and paper mills had a pulping capacity of 8,230 tons per day and owned 3,071,000 acres of timberland, which represented 18.7 percent of the state's total. These companies practiced intensive industrial forestry, attempting to maximize production from their own lands, leased lands, and lands managed for nonindustrial private owners (which Weyerhaeuser called its Tree Farm Family) to assure a reliable timber supply for their mills and pulping operations. Among these firms, Weyerhaeuser and IP stand out as the largest and, in some ways, the models. By the mid-1980s, Weyerhaeuser was the nation's largest lumber manufacturer and one of the biggest papermakers. It owned 3 million acres of forests in the South, principally in Oklahoma, Arkansas, North Carolina, and Mississippi, ranking second only to IP's 4.6 million acres. As one writer described it in 1985, "Weyerhaeuser has embraced the goal of higher forest productivity with particular fervor. Millions of its corporate dollars annually go into research on intensive silviculture in the South, and tens of millions into translating research results into forest management on the ground." The company referred to its efforts as "the Weyerhaeuser high yield forestry program." Some southern foresters called it the "Weyerhaeuser way."[27]

By the mid-1980s a working group of the Society of American Foresters looked back at silvicultural trends in the South since the 1930s and concluded that the primary developments were an emphasis on timber production, the natural regeneration and planting of pine on retired farm lands, and a sharp decline in the proportion of farmers owning commercial timberlands. There was also the reduction of pine harvesting rotations from about sixty years to around thirty. The group emphasized the fact that less than half of harvested pinelands were regenerated in pine and that hardwood growth far exceeded harvests. Looking toward the next thirty years, they predicted that an increasing area of forestlands would be better suited to hardwoods than pine, hardwood growth rates would decrease with increased harvests, most pine stands would be regenerated to pines, and pine harvest rotations would be increased from thirty to about forty-five years.[28]

The Forestry Productivity Committee of the Mississippi Forestry Association collaborated with a similar group from the Forest Industries Council to produce a 1979 study on the state's future timber supply. The report found that regeneration was not keeping pace with commercial forest timber production, noting that over a recent ten-year period pine growth in the state increased by only 16 percent while timber harvests and other softwood removals doubled. The biggest problem, the authors said, was on privately owned, nonindustrial lands. However, a U.S. Forest Service study for the period from 1948 through the late 1980s showed that softwood inventories in Mississippi had steadily increased (although they leveled off in the late 1980s) and that hardwood growing-stock volume had increased as well. In 1967 softwood growth more than doubled removals and in the next ten years exceeded removals by 56 percent. However, from 1977 to 1987 removals exceeded growth by 2 percent. Hardwood growth exceeded removals by 81 percent from 1977 to 1987.[29]

While Mississippi was again as green as in its earliest years, the problems that had devastated the earlier woods were not totally eliminated. For example, while public and private foresters and an increasingly enlightened public had fought courageously and somewhat successfully to stamp out the curse of woods fires and arson, the problems remained worrisome. At the end of World War II Governor Thomas L. Bailey told the legislature that the volume of timber in Mississippi had declined by at least one-eighth since 1940 and that one of the major contributing factors was fire. During the previous five years, he said, an average of 3.7 million acres of Mississippi forestland had burned, some 22 percent of the state's total forested area.

In 1956 the southern governors held a conference in New Orleans to address the issue. As Daniels put it, they wanted to "emphasize the fact that in these times setting fire to the woods is comparable to the poisoning of wells in the past" and "to emphasize the determination of their States to stop fires and treat woods arsonists like the criminals or idiotic enemies of the community which they are." The fact was that arsonists were rarely successfully prosecuted, even though the legal system and even Scripture said that they should be. As Allen noted in 1981, "Justice for woods burners has its biblical roots just as do many of the laws that today help sustain our free society." He cited Exodus 22:6: "If a fire break out, and catch in thorns, so that stacks of corn, or the standing corn, or the field, be consumed therewith; he that 'kindleth the fire shall surely make restitution.'"[30]

Still, said Daniels, in dealing with fire, "Prevention is the only effective procedure. Experienced foresters know that once a substantial fire gets started, no energy or equipment can quickly halt it. Until wind or rain takes the side of the fighters, blazing forests will jump the widest fire lanes and disregard the most desperate efforts of the most determined men. . . . [T]he foresters of States, counties, the United States, and, of course, the companies, are spending millions on fire prevention and suppression in the South. More could be profitably spent."[31]

Recent discussions of fire have taken on an ironic aspect. After treating fire as an unmitigated curse for decades, researchers and foresters found that fire was a necessary tool in certain situations in both pine and pine-hardwood forests.

As far back as 1912 Yale Professor Chapman had advocated the use of what would later be called prescribed burning in southern pine forests. In 1926 Chapman published his famous bulletin 16, which argued that the silvicultural use of fire to prepare seedbeds and control brown-spot needle blight was essential for the natural reproduction of longleaf pine. Chapman was generally derided and his ideas considered dangerous. However, some companies did utilize controlled burning. In 1945 and 1946 the Dantzler Lumber Company burned some 8,800 acres in Stone County to reduce the danger of destruction by wildfire. By burning this land, which had a past fire record of nearly 100 percent loss, Dantzler could focus its fire prevention and suppression measures on other lands, where it was able to cut its losses significantly. Fire was also used, as in the case of the Johns Manville company, "first, to destroy or reduce small hardwoods in predominantly hardwood areas as a prelude to planting or natural seeding, and second, [for] brush reduction in pure pine stands." A company report noted, "It is doubtful that pine would survive as an important tree species in our area over several generations without the use of fire or other artificial restocking measures." In the mid-1950s Johns Manville planned to burn about 3,500 acres of hardwood lands over a period of six years and a little less than 1,500 acres of pineland over five years. In 1946 A. D. Folweiler of the U.S. Forest Service said, "All fire in the forest no longer is regarded as detrimental. . . . Thus, there is an enormous educational task confronting the South—how to condition the average landowner in using fire so that it retains its status as a servant and does not become the master." Still, after decades of telling the public that fire was an unmitigated evil, the concept of controlled or prescribed burning was difficult to explain.[32]

One of the important stories of the modern Mississippi forest concerns the development of new technology and methodology in the growing, harvesting, and processing of timber. The major technological change of the period was the increasing use of coarse mill residues, slabs, and edgings and trimmings for pulp chips. One student termed it "the most important advance in southern pine sawmilling in decades." The technology was imported from Sweden, where machinery was developed to debark logs before sawing so that the slabs and edgings from lumber manufacturing were clean and, after chipping and screening, suitable raw material for pulp and paper. In the late 1940s a delegation of American lumbermen traveled to Sweden to examine the machinery, and in 1952 the first sawlog debarker, chipper, and screen was installed at the Southern Lumber Company in Warren, Arkansas. An installation at the W. T. Smith Lumber Company of Chapman, Alabama, soon followed. Not until 1956 did Mississippi lumber mills begin utilizing coarse sawmill residues for pulp chips. The Sanders Lumber Company of Meridian was one of the first to achieve complete utilization of its raw material. It produced lumber, sent the bark to the Ole Diz Charcoal Company at Pachuta, the shavings to Georgia-Pacific at Louisville, Mississippi, and the chips to Marathon (later American Can). As was often the case, a pulp and paper company, in this case Marathon, loaned the lumber firm the money to install its chipping and debarking machinery.

By 1959 southern pine sawmills and sawmill-planers produced 153,000 tons, with the larger mills—those producing more than 3 million board feet annually—producing 97 percent of the total. Between 1952 and 1960 at least one thousand southern mills installed debarking and chipping equipment. The peckerwood mills were completely frozen out of this market because of the high cost of debarking and chipping machinery and the waste of wood in their operations.

The new practices brought other changes as well, including the construction of chip-receiving and -storage facilities at the mills, the development of specialized railroad cars and trucks to haul the chips, and the advent of tree-length logging. The last change reflected the fact that since the entire tree could be used for either lumber or chips, it made sense to bring the entire tree into the mill to make that determination. Also in the

1950s, mechanized pulpwood-concentration yards began to appear, serving the pulp and paper industry, whose firms often operated the yards as markets for local wood producers. At these facilities wood could be delivered, scaled, mechanically unloaded from a truck, and loaded onto a railroad car within minutes. One of the first company wood yards placed into operation was the IP facility at Buckatunna, which opened in 1950.

By the mid-1960s some firms were experimenting with what were then called kerf-chip saws, which produced chips rather than sawdust in the process of sawing lumber. These machines became known as chipping head rigs, or Chip-n-Saws, after one particular brand whose registered trade name became generic in the industry. Some mills were introducing narrow-kerfed gang saws, which produced more lumber from a log than could be cut with a circular saw.[33]

Only two Mississippi mills had installed debarking and chipping machinery in 1956; by 1959, twenty-five mills, 22 percent of the total, had the equipment. By 1990 thirteen independent chip mills operated in Mississippi, some utilizing only hardwood, others exclusively pine, and some chipping both. There was also an increase in the use of mechanized and automatic equipment for lumber handling, including gang saws and automatic carriages in the mills; forklifts and straddle buggies in the yards; and power saws, tractors, side-loading trucks, and truck-mounted log loaders in the woods.[34]

By the 1990s other technological innovations transformed Mississippi's mills. Laser and optical scanners and computers determined log shapes and sizes and the best way to peel or saw them. Computers and optical scanners also controlled the edging and trimming of sawn lumber. Moisture and temperature sensors and computers controlled conditions in dry kilns. Thinner and more efficient saw blades increased the yield and quality of lumber. The first curve-sawing system was introduced in Mississippi, allowing the blades to follow the natural contours of sawlogs, thus increasing lumber quality and yield. These changes

combined to produce a healthy percentage increase in the output of wood products from harvested logs.[35]

During the past twenty years developments in logging have increased productivity and lowered logging costs in the South. Prior to the 1970s mills were forced to maintain large raw material inventories because the vagaries of weather, particularly wet weather, often interfered with timber harvesting. Improved year-round harvesting methods enabled mills to reduce their raw-material inventory levels, thereby changing mill operations. The construction of the St. Regis paper mill at Brookhaven introduced tree-length logging to Mississippi, and as Mississippi's mills moved from the utilization of short wood to tree-length timber, transport shifted from rail to trucks. The growing usage of chipping head rigs in lumber mills and the advent of chip mills led to the dominance of chips over roundwood in railroad shipments. The new logging equipment was expensive and pushed loggers to attempt to keep working, even in questionable weather, and probably contributed to logging site damage as well.[36]

One example of the ways in which equipment became faster and more productive is felling machines. Chainsaws became faster, lighter, and more powerful and fuel efficient. However, chainsaw felling, while still used, was often replaced by machines that could be driven directly to trees. These feller-bunchers had hydrostatic transmissions and could operate any one of a dozen felling attachments, thereby doing both jobs. Saw head attachments were commonly used in thinning cuts and in harvesting natural stands with mixed tree sizes. The advantages included productivity and the fact that these machines caused less damage to felled timber than did shears.

Rubber-tired skidders with improved grapples and wide tires that minimized site damage and enhanced machine performance also became common, as did mechanical delimbing equipment that often replaced delimbing with chainsaws. Similarly, machines that undertook debarking and chipping operations in the woods and others that produced precision cut-to-length logs also came into use. Harvester machines carried out both the felling and processing operations. Even transportation, which remained the most expensive part of logging, was improved with the use of lighter trucks and specially designed trailers with onboard scales to maximize payloads. Over the past forty years labor's productivity has increased by an estimated 750 percent because of the new technologies and methodologies.

In recent years there has been an emphasis on making machines more fuel efficient, ergonomically designed, safer, and less damaging to the forest. By the mid-1990s most Mississippi loggers felled trees with disc felling heads mounted on four-wheel drive, articulated carriers with rubber tires or on track-type vehicles for steep slopes or wet conditions. Three-wheeled vehicles with felling heads were used for thinning in plantations. Grapple skidders with rubber-tires (some as wide as sixty inches for use in wet weather) skid the trees with tops on to a loading dock, where they are topped and delimbed by a pull-through

delimber with knives. Knuckle-boom loaders pull the trees through the delimbers and load them onto trucks. The trees are topped by an automatic chainsaw. Some even more advanced technologies are in use, including Scandinavian harvesters and forwarders that minimize site damage and helicopter logging in some bottomlands. It is expected that computers and electronic and other sensors will make the logging machines of the future more productive, more environmentally sensitive, and easier to operate.[37]

Another technological development in forest management has been the increasing use of remote sensing technology. Film and video cameras, radar, and electro-optical scanners on airborne and spaceborne platforms have moved from the realm of the theoretical to the standard tool kits of many forest managers. Another weapon was added to this arsenal with the development of the Navstar global positioning system (GPS). Aerial photography for mapping became commonplace, with much of the technology developed by the military during World War II.

Navstar utilized a system of earth-orbiting satellites that offered continuous data and pro-

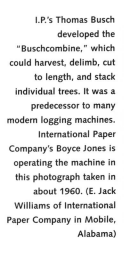

I.P.'s Thomas Busch developed the "Buschcombine," which could harvest, delimb, cut to length, and stack individual trees. It was a predecessor to many modern logging machines. International Paper Company's Boyce Jones is operating the machine in this photograph taken in about 1960. (E. Jack Williams of International Paper Company in Mobile, Alabama)

vided locational and boundary information at much lower cost than traditional ground surveys, which were labor intensive. Originally developed for use by the military, when completed the GPS would have eighteen satellites circling the earth around the clock. GPS receivers on the ground locked onto four satellites and recorded the data they were transmitting. The use of a GPS system enables forest managers to find sample points on photographs of otherwise featureless forests and to locate undocumented survey markers.

Among the uses of the photographic and satellite data are timber inventories, fire mapping, soil surveys, assessment and tracing of insect and disease epidemics, and evaluation of hurricane damage (as in the case of Hugo in 1989). The data generated by a GPS system works well in another new system, the geographic information system (GIS). The GIS is an electronic map that stores location data and descriptive information about features. A GPS system can feed a GIS system, which compiles, analyzes, and then presents a compilation of the information at its disposal in graphic form.[38]

The revival of hardwood forests and the development of technologies that created growing markets for their timber are important aspects of the modern greening of Mississippi. An important breakthrough was the U.S. Forest Products Laboratory's development of new semichemical and cold-soda processes that enabled hardwoods to produce quality pulps desirable for blending into fine bonds and book papers, corrugating board, newsprint, linerboard, food board, and food papers. Furthermore the high yields, as much as 90 percent of the dry weight of the wood, encouraged the use of such dense hardwoods as oaks for some paper products. The yield from the new processes was almost double that normally obtained from the sulfate process. During the period from the early 1950s to the mid-1960s, pulp and paper plants increased their use of southern hardwoods by six times. By the early 1960s 40 percent of the raw material for southern forest industries came from hardwoods. Also, a growing volume of hardwood was being used for building and in-

sulating boards, hardboards, and other fiberboards that could be fabricated without synthetic binders. Traditional hardwood markets in furniture, cabinetry, flooring, and other products continued to thrive. By the mid-1980s, 31 percent of the round pulpwood harvested in the South consisted of hardwoods.[39]

During the 1960s plywood producers and researchers at the Forest Products Laboratory developed efficient methods for producing plywood from second-growth southern pine. Southern states actively solicited new plants as municipalities and counties built, equipped, and leased manufacturing facilities and financed them with tax-exempt revenue bonds. The South also offered advantages in timber supply, lower freight costs resulting from proximity to markets, and cheaper labor over the plywood industry's old home in the Pacific Northwest. In 1963 a Georgia-Pacific plant in Fordyce, Arkansas, produced the first rotary-peeled, exterior-glued, structural plywood manufactured from southern pine, with other manufacturers soon to follow. In the early 1980s new plants producing wafer board and oriented strand board joined the southern panel board industry. By 1984 southern pine plywood production reached 9.7 billion square feet, nearly half of the national total.[40]

Scientific and technological change also transformed the naval-stores industry. At the turn of the century, rosin and turpentine were produced entirely by distilling gum from southern pines. However, the gum naval-stores industry has declined since the 1930s because of the cutting out of old growth timber, labor shortages, declining markets, and the development of alternative sources of supply. Starting in the 1920s steam distillation of stumps remaining from the logging of old-growth stands produced large quantities of rosin and turpentine. That production process reached its peak in the 1950s and has since declined to low levels. Since that time the drop in gum production and steam distillation has been offset by the recovery of tall oil and turpentine from the sulfate pulping process at southern pulp mills, which are now the primary sources of rosin and turpentine. In 1949 IP opened the first plant to produce high-quality rosin and fatty acids from tall oil by skimming off spent cooking liquors in the sulfate process. Since 1944 turpentine has been recovered from gases generated in the sulfate pulping process. By 1984 tall oil contributed 76 percent of total resin production, and sulfate turpentine accounted for 93 percent of the total production of turpentine. However, some traditional operations remained in Mississippi in the late 1970s, as second- and third-growth trees were worked for crude gum. There were no turpentine stills operating, and the processing was done in other states.[41]

In 1953 representatives from more than forty forest industries joined together to form the Southern Hardwood Forest Research Group. The group eventually included both companies and individuals. John A. Putnam of the Southern Forest Experiment Station and the Stoneville Research Center was elected chairman. The group sponsored regular field trips and a hardwood log and lumber grading course, which eventually settled in at the Louisiana Polytechnic Institute and utilized forestry students, U.S. Forest Service personnel, and staff members of the National Hardwood Lumber Association. During the field trips, J. S. McKnight said that the members discussed all sorts of topics, but "little mention has been made of pine. That worthy topic is left for other organizations and other times." A major step forward for hardwood research came in 1962 with the dedication at Stoneville of the Southern Hardwood Laboratory, an eighteen-thousand-square-foot facility with laboratories for seed, soils, plant physiology, plant pathology, and forest insect research. The complex includes administrative offices, a conference room-library, a photographic laboratory, and greenhouses covering 1,600 square feet.[42]

Hardwood advocates tend to feel overshadowed by the southern emphasis on pine, but some have a good sense of where the two woods fit in the modern scheme of things. At a 1960 meeting of the Southern Pulpwood Conservation Association in Atlanta, Philip A. Briegleb and McKnight summed things up well:

The hardwood forest of the South is a vast, valuable, heterogeneous, and comparatively neglected resource. To most people, the great southern pinery is the southern forest. . . . But the fact is that the southern forest is predominantly hardwood. Of the 193 million acres of forest land in the South, pines predominate on 92 million, hardwoods on 101 million acres. And overall, hardwoods make up 55 percent of the solid-wood volume of growing stock. Of course, hardwoods are now growing on extensive areas—totaling some 31 million acres in the South—where they do not belong. Here they are no credit to themselves, nor are they likely ever to be an asset for their owners. Conversion to pine is the prescription for such poor hardwood sites. Techniques for making this change in species have been developed by research and experience, and are now being applied vigorously by timberland owners over the South—particularly by the pulp and paper industry.[43]

Hardwood experts predicted the pulp and paper industry's demand for hardwoods would grow faster than its need for pine and noted that southern hardwoods were the nation's best, despite a history of poor management. Mississippi's hardwoods were representative of a decline in average tree size and quality across the South, but experts predicted that with intensive management, the batture lands along the Mississippi River would be especially productive sources for hardwoods, particularly cottonwood.[44]

Concerns about the conversion of hardwood lands to agricultural use remained intense and seemed especially apropos in the modern period. For several decades the total forested acreage in the South increased, partially because of the abandonment of farmland during the Great Depression and immediately after World War II. However, from the 1960s on, those trends reversed, with forests being cleared for agriculture. Hundreds of thousands of acres of former hardwood land in the Mississippi Delta were converted to soybean production, and projects like the Ross Barnett Reservoir claimed more.[45]

Conversely, Mississippi had some remarkable hardwood success stories. Crown Zellerbach Corporation planted cottonwood "sticks" in "rich Mississippi soil" at its Fitler Managed Forest near Vicksburg, where Crown Zellerbach had the world's largest cottonwood-planting program. The company annually planted about 500,000 cottonwoods from genetically improved stock derived through controlled breeding. The cottonwoods supplied hardwood pulp for Crown Zellerbach's paper mill in St. Francisville, Louisiana, which produced high quality coated printing paper.[46]

IP reported that "some hardwood trees, including twigs, branches, and bark, are chipped. . . . Such chips are being used for as much as 10 to 30 percent of the total mix at some pulp mills with no loss of value in the finished product." Speaking at a 1975 conference at Purdue University, C. Ronald Hunt, a senior project forester in hardwood research at IP's Southlands Experiment Forest, reported that "International Paper Co. has 10 of its 12 mills in the South using significant quantities of hardwood in its manufacturing processes, and the Company is therefore vitally interested in hardwood management."[47]

The utilization of hardwood chips by the pulp mills contributed to the solution of a long-standing problem in the southern forest-products industry. While there were various uses for hardwood and foresters who built their careers on the advocacy of hardwood and mixed pine-hardwood forests, many leaders and foresters of the southern pine-oriented industry had traditionally regarded hardwoods as intruders. These foresters had emphasized removal of the hardwoods so that the pine, which was historically more valuable, could be produced in greater volume. Of course one of the basic problems in forest management is the fact that decisions made today are based on projections of future needs and markets, and no one can be entirely sure of what those needs and markets will be.[48]

Another part of the effort to bolster hardwoods was the promotion of tree farms in the Delta. In the 1950s the Mississippi Forestry and Chemurgic Association published a pamphlet entitled *What Trees Mean to the Delta* that advised landowners that to enable Delta woodlands to produce a cash crop, they should keep fire out of their woods, cut selectively, keep cattle out of the forests, and consult professional foresters. The pamphlet said that 35 percent of the Delta was in forests and that only 1 percent was being properly managed or protected at a time when the state was cutting 20 percent more than it was growing. It said that 1.6 million acres of Delta land were "useful only for timber production."[49]

Partially because of the work of Putnam and his disciple, McKnight, as the industry moved into the 1970s and 1980s there was increasing recognition of the benefits of hardwood and/or mixed pine-hardwood forests not only for wood products but in terms of aesthetics, wildlife habitat, and recreation. It was also generally recognized that some sites were suitable only for hardwood production, while others favored pine. A rough rule of thumb was that watersheds, lowlands, river bottoms, and areas that were under water during part of the year were best suited to grow hardwoods, while the hilly, upland, dryer sites were better for pine. A forester or forest manager who tried to convert a natural hardwood area to pine was defying nature and common sense.[50] The emphasis on thorough utilization of the trees and the growing importance of hardwoods reflected changes in the forest-products industry during the 1960s and 1970s.

The increasing use of computers and sophisticated managerial concepts dominated the forest-products industry by the 1960s and 1970s. Net present value, financial maturity, stocking, site indexes, modeling, computer simulations, and other sophisticated concepts and tools made decisions even more difficult and subject to interpretation. Just like the pioneer industrial foresters of the earlier period, the managers and foresters of the 1970s and 1980s were faced with a range of choices, many of which could be made within the context of responsible forest practice. In the final analysis, when managing a forest property, common sense was still the best standard for judgment. What did the owner want from the property? What were the markets? What were the site conditions? What were the expenses? What actions were socially responsible?[51]

Regeneration of the forest through both natural reseeding and planting has been a focus of modern forest management. Genetic research and the development of "supertrees" have contributed to increased production, particularly on corporate lands. In 1955 the Southern Institute of Forest Genetics was established at Gulfport. Eventually three major tree-improvement cooperatives were created in the South as partnerships among universities, the forest-products industry, and government agencies. Forest genetics had practical results. In addition to the selectively bred, genetically improved cottonwood seedlings Crown Zellerbach planted in its Fitler Managed Forest, by 1973 the company had planted more than 325,000 acres with pine seedlings and had directly reseeded another 40,000 acres in Louisiana and Mississippi since the 1920s. The bulk of the reforestation stock consisted of nursery-raised, genetically improved bare-root seedlings. By the early 1970s forest-products companies generally considered seeding and planting more productive than natural regeneration.[52]

By 1968 IP planned to "put substantially all" of the company's lands into plantations and to reduce the rotation cycle from the existing forty- to fifty-year period down to twenty-five years. IP predicted that the combination of supertrees and the twenty-five-year cycle would double the productivity of its timberlands. Incidentally, IP reported that in fifteen years of research the company had "found only 308 trees in our southern forest with the same characteristics—faster growth, straightness of trunk, small crown, densely packed wood fibers. These are the parent stock for the first generation of supertrees." IP now predicted that within ten years, all of its planting would be supertrees and actively promoted what it called its "SuperTree Seedlings" for sale to private landowners.[53]

Despite the glamour of supertrees and the advent of pine plantations, by the mid-1980s 75 to 80 percent of the pine forests in the South were natural stands. Many environmentalists and some foresters advocated natural-stand management. Consulting forester L. Keville Larson observed that the respected former Bureau of Land Management chief Marion Clawson had noted that the "capacity of natural forest lands to regenerate timber stands and the capacity of timber to grow, even in the absence of man's help and often in spite of his wishes, tend to be overlooked or ignored." Larson argued that "[f]or many owners and situations . . . planting should be done only as a last resort."[54]

Allen experienced the evolution of beliefs about regeneration: "The site really is generally the determinant of what type of regeneration is called good forestry. . . . In . . . south Mississippi there are sites that are just disasters to direct seed . . . but over in Rankin County, Mississippi, Scott County, Mississippi, those flatlands are just absolutely great for direct seeding and seed trees. In fact, the United States Forest Service in Scott County has some of the best examples of good forestry I have ever seen where they leave six to ten seed trees to the acre, and it's just come back up like hair on a dog's back in time. And they use some direct seeding, too. . . . There are acceptable different methods of regeneration of timber. It's not all one way."[55]

During Allen's tenure as state forester in the early 1980s, the Mississippi Forestry Commission implemented a cooperative direct-seeding program with the forest-products industry. During the 1981–82 planting season 191,244 acres were planted and direct-seeded, the highest total in Mississippi's history. By the late 1980s Mississippi led the south-central states in artificial regeneration of hardwoods and in total acres of artificial regeneration, with 699,000 acres. However, by the same time period the Forest Service estimated that nearly 6 million of Mississippi's 16,072,000 acres of timberland needed treatment to improve productivity, including 1,098,000 acres of forest-industry land, 4,356,000 acres of other private land, and 367,000 acres of national-forest land. The Forest Service estimated that the investment in treatments would produce a return of 4 percent or more.[56]

Forest-products companies were concerned about and influenced by the unsettled conditions in the industry during the early 1980s. Corporate takeovers by raiders, high interest rates triggered by the inflation of the period, and the realization that fears of a timber famine had not materialized prompted changes in attitudes toward the value of timber holdings. As Ronald J. Slinn, vice president of the American Paper Institute, described the situation, "Rates of returns on . . . forest holdings often fell far below [the] internal hurdle rate [the minimum rate of return a corporation requires before it will invest in a particular project] for assets. Some companies put relatively large tracts of land on the market, hoping to capitalize on the national mood favoring ownership of real property. This would generate cash to invest in manufacturing plants or in other alternatives that would have a better return on invested capital. Profitability and responsibility to stockholders became compelling factors in determining individual corporate strategies and in ensuring fibrous raw material supplies."

The takeover aspect was particularly important in motivating companies to improve their economic defenses through restructuring or increasing cash flow. Some companies formed limited partnerships to separate forestry assets from the holdings of the parent company, thereby hoping to dissuade those who sought to acquire many undervalued forest assets in one stroke. Slinn argues that "the strong inflationary pressures of the early 1980s made owning real property a prudent step, and Wall Street focused fresh interest on pulp and paper companies: 'We believe that many forest products and paper company stocks are properly classified as undervalued asset situations, and this factor has increased their appeal to long-term investors and lenders.' Short-term investors and raiders found these kinds of companies appealing. Indeed, several companies adopted defensive measures to ward off takeovers."[57]

Another growing concern was wildlife and recreation, which became important considerations in some corporations' land management as early as the 1940s. For example, IP could and did convert some of these other products of the forest to profit, both monetary and indirect. By the late 1940s the company was providing game preserves and hunting leases for "the purpose of promoting good will toward the Company and interest in forest protection. . . . As a result of these leases . . . improved fire and trespass control will be obtained in addition to the benefit to the wildlife."[58]

John Tyler remembered that at IP during the 1940s and 1950s, "as far as game was concerned, we were very much interested in Mississippi in the game preserve which was on our lands up there. . . . And we cooperated with the State Game and Fish Commission on that." IP's wildlife experts at the Southlands research center conducted research on habitat and on "the interrelationships between various aspects of our forest-management programs and development of populations of wildlife of various desirable species. . . . In every area I-P feels that such cooperation in wildlife management and outdoor recreation at the state and local levels has become an important part of any modern program of industrial land management."[59]

By the 1960s, wildlife management and the provision of recreational opportunities had become serious business for some forest-products companies. Wildlife programs went through three stages. During the initial stage they were built around public use of existing game and fish resources. At that time, "little information was available on the biology of animals in managed forests or the improvement of habitat in plantations." During the second stage, the companies began to realize greater monetary returns from wildlife resources. The third phase, termed by some the "wildlife ecology stage," "began as a result of more intensive forestry practices and greater pressures for multiple use. Concern increased for non-game wildlife and non-consumptive forest recreation (hiking, canoeing, camping, bird-watching, etc.). Environmental concerns began to influence forest management decisions as heavily as recreational demands."[60]

By 1960 most of IP's lands and access roads were open to the public for hunting and fishing in season and for picnicking, hiking, canoeing, and other forms of outdoor recreation. By the mid-1970s nearly 1.3 million people visited the company's lands for recreational purposes during a one-year period. IP maintained forty-one rustic areas for picnics, boat-launching facilities, camping facilities, and nature trails. The company also opened its lands to organized groups that held national championships or field trials for fox hunters, archers, and bird dogs.[61]

In the mid-1970s 40 percent of IP's 5 million acres in the South were under some form of comprehensive wildlife management. As Darwin E. Fender, the director of land management for IP's Southern Kraft Division, reported in 1974, "18 percent is leased to hunting clubs; 12 percent is in company wildlife management areas where a fee is charged for hunting privileges and 10 percent is leased to the various states for state wildlife management areas. A significant amount of the remaining 60 percent will be put into intensive game management areas as habitats are improved and wildlife populations are increased." More than 90 percent of the South's industrially owned timberlands were open for public hunting and fishing by the 1970s, often in partnership with state fish and game commissions. In Mississippi the Masonite Corporation by 1975 had more than 215,000 acres of land in twenty-six counties that were open to the public for fishing, hunting, camping, hiking, and "other legitimate use."[62]

Other lands were set aside as nature preserves. Bowaters Paper Corporation developed the idea of "pocket wildernesses" of five hundred acres or less on their timberlands that were open to hikers. Champion International pioneered in the provision of easily accessible public hiking trails on their lands. In 1978 IP donated 457 acres of land in southwest Mississippi to the Nature Conservancy for public use as a nature area called Clark Creek Falls. The land is in a wooded area adjacent to the Mississippi River in Wilkinson County and contains seven waterfalls ranging in height from twenty to fifty feet.

The Nature Conservancy was also instrumental in the preservation of several other tracts, including more than thirty-two thousand acres purchased by the state for the Pascagoula River Wildlife Area and the Panther Swamp National Wildlife Refuge and the Mississippi Sand Hill Crane National Wildlife Refuge, purchased by the federal government from the Nature Conservancy, which had acquired the land through a donation from St. Regis. In December 1989 the organization purchased a pitcher-plant bog in southern Mississippi that contained a half dozen rare plant species and by that time was credited with preserving more than eighty-three thousand acres in Mississippi. Under the terms of Mississippi's Natural Heritage Act of 1978, IP listed nine parcels of company lands as "natural areas" in the winter of 1990, including a bald eagle nesting site in Harrison County, Foster's Creek in Copiah County, six "quaking bogs" in Harrison and George Counties, and Doby's Bluff in Clarke County. In 1999 IP donated a 1,700-acre tract in Moss Point and a 950-acre conservation easement along the Wolf River in Harrison County to the Conservation Fund.[63]

Many forest-products companies and other private timberland owners lease hunting rights to hunting clubs or individuals to generate income as well as discourage arson. By the late 1990s forestland managers were advocating leasing hunting rights to hunting clubs with the same rationales that had been offered by the pioneering foresters a half century earlier: hunting leases provided not only income but also protection for the land and goodwill within the community. Two executives of a forest-management company suggested, "Good clubs provide several additional sets of eyes on your property, offering protection against timber theft, road damage, dumping, arson, trespassing, and forest pests (such as pine beetles and beavers)." The vice president and general manager of the Masonite

Corporation's Southern Woodlands Division said that his company found the hunting clubs "extremely cooperative and conscientious in protecting the property against fire and trespass." Nelson remembered working with hunters during his days with Flintkote:

There had always been organized deer camps. They'd been doing that for years. Well, you're not going to interrupt that at all. So we just let them go right on doing that. . . . There would be four or five of those camps around. All of them would have a bunch of dogs. And the dogs would get lost and would turn up in the wrong camp. And there is nothing dearer to a guy than his hunting dog. . . . We'd just about stopped everything during hunting season, and we kept a radio truck around and . . . a lost dog would show up in some other camp's dogs, and a guy'd get on the radio and he'd say, "We got Old Blue over here." . . . And the same thing with turkey hunters. . . . They had camps. . . . It was a great excuse to get out into the woods and play poker and drink whiskey. . . . They would always have a couple of old black men around who were really good at barbecuing and make barbecue bull hogs, in great, big pits, you know. It was a real extravaganza. It went on for three or four days. And these people that you worked with like this, they were a great help in eliminating the fire situation. Also, when you worked with your neighbors . . . you'd find out who else would have some timber to sell.[64]

Of course private nonindustrial owners own most of Mississippi's forestland (71 percent in 1985). In addition to hunting on their own land, many of these owners leased hunting rights, usually on a per-acre basis. By the mid-1980s these leases sold for a range of from one dollar to eight dollars per acre, although there were a few cases where leases brought as much as thirty dollars an acre per year. The most hunted game species was the white-tailed deer, and in 1984 deer hunters spent an estimated $4 million on deer hunting, mostly on forested lands. The Mississippi Forestry Association actively encouraged landowners to make their lands available to the public for hunting and other forms of recreation. Some experts also encouraged landowners to maintain at least five mast-bearing oaks on each acre if they wanted to maintain a supply of game animals that fed on acorns, including deer, squirrels, wild turkeys, quail, and ducks. Another interesting development on private nonindustrial land was the program of Ducks Unlimited, the world's largest wetlands conservation organization, which planted approximately 10 million hardwood seedlings on more than thirty-four thousand acres in the river bottomlands of Arkansas, Louisiana, and Mississippi. Some funding was provided by the North American Wetlands Conservation Council, and seedlings were donated by IP and Weyerhaeuser. The restoration of the bottomland forests of the Mississippi alluvial valley would be a major boon for the migrating ducks, geese, and other birds of the Mississippi flyway.[65]

By the late 1980s Mississippi ranked third nationally in total wild turkey population, and wildlife experts were telling landowners that through proper management both timber and wildlife production were possible in most types of managed forests. Mississippi has one of the most active hunting populations in the nation. In 1989 about 37 percent of the population above the age of sixteen held hunting and/or fishing licenses, and many others hunted without possessing licenses. To cope with demands for hunting, some landowners joined together to form cooperatives to provide integrated wildlife and timber management on their lands.[66]

By the late 1990s wildlife had a major impact on Mississippi's economy. More than a million Mississippians sixteen years or older hunted, fished, or engaged in activities such as hiking, camping, photographing nature and wildlife, bird watching, feeding wildlife, and boating. According to the Forest and Wildlife Research Center at Mississippi State University, more than 505,000 Mississippians fished, more than 292,000 hunted, and another 742,000 engaged in "nonconsumptive activities." These recreationists pumped nearly a billion dollars annually into Mississippi's economy in the form of travel, equipment, licenses, landownership and leasing, contributions, and other services and items. Of course, out-of-state visitors added considerably to these figures.[67]

By the end of World War II there was increasing recreational and commodity usage in Mississippi's national forests. The forests had benefited from the "generally custodial" management style of the 1930s and early 1940s and had better stocking and growing stands of both softwoods and hardwoods. Now, "attention turned to the need to manage more intensively large areas of pine plantations, many of which already contained pulpwood or small sawtimber-size trees, and extensive second-growth natural stands of softwood and hardwood timber."

In the late 1940s Mississippi's pulp and paper companies competed for the purchase and control of timbered lands amidst growing concerns that production from industrial and small-ownership private lands would not be sufficient to meet the industry's needs. The pulp and paper companies also turned to the national forests to help meet their pulpwood requirements. While bemoaning the fact that dealing with the government would entail "restrictions placed on our land management," which were "onerous," and the "requirement that the Government could inspect J M books," which was "not desirable," a Johns Manville official reported that the company might well have to begin purchasing pulpwood from the Homochitto National Forest. He noted, "Competition for pulpwood on the Homochitto National Forest has already become so intense that we have been forced to bid so high on the last two sales that our cost of wood FOB cars will be higher than present market price." Nonetheless, in 1947 Johns Manville "signed the biggest pulpwood contract ever offered in the Homochitto National Forest."[68]

Mississippi's national forests clearly had an increasing supply of merchantable timber, and as the Forest Service saw it, "Managers previously worried about adequate stocking of desired species. Now they had to address stocking controls and thinning regimens and regeneration of second-growth stands now approaching maturity

to ensure sustained yields of timber in a steady flow. This meant working toward establishing a balanced system of age classes, classifying site quality for various lumber species, and applying prescribed silvicultural systems designed to achieve full productivity of those sites—all in keeping with management objectives that stressed multiple use of the resource. The changes in management emphasis and intensity that followed were questioned and even seen as controversial inside and outside the Forest Service." In 1961 the Forest Service proposed a ten-year plan that included more than doubling the harvest of sawtimber by the year 2000 and preparing facilities and programs to handle a nearly sixfold increase in recreational visits over the same period.[69]

Even-aged management and species selection became official policies in southern national forests in 1963. Before federal acquisition, many sites had evolved from softwood to hardwood cover because of frequent fires and insect and disease attacks. Now the Forest Service worked to bring back the pines through removal of hardwood species and regeneration cuts. These silvicultural practices brought loud protests from hunters, recreational users, and even some foresters. Growing pressure from a public that wanted more from the forests than timber for lumber and pulp mills was also part of the story.

The burgeoning environmental movement, concern about various silvicultural practices, particularly clear-cutting, and the increased use of national forests for recreation and aesthetic enjoyment created a different environment within which both public and private foresters had to work. However, Mississippi's environmental community was weaker than in many other parts of the nation. Also, the rigors of the hot and sultry climate plus the absence of grandiose scenic wonders placed less recreational pressure on the national forests of the Magnolia State than on those of, for example, the Rocky Mountain region.

By the 1950s the southern national forests contained more than 10 million acres of commercial forestland area, of which some 454,738 acres had been restored by planting or natural seeding and by prescribed burning. More than 4 million acres were pine forests, 338,999 acres were mixed pine and hardwoods, and 346,000 acres were bottomland hardwoods. Growth rates had improved markedly over a twenty-year period. Vegetation control, the use of herbicides, controlled burning, precommercial thinning, and the use of fertilizers became common practices.[70]

Ironically, the improvement of the commercial stands on national forests and the conversion of some sites from hardwood to pine triggered more controversies. Some interests wanted the lands, now that they had been restored and were commercially valuable, sold off and returned to the private sector. Wildlife interests were concerned that the conversion of lands from hardwoods to pine would harm the deer, squirrel, and turkey populations. There was also an increasingly vocal preservationist community, and by the 1980s some foresters felt that their purpose was to "save much of the nation's forests from being ruined, and . . . save the rest from being preserved."[71]

Some of the difficulties faced by land managers, public and private, in dealing with the citizenry had to do with perceptions—or, more properly, the public's misinterpretation of what it saw on the ground. Conversely, foresters were often insufficiently attuned to the public's perceptual sensitivity and landscape aesthetics. Both the Forest Service and the Bureau of Land Management were sufficiently concerned that in the mid-1970s they implemented programs to identify and classify scenic quality and place visual constraints on natural-resource management. However, the problem for resource managers was that the general public often simply did not understand what they were seeing or feeling. It was clear, however, that the public liked "natural" landscapes, and that "[t]o those who care about wildlife first, old-growth forests are both unique communities and special habitats for certain plants and animals. For people concerned with esthetics and recreation, old-growth forests

are pristine examples of the forest primeval." However, these are romantic ideals, for there is no generally accepted definition of exactly what an "old growth" forest is, and few if any of today's forests are unaltered by natural or human disturbances.[72]

The misconceptions were understandable, for a healthy and diverse forest is not always aesthetically pleasing to the public. In fact, as one writer put it, "Some practices that enhance biodiversity may work against those that promote visual quality or mitigate visual effects of forest harvesting." He called for moving beyond a "scenic esthetic" toward a more cerebral ecological aesthetic built around appreciation of the integrity of the evolutionary heritage and ecological processes of the land in the spirit of Aldo Leopold. Leopold taught, he said, "that the goodness of land management cannot be judged simply by how things look on the surface."[73]

Forest management on nonindustrial private lands and farms has long been a matter of concern to southern foresters and policy makers. As early as the 1930s companies such as IP and Champion were providing assistance to small landowners who would manage their timberlands responsibly. A 1951 Mississippi State College Agricultural Experiment Station bulletin dealing with private forest landowners in central Mississippi described the state's forest resources as "poorly managed." It concluded that in central Mississippi, "a vast improvement in timber management is needed" and suggested that increased public regulation of timber-management practices was necessary.[74]

As Robert G. Healy has noted, "The crucial variable in assessing the future of the South's timberland is the behavior of the nonindustrial private owners. Until recently, it was assumed that the most appropriate goal of forest policy was to find ways to make the nonindustrial owners adopt the intensive forestry practices of industry." From the post–World War II period on, concern about the supposed lack of productivity from these lands was a continuing topic of concern. In the late 1940s the Mississippi Forestry

Commission published a handbook on timber management that was designed to provide farmers with the basic information they needed to begin growing and marketing timber.[75]

Private forest-products companies as well as the U.S. Forest Service and state forestry agencies recently have strongly emphasized increasing forest management and timber production on such lands. One study indicated that landowners who consulted a forester provided for regeneration on 63 percent of their land, while those who did not attempted to reforest only 12 percent of their holdings. The conventional wisdom in the late 1970s was that future demands for timber would exceed supply, driving prices up to an unacceptable level, and that nonindustrial forestlands were poorly managed and producing far less timber than was possible. One study of nonindustrial private landowners by a large forest-products company found that the top six reasons, in order, that some of these owners were not interested in forest management were (1) it took too long to realize a profit; (2) the profit was too small; (3) they wanted to preserve their timber in a "natural" state; (4) it conflicted with other ownership goals; (5) they thought logging looked bad and harmed the land; and (6) they believed timber management was harmful to hunting.[76]

Mississippi was traditionally among the national leaders in agricultural conservation money used for forestry practices, and from 1957 to 1961 forestry-management practices were utilized on more than 250,000 acres in the state by more than 8,200 landowners. In 1960 the state legislature passed Senate Bill 1575, known as the Forestry Bank Law, which provided for loans to small landowners for the development of their woodlands. The Mississippi Forestry Commission was responsible for preparing management plans and administering the lands covered by these loans. By the end of 1961, 155 applications for loans had been processed, but the legislature repealed the program in 1964.[77]

Assistance in planting and the provision of timber-management plans for small landowners was also an important part of the restoration efforts on the denuded and gullied lands of the Yazoo–Little Tallahatchie Flood Prevention Project in north Mississippi. In the mid-1970s a program to improve the harvesting standards on project lands called the "Conservation Code of Good Practices" for wood producers was developed under the auspices of the Mississippi Forestry Association.[78]

From 1950 to 1980 concern about the productivity of nonindustrial private lands intensified as the consumption of most timber products in the United States rose. By 1978 softwood lumber use was 25 percent above the 1950 level. Pulpwood consumption quadrupled, and hardwood plywood use tripled during the same period, while softwood plywood use showed a sevenfold increase. Under this pressure, longleaf pine supplies declined. While the South's second forest contained longleaf stands that had mostly naturally reseeded, they depended on fire during the growth cycle. A combination of two factors inhibited natural longleaf regeneration. First, much of the former longleaf habitat was at one time converted to cropland and pasture. Once land has been cleared, longleaf does not compete well with more aggressive species. Ironically, the implementation of fire-protection policies also was a factor, for they allowed the invasion of longleaf sites by hardwoods and other, more aggressive, species of pine.[79]

Also, with the growing importance of pulp and paper companies, priorities changed. Lumber companies that preferred longleaf for high-quality logs and poles were replaced by paper companies that favored faster-growing species and turned away from longleaf toward genetically improved loblolly and slash pine. Loblolly and slash pine by the early 1990s accounted for 95 percent of all southern pine seedling production.[80]

In 1973 Congress created the Forestry Incentives Program to provide cost-sharing assistance for the improvement of privately owned timberland. The program was assigned to the U.S. Forest Service, which in turn delegated it to the Mississippi Forestry Commission. At the state level the Mississippi legislature in 1974 passed

Senate Bill 2200, creating the Forest Resource Development Program, administered by the forestry commission, whereby the state would share the landowner's cost for tree-planting and other forest-management practices.[81]

The Forest Resource Development Program was the second state-sponsored forestry assistance program in the nation. It was funded by a severance tax levied at the point of first processing. The tax doubled the existing severance tax on timber and timber products, with the additional income going to fund the development program. The remaining tax receipts were divided between the state general fund and the county from which the timber was harvested. The tax rate was raised again in 1981. The tax rate (except on poles, piling, and posts) was set on a per-unit basis rather than as a percentage of harvest value. The program sought to assist the owners of nonindustrial private timberland with the expenses of forestry practices through cost sharing. Most of the money was spent for pine regeneration, although some went to hardwood management. The money was spent only on practices or areas that were not funded by the federal Forestry Incentive Program, and during the period from 1976 to 1981 approximately twenty thousand acres were treated annually.[82]

The lack of adequate timber production and forest management on nonindustrial, private lands became a recurring topic in the *Journal of Forestry* beginning in the late 1970s. Despite the fact that by the mid-1980s these lands produced about 60 percent of the South's total softwood roundwood and 70 percent of its total hardwood roundwood, forest-products companies and public officials were concerned about what they considered underproduction. Forest-products companies, consulting foresters, and forest-management firms targeted these owners as buyers for such services.[83]

Many of these landowners did not consider timber production their top priority if a priority at all. Whereas at one time most private woodland owners were rural people who expected to derive some income from timber, in recent decades owners were more likely to be urbanites more interested in aesthetics, recreation, and wildlife than in timber. Much of this land was not under professional timber management. Various programs sponsored by the government and by forest-products companies attempted to bring these lands under professional management plans. In fact, a 1978 Forest Service study reported that based on various studies by other scholars, "It is now well documented that nonindustrial private owners have recognizable socioeconomic characteristics, objectives, and needs which do not always mesh with the forester's goal of increasing productivity from these lands."[84]

However, some critics questioned the conventional wisdom, pointing out, among other things, that predictions of a "timber famine" or shortage have been common throughout the twentieth century but that it has never occurred. Some also questioned the U.S. Forest Service's methods of forecasting. James M. Vardaman of Jackson, a consulting forester whose firm was one of the largest in the nation, with offices in eleven states, argued that in fact the small, private landowners were the best forest managers in society and that their decisions and practices were sensible and defensible. Vardaman said that many foresters and policy makers who judged the small private timberland owners knew little about them, their motives, and their decisions. Others agreed with Vardaman, pointing out that much of the information about these owners was badly outdated. One Georgia study showed that between 1936 and 1972, while there was room for improvement, private nonindustrial owners compared favorably with both industrial and public land managers in their performance.[85]

In 1977 President Jimmy Carter issued an environmental-issues message calling for measures to improve timber productivity on private lands. In response, the U.S. Forest Service's Southeastern Area of State and Private Forestry organized a task force to consider this problem. The group's report was written by Hamlin L. Williston, who was then a softwood-management specialist for the agency in Jackson. One of the problems in

Mississippi, Williston reported, was that fewer than half of private landowners surveyed thought of timber growing as a primary use of their forest. Some were more affluent and well educated than owners in the past, and a growing element bought land primarily for the pleasure of ownership and for recreation. Many did not live on the land but thought that timber harvests would interfere with their main purposes in owning their properties. Williston argued that consultation with professional foresters might convince such owners of the benefits of multiuse management. The task force recommended one hundred courses of action to increase the timber production of nonindustrial private lands. These proposals emphasized the need for information for and about the landowners, increased landowner-assistance programs, increased assistance from professional foresters, and a favorable government climate and policies for timber growers. Reflecting the continuing importance of the topic, in late 1983 a national forum on nonindustrial forestlands was held in St. Louis, with Mississippi's Allen serving as general chairman. The forum provided an environment where private landowners, industry representatives, academicians, and government representatives could exchange ideas and develop plans for promoting greater production on nonindustrial private timberlands.[86]

The Mississippi Forestry Commission joined in the 1970s efforts to promote increased tree planting by timberland owners. The agency increased seedling production, stepped up its assistance to small landowners, and even built twenty tree planters that were placed around the state to assist in the effort. The commission also began to publish stumpage prices to help small landowners who wanted to sell their timber. In 1982 the commission cooperated with the U.S. Forest Service in the writing and publication of a guide to assist private landowners in regenerating their timberlands.[87]

The forestry commission accomplished a good deal despite the fact that its workers were chronically underpaid and its programs often under-funded. Allen remembered that when he joined the commission as one of its first trained foresters, the agency was poorly equipped and understaffed. The commission was also victimized by excessive political interference in its activities. For example, State Forester Clifton B. Marlin worked well with Governor J. P. Coleman, although Coleman had favored two other men for the job. However, Marlin's situation deteriorated rapidly with the election of Ross Barnett in 1960. Marlin became convinced that "Governor Barnett was more interested in using the Forestry Commission as a job placement bureau to relieve some patronage pressure than he was in having a strong forestry program." Marlin resigned in 1961 and took a job on the faculty of the School of Forestry and Wildlife Management at Louisiana State University. John Squires, the manager of the Sears, Roebuck, and Company Forestry Division and an LSU graduate, praised Marlin and said that his departure would "retard the fine progress" that the commission had been making. Paul Y. Burns, director of the LSU School of Forestry, observed that "Mr. Marlin is leaving the state forestry commission in Mississippi because he has reached the limit of his endurance of political pressure on himself as head of a state organization. The Mississippi Forestry Commission has long been unstable politically, compared to forestry commissions in other states." Squires also argued that at the time he became national forest supervisor in Mississippi, the U.S. Forest Service did not work well with the Mississippi Forestry Commission in such areas as fire control, possibly because of professional jealousy on the part of the Mississippi state forester.[88]

In 1968 the Mississippi Chapter of the Gulf States Section of the Society of American Foresters sent a resolution expressing "deep concern" to Governor John Bell Williams over the appointment as state forester of a man without any training as a professional forester. W. D. Hagenstein, president of the Society of American Foresters, sent a letter to the same effect to the governor. Finally, in 1981, the Mississippi state legislature passed and Governor William Winter signed legislation initiated by the Mississippi Forestry Association that was designed to professionalize the commission and to eliminate political partisanship in its operations. Among the new requirements was that the state forester must have a forestry degree from an accredited school and be registered as a professional forester in Mississippi. The dean of the School of Forest Resources at Mississippi State University became an ex officio member of the commission with full voting rights, and one member was to be appointed to the commission from each congressional district. These appointees were required to be certified tree farmers or to derive most of their income from forest-related activities. Three other members were to be appointed at large, and they did not have to meet these requirements. The governor would no longer serve as a commission member. In 1988 the commission passed a resolution and petitioned Governor Ray Mabus to maintain the agency's independence.[89]

In 1978 Congress passed the Cooperative Forestry Assistance and Renewable Resources Extension Acts. The extension act broadened the concept of agricultural extension to include development of a plan for education of owners in management of renewable resources, but the measure was not even partially funded until 1983. The assistance act consolidated federal programs under one law, encouraged states to develop comprehensive forestry plans, and utilized block grants to states to implement approved plans. County foresters employed by the Mississippi Forestry Commission played an important role in taking forestry education and assistance to local landowners. By the early 1980s the commission had county foresters in all but eleven of Mississippi's counties, and some of those without county foresters were in the Delta, where there was a low percentage of timbered lands.[90]

Typical of private industrial efforts was IP's landowner-assistance program. In the late 1970s two IP representatives, Frank E. Taylor Jr., an area superintendent, and Connie G. Wilkerson, a forester, compiled a profile of private landowners

who participated in IP's landowner-assistance program in southeastern Mississippi. The age range of participants was wide, nearly half had inherited their property, and most of the inherited property had been in the family for more than fifteen years. Only 34 percent lived on the land, and some lived as far away as eight hundred miles. None of the landowners derived all of their income from the land, and 28 percent rarely received any forest income at all. The landowners were mostly retired, businesspeople, government employees, and professionals. The landholdings ranged from 40 to 2,258 acres in size, with an average of 225 acres. More than half the land was pineland, with hardwoods on poorly drained lowlands the next most common type. In addition to timber, the land was used for cattle grazing, hunting, investment, and recreation. The lands produced both pine and hardwood sawtimber and pulpwood. Boundary-line maintenance and controlled burning were both the most requested and most recommended management practices. The IP officials observed that the most badly needed actions appeared to be salvage cuts followed by reforestation. Two-thirds of the 119 landowners said they were willing to invest money in forest management, and 10 percent already had done so. Nearly all of these owners had participated in government cost-sharing programs. The survey found that the landowners had various motives in managing their forests, ranging from "higher needs" such as environmental and aesthetic considerations to "basic needs" such as income and financial security.[91]

In any case, small southern landowners must have been doing something right. Between 1952 and 1976 harvests from southern nonindustrial private forests increased by only 5 percent, while growth increased by 73 percent. The Mississippi Forestry Commission deserved some of the credit for this performance. In the fiscal year 1984 alone, the commission prepared more than two thousand management plans covering 147,712 acres for private nonindustrial landowners. Nearly eleven thousand landowners received assistance from the agency, and during the year about 11 percent of timber improvement and related work on private lands was performed by forestry commission crews.[92]

An interesting variation on the story of private landholdings is that of the Choctaw Reservation, which is scattered over some twenty-two thousand acres in eight east Mississippi counties. Much of the area was once cutover and abandoned timberland, and a timber-management program was developed during the 1950s by U.S. Forest Service foresters in cooperation with the Bureau of Indian Affairs. In the 1980s the Choctaws employed their first professional forester, the outdated management plan was replaced, and intensive timber management was implemented. By the late 1980s the land's timber and wildlife production was thriving, and in 1990 the Choctaws began offering public forestry and vending services to the outside community.[93]

One of the duties of the U.S. Forest Service was monitoring watershed protection, and in the 1940s this area became a focus in Mississippi. For years the light sandy soils in the watersheds of the Yazoo and Little Tallahatchie Rivers in north Mississippi had been eroding. The loss of soil and growth of gullies in the hilly country of the area accelerated and exceeded 100 million tons of soil washing out of the hills annually. There was annual flooding in the bottomlands, with 65 percent of the area affected as sterile sand washed across formerly fertile lands. In 1944 Congress passed a flood-control act authorizing the U.S. Department of Agriculture to implement flood-prevention measures in eleven large river basins, including the Yazoo and the Little Tallahatchie. By 1947 the Soil Conservation Service and the Forest Service were helping landowners plan and implement tree planting and other soil conservation measures to protect the land from floods. The Mississippi Forestry Commission cooperated closely with project foresters in the preparation of management plans and in marking timber for cutting. The commission, Mississippi Extension Service, Mississippi Forestry Association, U.S. Soil Conservation Service, and U.S. Forest Service all worked together to promote the implementation of management on the area's private forestlands. There were 142,000 acres of national forestland within the project area, and the Forest Service provided fire protection for these and neighboring lands.[94]

A U.S. forester described the Yazoo and Little Tallahatchie basins as an area "where the economy of whole worn and eroded sections had been changed by a flood-control and a watershed project which involved the planting of trees by the millions. Both were accompanied by additional plantings by rural people themselves, and both have made possible the combination of town and country work and income which shapes new possibilities in Southern living." His own comment was brief but eloquent: "The people were eager to participate."[95] The work in the Yazoo and Little Tallahatchie basins intensified from the late 1940s until the project was terminated in the mid-1980s.

The Yazoo–Little Tallahatchie Flood Prevention Project covered 4.2 million acres in north Mississippi and became one of the largest public endeavors in the state over four decades. It restored heavily eroded and gullied lands where for years sand and sediment had washed out of the hills into the stream channels and valleys. Local farmers described the area's creeks as being "too thick to drink, too thin to plow." Some estimated that the gullies were eroding at the rate of three hundred tons per acre per year. The project involved the construction of four large floodwater storage dams and straightening and enlarging the river channels below the dams. The rivers and dams were the Tallahatchie River (Sardis Dam), Coldwater River (Arkabutla Dam), Yocona River (Enid Dam), and Yalobusha River (Grenada Dam).

Reforestation of the land upstream sought to deal with eroded areas that one project official said were so bad that without treatment "the four big lakes might have filled up with silt." Tree planting began slowly under the auspices of the U.S. Soil Conservation Service in the late 1940s. In 1951 the U.S. Forest Service took over the planting responsibilities and soon shifted from using contract crews to its own employees. Over the

Eroded lands in the Yazoo–Little Tallahatchie Flood Prevention Project area. Courtesy Mississippi Forestry Commission, Jackson.

years the criteria with regard to which "critical" areas should be planted and which should be considered for "conversion" planting to other species changed. There was also a research component to the program, and in 1946 the Forest Service established the Oxford Research Center of the Southern Forest Experiment Station to conduct research in north Mississippi and west Tennessee. A 4,400 acre experimental forest was established within the Holly Springs National Forest.[96]

Despite the early difficulties, by 1962 over one-third of a million acres had been planted, and cull trees were deadened on more than 120,000 acres. By the mid-1980s some 835,893 acres were successfully reforested, and 918 million seedlings had been planted. The list of those actively involved testifies to the central importance of forests in Mississippi life—private landowners

(many of whom received no financial assistance), 4-H Clubs, Boy Scouts, Future Farmers of America, schools, the U.S. Forest Service, the U.S. Army Corps of Engineers, the Forest Hydrology Laboratory, forest industries, the Mississippi Forestry Commission, and the Young Adult Conservation Corps (funded by the U.S. Department of Labor). The preferred species for erosion control was loblolly pine, although some shortleaf was planted as a result of landowner preferences. Hardwoods were planted on the lower slopes and along stream bottoms. Black locust, which was used on erosion-control projects in other parts of the country, did not perform well on the Yazoo–Little Tallahatchie project lands. Much of the area was converted from "undesirable" hardwoods to pine through the use of girdling and chemicals, including 2,4,5-T and 2,4-D.[97]

The trees planted grew to merchantable size even faster than some people expected, and by the 1960s, despite the Forest Service's claim that the forests were "being re-established primarily for flood prevention and soil stabilization with timber production a secondary benefit," pulpwood from the area was being sold to the Tennessee River Pulp and Paper plant at Counce, Tennessee, and to other companies, including Bowaters, Gulf States, Gaylord, and IP. The construction by Champion International of a flake-board plant at Oxford in 1968 provided another market.

Much of the foresters' work in the Yazoo–Little Tallahatchie area consisted of implementing fire control so that the young forests had a chance of survival. As in other areas of Mississippi, the foresters found that fire prevention through educational campaigns was just as important as suppression. As a later assessment of the project put it, "Ingrained practices handed down for generations had to be eliminated or changed." Their efforts succeeded, for over the years both the number and severity of fires in the project area decreased dramatically.

By the mid-1980s the foresters' work was over, and the Yazoo–Little Tallahatchie Flood Prevention Project was shut down in 1985. The jobs of fire prevention and suppression, planting, and providing timber-management advice and information for the largely restored area were assumed by other agencies, such as the Mississippi Forestry Commission, the U.S. Soil Conservation Service, the U.S. Agricultural Stabilization and Conservation Service, the state extension service, and the Holly Springs National Forest. The cycle of total dependence on marginal agriculture had

been broken. It represented one of the most striking chapters in the greening of Mississippi.[98]

In 1954 Congress passed legislation enabling landowners to form watershed-management districts under a state law. The Mississippi legislature passed the requisite state law 1220. The cost of the watershed-protection work was shared by the landowners and the government. Watershed protection was extended to smaller streams in 1959 under Public Law 566. In that year the Mississippi Forestry Commission began planting on critically eroded areas along Muddy Creek, Indian Creek, and Ellison Creek. During the first three years of the program, the forestry commission planted 9.3 million seedlings on the critically eroded areas of ten small watersheds. A related problem by the summer of 1961 was the explosion of the state's beaver population, which caused floods that killed thousands of acres of timber. The Mississippi Forestry Commission, Mississippi Forestry Association, and various private companies and individuals conducted beaver-trapping demonstrations across the state and significantly reduced the problem.[99]

By the late 1990s Mississippi's forests had long recovered from the devastation suffered early in the century. Foresters and landowners were developing the fourth forest that would carry the state well into the twenty-first century. The forest-products industry was thriving, and the national forests were generally healthy, productive, and increasingly popular among the recreational public. Still, significant issues, large and small, philosophical and managerial, confronted Mississippi's citizens and forest managers as they approached the millennium.

9   The Path to the Future

Forests for Whom?

From the 1960s to the present, questions and issues regarding the treatment of forests have developed that transcend the old debates over proper seeding and harvesting methods, pest and fire control, and other traditional controversies. For both public and private foresters these matters have brought new anguish and soul searching to their professional lives. At the heart of these debates are the questions of, first, what constitutes a forest and what is its ultimate purpose, and, second, what are the respective rights of the landowner and the public in land management on both public and private lands? These issues are not close to a definitive resolution as the public and professional land managers struggle to establish the parameters of forest management for the twenty-first century.

While advocating the concept of multiple use during most of the twentieth century, the U.S. Forest Service emphasized timber production over such other values as recreation and aesthetics. Forests were seen essentially as timber farms, and a close, if sometimes rocky, relationship existed between the Forest Service and the forest-products industry. By the late 1980s the popular environmental movement was overwhelming the agency. An emphasis on personnel with broader perspectives altered the agency's traditional domination by commodity-oriented professional foresters. The agency was "greened" as biologists, ecologists, environmental specialists, and other scientists and social scientists, with no training in traditional forestry disciplines, rose to great influence. By the 1990s the agency had undertaken plans to drastically reduce timber harvests in national forests and had adopted the philosophy of ecological management as its operating credo. Aldo Leopold replaced Gifford Pinchot as the patron saint of the U.S. Forest Service, to the chagrin of many of its older forestry-trained employees.

The private sector was affected as well. Industrial foresters had long been aware of the need to be somewhat sensitive to the public because of their concern about government policies, taxes, and, particularly in an earlier era, the threat of woods arson. Thus, forest-products companies had made an effort to be involved in community affairs, to provide professional advice for small timberland owners, to help provide fire protection, and, later, to offer recreational opportunities on company-owned lands. Aware of the public's adverse reaction to the ugliness of clear-cuts, they used "screening," leaving strips of trees along roads to mask the clear-cuts' impact (although these strips also provided timber for hungry mills during wet weather, when it was difficult to get back into less accessible areas). However, despite these concerns, there was never any doubt in the minds of most industrial foresters that the ultimate criterion in managing forests was the owners' objectives and that owners could do essentially as they wished in managing private land. Doing what the owner wanted—usually, commodity production—was foresters' primary task, and those who failed to recognize that fact soon became unemployed foresters.

Implicit in this relationship was the idea that the private landowners, whether large companies or small independent citizens, could do as they wished with their land, their private property. Americans had long been accustomed to zoning laws, building codes, easements, government taking of private land through the process of eminent domain, and other restrictions on private landownership, but beginning in the 1960s things began to change. Most restrictions on private landownership had been on urban properties. Now a population that was increasingly urban, that was becoming more environmentally conscious (if not well informed), and that increasingly had the leisure time to recreate in rural forested areas began to assume that the general public had a legitimate voice in determining how private lands should be managed or whether they should be managed at all. The discussions were not couched in terms of classical political and economic philosophy. John Locke, Adam Smith, James Madison, and Alexander Hamilton seldom, if ever, were mentioned in the debates. But they went right to the heart of fundamental issues regarding the social compact, the legitimate role of government, and the limits, if any, of private property rights. It would be difficult if not impossible to compromise on these questions and issues, at least as long as the current generation of combatants remained involved. As one observer put it, "The right to own and use private property is at the heart of the traditional American social value system." Conversely, he noted, "private ownership means stewardship or trusteeship, not the right to do whatever one wants."[1]

As some experts pointed out, the lines between private and public ownership and between individual and industry ownership were blurring, and the public had strong feelings about the management and appearance of forests. Also, the public and some scientists were beginning to recognize that many of the noneconomic aspects of forests required management actions that transcended ownership boundaries, leading to the prediction that public and scientific pressure to modify forest management would not recognize old ownership parameters.[2]

Environmental awareness and activism have been on the rise in the United States since the 1960s. As distinguished historian Samuel P. Hays has noted, one of the key differences between old-style conservationists and the new environmentalists was that "[i]n forestry, conservation had stressed sustained-yield wood production while the environmental movement thought of the forest as an environment for home, work, and play rather than as a source of commodities. The environmental demand for wilderness designations and aesthetic management met with severe opposition from professional foresters interested primarily in wood production." By the 1990s opinion polls showed that most Americans considered themselves environmentalists, and tens of millions belonged to one or more environmental or conservation organizations. In 1989 the United States boasted more than 5,800 environmental organizations. By 1991 the forty-four largest groups had a collective membership of 15 million citizens (although that number does not take into account the fact that some people belong to more than one organization). Membership in these groups was stimulated by such events as publicity surrounding Earth Day in 1970, Secretary of the Interior James G. Watt's and the Reagan administration's attacks on environmentalism, and publicity concerning ecological problems and disasters such as the Exxon Valdez oil spill. In 1993 selected environmental organizations with memberships in excess of 80,000 included Defenders of Wildlife (80,000), the Natural Resources Defense Council (170,000), the Environmental Defense Fund (200,000), the Wilderness Society (310,000), the Nature Conservancy (588,000), the National Audubon Society (600,000), the Sierra Club (650,000), and the National Wildlife Federation (6,200,000).

In contrast, two of the leading resource professional organizations, the Soil and Water Conservation Society and the Society of American Foresters, had thirteen thousand and nineteen thousand members, respectively. Both groups lost members between 1980 and 1993, and they were the only natural-resource professional societies with more than ten thousand members. In 1989, according to the National Center for Charitable Statistics, 3,571 of 5,817 environmental, natural-resource, and animal-related organizations reported total assets of $6.7 billion to the Internal Revenue Service (and not all such groups are required to do so). The citizen environmental organizations directly affected policy in such areas as endangered-species protection, allowable harvests on public lands, timber exports, and forest-practice regulation, and they certainly contributed to the advent of ecosystem management as a forest-management philosophy. Some of these organizations grew to have full-time legal, scientific, and natural-resource professional staffs.[3]

By the 1960s the growing environmental movement was producing organizations, study groups, and writers who were critical of both forest-products companies, including their land and plant management, and public agencies, especially the U.S. Forest Service, which is the steward of vast acreages of U.S. public lands. Mississippi was not in the forefront of these activities, but its citizens and land managers could scarcely avoid awareness of the ideas that were changing the country. For example, in 1974 a group headed by Ralph Nader published a study of the pulp and paper industry in Maine, where seven large companies (Great Northern–Nekoosa, International Paper, Scott Paper, Diamond International, St. Regis Paper, Georgia-Pacific, and Oxford Paper, a division of Ethyl Corporation), owned roughly one-third of the state's land. The report severely criticized the industry for creating water and air pollution, for exploiting small landowners and woodcutters, and for having excessive political and economic influence in the state. The study group found this influence particularly troublesome, for none of the companies was headquar-

tered in Maine. The Nader report reflected the kinds of charges that critics increasingly leveled at large forest-products companies.[4]

A year later, Jack Shepherd published a devastating critique of the Forest Service's land-management policies. A wide-ranging attack, Shepherd's book especially targeted overcutting; clear-cutting, which he called "timber strip mining"; and the use of chemicals. Again, these matters formed part of Forest Service critics' standard litany. Also in the early 1970s well-known outdoor writer Michael Frome published a thoughtful study of the Forest Service in the modern era in which he criticized much of the Forest Service's approach. Although he was fired from the staff of *American Forests* for being excessively critical, his book was not a diatribe. It raised important issues in a balanced manner.[5]

Mississippi's environmental discussions have been lower key and less fractious than those in other parts of the country, for several possible reasons. First, many Mississippians, especially the whites who have generally controlled the political process, are quite conservative. They strongly support the free-enterprise system, especially the rights of private property owners to manage their properties as they see fit. Environmental laws or controls imposed by government, especially the federal government, do not go over well. The view of many conservative Mississippians was reflected in the words of Gene A. Sirmon, president of the Mississippi Forestry Association (MFA), who described the rise of "environmental mania," fueled by "wildlife groups, rainforest groups, and toxic waste groups . . . grass root groups and regional groups and direct action groups. All of them jockeying for positions to 'save the world.'" He concluded that the "so-called success" of "these preservation groups" resulted from the fact their opponents had not been well enough organized or effective in getting their message out to the public. Part of the problem, he said, was "loosely written" environmental laws that "liberal judges" could interpret broadly to "make it easy for these people to accomplish their objectives."[6]

Second, Mississippi is primarily a rural state. Most people live in rural areas, many of which are forested, and an old rule of thumb is that people often tend to undervalue those things that are most familiar. To some extent it may be true that rural Mississippians take their forests and their natural resources for granted. In any case, rural Mississippians are notoriously adverse to any sort of advice or control, real or perceived, from "outsiders." Urban sprawl, especially the migration of former urbanites to the environs of those forests, has created new tensions, perspectives, and issues. But it should also be remembered that many urbanites, whether in Jackson, Meridian, Biloxi, Vicksburg, Tupelo, Memphis, or New Orleans, are fairly recent arrivals from the rural regions. Many of them or members of their families still own land in the rural forested areas, and so they tend to lack the urban perspective of residents of New York, Chicago, or Los Angeles.

Furthermore, the educational level—and, some would argue, the level of sophistication—among some Mississippians is relatively low. For good or bad, those issues, leaders, and movements that are trendy in other parts of the country may not be particularly marketable in the Magnolia State. And with regard to specifics, many Mississippians have not held the environmental movement and its leaders in high regard. Mississippi is, after all, a state where leading politicians and civic leaders favored the use of nuclear devices to blast out the "divide cut" for the Tennessee-Tombigbee Waterway during the 1970s and 1980s. To call someone an environmentalist in Mississippi is not necessarily a compliment.[7]

Finally, the training of foresters shaped and influenced public opinion. While Mississippi has had a sizable number of professional foresters and forestry leaders who were trained outside the state, with the establishment of the School of Forestry at Mississippi State in 1954, the great majority of Mississippi's foresters were educated and acculturated within the state. And while Mississippi State has an excellent reputation among forestry schools, it has remained closely tied to the forest-products industry, which provides much of the school's funding, and the school has offered a very traditional curriculum and culture. Self-studies and accreditation teams from the Society of American Foresters (the accrediting agency for forestry schools) consistently commented on the school's strong emphasis on timber production and harvesting and recommended more attention to other forest values and environmental concerns.

In 1971 the Society of American Foresters' accreditation team reported, "The forestry students interviewed appeared to be rather conservative with only minimal concern for national environmental issues and other issues facing the profession. Unfortunately, little exposure to such issues is provided in the classroom experience of the student." The report also concluded, "The courses and course content appear too completely oriented to commercial timber production. While it is clear that the principal market for graduates is southern forest industry, a better awareness and integration of other forest products and services into their perspective and training seems in order." Noting that "[a]s a whole the outlook of staff and student was dedicated, conservative, but somewhat provincial," the report recommended more attention to "contemporary resource management and policy issues at the national level."

While generally praising Mississippi State's forestry program, the 1977 accreditation report said that the "visiting team . . . has a concern that the curriculum may not give adequate weight to forest resources other than timber" and recommended that the curriculum be reexamined with the possibility of "assigning more weight to non-timber forest resources." In 1987 the society's accreditation team was continuing to urge that the school should "[r]e-examine available courses in values other than timber." By the early 1990s the school had responded to these criticisms by adding a new elective course in forest ecology and the global environment. School officials also pointed out that they had added faculty members with training in disciplines other than traditional forestry and said that many courses now paid more attention to forest values other than timber production. Officials also argued that students with an interest in these areas could find what they wanted in the university's wildlife, fisheries, and biology programs. Still, Mississippi State—trained foresters were less likely than those from many other schools in different areas of the country to be influenced by the rise of environmental issues and the advent of ecosystem management, which became so fashionable elsewhere in the late twentieth century. However, by the late 1990s environmentalism and ecosystem management had become part of the milieu in which Mississippi's industrial foresters and forest-products companies operated. The state's implementation of the sustainable forestry initiative signified that national trends had significantly affected Mississippi.[8]

Organized environmentalism has been limited in Mississippi, and as a 1971 article in *Forest Industries* observed, "the voice of conservation or preservation has to date been less forceful, less demanding and often more reasonable than elsewhere." By the early 1990s, while the Nature Conservancy had more than 550,000 members nationally, Mississippi's membership base numbered only about 1,500. By the latter part of the decade Mississippi's environmental organizations remained quite weak. The Audubon Society, Nature Conservancy, and Sierra Club maintained professional staffs in the state, but only Sierra and Audubon were represented by regular, professional lobbyists in dealing with the legislature and other government agencies.

The Audubon Society's presence in Mississippi dates back to the early 1970s, and in the late 1990s the state had six chapters. Most, like the Jackson group, focused primarily on bird watching and related activities, and as one spokesman put it, consisted mostly of folks who were "old and don't like to rock the boat." By early 1999 the Sierra Club group in Jackson did not even hold meetings. The Nature Conservancy and National Wildlife Federation, which might be considered less aggressive than the other groups in

dealing with environmental issues on the national level, also maintained presences in the Magnolia State. The Mississippi Nature Conservancy, a branch of the international organization, established a field office in Jackson in 1989. Working with individuals, corporations, government, and foundations, the Conservancy is probably best known for purchasing lands that are ecologically significant or representative, and by the late 1990s the Conservancy's staff and volunteers monitored some thirty registered natural areas and twenty nature preserves in Mississippi.

One of the problems plaguing the Mississippi environmental movement was the fact that some of its leaders, sympathizers, and activists worked for state universities or other state agencies. Some complained anonymously that during Governor Kirk Fordice's conservative, antienvironmental administration, superiors had pressured these people to tone down their activism and rhetoric. They believed that U.S. Forest Service personnel in the state had encountered some of the same problems and had no doubt that the word had been sent down to silence them. Some claimed they had suffered direct persecution. These people were extremely distrustful of forest-products companies' efforts in such areas as the preservation of endangered species and protection of streams running through the forests, and one termed the industry's implementation of "best management practices" as "bogus," although he conceded that large companies and landowners probably did a better job in this area than small independents and many nonindustrial landowners because of the costs involved. There were also charges that the Forest Service in Mississippi had been excessively influenced by industry and had dragged its feet in working to add some vulnerable wildlife to the endangered-species list. The prime example cited was the dusky gopher frog, which was said to exist in Mississippi only around a pond on the de Soto National Forest. The frog was threatened by proposed timber harvesting in the immediate area and by a plan to sell recently clear-cut corporate lands on the border of the national forest to developers who intended to build a retirement community on the property.

Among the issues that seemed of most interest to Mississippi's environmentalists were protection of the red-cockaded woodpecker, the recent work of the international group Partners in Flight to cooperate with landowners and companies in protecting nesting sites for migrating birds, and a recent battle over efforts by the University of Mississippi to harvest timber on lands it owned in the southern part of the state. By 1998 the university had agreed to sell twenty-three thousand acres to the Forest Service, and environmentalists were lobbying for the establishment of special management guidelines on the grounds that the property contained some unique areas. At the national level the Audubon Society was involved in a campaign to restrict the construction and activities of chip mills. Cooperating groups in Arkansas, Tennessee, Alabama, North Carolina, and Missouri formed a group called the Dogwood Alliance to fight chip mills across the South, but there was no affiliated organization in Mississippi. While there were some 140 such mills in the South by the late 1990s, only sixteen to eighteen were located in Mississippi, and some were closing because of changing market conditions. However, many of the chip mills were concentrated along the Tennessee-Tombigbee Waterway, where they could ship chips by water to area mills and through Mobile to foreign markets, particularly Japan. Some critics found the clear-cutting of southern forests to supply chips to Japan particularly reprehensible.

The crux of the opponents' arguments in the chip mill controversy was that the mills promoted more and faster clear-cutting, with resultant devastation of the land and wildlife. Critics also charged that as hardwood forests were clear-cut to supply the chip mills, they were being replaced by pine plantations, which some termed "ecological deserts." Industry defenders responded that chip mills did not significantly affect timber-harvesting methods or schedules and that the environmentalists essentially did not want trees harvested at all. Industry spokesmen argued that

environmentalists had seized on the chip-mill issue as an emotional hot button. The arguments on both sides were directed toward the general public and political leaders, for it was unlikely that the minds of activists or spokespeople on either side would be changed by their opponents' reasoning.[9]

Other environmental issues have also caused concerns in Mississippi. Some citizens have begun to question the level and methods of timber harvests on national forests. There is growing interest in the impact of forest-site preparation on water quality and stream sedimentation. Other concerns include the impact of chemicals and harvesting on neighboring streams. Also, in a state with a strong hunting culture, the supply of wildlife is always a concern to many people. As the southern editor of a forest-industries magazine pointed out in the early 1970s, many sportsmen as well as environmentalists are skeptical of industry claims that wildlife populations have increased under timber management, arguing that while industry spokesmen equate deer populations with total wildlife populations, any ecosystem includes many species besides deer, and many of these populations are not increasing.[10]

However, even while rejecting or ignoring modern environmentalism, many Mississippians, especially professional foresters, accepted and promoted the ideals of progressive, utilitarian, conservation and sustained-yield management as preached by Pinchot and the fathers of the industrial-forestry movement. These foresters considered themselves advocates of Pinchot's philosophy of conservation as "wise use," although they certainly disagreed heatedly with his advocacy of extensive federal regulation or ownership of the nation's forests. Their antagonists in the environmental community they labeled preservationists who would simply lock up the forest resources, especially timber. Most would have fit comfortably into Paul Ehrlich's 1970 description of a "culture which traditionally sees man's proper role as dominating nature, rather than living in harmony with it. It is a culture which equates 'growth' and 'progress' and considers both as self-evidently desirable." And like a pioneering environmentalist profiled in Champion International's company magazine, many believed that "[w]e have raised a whole generation of people who are misinformed about the facts of the environment" and that there was a need for "a more deliberate approach to environmental problems."

Some industrial foresters viewed themselves as environmentalists as they worked to maintain Mississippi's forest base. And forest management was not the only story they wished to tell. For example, one of the old landmarks of southern lumber operations was the "wigwam burner," where the wastes of the sawmilling process were burned, sometimes creating air-pollution problems. The invention of the sawlog debarker made it possible to convert milling residues such as slabs and edgings into clean chips for the region's pulp mills, condemning the wigwam burner to obsolescence. By the mid-1970s these residues constituted more than 27 percent of total pulpwood production, the equivalent of adding 13.5 million acres of productive timberlands to the southern resource base. Thus, said the industrial forester, both the industry and society won from a profit as well as an environmental standpoint.

Longtime Mississippi forester Richard C. Allen emphasized the role of trees in absorbing carbon dioxide and producing oxygen. He argued in 1974 that it took 78 trees to maintain the atmospheric balance for every person in the United States, 20 trees to control the polluting effects of a car driven sixty miles a day, and 100,000 trees to offset the pollution created by a jet making one round trip per day from New York City to Los Angeles. Said Allen, "Just think what our tree planting program is doing to provide clean air!"[11]

However, while professional foresters often talked about public misconceptions, concern for environmental values, and sympathy for some ecological issues, it was clear that many foresters and others in the forest-products industry had barely veiled (if veiled at all) contempt for environmental leaders, organizations, and issues. These industry insiders also emphasized that, in

their opinion, many environmentalists and citizens confused conservation with preservation. In the early 1990s MFA President Jerry Perkins actively defended clear-cutting on both silvicultural grounds and as a means of creating diverse habitat for wildlife. Tom Monaghan, another MFA president and a member of the Mississippi State University School of Forestry faculty, compared the battle between the "forestry community" and "preservationists and other 'radical' environmental groups" to the conflict between the United States and Saddam Hussein. The enemy, he said, "are committed to their cause, have a large self-equipped 'army,' and have modern media 'weapons' at their disposal." He concluded that the conflict was not "a battle between destruction and preservation as some would have the public believe. It is a battle between wise use and restricted use. Unfortunately, the restricted use side relies on emotionalism and sensationalism." While members of the forest-products industry, the forestry community, and many private landowners undoubtedly felt beleaguered, these words were decidedly not the language of reason or compromise.[12]

Conversely, in 1990 the MFA invited Thomas M. Pullen Jr., a longtime environmentalist, to address its annual meeting on the topic of environmental concerns about forestry in Mississippi. While calling for moderation, Pullen pointed out that to much of the general public, forest-products-industry advertising often seemed like propaganda, and he suggested a variety of ways that the industry could become more environmentally sensitive. The ultimate question, he said, was "Are we making it better than it was when we found it?" In the Mississippi forestry community, Allen was a voice for aggressive moderation, telling a 1974 meeting of the Southern Forest Industries, "We've got to let people know that we are environmentalists." Allen explained his feelings in detail:

The forestry profession had a much earned reputation during the 30's, 40's, 50's, and the first four or five years of the 60's. . . . [W]e were the protector of a precious resource. We were against fire, adverse taxation, over-cutting, and anything that endangered the emergence of the second forest. Then came the radical environmentalists of the 1960's who accused us of mismanagement of those forests. Some foresters became negative reactors to this criticism, defensive of proven practices so good in the past—rather than positive action to a situation that merits *some* changes but recognizes that quality environment for living is compatible with growing crops of timber to maintain jobs—and resulting products of this labor—so citizens can earn a living, *can eat*—to be able to sustain life. . . . We need to let our public know that we agree with the needs for clean air, good hunting and fishing, camping. We love to breathe, fish, hunt and camp as well as anyone else. We have got to let our public know what good environmentalists we are, and we don't have to be defensive about our profession. Foresters were the *original* environmentalists! We need to get these people who are so called "rabid radical environmentalists" helping us to grow trees.[13]

Restrictions on the rights of private landowners were at the heart of much opposition to the environmental movement and policies. After reciting examples of how environmental policies restricted landowners' activities, MFA President John O. Moore appropriated the label "environmentalist" and warned that "we must stand up and be heard—the preservationists are . . . reporting only one side of a situation, and that is not the side of environmentalists or the forestry community." The MFA opposed the passage of a bill to establish a natural and scenic waterways system to protect such waterways and define prohibited activities in or near them in 1993 and a 1995 effort to designate a Mississippi River Heritage Corridor. Both efforts triggered MFA concerns about restrictions on private property rights.[14]

The theme of the MFA's 1992 annual meeting was, as G. Stephen Parker of the conservative Southeastern Legal Foundation put it, "how to protect the rights of property owners in the face of increasing regulatory activity, and in the face of increasing public demand for government at all levels to 'do more' to protect the environment." He observed that groups such as the Sierra Club, Natural Resources Defense Council, the National Wildlife Federation, and Environmental Defense Fund maintained legal staffs and used public-interest law to "promote the interests of their constituency, or more accurately, of their current leadership."[15]

The association also brought in Bruce Vincent, a Montana logger and activist, who recited a horror story concerning what had happened in his region and who warned that "the preservationist program for America is threatening . . . every rural area in our nation." He went on to argue that "[t]here is a thin line between environmental sensitivity and environmental insanity. When we have a society that calls Earth First! an environmental group, we have crossed that line. . . . Folks, these guys are criminals. We have gone so far that our media call them environmentalists." The speaker's style and message fit comfortably into the general habit within the forestry community of demonizing the environmental movement.[16]

By 1993 MFA president Larry Tyner portrayed the environmental battle as one of "ideas and principles that go to the very heart of the fundamental values of our society. . . . There are organizations that paint private property rights as an enemy of the environment. They are intensely creating the perception that it is 'politically incorrect' to advocate protection of private property rights!" He argued that property owners should be compensated for losses incurred as a result of the enforcement of environmental laws on their property and theorized that under such policies the "special-interest groups" would lose a lot of public support. "The public may be willing to pay for the 'taking' of private property to save the eagle or the red-cockaded woodpecker," he said, "but may *not* be willing to pay for the 'taking' of private property to save a rat or some minimally differentiated or not particularly unique aquatic life." "Until the public sees that cost and has to pay for it," he concluded, "the outcome of current debate on amending the Endangered Species

Act and other environmental issues will be skewed, unreasonable and unbalanced!" In 1994 the Mississippi legislature passed a law that made the state the first in the nation to "empower an owner with the right to file suit against the state for inverse condemnation due to governmental action that significantly reduces the value of the property." The law obviously had profound implications in the area of environmental legislation.[17]

Reflecting the state's conservatism, in late 1997 Governor Fordice announced the organization of a wildlife group that he said would steer clear of liberal agendas. Based in Stoneville, Wildlife Mississippi was supposed to encourage private landowners to practice conservation techniques that would improve hunting and fishing, including the reversion of marginal croplands to wetlands. Fordice said of the organization, "We are reinventing conservation so that we may go about the business of living and working in Mississippi in a manner that accommodates fish and wildlife resources. Wildlife Mississippi will be one of the few organizations anywhere in America focusing not on legal coercion or a liberal political agenda." Wildlife Mississippi's executive director said that the group would stay away from "stances on specific issues" and cooperate with the Mississippi Wildlife Federation and the Nature Conservancy to secure state funding for setting aside private lands for habitat conservation.[18]

But across the nation old-fashioned conservation lost out among the general populace to the newer concepts of environmentalism. The "gospel of ecology" replaced the "gospel of efficiency" nationally, if not in Mississippi. Environmental issues became increasingly important in foresters' professional lives as they entered the age of ecosystem management. Foresters have become professionally preoccupied with increasing their sensitivity to environmental issues and with making sure that environmental activists, managers trained in new fields such as environmental studies, and others with an interest in forest issues but no formal training in traditional silvicultural practice have not pushed aside or marginalized foresters in debates about land

management. The issues divided the forestry profession, for foresters trained in the past had been primarily oriented toward land management that emphasized timber production, while their newer and younger colleagues often came out of programs with broader foci. While the issues and conflicts had been around for years (although the terminology might have changed), the debates reached a crescendo in the 1990s. Public foresters, in particular, found themselves in the eye of the storm.[19]

Before the term *ecosystem management* came into vogue, the trendy phrase for the new approach to forestry was *holistic (new) forestry*. While writers disagreed on particulars, the term referred to an approach that would reduce energy usage, pesticides, and artificial fertilizers in the forest environment. However, many foresters found nothing particularly innovative in the concept, for as Timothy O'Keefe noted, "I have concluded that there is nothing that is in any way significantly different from good, sound multiple-use forest management." Unless foresters wanted a new "public relations gimmick," said the critic, "I see very little value in adding another term which essentially means the same thing as our traditional and very effective, concept of multiple-use management."[20]

However, O'Keefe also conceded that some equated new forestry with management of forests on an uneven-stage stand basis and traditional forestry with even-aged management. Art Nelson remembered that the public was out in front of the foresters, even in the age of multiple use: "I'll never forget the first time I tried to explain what multiple use was to a native Mississippian years ago. When I finished he said, 'Why h---man, we've been doing that around here long before you ever came along.' And so they have. Southerners know that the harvesting, growing, and harvesting again of tree crops has enhanced rather than diminished multiple-use opportunities."[21]

Much of the philosophical debate occurred within the Forest Service and spread to the private sector. As the *Journal of Forestry* noted in an introduction to a 1990 article, "If some have doubted that major changes were coming in the practice of forestry, the recent embracement by the USDA Forest Service of Jerry Franklin's once radical and unpopular 'new forestry' must serve as a major confirmation. 'New forestry' . . . is still being defined, and its implications for forest practice are somewhat dimly perceived." Many foresters were and are convinced that their traditional practice of sustained-yield, multiple-use forest management was fully consistent with ecological principles and the new management philosophies. As Forest Service veteran Karl F. Wenger put it,

Many people, perhaps most, do not make the connection between the paper and wood products they need and use and the timber harvesting they are being told is bad for "the ecology." We know, but the public clearly does not, that some tree species are not only more beautiful but also more useful and faster growing than others. Most people think that one species is just as good as another and see no reason for the apparently drastic treatments usually needed to favor more desirable species. They believe that lack of disturbance is the most desirable and beneficial forest condition. They do not know that the undisturbed forest floor is the poorest of all seedbeds for natural regeneration. Or that planted seedlings are unlikely to survive on an unprepared site. Or that unbroken hardwood high forest is the poorest of all wildlife habitats. Or that severe, widespread disturbance was normal in "virgin" North American forests before Europeans arrived.[22]

By 1992 the term *new forestry* was old and *ecosystem management* was hot, with the Forest Service announcing that ecosystem management would be adopted throughout the national forests. In 1989 the Forest Service began to manage the forests under its "New Perspectives" program, which sought to expand the traditional focus on sustainable multiple use by focusing attention on broader ecological and social needs. This program reflected the agency's response to a public that shifted its concern from an emphasis on "what we remove from the land to a deep interest and concern for what is left remaining on the land." Three years later the Forest Service moved toward "managing ecosystems to sustain both their diversity and productivity . . . the foundation for sound multiple-use, sustained-yield management." Dale Robertson, chief forester of the U.S. Forest Service, said of New Perspectives, "We must blend the needs of people and environmental values in such a way that the national forests and grasslands present diverse, healthy, productive, and sustainable ecosystems." The Bureau of Land Management and the Department of the Interior made the same decision. The bureau defined ecosystem management as "the skillful use of ecological, economic, social, and managerial principles in managing ecosystems to produce, restore, or sustain ecosystem integrity and desired conditions, uses, products, values, and services over the long term."

The Society of American Forester's *Task Force Report on Sustaining Long-Term Forest Health and Productivity* focused attention on the question of whether a holistic approach to land management would work while allowing forests to produce the products that the public wanted at a reasonable cost. The report also considered the possibility that sustained-yield management with a focus on all forest values actually was ecosystem management by another name. By 1994 the Forest Service defined ecosystem management as "the use of an ecological approach that blends social, physical, economic, and biological needs and values to assure productive, healthy ecosystems." Reflecting the consuming interest in the subject, the *Journal of Forestry* devoted its entire August 1994, issue to discussions of ecosystem management.[23]

Whereas Pinchot was the patron saint of multiple use, the great Wisconsin forester, teacher, wildlife biologist, and philosopher Aldo Leopold was the hero of those who advocated ecosystem management. By the middle of the 1980s the *Journal of Forestry* featured a section of Leopold's writings, including his definition of a land ethic, plus an article calling for inclusion of a land ethic in the Society of American Foresters' Code of Ethics. In 1990 Alan G. McQuillan, director of the Wilderness Institute, asked whether Leopold's land ethic and multiple-use forest management on forest reserve lands were compatible, concluding that accommodation could be reached only if lands were divided between "developers" and "preservationists."[24]

Assessing Leopold's influence, Hal Salwasser said, "More than 40 years ago . . . Aldo Leopold said that people should take care of the land as a 'whole organism' and try to keep all the cogs and wheels in good working order. If we humans did this, he implied, the productivity and renewability of land for the many things we value (for example, timber yield, water quality, wildlife, scenery, and livestock forage) would fare well. What Leopold had in mind was to sustain the diversity and productivity of ecosystems while meeting people's needs for livelihood. Lately, natural resource scientists and managers in the United States have begun to call this process ecosystem management. It encompasses, or is directly linked to, several other concepts such as biodiversity, conservation, sustained yield of multiple uses, ecosystem health, and sustainable development in general."[25]

While Leopold never actually used the term *ecosystem management,* he did introduce the "conservation esthetic." He promoted a philosophy based on recognition of ecological processes and emphasized the importance of ecological states as well as production and consumption. He was concerned about maintaining sustainable resources. In 1992 members of the Society of American Foresters voted to modify its Code of Ethics to include a land ethic, with the preamble stating, "Stewardship of the land is the cornerstone of the forestry profession," and Canon 1 avowing, "A member will advocate and practice land management consistent with ecologically sound principles." This was a significant step for a profession that had been traditionally oriented toward utilitarian resource management in the spirit of Pinchot.[26]

In 1993 Lloyd C. Irland neatly summed up the debate over precisely what ecosystem management is and is not: "Some people view ecosystem management (EM) as a new Golden Age in which there is much less cutting; no clearcutting; no chemicals; fewer people; and no multinational corporations. Still others tell us that 'we've been doing it all along; we just need to explain it better.' Ecosystem management certainly poses a new paradigm for managing forests. For example, its focus on landscape conditions and trends changes our approach to ownership distinctions. Its focus on ecosystem integrity instead of predictable timber outputs produces uncertainties about wood supply, reliability, and costs." Definition of ecosystem management has been part of the problem. Thomas A. More, a forest service employee, called it a "'fuzzy,' questionable concept," and observed, "The core of the problem seems to be a deep-seated yearning for a precise definition, something that will specify exactly what ecosystem management is—and what it is not. 'If only we could define it!' is heard in all quarters from professional meetings to informal discussions."[27]

Many land managers were deeply concerned about the onset of ecosystem management. Irland noted, "Many southeastern . . . landowners are cutting their timber while they still can. Private owners are reluctant to pay taxes for years to grow larger sawtimber and take the risk that an extended area around a potential woodpecker den tree . . . will become the property of the sovereign state." Also, said another article, "the problem or problems that ecosystem management is supposed to solve are not clear. . . . This confusion about what ecosystem management is supposed to do has hampered the forestry community's debate on the legitimacy of this natural resource management paradigm."[28]

Some foresters' fears and prejudices were reflected in the words of William R. Maxey, who bemoaned the fact that the Forest Service had reduced the number of foresters in management and replaced them with landscape architects, botanists, archaeologists, and engineers, as the agency became, in his words, "excessively 'green' and politically correct." Criticizing those who were opposed to timber harvests on public lands, Maxey termed their weapons "emotionalism and pseudo-science" and said, "If not one 'endangered species,' any other furry or feathered critter would be the ploy to persuade the uninformed that trees should not be cut." He concluded, "The preservationist's mission has little to do with saving species and everything to do with stopping timber harvests. This vocal, well-funded minority is undermining the fiber of our nation's greatness: the free enterprise system and the right to truly own property." To correct these trends, Maxey advocated putting foresters back in charge of forest management and changing "all of the schools of environmental science back to colleges of forestry led by directors whose primary areas of expertise are in forest management."[29]

Conversely, Andrew Colaninno, a Forest Service district ranger who helped "manage the world's largest population of red-cockaded woodpeckers," equated the loss of species to the destruction of a great library whose works (genetic codes) have not yet fully been read and understood. In 1998 Sirmon seemed to be fighting a battle that was already over when he criticized the draft report of a committee of scientists providing scientific and technical advice on Forest Service land-management planning guidelines and procedures. The report, he said, "tries to establish ecosystem management as the paradigm under which national forests will be managed in the future. The approach stresses a shift to forest 'conditions' rather than outputs. . . . It is apparent the committee is biased toward preservation values rather than conservation and consumptive uses of our natural resources."[30]

Priorities will ultimately determine whether both resource managers and the public make a genuine transition from the values and emphases of progressive conservation and sustained-yield, product-oriented management to the ecosystem-management philosophy. As Hanna J. Cortner put it, "A true paradigm shift will require significant changes in values, including attitudes defining the relationships of humans to nature. . . . Changing values and attitudes will need to become manifest in behavior; for example, practices that value biodiversity over board-feet."[31]

An identity crisis was truly occurring in the forestry profession, and by the mid-1990s, with the rush of many resource managers and environmental groups to the banner of ecosystem management, the Society of American Foresters felt it necessary to reaffirm its commitment to private-sector forestry, the rights of private landowners, and multiple use-sustained yield forest management. Mississippi foresters were also concerned with professionalism. In 1977 the state legislature passed the Foresters' Registration Act, which regulated the practice of forestry and required the registration of its practitioners. During the law's first five years, nearly one thousand foresters were registered.[32]

However, even as ecosystem management and the "new forestry" became the operating principles of the U.S. Forest Service and some foresters and land managers, others wanted to go even farther, advocating, as did Chris Maser in his controversial book *The Redesigned Forest,* not only an ecological approach to forest management without an anthropocentric orientation but also an emphasis on "restoration forestry" with the maintenance of original, unmanaged forests as well as the inclusion of old-growth rotation in management cycles. However, as forester and historian Douglas W. MacCleery has pointed out, restoration forestry has some problems in terms of what is being restored. As MacCleery asks, "What conditions should ecosystems be restored to? For example, will we try to bring them back to conditions before modern fire control? Or to conditions before European settlement? If to the latter, should we try to restore the landscape to its condition before or after the holocaust of Old World diseases decimated native peoples? It's not an option to go back to conditions before people inhabited North America: It would be tough to get the continental glaciers to come back."[33]

National forests traditionally have been managed under the multiple-use philosophy, which defined conservation on the Pinchot "wise use" model. The Creative Act of 1891 and the Organic Administration Act of 1897 emphasized protection of waterflows as much as furnishing a continuing supply of timber. While some people, both within and outside of the U.S. Forest Service, have criticized this philosophy, virtually from the beginning the Forest Service included within its definition of multiple use the growth, harvest, and sale of timber to private forest-products industries. Some critics say that this emphasis has neglected such other uses as recreation, watershed protection, and scenic preservation or aesthetics.

The Multiple Use And Sustained Yield Act of 1960 gave the congressional stamp of approval to what had, in effect, been Forest Service policies for years, although the measure added wildlife, fish, recreation, and range to the original purpose of managing the forests for water and timber. The 1960 act said that each purpose should receive equal consideration in forest management so that "all the various renewable surface resources of the national forests . . . are utilized in the combination that will best meet the needs of the American people."[34]

Timber harvesting was once relatively unimportant, but World War II and the postwar housing boom propelled the annual harvest to 11 billion board feet by 1965, where it remained until 1990. In the early 1980s, because of increasing national consumption of timber for construction and paper, some were pushing for increased softwood harvesting in national forests. This issue was important for Mississippi, since by 1988 timber sales from the state's national forests were the largest in the eastern two-thirds of the nation, with sales of 244 million board feet valued at almost $21 million. In 1991, although Mississippi's national forests constituted only 1/191 of the total national forest acreage, they ranked fifth nationally in the return of receipts to the national treasury from the balanced resource programs.[35]

The largest part of the return was from timber harvests, and by 1996 Mississippi led the nation in timber sales from national forests. However, since 1990 harvests have declined because of op-

position by environmental groups, public pressure, and management to protect endangered species. The National Forest Products Association, concerned about the continued availability of timber from southern national forests, established a Public Timber Council Regional Office in Atlanta. The association argued that through lawsuits and challenges, environmental groups were seeking to block harvests so that they could promote "recreational and aesthetic values as the dominant management objectives for southern and eastern national forests."[36]

Some observers found the environmentalists' approach perfectly acceptable. Analyzing the history of the Organic Act of 1897, John Fedkiw described the national forests as "resilient and responsive to management." He went on to say that although the forests' "management direction has changed a great deal since World War II, and especially since 1990, the uses remain much the same as they were when the Organic Act became law." Fedkiw noted that both timber harvests and land available for harvest had dropped significantly and observed that "national forest management emphasis has shifted from maintaining ecosystems for production to maintaining and restoring ecosystems for their environmental services." However, he conceded that "the greatest weakness in the national forest management setting lies in the lack of a national consensus about the optimum use and management of national forests, the diversity of user and public interests, and the nature of our democratic system and processes."[37]

By 1994 the Mississippi national forest timber harvest was down significantly, and because of concerns about the decline, members of the forest-products industry formed the Mississippi Federal Timber Council (MFTC). The organization originally included forty-one members ranging from large corporations to small wood dealers and operated under the umbrella of the MFA. The MFTC hired as its consultant Gene A. Sirmon, who had recently retired from a long career with the Forest Service, the last part as acting supervisor of Mississippi's national forests.

The organization was designed to represent the industry in the national forest-planning process, in the political arena, and in relations with other organizations concerned about resource issues on public lands. Said the MFTC, "Industry must take a cue from environmental groups and get involved in the early stages of forest planning and follow the process all the way through." The council also began to work toward a coalition of organizations affected by the level of timber sales from national forests, and during 1994 the Mississippi Association of Supervisors, the Mississippi School Board Association, the Mississippi Loggers Association, and the MFA and other organizations created the Mississippi Public Lands Coalition to fight further reductions in timber harvests.[38]

Timber sales were affected by Forest Service efforts to protect the endangered red-cockaded woodpecker. The Sierra Club threatened to sue the Forest Service, charging that woodpecker populations in the national forests were declining because of "inadequate management practices for protecting" the bird. In 1989 the new forest supervisor for the Mississippi national forests, Kenneth R. Johnson, cited protecting the woodpecker as the most important issue affecting the timber supply.[39]

By the 1980s Forest Service critics were charging that the agency was selling timber at below cost, although others disputed the figures and calculations. The principal law governing below-cost sales and Forest Service timber practices in general is the National Forest Management Act of 1976, and by the late 1980s the legality of the sales remained largely unresolved and untested. In fact, some experts argued that a definitive answer to the question was unlikely and that the issue should remain a matter of administrative discretion. One of the major problems is that of separating timber management and harvest costs from other multiple-use common expenses. The Society of American Foresters, with its own members divided and grappling with a definition of a below-cost sale, issued a position statement condoning below-cost sales if they were part of a "land-use forest-management 'activity package' that may include negative cash-flow projects."[40]

Since the 1970s the attitudes of many people toward national forest management and use have been changing. The Forest Service as well as forest-products companies and private foresters, now had to operate within a new philosophical and legal climate. In 1970 the passage of the National Environmental Policy Act meant that the Forest Service had to assess and document the environmental impact of its decisions. The 1972 amendments to the Water Pollution Act (the Clean Water Act) required evaluation of discharges from nonpoint sources (such as runoff from forestland). Following the passage of the Water Quality Act of 1987, which emphasized the control of nonpoint sources of pollution, the MFA's Environmental Affairs Committee developed a handbook of voluntary forest management techniques, called Best Management Practices, for the guidance of the Mississippi forestry community. The National Forest Management Act of 1976 established new guidelines for land management and use and required the Forest Service to prepare detailed management plans for each national forest on a ten- to fifteen-year cycle. These changes gave the general public additional opportunities to be involved in management decisions at a time when many people were moving toward greater environmental consciousness.[41]

As part of its response to these new pressures, the Forest Service undertook a survey of cultural resources, defined as "sites, artifacts, structures or features which remain from human activity in the past." For Mississippi, sites older than fifty years and structures built prior to World War II qualified as "cultural resources." By the time of the mid-1980s land and resource management plan, only about 7 percent of Mississippi's national forests had been inventoried. Most of the 250 sites identified were classified as insignificant, with only one, the Owl Creek Mounds in the Trace Unit of the Tombigbee National Forest, listed on the National Register of Historic Places. Three other sites, including the Dowling Bayou

Complex and Riley site in the Delta National Forest and a site in the Ackerman Unit of the Tombigbee National Forest, were deemed "potentially significant." Forest managers voiced their commitment to protecting significant cultural sites, and they had provided for "enhancement," meaning the dissemination of information and provision of signs and self-guided trails or other measures at nine additional sites.[42]

A 1977 American Forest Institute survey asked people to choose between increasing timber harvests and sales from national forests or preserving the trees in their natural state. Sixty-two percent chose preserving trees, and 28 percent wanted increased timber sales. The same survey showed that 46 percent of respondents indicated that the present amount of wilderness was "about right," while 32 percent said it was "too little." A 1982 survey revealed significant displeasure with forest-management practices, identifying the following as the worst abuses: clear-cutting (43 percent), use of insecticides (37 percent), use of herbicides (36 percent), thinning (25 percent), controlled burning (20 percent), and reforestation (20 percent). More than 50 percent thought insecticide use should be more strictly regulated, with many fearing the contamination of water supplies.[43]

Pressure on forest managers increased as urbanites moved to forested rural areas. Many who stayed in the cities became more environmentally conscious. Urbanites flee the cities and take up residence on the borders of national or privately owned forests, apparently thinking that the stately trees within their areas will remain untouched indefinitely. They are horrified and furious when the Forest Service or private landowners contract to thin and even clear-cut some of these areas for timber-stand improvement or timber sales.

As early as 1971 the Mississippi Forestry Commission initiated a rather benign program to reach urbanites. The commission established an urban forestry program, primarily to provide information and advice about insects and diseases that affected shade trees in the towns and cities.

By the mid-1980s demographers were predicting that by the turn of the twenty-first century, half of Mississippi's population would be concentrated in eighteen of the state's eighty-two counties. It was expected that many of the people in these urban areas would still own commercial timberland in rural regions. Thus the forestry commission increased its urban forestry programs to provide technical assistance to urban absentee timberland owners and to increase the urban public's knowledge of forestry's contributions and needs. In 1984 residents of the capital city formed the Jackson Area Absentee Forest Landowner Association. The commission also assisted more than one hundred Mississippi towns in developing and maintaining nature trails and arboretums; staging Arbor Day and community tree-planting programs; and dealing with insects, disease, and other urban forestry problems. By 1987 Laurel, Biloxi, and Tupelo had become tree cities under the Arbor Day Foundation's Tree City USA program, and by 1991 Mississippi had thirteen Tree City USA communities.[44]

In 1990 a national program called "America the Beautiful" was created under that year's farm bill. President George Bush pledged to plant 1 billion trees annually in the United States, and in 1991 $21 million was appropriated for urban and community forestry, followed by $24 million in 1992. Mississippi received $290,000 the first year and $305,000 the second. The money was used to fund the administrative and program expenses for the Mississippi Forestry Commission, to develop a statewide urban forestry council, and to fund projects through a competitive matching-grant program. Some twenty-three communities and organizations initiated projects during the first round of funding. Various corporations also provided funding for urban tree-planting programs. By this time the U.S. Forest Service was also actively promoting urban and community forestry programs.[45]

The problems of urban encroachment on forests are not confined to national forests. In 1982 Henry Vaux, chair of the California State Board of Forestry, coined the term *urban-forest interface* and warned of the growing conflicts between residential development in and near forests and forest management. Researchers in the late 1980s and early 1990s found that national-forest supervisors and district rangers identified the problems associated with the wildland/residential/urban interface as among their top emerging issues. Much of their attention was focused on fire protection for homes built on forested lands. Other problems include the management of increased recreational usage, pollution of forest streams from septic and sewer systems, disturbances to wildlife and loss of habitat to development, conflicts between domestic pets and wildlife, and demands for the suppression of predatory wildlife to protect pets. There are also public objections to timber harvesting on aesthetic grounds, public objections to the use of pesticides, and concerns about logging traffic on rural roads.[46]

The pressures are growing. Between 1970 and 1980, populations in the nation's nonmetropolitan counties grew by an average of 13.4 percent, while populations in rural counties influenced by the presence of a national forest grew by 23.4 percent. New residents often have different values than did the previous rural dwellers. For example, by the mid-1990s both the percentage and the absolute number of adult Mississippians who hunted was on the decline, and some argued that this phenomenon diminished people's connection with the natural environment. Urban populations typically place less value on the commercial use of the forest and a much higher emphasis on aesthetics. The problem for forest managers becomes that of balancing the traditional uses of the land with the new values. While these problems are not yet as acute in Mississippi as in other states with larger urban centers, even the Magnolia State is in the early stages of feeling these strains. The recent controversy in the Holly Springs National Forest is a case in point.[47]

The Holly Springs National Forest sold 20 to 40 million board feet of timber annually for years, with little or no controversy, until the Forest Service announced plans for harvesting hardwood, pine pulpwood, and sawtimber on a 1,251-acre area that would call for two clear-cuts in 1998. In March 1998 the *Memphis Commercial Appeal* ran a front-page story under the headline, "Chain Saws Buzzing in Miss. Forest Sound Like Massacre to Ex-Urbanites." Nearby residents formed "Citizens for Holly Springs National Forest" and lobbied for a moratorium on clear-cutting until further studies were done.

District Ranger Gary Yeck attributed the developing controversy to the influx of new residents from Memphis and other cities. Said Yeck, "I think they look at the woods differently than I look at the woods. They have different values, different ideas of how their land should be managed, and they're expressing that. . . . They moved from the city to live near the forest, and they don't want the forest cut." Under pressure, the Forest Service backed off plans for clear-cuts but intended to go ahead with thinning and commercial harvests, leaving ten to fourteen trees per acre in some areas for natural reseeding.

The environmentalists' positions in the Holly Springs controversy offered a textbook example of the modern debate over national-forest management. They argued that the forest's management plans emphasized timber production at the expense of such other uses as wildlife habitat, recreation, and water quality. The environmentalists emphasized that the cutting posed a particular threat to songbirds, which the activists claimed required a large expanse of forest habitat. The environmentalists also pointed to the fact that the headwaters of the Wolf River, a stream that wanders through rural north Mississippi and west Tennessee before entering the Mississippi River at Memphis, are in the Holly Springs National Forest. The Wolf River, they said, was increasingly popular with recreationists, and recreation provided a greater economic return to the area than logging.

Local environmentalists also received assistance from groups and individuals outside the area, including an Indiana-based organization called Heartwood. Said Scott Banbury, president of the Memphis Audubon Society, "The environmental assessment [the Forest Service] produced on their timber production has not adequately addressed the other values of the forest." Heartwood's Joe Glisson argued that the Holly Springs National Forest was being transformed with the help of large amounts of herbicides from a mixed forest to a tree farm of pines. He said that managers had failed to fulfill the conditions of the 1976 National Forest Management Act by not monitoring the cumulative effects of timber harvesting and failing to conduct an adequate inventory of wildlife. "Holly Springs has never had any scrutiny from outside the agency, and therefore they just haven't bothered to fulfill the requirements of the law," he stated.

Heartwood's position reflected its interpretation of legislation enacted in the 1970s. The 1970 National Environmental Policy Act required environmental analysis of the impacts of resource management decisions and provided for public review of the supporting environmental impact statements. As a later Forest Service publication put it, "This requirement afforded interested parties additional opportunities to criticize and oppose timber management activities, particularly those involving timber sales perceived to affect other resource uses adversely."[48]

The other law invoked by the opponents of the Holly Springs clear-cuts was the National Forest Management Act of 1976. In 1974 Congress enacted the Forest and Rangeland Renewable Resources Planning Act (RPA) which directed the Forest Service to assess the renewable resources in all national forests. The law was amended by the National Forest Management Act of 1976, which required assessments of renewable resources at the end of 1975, to be updated in 1979, and every tenth year thereafter. The Forest Service was also to develop a renewable-resources program to cover the four-year period after October 1976 and the following four decades. These assessments and programs were to be reflected in the Southern Region's 1982 final environmental impact statements and resource planning standards and guidelines and in

the land and resource management plans of the various forests.[49]

The 1976 legislation required the Forest Service to establish guidelines for managing the forests so that timber would be harvested only where specified by the act. It spelled out the conditions under which clear-cutting, seed-tree cutting, and other cuts designed to regenerate even-aged stands of timber could occur. Each national forest was now required to have a comprehensive resource management plan, and all existing timber-management plans had to be incorporated into the new plans developed under the RPA and the National Forest Management Act. By the mid-1980s land and resource management plans had been approved and implemented in all of Mississippi's national forests.[50]

Across the country timber sales were challenged by various private interests and citizens "who view timber sales as being in conflict with other resources and uses they regard as more important or valuable than timber production." Nonetheless, in the late 1980s timber sales continued at a level slightly higher than they had been in 1970. By that time some 95 percent of national forest areas were classified as commercial forestland, and the U.S. Forest Service considered roughly 75 percent of national forestland in the South suitable for timber production. The land and resource management plan for the Mississippi national forests listed among the management objectives an effort to "accelerate the harvest of pine sawtimber," which would be accomplished through clear-cutting. Forest Service spokesmen boasted of cutover, burned-over, and understocked lands restored to health and noted that "even with the extensive use of clearcutting for regenerating both pine and hardwood stands, the proportion of commercial forest land in pine and that in mixed pine and hardwood types has been relatively stable since 1952."[51]

Regional forester Gary Yeck expressed the hope that he could meet with the critics, walk the woods with them, and reach a mutually satisfactory understanding regarding the management of the Holly Springs National Forest. He observed that the environmentalists perhaps misunderstood the situation, noting that some areas they considered hardwood sites would be pine-dominated at maturity. He denied that the forest was to become a pine monoculture and said that there had been "very little" conversion of hardwood areas into pine stands.

Yeck reported that the Holly Springs National Forest featured a rich mosaic of mixed forest cover and open areas, which combined to offer excellent wildlife habitat. Clear-cutting, he said, was used only where existing trees would not provide enough seed for regeneration. In such cases, he stated, "If we want to get that stand of trees back and we don't have a seed source . . . then we'll clearcut and plant." He also noted that some of the forest's trees were past their prime and would be gone "whether we do anything or not." Yeck concluded, "We're trying to steward this land for the American public. The most controversial thing we do is cut trees."

In the meantime the MFTC called a meeting of local government and school officials, business leaders, and community and industry leaders at Wall Doxey State Park to inform them that the MFTC believed Heartwood was "gearing up for a major assault on the Holly Springs and perhaps all the national forests in Mississippi." The council hoped to encourage local leaders to "become involved and hopefully counteract some of the pressure on the Forest Service to stop timber sales." In November 1997 the Friends of the Holly Springs National Forest and Heartwood submitted a notice of intent to the secretary of the interior indicating that they intended to file a lawsuit to stop the proposed cutting in the Holly Springs National Forest. The groups claimed that the proposed harvest violated the Endangered Species Act by impacting the Indiana bat's habitat. According to the Forest Service, the last known sighting of an Indiana bat in Mississippi was more than thirty years earlier and some fifty miles from the Holly Springs National Forest.[52]

Yeck's efforts at compromise were unsuccessful. He revised the original environmental assessment and incorporated many of the opponents'

objections, including the elimination of clear-cutting, increasing the acreage of seed-tree (natural) regeneration, reducing the volume of timber to be harvested by 19 percent, and reducing site-preparation activities, including the use of herbicides. Nevertheless, at least four organizations, including the Memphis Audubon Society; Heartwood; Wildly, of Montgomery, Alabama; and Citizens for the Holly Springs National Forest, of Oxford, Mississippi, filed administrative appeals with the regional forester in Atlanta. Wildly also filed an appeal of a proposed timber sale on eight thousand acres of pine plantations on the Homochitto National Forest, claiming that the harvests would degrade water quality. By early 1999 several environmental groups had filed suit in federal court to stop the Forest Service from conducting timber sales in Holly Springs and all other national forests in Mississippi, and school boards and county governments in several counties were preparing to intervene in opposition to the suits. After denying these groups permission to intervene in the suit in March 1999, the Northern District Court in Oxford reconsidered the case and granted intervenor status to the Holly Springs Area School Board Associations and boards of supervisors.[53]

One is left with the impression of two well-meaning sides, both believing deeply in the propriety of their positions. Visual perceptions and misconceptions undoubtedly formed part of the problem. Also, some foresters had long believed that their profession had not done an adequate job of communicating with urban dwellers and addressing their concerns. At a 1984 professional meeting, Nelson argued that one of the problems foresters and landowners faced was that they were now dealing with an urban population that "viewed the forest more from a recreational standpoint than from a production standpoint" and with political leaders who reflected those views and had little or no direct knowledge of forests or the benefits of forest management.[54] Like his old colleague, Allen, Nelson espoused a more positive and less shrill approach to dealing with environmental issues and criticisms than did many other industry spokespeople.

Controversies and debates over forest policy continue today, just as they always have and probably always will. For example, as of 1998, the U.S. Forest Service continued to operate under the 25 percent rule, under which the county from which national-forest timber is cut and sold receives one-fourth of the revenue. This money is a major source of income for rural counties in timber country and helps to lessen the local tax burden. Over the past decade the revenues from timber sales have decreased by as much as two-thirds as a result of reduced harvesting. The reduced harvests were linked in part to management practices designed to protect red-cockaded woodpecker habitat, and in 1994 county boards of supervisors in Mississippi's De Soto National Forest area met to discuss the Declining sales and to consider forming a coalition of counties with national forestlands to consider their common interests. In the fall of 1995 the Mississippi Public Lands Coalition, the Mississippi Association of School Boards, and the Mississippi Association of Supervisors agreed to jointly spend between fifteen and forty thousand dollars to appeal the Forest Service's red-cockaded woodpecker environmental impact statement.

Some observers expect that under pressure from environmentalists to further restrict harvests and manage the national forests with greater emphasis on other forest uses such as recreation, watershed protection, and esthetic enjoyment, timber harvests will be even more severely restricted in the future. The Forest Service proposes that by 2005 the 25 percent rule be dropped in favor of fixed annual payments to counties at their current levels. Environmentalists favor the plan, believing that it will not only reduce cutting in the forests but also will cut down on the influence of local politicians, whom they regard as valuable members and allies of the timber lobby. The new plan is controversial. It must be approved by Congress, and strong opposition from timber states is expected. This controversy is only one of many debates on the environmental horizon.[55]

Some foresters are predictably outraged by the actual and proposed reductions. As Michael C. Thompson observed, "The allowable cut on the National Forest System has collapsed. . . . The national forests must once again make a significant contribution to the nation's wood supply through more intensive forest management on a larger timberland base. This was one of the major reasons the forests were established in the first place." Others argued, however, that the Forest Service, by selling timber from the national forests at below cost, was mistreating the general citizenry to help the forest-products industry. Some within the agency, as well as many outside observers, questioned the critics' figures. As the debates raged, harvests on the Mississippi national forests were virtually halted in 1998 because of a lack of funding for timber-sale preparations. In fact, Mississippi's national forests ranked forty-first among the nation's timber-producing forests in funding for sales, some 25 percent below the next lowest state.[56]

In addition to growing pressure and criticism from society, the ideas and lobbying of an internal group affected the Forest Service beginning in the late 1980s. A group of employees emerged that was dedicated to the reform of the Forest Service and the conversion of its land-management philosophy from an emphasis on commodity production to the promotion of ecological integrity. In 1989 these men and women founded the Association of Forest Service Employees for Environmental Ethics. A 1996 study indicated that the 450 association members, a small minority within the Forest Service, are far more likely to identify with Leopold's land-ethic philosophy than are their fellow employees, who tend to be more attuned to Pinchot's values. In general, foresters, engineers, and range managers tend to be closer to the Pinchot model than do biologists, hydrologists, and landscape architects. This schism is significant, for the percentage of nonforesters with views closer to the Leopold model is rising in the Forest Service, and they are moving up the organizational ladder. From 1985 to 1993 the percentage of foresters, engineers, and range managers in the Forest Service dropped from 66 to 51 percent, while the number of biologists, hydrologists, and landscape architects rose from 10 to 15 percent. Most important, members of the latter group are rising to the top of the agency, as evidenced by the ascension of fisheries biologist Michael Dombeck as chief forester in the late 1990s. As the authors of a 1996 study concluded, "newer employees whose backgrounds are often outside the forestry profession are infusing the agency with non commodity values based on environmental and ecological concerns."[57]

In 1991 Robertson said,

The Forest Service has been changing very rapidly, I think, over the last three or four years, and for several reasons, not only because of new people in the Forest Service, but also because people outside the Forest Service are debating the role of the national forests and how they ought to be managed. . . . The old-growth issue has been successfully taken by environmental groups from just old trees to old-growth ecosystems. So if you really look at what's coming out of research and the thinking of the last five years, we've got to look at the forest much more broadly. We've got to look at the forest as an ecosystem, and we've got to somehow look at all the values in the forest—not just the trees, timber, but not exclusive of timber either—to try to determine how we perpetuate all those values through time in a managed forest. . . . The conflict comes where we've got special interest groups still looking at it piece by piece, and they're very vocal, with strong constituent special interest groups behind them.[58]

In 1991 Tom Mills, the acting associate director for programs and legislation in the Forest Service's Washington office, said that the Forest Service would emphasize four things over the next few years: (1) enhancement of recreation, wildlife, and fisheries resources; (2) environmentally acceptable commodity production; (3) expansion of scientific knowledge about natural-resource systems; and (4) responding to global resource issues. In 1994 an interdiscipli-

nary group of scholars and Forest Service personnel gathered at Grey Towers, Pinchot's home, to discuss the agency's effort to reinvent itself.[59]

Controversies over Forest Service philosophy and land management will undoubtedly continue into the future. Nonetheless, particularly when the lands with which they started are considered, the Forest Service's performance has been impressive. As their spokespersons see it, "From a public-use standpoint, probably the most significant impact of the southern national forests on the South's timber resources and future management of those resources has been and is the demonstrated capability of properly managed forestlands to produce large volumes of high-quality timber in combination with other forest resources. Providing over 23 million visitor-days of recreation annually for hunters, fishermen, sightseers, hikers, campers, and other users of the forests' nontimber assets; the critical habitat for several threatened, endangered, and sensitive plant and animal species; wilderness and natural areas; research areas; water for domestic and industrial uses; forage for domestic animals; and timber, these forests are examples of successful multiple-use, sustained-yield forest resource management."[60]

Another recent recurring battle of the environmental cause has concerned protection of endangered species. Some critics question whether some species are worth protecting or restoring at all. They fail to see the snail darter's, spotted owl's, or red-cockaded woodpecker's importance to society. In fact, most people value wildlife, and economists have identified two kinds of values—use and intrinsic. Use values include wildlife uses such as hunting and fishing that diminish the population as well as nonconsumptive use values such as photography or bird watching. Intrinsic values include the inherent value of an animal's existence, even for people who do not expect directly to use the resource. Other intrinsic values include the option value, held by people who may not presently use the resource but may want to do so in the future, and the bequest value, held by those who want to assure the existence of wildlife populations for future generations. Finally, of course, there are those who simply think that wildlife has as much a right to inhabit the planet as humans and that people should protect what they have and restore what they have diminished. In 1973 Congress passed and the president signed the Endangered Species Act. It is designed to provide for the conservation and preservation of endangered and threatened species and the ecosystems on which they depend.[61]

Southern forests contain several endangered plants and animals, and while the South has not had controversies with the intensity and vitriol of those in other sections, such as the spotted-owl battles in the Pacific Northwest, Dixie has had at least one high-profile endangered species: the red-cockaded woodpecker. At least three-fourths of the total population, more than two thousand colonies, lives in the piney woods of national forests in the Carolinas, Florida, Alabama, Louisiana, Texas, and Mississippi. Some environmentalists and experts claim that the official figures on woodpecker populations are unreliable and overstated. These advocates sharply criticize clear-cuts, even-aged management, and short harvest rotations on both forest-industry lands and national forests, arguing that these practices are inimical to the bird's habitat and survival. The bird's defenders basically believe that the economics of timber management have been far more important to both public and private forest managers than has protection of the red-cockaded woodpecker.

In the late 1980s, the Forest Service planned to manage its pinelands with recognition that the woodpecker needed 125 acres of thirty-year-old or older stands, or "foraging habitats," to sustain a colony. The Forest Service would modify harvesting methods within three-quarters of a mile of woodpecker colony sites where there were populations of less than 250 colonies. The birds nest inside living pine trees, and a producing colony consists of three or four birds, including a breeding pair and one or two helpers, although some colonies contain only males. By the early 1990s an effort was under way in the Homochitto National Forest to return some pine areas to their original open conditions, as they were "when the Indians lived here and regularly burned the pine forests," thereby creating an ecosystem that would accommodate the needs of the red-cockaded woodpecker. While these efforts were under way in all national forests in the southeast, a wildlife biologist in the Homochitto said that the effort there was "much more advanced . . . than on any other of the national forests."

The policy generally eliminated clear-cuts within three-quarters of a mile of colonies on proposed timber sale areas. Clear-cutting would be replaced by an emphasis on thinning existing stands, with the oldest, hardiest, and most suitable of the trees left for the birds. The agency hoped to double the national red-cockaded woodpecker population. By the late 1980s officials claimed that some 250,000 acres of mature timber in the southern national forests were being managed in a way designed to protect the woodpeckers.

However, the Sierra Club found the policy wanting, threatening lawsuits and charging that woodpecker populations in the national forests were declining because of "inadequate management practices for protecting" the bird. On the other side of the issue, in December 1990, the Forest Service Timber Purchasers' Council filed a lawsuit against the Forest Service, charging that it had illegally instituted the harvesting plan on woodpecker habitat without following the established legal procedures and allowing public participation in the decision-making process. The MFTC argued that the Forest Service's management measures "far exceed the woodpeckers' needs," and although "trying very hard not to portray an image of opposing the protection and recovery of the bird," termed the government's policies "extreme measures."[62]

Mississippi's national forests by the 1980s also were being managed to protect several other endangered or sensitive species of plants and animals, among them the Mississippi sandhill crane,

American alligator, eastern indigo snake, and gopher tortoise. Gopher tortoise management occurred mostly on 13,265 acres of the De Soto National Forest. The plant species included the needle palm, beak rushes, southern yellow orchid, prairie clover, loblolly bay or black laurel, Juneberry holly, and little floating heart. In the late 1990s the Louisiana quillwort, a rare and endangered plant previously believed to exist only on private lands in Louisiana, was found in at least twenty-five locations in the De Soto National Forest and placed under a recovery plan. Sensitive invertebrates and vertebrates included crayfish, southern hog-nose snakes, black pine snakes, and rainbow snakes. The only sensitive fish listed were the Yazoo darter, bluenose minnow, and the least madtom. In March 1986 the U.S. Fish and Wildlife Service was petitioned to list as an endangered species the Louisiana black bear, whose habitat was in Louisiana, the Yazoo River basin, and the loess bluffs of Warren County south through Wilkinson County, Mississippi. Both Louisiana and Mississippi put the bear on their state endangered-species lists, and a coalition of private companies, organizations, and state agencies from Arkansas, Texas, Louisiana, and Mississippi united to form the Black Bear Conservation Committee to develop a restoration plan.[63]

Private forest-products companies also responded to the concern about wildlife and endangered species. In 1993 International Paper Company announced a habitat conservation plan for the gopher tortoise, which was a threatened species when found west of the Tombigbee River in Mississippi and Alabama. The plan was endorsed by the U.S. Fish and Wildlife Service and was expected to be the first of its kind in the nation. International Paper also maintained streamside management zones along the Pearl River drainage system in Mississippi and Louisiana and expected to protect the habitat for the ringed sawback turtle through the protection of water quality by the use of Best Management Practices. The company also joined the U.S. Fish and Wildlife Service in developing a plan to protect

the Red Hills salamander. Georgia-Pacific cooperated with the U.S. Fish and Wildlife Service to protect the red-cockaded woodpecker on its lands. Some companies created more edge territory by leaving natural hardwood drains and creek bottoms between their site-preparation areas. This procedure was not totally altruistic, for as one company official observed, "Many of these areas are going to come back in hardwoods anyway and it's a waste of money to try to convert them."[64]

Owners of nonindustrial private forestlands were understandably concerned about the impact of endangered-species legislation and protection on their investments. To allay their fears and provide management guidance, the various southern regional chapters of the Society of American Foresters, including the Mississippi chapter, prepared and endorsed a January 1992 paper discussing the problem and recommending various actions. The society essentially encouraged landowners and public officials to cooperate in finding solutions while recognizing that "humans have a legitimate biotic right to compete with other species for goods and services from the land." Some environmentalists expressed a good deal of skepticism concerning the legitimacy of concerns about endangered species among forest-products companies, private landowners, and even the Forest Service.[65]

For example, John W. Thompson, who had managed the Johns Manville industrial forests in Mississippi, became an avid bird watcher following retirement and an activist in the campaign to save the red-cockaded woodpecker. He noted that he was considered a radical or traitor by many of his former colleagues and commented bitterly on forest-industry attitudes and practices. In 1987 he noted that the bird's "decline on private lands in the last 15 years has been alarming, particularly on industry lands." He also reported that "[i]ndustry has been particularly cynical." To support this claim he noted that the former wildlife manager for the Southern Kraft Division of International Paper said that he believed every red-cockaded woodpecker colony on the company's land, except for a few at the Bainbridge, Georgia, research forest, had been destroyed. In trying to persuade Nelson to join the bird's cause, Thompson wrote, "The antagonists think that the advocates for saving RCW are a bunch of extremists, and it will make them think to see a dirt forester in the bird's corner."[66]

Conversely, some experts believed that as more land was managed for species protection or outright preservation, reasonable approaches would keep both timber advocates and environmentalists and preservationists happy. The solutions lay in managing different lands for different purposes and in utilizing technologies for tree improvement; better matching of species and seed sources with sites; and improvement of site preparation, weed control, and fertilization to boost productivity on those lands managed for timber. Also needed, according to these experts, were better use and conversion at manufacturing plants and increased use of recycled fiber.[67]

Debates about forest management among both the general public and professionals are often influenced by basic research undertaken by public agencies and universities. Federal funding for research in forestry schools is provided through the McIntire-Stennis program administered by the U.S. Department of Agriculture Cooperative State Research Service. Created under the McIntire-Stennis Cooperative Forest Research Act of 1962, this program significantly increased federal funding to land grant and other state forestry schools for research and training. Funds are also available through the Forestry Competitive Grants Program, with the money coming from the Forest Service and the program administered by the Cooperative State Research Service. The increased funding for university research has assisted Mississippi State University's work in wood preservation and timber harvesting.[68]

In 1974 the Forest and Rangeland Renewable Resources Research Act replaced earlier legislation providing for forestry research, and this law remains the authorization for conducting research inventories. This legislation mandated that over a fifty-year period, forest, rangeland, and associated resources (public and private) should be assessed on a ten-year cycle, with updates every five years. This law went farther than earlier research legislation by broadening the inventory's scope to include all of the resources and values of forests, not simply the timber. Other aspects surveyed would include land use, vegetation structure, and forest health. There would be five-year programs for the Forest Service, including annual progress reports.

In 1976 the act was amended by the National Forest Management Act (NFMA). The National Forest Management Act required ten-year interdisciplinary forest plans for each of the administrative units in all of the national forests. The idea was that on the basis of these ten-year surveys, the Secretary of Agriculture could direct the U.S. Forest Service to implement appropriate policies, and the President would provide Congress with a Presidential Statement of Policy, which they could discuss and perhaps modify. Forest Service policies would be recommended for all forested lands, but enforced only on lands administered by that agency.

The 1989 assessment showed that three forest uses or demands were increasing at an accelerated rate: recreation, hardwood timber, and wildlife and fish use. By the 1990s there were efforts to broaden the Forest Inventory and Analysis to expand information on ecosystems and view the forest in its broadest sense. The research program began to take an ecological approach to the inventory and analysis of forests.[69]

In 1991 the Southern Forest Experiment Station's Forest Inventory and Analysis Unit began a two-phase program for the 1993 RPA update. It mapped the distribution of forests in the United States and developed a forest density map showing the percent of forest per unit area. These maps were prepared using digital analysis of advanced very high resolution radiometer (AVHRR) weather satellite data and map and field information from across the country. The first phase of the project developed and tested the data analysis procedures for the mid-South states, including Mississippi.

Prior to this effort, the primary source for forest-cover distributions in the United States was the forest-types map published in the *National Atlas* and other related works. The atlas was compiled by the U.S. Geological Survey, based on older forest-type maps and data supplied by the Forest Service. Forest distribution and transitional and overlapping zones between forest types were not well represented. The new map updates the 1967 major-forest-types map and depicts the location of major forest types in the mid-South as of 1991. It also shows land-use patterns and helps to determine shifts in forest-type distributions between 1967 and 1991.

The 1991 maps showed two major changes for Mississippi. First, the 1967 map showed loblolly-shortleaf pine forests covering part of the Blackbelt Prairie, an arc of mostly unforested land stretching from northern Mississippi to southeastern Alabama. The high base saturation and acidity of the soils in this area are unfavorable for southern pines, and the 1991 maps do not show these forests. The AVHRR cover-type maps also show that large areas of the bottomlands in the Mississippi alluvial plain had been converted from oak-gum-cypress forests to nonforest (agricultural) uses since 1967.[70]

Another continuing area of public controversy for forest managers has been the use of chemicals. A serious but sporadic problem for growers of southern pines is the pine bark beetle or southern pine beetle. The onset of beetle infestations cannot be effectively predicted, despite ongoing work by entomologists, foresters, and other scientists. To try to deal with the problem, forest researchers are looking at forest type, tree size and age, and stand density in an attempt to identify stands where abundant food and habitat are favorable for beetle reproduction. Another technique is to use infrared aerial photographs to identify forests with stands that have favorable characteristics for beetle infestations. The hope is that instead of treating beetle infestations on an ad hoc basis when they appear, a strategy that often is not especially successful, integrated pest management will become an integral part of forest management and bring greater success. Other significant diseases and insect pests that plague southern forests are fusiform rust, root rot, pitch canker, little-leaf disease, and tipmoth.[71]

New pesticides and herbicides were developed during the 1940s. Federal funding for pest and disease control was provided through the Forest Pest Control Act of 1947, which has been administered by the Forest Service since 1954. Chemicals have been widely used by forest managers, sometimes with controversial results. One of the greatest debates centered on 2,4,5- trichlorophenoxy acetic acid (2,4,5-T), a member of the phenoxy herbicide group noted for killing broadleaf plants while most grasses and coniferous trees were fairly resistant. The chemical was widely used in site preparation and control in conifer plantings.

During the Vietnam War, however, a mixture of 2,4-D and 2,4,5-T was widely used as a defoliant under the name Agent Orange. Charges of damage to humans, animals, and plant life led to controversy and scientific investigations of Agent Orange. All chemicals came under public scrutiny. And indeed, the public was already becoming aroused because of the publicity surrounding Rachel Carson's 1962 book, *Silent Spring*. Research indicated that 2,4,5-T caused birth defects in rats and mice, because of a byproduct of the manufacturing process called dioxin, or TCDD. The problem was exacerbated by the fact that TCDD, one of the most toxic chemicals known, could not be entirely eliminated from the 2,4,5-T manufacturing process.

While manufacturers succeeded in drastically reducing the percentage of dioxins, safety questions persisted. Late in 1969 and early in 1970, Environmental Protection Agency administrator William D. Ruckelshaus banned the use of 2,4,5-T for a variety of purposes, including on forests, rangelands, and rights-of-way. Dow Chemical Company fought the ruling, but it was upheld in court in 1973. However, Dow, the agency, the Environmental Defense Fund, and the U.S. Department of Agriculture undertook testing in an attempt to more definitively examine the relationships between 2,4,5-T and TCDD and safety and long-term health effects. The ban ultimately was lifted.[72]

The Journal of Forestry reported that 2,4,5-T was "to forest pesticides what Ali is to boxing—the meanest and the greatest." The magazine said that "T, as the chemical is affectionately known to applicators," was extremely potent in killing broadleaf plants that invaded conifer sites but was harmful when it drifted onto nontarget crops. It was cheap, under fifty dollars an acre with aerial application, and could produce as much as a 40 percent increase in timber volume at the time of harvest. It also pointed out the level of dioxin in the notorious Agent Orange was much higher than in T and that, in any case, the effects of the defoliant used in Vietnam were turning out to be less than once thought, according to a National Academy of Sciences study. Furthermore, said the *Journal of Forestry* article, the levels of dioxin found in the soil were very limited, and the chemical degraded fairly quickly. The article essentially urged common sense and balance in determining whether T should be licensed for use in forest applications. A study entitled *The Phenoxy Herbicides*, the second edition of which was issued by the Council for Agricultural Science and Technology in 1978, concluded, "The evidence indicates that the TCDD contaminant in 2,4,5-T and silvex, is well below levels hazardous to humans and other organisms."[73]

Nearly a decade later an article in the *Journal of Forestry* put the controversy into perspective: "All the King's Horses and All the King's Men: 2,4,5-T was the best tool of all; yet 2,4,5-T had a very great fall. All of the facts midst all of the din couldn't put 'T' back together again." This article came in the wake of the Environmental Protection Agency's decision to cancel the use of 2,4,5-T and of silvex, a chemical analog of T, on January 30 and February 11, 1985. The article argued that the ban resulted from the cumulative effects of activism, litigation, antiherbicide violence, and contradictory science that raised questions concerning the role of government in pesticide regulation and the integrity of industry-funded science. The public concluded that with all the smoke, there must be fire. According to the article, "Campaigns by environmental interest groups, publicity about industrial accidents, occasional careless applications by herbicide users, inflammatory news reporting, and the legacy of Agent Orange forced EPA to regulate on the basis of political pressure rather than scientific protocol." The end result, said the authors, was that, the "consequences of the herbicide issue went far beyond the removal of 2,4,5-T and silvex from the marketplace. Confidence in the entire regulatory process was shaken, and respect for the analytical capabilities of EPA diminished. Foresters were deprived of a valuable management tool. Chemical manufacturers became less inclined to develop new products tailored to forestry because of the inordinate concern over such applications. The credibility of forest managers suffered from a perception that they had used improper methods. These perceptions, in turn, led to protests and litigation over various management decisions."

However, the article said, the results were not all bad. They pointed to the development of more effective substitutes and alternative methods. Furthermore, "More thorough evaluations of site conditions have helped confine vegetation-management treatments to areas where they are most needed. More intensive site preparation has also been used to reduce the need for follow-up release treatments. The issue has heightened awareness of the importance of safety and stewardship in using pesticides." Other studies noted that after the ban on 2,4,5-T and because of pressure from environmental groups, foresters relied on mechanical methods of vegetation and pest control but soon returned to an interest in chemicals for site preparation because of the expense of mechanical methods and the development of effective alternative herbicides.[74]

The Forest Service carries out control projects including spraying and tree removal on federal lands and cooperates with the Mississippi Forestry Commission on private lands. Because of recent environmental concerns about chemicals, foresters have turned to biological and cultural controls to treat pests and disease. The controversies over chemicals will not disappear, despite safety certifications by the federal government or educational efforts by foresters and chemical companies. In 1998 the Earthwatch Institute, a Massachusetts-based nonprofit organization that helps scientists get volunteers for research, joined a group of professors from the University of Mississippi to study the impact of agricultural chemicals on the people of the Delta. It is reasonable to assume that similar efforts in forested areas where herbicides and other chemicals are applied will occur in the future.[75]

Conversely, chemical companies tout the safety and effectiveness of the new generation of herbicides. For example, American Cyanamid claims that its imidazolinone herbicide marketed under the name Arsenal is not only effective in site preparation, herbaceous weed control, and release of conifer stands but has "little risk to mammals, birds and fish," because it is "rapidly excreted from animal systems and does not bioaccumulate." The company also says that the herbicide enhances the supply of wildlife food plants and habitat, including that of bobwhite quail and white-tailed deer. President Bill Clinton honored an American Cyanamid scientist with the National Medal of Technology for the "discovery and commercialization of environmentally friendly herbicides." Obviously sensitive to public concerns about chemicals and pesticides, both chemical and forest-products companies recently have produced sophisticated promotional brochures to convince the public of their ethics and of the safety of the chemicals they produce and use.[76]

One of the most dramatic, if often misunderstood, issues of recent years has been the continuing controversy over clear-cutting. There is little disagreement that the early period after a clear-cut is aesthetically disastrous. In a 1971 speech Allen observed, "Clearcutting gives me a bad gut feeling. It's too reminiscent of the old 'cut out and get out' days." But is clear-cutting necessary to

manage a forest responsibly? Is clear-cutting preferable to selective cutting in certain situations? Should the general public have a voice in determining the use of clear-cuts, especially on public lands? One old timer from Chunky, in east Mississippi, brought a lifetime of experience and family memories to a 1991 interview. His father, brother, and grandfather had been loggers and mule drivers, working for the Cotton States Lumber Company, and he stated, probably erroneously, "The private people wouldn't have clear cut . . . back then like they do now." And he had an interesting theory concerning the use of clear-cutting in the modern era: "I'll tell you one reason why they clear cut now. It's the machinery they use. They have to. See, one time they had mules and little smaller tractors where they could cut the trees down and pull the timber straight and sell it down to a certain inch. And so they quit doing that, and they just buy it all."[77]

Prominent Philadelphia, Mississippi, lumberman Tom DeWeese remembered that his father cut out in 1929 and said that "the timber was all gone." DeWeese, interviewed in 1991, was amazed that "in recent years they were producing more timber and lumber in this area here by far than they did in the 20's and 30's and 40's and 50's. And I don't understand it. . . . I knew the country. I knew the timberlands, and I thought it was about all gone, and they're cutting more today than they ever have." A lumberman who operated along the Mississippi-Alabama border noted in 1991 that the "timber companies and the papermills have decided that [clear-cutting is] the best, and it looks mighty rough the first 4 or 5 years, but after that it looks better every year. We have some that's 25 or 30 years old. It looks fine. . . . It was clear cut."[78]

Charles A. Connaughton, a longtime forester with the U.S. Forest Service, acknowledged in 1970 environmentalists' and even some foresters' general opposition to clear-cutting. However, he defended the practice as a necessary and appropriate silvicultural tool in certain situations. While conceding that clear-cutting was not always appropriate and that there were unwise uses of the practice in the past that gave clear-cutting and foresters a bad name, he argued that it was still a useful and sometimes necessary practice. He did advise using thorough efforts to minimize aesthetic and environmental damage when using clear-cutting. Even so, he conceded, the appearance of a clear-cut could be harsh to the untrained eye. Most citizens certainly were not trained foresters, and Senator Gail McGee of Wyoming reflected growing public concern and pressure when he called for a moratorium on clear-cutting in all national forests in 1972.[79]

In the same period a conservation specialist for the Oregon school system compiled papers on clear-cutting by the deans of various forestry schools in different parts of the country. The dean of the Duke University School of Forestry contributed an article on clear-cutting in public forests of the southern pine region. Like most other foresters of the period, he defended clear-cutting but urged the use of practices to reduce its aesthetic and environmental impacts. In its management plan for Mississippi's forests in the 1980s, the Forest Service did exactly that. The plan referred to the cuts as regeneration cuts and said that they should be limited in size to eighty acres for pines and forty for other species. They should also be at least three hundred feet apart and not adjacent to earlier harvests until those lands had recovered. The plan noted that clear-cutting would be the preferred method of harvesting in Mississippi's national forests. Forest-products companies defended even-age management and clear-cutting, arguing that these practices produced superior and healthier forests, abundant and flourishing wildlife, and a healthy aquatic environment.[80]

Industry spokespersons sometimes stridently defended clear-cutting. In 1973 President Richard M. Nixon received and endorsed a report from a special panel that recommended increased harvesting on national forests. The policy was enthusiastically endorsed by conservative syndicated newspaper columnist James J. Kilpatrick, who noted the Sierra Club representatives' "Pavlovian" negative reaction and concluded, "It would

be folly to pursue the policy of letting the trees grow up and rot." When the editor of the *Paducah (Kentucky) Sun Democrat* disagreed with the report and with Kilpatrick while condemning the impact of clear-cutting and replacement of mixed hardwood forests with "controlled" forests of pine and other species, a quick response emanated from Benton H. Box, the executive vice president of the Southern Forest Institute (which grew out of the Southern Pulpwood Conservation Association in 1969).

Box questioned the editor's "apparent hostility toward the private enterprise system as evidenced in your attacks on the forest products industries," defended clear-cutting as "a practice that is generally accepted by professional forest managers as vital to the regeneration of many forest types," and concluded, "If we are to enjoy the 'luxury' of having millions of acres locked up in wilderness areas most people will never see, then let us be sure that the acres remaining in timber production are as well managed as possible for the many products we depend on." The association's chief forester praised newspaper writers who supported clear-cutting and "quit 'buying' environmental pronouncements on face value," expressing his hope that "the public will continue to be interested in developing the forests after the hysteric glamour has faded."[81]

Clear-cutting was not a new issue. As early as 1940 the Southern Pulpwood Conservation Association had grappled inconclusively with the issue, but by the early 1970s the organization soundly endorsed the practice, although recognizing some legitimate objections to clear-cutting as it was sometimes practiced, especially on non-industrial privately owned lands. In 1975 the Gulf States Section (Texas, Louisiana, Mississippi) of the Society of American Foresters endorsed clear-cutting as an acceptable management tool. However, clear-cutting procedures changed between the 1960s and mid-1980s as a result of experience, research, and public pressure. In particular, research on several wildlife species had supported such modifications as reduction of the size of cuts, irregular shapes more harmonious with natural stand boundaries, scattering cuts to create a mosaic pattern, the use of intermediate thinnings, and prescribed burning. Some wildlife experts also recommended the preservation of tree cavities in dead, dying, or living trees. These cavities, called snags, provide essential habitat for at least eighty-five species of birds, forty-nine species of mammals, and numerous insects, reptiles, and amphibians. Some experts believed that clear-cutting was critical for intensive pine-plantation management and rehabilitation of hardwood stands that had been high-graded. These foresters also argued that the public opposition to clear-cutting did not represent a desire to see timber harvesting totally banned. In fact, most of the general public and nonindustrial forest landowners surveyed in an early 1990s study believed that harvesting could improve the forest's health.[82]

In 1991 Mills said that the U.S. Forest Service was planning fewer clear-cuts in the future and was proposing a 25 percent reduction under the RPA program. He said that he thought adequate timber output could be achieved without clear-cuts and concluded, "If what we normally do is project ourselves as a bunch of tree farmers like corn farmers, then we're going to keep clearcutting. But we'd better figure out a different way to do it, because that's not what the public wants. . . . [S]omething we have to do as a profession is to be more sensitive to what the public is asking for in the management of its lands."[83]

While most foresters today agree that clear-cutting is an acceptable—even, in some cases, preferred—silvicultural practice, they also agree that prompt regeneration efforts should follow. Beyond the aesthetic considerations, much of the controversy about clear-cutting stems from the fact that reseeding or replanting is often ignored, especially on small, privately owned, nonindustrial tracts. This failure leads to reversion of the land to low-quality hardwoods and to serious erosion, particularly in hilly areas. Small landowners' temptation to clear-cut their land, without provision for regeneration, is strong. Many are old and poor, and they are often offered twice as

much for clear-cut wood as for thinned wood. Also, as they die their heirs want to get as much as possible out of their inheritance, and land and timber are worth more sold separately than as a unit. Their timber is actively solicited by procurement people for forest-industry plants and mills, pulpwood dealers, and independent loggers and pulpwood cutters, all of whom depend on wood acquisitions to keep their firms operating.

Sometimes a potential conflict of interest exists for large forest-products companies, such as Georgia-Pacific, International Paper, Louisiana-Pacific, Westvaco, and Weyerhaeuser, all of whom provide management assistance to small Mississippi landowners. These companies are also major consumers of the timber grown on these lands. Also, since land prices have exploded since the late 1960s, with some tracts bringing ten times as much as they did then, buyers often seek to offset some of the purchase price with an immediate timber sale. Some are affluent city folk with rural backgrounds who have little interest in tree farming and want to clear the land for pastures and become cattle-raising gentleman farmers.[84]

Like the controversies surrounding clear-cutting, debates over fire management continue to rage today and are likely to remain hot well into the foreseeable future. Although some foresters had long believed that fire had an appropriate role in southern forest management, for decades the U.S. Forest Service and most professional foresters classified all woods fires as bad, although there were satisfactory experiments with controlled burning in southern national forests in the 1930s and the practice was approved for general use in Forest Service Region 8 in 1943. By the late 1960s prescribed burning was common across the region, however, as many professional foresters returned to the older idea that prescribed burns and even natural fires are helpful and worthwhile in certain situations. Fires reduce flammable materials that fuel destructive wildfires, and, as southern natives had always believed, they benefit grazing by stimulating grass growth in the spring. Also, in areas where pine growth is preferred, the fires suppress unwanted hardwoods and other vegetation.

Prescribed burning is a difficult concept for the public to accept after having been bombarded for decades by Smokey Bear and Woodsy Owl's warnings of the evils of all fire. Some foresters and administrators fear that their long struggle against wildfires will be compromised. However, in 1977 the basic fire policy on national forest-lands was changed. Fires would be evaluated and treated according to their economic and social cost. Also prescribed burning, where and when appropriate, was implemented. By the 1980s the Forest Service treated several million acres annually with prescribed burns. Later, a stunned public looked on with horror at the raging fires and charred forests of Yellowstone in 1988. However, most foresters saw a healthier forest in the wake of the fires, as decades' worth of accumulated understory and ground debris in the wake of fire exclusion and suppression was now finally removed.[85]

The most common objective of prescribed burns was reduction of the fuel hazard. Wildlife habitat maintenance, control of undesirable species, and understory thinning were other uses. Besides the traditional fears about prescribed burns getting out of control and becoming wild-fires, in the modern world air quality has been a concern. However, as a 1986 Society of American Foresters study concluded, "Prescribed fire in pine forests reduces the risk of wildfires, improves habitats for game and timber, reduces diseases, reduces hardwood competition, and increases forage. . . . [C]ompetent use of fire is an environmentally and economically acceptable way to maintain pine." The study did acknowledge the problems of smoke pollution and fires getting out of control.[86]

There is another way to look at the air-quality situation. Wildfires burning out of control create tremendous atmospheric pollution, so controlled burns that reduce the fuel for wildfires create a net savings in terms of pollution. The key is for prescribed burns to be done correctly—that is, to exercise smoke management. To do so, schools

for control burners have been held across the South, scholarly research and symposia have been devoted to the topic, and the fire school in Florida has conducted continuing research on the topic.[87]

By the 1980s prescribed burning, which had long been an accepted management practice in south Mississippi, especially on national forest and industry lands, became more common in the northern part of the state as well. It was used on the Holly Springs National Forest for litter reduction, site preparation, and wildlife habitat improvement, with the average annual amount of prescribed burning rising from two hundred acres in 1974 to more than nine thousand acres by 1983. From 1981 to 1983 the Mississippi Forestry Commission had an average prescribed burn of 4,171 acres, mostly on private lands.[88]

Prescribed burning and even wildfires are today accepted on some lands and under certain conditions. But there are still situations in which wild or incendiary fires cannot be tolerated by the landowner or by society. Fire control remains a major job for public and private foresters. Mississippi's public foresters got a huge boost in 1998 when the Mississippi legislature approved $3.5 million in additional funding for the Mississippi Forestry Commission to update its fire-fighting equipment, much of which dates from the early 1970s. The commission plans to purchase eighty-one crawler tractors and 112 transport trucks (each fire unit consists of one of each) by 2003. In 1998 the commission had 237 tractors.[89]

Another issue that has cropped up periodically over the past several decades is concern about the timber supply. Warnings of a timber shortage or famine go far back in history. Pinchot and President Theodore Roosevelt popularized the phrase *timber famine* early in the twentieth century, but the same ideas were widely circulated even before that time. The Capper Report of 1920, the U.S. Forest Service in the 1930s, and the 1950s Forest Service report *Timber Resources for America's Future* all referred in various ways to the idea that the nation was facing a severe timber shortage. However, in the 1960s and into the 1970s the increasing supplies of both softwood and hardwood timber inventories in the South led one economist to ask, "Who's Going to Use All This Wood?"[90]

During the 1970s concerns about the nation's timber supply, especially softwoods, resurfaced, and these concerns survived into the 1990s. By the mid-1990s hardwood annual growth in the South still exceeded removals by a substantial margin, but softwood growth did not. Mississippi reflected southern patterns. U.S. Forest Service data for 1987 showed that Mississippi had an inventory of 9.09 billion cubic feet of softwood, growth of 509 million cubic feet, and removals of 520 million cubic feet. The hardwood inventory was 10.34 billion cubic feet, with growth of 436 million cubic feet and removals of 241 million cubic feet. However, the Mississippi Delta was the only area in the South where hardwood forests were decreasing in volume. The economic pressure on southern forests was a product of increasing foreign and domestic demands for forest products as well as of the substantial reduction of harvests on public lands in the West.[91]

The U.S. Forest Service, despite its movement toward less emphasis on timber production and adoption of ecosystem management, showed that it still had a strong inclination toward viewing forests as commodity producers as it pushed the concept of the fourth forest to publicize and promote the need for accelerated timber growth in the South. The Mississippi Forestry Commission promoted the "Pathways for Forestry in Mississippi" development program, including the conversion of marginal cropland to forests. The state's growing furniture- manufacturing industry was emphasized as an important market for hardwoods.[92]

By the mid-1990s hardwood annual growth in the South still exceeded removals by a substantial margin, but softwood growth did not. From 1950 to 1980 the consumption of most industrial timber products in the United States rose, and by 1978 softwood lumber use was 25 percent above the 1950 level. Pulpwood consumption quadrupled, and hardwood plywood use tripled during the same period, while softwood plywood use showed a sevenfold increase. Also, as noted earlier, with the growing importance of pulp and paper companies, priorities changed. Lumber companies that preferred longleaf for high-quality logs and poles have been replaced by paper companies that favor faster-growing species and have turned away from longleaf toward genetically improved loblolly and slash pine. Loblolly and slash pine in the early 1990s accounted for 95 percent of all southern pine-seedling production.[93]

By the late 1980s one U.S. Forest Service researcher attributed the "pine decline" in the South's fourth forest to four factors: a continuing decline in the area of timberland, inadequate regeneration after harvesting on nonindustrial private land, a sharp increase in tree mortality (much of it resulting from attacks by pine bark beetles), and reductions in growth rates. Some studies indicated that the decline in growth rates resulted in part from nutrient losses associated with logging and the resultant diminution of site quality in pine plantations.

While cropland in the South declined from 1945 to 1965, with much of the land seeded to trees, especially southern pines, from 1965 to 1985 the soybean boom brought another increase in cropland. Extensive areas of timberlands were converted to cropland and urban development. By the mid-1980s the amount of cropland was again decreasing, but so was timberland, as areas were diverted to urban and other uses. About one-third of the loss resulted from the clearing of bottomland hardwood sites, but most of the decline was in pine stands. One researcher predicted that the decline in timber volume on nonindustrial private lands would force the forest-products industry to rely more heavily on hardwoods and on its own lands, especially pine plantations. However, rather than an expansion of industry-owned timberlands, the trend moved toward more extensive ownership by nonforest corporations, such as realty firms, utility companies, hunting clubs, banks, insurance companies, and timberland companies that did not own mills. These lands would be managed through long-term timber leases.[94]

Concerned about the apparent downward trend in the net annual growth of softwood timber in the South by the late 1980s, the U.S. Forest Service, several states, the forest industries, universities, and other interested parties undertook a study that produced the 1988 publication *The South's Fourth Forest*. A massive overview of various aspects of the historical and current forest situation of the South, it was accompanied by a slick booklet designed to summarize and promote the conclusions and recommendations contained in the large volume. The effort was heavily geared toward commodity timber production, noting the central importance of timber to the southern economy and lifestyle and predicting that timber demands would be even greater in the future. It also recorded the dramatic increases in consumption of various types of timber from 1962 to 1984 as well as the continuing importance of fuelwood.[95]

The study identified the major concerns about the South's forest future from the vantage point of the late 1980s. The most serious problems listed were (1) the lack of adequate regeneration of pine stands after harvest, especially on nonindustrial private lands; (2) an increase in the volume of mortality and cull trees in softwood stands, mostly because of attacks by pine bark beetles and suppression of overtopped trees due to increasing stand age; and (3) the conversion of timberland to cropland, pastures, and urban or other nontimber uses. The Forest Service noted that since the early 1960s, the area of timberland in the South had declined from 197 million to 182 million acres, with one-third of the loss stemming from the conversion of hardwood bottomlands to cropland in the Mississippi Delta. Most of the loss was from pine stands on nonindustrial private lands.

If southern timber production was not increased, what would be the result? In an interesting attempt to turn environmental arguments into a defense of timber harvesting, the Forest Service said that declining timber production would force manufacturers and consumers to turn to substitute products, such as concrete, steel, aluminum, and plastic: "As production of these substitutes is stepped up, more and more nonrenewable resources, including the ore and fossil fuels used in their production, will be removed from the Nation's finite supply." In addition, said the Forest Service, "the mining, industrial processing, and power generation associated with increased use of timber substitutes will result in more air and water pollution." Some scientists believed that air pollution contributed to forest declines, although these connections had not been firmly established.

The Forest Service also emphasized the loss of jobs if the situation did not improve and said that total employment was increased by about 2.3 jobs for each job in the lumber and wood-products industry and 2.6 jobs for each job in the pulp and paper industry. What did the Forest Service advocate to solve these problems? Large increases in management programs, with a particular emphasis on regeneration. However, by the late twentieth century the forest-products industry utilized the available timber far more fully than in the past. Lumber and plywood trimmings, once burned as waste, are today processed into chips for pulping. Other wood residues that were also formerly burned are now converted into such finished products as roofing material, particleboard, ground cover, insulation, hardboard, chemicals, fuels, charcoal, and concrete additives. Thus, in addition to achieving more thorough and efficient utilization of timber, the solid-waste disposal problem is lessened.[96]

In recent years forest-products companies as well as both industrial and public foresters have been greatly concerned about public perceptions of their land stewardship. They have mounted public-relations and educational initiatives to tell their stories to the general public. Foresters have rather consistently cried that they are misunderstood, that much of the public criticism of industry and national forest-management practices is based on lack of knowledge. Industry leaders and spokespersons have sometimes seemed almost paranoid in their reactions to environmentalist critics. Trade associations like the Southern Forest Institute monitored and responded to articles and other materials dealing with environmental and other industry issues. They also reproduced and distributed "industry-friendly" articles like a 1970 feature in the *Arkansas Gazette* that compared "recently converted ecologists" to "erstwhile sinners who, having responded to the persuasion of a powerful evangelist, are likely to conclude that the world is considerably more wicked than they formerly suspected."[97]

Conversely, by the 1970s the Southern Forest Institute's chief forester, Donald W. Smith, admitted that "we have made mistakes; and we hope we have learned from these mistakes." He noted that foresters and industry members tended to talk to themselves rather than the public and said that "we must recognize that we have a problem." He urged industry people to join community environmental organizations and "encourage all the conservation groups, as diverse as they are and as extreme as they are, to sit down and attempt a dialogue to discover what we can agree on, not what we disagree on." Smith also admitted that "our biggest problem may be to live with our past mistakes, because there is no question that what we said in the past has often been different from what we did." However, he continued in the tradition of past industry spokespeople by attacking the "misinformation" about the industry in the press and environmental organizations, and he called for a renewed effort to get the forest-product industry's message out to the public. While there was talk about past "mistakes," the message still seemed to be that the industry had simply failed to communicate its truth to the general populace.[98]

However, the industry periodically examined its own standards and practices. In 1972 the American Pulpwood Association's Environmental Protection Committee undertook a study to "examine our current practices . . . and from this assessment develop new policies and guidelines to apply improved forest practices." Among the topics considered were clear-cutting, planting and seeding, harvesting, prescribed burning, fertilization, herbicides and pesticides, wildlife, and water management. In each category the study recommended various "improved practices," and it listed nineteen separate practices that companies should implement.[99]

To deal with the industry's "image problem," the MFA, the Mississippi Forestry Commission, and the state's national forests implemented Project Learning Tree (PLT), one of the most popular programs dealing with forests and environmental issues in Mississippi today. Created and led in Mississippi by William C. Colvin, the commission's longtime information-education director, the program was far removed from the time when an earlier state forester could not even bring himself to utter the word *environmentalism* without sputtering.

The program originated in 1973 through a partnership between the American Forest Council and the Western Regional Environmental Council in the Rocky Mountain region. The project takes environmental education into schools and civic organizations in a manner that is favored by many professional foresters and forest-products companies and organizations. As one Georgia-Pacific forester in Florida put it, the program "helps people see the cycle of the forest, not just a snapshot. Instead of just seeing death [on a logging truck], teachers and students see life and death and life again. They can see trees not just as a resource but as a renewable resource."[100]

PLT came to Mississippi largely as a result of the efforts of Colvin and MFA Executive Vice President Bob Izlar. The money to initiate the program came from the MFA, which provided unused funds from a Tennessee Valley Authority conservation-education grant. Colvin became the state coordinator, and the first leadership training workshop was held in November 1987. The Mississippi program was recognized by the national PLT program as the outstanding new program for that year. By March 1998 Mississippi's PLT had trained 8,127 educators and was conducting about fifty workshops annually with about twenty educators per session.

Colvin summed up the program's impact in 1998 when he said that "we have established solid new credibility with the educational community as a result of foresters dealing one-on-one, close up and personal, with the attitudes (good or otherwise) of educators who are often being led in their environmental education thinking and teaching by unscientific rhetoric, half-truths and media over-kill with regard to the condition of ours and the world's environment. Most teachers are amazed when they learn that our state has over two million more acres in trees now than in the 1960s and that we are definitely not 'running out of trees!'" In fact, in 1991 E. R. Coleman, a longtime resident of Noxapater whose father "was a sawmill man," commented, "There's more trees now than it was when it was virgin timber. More pine."[101]

Nationally, PLT promoted a hands-on, interdisciplinary approach to environmental education to fulfill this mission: "PLT uses the forest as a 'window into the world' to increase students' understanding of our complex environment; stimulate critical and creative thinking; develop the ability to make informed decisions on environmental issues; and instill the confidence and commitment to take responsible action on them." By 1998 more than 500,000 educators had been trained in the program and more than 25 million students in the United States and several foreign countries had received PLT instruction. PLT holds two-day workshops to train facilitators, who are then certified to conduct workshops in their home regions. Among the 250 facilitators in Mississippi were volunteers from the Mississippi Forestry Commission, the federal government, and forest-products companies.[102]

In the 1990s the forest-products industry adopted another program designed to improve not only forest productivity and logging and manufacturing processes but also the industry's image. The campaign was developed by the American Forest and Paper Association (formerly American Forest Council), the trade association for companies that produced about 95 percent of the paper and 60 percent of the lumber in the nation. By the early 1990s these companies were concerned about their public image in environmental areas and the "diminishing success of the industry in public policy debates on forestry and other issues."[103]

The industry commissioned a study of its image in 1992, interviewing representatives from the media, environmental organizations, political parties, educational institutions, the industry, and others. The study found that whereas industry leaders (and industrial foresters) had always tended to blame their image problems on a lack of public knowledge, those interviewed "believed industry did not have a communications problem, but rather a behavioral problem." According to one study in the early 1990s, "The forest products industry has little credibility with the general public. Public and media attitudes toward industry range from mild cynicism to open hostility." The authors concluded, "To change this negative view will require a shift in corporate attitude and communications style—from guarded, self-serving hyperbole to a genuinely open, vulnerable model that sincerely seeks to serve the broader interests of society and the environment."[104]

By this time the movement toward greening the forest-products industry through public pressure was well under way. Some experts in this country predicted that customers would be willing to pay premium prices for "green-certified" wood products, and some producers argued that the approach would assure a continuing supply of timber and represented a middle ground between environmental groups and industry. Retailers such as Home Depot and Wal-Mart were introducing "green certification" into their operations, with documented assurances to retail customers that the wood products in their stores were produced in an environmentally and politically responsible manner that would guarantee sustainability of the forests and fair treatment of local populations in the forested areas. However, critics noted that certified products did not perform better than uncertified ones and doubted that consumers would be willing to pay premium prices to salve their consciences.

The National Hardwood Lumber Association's newsletter, *Greenspeak,* said, "The forest products industry is hearing a lot about this new marketing tool, which seems to be retailer driven." Conversely, the association pointed out that the Forest Stewardship Council, a body set up to establish worldwide standards for good forest management, included little representation from industry, the U.S. Forest Service, or the governments of producing countries.

The process at Home Depot was not fast enough for environmentalists, who in 1998 picketed the "biggest old-growth retailer in the world" in seventy cities and offered "rain forest tours" through its stores, spotlighting products from old-growth forests, including Douglas fir lumber. On other fronts a number of major companies, including Mitsubishi, Kimberly-Clark, Nike, Levi Strauss, and Andersen Corporation, agreed not to use or to scale back their use of rain-forest wood fiber. Canada's MacMillan Bloedel agreed to stop clear-cutting and to stay out of coastal rain forests. In Great Britain the largest supplier to the home maintenance market announced that it would no longer purchase timber from clear-cuts, whatever the reason for the harvest, and announced that it preferred "forest products from small-scale, community-based forest activities where the forest owner takes an active role in the management decisions, the harvesting and the manufacture of forest products."[105]

Across the country, trade associations, professional societies, and private organizations were developing green certification programs for forest management. One such group, the Forest Partnership of Burlington, Vermont, established a set of criteria delineating the differences between what it termed "common industry practices" or "sustained-yield forestry" and "forest-friendly practices" or "sustainable forestry." In sustained-yield forestry, said the group, "clearcutting is common and on a wide scale." "Regeneration," the organization said, is "often by mechanical means." It noted that "[s]ingle-species plantations" are "often favored," and "[c]hemicals [are] often used to control growth." Sustained-yield forestry's "[g]oal is sustained-yield of wood fiber," while the "[r]ights of local peoples [are] often given low priority." "Management plans [are] not mandatory," and "[h]igh-grading (taking the best trees) is common." Finally, according to the Forest Partnership, "Manufacturing inefficiencies are common," and there was "[n]o system for enforcing standards."[106]

In contrast, the Forest Partnership said that in sustainable forestry, clear-cutting was infrequent and on a small scale, and regeneration was generally by natural means. Mixed-species forests were always favored, and chemicals were not favored or normally required. The goal of sustainable forestry, according to the group, was "the overall health of the forest," and "[l]ocal people's rights are always a high priority." The organization said that under this approach, long-term plans were mandatory and high-grading was not acceptable. Finally, the Forest Partnership observed, "Manufacturing efficiency is vital," and "[i]ndependent certification is mandatory."[107]

The MFA was concerned about the future for small, nonindustrial landowners who grew much of the timber that supplied the forest-products industry. "If the Green Certification concept becomes widely accepted in domestic and international markets," said the MFA, "private forestland owners in the South could find themselves with fewer buyers for their timber in the future." The reason? The MFA pointed out that "[m]any of the forest practices common in the South are not viewed favorably by certification groups."[108]

Still, there was an economic upside. Some analysts argued that the "'greening' of consumerism offers proactive forest products companies an opportunity to capitalize on the fact that trees are the most environmentally benign raw material for many consumer products—the forest resource is renewable; forest-derived products have lower energy costs than products made from competing materials; and wood products sequester carbon dioxide." Some of Mississippi's pioneer foresters had made exactly these arguments for years.[109]

The American Forest and Paper Association set out to solve the industry's image and behav-

ioral problems in 1994 by adopting a set of standards called the "Sustainable Forestry Initiative."
The initiative involved a commitment to use and
renew the forests in a responsible environmental
manner that would ensure the availability of
these resources for future generations. To maintain membership in the association, forest-products companies were required to implement a
number of practices relating to reforesting after
harvest; the protection of water quality; the enhancement of habitat diversity and quality for
wildlife; the minimization of visual impacts of
clear-cuts and other harvests; the enhancement
of landscape diversity; the special treatment of
lands of ecologic, geologic, or historical significance; the improvement of forest utilization; the
prudent use of chemicals; the promotion of the
program among employees, nonindustrial private
landowners, and loggers; the responsible monitoring and reporting of their compliance efforts;
and attempts to include the public in the sustainable forestry initiative.[110]

Interestingly, in addition to a commitment to
reduce the "risk and occurrence of wildfires," to
"promote and utilize integrated pest management," and to "encourage forest health and productivity research," the sustainable-forestry
program's public-policy goals included "help to
implement appropriate ecosystem management
on federal lands." Said the guidelines, American
Forest and Paper Association "members will work
with Congress and public agencies to appropri-
ately define and implement active ecosystem
management on all National Forest System and
Bureau of Land Management lands." Private firms
quickly began to endorse the Sustainable Forestry
Initiative and to issue slick promotional brochures
to make sure that they got public credit for their
efforts. In Mississippi the Cooperative Extension
Service at Mississippi State issued an attractive
portfolio of information on sustainable forestry
and other management practices with the sponsorship of several forest-products companies.[111]

The MFA endorsed the sustainable-forestry
program in April 1995. In Mississippi the program
would be spearheaded by the MFA in close cooperation with the College of Forest Resources at
Mississippi State University, the Mississippi
Forestry Commission, the Mississippi Loggers Association, the U.S. Forest Service, the Mississippi
Cooperative Extension Service, logging contractors, and forest-resource companies. The MFA
defined the Sustainable Forestry Initiative as "a
comprehensive program of forestry and conservation practices designed to ensure that future
generations of Americans will have the same
abundant forests that we enjoy today." It went
on to say that the program "is a land stewardship
ethic which integrates the growing, nurturing,
and harvesting of trees for useful products with
the conservation of soil, air, and water quality,
wildlife and fish habitat, and aesthetics." In Mississippi, extensive efforts were undertaken to
promote the program among nonindustrial private landowners and loggers.

To bring the loggers up to speed in the implementation of the environmental guidelines, the
extension division of the Mississippi State University Department of Forestry, the Mississippi Loggers Education Council, and the Mississippi
Loggers Association developed a training program. By the summer of 1998 more than five
thousand loggers had attended training sessions,
and more than 1,300 wood-supplying firms had
participated in the workshops. To educate its
members and promote the Sustainable Forestry
Initiative, the MFA dedicated the entire spring
1996, issue of its journal, *Tree Talk,* to the sustainable-forestry issue and utilized various techniques
around the state to publicize the program. The effort clearly succeeded, for by the fall of 1998 at
least one timber company mailed an advertise-
ment to MFA members announcing that it would
thin and/or clear-cut timber and that it was "Certified in Sustainable Forestry Initiative."[112]

Beyond the obvious importance of the goals
of the sustainable-forestry program, two things
set it apart from earlier industry efforts at image
making. First, there was a monitoring process
whereby to remain members of the American
Forest and Paper Association, companies had to
report their compliance efforts to the association.
Second, the progress of the entire program would
be annually evaluated by "outside experts" in a

public report. The "independent expert review panel" consisted of representatives from several state forestry departments, universities, environmental organizations, and federal agencies, including the Forest Service and the Environmental Protection Agency. The chairman was Paul Hansen, the executive director of the Izaak Walton League of America. None of the more aggressive environmental organizations, such as the Sierra Club, Wilderness Society, or Greenpeace, were represented.

While by 1998 the review panel generally praised efforts to implement the program, Hansen confessed to "trepidation" about participating and observed, "Along with the rest of the nation, and much of the world, I am waiting to see how committed the forest products industry will be to strengthening the performance measures relating to good stewardship—such as water quality, wildlife habitat, and biodiversity." "There are those who tell me that the SFI program is a panacea," he said, "and others that claim it is nothing but a public relations scam." However, he concluded, "Both are wrong. It is an innovative effort that has begun to make an important difference in how we manage and harvest trees throughout an enormous portion of the nation's commercial forests." The major accomplishments, Hansen said, were in logger education and educational outreach to private, nonindustrial forest owners. The most significant challenge was the development of credible verification procedures to evaluate improved forest practices. In other words, as the forest-products industry approached the end of the century, it had an environmental image problem, it was moving in a positive manner to correct that problem, and the jury was still out with regard to the success of that effort. The industry itself acknowledged that it had a way to go. A 1995 informational pamphlet produced by the American Forest and Paper Association reported, "Many forest and paper companies have followed some of these Forestry Principles, but no

company has followed all of them." Nevertheless, the Sustainable Forestry Initiative program represented a recognition by the industry that it now had to work with the public in maintaining healthy and productive forests for future generations.[113]

It is clear that the forest will remain a central factor in Mississippi's economic and social life in the twenty-first century. By 1998 62 percent of Mississippi's land, 18.5 million acres, was forested, and the amount of forestland had remained stable for four decades. One in four manufacturing jobs in the state, 10 percent of all jobs in Mississippi, were in the forest-products industry. By 1993 the annual value of Mississippi's timber harvest was more than $1 billion. It is also apparent that debates about the rights and limits of private forest ownership, about the proper management of private and national forests, and about the propriety and efficacy of various silvicultural practices will remain prevalent. The Sustainable Forestry Initiative program and Project Learning Tree reflect the forest-products industry's concern about issues and public perceptions, as do the mountains of promotional materials they issue to convince the public that they are responsible stewards of the land. The growth of environmental organizations and groups like the Dogwood Alliance, as well as activities such as the legal challenges to timber harvests on Mississippi's national forests, reflect different views toward forest ownership and management among some segments of the citizenry. Whatever the resolution of these issues, it is safe to predict that in the future the general public will have a greater interest and voice in both private and public forest management than was the case during most of the twentieth century. Mississippians can take pride in the fact that a resource that was so mistreated that it was considered exhausted in the early twentieth century has been restored by nature and humans to occupy a central role in the life and economy of the Magnolia State on the threshold of the next millennium.[114]

Notes

Chapter 1

1. "Mississippi Forest Facts" (Jackson: Mississippi Forestry Association, 1997); *Land and Resource Management Plan: National Forests in Mississippi* (n.p.: U.S. Department of Agriculture, Forest Service, Southern Region, Mississippi, n.d.), 1-3, 1-4, 2-3; James E. Fickle, "Mississippi Forests," in *Encyclopedia of American Forest and Conservation History*, ed. Richard C. Davis (New York: Macmillan, 1983), 2:136–37; Mississippi Automated Resource Information System, *Forest Cover Types* (Jackson: Mississippi Forestry Commission, 1997), forest cover derived by the U.S. Forest Service from digital AVHRR satellite imagery. A useful source describing for young readers the origins, succession, utilization, and conservation of southern forests, with a section on Mississippi, is Everett F. Evans and Roy L. Donahue, *Our South: Its Resources and Their Uses* (Austin, Tex.: Steck, 1949), 251–67, 279–82, 298–321. Joe L. McDonald, "Mississippi's Forests: A Historical Sketch," is a fifty-two-page unpublished, typewritten manuscript in the files of the Mississippi Forestry Commission, Jackson (hereafter cited as MFC Files). This manuscript covers the period from the precolonial era to the 1970s.

2. An excellent brief description of the evolution of the southern forested landscape and the impact of early humans is Edward Buckner, "Prehistory of the Southern Forest," *Forest History Today* (1996): 38–40 (reprinted from *Forest Farmer* 54 [July–August 1995]). Another good overview, not confined to the South, that also considers the question of why the mythology about the "forest primeval" developed and was maintained is Douglas W. MacCleery, "When Is a Landscape Natural?" *Forest History Today* (1998): 39–41 (reprinted from *Minnesota Volunteer* [September–October 1996]). See also MacCleery's *American Forests: A History of Resiliency and Recovery* (Durham, N.C.: Forest History Society, 1993), 3–8 (originally published in

1992 by the U.S. Forest Service as FS-540). The entire September 1992 issue of the *Annals of the Association of American Geographers* is devoted to the subject of "The Americas before and after 1492: Current Geographical Research," under the guest editorship of Karl W. Butzer. See also Jerome A. Jackson, "The Southeastern Pine Forest Ecosystem and Its Birds: Past, Present, and Future," in *Bird Conservation 3* (Madison: University of Wisconsin Press, 1989), 119–59.

3. Calvin Martin, "Fire and Forest Structure in the Aboriginal Eastern Forest," *Indian Historian* 6 (summer 1973): 23. It is interesting that in 1951 one writer said that a squirrel might have gone from Maine to Louisiana by jumping "from one giant tree to the next." Indeed, in 1950 another writer said that a squirrel might have traveled a lifetime without coming down out of the white pines of the Northeast (Gordon M. Day, "The Indian as an Ecological Factor in the Northeastern Forest," *Ecology* 34 [April 1953]: 329). This metaphor has been used frequently to describe heavily forested environments in various societies. For example, S. T. Bindoff quotes an "old rhyme found, in varying forms, in many districts: From Blacon Point to Hillbree, A squirrel may jump from tree to tree" (*Tudor England* [Harmondsworth, Middlesex: Penguin Books, 1950], 9–10). Another example of the propagation of the concept of a continuous forest is James Elliott Defebaugh's *History of the Lumber Industry of America.*. Defebaugh, the editor of the influential trade journal *American Lumberman*, said, "What is now the United States presented an almost solid and continuous forest from the Atlantic to the Mississippi River and in places still farther west" (*History of the Lumber Industry of America* [Chicago: American Lumberman, 1906–7], 1:8). See also Gilbert Chinard, "The American Philosophical Society and the Early History of Forestry in America," *Proceedings of the American Philosophical Society* 89 (July 18, 1945):

444–88; Anthony N. Penna, *Nature's Bounty: Historical and Modern Environmental Perspectives* (Armonk, N.Y.: Sharpe, 1999), 21–22.

4. "A Reporter at Large, the Ancient Forest," *New Yorker* (May 14, 1990): 46; Frank B. Pittman, "Mississippi's Forests of Yesteryear," *Forest Farmer* (April 1963): 24; Thomas D. Clark, *The Greening of the South: The Recovery of Land and Forest* (Lexington: University Press of Kentucky, 1984), xi, xiv; Zebulon W. White, "Loblolly Pine: With Emphasis on Its History," in *Proceedings of the Symposium on the Loblolly Pine Ecosystem (West Region), Jackson, Mississippi, March 20–22, 1984,* ed. Bob L. Karr, James B. Baker, and Tom Monaghan (Starkville: Extension Service of Mississippi State University, 1984), 8–9; W. M. Denevan, "The Pristine Myth: The Landscape of the Americas in 1492," *Annals of the Association of American Geographers* 82 (September 1992): 369. See also Karl W. Butzer, "The Americas before and after 1492: An Introduction to Current Geographical Research," *Annals of the Association of American Geographers* 82 (September 1992): 347–48. Even longtime lumber journalist James Boyd, associate editor of *Southern Lumberman,* could not resist the hyperbole. Said Boyd in 1880, "the South was a virgin forest untouched by man, except along streams at some points on the few railroads that had been built and on others that were being constructed" ("Fifty Years in the Southern Pine Industry," *Southern Lumberman* 144 [December 15, 1931]: 59). Some writers do not perpetuate these romantic stereotypes. For example, see Robert G. Healy, *Competition for Land in the American South: Agriculture, Human Settlement, and the Environment* (Washington, D.C.: Conservation Foundation, 1985), 78–79.

5. Martin, "Fire and Forest Structure," *Indian Historian* 6 (fall 1973): 38–39; (summer 1973): 23, 24. While pointing out Native Americans' use of fire and forest products and talking about their farming activities, Thomas C. Croker Jr. argues that the "Indians' clearings for gardens and field crops rarely encroached on the longleaf pine forests. . . . On balance, the Indians did not materially change the character of the virgin forest" ("The Longleaf Pine Story," *Journal of Forest History* 23 [January 1979]: 34).

6. J. Baird Callicott, "A Brief History of the American Land Ethic since 1492," *Forest History Today* (1995): 16; Denevan, "Pristine Myth," 370; M. J. Bowden, "The Invention of American Tradition," *Journal of Historical Geography* 18 (1992): 3–26. Denevan disagrees with this interpretation, arguing that "the 'invention' of an earlier wilderness is in part understandable and is not simply a deliberate creation which ennobled the American enterprise" ("Pristine Myth," 380).

7. Stephen H. Spurr, *Forest Ecology* (New York: Ronald Press, 1964), 290. Scientists are not consistent in their use of the term *virgin forest.* For example, despite what Spurr says, the authors of a preface to a set of papers on the role of fire in the conifer forests of western and northern North America refer to "large blocks of virgin forest" and specifically to the Boundary Waters Canoe Area as constituting "the last sizable area of virgin forests in the Great Lakes region, in fact in the entire area east of the Rocky Mountains." They seem to assume that forests that have "not been converted to saw timber and pulpwood by this time" are by definition virgin forests (H. E. Wright and M. L. Heinselman, preface to "The Ecological Role of Fire in Natural Conifer Forests of Western and Northern North America," *Quaternary Research* 3 [October 1973]: 317). Douglas MacCleery argues that after the decimation of the Native American populations by the diseases brought to the New World by Europeans, there was a two- to three-century period during which the Indian agricultural lands reforested before the permanent European-American settlers began to move through the Appalachian gaps. Thus, he says, the "pioneers found landscapes that looked more 'pristine' than they had in more than 1, 000 years" ("When Is a Landscape Natural?" 40–41).

8. William Cronon, *Changes in the Land: Indians, Colonists, and the Ecology of New England* (New York: Hill and Wang, 1983), 9–11.

9. Spurr, *Forest Ecology,* 275–80. Another useful tool, particularly in interpreting the record of historic forests, is the use of aerial photography. See Stephen H. Spurr, *Photogrammetry and Photo-Interpretation: With a Section on Applications to Forestry* (New York: Ronald Press, 1960), 455. Scholars have also developed computer simulation programs that "reconstruct" old forests and project their development under different management strategies. See Daniel B. Botkin, *Discordant Harmonies: A New Ecology for the Twenty-First Century* (New York: Oxford University Press, 1990), 117–20.

10. Spurr, *Forest Ecology,* 281–82; Thompson Webb III, "The Past 11,000 Years of Vegetational Change in Eastern North America," *Bioscience* 31 (July–August 1981): 501–6. Some scholars have altered their views of the traditional division of Pleistocene glaciation into four periods as a result of studies of ocean cores. These scholars now argue that there were sixteen or seventeen cold periods that cannot be correlated with the four-period sequence.

11. Spurr, *Forest Ecology,* 281–82, 287–88, 277; Don Burdette, "The Southern Forests: A Legacy of Nations, Part 1," *Alabama's Treasured Forests* 14 (fall 1995): 27; Hazel R. Delcourt and Paul A. Delcourt, "Quaternary Palynology and Vegetational History of the Southeastern United States," in *Pollen Records of Late-Quaternary North American Sediments,* ed.

Vaughn M. Bryant Jr. and Richard G. Holloway (Dallas: American Association of Stratigraphic Palynologists Foundation, 1985), 20.

12. Hazel R. Delcourt, Paul A. Delcourt, and Elliott C. Spiker, "A 12,000-Year Record of Forest History from Cahaba Pond, St. Clair County, Alabama," *Ecology* 64 (August 1983): 874–87. For an example of using the field notes of early surveyors employed by the U.S. General Land Office to reconstruct the composition of primeval forest communities, see Hazel R. Delcourt, "Reconstructing the Forest Primeval, West Feliciana Parish, Louisiana," *Melanges* 10 (December 17, 1975): 1–13.

13. James Axtell, *The Indians' New South: Cultural Change in the Colonial Southeast* (Baton Rouge: Louisiana State University Press, 1997), 1; "Bering Land Bridge Theory of How First Americans Arrived May Be False," *Memphis Commercial Appeal,* February 17, 1998, A2. For other opinions regarding the dates for migration across the land bridge, see James A. Brown, "America before Columbus," in *Indians in American History: An Introduction,* ed. Frederick E. Hoxie (Arlington Heights, Ill.: Harlan Davidson, 1988), 22–23, 25; Walter L. Williams, "Southeastern Indians before Removal: Prehistory, Contact, Decline," in *Southeastern Indians since the Removal Era,* ed. Walter L. Williams (Athens: University of Georgia Press, 1979), 4–5; and John A. Walthall, *Prehistoric Indians of the Southeast: Archaeology of Alabama and the Middle South* (University, Ala.: University of Alabama Press, 1980), 20–25. A good indication of how archaeological opinion has changed over the past three or four decades is William G. Haag's 1955 statement that "[w]hen ice stood along the Missouri-Ohio river line for the last time and was about to begin to retreat northward in a gradually warming world, Mississippi was without human inhabitants. However, nowhere else in North or South America were there any inhabitants, for this is thought to have been 25,000 to 35,000 years ago, and there is nothing to suggest that man was in the New World so long ago" ("A Prehistory of Mississippi," *Journal of Mississippi History* 17 [April 1955]: 82–83). With equal confidence another recent writer asserts that "it has not been ascertained with certainty when or from where man first arrived in the South. . . . [N]ot ruling out intrusions from Europe, Africa, or the Orient, there is a consensus, or nearly so, that man crossed the ice bridge over the Bering Strait and spread over much of North and South America." Furthermore, "Recent archaeological evidence suggests the traditional date of twenty thousand years ago is possibly too late and that man first crossed the Bering Strait perhaps forty thousand or more years ago. The latest archaeological excavations in the Eastern woodlands have supported this theory" (J. Leitch

Wright Jr., *The Only Land They Knew: The Tragic Story of the American Indians in the Old South* [New York: Free Press, 1981], 2).

14. James A. Brown, "America before Columbus," 23; Charles H. McNutt, ed., *Prehistory of the Central Mississippi Valley* (Tuscaloosa: University of Alabama Press, 1996), 189; J. Leitch Wright, *Only Land They Knew,* 3.

15. J. Leitch Wright, *Only Land They Knew,* 3. See also James A. Brown, "America before Columbus," 38; Burdette, "Southern Forests, Part 1," 27; Walter L. Williams, "Southeastern Indians," 5; and Haag, "Prehistory," 85–86. For brief descriptions of prehistoric humans' use of fire, see A. J. Kayll, "Use of Fire in Land Management," in *Fire and Ecosystems,* ed. T. T. Kozlowski and C. E. Ahlgren (New York: Academic Press, 1974), 485–87; and Verna R. Johnston, "The Ecology of Fire," *Audubon* 72 (September 1970): 78, 81. Johnston argues that prehistoric people probably knew how to make fire when they crossed the land bridge into North America.

16. J. Leitch Wright, *Only Land They Knew,* 3–4; James A. Brown, "America before Columbus," 38; Walter L. Williams, "Southeastern Indians," 5; Burdette, "Southern Forests, Part 1," 27; Jesse E. Jennings, "Chickasaw and Earlier Indian Cultures of Northeast Mississippi," *Journal of Mississippi History* 3 (July 1941): 155–226; Walthall, *Prehistoric Indians,* 106–7, 149–50; and Haag, "Prehistory," 91–100. For descriptions of the early development of agriculture among prehistoric Native Americans, see Dean R. Snow, "The First Americans and the Differentiation of Hunter-Gatherer Cultures," in *The Cambridge History of the Native Peoples of the Americas,* ed. Bruce G. Trigger and Wilcomb E. Washington, vol. 1, pt. 1, *North America* (Cambridge: Cambridge University Press, 1996), 162–63; James A. Brown, "America before Columbus," 42; and J. Leitch Wright, *Only Land They Knew,* 6–9.

17. Walter L. Williams, "Southeastern Indians," 6–7; James A. Brown, "America before Columbus," 38; Burdette, "Southern Forests, Part 1," 27; Haag, "Prehistory," 100–107; J. Leitch Wright, *Only Land They Knew,* 6–7; and Walthall, *Prehistoric Indians,* 185–200, 211–26.

18. Day, "Indian as an Ecological Factor," 341. Aerial photographs are useful tools for recognizing and locating archaeological sites; see Spurr, *Photogrammetry,* 338–39.

19. James Adair, *The History of the American Indians; Particularly Those Nations Adjoining to the Mississippi, East and West Florida, Georgia, South and North Carolina, and Virginia* (London, 1775; reprint, with an introduction by Robert F. Berkhofer Jr., New York: Johnson Reprint Corporation, 1968), 405–6.

20. Ibid., 406–7.

21. Charles Hudson, *The Southeastern Indians* (Knoxville: University of Tennessee Press, 1976), 276; Stephen J. Pyne, *Fire in America: A Cultural History of Wildland and Rural Fire* (Princeton: Princeton University Press, 1982), 71–72; J. Leitch Wright, *Only Land They Knew*, 7–10. Although not dealing directly with the South or Mississippi, four articles on the "Indian Fire" issue in *Proceedings—Symposium and Workshop on Wilderness Fire (Missoula, Montana, November 15–18, 1983)*, General Technical Report INT-182 (Ogden, Utah: U.S. Department of Agriculture, Forest Service, Intermountain Forest and Range Experiment Station, 1985) are useful sources. The articles deal with the extent of Indian burning, reasons for burning, the ecological and management effects of burning, and the relevance of past Indian fires to current fire-management programs.

22. Hudson, *Southeastern Indians*, 276–77. For the use of fire by Native Americans in "directly manipulating the environment" in California, see Thomas C. Blackburn and Kat Anderson, eds., *Before the Wilderness: Environmental Management by Native Californians* (Menlo Park, Calif.: Ballena Press, 1993), 15–26.

23. Delcourt and Delcourt, "Quaternary Palynology," 21; Margaret B. Davis, "Phytogeography and Palynology of Northeastern United States," in *The Quaternary of the United States: A Review Volume for the Seventh Congress of the International Association for Quaternary Research*, ed. H. E. Wright Jr. and David G. Frey (Princeton: Princeton University Press, 1965), 382.

24. Pyne, *Fire in America*, 75.

25. Michael Williams, *Americans and Their Forests: A Historical Geography* (Cambridge: Cambridge University Press, 1989), 45, 47. One recent study concludes that the "longleaf pine ecosystem is distinguished by open, park-like, 'pine-barrens,' which are composed of even-aged and multi-aged mosaics of forests, woodlands, and savannas, with a diverse groundcover dominated by bunch grasses and usually free of understory hardwoods and brush. Longleaf pine is the key tree species in a complex of fire-dependent forest ecosystems long native to the southeastern United States. Its existence was dependent on periodic fire, to which it is adapted while most of its potential competitors are not. . . . The ecological persistence of pine barrens is a product of long-term interactions among climate, fire, and the traits of key plants. Regional dominance by southern pines began to redevelop about 10,000 years ago with a warming trend following retreat of the last continental ice sheet. The modern longleaf pine-turkey oak (Quercus laevis) forests were established in north Florida about 7,800 years ago, and over the next 4,000 years reinvaded the rest of the Southeast. The forests of the southeastern United States, as found in historic times, were apparently in place about 5,000 years ago, with pollen records indicating 65% pine and 15% oak plus most other elements of the modern forest. Undoubtedly, these forests included extensive longleaf pine stands much like those found by the first European travelers in the region" (J. Larry Landers, David H. Van Lear, and William D. Boyer, "The Longleaf Forests of the Southeast: Requiem or Renaissance?" *Journal of Forestry* 93 [November 1995]: 40).

26. Michael Williams, *Americans and Their Forests*, 47–48. For a brief overview of evolving theories regarding the ecological role of fire in forest succession, see H. E. Wright and M. L. Heinselman, "Ecological Role," 317–28.

27. Pyne, *Fire in America*, 84–85. See also Erhard Rostlund, "The Myth of a Natural Prairie Belt in Alabama: An Interpretation of Historical Records," *Annals of the Association of American Geographers* 47 (December 1957): 392–411. Consistent with the later white belief that fire was bad, some writers have been extremely critical of the Native Americans' burning practices. For example, reflecting the belief of the time that forest burning was an unmitigated evil, a U.S. Forest Service official wrote in the early twentieth century, "The Indian is by nature an incendiary, and forest burning was the . . . Indian's besetting sin" (Hu Maxwell, "The Use and Abuse of Forests by the Virginia Indians," *William and Mary Quarterly*, 1st ser., 19 [October 1910]: 86). Unlike most scholars writing today, Emily W. B. Russell in a study of Indian-set fires in the northeastern United States concludes that "the frequent use of fires by the Indians to burn the forests was probably at most a local occurrence," although she concedes that the Indians' "use of fire for many purposes did . . . increase the frequency of fires above the low levels caused by lightning, and thus had some effect on the vegetation" ("Indian-Set Fires in the Forests of the Northeastern United States," *Ecology* 64 [February 1983]: 78–88). By contrast, E. V. Komarek says, "When man became a member of the southeastern ecosystems some 20,000 years ago he became another 'fire agent' [who] was not limited to specific and short periods of ignition. . . . [M]an may have set in motion other ecological changes of which we are not even aware" ("Effects of Fire on Temperate Forests and Related Ecosystems," in *Fire and Ecosystems*, ed. Kozlowski and Ahlgren, 253). Stephen H. Spurr agrees with Komarek: "It is impossible to overestimate the effect of human activity on the forests of the world, whether by civilized or by prehistoric uncivilized man," says Spurr. "The character of the vegetation of a large part of the world has been greatly altered by extensive burning" (*Forest Ecology*, 299).

28. Day, "Indian as an Ecological Factor," 340; Douglas H. Ubelaker, "Prehistoric New World Popula-

tion Size: Historical Review and Current Appraisal of North American Estimates," *American Journal of Physical Anthropology* 45 (November 1976): 661, 665; James A. Brown, "America before Columbus," 42; Alfred W. Crosby, *Ecological Imperialism: The Biological Expansion of Europe, 900–1900* (Cambridge: Cambridge University Press, 1986), 211. See also J. Leitch Wright, *Only Land They Knew,* 22–25. Geographers place the figures at a much higher level: Kirkpatrick Sale, *The Conquest of Paradise: Christopher Columbus and the Columbian Legacy* (New York: Alfred A. Knopf, 1990; reprint, New York: Plume, 1991), reports that at the time of "discovery" (when the population of Europe outside of Russia was between 60 and 70 million), there were an estimated 7 to 18 million people north of Mexico, most of them in the Mississippi basin and along the Atlantic coast. Henry Dobyns, in his controversial work *Their Numbers Became Thinned: Native American Population Dynamics in Eastern North America* (Knoxville: University of Tennessee Press, 1983), 42, 298, argued for the higher figure for the area north of civilized Mesoamerica in the early sixteenth century, which he said might even be an underestimate. Sale concludes that in his view a figure of about 15 million is about right and that in any case "pre-Columbian North America was fairly densely populated, as such cultures go, and certainly was not the empty wasteland and untouched wilderness that Europeans took it to be" (*Conquest of Paradise, 315–16*). Denevan places the total for North America at the time of contact as 3.8 million ("Pristine Myth," 370–71). He says that by 1800 the population dropped to 1 million, a 74 percent decline. For purposes of comparison, by 1750 there were about 1.3 million Europeans and slaves in North America. See also Alfred W. Crosby, *The Columbian Exchange: Biological and Cultural Consequences of 1492* (Westport, Conn: Greenwood Press, 1972).

29. Michael Williams, *Americans and Their Forests,* 48–49.

30. Walthall, *Prehistoric Indians,* 247. For an account of the explorers and the southern forests they traversed, see Laurence C. Walker, *The Southern Forest: A Chronicle* (Austin: University of Texas Press, 1991), 1–32.

31. Hudson, *Southeastern Indians,* 102–7; Walthall, *Prehistoric Indians,* 247–48.

32. Alfred W. Crosby, *Ecological Imperialism,* 212–14. Some scholars dispute the idea of epidemic disease, not denying that there was disease but postulating that it advanced in a more sporadic pattern. See Robert L. Blakely and Bettina Detweiler-Blakely, "The Impact of European Diseases in the Sixteenth-Century Southeast: A Case Study," *Midcontinental Journal of Archaeology* 14 (1989): 62–89.

33. Walter L. Williams, "Southeastern Indians," 7; J. Leitch Wright, *Only Land They Knew,* 25; Haag, "Prehistory," 107.

34. Walthall, *Prehistoric Indians,* 248.

35. William A. Love, "Route of de Soto's Expedition through Lowndes County, Mississippi," *Publications of the Mississippi Historical Society,* centenary ser., 4 (1921): 270, 273; W. A. Evans, "The Route of de Soto across Monroe County, December 1540," *Journal of Mississippi History* 2 (April 1940): 71–78; Walthall, *Prehistoric Indians,* 251; Carl Ortwin Sauer, *Sixteenth Century North America: The Land and the People as Seen by the Europeans* (Berkeley: University of California Press, 1971), 184. For the latest published work on the de Soto expedition and its contacts with Native Americans, see Charles Hudson, *Knights of Spain, Warriors of the Sun: Hernando de Soto and the South's Ancient Chiefdoms* (Athens: University of Georgia Press, 1997). Evans's account is based largely on the work of the U.S. de Soto Commission, which was headed by Dr. John R. Swanton of the Smithsonian Institution. Created under a resolution of Congress in 1935, the commission published its conclusions regarding de Soto's route in *Final Report of the United States de Soto Expedition Commission,* 76th Cong., 1st sess., 1939, House Doc. 71.

36. Hudson, *Southeastern Indians,* 114–16.

37. J. Leitch Wright, *Only Land They Knew,* 24; Walthall, *Prehistoric Indians,* 249.

38. Sauer, *Sixteenth Century North America,* 282–83; Michael Williams, *Americans and Their Forests,* 42.

39. Sauer, *Sixteenth Century North America,* 184–85; Axtell, *Indians' New South,* 22.

40. Walthall, *Prehistoric Indians,* 249–51; Hudson, *Southeastern Indians,* 116–18; J. Leitch Wright, *Only Land They Knew,* 24.

41. John K. Bettersworth, *Mississippi: A History* (Austin, Tex.: Steck, 1959), 54–58, 61–64.

42. D. Clayton James, *Antebellum Natchez* (Baton Rouge: Louisiana State University Press, 1968), 3–12; Nell Angela Heidelberg, "The Frontier in Mississippi" (master's thesis, Louisiana State University, 1940), 11–13; Neal Salisbury, "Native People and European Settlers in Eastern North America, 1600–1783," in *Cambridge History,* ed. Trigger and Washington, vol. 1, pt. 1, *North America,* 441–43. John K. Bettersworth says, "A few of the Natchez escaped to live with the Chickasaws, but the remainder were taken as slaves to New Orleans and eventually were sold in Santo Domingo" (*Mississippi,* 82). In a letter written in 1770, Peter Chester, the British governor of West Florida, reported that "the remaining few" Natchez "do not exceed one hundred men who are about one half incorporated with the Nation of Creeks and the other

half with the Cherokees, and [they are] now . . . inter-married and connected with those Nations" (Chester to the Earl of Hillsborough, Pensacola, September 26, 1770, in Mrs. Dunbar Rowland, "Peter Chester: Third Governor of the Province of West Florida under British Dominion, 1770–1781," *Mississippi Historical Society Publications,* centenary ser., 5 [1925]: 18–19).

43. Bettersworth, *Mississippi,* 82, 86; Alexander More, ed., *Nairne's Muskhogean Journals: The 1708 Expedition to the Mississippi River* (Jackson: University Press of Mississippi, 1988), 3–4.

44. "An Account of the Customs, Humers, and Present State of the Chicasaws to Ralph Izard Esquire for the use of the Board of Commissioners, April 12, 1708," and letter to Robert Fenwick, April 13, 1708, both in *Nairne's Muskhogean Journals,* ed. More, 47, 52–53.

45. Letter to Robert Fenwick, April 13, 1708, in ibid., 54–55.

46. Ibid., 57–58, 60.

47. Perier and De La Chaise to the directors of the Company of the Indies, New Orleans, January 30, 1729, in *Mississippi Provincial Archives, 1701–1729: French Dominion,* ed. Dunbar Rowland and Albert Godfrey Sanders (Jackson: Press of the Mississippi Department of Archives and History, 1929), 2:616–17.

48. Perier and De La Chaise to the directors of the Company of the Indies, New Orleans, March 25, 1729, and Superior Council of Louisiana to the general directors of the Company of the Indies, New Orleans, February 27, 1725, in ibid., 627, 403.

49. Bienville, memoir on Louisiana, ca. 1725–26, in *Mississippi Provincial Archives, 1704–1743: French Dominion,* ed. Dunbar Rowland and Albert Godfrey Sanders (Jackson: Press of the Mississippi Department of Archives and History, 1932), 3:531, 522.

50. King of France, memoir to Bienville, Marly, February 2, 1732, and king to Bienville and Salmon, Marly, February 2, 1732, in *Mississippi Provincial Archives, 1704–1743,* ed. Rowland and Sanders, 3:545–46, 570; Croker, "Longleaf Pine Story," 35.

51. Bienville and Salmon to Maurepas, New Orleans, May 12, 1733, March 20, 1734, April 16, 1736, all in *Mississippi Provincial Archives, 1704–1743,* ed. Rowland and Sanders, 3:601–2, 638, 685.

52. Seymour Feiler, trans. and ed., *Jean-Bernard Bossu's Travels in the Interior of North America, 1751–1762* (Norman: University of Oklahoma Press, 1962), ix, 194–95, 196–97.

53. Alfred W. Crosby, *Ecological Imperialism,* 215; Cronon, *Changes in the Land,* 90–91.

54. Alfred W. Crosby, *Ecological Imperialism,* 213. Pyne offers a quite different interpretation of the expansion of the buffalo's range, arguing that at the time of European discovery, the dominant vegetation type in America was grassland or open-forest savannah, which had been fostered by anthropogenic fire. In fact, "when broadcast burning was suppressed as a result of European settlement, the land spontaneously reverted to forest." This grassland "reflected the penetration of nomadic hunting culture enlarging the range of their prey," and he argues that by A.D. 1000 the buffalo crossed the Mississippi River and that "[b]y the sixteenth century the buffalo entered the South. . . . This expansion could have been accomplished only through a change in habitat, partly due to climate, but largely achieved through the application of anthropogenic fire" (*Fire in America,* 75–76). See also Erhard Rostlund, "The Geographic Range of the Historic Bison in the Southeast," *Annals of the Association of American Geographers* 50 (December 1960): 395–407.

55. Walter L. Williams, "Southeastern Indians," 10, 12–13; Salisbury, "Native People and European Settlers," 426, 428–29, 433–34; Charles M. Hudson Jr., "Why the Southeastern Indians Slaughtered Deer," in *Indians, Animals, and the Fur Trade: A Critique of Keepers of the Game,* ed. Shepard Krech III (Athens: University of Georgia Press, 1981), 169–70.

56. Bettersworth, *Mississippi,* 84, 89–90.

57. D. Clayton James, *Antebellum Natchez,* 12–13; Arthur H. DeRosier Jr., *The Removal of the Choctaw Indians* (Knoxville: University of Tennessee Press, 1970), 16–17; Salisbury, "Native People and European Settlers," 449; Charles Stuart to Peter Chester, n.d., in Mrs. Dunbar Rowland, "Peter Chester," 46.

58. Bettersworth, *Mississippi,* 100; D. Clayton James, *Antebellum Natchez,* 13, 14.

59. Mrs. Dunbar Rowland, "Peter Chester," 6, 8; Peter Chester to Earl of Hillsborough, Pensacola, August 28, 1771, in Mrs. Dunbar Rowland, "Peter Chester," 56. In a 1771 letter the governor of West Florida talks about the activities of unscrupulous whites among the Creeks, Choctaws, and Chickasaws and refers to such whites as "Crackers and Stragglers who come from the back settlements of Georgia, Carolina and Virginia into the Indian Country" (Peter Chester to Earl of Hillsborough, Pensacola, March 9, 1771, in Mrs. Dunbar Rowland, "Peter Chester," 39.

60. Peter Chester to Earl of Hillsborough, Pensacola, September 26, 1770, in ibid., 19, 20, 23, 24.

61. John McIntire to Peter Chester, Fort Natchez, July 19, 1770; deposition of Daniel Huay, August 20, 1770, both in ibid., 25–26, 26–27; Pittman quoted in D. Clayton James, *Antebellum Natchez,* 16.

62. Edward Mease, "Narrative of a Journey through Several Parts of the Province of West Florida in the Years 1770 and 1771," in Mrs. Dunbar Rowland, "Peter Chester," 58–65.

63. Ibid., 65–76.

64. Ibid., 77–79.

65. Ibid., 79–80.

66. Ibid., 80–81.

67. Ibid., 82–83.

68. Ibid., 83–87.

69. Ibid., 87–90.

70. "An Attempt towards a Short Description of West Florida," in ibid., 171–72.

71. Ibid., 172.

72. Ibid., 175–76.

73. Robert F. Berkhofer Jr., introduction to Adair, *History*, v.

74. Adair, *History*, 284, 308, 359–60.

75. Ibid., 360–61.

76. Ibid., 458, 461–62.

77. D. Clayton James, *Antebellum Natchez*, 18, 25–29; Bettersworth, *Mississippi*, 102–4.

78. D. Clayton James, *Antebellum Natchez*, 57–58, 62; Bettersworth, *Mississippi*, 105.

79. "Report of Sir William Dunbar to the Spanish Government at the Conclusion of His Services in Locating and Surveying the Thirty-First Degree of Latitude," *Mississippi Historical Society Publications* 3 (1900): 188–89, 191–92.

80. Ibid., 192, 193.

81. Ibid., 193–94.

82. Ibid., 200–201.

83. Ibid., 201–5.

84. Mark van Doren, ed., *The Travels of William Bartram* (New York: Dover Publications, 1928), 328, 404.

85. John Francis McDermott, foreword to Francis Baily, *Journal of a Tour in Unsettled Parts of North America, in 1796 and 1797* (Carbondale: Southern Illinois University, 1969), vii; Baily, *Journal*, 179, 153. Major Samuel S. Foreman traveled to Natchez in 1790 and reported, "Boards were scarce, and I do not remember of seeing any saw or grist-mills in the country." (*Narrative of a Journey down the Ohio and Mississippi in 1789–90*, quoted in Dunbar Rowland, *History of Mississippi: The Heart of the South* [Chicago: S. J. Clarke Publishing, 1925], 1:309).

86. Baily, *Journal*, 171–72.

87. Ibid., 196.

88. Ibid., 1, 203.

89. Ibid, 203.

90. Ibid., 210–11.

91. Ibid., 217, 218.

Chapter 2

1. Bettersworth, *Mississippi*, 121–22; D. Clayton James, *Antebellum Natchez*, 75–76.

2. Bettersworth, *Mississippi*, 129–30, 168, 172–74; Rowland, *History of Mississippi*, 1:409, 471, 509–10, 555–56, 579–80; Michael D. Green, "The Expansion of European Colonization to the Mississippi Valley, 1780–1880," in *Cambridge History*, ed. Trigger and Washington, vol. 1, pt. 1, *North America*, 519–20, 522. For a detailed discussion of the fraud and chicanery involved in the negotiation and administration of the Treaty of Dancing Rabbit Creek, see Franklin L. Riley, "Choctaw Land Claims," *Mississippi Historical Society Publications* 8 (1904): 345–95.

3. James Hall, *A Brief History of the Mississippi Territory, to Which Is Prefixed, a Summary View of the Country between the Settlements on Cumberland-River and the Territory* (Salisbury, 1801; reprinted in *Mississippi Historical Society Publications* 9 [1906]: 540, 541, 542–43). Arguments concerning the extent of "savagery" or "civilization" among the Native Americans of this period ushered in disputes that persist in various incarnations to the present. One of the more recent controversies concerns the ecological "consciousness" and impact of North Americans, particularly of the pre-Columbian period. In the latest variation of the "noble savage" theories of nineteenth-century romantic writers, some students since the 1960s have argued that American natives were ecological models who lived in harmony with nature. Other scholars have counterattacked, describing these romantic people of nature as the "Nevawas" (Sale, *Conquest of Paradise*, 317–24). See also Calvin Luther Martin, *The Way of the Human Being* (New Haven: Yale University Press, 1999) and Shepard Krech III, *The Ecological Indian: Myth and History* (New York: Norton, 1999). With regard to "civilization," insomuch as it can be defined by such practices of "civilized" societies as settled communities engaged in "improving" the land by clearing fields and planting crops, modern scholars believe that the Native Americans of the Eastern Woodlands in the pre-Columbian period were "civilized." As R. Douglas Hurt argues, "By the time of Spanish exploration the southern Indians had engaged in farming for a long time, and they possessed a well-developed agricultural economy." He also notes, "By the mid eighteenth century, agriculture also was important for the Cherokee, Choctaw, Chickasaw, and Creek, who cultivated small private gardens and large communal fields." Hurt says that the Indians cleared fields by girdling trees and removing brush with the help of axes, fire, and mattocks but, "[n]o one can state with certainty how much acreage these farmers cultivated." Hurt also discusses at length the attitudes of the various European colonizing powers toward Indian land rights and titles (*Indian Agriculture in America: Prehistory to the Present* [Lawrence: University Press of Kansas, 1987], 27, 32, 39, 77–95). See also William E. Doolittle, "Agriculture in North America on the Eve of Contact: A Reassessment," *Annals of the Association of American Geographers* 82 (September 1992): 386–401; and Butzer, "Americas before and after 1492," 348–50.

4. Hall, *Brief History,* 543, 544.

5. Ibid., 552–54.

6. Ibid., 566, 557, 561.

7. Thomas Fenton to postmaster general [Gideon Granger], June 27, 1802, in *The Territorial Papers of the United States,* vol. 5, *The Territory of Mississippi, 1798–1817,* ed. Clarence Edwin Carter (Washington, D.C.: U.S. Government Printing Office, 1937); Everett Dick, *The Dixie Frontier: A Social History of the Southern Frontier from the First Transmontane Beginnings to the Civil War* (New York: Capricorn Books, 1964), 337; Ephraim Kirby to the president [Thomas Jefferson], May 1, 1804, in *Territorial Papers,* ed. Carter, vol. 5.

8. Jesse D. Jennings, ed., "Notes and Documents: Nutt's Trip to the Chickasaw Country," *Journal of Mississippi History* 9 (January 1947): 37–39.

9. Ibid., 40. Nutt crossed the line near Smith's Stand, known also by various other names. It was north of the extinct town of Rocky Springs on the Natchez Trace at the Claiborne–Hinds County line.

10. Ibid., 41–43, 44.

11. Ibid., 45.

12. Ibid., 45–46.

13. Ibid., 47, 48–49, 53. According to John H. Peterson Jr., "The prosperity of the Choctaws in the decades preceding removal was based on an expanded agricultural base which began to develop in the middle of the eighteenth century. While the dependence of the aboriginal Choctaws on agriculture may be overemphasized, it is clear that by the second half of the eighteenth century traditional subsistence agriculture was supplemented by European grains and garden vegetables, horses, cattle, hogs, and domesticated fowl. By the nineteenth century cattle herds were extensive, and the Choctaws began to grow cotton and produce their own clothing. The establishment of a United States trading post at Fort Stevens on the Tombigbee River (near the Choctaws) in 1802 intensified trade. . . . As trade increased, public inns were erected along major travel routes through Choctaw territory, usually under the ownership of whites or Choctaws of mixed heritage. . . . Change accelerated after 1818, when the Choctaws invited missionaries to establish schools in their country and . . . [b]y 1830 there were eleven schools among the Choctaws and twenty-nine teachers" ("Three Efforts at Development among the Choctaws of Mississippi," in *Southeastern Indians,* ed. Walter L. Williams, 143). Modern scholars endorse Nutt's observations that the scarcity of game resulted from the European introduction of the fur and game trade. For example, R. David Edmunds argues, "Although the Choctaws originally had sustained themselves through hunting and horticulture, by the middle of the eighteenth century they had become so enmeshed in the European trading system that much of their economy was based on their ability to supply deerskins to British merchants. . . . [B]y 1800

they had so depleted the deer population in Mississippi that they could no longer provide the hides needed to purchase necessities." ("National Expansion from the Indian Perspective," in *Indians in American History,* ed. Hoxie, 166). See also Walter L. Williams, "Southeastern Indians," 13; and Hudson, "Why the Southeastern Indians Slaughtered Deer," 158–59, 162–63.

14. Jennings, ed., "Notes and Documents," 55–56.

15. "Letter XXVII. Natchez, Mississippi Territory, April 6, 1808," in Christian Schultz, *Travels on an Inland Voyage through the States of New York, Pennsylvania, Virginia, Ohio, Kentucky and Tennessee, and through the Territories of Indiana, Louisiana, Mississippi and New Orleans; Performed in the Years 1807 and 1808; Including a Tour of Nearly Six Thousand Miles* (New York: Isaac Riley, 1810), 128.

16. Ibid., 139, 186.

17. Ibid., 181–82.

18. Ibid., 187–88.

19. F. Cuming, *Sketches of a Tour to the Western Country, through the States of Ohio and Kentucky; a Voyage Down the Ohio and Mississippi Rivers, and a Trip through the Mississippi Territory and Part of West Florida* (Pittsburgh: Cramer, Spear, and Eichbaum, 1810), 284, 288, 290, 293.

20. Ibid., 298–99, 301, 303.

21. Ibid., 321, 322.

22. Ibid., 322, 323.

23. Ibid., 323.

24. "Autobiography of Gideon Lincecum," *Mississippi Historical Society Publications* 8 (1904): 468.

25. Ibid., 469. The same sort of "selective cognition" was displayed by "A Descendent of One of the First Settlers" who some sixty years after the fact described how he, at the age of twelve, had traveled with his family from south Mississippi through "a wild, trackless, savage territory," to their new home on the Big Hatchie River of West Tennessee in the early nineteenth century. His mother, grandmother, and the young children traveled in a "carryall (ambulance it would be called now-a-days)," which was "a sleeping apartment, as well as traveling vehicle; long and broad, deep sides and high back, with heavy leather curtains, lined with thick, green baize, when closely buttoned down, and bed made up in it, was comfortable enough for an emperor's wife." They traveled through "country which . . . was slightly rolling, wood principally oak and hickory, devoid of tangled undergrowth." This description scarcely sounds like a journey through a "trackless, savage territory" (*Old Times in West Tennessee* [Memphis: W. G. Cheeney, 1873]: 8–9).

26. "Autobiography of Gideon Lincecum," 470, 471.

27. Ibid., 479, 485, 517–19.

28. Adam Hodgson, *Remarks during a Journey through North America in the Years 1819, 1820, and 1821* (New York: Samuel Whiting, 1823), n.p.

29. Ibid.

30. Ibid.

31. Paul Wilhelm, Duke of Wurttemberg, *Travels in North America, 1822–1824*, trans. W. Robert Nitske, ed. Savoie Lottinville (Norman: University of Oklahoma Press, 1973), xiii–xxviii, 131–33.

32. Ibid., 138, 142–43.

33. Excellent accounts of the Indians in Mississippi and their removal include J. Leitch Wright, *Only Land They Knew*, and DeRosier, *Removal of the Choctaw Indians*.

34. E. L. Jones, "Creative Disruptions in American Agriculture, 1620–1820," *Agricultural History* 48 (October 1974): 515.

35. Spurr, *Forest Ecology*, 291. There has traditionally been a tendency to overstate the percentage of the state that was forested at the time of early European settlement. For example, a 1936 study compiled for the State Planning Commission and State Forestry Commission reported, "The area of Mississippi is 29,671,680 acres. The state was originally nearly all covered with timber. . . . The timbered area . . . originally covered an area estimated to be 28,800,000 acres" (Rowan D. Crews, comp., "Economic Report on Forestry in Mississippi," unpublished report in MFC Files, 1). There are those who believe there was a very significant loss of forest cover over time. One such study, which is not specific to Mississippi, says that in the area from the 47th parallel in Canada to the coastal plain of the Carolinas and from the Atlantic to the Mississippi, there were 431 million acres of forest at the beginning of European settlement and that today only 19.9 million acres, or 4.4 percent, remains (James E. Greenway Jr., *Extinct and Vanishing Birds of the World* [New York: Dover Publications, 1967], 37). These figures are hard to accept, given the fact that Mississippi alone has roughly 18.5 million acres of forest today.

36. Roderick Nash, *Wilderness and the American Mind*, 3d ed. (New Haven: Yale University Press, 1982), 7.

37. Timothy Flint, *A Condensed Geography and History of the Western States or the Mississippi Valley* (1828; Gainesville, Fla.: Scholars' Facsimiles and Reprints, 1970), 497.

38. Ibid., 198–99, 502.

39. Ibid., 503, 504.

40. Ibid., 506, 509.

41. *View of the Valley of the Mississippi; or, The Emigrant's and Traveller's Guide to the West* (Philadelphia: H. S. Tanner, 1832), 247–48, 30, 32.

42. Ibid., 249.

43. Ibid., 250, 254.

44. Michael Williams, *Americans and Their Forests*, 129–30. For an overview of the pioneers' forest, see Laurence C. Walker, *Southern Forest*, 33–87.

45. Benjamin L. C. Wailes, *Report on the Agriculture and Geology of Mississippi, Embracing a Sketch of the Social and Natural History of the State* (Philadelphia: E. Barksdale, 1854), 128.

46. Mrs. Dunbar Rowland, "Peter Chester," 77–78; Heidelberg, "Frontier in Mississippi," 13–16.

47. Heidelberg, "Frontier in Mississippi," 16, 17; John F. H. Claiborne, *Mississippi, as a Province, Territory and State, with Biographical Notices of Eminent Citizens* (Jackson: Power and Barksdale, 1880), 140; John Hebron Moore, *Agriculture in Ante-Bellum Mississippi* (New York: Bookman Associates, 1958), 15–16.

48. John Hebron Moore, *Agriculture*, 21–22.

49. Dick, *Dixie Frontier*, 74, 63–64. See also Paul Wallace Gates, "Private Land Claims in the South," *Journal of Southern History* 22 (May 1956): 183–204. The survey records can be valuable sources in reconstructing the history of the forest but must be used with caution. See Eric A. Bourdo Jr., "A Review of the General Land Office Survey and of Its Use in Quantitative Studies of Former Forests," *Ecology* 37 (October 1956): 754–68; Spurr, *Forest Ecology*, 295–96, and Malcolm J. Rohrbaugh, *The Land Office Business: The Settlement and Administration of American Public Lands, 1789–1837* (New York: Oxford University Press, 1968). See also Delcourt, "Reconstructing the Forest Primeval," 1–13.

50. Dick, *Dixie Frontier*, 64–65; Heidelberg, "Frontier in Mississippi," 33; Mary J. Welsh, "Recollections of Pioneer Life in Mississippi," *Mississippi Historical Society Publications* 4 (1901): 351.

51. Welsh, "Recollections," 65, 66–68; Clarence Edwin Carter, ed., *The Territorial Papers of the United States*, vol. 6, *The Territory of Mississippi, 1809–1817* (Washington, D.C.: U.S. Government Printing Office, 1938), 646–47.

52. Dick, *Dixie Frontier*, 68–69.

53. Ibid., 71–72, 76; Riley, *Choctaw Land Claims*, 353–55; Edwin A. Miles, *Jacksonian Democracy in Mississippi* (Chapel Hill: University of North Carolina Press, 1960), 118.

54. Dick, *Dixie Frontier*, 2; Charles D. Lowery, "The Great Migration to the Mississippi Territory, 1798–1819," *Journal of Mississippi History* 30 (August 1968): 178; E. L. Jones, "Creative Disruptions," 514.

55. Heidelberg, "Frontier in Mississippi," 20–21, 30; *Census of the United States, 1810: Aggregate Amount of Each Description of Persons within the United States of America, and the Territories Thereof, Agreeably to Actual Enumeration Made According to Law, in the Year 1810* (Washington, D.C., 1811; reprint, New York: Norman Ross, 1990); Lowery, "Great Migration," 180.

56. John Hebron Moore, *Agriculture*, 37–39; Michael Williams, *Americans and Their Forests*, 60. In the winter of 1853–54 Frederick Law Olmsted traveled in the South. While in Mississippi, he noted, "I passed during the day four or five large plantations, the hillsides gullied like icebergs, stables and negro-quarters all abandoned, and given up to decay." The culprit was

erosion, and "from the cause described [the land's] productiveness rapidly decreases" (*A Journey in the Back Country: In the Winter of 1853–4,* 2 vols. [New York: G. P. Putnam's Sons, 1907], 1:10–11). The Log Hall Plantation, discussed below, offers a good example of the overuse of the land: "This big cut has been in cultivation about 9 years, with 8 consecutive cotton crops taken off" (Franklin L. Riley, "Diary of a Mississippi Planter, January 1, 1840, to April 1863," *Mississippi Historical Society Publications* 10 [1909]: 364).

57. Riley, "Diary," 305, 312–14.

58. Dick, *Dixie Frontier,* 25; "Autobiography of Gideon Lincecum," 470, 471.

59. Welsh, "Recollections," 347–48, 349, 350.

60. Edward M. Steel Jr., "A Pioneer Farmer in the Choctaw Purchase," *Journal of Mississippi History* 16 (October 1954): 232, 237.

61. Heidelberg, "Frontier in Mississippi," 53–54; *Census for 1820* (Washington, D.C.: Gales and Seaton, 1821); *Abstract of the Returns of the Fifth Census,* 22d Cong., 1st sess., 1832, House Doc. 263, 36.

62. Robert Bowman, "Early History and Archaeology of Yazoo County," *Mississippi Historical Society Publications* 8 (1904): 427–30.

63. Willie D. Halsell, "Migration into, and Settlement of, Leflore County, 1833–1876," *Journal of Mississippi History* 9 (October 1947): 220, 222.

64. Michael Williams, *Americans and Their Forests,* 118–20; *The Seventh Census of the United States: 1850* (Washington, D.C.: Robert Armstrong, 1853), 456.

65. *Abstract of the Returns of the Fifth Census,* 36; *Historical Statistics of the United States: Colonial Times to 1970,* pt. 1 (Washington, D.C.: U.S. Government Printing Office, 1975), 30; John Hebron Moore, *Agriculture,* 180; William K. Scarborough, "Heartland of the Cotton Kingdom," in *A History of Mississippi,* ed. Richard Aubrey McLemore, 2 vols. (Hattiesburg: University and College Press of Mississippi, 1973), 1:325.

66. Michael Williams, *Americans and Their Forests,* 133, 138–39; David E. Schob, "Woodhawks and Cordwood: Steamboat Fuel on the Ohio and Mississippi Rivers, 1820–1860," *Journal of Forest History* 21 (July 1977): 124; Sam H. Schurr and Bruce C. Netschert, *Energy in the American Economy, 1850–1975: An Economic Study of Its History and Prospects* (Baltimore: Johns Hopkins Press for Resources for the Future, 1960), 50n. A cord is a cubic measure of wood, 8 feet by 4 feet by 4 feet, or 128 cubic feet.

67. Flint, *Condensed Geography,* 498; *View of the Valley,* 250; Michael Williams, *Americans and Their Forests,* 153–55.

68. Schob, "Woodhawks and Cordwood," 124, 126, 129–30.

69. Ibid., 126–27; Michael Williams, *Americans and Their Forests,* 153–55; Charles MacKay, *Life and Liberty in America; or, Sketches of a Tour in the United States and Canada, in 1857–8,* 2 vols. (London, 1859), 1:159. For detailed descriptions of Mississippi's lands and forests in 1860, see Eugene W. Hilgard, *Report on the Geology and Agriculture of the State of Mississippi* (Jackson, Miss.: E. Barksdale, 1860).

Chapter 3

1. James H. McClendon, "The Development of Mississippi Agriculture: A Survey," *Journal of Mississippi History* 13 (April 1951): 81.

2. John Hebron Moore, *Andrew Brown and Cypress Lumbering in the Old Southwest* (Baton Rouge: Louisiana State University Press, 1967), vii–viii.

3. D. Clayton James, *Antebellum Natchez,* 3–12; Heidelberg, "Frontier in Mississippi," 11–13; Nollie Hickman, *Mississippi Harvest: Lumbering in the Longleaf Pine Belt, 1840–1915* (University: University of Mississippi, 1962), 15; Superior Council of Louisiana to the general directors of the Company of the Indies, New Orleans, February 27, 1725, in *Mississippi Provincial Archives, 1701–1729,* ed. Rowland and Sanders, 2:403.

4. Bienville, memoir on Louisiana, ca. 1725–26; king of France, memoir to Bienville, Marly, February 2, 1732; and king of France to Bienville and Salmon, February 2, 1732, all in *Mississippi Provincial Archives, 1704–1743,* 3:531, 545–46, 570.

5. Bienville and Salmon to Maurepas, New Orleans, May 12, 1733, March 20, 1734, April 16, 1736, all in ibid., 3:601–2, 638, 685.

6. John A. Eisterhold, "Lumber and Trade in the Lower Mississippi Valley and New Orleans, 1800–1860," *Louisiana History* 13 (winter 1972): 71; John Hebron Moore, *Andrew Brown,* 3–6.

7. Eisterhold, "Lumber and Trade," 71–72; D. Clayton James, *Antebellum Natchez,* 12–13; Thomas Hutchins, *An Historical Narrative and Topographical Description of Louisiana and West Florida* (Philadelphia, 1784), 38–39; Hickman, *Mississippi Harvest,* 16; Charles S. Sydnor, *A Gentleman of the Old Natchez Region: Benjamin L. C. Wailes* (1938; reprint, Westport, Conn.: Negro Universities Press, 1970), 10.

8. Bettersworth, *Mississippi,* 100; Hickman, *Mississippi Harvest,* 16; Hutchins, *Historical Narrative and Topographical Description,* 62.

9. Eisterhold, "Lumber and Trade," 71–72. Some of these rafts were enormous. Eisterhold describes an 1819 case in which a 180,000-board-foot cypress raft was taken from Catahoula Parish, Louisiana, just across the river from the area between Natchez and Port Gibson, to

New Orleans. He says that some rafts were larger than 200,000 board feet in size (73, 85). A board foot (BF) of timber or lumber is one foot by one foot by one inch. Twelve BF equal one cubic foot. The metric equivalent of one cubic foot is 0.02832 cubic meters.

10. Ibid., 90–91.

11. Schultz, *Travels*, 188.

12. Rowland, *History of Mississippi*, 1:309; Eisterhold, "Lumber and Trade," 84.

13. Samuel Brown to Governor Holmes, Percyfield, June 24, 1811, in *Territorial Papers*, ed. Carter, 6:206–7.

14. Thomas Freeman to secretary of the treasury, Surveyors Office, Washington, Mississippi Territory, July 9, 1811, in ibid., 6:205–6.

15. Nehemiah Tilton to Edward Tiffin, Land Office west of Pearl River, July 1, 1814, and Governor Holmes to Mr. Taylor, September 17, 1811, both in ibid., 6:625, 224.

16. Eisterhold, "Lumber and Trade," 85; Bowman, "Early History," 430.

17. Eisterhold, "Lumber and Trade," 76–77; Hickman, *Mississippi Harvest*, 16.

18. Hickman, *Mississippi Harvest*, 17.

19. *View of the Valley*, 31–32, 249–50.

20. John Hebron Moore, *Andrew Brown*, 22–23.

21. Ibid., 25–27, 30–35.

22. John Hebron Moore, *Andrew Brown*, 37–44; M. B. Peabody, "125 Years of Sawmilling," *Southern Lumberman* (December 15, 1956).

23. D. Clayton James, *Antebellum Natchez*, 207–8; John Hebron Moore, *Andrew Brown*, 103–4.

24. John Hebron Moore, *Andrew Brown*, 12, 19, 26–28, 34, 40–42, 51–59, 82–97, 111, 117–18, 126, 130–48, 153–55; D. Clayton James, *Antebellum Natchez*, 207; Hickman, *Mississippi Harvest*, 40–41.

25. Bowman, "Early History," 429–30; Hickman, *Mississippi Harvest*, 34; Eisterhold, "Lumber and Trade," 87.

26. Willie D. Halsell, "Migration into, and Settlement of, Leflore County in the Later Periods, 1876–1920," *Journal of Mississippi History* 10 (July 1948): 229, 248; Welsh, "Recollections," 345.

27. *Digest of Accounts of Manufacturing Establishments in the United States and of Their Manufactures* (Washington, D.C.: Gales and Seaton, 1823).

28. *Statistics of the United States of America: The Sixth Census, June 1, 1840* (Washington, D.C.: Blair and Rives, 1840), 262–65.

29. Hickman, *Mississippi Harvest*, 1–2; "Map of Mississippi Showing the Distribution of the Pine Forests, 1881," in Hickman, *Mississippi Harvest*, following p. 100. Hickman's description (3–4) of the longleaf cover does not precisely agree with this map. He also refers to the "sixteen pine counties" (8).

30. Heidelberg, "Frontier in Mississippi," 43, 44; Hickman, *Mississippi Harvest*, 2, 6; Nollie W. Hickman, "Logging and Rafting Timber in South Mississippi, 1840–1910," *Journal of Mississippi History* 19 (July 1957): 154. For a 1903 description of the longleaf forests of East Texas, which were much like those of south Mississippi, see William B. Howard, "Bureau Work in Texas," *Forestry Quarterly* 1 (April 1903): 113–14: "The thing which impresses one especially is the park-like appearance and exclusive character of the Longleaf Pine forest. . . . This peculiar park-like appearance is undoubtedly due to the high-light requirement of the species. After a Longleaf stand has started no younger generation can appear under the shade of the original stand. Gradually the stand thins itself, and when maturity is reached it is composed of comparatively uniform sized trees."

31. Hickman, *Mississippi Harvest*, 13; Hilgard, *Report*, 361.

32. J. F. H. Claiborne, "A Trip through the Piney Woods," *Mississippi Historical Society Publications* 9 (1906): 487, 514, 515–16, 521, 522.

33. Ibid., 523–24.

34. Ibid., 528–30; Hickman, *Mississippi Harvest*, 7; L. A. Besancon, *Besancon's Annual Register of the State of Mississippi* (Natchez: n.p., 1838), 190.

35. Tenth Census 1880 [I] *Population* (Washington, D.C.: U.S. Government Printing Office, 1883), 67–68; Hickman, *Mississippi Harvest*, 7 (cites U.S. Census, Tenth Census, 1880, [I] *Population*, 67–68; and Besancon, *Besancon's Annual Register*, 190).

36. Hickman, *Mississippi Harvest*, 3.

37. Michael Williams, *Americans and Their Forests*, 147; Thomas D. Clark, "The Impact of the Timber Industry on the South," *Mississippi Quarterly* 25 (spring 1972): 149–50. See also Michael Williams, "Products of the Forest: Mapping the Census of 1840," *Journal of Forest History* 24 (January 1980): 4–23. For a very brief encapsulation of some of the topics in Williams's massive book covering American forests from the age of European contact through the rise of lumbering and other forest uses down to the present, see Michael Williams, "The Clearing of the Forests," in *The Making of the American Landscape*, ed. Michael P. Conzen (Boston: Unwin Hyman, 1990), 146–68.

38. Michael Williams, *Americans and Their Forests*, 146.

39. Ibid., 152.

40. Ibid., 156–57.

41. Ibid., 160–61.

42. Hickman, "Logging and Rafting Timber," 154–55; Hickman, *Mississippi Harvest*, 17–18.

43. Eisterhold, "Lumber and Trade," 78–79.

44. Hickman, *Mississippi Harvest*, 18.

45. Ibid., 18–19.

46. Eisterhold, "Lumber and Trade," 79–80; Hickman, *Mississippi Harvest*, 19.

47. Eisterhold, "Lumber and Trade," 79–80; Hickman, *Mississippi Harvest*, 18–20. For another brief account of the history of the H. Weston Lumber Company, see "H. Weston Lumber Company" (typewritten collection description, H. Weston Lumber Company Records), Special Collections, J. D. Williams Library, University of Mississippi, Oxford (hereafter cited as Weston Lumber Company Records), 1–2.

48. Hickman, *Mississippi Harvest*, 20, 21.

49. Ibid., 21–22.

50. Ibid., 22–23.

51. Ibid. 23.

52. Ibid., 24–25, 41.

53. Ibid., 25, 31–32; Eisterhold, "Lumber and Trade," 87.

54. Hickman, *Mississippi Harvest*, 28–29.

55. Ibid., 29–30. For the story of the early mill operators in the Bayou Bernard area and the growth of the town of Handsboro, "one of the first Mississippi towns that grew directly out of the lumber industry," see also John Peter Switzer, "Handsboro: A South Mississippi Town, 1840–1920" (master's thesis, University of Southern Mississippi, 1985). Switzer says that the area's mills, which were prospering on the eve of the Civil War, declined from 1865 to 1920 because of a lack of capital, as the size of investments, mills, and landholdings in the industry became much larger in the late nineteenth century. The area was also hurt by labor problems, the depletion of local timber, and the construction of railroads that facilitated the rise of large interior mills in Mississippi. Also, the Gulf and Ship Island Railroad, which was originally to run through Handsboro and terminate in Mississippi City, was instead built to Gulfport, and Handsboro was completely bypassed. A spur initially carried lumber from Gulfport to Handsboro, where it was loaded onto oceangoing ships, but the completion of a deep-water channel from Ship Island to Gulfport eliminated the need for the Handsboro connection. Switzer concludes, "When the railroad bypassed Handsboro so did the lumber industry, thus ending Handsboro's chance of economic independence." In 1966 Handsboro was annexed by the city of Gulfport.

56. Hickman, *Mississippi Harvest*, 34.

57. Eisterhold, "Lumber and Trade," 41, 80–84; Hickman, *Mississippi Harvest*, 41.

58. Hickman, *Mississippi Harvest*, 34–38.

59. Ibid., 38–40.

60. Ibid., 30–31.

61. Ibid., 33–34.

62. Ibid., 32–33.

63. Eisterhold, "Lumber and Trade," 86; Hickman, "Logging and Rafting Timber," 164; Hickman, *Missis-*

sippi Harvest, 25–26; *Manufactures in the Several States and Territories for the Year Ending June 1, 1850: Abstract of the Statistics of Manufactures, According to the Returns of the Seventh Census* (n.p., n.d.), 73.

64. Hickman, *Mississippi Harvest*, 26.

65. Eisterhold, "Lumber and Trade," 90.

Chapter 4

1. Peabody, "125 Years of Sawmilling," 193–94.

2. Jeffrey A. Drobney, *Lumbermen and Log Sawyers: Life, Labor, and Culture in the North Florida Timber Industry, 1830–1930* (Macon, Ga.: Mercer University Press, 1997), 16–17; Robert S. Maxwell and Robert D. Baker, *Sawdust Empire: The Texas Lumber Industry, 1830–1940* (College Station: Texas A&M University Press, 1983), 19; *Ninth Census*, vol. 3, *The Statistics of the Wealth and Industry of the United States* (Washington, D.C.: U.S. Government Printing Office, 1872), 612. In 1870 Mississippi's sawmills utilized 192 steam engines (*Thirteenth Census of the United States Taken in the Year 1910*, vol. 10, *Manufactures, 1909* [Washington, D.C.: U.S. Government Printing Office, 1913], 502).

3. Michael Williams, *Americans and Their Forests*, 168, 201–2; Drobney, *Lumbermen and Log Sawyers*, 19–20; Maxwell and Baker, *Sawdust Empire*, 19. Brief treatments of the southern lumber industry and its workers appear in Edward L. Ayers, *The Promise of the New South: Life after Reconstruction* (New York: Oxford University Press, 1992), 123–31; and Edward L. Ayers, *Southern Crossing: A History of the American South, 1877–1906* (Oxford: Oxford University Press, 1995), 65–68. A far more comprehensive treatment is Laurence C. Walker, *Southern Forest*, 88–145.

4. Michael Williams, *Americans and Their Forests*, 168, 202.

5. Peabody, "125 Years of Sawmilling," 194; Milton A. Nelson, "The Lumber Industry of America," *American Monthly Review of Reviews* 36 (November 1907): 570.

6. Michael Williams, *Americans and Their Forests*, 169; *A Compendium of the Ninth Census (June 1, 1870)* (Washington, D.C.: U.S. Government Printing Office, 1872), 918; M. B. Newton Jr., "Water-Powered Sawmills and Related Structures in the Piney Woods," in *Mississippi's Piney Woods: A Human Perspective*, ed. Noel Polk (Jackson: University Press of Mississippi, 1986), 160–61.

7. Michael Williams, *Americans and Their Forests*, 168–69.

8. Archer H. Mayor, *Southern Timberman: The Legacy of William Buchanan* (Athens: University of Georgia Press, 1988), 45–46; Kenneth L. Smith,

Sawmill: The Story of Cutting the Last Great Virgin Forest East of the Rockies (Fayetteville: University of Arkansas Press, 1986), 25; Michael Williams, *Americans and Their Forests,* 261; Hickman, *Mississippi Harvest,* 175–76.

9. Mayor, *Southern Timberman,* 47–48.

10. Drobney, *Lumbermen and Log Sawyers,* 20; Kenneth L. Smith, *Sawmill,* 25–26; Michael Williams, *Americans and Their Forests,* 261–62.

11. Drobney, *Lumbermen and Log Sawyers,* 48–49, 51; Kenneth L. Smith, *Sawmill,* 26–27; Michael Williams, *Americans and Their Forests,* 261.

12. *From Tree to Trade* (Kansas City: Long-Bell Lumber Company, 1920), 12, 17–18. Good, brief descriptions of the machinery and processes of sawmilling appear in Nelson Courtland Brown and James Samuel Bethel, *Lumber,* 2d ed. (New York: John Wiley and Sons, 1958); Richard W. Massey Jr., "A History of the Lumber Industry in Alabama and West Florida, 1880–1914" (Ph.D. diss., Vanderbilt University, 1960), 155–73; and Drobney, *Lumbermen and Log Sawyers,* 93–102.

13. Hickman, "Logging and Rafting Timber," 157–58.

14. For a good description of early logging procedures and transactions, see J. Roland Weston, "Sunken Logs and Logging Brands of the Lower Pearl River Valley," *Journal of Mississippi History* 5 (April 1943): 83–86. See also Stanley Horn, *This Fascinating Lumber Business* (Indianapolis: Bobbs-Merrill, 1943), 123–26.

15. Weston, "Sunken Logs," 83–84; Hickman, "Logging and Rafting Timber," 158–60; David Wilburn Higgs, "Eastman, Gardiner and the Cohay Camps: A Mississippi Lumber Empire, 1890–1937" (master's thesis, Mississippi College, 1991), 14; Michael Williams, *Americans and Their Forests,* 251; Hickman, *Mississippi Harvest,* 104.

16. Higgs, "Eastman, Gardiner," 14–15; Hickman, "Logging and Rafting Timber," 158–60; Art Nelson, "The Lindsey Eight-Wheel Wagon," *Tree Talk* 17 (summer 1995): 24. For other brief accounts of the Lindsey eight-wheeled wagon, see Pauline L. Hester, *Yesteryears: Steppingstones to Tomorrow* (Laurel, Miss.: n.p., 1976), 24–25; and John Carroll Eudy, "A Mississippi Log Wagon," *Journal of Mississippi History* 30 (May 1968): 143–50.

17. Michael Williams, *Americans and Their Forests,* 251–52.

18. Ibid., 218; Weston, "Sunken Logs," 83.

19. Sydnor, *Gentleman,* 273–74.

20. John Hebron Moore, "Railroads of Antebellum Mississippi," *Journal of Mississippi History* 41 (February 1979): 53–56.

21. Ibid., 71–75; Charles Ripley Johnson, "Railroad Legislation and Building in Mississippi, 1830–1840," *Journal of Mississippi History* 4 (October 1942): 195–206. Service on the Ponchartrain Railroad began in 1831 with horse-drawn cars.

22. John Hebron Moore, "Railroads," 77–80; Bettersworth, *Mississippi,* 353–54.

23. John Hebron Moore, "Railroads," 78–79; U.S. Department of Commerce and Labor, Bureau of Corporations, *The Lumber Industry,* pt. 1, *Standing Timber* (Washington, D.C.: U.S. Government Printing Office, 1913), 226.

24. Michael Williams, *Americans and Their Forests,* 212, 253–54.

25. Sammy O. Cranford, *The Fernwood, Columbia and Gulf: A Railroad in the Piney Woods of South Mississippi* (New York: Garland Publishing, 1989), 10–13.

26. Hickman, *Mississippi Harvest,* 158–59.

27. Hickman, *Mississippi Harvest,* 157, 186; Michael Williams, *Americans and Their Forests,* 255; Switzer, "Handsboro," 82.

28. Bettersworth, *Mississippi,* 353–54, 392; Michael Williams, *Americans and Their Forests,* 255–56; Hickman, *Mississippi Harvest,* 156–59. The critical and continuing importance of railroads was demonstrated much later, in the late 1940s, when Johns Manville built an insulating board plant on the Mississippi Central Railroad outside the switching limits of Natchez. It cost the company less to ship pulpwood 150 miles on the Mississippi Central from Hattiesburg to its plant than it did to ship from Fayette on the Illinois Central, which was only twenty-three miles away (John W. Thompson, "History of the Johns Manville Timberlands in Southwest Mississippi," manuscript in Johns Manville Timberlands Records, Special Collections, Louisiana State University, Baton Rouge [hereafter cited as Johns Manville Records], box 1, folder 1).

29. Cranford, *Fernwood, Columbia, and Gulf,* 11–12, 16–17, 19–20; James Boyd, "Fifty Years," 62–63; Clark, "Impact of the Timber Industry," 156; Art Nelson, "Tie Hackers," *Tree Talk* 16 (fall 1994): 14; Art Nelson, "Forest History: Railroads Encouraged Mississippi Forestry," *Tree Talk* 15 (winter 1993): 31. The annual and biennial reports of the Railroad Commission of the state of Mississippi are excellent sources for the history of early railroads in the state. In Mississippi narrow-gauge logging railroads or trams were often called dummy lines. The term originated in the fact that many dummy lines utilized condensing locomotives rather than ones with a noisy stack; thus, they were silent, or dummy, lines (Charles A. Heavrin, *Boxes, Baskets, and Boards: A History of Anderson-Tully Company* [Memphis: Memphis State University Press, 1981], 163). For an interesting contemporary assessment of the effect of railroad wood usage on the forests, see Charles S. Sargent, *Report on the Forests of North America* (Washington, D.C.: U.S. Government Printing Office, 1884), 493. Sargent says that the real damage from this usage

was that ties were cut from vigorous young trees, which therefore did not grow to more productive maturity.

30. Cranford, *Fernwood, Columbia, and Gulf,* 2–10.

31. Williams, *Americans and Their Forests,* 256; Hickman, *Mississippi Harvest,* 215–16; James W. Silver, "Paul Bunyan Comes to Mississippi," *Journal of Mississippi History* 19 (April 1957): 96–97. The James L. Moreton file in the Mississippi Forestry Association Records in the Special Collections, Mitchell Memorial Library, Mississippi State University, Starkville (hereafter cited as MFA Records) contains typewritten essays on the Hartman, Keystone, and Hamilton, Hoskins, and Company firms. The essays were apparently intended for inclusion in Gilbert H. Hoffman's book, *Dummy Lines through the Longleaf: A History of the Saw Mills and Logging Railroads of Southwest Mississippi* (Oxford: University of Mississippi, Center for the Study of Southern Culture, 1992). A recent publication by Hoffman is *Steam Whistles in the Piney Woods: A History of the Sawmills and Logging Railroads of Forrest and Lamar Counties Mississippi,* vol. 1, *The Newman and Tatum Lumber Companies and the Mills at Lumberton* (Hattiesburg, Miss.: Longleaf Press, 1998).

32. Michael Williams, *Americans and Their Forests,* 258; Hickman, *Mississippi Harvest,* 163–64. The shay was a low-speed steam locomotive that was invented by Ephraim Shay of Michigan in the late nineteenth century. The shay had several advantages over traditional rod-driven locomotives. The traditional locomotive had power applied directly to rigid driving wheels, which applied a great deal of friction to the tracks and were thus very destructive when used on the light and temporary trackage of a lumbering road or spur. In contrast, the shay transmitted power from upright cylinders by means of a crankshaft fastened with flexible couplings to a pinion, a line, or driveshafts on one side of the locomotive. The pinion shafts were usually joined in several places by means of universal joints and transferred power to worm-geared wheels on one side of the locomotive by means of beveled gears. The driven wheels were fastened to an axle that coupled them with their partners on the other side of the machine. The gear-driven mechanism with the universal joints gave the shay locomotive more traction and pulling power and a degree of flexibility that allowed it to safely sway back and forth as it negotiated the grades, sharp curves, and constant undulations that characterized logging tramways. Another advantage of the shay locomotive was its boiler design, which allowed it to negotiate grades of as much as 10 percent while maintaining a safe water level in the boiler. The shay locomotives could pull incredible loads at a top speed of ten to twelve miles per hour. Early foresters learned to construct the tracks, usually by laying ties on an unpre-

pared roadbed and then loosely spiking the rails to the ties. Then a shay locomotive was "walked" over the rails, working them into a "negotiable" position, and only then were they firmly spiked to the ties (Michael Koch, *The Shay Locomotive: Titan of the Timber* [Denver: World Press, 1971], 25, 32; conversation with Arthur W. Nelson Jr., March 12, 1999).

33. Michael Williams, *Americans and Their Forests,* 244–45, 247, 258; Hickman, "Logging and Rafting Timber," 163, 167, 172.

34. Michael Williams, *Americans and Their Forests,* 248–50; Heavrin, *Boxes, Baskets, and Boards,* 89, 98–103.

35. Michael Williams, *Americans and Their Forests,* 193.

36. Ibid., 224, 228–29.

37. Defebaugh, *History,* 2:iii.

38. Michael Williams, *Americans and Their Forests,* 238, 244; Rowland, *History of Mississippi,* 2:545; James Boyd, "Fifty Years," 61; Sargent, *Report,* 487; *Twelfth Census of the United States Taken in the Year 1900,* vol. 9, *Manufactures,* pt. 3 (Washington, D.C.: U.S. Census Office, 1902), 839; *Fourteenth Census of the United States Taken in the Year 1920,* vol. 10, *Manufactures, 1919* (Washington, D.C.: U.S. Government Printing Office, 1923), 437; W. Watson Davis, "The Yellow Pine Lumber Industry in the South," *American Monthly Review of Reviews* (April 1904): 29. The copy of Boyd cited is a mimeographed typescript in the possession of author. The pagination is not the same as in the original journal. Copies of this typescript are available in the MFC Files and the Forest History Society in Durham, North Carolina (hereafter cited as FHS).

39. Edgar C. Scott Jr., "The St. Louis Lumber Market: An Historical Sketch," *Southern Lumberman* 193 (December 15, 1956); James Boyd, "Fifty Years in the Southern Pine Industry, Part 2," *Southern Lumberman* 145 (January 1, 1932): 51–53, 61. The copy of Boyd cited is a mimeographed typescript in the possession of author. The pagination is not the same as in the original journal. Copies of this typescript are available in the MFC Files and the FHS. Much of Boyd's material is quoted from information on Mississippi compiled by Dr. Charles Mohr for inclusion in Sargent, *Report.* There are some slight discrepancies between Boyd's quotations and the originals in Sargent.

40. Michael Williams, "Industrial Impacts on the Forests of the United States, 1860–1920," *Journal of Forest History* 31 (July 1987), 108; U.S. Department of Commerce and Labor, Bureau of Corporations, *Standing Timber,* 36–37.

41. James Boyd, "Fifty Years," 63; James E. Fickle, *The New South and the "New Competition": Trade Association Development in the Southern Pine Industry* (Urbana: University of Illinois Press, 1980), 179–96.

42. James Boyd, "Fifty Years," 65–66; Fickle, *New South,* 19–20, 179–80, 186–89.

43. Drobney, *Lumbermen and Log Sawyers,* 24–25; Maxwell and Baker, *Sawdust Empire,* 21; Michael Williams, *Americans and Their Forests,* 239–40; Hickman, *Mississippi Harvest,* 155–56. The figures from various sources, and even within sources, are often contradictory. For example, the 1900 Census on Manufactures credits Mississippi with 844 establishments capitalized at $17,337,538 (*Twelfth Census,* vol. 9, pt. 3, p. 809).

44. Hickman, *Mississippi Harvest,* 154.

45. Jo Dent Hodge, "The Lumber Industry in Laurel, Mississippi, at the Turn of the Nineteenth Century," *Journal of Mississippi History* 35 (November 1973): 372; Nollie Hickman, "The Lumber Industry in South Mississippi, 1890–1915," *Journal of Mississippi History* 20 (October 1958): 218; Hickman, *Mississippi Harvest,* 184–85; "How Our Garden Grows; or, A Story of Mississippi's Lumber Industry," *Mississippi Magic* (spring 1972): 3. In 1911 nearly 380,000,000 board feet of pine lumber was exported through Gulfport.

46. Fickle, *New South,* 2; Paul Wallace Gates, "Federal Land Policy in the South, 1866–1888," *Journal of Southern History* 6 (August 1940): 304.

47. Fickle, *New South,* 2–3; Gates, "Federal Land Policy," 305–12; C. Vann Woodward, *Origins of the New South, 1877–1913* (Baton Rouge: Louisiana State University Press, 1951), 115–16; Hickman, *Mississippi Harvest,* 69–71.

48. Clark, *Greening,* 14, 15; Fickle, *New South,* 3; Gates, "Federal Land Policy," 311–14; Hickman, *Mississippi Harvest,* 71–72; U.S. Department of Commerce and Labor, Bureau of Corporations, *Standing Timber,* 183, 256–58. One source tells of another means whereby valuable southern timberlands were acquired for practically nothing. When reserves were being set aside in the West (eventually becoming the national forests), the "Forest Lieu Act allowed settlers or owners inside the gross area of a reserve to exchange this land for vacant land elsewhere." Thus, "[c]ut over or arid and virtually worthless land inside the reserves was picked up and used as trading stock for valuable pine lands in the South. . . . In a visit to Crossett last year, I was shown the vault where abstract and land records are kept. We pulled out an abstract file at random and looked at the original entry. Lo and behold! Eighty acres in Morehouse Parish had been obtained by a predecessor in title of the present owner through exchange of eighty acres in the Black Hills Reserve of South Dakota" ("A Few Interesting Items on Lands Involved in Sale from Johns Manville Products Corporation to Rex Timber Corporation, December 10, 1971," Johns Manville Records, box 1, folder 3; J. W. Thompson, the chief forester of the Johns Manville timberlands, probably wrote this booklet).

49. U.S. Department of Commerce and Labor, Bureau of Corporations, *Standing Timber,* 184–85, quoting James D. Lacey before the Committee on Ways and Means of the House of Representatives, November 20, 1908. Lacey helped to put together the timber holdings that supported the mill of the Great Southern Lumber Company of Bogalusa, Louisiana, just over the Mississippi border. The Great Southern drew from timber in both Louisiana and Mississippi and was at one time considered the largest sawmill in the South, if not the nation and the world (Michael Curtis, "Early Development and Operations of the Great Southern Lumber Company," *Louisiana History* 14 [fall 1973]: 350–52). As noted earlier, an excellent detailed description of Mississippi's forests in 1880 prepared for the U.S. Census of that year by Dr. Charles Mohr appears in Sargent, *Report,* 530–36. The James D. Lacey Company of Chicago, with offices in New York City, became "foremost in timberland trading and timber estimates. All the early foresters either worked for the Forest Service or cruised timber for Lacey" ("A Few Interesting Items"). For a brief overview of Lacey's life and career, see "James D. Lacey," in *American Lumbermen: The Personal History and Public and Business Achievements of One Hundred Eminent Lumbermen of the United States* (Chicago: American Lumberman, 1905), 235–38.

50. *Chattanooga Tradesman,* May 1, 1886, 16, cited in C. Vann Woodward, *Origins,* 118; Jo Dent Hodge, "Lumbering in Laurel at the Turn of the Century" (master's thesis, University of Mississippi, 1966), 13; Fickle, *New South,* 3–4; Michael Williams, *Americans and Their Forests,* 241; Gates, "Federal Land Policy," 314–16, 328; Horn, *Fascinating Lumber Business,* 102; Hickman, *Mississippi Harvest,* 159; Hickman, "Lumber Industry," 212. One promoter boasted, "The Supply of Timber [in the South] is inexhaustible . . . and is being bought in large tracts by lumbermen" (A. H. Harrison Jr., *How to Get Rich in the South* [Chicago: n.p., 1888]).

51. R. S. Kellogg, *The Timber Supply of the United States* (Washington, D.C.: U.S. Department of Agriculture, Forest Service, 1907), 7–10.

52. James Boyd, "Fifty Years," 66; James Boyd, "Fifty Years, Part 2," 59. See also William B. Greeley, *Some Public and Economic Aspects of the Lumber Industry,* pt. 1 of *Studies of the Lumber Industry,* U.S. Department of Agriculture Report 114 (Washington, D.C.: U.S. Government Printing Office, 1917); and William G. Robbins, *American Forestry: A History of National, State, and Private Cooperation* (Lincoln: University of Nebraska Press, 1985), 31–33. For the life of Robert Alexander Long, see Lenore K. Bradley, *Robert Alexander Long: A Lumberman of the Gilded Age* (Durham,

N.C.: Forest History Society), 1989; and "Robert A. Long," in *American Lumbermen*, 375.

53. Fickle, *New South*, 6; Hodge, "Lumbering in Laurel," 13, 21; Hodge, "Lumber Industry," 363–64; Hickman, *Mississippi Harvest*, 179–80; James Boyd, "Fifty Years, Part 2," 58; Clark, *Greening*, 15; Gates, "Federal Land Policy," 326. See also Hester, *Yesteryears*, 19–22, and Higgs, "Eastman, Gardiner," for the story of Kamper and Eastman-Gardiner. Eastman-Gardiner is also described in *Twentieth Century Coast Edition of the Biloxi Daily Herald* (Biloxi: Biloxi Daily Herald Printery, n.d.), 95–98 (copy in Lauren Rogers Museum of Art, Laurel, Miss.). For sketchy accounts of many of the early Mississippi mills, see "Reminiscences of Saw Milling in Mississippi," *St. Louis Lumberman* (July 1902): 51. When Congress created new states out of the public domain, it reserved for itself the management and disposal of the public lands within their borders. However, it granted land to the states for various purposes, among which was to aid in the development of public schools. Lands granted for this purpose were called school lands. For a brief overview of the life and career of Stimson Gardiner, see "Stimson B. Gardiner," in *American Lumbermen*, 315–18.

54. Ralph W. Hidy, Ernest Hill, and Allan Nevins, *Timber and Men: The Weyerhaeuser Story* (New York: Macmillan, 1963), 208–9.

55. Nollie W. Hickman, "The Yellow Pine Industries in St. Tammany, Tangipahoa, and Washington Parishes, 1840–1915," *Louisiana Studies* 5 (summer 1966): 81–82; Hickman, *Mississippi Harvest*, 136, 170, 176–77; Clark Forrest Jr., "The Denkmanns: A Pioneer American Lumbering Family and Their Florida Parishes Operations," *Southeast Louisiana Historical Association Papers* 8 (1981): 28.

56. Fickle, *New South*, 5; Gates, "Federal Land Policy," 317; Michael Williams, *Americans and Their Forests*, 241, 243; L. O. Crosby Jr., *Crosby: A Story of Men and Trees* (New York: Newcomen Society in North America, 1960), 12. For a firsthand account of a girlhood in the longleaf area of Marion County in the early twentieth century, of the devastation of "cut out and get out" lumbering, and of the mysterious northerner named Blodgett who controlled much of the land in the area, see Eva V. Beets, "Marion County Forestry History," in MFA Records. Ms. Beets's memoir was edited by Christine Wilson and published as "Growing Up in Marion County: A Memoir by Eva Davis Beets," *Journal of Mississippi History* 48 (August 1986): 199–213.

57. Fickle, *New South*, 6; R. E. Appleman, "Timber Empire from the Public Domain," *Mississippi Valley Historical Review* 26 (September 1939): 193; Michael Williams, *Americans and Their Forests*, 242; Gates, "Federal Land Policy," 319–25.

58. Hickman, "Lumber Industry," 215; Fickle, *New South*, 7; Gates, "Federal Land Policy," 327–30; Michael Williams, *Americans and Their Forests*, 243, 263, 278–79.

59. Hickman, "Lumber Industry," 215.

60. Fickle, *New South*, 7; Hidy, Hill, and Nevins, *Timber and Men*, 290, 301; Hickman, *Mississippi Harvest*, 166–67; Hickman, "Lumber Industry," 216; Sargent, *Report*, 531.

61. Hickman, *Mississippi Harvest*, 167–68, 172–77; Sargent, *Report*, 531–32; James Boyd, "Fifty Years, Part 2," 50; J. E. Bryan Jr., "Forest History—L. N. Dantzler Lumber Company," MFA Records, 1–10. The Dantzler firm was said to hold the second-oldest charter of any corporation in Mississippi. In 1949 the firm closed its last sawmill and became the largest industrial tree farmer in the state before selling out to IP in 1967 ("Mayers Dantzler," *Newsletter, Mississippi Society of American Foresters* 5 [March 1983]: 11). See also *Twentieth Century Coast Edition*, 99–100.

62. James Boyd, "Fifty Years, Part 2," 54. For an account of life and work in the mills, woods, and towns of the Central Lumber Company, see Bettye Jo Wolfkiel, "Towns That Crept across America," James L. Moreton File, MFA Records, 8–11. For descriptions of the Moretons' Celco, Lucien, and Quentin mills, see Charley Walker, interview, September 10, 1974, MFA Records.

63. James Boyd, "Fifty Years, Part 2," 55–56.

64. Ibid., 54–55.

65. Ibid., 56–57.

66. Hickman, *Mississippi Harvest*, 175–77; James Boyd, "Fifty Years, Part 2," 51–52.

67. Hickman, *Mississippi Harvest*, 182; James Boyd, "Fifty Years, Part 2," 57.

68. Hickman, *Mississippi Harvest*, 177–78, 178–79; James Boyd, "Fifty Years, Part 2," 59; Hodge, "The Lumber Industry," 365.

69. Hickman, *Mississippi Harvest*, 178–79; Hodge, "Lumber Industry," 365; James Boyd, "Fifty Years, Part 2," 57–58. For brief descriptions of the Gilchrist-Fordney, Wausau-Southern, and Marathon lumber companies in Laurel, see Hester, *Yesteryears*, 25. For the history of Laurel and Jones County, see Suzanne Spell, "A History of Jones County, Mississippi" (master's thesis, Mississippi College, 1961).

70. James Boyd, "Fifty Years, Part 2," 58–59; Jim Fisher, *Gilchrist: The First Fifty Years* (Bend, Ore.: Oregon Color Press, 1988), 11, 13, 15, 17; *Twentieth Century Coast Edition*, 98–99.

71. Ibid., 59. For a contemporary illustrated article on the Sumter Lumber Company, see "Ample Timber Supply ahead of These Operations," *American Lumberman* (June 14, 1924).

72. Tom DeWeese, interview by Judy Ryals, May 29, 1991, in *The Timber Industry in the Great Depres-*

sion: *An Oral History Project of the Lauderdale County Department of Archives and History, Inc., and Meridian Community College* (Meridian, Miss.: Lauderdale County Department of Archives and History, 1991), 368–69.

73. DeWeese, interview by Ryals, 60; Thomas A. De-Weese, interview conducted for Weyerhaeuser Company Archives by Linda Edgerly, November 28, 1979, MFA Records, 2; Davis L. Fair Jr., interview by Bobbie Jean Dickinson, September 6, 1988, MFA Records.

74. Hickman, *Mississippi Harvest,* 180–82; James Boyd, "Fifty Years, Part 2," 57–58; *Newman* (n.p., n.d.; reprinted from *American Lumberman* [May 16, 1925]), 3–16, copy in James L. Moreton File, MFA Records). In the 1920s King W. Bridges, the assistant general sales manager of the J. J. Newman Lumber Company at its Brookhaven general sales office, wrote an illustrated and detailed account of the lumber industry from raw material to finished product. It was published in *American Lumberman* and reprinted as a booklet entitled *The Lumber Industry from Tree to Trade* (copy in James L. Moreton File, MFA Records). In 1900 Newman registered a trademark with the U.S. Patent Office for an African American woman composed of pine tree parts over the inscription "Mrs. Sippi Long Leaf" ("U.S. Patent Office, J. J. Newman Lumber Company, of Hattiesburg, Mississippi, Trade-Mark for Lumber," copy in James L. Moreton File, MFA Records).

75. James Boyd, "Fifty Years, Part 2," 60.

76. "Glimpses of the Mills that Make 'SI Pine,'" *American Lumberman* (October 20, 1917): 40; James Boyd, "Fifty Years, Part 2," 59.

77. James Boyd, "Fifty Years, Part 2," 50; Sargent, *Report,* 533–34.

78. Heavrin, *Boxes, Baskets, and Boards,* 53, 76–77, 115–16, 118–19; Halsell, "Migration, 1876–1920," 249–50, 254; *Southern Forestry: A Study of the South's Renewable Natural Resource* (Chicago: Research and Development Bureau, Illinois Central Railroad, 1944), 60, copy in MFA Records. See also Charles W. Crawford, "A History of the R. F. Learned Lumber Company, 1864–1945" (Ph.D. diss., University of Mississippi, 1968).

79. Silver, "Paul Bunyan," 93–94, 96, 119.

80. Samuel Nickey Sr., interview by John Larson, Memphis, December 1953, 5, 8–9, copy in FHS.

81. Fickle, *New South,* 8; James Boyd, "Fifty Years," 64; Hickman, *Mississippi Harvest,* 202. Works dealing with these organizations include James W. Silver, "The Hardwood Producers Come of Age," *Journal of Southern History* 23 (November 1957): 427–53; Stanley F. Horn and Charles W. Crawford, "Perspectives on Southern Forestry: The *Southern Lumberman,* Industrial Forestry, and Trade Associations," *Journal of Forest History* 21 (January 1977): 18–30; and Fickle, *New South,* 7–23.

Chapter 5

1. R. C. Fraunberger, "Lumber Trade Associations: Their Economic and Social Significance" (master's thesis, Temple University, 1951), 21; Fickle, *New South,* 7; Gates, "Federal Land Policy," 327; Hidy, Hill, and Nevins, *Timber and Men,* 305–7; U.S. Department of Commerce and Labor, Bureau of Corporations, *Standing Timber,* 40.

2. U.S. Department of Commerce and Labor, Bureau of Corporations, *Standing Timber,* 41, 62.

3. Ibid., 46–47. For more information on Doyle and Scribner, see Harold C. Belyea, "A Postscript on the Lost Identity of Doyle and Scribner," *Journal of Forestry* 51 (May 1953): 326–29. For a good description of the cruising methods of the well-known southern forestry consulting firm of Pomeroy and McGowan during the 1930s and 1940s, see Zebulon W. White, interview by author, May 17, 1991.

4. U.S. Department of Commerce and Labor, Bureau of Corporations, *Standing Timber,* 48–49.

5. James Boyd, "Fifty Years," 60.

6. U.S. Department of Commerce and Labor, Bureau of Corporations, *Standing Timber,* xvii, xix.

7. Ibid., xxi, xxii.

8. Ibid., 1, 65, 26.

9. Ibid., 186, 188, 195–96. James Boyd's figures on the amount and prices of stumpage in the South during the late nineteenth and early twentieth centuries are derived from U.S. Census reports, the Bureau of Corporations report, and compilations by the Yellow Pine Manufacturers' Association, the Southern Pine Association, the *American Lumberman,* and other sources ("Fifty Years," 60–61).

10. U.S. Department of Commerce and Labor, Bureau of Corporations, *Standing Timber,* 36, 38. This sentiment would certainly have been endorsed by M. A. Dees, the editor of the *Pascagoula (Mississippi) Chronicle Star,* whose family had a background in the lumber business. In 1893 Dees published a historical overview of the lumber industry along the Gulf Coast that was basically a chronicle of all of those who had failed in trying to make a living out of sawmilling. Dees concluded that these people would have been better off if they had left the timber standing and wound up with a sad epitaph: "But why should I continue to recount failures. It is plain that we have only to think of any saw mill and finally find it a failure. These failures were not because our mill men have been poor business men. Our mill men as a rule, have been of the best. . . . It would seem that all mill men's worldly creed should be; 'Eat, drink and be merry, for to-morrow we are busted'" ("A Retrospective View of Our Saw Mill Business," *Pascagoula (Mississippi) Chronicle Star,* November 20, 1893, typewritten extract by

Harry H. McDonald Sr., copy in William Colvin Files, MFC).

11. U.S. Department of Commerce and Labor, Bureau of Corporations, *Standing Timber,* 11, 74–75, 77, 183.

12. Ibid., 11, 75–76.

13. Ibid., 284, 32.

14. Ibid., 11, 16, 21, 24, 28, 36.

15. Ibid., 109, 121, 154.

16. Ibid., 35.

17. Ibid., 35–36.

18. Ibid., 278–79; *American Lumberman,* February 15, 1902, July 13, 1907.

19. U.S. Department of Commerce and Labor, Bureau of Corporations, *Standing Timber,* 79–80, 82, 88–92.

20. Ibid., 35, 4.

21. A. M. Muckenfuss, "The Development of Manufacturing in Mississippi," *Mississippi Historical Society Publications* 10 (1903): 164–65.

22. Asa S. Williams, "Logging by Steam," *Forestry Quarterly* 6 (March 1908): 1–4; Michael Williams, *Americans and Their Forests,* 216. For a brief description of railroad logging, see Thomas Caldwell Croker Jr., *Longleaf Pine: A History of Man and a Forest,* Forestry Report R8-FR 7 (Washington, D.C.: U.S. Department of Agriculture, Forest Service, Southern Region, 1987), 11. See also John E. Hyler, "Log Handling: Historical and Present Skidding Practices," *Southern Lumberman* (December 15, 1956): 60, 64, 66, 68, 70. Hyler has some material on early skidding practices and machinery, although he focuses on the period following the age of steam skidding. A recent work is Ken Drushka and Hannu Konttinen, *Tracks in the Forest: The Evolution of Logging Machinery* (n.p.: Timberjack Group, 1997). For an example of the floating operations, see Zollie O. Bourne, interview by Bobbie Jean Dickinson, March 14, 1990, MFA Records, 8–9; Jimmy W. Cox, "Production Line: Ever Seen a 'Floating Sawmill?'" *Columbia (Mississippi) Columbian Progress,* March 31, 1990, copy in MFA Records; and Charles S. Jordan Jr., interview by Bobbie Jean Dickinson, March 14, 1990, MFA Records. These sources describe a floating mill constructed in 1910 that worked along the Pearl River until 1917.

23. Asa S. Williams, "Logging by Steam," 5.

24. Ibid., 5–6.

25. Ibid., 6.

26. Ibid., 6–8.

27. Ibid., 9–11, 15.

28. Ibid., 22, 24–28.

29. Ibid., 29.

30. Wilson Compton, "Forestry under the Free Enterprise System," *American Forests* 66 (August 1960): 51; Greeley, *Some Public and Economic Aspects,* 14–16; Robbins, *American Forestry,* 31–33; Harold K.

Steen, *The U.S. Forest Service: A History* (Seattle: University of Washington Press, 1976), 112–13.

31. *From Tree to Trade,* 12.

32. Curtis, "Early Development," 34. J. R. Weston, "History of Forestry in Southwest Mississippi," Mississippi Department of Archives and History, Jackson (hereafter cited as MDAH); Winifred C. Turner, "The Industrial Folly," *Southern Conservationist* (April 1939), unpaginated typescript copy in MFC Files. Edward Hines was elected president of the National Lumber Manufacturers' Association in 1909. The Edward Hines Lumber Company fit the stereotypical pattern of the lumber industry, because it moved south as the northern woods were cut over and then moved on to the West Coast after depleting the Mississippi forests. For a laudatory account of Hines's life and career until 1909, see *American Lumberman* (July 24, 1909): 1, 42–43.

33. N. F. McGowin, "Private Forestry in the South," in *Proceedings of the Golden Anniversary Meeting of the National Lumber Manufacturers' Association at St. Louis, Missouri* (Washington, D.C.: National Lumber Manufacturers' Association, 1952), 49; James Boyd, "Fifty Years," 66; P. N. Howell, "Early Timber Operations Defended by P. N. Howell," *Conservation News* (November 17, 1948): n.p., copy in MDAH; Michael Williams, *Americans and Their Forests,* 280. By the 1960s the Edward Hines Lumber Company again had mills in Mississippi, and on the company's seventy-fifth birthday in 1967 an advertising department news release credited Hines as a pioneer in sustained-yield forest management. According to the release, after World War I, "Edward Hines was about to realize his life-long dream of no longer treating lumber as a resource to be 'mined,' but as a crop for harvesting season after season. As early as 1920, he had stated, 'There is no good reason why reforestation cannot be undertaken, and the lumber business be made as perpetual in America as the growing of wheat.'" Hines put his ideas into operation in the Ponderosa pine stands in and around the Malheur National Forest in Oregon in 1928. Said the company release, "The multiple-use forest came into being permitting wildlife to flourish, creating recreational opportunities for today and tomorrow, and offering a sustained harvest of the finest lumber. Oregon soon became the leading lumber-producing state and Hines made a solid contribution to woodland conservation" ("Forest to Factory to You, Edward Hines Lumber Co., Seventy-Fifth Year," news release, FHS).

34. James Boyd, "Fifty Years," 66.

35. Charles S. Keith, "The Trust Question as Relating to the Lumber Industry," in *The American Lumber Industry: Official Report, Tenth Annual Convention, National Lumber Manufacturers' Association* (Chicago: National Lumber Manufacturers' Association, 1912),

92; Michael Williams, *Americans and Their Forests,* 230, 129.

36. Asa S. Williams, "Logging by Steam," 30.

37. Nelson White Sr., interview by Leigh Ann Smith, April 1, 1991, in *Timber Industry in the Great Depression,* 410–11.

38. James Boyd, "Fifty Years," 66; Howell, "Early Timber Operations," n.p.; Croker, *Longleaf Pine,* 11.

39. Clark, *Greening,* 4; *Hattiesburg American,* July 4, 1976, n.p., clipping in William Colvin Files, MFC. Wilson Compton, longtime general manager of the National Lumber Manufacturers' Association, later remembered that "the larger sawmills were moving from one region to another like threshing machines through fields of ripe wheat" ("Forestry," 51).

40. McGowin, "Private Forestry," 46–47; Gavin Wright, *Old South, New South: Revolutions in the Southern Economy since the Civil War* (New York: Basic Books, 1986), 161. For a discussion of efforts to sell cutover lands for agricultural use, see Fickle, *New South,* 243–45.

41. Jeff D. Hughes Jr., interview by author, August 1989; Zebulon White, interview; J. Walter Myers Jr., *Opportunities Unlimited: The Story of Our Southern Forests* (Chicago: Illinois Central Railroad Agricultural Department, 1950), 66.

42. Nollie Hickman says that Henry Weston and his sons and the L. N. Dantzler Company were exceptions to the rule, being "especially sensitive to the welfare of their employees" and "paternalistic in its policies," respectively (*Mississippi Harvest,* 234). Other owners and companies undoubtedly also treated their employees better than did most firms.

43. Hickman, *Mississippi Harvest,* 235, 240, 242–43, 246–49; Annie Louise D'Olive, "Reminiscences of Ten Mile: A South Mississippi Saw Mill Town," *Journal Of Mississippi History* 39 (May 1977): 176; Weston, "Sunken Logs," 84; Silver, "Paul Bunyan," 107–9; Hickman, "Logging and Rafting Timber," 162; Nollie W. Hickman, "Black Labor in Forest Industries of the Piney Woods, 1840–1933," in *Mississippi's Piney Woods: A Human Perspective,* ed. Noel Polk (Jackson: University Press of Mississippi, 1986), 87.

44. D'Olive, "Reminiscences," 173–74; Hickman, "Lumber Industry," 220–21; Hodge, "Lumber Industry," 372; Hickman, *Mississippi Harvest,* 240–42, 245–47; Hickman, "Black Labor," 86. A resident of Dushau, a Gilchrist-Fordney logging camp about sixty miles north of Laurel, remembered the "quarter" where the black people lived: "I do not know much about the this section of town as I was never allowed to go there" (Elise Graham, "Dushau Days," typewritten manuscript in Lauren Rogers Museum of Art, Laurel, Miss., 3).

45. Hickman, *Mississippi Harvest,* 245–46; D'Olive, "Reminiscences," 173.

46. Silver, "Paul Bunyan," 109; Hickman, *Mississippi Harvest,* 241–42.

47. Hickman, "Lumber Industry," 221; Hickman, *Mississippi Harvest,* 241–43; Dees, "Retrospective View."

48. Hickman, *Mississippi Harvest,* 244–45.

49. Asa S. Williams, "Logging by Steam," 29.

50. R. H. Price to P. A. Bloomer, June 10, 1919, Louisiana Long Leaf Lumber Company Records, Louisiana State Archives, Baton Rouge (hereafter cited as 4L Records), box 12. For a discussion of labor conditions and developments in the southern pine industry during World War I and into the mid-1920s, see James E. Fickle, "Management Looks at the 'Labor Problem': The Southern Pine Industry during World War I and the Postwar Era," *Journal of Southern History* 40 (February 1974): 61–76.

51. Hickman, *Mississippi Harvest,* 234–38; Hickman, "Black Labor," 82–83.

52. Hickman, *Mississippi Harvest,* 239–40.

53. For information on the operators' association and on labor troubles bordering on Mississippi, see Curtis, "Early Development," 347–68; Amy Quick, "The History of Bogalusa, the 'Magic City' of Louisiana" (master's thesis, Louisiana State University, 1942); Huey Latham Jr., "A Comparison of Union Organization in Two Southern Paper Mills" (master's thesis, Louisiana State University, 1962); Fickle, "Management Looks at the 'Labor Problem, '" 62–63, 72–73; and Stephen H. Norwood, "Bogalusa Burning: The War against Biracial Unionism in the Deep South, 1919," *Journal of Southern History* 63 (August 1997): 591–628; Southern Lumber Operators' Association to members, April 8, 1922, 4L Records, box 15. Much of the material concerning the Southern Lumber Operators' Association and its subscribers is included in an article by James E. Fickle entitled "Comfortable and Happy? Louisiana and Mississippi Lumber Workers, 1900–1950," *Louisiana History* 40 (fall 1999): 407–32.

54. Southern Lumber Operators' Association to members, November 28, May 5, June 28, 1923, 4L Records, box 16.

55. Elwood R. Maunder, "Go South, Young Man: An Interview with J. E. McCaffrey," *Forest History* 8 (winter 1965): 6–7.

56. "Report on the Exodus of South's Negro Labor," and "Labor Report for Mr. Berckes, June 15, 1923," both in Southern Pine Association Records, Louisiana State University Archives, Baton Rouge (hereafter cited as SPA Records), box 93a; C. H. Lewis Jr., "Crosby Lumber Company . . . as I Remember: Sept. 1939 thru April 1941," MFA Records, 8; Gavin Wright, *Old South, New South,* 162.

57. Silver, "Paul Bunyan," 108, 107; Hickman, "Lumber Industry," 222.

58. D'Olive, "Reminiscences," 175–76; Weston, "Sunken Logs," 84; Hickman, "Black Labor," 84; Al Brown, "This I Remember," *Gulf Coast Lumberman* 1 (November 1963): 28.

59. Kenneth L. Smith, *Sawmill,* 136–37; D'Olive, "Reminiscences," 176–77.

60. Weston, "Sunken Logs," 84; Silver, "Paul Bunyan," 101–2; Hickman, "Logging and Rafting Timber," 160–61. The quotation is from *From Tree to Trade,* 9–12. The information concerning the terms for woods workers is from Ruth A. Allen, *East Texas Lumber Workers: An Economic and Social Picture, 1870–1950* (Austin: University of Texas Press, 1961), 38; Mayor, *Southern Timberman,* 38–41, 241; *Forestry Terminology: A Glossary of Technical Terms Used in Forestry* (Washington, D.C.: Society of American Foresters, 1950), 33; John Reed Tarver, "The Clan of Toil: Piney Woods Labor Relations in the Trans-Mississippi South, 1880–1920" (Ph.D. diss., Louisiana State University, 1991), 1:1; and Whiteford L. Baker, *Eastern Forest Insects,* U.S. Department of Agriculture, Forest Service Miscellaneous Publication 1175 (Washington, D.C.: U.S. Government Printing Office, 1972), 203. The "flatheads" were named for the flatheaded beetle, or sawyer beetle, that laid eggs in or under the bark when a pine tree was cut. The eggs hatched white grubs with a flat brown head that cut out the inner bark of the tree and ate it. Since both the grub and the man cut pine, both were "flatheads," according to Allen. Tarver, citing Baker, says that the sawyer beetle made a noise that resembled that of the drag teeth of a two-man crosscut saw bucking pine logs. The suggestions for the implementation of "scientific management" are from Edward A. Braniff, "Scientific Management and the Lumber Business. A Possible Field for Foresters," *Forestry Quarterly* 10 (1912): 9–14. Another writer in the same journal suggested that "scientific management" could be used to improve the performance of foresters in the U.S. Forest Service (see Karl W. Woodward, "The Application of Scientific Management to Forestry," *Forestry Quarterly* 10 [1912]: 407–16). For a description and evaluation of Taylorism, or scientific management, see Glenn Porter, *The Rise of Big Business, 1860–1920,* 2d ed. (Arlington Heights, Ill.: Harlan Davidson, 1992), 106–8; Bourne, interview, 4–5. For a firsthand description of the work of a log scaler and loggers for the Crosby Lumber Company in the late 1930s, see C. H. Lewis Jr., "Crosby Lumber Company," 8–9.

61. Carl McIntire, "Lumber Camp Towns Lived with Tragedy," *Jackson (Mississippi) Clarion-Ledger,* October 28, 1979. A similar account from a Gilchrist-Fordney logging camp appears in Graham, "Dushau Days," 18.

62. Asa S. Williams, "Logging by Steam," 29, Luther Wade, interview by Bobbie Jean Dickinson, May 19, 1989, MFA Records; McIntire, "Lumber Camp Towns." The Wade interview also contains information about logging camps, commissaries, and other details of life and work in the early logging business.

63. Hickman, "Lumber Industry," 222; Hickman, *Mississippi Harvest,* 251; Gavin Wright, *Old South, New South,* 161. Wright says that the logging camps were "isolated, temporary affairs" and quotes a source who says that the great majority of the workers were "single, homeless, and possessionless." McIntire, "Lumber Camp Towns," contains reminiscences and descriptions by residents of the Eastman-Gardiner Lumber Company logging camps of Cohay I and Cohay II, the Great Southern Lumber camp in Copiah County between Rockport and Stronghold, the Wisner camp, the Brady camp south of Summerland, and Guitano in Jones County. Contrary to Wright's source, the inhabitants of many logging camps included women and children.

64. Hodge, "Lumber Industry," 373; Hickman, *Mississippi Harvest,* 251–52. For a description of a Gilchrist-Fordney camp, see Graham, "Dushau Days," 1–3.

65. Silver, "Paul Bunyan," 104.

66. Ibid., 106.

67. Ibid., 107.

68. Hodge, "Lumber Industry," 374–75. See also Higgs, "Eastman, Gardiner."

69. D'Olive, "Reminiscences," 176; For an account of early-twentieth-century life in three small south Mississippi sawmill towns—Richton in Perry County, Clyde in Lamar County (a company town), and Avera in Greene County—see "Forest History by George Huff McBride, Ellisville, Mississippi," January 11, 1990, MFA Records. Some sawmill workers and their families moved from town to town to find employment. One sawmill town resident remembered living in Stevenson (Foster Creek Lumber Company); Lumberton (Hinton Brothers Lumber Company); Meehan Junction (Cotton State Lumber Company); Lyman (Ingram Day Lumber Company); Fernwood (Fernwood Lumber Company); Garyville, Louisiana (Lyons Lumber Company); Bogalusa, Louisiana (Great Southern Lumber Company); Louisville, Mississippi (Fair Lumber Company); Picayune (Crosby Lumber Company); Quitman (Long-Bell Lumber Company); Golden (Golden Lumber Company); Gloster (Will Robinson Lumber Company); Bruce (Fair Lumber Company); and Wiggins (Finkbine Lumber Company). Her father also worked in D'Lo, Lake, Electric Mills, and Bude while the family lived in Biloxi. The interview contains descriptions of some of the sawmill towns, of "snaking" logs out of the woods with mules and oxen, and of naval-stores operations in south Mississippi (Mrs. O. M. Smith [Alice Blanche Seale], interview by Bobbie Jean Dickinson, May 12, 1989, MFA Records).

70. D'Olive, "Reminiscences," 174–75.

71. Sargent, *Report,* 531; Rowland, *History of Mississippi,* 2:545.

72. Croker, *Longleaf Pine,* 11; *The South's Fourth Forest: Alternatives for the Future,* Forest Resources Report 24 (Washington, D.C.: U.S. Department of Agriculture, Forest Service, 1988), 32–33. *Naval stores* refers to tar, pitch, resin, and turpentine. The term is derived from the time when wooden vessels were caulked with pine tar and pitch. Resin and turpentine are distilled from gum extracted from pine trees and combined with other chemicals used in the production of adhesives, carbon paper, gasoline additives, lubricants, inks, and detergents. For a brief account of the industry in Mississippi, see Art Nelson, "Naval Stores: A Forgotten Era in Mississippi's Forest History," *Tree Talk* 16 (summer 1994): 30. For the history of one family active in Mississippi's naval-stores business during much of the first half of the twentieth century, see Albert M. Joyner, interview by Bobbie Jean Dickinson, November 28, 1988, MFA Records. Another recollection by a woman who worked in the industry is Helen McDaniel, interview by Bobbie Jean Dickinson, March 15, 1990, MFA Records. See also Croker, "Longleaf Pine Story," 35–37; and Carroll B. Butler, *Treasures of the Longleaf Pines: Naval Stores* (Shalimar, Fla.: Tarkel Publishing, 1998).

73. Croker, *Longleaf Pine,* 11; Hickman, "Black Labor," 87–89. For the history of the Newton Naval Stores Company of Wiggins, the Newton family, and a description of the work and processes involved in manufacturing naval stores, see J. B. Newton, interview by Bobbie Jean Dickinson, December 13, 1988, MFA Records. See also "A Veteran of the Naval Stores Industry: For Fifty-Five Years Mr. J. B. Newton Has Been Actively at Work in It," *Savannah Weekly Naval Stores Review and Journal of Trade* (1927): 12, clipping in MFA Records.

74. "Southern Pine and Total Lumber Production—1869 to Latest Available Year," report, Southern Forest Products Association, New Orleans, SPA Records.

75. *Lumber Trade Journal* 67 (November 15, 1915): 19; Hickman, "Lumber Industry," 222–23.

76. Hickman, "Lumber Industry," 220; James Street, *Look Away! A Dixie Notebook* (New York: Viking, 1936), 114–15, quoted in John H. Napier III, "Piney Woods Past: A Pastoral Elegy," in *Mississippi's Piney Woods: A Human Perspective,* ed. Noel Polk (Jackson: University Press of Mississippi, 1986), 22. In 1924 one Louisiana sawmill town was relocated to Arizona amid large stands of virgin western pine (H. H. Chapman, "Why the Town of McNary Moved: A Tragedy of the Southern Pines and a Parallel Which Carries Its Own Lesson," *American Forestry* 30 [October 1924]: 589–92, 626). A 1937 Mississippi Forestry Commission report referred to these "[a]bandoned sawmills with their accompanying 'relief roll' villages" (*The Forest Situation in Mississippi* [Jackson: Mississippi Forestry Commission in Cooperation with U.S. Forest Service, 1937, copy in MFC Files], 5).

77. William Faulkner, *Light in August* (1932; New York: Modern Library, 1950), 4; William Faulkner, "The Bear," in *"Go Down Moses" and Other Stories* (London: Chatto and Windus, 1942), 227–29.

78. D'Olive, "Reminiscences," 184. For life in the Central Lumber Company's Mississippi sawmill towns and in the town of D'Lo, see Wolfkiel, "Towns," 7–12.

79. C. V. Clarke, "Looking Backward," *The Conservationist* (August 1940): n.p., typewritten copy in William Colvin Files, MFC.

80. *Voices from the South: Recollections of Four Foresters* (Santa Cruz, Calif.: Forest History Society, 1977), 38.

Chapter 6

1. "The Lumber Industry Speaks," *Journal of Forestry* 37 (November 1929): 759.

2. J. B. White, "Lumbermen and Conservation," *American Forestry* 19 (April 1913): 259; "Is Forestry Practical?" *American Forestry* 17 (July 1911): 425–26.

3. *Voices,* 97; Jonathan Daniels, *The Forest Is the Future* (New York: International Paper Company, 1957), 7.

4. C. B. Sweet, "Long-Bell Experimental Farm," *American Forestry* 18 (October 1912): 668; *From Tree to Trade,* 15; Fickle, *New South,* 243–44. A 1944 Illinois Central Railroad publication described the Southern Settlement and Development Organization as "a railroad agency" (*Southern Forestry,* 4). See also "State-Wide Activities of a State-Wide Organization, Mississippi Landowners Association," SPA Records, box 37B. The cover of this pamphlet lists the organization's objectives as better living conditions, better schools, farm ownership, better roads, enlargement of the livestock industry, propagation of grass and forage crops, extensive drainage, utilization of Mississippi's 20 million acres of idle land, and land settlement.

5. *From Tree to Trade,* 46; Joseph S. Weston to Steve Corbitt, July 10, 1997, copy in possession of author.

6. Fickle, *New South,* 243–45; John C. Barber, "Forestry in the Midsouth," *Journal of Forestry* 74 (August 1976): 505–6; Philip C. Wakeley, "F. O. ('Red') Bateman: Pioneer Silviculturalist," *Journal of Forest History* 20 (April 1976): 93; Lucile Kane, "Selling Cut-Over Lands in Wisconsin," *Business History Review* 28 (September 1954): 236–48; "Good Forests or Bad Farms?" *American Forests and Forest Life* 21 (December 1925): 740.

7. L. K. Pomeroy, "Applications of German Forestry to Conditions in the South," *Journal of Forestry* 30 (January 1935): 16–19; Warren B. Bullock, "Paper and Pulp Mills' Industrial Forestry Program," *Southern Pulp and Paper Manufacturer* (January 11, 1960): 46. For the story of forestry in the South, see Laurence C. Walker, *Southern Forest,* 170–226.

8. Robert Pogue Harrison, *Forests: The Shadow of Civilization* (Chicago: University of Chicago Press, 1992), 121–23; Clark, "Impact of the Timber Industry," 162. The Forest History Society has recently reissued Schenck's history of the Biltmore Forest School. See Carl Alwyn Schenck, *Cradle of Forestry in America: The Biltmore Forest School, 1898–1913,* ed. Ovid Butler, intro. Steven Anderson (Durham, N.C.: Forest History Society in cooperation with the Cradle of Forestry in America Interpretive Program and the Forest Service History Program, 1998).

9. *Voices,* 1–3.

10. George Perkins Marsh, *Man and Nature; or, Physical Geography as Modified by Human Action* (New York: Scribner, 1864); Henry Clepper, *Professional Forestry in the United States* (Baltimore: Johns Hopkins University Press for Resources for the Future, 1971), 14–15; Thomas R. Cox, Robert S. Maxwell, Phillip Drennon Thomas, and Joseph J. Malone, *This Well-Wooded Land: Americans and Their Forests from Colonial Times to the Present* (Lincoln: University of Nebraska Press, 1985), 144–46; Thomas R. Cox, "The Stewardship of Private Forests: The Evolution of a Concept in the United States, 1864–1950," *Journal of Forest History* 25 (October 1981): 188. See also Callicott, "Brief History," 16–17. For a brief treatment of Marsh, see Arthur A. Ekirch Jr., *Man and Nature in America* (New York: Columbia University Press, 1963), 70–80.

11. Clark, *Greening,* 42; John C. Shideler and Robert L. Hendricks, "The Legacy of Early Ideas of Conservation: Tracing the Evolution of a Movement," *Journal of Forestry* 89 (October 1991): 21–23; Sally K. Fairfax, "Riding into a Different Sunset: The Sagebrush Rebellion," *Journal of Forestry* 79 (August 1981): 516–17; Samuel P. Hays, *Conservation and the Gospel of Efficiency: The Progressive Conservation Movement, 1890–1920* (1959; New York: Atheneum, 1969), 261–76. See also Callicott, "Brief History," 16–17. For an interesting overview of the rise of forestry and of the forest-products industries, see Compton, "Forestry," 26–27, 50–54. Compton was the longtime general manager of the National Lumber Manufacturers' Association, and his remembrances of his dealings with Pinchot are revealing.

12. Thomas R. Cox, Maxwell, Thomas, and Malone, *Well-Wooded Land,* 184; Fickle, *New South,* 249–50; Char Miller, "Sawdust Memories: Pinchot and the Making of Forestry History," *Journal of Forestry* 92 (February 1994): 9. See also Martin Nelson McGeary, *Gifford Pinchot, Forester-Politician* (Princeton: Princeton University Press, 1960); and T. H. Watkins, "Father of the Forests," *Journal of Forestry* 90 (January 1992): 12–15. Miller argues that Pinchot had the greatest influence in shaping the U.S. Forest Service as an indigenous American institution. Ben W. Twight thinks that Bernhard Fernow had the greater influence and modeled the agency on the Prussian model. See Ben W. Twight, "Bernhard Fernow and Prussian Forestry in America," *Journal of Forestry* 88 (February 1990): 21–25; Ben W. Twight, "'Fernow' Author Responds," *Journal of Forestry* 89 (March 1991): 25–27; and Char Miller, "The Prussians Are Coming! The Prussians Are Coming! Bernhard Fernow and the Roots of the USDA Forest Service," *Journal of Forestry* 89 (March 1991): 23–27, 42. A standard biography of Fernow is Andrew Denny Rodgers, *Bernhard Eduard Fernow: A Story of North American Forestry* (Princeton: Princeton University Press, 1951). See also Pomeroy, "Applications," 16–19; and Franz Heske, *German Forestry* (New Haven: Yale University Press, 1938).

13. Fred Gragg, interview by author, September 1, 1989.

14. Clark, *Greening,* 39.

15. Max Rothkugel, "Forest Management in Southern Pines," *Forestry Quarterly* 5 (March 1907): 1; *Voices,* 4–5; A. E. Wackerman, "Sustained Yield Forestry in the Southern Pine Region," *Journal of Forestry* 33 (March 1935): 231–36. Rothkugel reported on his experiences working for eighteen months as a forester for a lumber company logging loblolly pine and other species near Charleston, South Carolina. Fire prevention and control occupied most of his time, although he regarded hogs as "ten times worse than fire." For an overview of the development of forestry on private lands, including industrial forests, see Thomas R. Cox, "Stewardship," 188–96. The observations of a famous forester regarding the development of industrial forestry appear in David T. Mason, "Changing Economic Conditions and Forest Practices on Privately Owned Lands," *Journal of Forestry* 51 (November 1953): 803–8. Wackerman provides an excellent brief description of the development of sustained-yield operations in the southern lumber industry.

16. *Voices,* 7.

17. Clark, *Greening,* 10–11, 39–40. See also Sargent, *Report,* 530–36. Mohr prepared the section on the South for the 1880 census, and these pages cover Mississippi.

18. *Voices,* 41, 224; Henry Clepper, "Industrial Forestry in the South," *Forest Farmer* (August 1969): 13, clipping in General Files, International Paper Company, Dallas, Tex. (hereafter cited as IP Files). These files were broken up and placed in various other IP facilities in 1997. The standard source on Herty is Germaine M.

Reed, *Crusading for Chemistry: The Professional Career of Charles Holmes Herty* (Athens: University of Georgia Press, 1995).

19. Roy R. White, "Austin Cary, the Father of Southern Forestry," *Forest History* 5 (spring 1961): 3–4; *Voices,* 41. See also Roy Ring White, "Austin Cary and Forestry in the South" (Ph.D. diss., University of Florida, 1960).

20. *Voices,* 123–24.

21. Frank Heyward, *History of Industrial Forestry in the South: William B. Greeley Lectures in Industrial Forestry* (Seattle: University of Washington College of Forestry, 1958), 28.

22. *Voices,* 4, 5.

23. Clepper, *Professional Forestry,* 244–45; Heyward, *History of Industrial Forestry,* 33. The survey reported that Mississippi had 18,295,000 acres of forest and 31,290,000,000 board feet of merchantable timber, with loblolly and shortleaf pine representing the largest species category (Crews, comp., "Economic Report," 2; this report was prepared in 1936 for the State Planning Commission and the State Forestry Commission; the statistics on forests and timber are taken from the U.S. Forest Service).

24. *Voices,* 125–27.

25. Elwood R. Maunder and Elwood L. Demmon, "An Interview with Reuben B. Robertson, Trailblazing in the Southern Paper Industry," *Forest History* 5 (spring 1961): 7; *Champion Magazine* 8 (1981): 9, 37–40.

26. Franklin B. Hough, *Report upon Forestry,* vols. 1–3 (Washington, D.C.: U.S. Government Printing Office, 1878–80); Robert K. Winters, ed., *Fifty Years of Forestry in the U.S.A.* (Washington, D.C.: Society of American Foresters, 1950), 3; *South's Fourth Forest: Alternatives,* 39.

27. Thomas R. Cox, Maxwell, Thomas, and Malone, *Well-Wooded Land,* 194; *South's Fourth Forest: Alternatives,* 40. See also "State Forestry in the South," *Forest History* 16 (October 1972): 50–53.

28. Steen, *U.S. Forest Service,* 173; *South's Fourth Forest: Alternatives,* 41.

29. Winters, *Fifty Years of Forestry,* 4–5, 7; Clepper, *Professional Forestry,* 31–38, 124–26, 28; Henry Clepper, "The Ten Most Important Events in American Forestry," *American Forests* (October 1955): 53. For Biltmore, see also Harley E. Jolley, "The Cradle of Forestry: Where Tree Power Started," *Forest History Today* (1998): 18–20. For the New York State College of Forestry, see James Lassoie, Raymond Oglesby, and Peter Smallidge, "Roots of American Forestry Education: Trials and Tribulations at Cornell University," *Forest History Today* (1998): 21–25. For Yale, see Edith Nye Macmullen, "Planting the Seed: The Origins of the Yale Forest School," *Forest History Today* (spring 1999): 11–16. See also Henry Clepper, "The History of Forestry Education in America and the Problems of Writing It," in Society of American Foresters Records, Forest History Society, Durham, North Carolina (hereafter cited as SAF Records), box 167.

30. Winters, *Fifty Years of Forestry,* 9–12.

31. Clepper, *Professional Forestry,* 207–8. The *Journal of Forestry* publishes reports on the enrollments and number of graduates of U.S. forestry schools. These reports and earlier summary compilations cover the period since 1900. For representative examples, see Cedric H. Guise, "Statistics from Schools of Forestry for 1939: Degrees Granted and Enrollments," *Journal of Forestry* 38 (March 1940): 241–46; Cedric H. Guise, "Statistics from Schools of Forestry for 1945: Degrees Granted and Enrollments," *Journal of Forestry* 44 (February 1946): 110–14; Gordon D. Marckworth, "Statistics from Schools of Forestry for 1954: Degrees Granted and Enrollments," *Journal of Forestry* 53 (April 1955): 256–61; Gordon D. Marckworth, "Statistics from Schools of Forestry for 1965: Degrees Granted and Enrollments," *Journal of Forestry* 65 (March 1966): 178–84; and Ronald R. Christensen, "Forestry School Enrollment and Degrees Granted, 1971–1981," *Journal of Forestry* 81 (October 1983): 660–62.

32. *Voices,* 3; Richard Allen, interview by author, August 31, September 2, 1989.

33. Richard Allen, interview; Art Nelson, "Art, How'd You Get in This Business Anyway?" *Tree Talk* 19 (fall 1997): 50; A. W. Nelson Jr., "A Story Is to Be Told," *The Unit* 100 (March 1964): 5; Jean Firestone, "Art Nelson: A Shining Light for Forestry," *Forestry Forum* 6 (summer 1992): 22.

34. Weston, "History of Forestry," 3, 9; James W. Craig to Jason N. Kutack, July 5, 1988, MFA Records, box 50; Art Nelson, "Focus on Pioneer Forestry Consultants," *Tree Talk* 15 (summer 1993): 14; "The History of Forestry in Mississippi," unpublished manuscript in MFC Files, 24, 29. The authorship of this manuscript is cloudy. Some Forestry Commission employees say it was begun in the 1960s by MFC information specialist and pilot Bob Church and was continued for the next few years by several staff members. From 1975 until 1984 it was written by William Colvin, the MFC's information and education director. All copy was approved by the state foresters who served during the period covered by the document. However, materials in the Dick Allen File of the MFA Records indicate that the portion covering the years from 1926 through 1971 was done by Church and the period from 1972 through 1982 by longtime MFC secretary Bobbie Jean Dickinson. Most of the H. Weston Lumber Company records, including company materials and family papers, are in the Special Collections, J. D. Williams Library, University of Mississippi, Oxford. Most of the early materials were destroyed in a fire at the north mill, company offices, and

store at Logtown on October 26, 1900. From 1912 on the records are fairly complete. By the late 1940s the company's operations had virtually ceased, and in the early 1950s the holdings were sold to IP (Joseph S. Weston to Steve Corbitt, July 10, 1997, copy in possession of author; "H. Weston Lumber Company," description of the Weston Lumber Company Records).

35. Weston, "History of Forestry," 8–9; Ray M. Conarro, *The Beginning: Recollections and Comments* (n.p.: U.S. Forest Service, Southern Region, 1989), 8; "History of Forestry in Mississippi," 2–3.

36. Pittman, "Mississippi's Forests of Yesteryear," 25; Arthur W. Nelson Jr., "Posey Howell: Mississippi's First Forester," *Tree Talk* 9 (fall 1987): 9; J. E. Bryan Jr., "Forest History," 11, MFA Records. For an excellent photograph of Posey Howell and a slightly different version of the wild hog story, see "The Father of Mississippi Forestry," in *The Great Southern Tree Crop: A Report to the People of the South for the Year 1947—by Southern Kraft Division of International Paper Company* (n.p.: IP, n.d., copy in MFA Records), 7.

37. Arthur W. Nelson Jr., interview by Wayne Flynt and Warren Flick, November 8, 1978, copy in possession of author; *Voices,* 128. Joseph E. McCaffrey, who was in charge of woodlands for the Southern Kraft Division of IP and who was a company vice president, tells a similar story. McCaffrey attended the New York Ranger School in 1915 and 1916 said that one of his professors told him, "The Southern pine region one day will have all the paper industry or a large portion of it. They've got climate, rainfall and soil. If I were you, I'd go South" (Maunder, "Go South, Young Man," 3).

38. R. D. Forbes, "Essential Requirements for the Practice of Forestry," in *Protection for Buyers of Pine: Annual Meeting Report of the Southern Pine Association, 1921* (New Orleans: Southern Pine Association, 1921), 155–56, copy in SPA Records, box 85B; Sargent, *Report,* 490.

39. William B. Greeley, "The Business of Growing Trees," in *A Decade of Service: Official Report of the Tenth Annual Meeting of . . . the Southern Pine Association . . . March 24 and 25, 1925,* 69, SPA Records; Thomas R. Cox, "Stewardship," 192; William G. Robbins, *Lumberjacks and Legislators: Political Economy of the U.S. Lumber Industry, 1890–1941* (College Station: Texas A&M University Press, 1982), 10–12, 17. In 1910 R. S. Kellogg of the U.S. Forest Service said, "The conservationist is no idle theorist. He believes in use, but not in abuse. Granted that the forest must be made of the greatest possible use, but that this use must not be destructive, that we may cut the trees from year to year, but that the forest must exist forever" ("Perpetuating the Timber Resources of the South," *American Forestry* 16 [January 1910]: 6). For a brief overview of the background and development of these pioneering efforts,

see Clepper, "Industrial Forestry," 12–14; and Barber, "Forestry," 505–11. For an overview of the management of U.S. industrial forests during the late nineteenth and early twentieth centuries, see Michael Williams, "Industrial Impacts," 108–21.

40. Fickle, *New South,* 242–43; *Proceedings of the Second Southern Forestry Congress* (Durham, N.C.: Seeman Printery, 1920), 70. For a brief description of the development of industrial forestry in the South, see *Southern Forestry,* 55–61. The forestry activities of Hardtner at Urania, the Great Southern in Louisiana, and Crossett in Arkansas are treated concisely in Robert S. Maxwell, "The Impact of Forestry on the Gulf South," *Forest History* 17 (April 1973): 31–35.

41. Clark, *Greening,* 55; Clark, "Impact of the Timber Industry," 161; Art Nelson, "Sustainable Forestry," *Tree Talk* 18 (spring 1996): 30.

42. Fickle, *New South,* 243, 246–47; Stanley Todd Lowry, "Henry Hardtner, Pioneer in Southern Forestry: An Analysis of the Economic Bases of His Reforestation Program" (master's thesis, Louisiana State University, 1956), 57–72. See also E. L. Demmon, "Henry Hardtner," *Journal of Forestry* (December 1955): 885–86. Hardtner was absolutely right in his recognition of the need to keep hogs out of the pine forests during the early years of growth. However, over the years it became generally recognized that grazing of cattle, sheep, and hogs in a commercial forest was feasible and desirable if properly managed. As the chief of the Division of Range Management for the U.S. Forest Service put it in the early 1950s, "Range livestock grazing is . . . a mixed blessing in southern forests. Grazing reduces the fire hazard and yields cash returns. . . . It has caused damage to tree reproduction mainly from hogs and sheep, and under some circumstances from cattle. . . . [R]esearch and experience during recent years have shown that integrated management is necessary. . . . The proper management of livestock is integrated with forest practices. Cattle grazing is preferred and is restricted to late spring and summer use, and numbers must be controlled to prevent damage to pine seedlings and to insure adequate animal nutrition. . . . Grazing use by hogs is not recommended until at least fifteen years after the establishment of a plantation" (Walt L. Dutton, "Forest Grazing in the United States," *Journal of Forestry* [April 1953]: 248–51). See also T. E. Maki and William F. Mann Jr., "Some Effects of Sheep Grazing on Longleaf Pine," *Journal of Forestry* (April 1951): 278–81.

43. Fickle, *New South,* 253; Clepper, *Professional Forestry,* 238; Clark, *Greening,* 57; Philip C. Wakeley, "The Adolescence of Forestry Research in the South," *Journal of Forest History* 22 (July 1978): 141–42. Charles Goodyear's book on Bogalusa mentions Hardtner's work at Urania but does not discuss Sullivan's trip

to inspect Hardtner's operations (*Bogalusa Story* [Buffalo, N.Y.: privately printed, 1950]). For another account of the activities of Hardtner, Great Southern, and other pioneering Louisiana forestry leaders, see Edward F. Kerr, "Louisiana's State Story, Part 1," *American Forests* (April 1953): 24–26, 55; and Edward F. Kerr, "Louisiana's State Story, Part 2," *American Forests* (May 1953): 22–24, 47. For a popular account of Great Southern, see Jerry L. Myrick, "History of the Great Southern Lumber Company," *Bogalusa (Louisiana) Daily News,* January 24–February 12, 1991. An illustrated contemporary description of the company and its Bogalusa facilities appears in "The Largest Lumber Manufacturing Proposition in the World," *American Lumberman* (July 4, 1908): 53–68. A good account of Great Southern's early years, including its reforestation efforts, appears in Curtis, "Early Development," 347–68. Curtis says that the Goodyears originally planned to build their mill on Ten Mile Creek near Columbia, Mississippi, but were deterred by difficulty in purchasing land and by the "more important" fact that "Mississippi laws prohibited the establishment of a corporation with real property value of more than one million dollars" (351–52).

44. P. M. Garrison, "Building an Industry on Cut-Over Land," *Journal of Forestry* 50 (March 1952): 185–87; Croker, *Longleaf Pine,* 12; Zebulon White, interview. A dibble is a spadelike tool used to prepare planting holes for seedlings. The blade is of heavy, sharp steel, about three or four inches wide, and about six inches long. The dibble is stuck in the ground, and when it is removed, the seedling is placed in the opening. Another dibble insertion presses the soil against the root. Hand planting was often done by crews, with a man operating the dibble and a boy placing the seedlings in the ground. Great Southern used crews of twenty with a foreman for each crew. The company would assign as many as fifteen to twenty crews to a job, and each crew could plant about forty acres a day, with roughly one thousand seedlings to each acre (Curtis, "Early Development," 365). Wakeley became employed by the Southern Forest Experiment Station in 1924 and was assigned to work at Bogalusa, where the station had centered its seed, nursery, and planting research. For his descriptions of the early planting efforts of Great Southern and of the station, see Philip C. Wakeley, "The Ups and Downs of Pioneer Planting Research in Louisiana—Problems in the Design and Analysis of Planting Trials," *Forestry Chronicle* 43 (June 1967): 135–44. For additional accounts of the Bogalusa story, see Paul M. Garrison and Thurman E. Bercaw, "The Gaylord Story, Part 1," *Forest Farmer* (November 1953): 8–9, 19–20, 26; Paul M. Garrison and Thurman E. Bercaw, "The Gaylord Story, Part 2," *Forest Farmer* (December 1953): 8–9, 18, 20; J. Harold Foil, "The

Gaylord Pine Plantation and Forestry Policy," *The Lumberman* (April 1950): 89; "The 100 Millionth Tree," *American Forests* (April 1954): 23; Erle Kauffman, "They Had Faith in the Land," *American Forests* (March 1950): 6–11; Philip C. Wakeley, "The South's First BIG Plantation," *Forests and People* (2d quarter 1973): 26–28, 30–31; Garrison, "Building an Industry," 185–87; Wakeley, "F. O. ('Red') Bateman," 91–99; and Vertrees Young, "History of Gaylord Plantations," *The Unit* (July 1952): 19–23. *The Unit* was a publication of the Southern Pulpwood Conservation Association. Another account, with a particular emphasis on what the author calls Bateman's "genius," appears in Wakeley, "Adolescence," 142–44.

45. Richard Allen, interview. For a brief description of the development of industrial forest management in the South and particularly the work of the early lumber companies and pulp and paper operations that pioneered in the adoption of enlightened practices, see William M. Bailey, "Industry's Effect on Forest Management," in *Proceedings, Society of American Foresters Meeting, Washington, D.C., 1960* (Washington, D.C.: Society of American Foresters, 1960). Bailey was an IP employee. Other materials dealing with Crossett include R. R. Reynolds, *The Crossett Story: The Beginning of Forestry in Southern Arkansas and Northern Louisiana,* General Technical Report SO-32 (New Orleans: U.S. Department of Agriculture, Forest Service, Southern Forest Experiment Station, 1980); S. V. Sihvonen, "Utilization—The Key to Better Forestry at Crossett," *Proceedings of the Society of American Foresters Meeting, "Forestry Faces Forward," Memphis, Tenn., 1956* (Washington, D.C.: Society of American Foresters, 1956), 138–41; James B. Baker, "The Crossett Farm Forestry Forties after Forty-One Years of Selection Management," *Southern Journal of Applied Forestry* 10 (November 1986): 233–37; R. R. Reynolds, "Twenty-Nine Years of Selection: Timber Management on the Crossett Experimental Forest," Research Paper SO-40 (New Orleans: U.S. Department of Agriculture, Forest Service, Southern Forest Experiment Station, 1969); R. R. Reynolds, "Eighteen Years of Selection: Timber Management on the Crossett Experimental Forest," Technical Bulletin 1206 (New Orleans: U.S. Department of Agriculture, Forest Service, 1959); and R. R. Reynolds, "Fifteen Years of Management on the Crossett Farm Forestry Forties," Occasional Paper 130 (New Orleans: U.S. Department of Agriculture, Forest Service, Southern Forest Experiment Station, 1953). For a brief overview of the pulp and paper industry's forestry activities from the time of its origins in the Northeast until the end of the 1950s, see Warren B. Bullock, "Paper and Pulp Mills' Industrial Forestry Program," 46, 48, 50, 52. See also Penna, *Nature's Bounty,* 38–39.

46. Weston, "History of Forestry," 1, 4.

47. Ibid., 2, 3.

48. "Preliminary Report of the Present Condition and Future Possibilities of the Holdings of the H. Weston Lumber Company, Logtown, Mississippi, Vitale and Rotherty Forest Engineers, June 12, 1923," 3, 20, 28–30, copy in Weston Lumber Company Records, box 29. In the area of fire protection, the report recommended keeping the timberlands in solid blocks to ease the problems of patrolling and reported that Great Southern found that it could patrol 100,000 acres with six men for six months at a cost of two thousand dollars. In 1926 Demmon, acting director of the Southern Forest Experiment Station, included the Weston Lumber Company and the Tatum Lumber Company of Hattiesburg on a "List of Lumber Companies Practicing Forestry" (E. L. Demmon to Shirley W. Allen, December 1, 1926, SAF Records, box 26).

49. Joseph S. Weston to Steve Corbitt, July 19, 1997, copy in possession of author; Weston, "History of Forestry," 5; *American Forestry* 28 (June 1920); "Resolution of the Board of Directors of the H. Weston Lumber Company, Logtown, Mississippi, August 16, 1933," Weston Lumber Company Records, box 42.

50. DeWeese, interview by Ryals, 357–58. An excellent source for the history of the DeWeese Lumber Company is DeWeese, interview by Edgerly. Among the interesting stories in this oral history is an account of how Ab DeWeese, the company founder, wrote a letter to the local newspaper in 1923 opposing the Ku Klux Klan at a time when the organization was very powerful (DeWeese, interview by Edgerly, 35). See also "Brief History of A. DeWeese Lumber Company, Inc., November 5, 1965," MFA Records.

51. DeWeese, interview by Ryals, 359, 361, 370–71. Tom DeWeese remembered that during the Great Depression his father divided up land among his employees and helped each of them build a house and barn. Tom said that his father died "with a safe full of unpaid notes and mortgages. . . . He would never foreclose on one of them" ("Forest History Project Traces Industry's Growth," *Tree Talk* 11 [spring 1989]: 21–22). Examining the records of many lumber companies and officials and the secondary accounts of some writers, it is easy to lose track of the fact that in some companies, genuine warm feelings existed between employees and employers and managers. In some cases company owners and officials, while often paternalistic, had real concern and affection for their employees. The DeWeese effort to help workers and keep the company operating during the Great Depression seems to be such an example. Some three decades later, ironically, in the same town, there was another. The Molpus Lumber Company of Philadelphia suffered a disastrous fire, and its facilities were badly underinsured. The company's

workers pitched in to help rebuild to salvage their jobs and to help the Molpus family. For the history of the Molpus Lumber Company see Dick Molpus, interview by Bobbie Jean Dickinson, October 11, 1988, MFA Records; and "Diversification Marks Molpus Progress Here," *Philadelphia (Mississippi) Neshoba Democrat,* August 6, 1981. For treatment of some aspects of the lumber industry and the Great Depression, see William G. Robbins, "The Great Experiment in Industrial Self-Government: The Lumber Industry and the National Recovery Administration," *Journal of Forest History* 25 (July 1981): 128–43; and Fickle, *New South,* 117–54.

52. "Crosby Lumber Company, Crosby, Mississippi, October 15, 1940," FHS; C. H. Lewis Jr., "Crosby Lumber Company," 10. Earlier, in the late 1920s, L. O. Crosby tried to rehabilitate his cutover lands by introducing new crops, including peaches, lemons, satsumas, and tung trees (L. O. Crosby Jr., *Crosby,* 14–15). See also "Chemurgy in Action: Tung— Mississippi's Newest Crop Blossom Time—April 1–20," *Mississippi Forest Facts* 2 (March 1943): 3. According to this article, tung oil was used in the manufacture of high-grade paints, enamels, varnishes, wallboard, linoleum, baking enamels, cement paints, plastics, drying salts, elastic products, flat coatings, glycerin compounds, insulating compounds, japans, lacquers, rustproof compounds, ink, vulcanizing compounds, lining for cans, waterproofing agents, concrete coatings, soaps, brake linings, tanning leather, and automobiles.

53. John M. Coates, *Masonite Corporation: The First Fifty Years* (New York: Masonite, USA, 1975), 2–11, 15, 26–27, 38–41. For brief versions of the Masonite story, see Hester, *Yesteryears,* 26–27; and *Southern Forestry,* 59. For an account of the process for producing Masonite, see William H. Mason, "Pulp and Board from Steam Exploded Wood," originally printed in *Paper Trade Journal* (February 24, 1927), copy in Business and Industry Records, Lauren Rogers Museum of Art, Laurel, Miss., box 3. The Rogers Museum also houses Mason's personal handwritten notebook or diary from the period he was developing his manufacturing process. Consulting forester Hall, based in Hot Springs, Arkansas, became a significant figure in Mississippi forest history. In addition to working with Masonite, in 1928 he was employed by the Sumter Lumber Company of Electric Mills to recommend the treatment of their cutover lands, and he suggested a program of fire protection, one of the first in that part of the state. He also worked with the group that prepared the outlines of the 1940 Timber Severance Tax Law, and he began the purchase of land and development of a forestry program for the Flintkote Company in the same year (Arthur W. Nelson Jr., "William L. Hall: A Pioneer Forester," *Forestry Forum* 8 [summer 1994]: 18–19).

54. *South's Fourth Forest: Alternatives*, 37. This material is from chap. 2 of the report, which was written by Dennis M. Roth, H. R. Josephson, and Harold K. Steen. One of the oldest, and at one time the largest, of Masonite's wood suppliers was the Richton Tie and Timber Company, owned by the Stevens family of Richton. For the story of the family and the company, see "The Stevens Way—The Right Way," *Gun Shots* (May 1947): 11–15; Ben M. Stevens Jr., interview by Bobbie Jean Dickinson, May 17, 1989, MFA Records. For the story of A. L. "Runt" Moser, a longtime Richton Tie and Timber Company employee, see the *Gun Shots* article and "A. L. Moser Forest History Questionnaire, March 23, 1989," in MFA Records. The Richton Tie and Timber Company, like many other southern pine lumber and pulpwood producers, utilized German prisoner-of-war laborers during World War II. For this story see Stevens, interview; and James E. Fickle and Donald W. Ellis, "POWs in the Piney Woods: German Prisoners of War in the Southern Lumber Industry, 1943–1945," *Journal of Southern History* 56 (November 1990): 695–724.

55. DeWeese, interview by Ryals, 362–63. For a description of the methods and technology of both logging and lumbering by the Crosby Lumber Company at the end of the 1930s, see C. H. Lewis Jr., "Crosby Lumber Company," 13–17. At the beginning of the 1990s at least one Smith County firm was still using horses in its logging operation. See Ed Brown, "Still Logging the Old-Fashioned Way," *Forestry Forum* 3 (winter 1989–90): 18. At about the same time, a man was still using mules to haul pulpwood from the logging sites to the wood yard around Louisville, Mississippi. See "Where There's a Will There's a Bill . . . and a Jenny, and a Jack, and a Maude," *Forestry Forum* 1 (December 1987): 14. One of the recurring problems in the woods was logging crews' tendency to leave higher stumps than the companies preferred, thus wasting timber. The reason for this practice was not surprising, for as a resident of an Eastman-Gardiner logging camp remembered, "It made a man quite stooped if he had to bend over all day long on a saw to leave a short stump" (McIntire, "Lumber Camp Towns").

56. Edgar Pope, interview by Judy Ryals, March 30, 1991, in *Timber Industry in the Great Depression*, 374; Southern Pine Association Release, May 29, 1945, copy in 4L Records, box 32.

57. Ernest Lamb, interview by Greg Williams, March 3, 1991, in *Timber Industry in the Great Depression*, 442; Arthur W. Nelson Jr., "The Development of Forest Practices in Mississippi and Louisiana in the Period 1940–1960," 16–17, unpublished paper revised and edited by James E. Fickle, copy in possession of author. For the twentieth-century development of logging technology, see Drushka and Konttinen, *Tracks in the Forest*. A work covering the same subject but with a geographical focus on eastern Canada is C. Ross Silversides and Richard A. Rajala, *Broadaxe to Flying Shear: The Mechanization of Forest Harvesting East of the Rockies* (Washington, D.C.: National Museum of Science and Technology, 1997).

58. *Forest Situation*, 8, 12; Richard C. Allen, interview by author, September 6, 1988, MFA Records, 16–17. The groundhog mills cut much of the lumber that was used for home building and other construction in rural areas. For the story of one of these operations in Walthall County, see "Groundhog Mills," *Forestry Forum* 3 (winter 1989–90): 20–21. For another of these small operations that ran in Neshoba County from the early twentieth century until about the 1930s, see Raymond Griffin, interview by Bobbie Jean Dickinson, May 4, 1989, MFA Records. Another small mill near Mize, the Cooley Brothers Lumber Company, cut the areas left by the bigger companies like Eastman-Gardiner that used railroad logging in the early twentieth century. For the story of this and similar companies, see W. L. Richardson, interview by Bobbie Jean Dickinson, May 19, 1989, MFA Records. P. N. Howell uses the term *pepper box sawmill* in "Forest Conservation vs. Forest Destruction in Mississippi," *Mississippi Forest Facts* (May 1947): 1, 4.

59. Olin Terrill Mouson, "The Social and Economic Implications of Recent Developments within the Wood Pulp and Paper Industry in the South" (Ph.D. diss., University of North Carolina, 1940), 104–13; Jack Porter Oden, "Development of the Southern Pulp and Paper Industry, 1900–1970" (Ph.D. diss., Mississippi State University, 1973), 1–25. See also Frank Colburn Bowler, *It Began with the Wasps!* (New York: Newcomen Society of England, American Branch, 1949). For an excellent brief discussion of the origins and technology of papermaking as well as the development of the industry in the United States until the beginning of the post–World War II era, see Joseph Otto Pecenka, "A Financial Analysis of Selected Major Pulp, Paper, and Paperboard Producers, 1947–1964" (Ph.D. diss., University of Illinois, 1967), 16–36. The technology of the kraft pulping process is discussed in Pede J. Kleppe, "The Process of, and Products from, Kraft Pulping of Southern Pine," *Forest Products Journal* 20 (May 1970): 50–59.

60. Quoted in Oden, "Southern Pulp and Paper Industry," 24; *South's Fourth Forest: Alternatives*, 71. For the early history of the industry in the South, see also Mouson, "Social and Economic Implications," 127–41; and H. J. Malsberger, "Seventy-Five Year History of the Wood-Pulp and Paper Industry in the South," *Southern Lumberman* (December 15, 1956): 182–84. The industry's origins in Alabama are discussed in Harry M. Roller Jr., "The Pulp and Paper Industry in the Southwest Al-

abama Forest Empire," *Journal of the Alabama Academy of Science* (January 1959): 67–72; and Sara Walls and William C. Vail, "Forty-five Years of Papermaking," *Forest Farmer* (November 1974): 10–11, 14–16. For a brief overview of the development of the pulp and paper industry in the South, see Art Nelson, "Pages from Art Nelson's Notebook: Cellulose, the Chemical That Grows," *Tree Talk* 19 (spring 1997): 30.

61. Oden, "Southern Pulp and Paper Industry," 23–24.

62. Ibid., 25. For an account of the Roanoke Rapids mill, see "Kraft Industry in United States Celebrates Fiftieth Birthday This Month," *Southern Pulp and Paper Manufacturer* (February 10, 1959): 22–23.

63. J. Finley McRae, *Paper Making in Alabama* (New York: Newcomen Society in North America, 1960), 1–10; Oden, "Southern Pulp and Paper Industry," 1–33; *International Paper Company after Fifty Years* (New York: International Paper Company, 1948), 66; C. F. Evans, "A Saga of Southern Pine; in Which Paper-Making and Forestry Are Seeking a Common Meeting Ground," *American Forests* 48 (September 1942): 404; A. W. Pesch, "An Example in Mississippi of How Science Has Aided in the Development of a Great Industrial Asset," *Journal of Mississippi Academy of Science* 4 (1948–50): 98–103; *South's Fourth Forest: Alternatives,* 71; "Moss Point IP Mill Is Still the Heart of Community—Making Paper and Friends," *Forestry Forum* 9 (fall–winter 1995): 18–20. For a description of the technology of the various papermaking processes, see Mouson, "Social and Economic Implications," 114–26.

64. W. L. McHale, "The Paper Industry and the Southland Mill," *Journal of Forestry* 50 (July 1952): 536–38; *This Is Champion: A Proud Name in American Industry* (Hamilton, Ohio: Champion Paper and Fibre Company, 1959), 55; *South's Fourth Forest: Alternatives,* 71. Earlier considerations of the feasibility of making newsprint from southern pine included those of the Great Southern Lumber Company of Bogalusa, Louisiana, during the 1920s. See "Memorandum of Conference Held at Office of Great Southern Lumber Company, New York City, N.Y., Wednesday, September 16, 1925," Weston Lumber Company Records, box 95. See also Jack P. Oden, "Charles Holmes Herty and the Birth of the Southern Newsprint Paper Industry, 1927–1940," *Journal of Forest History* 10 (April 1977): 76–89; and the chapter on the Southland mill in Reed, *Crusading for Chemistry,* 334–69.

65. Eleanor Amigo and Mark Neuffer, *Beyond the Adirondacks: The Story of St. Regis Paper Company* (Westport, Conn.: Greenwood Press, 1980), 135; Earl Porter, interview by Elwood R. Maunder and Joe Miller, October 1963, FHS, 49–52.

66. *South's Fourth Forest: Alternatives,* 71.

67. Oden, "Southern Pulp and Paper Industry," 66–68, 76, 91.

68. C. F. Evans, "Saga of Southern Pine," 404; Oden, "Southern Pulp and Paper Industry," 73–74.

69. *Voices,* 91–92. At the 1951 Biloxi meeting of the Society of American Foresters, Eldredge provided an excellent brief historical overview of the southern forests from the age of discovery through the arrival of the pulp and paper industry. See Inman F. Eldredge Sr., "Southern Forests, Then and Now," *Journal of Forestry* 50 (March 1952): 182–85. See also Barber, "Forestry," 505–11; and Croker, "Longleaf Pine Story," 32–43.

70. *Voices,* 92–93.

71. Maunder and Demmon, "Interview with Reuben B. Robertson," 12.

72. *South's Fourth Forest: Alternatives,* 72.

73. Oden, "Southern Pulp and Paper Industry," 99; Vertrees Young to Harry Malsberger, March 26, 1947; Malsberger to Young, March 31, 1947; "Memorandum," May 2, 1947, all in Southern Pulpwood Conservation Association Records in files of American Forest Council, Atlanta (hereafter cited as SPCA Records). For another contemporary view of the timber supply in the South and the needs of forest-products industries, see W. E. Bond, "The Integration of Forest Industries in the Southeastern United States," *Journal of Forestry* 36 (June 1938): 549–54.

74. Oden, "Southern Pulp and Paper Industry," 100–101; Mouson, "Social and Economic Implications," 223.

75. "Region within Mississippi That the Development of the Pulp and Paper Industry Is Possible," undated map with imprint of Mississippi State Planning Commission, copy in MFC Files; Oden, "Southern Pulp and Paper Industry," 102.

76. Oden, "Southern Pulp and Paper Industry," 102–4; Arthur W. Nelson Jr., "The South's Third Forest: Implications for the Future," speech presented for the S. J. Hall Lectureship in Industrial Forestry, April 13, 1976, University of California, Berkeley, College of Natural Resources, Department of Forestry and Resource Management, copy in possession of author; "Woodlands History, Final Draft (WGC)," 97, manuscript in IP Files. See also H. F. Smith, *Primary Wood-Products Industries in the Lower South,* Forest Survey Release 51 (New Orleans: U.S. Department of Agriculture, Forest Service, Southern Forest Experiment Station, 1940). For a description of the methodology and progress of the Southern Forest Survey, see I. F. Eldredge, "The Southern Forest Survey," Occasional Paper 31 (New Orleans: U.S. Department of Agriculture, Forest Service, Southern Forest Experiment Station, 1934). See also *Basic Data on Forest Area and Timber Volumes from the Southern Forest Survey, 1932–1936,* Forest Survey Release 54 (New Orleans: U.S. Department of Agriculture,

Forest Service, Southern Forest Experiment Station, 1946).

77. Oden, "Southern Pulp and Paper Industry," 105; W. J. Damtoft, "President's Annual Report," Southern Pulpwood Conservation Association, Fifth Annual Meeting, SPCA Records; C. F. Evans, "Saga of Southern Pine," 404–6; *South's Fourth Forest: Alternatives,* 73; "Paper Mills and Timber," *Southern Lumberman* (January 15, 1943): 26; "Woodlands History," 62–66; E. A. Sterling to J. W. Thompson, July 16, 1948, Johns Manville Records, box 16. Some companies' failure to join the SPCA in the early period may not have reflected any opposition to or disinterest in its conservation programs. The companies may have been motivated by the fact that one of the large SPCA member firms was operating under a consent decree involving alleged violations of federal wage and hours laws and that attorneys advised against close association with that company at that time.

78. Arthur W. Nelson Jr., "South's Third Forest"; "First Statement of the First President of the Southern Pulpwood Conservation Association to Its Directors, Officials, and Invited Guests," April 18, 1939, SPCA Records; Arthur W. Nelson Jr. to James E. Fickle, February 23, 1993, copy in possession of author; Zebulon White, interview. In the letter, Nelson says that the SPCA forestry effort "did more to get forestry practiced on the ground than any other program because it was associated with harvesting which did or would produce income. . . . This program, coupled with the efforts of others, effectively reversed timber depletion and led to enough new growth to support new pulp and paper mills. . . . This is the first time in man's long history that a declining resource trend has been reversed and turned around." The Jackie Davis books bore such titles as "How Does the Tree Crop Grow?" "Who Lives on the Forest Farm?" "How Trees Put the Rain to Work," "The Crop That Did Not Fail," "How Money Grows on Trees," "The Little Trees That Went to School," "The Trees That Are Marked for Market," and "How Money Goes Up in Smoke." The books were sixteen pages in length and seem rather primitive by the standards of today's publications, but in fact similar modern books for children such as Weyerhaeuser's 1991 "Forest Fun" and "Smokey Bear's Story of the Forest," issued by the U.S. Forest Service in 1977, are not much better. Copies in possession of author.

79. Richard Allen, interview. Dexter earned his forestry degree from the University of Montana in 1922 and later worked with both state and federal agencies and in the private sector. He later lived in Corinth and was actively involved in the formation of Tennessee River Pulp and Paper Company at Counce, Tennessee, which drew a lot of its pulpwood from north Mississippi. See "SAF Honors A. K. Dexter," *Tree Talk* 3 (sum-

mer 1980): 24. For an overview of forestry activities in the southern pulp and paper industry, see H. J. Malsberger, "The Pulp and Paper Industry in the South," *Journal of Forestry* 54 (October 1956): 639–42. An early contemporary view of the industry with interesting projections of its future importance appears in D. H. Killeffer, "Paper Goes South," *Industrial and Engineering Chemistry* 30 (October 1938): 1110–15.

80. "Woodlands History," 56. See also Frank Hayward Jr. to S. F. Horn, December 31, 1942; Frank Hayward Jr., "Room for All," 1941; and "Sterling and Heyward Refute Criticisms against Pulp Mills" (reprint from *Southern Lumber Journal* [December 1939]), all in SPCA Records.

81. *Voices,* 222; "Executive Committee Meeting, Southern Pulpwood Conservation Association, June 22, 1948," minutes in SPCA Records; "Paper Mills and Timber," 26.

82. Vertrees Young, "Problems and Opportunities Common to the Lumber and Pulp Industries," speech at the annual meeting of the Southern Pine Association, April 5, 1948, SPA Records. In the early days of the pulp and paper industry, stretching into World War II, there was another method of calculating the amount of pulpwood harvested. Loggers cutting pulpwood stacked five-foot-long logs into "pens" to a height of six feet. Four "pens" were considered a "cord," equaling 128 cubic feet. Five "pens" made up a "unit" of 160 cubic feet. "Cords" were commonly used in the North, where four-foot logs were the norm, and "units" were used in the South, where five-foot lengths were the norm. The increasing use of tree-length logging after the war generally ended "penning" (Art Nelson, "Pages from Art Nelson's Notebook," *Tree Talk* 17 [fall 1995]: 12; Fickle and Ellis, "POWs in the Piney Woods," 695–724).

83. A. M. Dantzler, interview, July 27, 1973, MDAH; "Woodlands History," 9.

84. "Instructions, Tables, Cutting Rules, and Specifications for the Cutting and Selling of Pulpwood," 3, report prepared by U.S. Forest Service and the Mississippi Agricultural Extension Service, March 1938, copy in Johns Manville Records, box 11; "Woodlands History," 61–62; E. A. Sterling to J. W. Thompson, July 16, 1948, Johns Manville Records, box 16.

85. *Voices,* 141, 144, 194; Arthur W. Nelson Jr., "Development of Forest Practices," 12; Louis T. Stevenson, "Southern Pulp and Paper Industry—1951 Model," *Thirteenth Annual Review Number* (October 1, 1951): 170.

86. Warren A. Flick, "From the Woods to the Mill," 1–2, paper in possession of author. For a detailed discussion of the wood-dealer system, see Warren A. Flick, "The Wood Dealer System in Mississippi: An Essay in Regional Economics and Culture," *Journal of Forest History* 10 (July 1985): 131–38. An excellent descrip-

tion of the mechanics and parameters of the pulpwood market in the late 1930s appears in "Instructions, Tables, Cutting Rules, and Specifications." For the experience of the Richton Tie and Timber Company as part of the wood-dealer, system see Stevens, interview.

87. Amigo and Neuffer, *Beyond the Adirondacks,* 86, 99–101, 136–37.

88. "Ten Years on the Flintkote Forest: The Story of the Development of the Forest from the Period 1941–1951," November 1952, Special Collections, Mitchell Memorial Library, Mississippi State University, Starkville; W. B. Greeley, "Industrial Forestry," in *Fifty Years of Forestry in the U.S.A.,* ed. Robert K. Winters (Washington, D.C.: Society of American Foresters, 1950), 249; "Reference and Excerpts Files for Fifteen-Year History of Association," SPCA Records.

89. Clepper, "Industrial Forestry," 13–14.

90. Ibid., 14. A. S. Todd Jr. and James G. Yoho argue that substantial progress in southern forestry did not occur until "the kraft paper mills began to spring up in the 1930's" ("Forestry in the Southern Economy," *Journal of Forestry* 60 [October 1962]: 703). Inman F. Eldredge Sr. argued that the movement of pulp- and papermakers into the South started "a surge in forestry" and noted that the industry purchased timberland "almost entirely from owners who had no intention of practicing forest management and . . . put this area under the care of professional foresters for continuous production" ("The Progress and Problems of Southern Forestry," *Journal of Forestry* 54 [October 1956]: 627–28).

91. Oden, "Southern Pulp and Paper Industry," 144, 173; John W. Thompson, "History of the Johns Manville Timberlands," 1–3. Upon retirement Thompson lived in Jekyll Island, Georgia, and became highly critical of the environmental attitudes and actions of the forest-products industry and professional foresters. An avid birdwatcher, Thompson became passionately involved in efforts to save the red-cockaded woodpecker and corresponded under the letterhead "Red-Cockaded Woodpecker Conservation." See Thompson correspondence in John Pete Switzer File, MFA Records. See also "A Few Interesting Items."

92. Oden, "Southern Pulp and Paper Industry," 177, 180–81.

93. "Board of Directors Meeting, Southern Pulpwood Conservation Association, April 30, 1952," minutes in SPCA Records; E. A. Sterling to J. W. Thompson, September 28, 1948; E. A. Sterling to D. R. Seip, August 3, 1948; John W. Thompson, "Forest Land Purchase—Mississippi," July 18, 1947; and John W. Thompson, "Timberland Acquisition," November 3, 1947, all in Johns Manville Records, box 16. Ernest A. Sterling was one of the earliest graduate foresters in the United States, earning his degree from the State University of

New York forestry school at Cornell in 1902. Sterling was a pioneering consulting forester, working for a time as the New York manager for the famous timberland trading and estimating firm James D. Lacey Company. He began working for Johns Manville in 1937, directing its timberland acquisition program in Virginia (John W. Thompson, "History of the Johns Manville Timberlands," 3).

94. "Timberland Acquisition at Natchez," October 18, 1948; E. A. Sterling, "Supplemental Comments on Natchez Pulpwood Resources," October 18, 1948; E.A.S. to J. W. Thompson, October 30, 1948; all in Johns Manville Records, box 16.

95. E. A. Sterling and John W. Thompson, "Summary of the Timberland and Pulpwood Situation at Natchez," May 12, 1948, Johns Manville Records, box 16; Fred Gragg, "An Explanation of Forest Landownership of Pulp and Paper Industry," *The Unit* 63 (May 1956): 25; Thomas J. Straka and James E. Hotvedt, "Timberland Ownership by Southern Companies," *Southern Pulp and Paper* (December 1984): 17–19.

96. *Problems and Criticisms Concerning Forest Land Ownership of Southern Pulp and Paper Industry and Proposed Plan of Action to Present Industry Facts* (Atlanta: Southern Pulpwood Conservation Association, 1957), 1, copy in SPCA Records.

97. *South's Fourth Forest: Alternatives,* 73; "1974 Was a Record Year for Pulpwood Production in the South," *Forestry News* 13 (March 1976): 4.

98. *Voices,* 57, 58.

99. John W. Thompson, "Comments on Item III of Report on Pulpwood Land—Jarrett and Natchez dated November 1, 1948," November 8, 1948; R. F. Bower, "Wood Procurement—Mississippi," August 12, 1946; and John W. Thompson to D. R. Seip, February 4, 1947, all in Johns Manville Records, box 16.

100. E. A. Sterling, "Memorandum for Mr. A. R. Fisher," August 10, 1948; and H. H. Howard Jr., "Pulpwood Situation, Sontag, Mississippi," March 15, 1948, both in Johns Manville Records, box 16; Maunder and Demmon, "Interview with Reuben B. Robertson," 12. The methodology of growing and selling pulpwood in the past and present is described in Flick, "Wood Dealer System," 131–38; Chris Bolgiano, "From Rags to No. 1: The Pulpwood Market in the 1980s," *American Forests* (January–February 1987): 16–19, 57–60; and A. I. Jeffords Jr., "Trends in Pine Pulpwood Marketing in the South," *Journal of Forestry* 54 (July 1956): 463–66.

101. Roller, "Pulp and Paper Industry," 70.

102. Conarro, *The Beginning,* 1–2. See also Don M. Bolinger, "For the People and by the People—Establishment of Our National Forests," *Tree Talk* 13 (summer 1991): 14–16. See also *Mississippi National Forests* (Jackson: U.S. Forest Service, Mississippi National Forests, [1935?], copy in MFA Records). In 1907 Presi-

dent Theodore Roosevelt established the first national forest east of the Great Plains. The Arkansas (Ouachita) National Forest contained a large area of shortleaf pine and was the first national effort to provide for the continuation of timber crops in the South (Barber, "Forestry," 507).

103. Conarro, *The Beginning*, 2–3; "History of Forestry in Mississippi," 14.

104. Conarro, *The Beginning*, 6; "Alton B. Farris, Sr. Autobiography," MFA Records, box 50. See also Frank A. Albert, "Rebuilding a Southern Forest," *Tree Talk* 14 (spring 1992): 18–19, 24, for a Forest Service description and assessment of the reforestation effort on the Bienville National Forest. Looking back on the situation many years later, Farris said, "In my humble opinion, the Forest Service is one agency of the Government that does a good job managing our forests and they are to be commended for their efforts. If they had not bought and own this land today, it would have been cut-over many years ago and possibly not a great deal of timber left except largely undesirable species and undergrowth" ("Alton B. Farris, Sr. Autobiography").

105. Conarro, *The Beginning*, 8, 9.

106. Ibid., 13, 14.

107. Ibid., 14–15; "History of Forestry in Mississippi," 14.

108. Conarro, *The Beginning*, 16; Sharon S. Young and A. P. Mustian Jr., *Impacts of National Forests on the Forest Resources of the South*, Miscellaneous Publication 1472 (n.p.: U.S. Department of Agriculture, Forest Service, 1989), 26.

109. Sharon S. Young and Mustian, *Impacts*, 20, 22–23.

110. Ibid., 24–26.

111. Ibid., 29, 26.

112. "History of Forestry in Mississippi," 14–15; John W. Squires, interview by James W. Craig, July 21, 1987, MFA Records. The Squires interview contains a great deal of material concerning the condition, policies, and personnel of Mississippi's national forests during the 1940s and 1950s.

113. William E. Shands and Robert G. Healy, *The Lands Nobody Wanted* (Washington, D.C.: Conservation Foundation, 1977); Alfred A Wiener, *The Forest Service Timber Appraisal System: A Historical Perspective, 1891–1981* (Washington, D.C.: U.S. Department of Agriculture, Forest Service, 1982), ii; R. M. Conarro, *Little Red Riding Hood and the Red Fire Wolf* (Atlanta: Regional Forester, Southern National Forest Region, n.d., copy in MFA Records, box 51); Hugh S. Redding, "The Progress of Forestry as a Science and the Objectives of the Mississippi National Forests," *Mississippi Forest Facts* 4 (April 1944): 4.

114. Marian Clawson and Roger Sedjo, "History of Sustained Yield Concept and Its Application to Devel-

oping Countries," in *History of Sustained-Yield Forestry: A Symposium,* ed. Harold K. Steen (Santa Cruz, Calif.: Forest History Society, 1984), 7; *South's Fourth Forest: Alternatives,* 328.

115. George L. Drake, "The U.S. Forest Service, 1905–1955: An Industry Viewpoint," *Journal of Forestry* 53 (February 1955): 116–20. For the Forest Service chief's brief evaluation of the agency's first half century, see Richard E. McArdle, "The Forest Service's First Fifty Years," *Journal of Forestry* 53 (February 1955): 99–10.

Chapter 7

1. *South's Fourth Forest: Alternatives,* 73.

2. "History of Forestry in Mississippi," 17–18, 20; Arthur W. Nelson Jr., "South's Third Forest"; "Forest Program Will Be Enacted, Board Predicts," *New Orleans Times- Picayune,* September 1, 1938; "New Severance Tax Goes into Effect," *The Conservationist* (July 1940); "Severance Tax," *Southern Conservationist* (December 1939); "Report of Joint Committee of the Mississippi Legislature on the Study of Forestry," in *Journal of the Senate of the State of Mississippi,* extraordinary session, Jackson, July 6–August 20, 1938 (Jackson: Hederman Brothers, 1938); Hickman, *Mississippi Harvest,* 266. For a detailed discussion of forest taxation, see Bruce Van Zandt, "Timber Taxation," *The Conservationist* (September 1940). See also James C. Fortson and Leon A. Hargreaves, "Capital Gains Taxation and the Industrial Forests of the South," *Journal of Forestry* 72 (June 1974): 345–48; and William K. Condrell, "How Has Taxation Affected the Growth of the Forest Products Industries," paper presented at the Harvard-Yale Conference on the History of the Forest Products Industries, May 17–18, 1966, Cambridge, Mass., copy in SAF Records, box 45. For the same subject, specifically in Mississippi, see Ronald Craig, "The Past and Future of Forest Taxation in Mississippi," *The Conservationist* (January 1941). The timber-harvesting law did not prove totally effective.

3. *South's Fourth Forest: Alternatives,* 65; Arthur W. Nelson Jr., "South's Third Forest."

4. Roy V. Scott, "American Railroads and the Promotion of Forestry," *Journal of Forest History* 23 (April 1979): 75–78, 81; Art Nelson, "Forest History," 31; Mississippi Forestry Commission booklet, title page missing, [1944?], 11, copy in William Colvin Files, MFC (hereafter cited as MFC booklet). For information concerning the life, training, and experience of longtime Mississippi forester John G. Guthrie as an Illinois Central Railroad Agricultural Department forester, see John G. Guthrie, interview by Bobbie Jean Dickinson, June 6, 1989, MFA Records.

5. MFC booklet, 20; "History of Forestry in Mississippi," 4–6; John C. Barber, *Impacts of State and Private Programs on Forest Resources and Industries in the South,* Forest Resource Report 25 (Washington, D.C.: U.S. Department of Agriculture, Forest Service, 1989), 22–23; "Early Forestry History in the Magnolia State," *Forestry News* 13 (March 1976): 6. This article says that the Federation of Women's Clubs emphasized growing and care of trees on cutover lands and prepared and distributed literature on the subject. The members also met with citizens' groups and legislative committees to lobby their cause. For additional information on Mrs. G. H. Reeves, see "Our First Lady of Forestry Featured in Bicentennial Book," *Forestry News* 13 (October 1976): 1. For a brief overview of state forestry in the United States, see Austin F. Hawes, "Forty Years of State Forestry," *Journal of Forestry* 39 (February 1941): 95–99.

6. "History of Forestry in Mississippi," 7–8; Barber, *Impacts,* 23; J. B. Bishop, acting secretary, State Forestry Commission, to Roy L. Hogue, June 2, 1926, MFA Records, box 51.

7. "History of Forestry in Mississippi," 8–9; Barber, *Impacts,* 23; Barber, "Forestry," 506–7.

8. "History of Forestry in Mississippi," 8–11, 21, 32, 41, 50.

9. Ibid., 15, 31, 11–12; "Early Forestry History," 6.

10. Clepper, "Ten Most Important Events," 101–2; "History of Forestry in Mississippi," 14, 18; Sharon S. Young and Mustian, *Impacts,* 29–31; "History of the 4441st Company, USFS/CCC, Camp Miss. F-24," MFA Records; Pope, interview, 380–81; Marie King, interview by Bobbie Jean Dickinson, May 16, 1989, MFA Records. For a brief overview, see "The Civilian Conservation Corps: The New Deal's Most Popular Program," *Forest History Today* (1996): 30–33. See also Leslie Alexander Lacy, *The Soil Soldiers: The Civilian Conservation Corps in the Great Depression* (Radnor, Pa.: Chilton Book Company, 1976); and John A. Salmond, *The Civilian Conservation Corps, 1933–1942: A New Deal Case Study* (Durham, N.C.: Duke University Press, 1967). For the story of a pioneering Mississippi conservationist who worked as a superintendent with the Abbeville CCC camp, see Jean Firestone, "Hiram O. Jones," *Forestry Forum* 3 (winter 1989–90): 16–17. For brief summaries of CCC activities in Mississippi, see Perry H. Merrill, *Roosevelt's Forest Army: A History of the Civilian Conservation Corps, 1933–1942* (Montpelier, Vt.: Perry H. Merrill, 1981), 142–44; and Victor B. MacNaughton, "A Yankee Grows in Dixie," *Maine Forester* (1969): 103. Another brief account of work in the Mississippi CCC camps appears in W. S. Mauldin Jr., interview by Bobbie Jean Dickinson, May 18, 1989, MFA Records.

11. Barber, *Impacts,* 43–46.

12. E. C. Burkhardt, "Hardwoods and the Man Who Showed Us How to Manage Them," *Forest Farmer* (March 1986): 25; Ed Kerr, "Thanks Sid," *Journal of Forestry* 88 (August 1990): 50; L. C. Maisenhelder and J. S. McKnight, "Southern Hardwood Research: Past—Present—Future," *Southern Lumberman* (December 15, 1962); J. S. McKnight and John A. Putnam, "Logging Cut-Over Stands of Bottomland Hardwoods," *Southern Lumberman* (December 15, 1952); "History of Forestry in Mississippi," 15–16; "John A. Putnam Elected Fellow," *Newsletter, Gulf States Section, Society of American Foresters* 4 (winter 1964): 11–12; I. F. Eldredge, "What Are We Going to Do with Our Hardwoods?" Occasional Paper 82 (New Orleans: U.S. Department of Agriculture, Forest Service, Southern Forest Experiment Station, 1939); J. S. McKnight, "Hardwood Research in the South," *Journal of Soil and Water Conservation* 19 (March–April 1964): 77–78. One writer dates the beginning of "[r]esearch on bottomland hardwood forests" to 1937, when "a Mississippi State University forester established some test plantings." The author stated, "Two years later, in 1939, the U.S.D.A. Forest Service, Southern Forest Experiment Station, joined with the university and started field studies on managing hardwood stands and establishing cottonwood plantations" (John Stanturf, "Bottomland Hardwood Research Center," *Tree Talk* 20 [summer 1998]: 17). For personal reminiscences of early forestry research in the South, particularly by the Southern Forest Experiment Station, see Wakeley, "Adolescence," 136–45.

13. McKnight, "Hardwood Research," 77.

14. "History of Forestry in Mississippi," 16–17; "Frank Pittman: MFA's First Executive," *Tree Talk* 9 (fall 1987): 15; J. Walter Myers Jr., *Impact of Forestry Associations on Forest Productivity in the South,* Miscellaneous Publication 1458 (n.p.: U.S. Department of Agriculture, Forest Service, 1988), 10; "Forestry Receives Consideration by Mississippi Law Makers," *Mississippi Forest Facts* 4 (April 1944): 1; R. S. McFarlane, "Forestry Text Book Report," *Mississippi Forest Facts* 9 (October 1944): 1; "Keep Mississippi's Forest Green," *Mississippi Forest Facts* (January 1946); "Let's Look at Our Forest," *Mississippi Forest Facts* (September 1946): 1; Squires, interview. Squires was the onetime supervisor of the state's national forests and was longtime chief forester for Sears, Roebuck, and Company, which owned fifty thousand acres of land in Mississippi. Between August 1, 1940, and November 1941 the Mississippi Forestry Association changed its name to the Mississippi Forestry and Chemurgic Association. For an explanation of chemurgy, see Elizabeth M. Stone, "Chemurgy's First Agent—Wood," *Mississippi Forest Facts* (December 1946): 1–3. By 1998 the MFA's membership included ninety-two associate members, forty-

one banks and financial institutions, four chip mills, eighty-one consultants, eleven equipment suppliers, thirty-one hunting clubs, 1,923 individuals, two lifetime members, sixteen "other manufacturers," three plywood companies, seventeen pulp and paper companies, forty-four sawmill-treating plants, 415 timberland owners, six utilities, two "veneer and others," and sixty-three wood dealers and suppliers ("Mississippi Forestry Association Member Totals by Category," copy in possession of author). In a letter to Bobbie Jean Dickinson, John W. Thompson remembered that during the 1950s, when the Mississippi legislature considered taxing large timberland holdings or limiting their size, "We worked on this through the Mississippi Manufacturers' Association because we wanted to keep MFA as mainly a nonindustrial owner association." Writing to Art Nelson, Thompson recalled, "We ran the work on this through the Mississippi Manufacturers Association because we felt it was an industry problem, not of special concern by smaller landowners comprising the bulk of MFA members" (Thompson to Bobbie Jean Dickinson, April 12, 1989; and Thompson to Nelson, October 24, 1987, both in MFA Records).

15. "Woodlands History," 13.

16. Thomas R. Cox, Maxwell, Thomas, and Malone, *Well-Wooded Land,* 210; Clark, *Greening,* 48, 67. For a contemporary discussion of the problems facing southern foresters in the 1940s, see Joseph C. Kircher, "Forestry Needs of the South," *Journal of Forestry* 40 (February 1942): 95–99.

17. Albert E. Cowdrey, *This Land, This South: An Environmental History* (Lexington: University Press of Kentucky, 1983), 114; Croker, *Longleaf Pine,* 13.

18. Nelson, interview; Richard Allen, interview. See also Lee M. James, William P. Hoffman, and Monty A. Payne, *Private Forest Landownership and Management in Central Mississippi,* Bulletin 33 (Starkville: Agricultural Experiment Station, Mississippi State College, 1951), 33. In 1947 the Forestry Department of the Southern Pine Association reported, "Wide variation exists today in the type of cutting practices employed by Southern Pine manufacturers. Many operators have put into effect conservative cutting practices designed to assure continuous production of timber. Many more, however, are still employing heavy cutting methods giving little consideration to future crops. These conditions apply to practices employed on company-owned lands as well as on other private holdings" (memorandum from W. C. Hammerle to H. C. Berckes, January 8, 1947, SPA Records, box 12B). There is a good exposition of the of the pulp and paper industry's contributions to southern forestry and the current status of the industry in F. C. Gragg, "Present and Potential Economics of Southern Forests," in *Proceedings of the Society of American Foresters Meeting, October 21–24, 1962*

(Washington, D.C.: Society of American Foresters, 1963), 2–5.

19. Heyward, *History of Industrial Forestry,* 33; Barber, "Forestry," 507.

20. Richard Allen, interview; Nelson, interview.

21. Gragg, interview; Nelson, interview; "The Lumber Industry Looks at Forestry," *Journal of Forestry* 36 (April 1938): 363–64.

22. *Voices,* 6–7.

23. Nelson, interview.

24. Hughes, interview; Richard Allen, interview; Jonathan Daniels, *Forest Is the Future,* 37.

25. John Tyler, interview by author, August 31, 1989; Richard Allen, interview. A 1960s Louisiana Forestry Commission study confirmed the validity of the views of foresters like Tyler and Allen that personal contact with area residents was a key to controlling incendiary and wild fires. See M. L. Doolittle and G. D. Welch, "Fire Prevention in the Deep South: Personal Contact Pays Off," *Journal of Forestry* 72 (August 1974): 488–90.

26. Hughes, interview; Robert M. Nonnemacher, interview by author, August 30, 1989. The importance of community relations in the work of the forester is emphasized in an unpublished 1955 paper by Glen R. Durrell (head of the Forestry Department at Oklahoma A&M College), "The People Side of the Large Scale Forestry Operation," copy in possession of author; and in Fred L. Palmer, "Public Relations and the Forester," *Journal of Forestry* 51 (May 1953): 334–37. For a lavishly illustrated account of a 1947 week in the working life of Nonnemacher, then an IP conservation engineer (forester) working Mississippi and the Florida parishes of Louisiana, see *Great Southern Tree Crop,* 3–18.

27. Jonathan Daniels, *Forest Is the Future,* 48–49. As late as 1979 about 60 percent of all wildfires in Mississippi occurred in the southern part of the state, and most resulted from arson. In that year two Wiggins banks offered a one thousand dollar reward for information leading to the arrest and conviction of malicious woods burners in Stone County. The MFA also offered a five hundred dollar reward on a statewide basis ("Wiggins Banks Offer Forest Fire Reward," *Tree Talk* 1 [winter 1979]: 15). An examination of MFC fire records for the period from the mid-1930s until the mid-1980s reveals invariably that by far the largest number of fires whose cause could be determined were set by incendiaries. These annual fire reports are found in the MFC files in Jackson and in Special Collections, Mitchell Memorial Library, Mississippi State University, Starkville.

28. "Crosby Lumber Company"; "An Oral History with Mr. L. O. Crosby, Jr., Industrialist and Native Mississippian," Mississippi Oral History Program of the University of Southern Mississippi, vol. 155, 1980.

29. Pyne, *Fire in America,* 143; Wakeley, "F. O. ('Red') Bateman," 92; Croker, "Longleaf Pine Story," 40.

30. John P. Shea, "'Our Pappies Burned the Woods' and Set a Pattern of Human Behavior in Southern Forests That Calls for New Methods of Fire Prevention," *American Forests* (April 1940): 159–62, 174.

31. George R. Fahnestock, "Southern Forest Fires: A Social Challenge," Preliminary Report 2 (Starkville: Social Science Research Center, Mississippi State University, in cooperation with Southern Forest Experiment Station, 1964); Alvin L. Bertrand and Andrew W. Baird, *Incendiarism in Southern Forests: A Decade of Sociological Research,* Mississippi Agricultural and Forestry Experiment Station Bulletin 838 (Starkville: Mississippi State University Agricultural and Forestry Experiment Station, 1975); M. L. Doolittle and M. L. Lightsey, *Southern Woods-Burners: A Descriptive Analysis,* Research Paper SO-151 (New Orleans: U.S. Department of Agriculture, Forest Service, Southern Forest Experiment Station, 1979). See also M .L. Doolittle, Francis Eller, and Robert S. Jackson, *Strategies for Reducing Incendiary Fire Occurrence in the South* ([New Orleans]: U.S. Department of Agriculture, Forest Service, Southern Forest Experiment Station, 1976). Ironically, even as Shea was writing, scientific evidence was accumulating that indicated that controlled burning would in fact provide some of the benefits for forest regeneration and wildlife habitat that folklore had claimed. See E. L. Demmon, "The Silvicultural Aspects of the Forest-Fire Problem in the Longleaf Pine Region," *Journal of Forestry* 33 (March 1935): 323–31; Leroy Watson Jr., "Controlled Burning and the Management of Longleaf Pine," *Journal of Forestry* 38 (January 1940): 44–47; N. G. T. Simerly, "Controlled Burning in Longleaf Pine Second-Growth Timber," *Journal of Forestry* 54 (July 1956); W. G. Wahlenberg, "Effect of Fire and Grazing on Soil Properties and the Natural Reproduction of Longleaf Pine," *Journal of Forestry* 33 (March 1935): 331–38; S. W. Greene, "Relation between Winter Grass Fires and Cattle Grazing in the Longleaf Pine Belt," *Journal of Forestry* 33 (March 1935): 338–41; and Herbert L. Stoddard, "Use of Controlled Fire in Southeastern Upland Game Management," *Journal of Forestry* 33 (March 1935): 346–51. See also John P. Shea, *Man-Caused Forest Fires: The Psychologist Makes a Diagnosis* ([Washington, D.C.]: U.S. Forest Service, 1939); and John P. Shea, *Getting at the Roots of Man-Caused Forest Fires,* Fire Prevention Studies Series A (Washington, D.C.: U.S. Department of Agriculture, Soil Conservation Service, 1940).

32. Hughes, interview; Clark, "Impact of the Timber Industry," 161. On the same subject, see also Nelson, interview.

33. Bertrand and Baird, *Incendiarism,* 8–9. The counties in south Mississippi with very high rates were Lincoln, Lawrence, Jefferson Davis, Covington, Jones, Amite, Pike, Walthall, Marion, Lamar, Forrest, Perry, Pearl River, Stone, George, Hancock, Harrison, and Jackson.

34. Coburn L. Weston, interview, September 27, 1973, transcript in MDAH; Pittman, "Mississippi's Forests of Yesteryear," 24–25.

35. Pyne, *Fire in America,* 143; Anna C. Burns, *A History of the Louisiana Forestry Commission* (Natchitoches: Louisiana Studies Institute, Northwestern State College, 1968), 94; A. D. Folweiler, "Forest Fire Prevention by a State Forestry Agency," in *Modern Forest Fire Management in the South: Proceedings of the Fourth Annual Forestry Symposium* (Baton Rouge: School of Forestry and General Extension Division, Louisiana State University, 1955), 2; Thomas R. Cox, Maxwell, Thomas, and Malone, *Well-Wooded Land,* 211; M. L. Doolittle, *Forest Fire Occurrence in the South, 1956–1965* (New Orleans: U.S. Department of Agriculture, Forest Service, Southern Forest Experiment Station, n.d.); Myers, *Impact of Forestry Associations,* 8.

36. *Journal of Forestry* 40 (February 1942): 93–94; *South's Fourth Forest: Alternatives,* 43. On the same subject, see Nelson, interview; Art Nelson, "Pages from Art Nelson's Notebook: Fire—The Forester's Dilemma," *Tree Talk* 18 (fall 1996): 45; and Nonnemacher, interview. The authors of a standard text on forest-fire control argue that it "is an essential part of professional forestry in the United States" and note, "Scientific European forestry almost ignores the control of fire as an important part of the forester's job and gives scant attention to what happens to silvicultural systems when fire intervenes. Professional forestry training in this country [was] influenced strongly by European traditions. . . . The effect of this has been that many young foresters have found themselves on a job of which four-fifths was protection of the forest from fire, but with their training in inverse ratio" (A. D. Folweiler and A. A. Brown, *Fire in the Forests of the United States* [St. Louis: privately printed, 1946], i, 3). In a 1956 article tracing the development of forest-fire protection in Dixie, Louisiana state forester James E. Mixon identified the "advent of pulp mills in the South" as one of the five major events in the history of southern forest protection ("Progress of Protection from Forest Fires in the South," *Journal of Forestry* 54 [October 1956]: 649–52). In 1944 the SPA Conservation Committee argued, "The control of forest fires still remains the South's basic forestry problem, primarily due to the complications of land ownership and the inherent apathy of the general public" ("Conservation Committee Report to the Board of Directors, Southern Pine Association, October 25, 1944," SPA Records, box 71B).

37. Pyne, *Fire in America,* 155–56; Richard C. McArdle, "History of Forest Fire Prevention in the United States" (master's thesis, University of Michigan, 1952), 18–34; Folweiler and Brown, *Fire in the Forests,* 8–12; Clare W. Hendee, "Forest Fire Prevention—Progress and Prediction," *Journal of Forestry* 60 (June 1962): 380–84; A. W. Hartman, "Wildfire Today in Southern Forests, "in *Modern Forest Fire Management in the South: Proceedings of the Fourth Annual Forestry Symposium* (Baton Rouge: School of Forestry and General Extension Division, Louisiana State University, 1955), 9–16.

38. Myers, *Impact of Forestry Associations,* 8–9; Erle Kauffman, "The Southland Revisited, Part 1," *American Forests* (August 1955): 36, 38–40; "New Forestry Project to Be Launched," *American Forests and Forest Life* 34 (August 1928): 455–56; Barber, *Impacts,* 34; *South's Fourth Forest: Alternatives,* 45; "J. Brooks Toler (1906–1949)," *Journal of Forestry* 47 (November 1949): 920.

39. W. Cullen Valentine, "Fire-Fighting Equipment Was Made . . . Not Born!" *Forests and People* (2d quarter 1954): 23–25, 42–43; W. Cullen Valentine, "From Fire Flaps to Superplows," *Forests and People* (1st quarter 1963): 40–41, 102–3; Lucy W. Cole and Harold F. Kaufman, *Socio-Economic Factors and Forest Fires in Mississippi Counties,* Preliminary Report 14 (State College: Social Science Research Center, Mississippi State University, in cooperation with U.S. Department of Agriculture, Forest Service, Southern Forest Experiment Station, 1966), 10–11; "Early Forestry History," 7.

40. "History of Forestry in Mississippi," 8–10, 12–13; Barber, *Impacts,* 23, 38, 50–51; Barber, "Forestry," 506–7; Crews, comp. "Economic Report," 7; Warren Nicke, "De Woods of Pine," *Forest Facts* 14 (December 1942): n.p.

41. Earl Porter, "A History of Forest Fire Prevention on International Paper Company Southern Timberlands in the Past 35 Years," *Journal of Forestry* 66 (August 1968): 619; "History of Forestry in Mississippi," 13; A. K. Dexter, "Mississippi Fire Finder," *Journal of Forestry* 34 (December 1936): 1067–68; Mixon, "Progress of Protection," 649–52.

42. Art Nelson, "Pages from Art Nelson's Notebook: Fire," 45; Nelson, interview; Art Nelson, "Early Radio Days," *Forest History Today* (1996): 28–29 (reprinted from *Tree Talk* 17 [spring 1995]). Other east Mississippi firms that pioneered in the use of two-way radios were A. DeWeese Lumber Company, D. L. Fair Lumber Company, and Barge Timberlands. For a good brief summary of 1943 fire-fighting techniques, see *Notebook for Forest Fire Wardens* (n.p.: U.S. Department of Agriculture, Forest Service, Southern Region, 1943, copy in MFA records).

43. Arthur W. Nelson Jr., "Development of Forest Practices," 4–6, 16.

44. "History of Forestry in Mississippi," 13–14; Jack Hollingsworth, interview by Bobbie Jean Dickinson, November 7, 1989, MFA Records. For maps showing the erection dates, manufacturers, and types of towers as of 1981, see Henry Orville Stewart File, MFA Records. As of January 1981 the state had 190 towers, 34 of them owned by "cooperators," and there were 192 state fire-suppression units. During World War II, when metal was scarce, James R. Clark, logging superintendent of the Crosby Lumber Company, designed a ninety-foot creosote pole fire tower. A picture of this tower appears in "Observation Towers Essential to Fire Protection," *Mississippi Forest Facts* 11 (February 1944): 4.

45. "History of Forestry in Mississippi," 17; "Protection Can Only Be Had by Concerted-Organized-Effort," *Mississippi Forest Facts* 6 (July 1943): 1; MFC booklet, 21; Vertrees Young to Harry Malsberger, March 26, 1947, SPCA Records. For a graph showing the acreage of federal lands protected, state and private lands protected, and state and private lands unprotected for each state at the end of 1944, see *Mississippi Forest Facts* (March 1946): 4.

46. Tyler, interview; Gragg, "Explanation," 30. For an MFC forester's account of the evolution of fire-fighting equipment and techniques from 1944 to 1967, see Robert P. Hansford, interview by Bobbie Jean Dickinson, June 24, 1989, MFA Records.

47. Dantzler Lumber Company, Annual Report, 1946, Dantzler Lumber Company Records, Special Collections, Mitchell Memorial Library, Mississippi State University, Starkville (hereafter cited as Dantzler Records); Zebulon W. White, "Loblolly Pine," 15; Myers, *Opportunities Unlimited,* 26; Joe McDonald, "MFC Still Waging War on Destructive Fires," *Forestry News* 13 (March 1976): 8; "Report on Big Red," Personal History File of Carsie Alexander Boxeman Sr., MFA Records, box 50. "Big Red" was preceded in 1949 by an even bigger fire that consumed more than 120,000 acres of woodlands in Yazoo County's Panther Creek Swamp ("Delta Fire Scorched 120,000 Acres in '49," *Forestry News* 13 [March 1976]: 11).

48. Squires, interview.

49. Nelson, interview; E. R. Toole and J. S. McKnight, "Fire and the Hapless Hardwood," *Southern Lumberman,* 181–82; E. Richard Toole and J. S. McKnight, "Fire Effects in Southern Hardwoods," both in IP Files; Art Nelson, "Pages from Art Nelson's Notebook: Fire," 45–46. Thomas R. Cox also cites this poem in an article on the history of private forest management ("Stewardship," 194). See also *South's Fourth Forest: Alternatives,* 77–78; and Carlton N. Owen, "Integrating Wildlife and Loblolly Pine Management," in

Proceedings, ed. Karr, Baker, and Monaghan, 233. Nelson provides a good brief overview of the issues and problems involved as foresters and the public moved from an emphasis on total fire suppression to the understanding that controlled or "prescribed" fires or "burns" were needed in certain situations.

50. "Proposed Forest Program for the Southern Johns Manville Corporation at Natchez, Mississippi," and "Forestry Program—Natchez Tentative Outline," May 3, 1948, both in Johns Manville Records, box 16; John W. Thompson, "History of the Johns Manville Timberlands," 5–7. One of the problems and ironies facing foresters as they attempted to overcome the wildfire problem in the South was the fact that fire could be a valuable silvicultural tool if it came at the right point in the growth cycle and was controlled. The difficulty was in distinguishing between wildfire and incendiary fire on one hand and prescribed burning on the other. Among the significant literature dealing with the efficacy and techniques of prescribed burning are Hugh E. Mobley, "Smoke Management Essential Part of Prescribed Burns in Forests," *Forest Farmer* (February 1982); Ragnar W. Johansen, "Aerial Ignition for Speed and Control with Prescribed Burns," *Forest Farmer* (March 1984); David Bruce, "Mortality of Longleaf Pine Seedlings after a Winter Fire," *Journal of Forestry* 52 (June 1954): 442–43; Demmon, "Silvicultural Aspects," 323–31; Wahlenberg, "Effect of Fire and Grazing," 331–38; Raymond M. Conarro, "The Place of Fire in Southern Forestry," *Journal of Forestry* 40 (February 1942): 129–31; Simerly, "Controlled Burning," 671–73; Leroy Watson Jr., "Controlled Burning," 41–47; Robert W. Cooper, "Prescribed Burning," *Journal of Forestry* 73 (December 1975): 776–80; Von J. Johnson, "Prescribed Burning: Requiem or Renaissance?" *Journal of Forestry* 82 (February 1984): 82–91; Hugh E. Mobley, "Fire as a Tool in Young Pine Management," *Proceedings, Symposium on Management of Young Pines 1974, Sponsored by Southeastern Area State and Private Forestry, Southern and Southeastern Forest Experiment Stations, U.S. Department of Agriculture, Forest Service* ([New Orleans: U.S. Department of Agriculture, Forest Service, 1974]), 234–42; A. B. Crow, "Use of Fire in Southern Forests," *Journal of Forestry* 71 (October 1973): 629–32; Daniel W. Lay, "Effects of Prescribed Burning on Forage and Mast Production in Southern Pine Forests," *Journal of Forestry* 54 (September 1956): 582–84; and Hugh E. Mobley, "Prescribed Burning Reduces Fire Hazard, Promotes Regeneration and Wildlife Habitat," *Forest Farmer* (February 1982): 6–7, 15–16.

51. "Forest Fire Protection Plans and Proposals, October 23, 1951," Johns Manville Records, box 22. In 1947 Johns Manville's losses were 3.7 percent of its protected acreage, compared with 1.2 percent for Crosby Lumber Company, 1.1 percent for Flintkote, and .12 percent on the Homochitto National Forest. Incendiary fires were the leading identifiable category ("Fire Protection—Mississippi, May 15, 1947," Johns Manville Records, box 22).

52. "The Yazoo–Little Tallahatchie Flood Prevention Project," *Forestry Forum* (September 1989): 15–16; Cole and Kaufman, *Socio-Economic Factors,* 10–11; *South's Fourth Forest: Alternatives,* 46; *Forest Situation.*

53. Richard Allen, interview. The Central Fire Control Association was formed by citizens and landowners with some 1 million acres of forested lands in Leake, Madison, Rankin, and Scott Counties. The association employed two local men as fire wardens and conducted fire-prevention campaigns in the local community and schools ("New Activities in Forest Fire Control," *Forest Facts* 15 [January 1943]: n.p.; "Private Citizens Group Cooperatively Control Fires," *Mississippi Forest Facts* [November 1947]: 1, 3).

54. James M. Vardaman, "Prospectus E. L. Bruce Co. (Incorporated) Mississippi Timberlands," March 15, 1963, Johns Manville Records, box 21, folder 841.

55. Richard Allen, interview.

56. "History of Forestry in Mississippi," 23–24. In California and Oregon World War I ace Henry H. "Hap" Arnold and some members of the Army Air Service undertook aerial fire patrol of the national forests with a Forest Service observer in each plane in 1919. Observers dropped messages in special cans or by small parachutes to lookouts who had telephones. Aerial fire patrollers also employed carrier pigeons until radios were installed in the planes in 1920. There were also tests of dirigibles and contact with the Army Chemical Warfare Service about the possible use of foams, froths, and other retardants. The program ended in 1922 (Pyne, *Fire in America,* 439–40).

57. Tyler, interview. Jimmy Clark and Charlie Robinson flew fire patrol for the Crosby Lumber Company in southwest Mississippi, and L. N. Dantzler hired Sonny Holleman to fly in the early 1950s, cutting fire losses from about thirty-five or forty thousand acres a year down to five thousand acres the first year. According to John G. Guthrie, there were as many fires as before, but they were much smaller. Dantzler eventually cut its losses to 2 percent a year "which was phenomenal at that time" (Guthrie, interview, 17). There are some variations in different accounts of early aerial fire detection. C. H. Lewis Jr. argued that he and Ralph Taggart began to fly the first fire patrol for the Crosby Lumber Company in its J-3 Piper Cub, which was soon joined by another company plane, a Bellanca Cruisaire. According to Lewis, the Johns Manville Company, Gloster Lumber Company, Fernwood Industries, and the U.S. Forest Service purchased fire-detection service from Crosby, and the "Texas Forest Service sent observers to Crosby

and soon thereafter began replacing Texas fire towers with airplanes. . . . Airplanes have largely replaced towers for fire detection across the South . . . and it all started at Crosby, Mississippi" (Charlie Lewis to Art Nelson, December 31, 1991, MFA Records). For Allen's recollections of Tyler's activities, see Richard Allen, interview.

58. John F. Tyler to S. E. Fogelberg, May 29, 1950; Tyler to Fogelberg, May 30, 1951, both in IP Files; "History of Forestry in Mississippi," 23–24.

59. "History of Forestry in Mississippi," 25–26.

60. John Tyler, "Use of the Airplane in Forest Fire Control," paper presented at the 1954 annual meeting, Woodlands Division, International Paper Company; John S. Tyler to Earl Porter, January 19, 1955, and Tyler to J. E. McCaffrey, April 14, 1955, all in IP Files.

61. John Tyler and C. H. Lewis, "Air Patrol for Better Detection and Protection in the South," *Journal of Forestry* 51 (June 1953): 444–46; A. B. Crow to John Tyler, February 28, 1955, IP Files.

62. "History of Forestry in Mississippi," 20, 22, 25, 28, 30–31, 35–36, 39, 42, 51, 54; Cole and Kaufman, *Socio-Economic Factors,* 1, 22; "1979 Forest Fires Down in South, Up in State," *Tree Talk* 3 (fall 1980): 36; McDonald, "MFC Still Waging War," 8–9; Henry Clepper, *Crusade for Conservation: The Centennial History of the American Forestry Association* (Washington, D.C.: American Forestry Association, 1975; also published in *American Forests* 81 [October 1975]). The figures on state expenditures on forestry and fire control sometimes differ from source to source. For example, a 1948 report compiled by the Southern Pine Association from figures supplied by state foresters reported that Mississipi state appropriations for all forestry purposes were $15,000 in fiscal year 1937–38, $55,000 in 1942–43, and $463,881 in 1947–48. This figure represented an incredible 2992.5 percent increase over a ten-year period (Southern Pine Association to Southern Group of State Foresters, January 9, 1948, SPA Records, box 53A).

63. *Elementary Forestry for Mississippi* (Jackson: Mississippi Forestry Commission, 1945), 79.

64. "History of Forestry in Mississippi," 38; L. H. Molloy to John Thompson, December 4, 1951, Johns Manville Records, box 16. See also M. L. Doolittle and G. D. Welch, *Fire Prevention,* 488–90.

65. "A Report of the Activities of the Woodlands Department, Year of 1951," Southern Kraft Division of International Paper Company, 24, copy in IP Files; Hughes, interview; J. E. Bryan Jr., "Forest History," 35.

66. Richard Allen, interview.

67. Gragg, interview. Wildfire remains a constant threat to forest-products companies. The hot summer of 1985 provided a recent reminder to southern foresters that they must remain ever vigilant and pre-

pared to deal with wildfires. See Bruce Jewell, "Wildfire—The South's Worst Season," *Forest Farmer* (November–December 1985): 20–22.

68. O. G. Tracewitz, interview by author, October 5, 1989; *South's Fourth Forest: Alternatives,* 47. For statistics on the number of fires, acres burned, percentage burned, average size in acres, and fires per million acres on protected Mississippi lands from 1927 through 1973 and on unprotected acreage from 1927 through 1940, see tables in Henry Orville Stewart File, MFA Records.

69. George H. Hepting, "Forest Disease Research in the South," *Journal of Forestry* 54 (October 1956): 656–60.

70. See R. A. Schmidt, A. E. Squillace, and B. F. Swindel, "Predicting the Incidence of Fusiform Rust in Five- to Ten-Year-Old Slash and Loblolly Pine Plantations," *Southern Journal of Applied Forestry* (November 1979): 138–40; G. D. Geron and W. L. Hafley, "Impact of Fusiform Rust on Product Yields of Loblolly Pine Plantations," *Southern Journal of Applied Forestry* (December 1988): 226–31; Ellis V. Hunt Jr. and J. David Lenhart, "Fusiform Rust Trends in East Texas," *Southern Journal of Applied Forestry* (October 1986): 215–16; Eugene Shoulders and Warren L. Nance, *Effects of Fusiform Rust on Survival and Structure of Mississippi and Louisiana Loblolly Pine Plantations,* Research Paper SO-232 (New Orleans: U.S. Department of Agriculture, Forest Service, Southern Forest Experiment Station, n.d.); Harry P. Powers Jr. and John R. Kraus, "Research May Soon Produce Planting Stock Resistant to Fusiform Rust," *Forest Farmer* (October 1982): 6–7; and H. R. Powers Jr. and S. J. Rowan, "Influence of Fertilization and Ectomycorrhizae on Loblolly Pine Growth and Susceptibility to Fusiform Rust," *Southern Journal of Applied Forestry* (May 1983): 101–3; *South's Fourth Forest: Alternatives,* 54.

71. Leon Brown, "Little Bug That Spells Big Trouble," *Forest Farmer* (September 1989): 11–13; Barber, *Impacts,* 68–69, 80–82; R. C. Froelich, T. Miller, and R. P. Belanger, "An Evaluation of Methods for Assessing Impacts of Pests on Forest Productivity," paper presented at IUFRO Forest Growth Modeling and Prediction Conference, Minneapolis, Minn., August 24–27, 1987.

72. "History of Forestry in Mississippi," 26–27, 42.

73. Hamlin L. Williston, *Southern Pine Management Primer* (New York: Vantage Press, 1987), 73.3; Nelson, interview. See also Art Nelson, "Land Lines: Determining Property Lines a Challenge," *Tree Talk* 16 (spring 1994): 33.

74. Hughes, interview. For a description of the lives and work of the early government surveyors, see Dwight L. Agnew, "The Government Land Surveyor as a Pioneer," *Mississippi Valley Historical Review* 28 (December 1941): 369–82.

75. Nelson, interview. For a Crosby Lumber Company forester's description of the methods and problems of running and establishing land lines and boundaries, see C. H. Lewis Jr., "Crosby Lumber Company," 11–12.

76. *Status of Timber Trespass on Pulp and Paper Company Lands,* Technical Release 58- R24 (n.p.: American Pulpwood Association, 1958).

77. Richard Allen, interview.

78. Ibid; Jonathan Daniels, *Forest Is the Future,* 45.

79. Gragg, interview.

80. "Oral History with Mr. L. O. Crosby Jr."; Stanley Shannon, interview by Wallace Dearing, April 30, 1991, in *Timber Industry in the Great Depression,* 66–67.

81. Tracewitz, interview.

82. Gragg, interview; "A True Story of Mississippi's Oldest Pine Plantation," *Mississippi Forest Facts* 2 (March 1943): 1.

83. *A Statistical History of Tree Planting in the South, 1925–1979,* Miscellaneous Report SA-MR8 (Atlanta: U.S. Department of Agriculture, Forest Service, 1980), 19; M. D. Mobley and Robert N. Hoskins, *Forestry in the South* (Atlanta: Turner E. Smith, 1956), 347; Samuel Trask Dana, *Forest and Range Policy: Its Development in the United States* (New York: McGraw-Hill, 1956), 303. See James H. Miller and Bruce Zutter, "A Region-Wide Study of Loblolly Pine Seedling Growth Relative to Four Competition Levels after Two Growing Seasons," paper presented at Southern Silvicultural Research Conference, Atlanta, November 4–6, 1986; and Eugene Shoulders, *Site Characteristics Influence Relative Performance of Loblolly and Slash Pine,* Research Paper SO-115 (New Orleans: U.S. Department of Agriculture, Forest Service, Southern Forest Experiment Station, 1976).

84. Kauffman, "Southland Revisited, Part 1," 36; *South's Fourth Forest: Alternatives,* 48–50. For the tree-planting record, including annual planting and seeding, in the South and in Mississippi from 1925 through 1979, see *Statistical History.*

85. Jonathan Daniels, *Forest Is the Future,* 39, 41. For the story of the development of tree-planting machines, see Fred B. Trenk, "Evolution of Modern Tree Planting Machines," *Journal of Forestry* 61 (October 1963): 726–30; Roy V. Scott, "American Railroads," 72–81; and "Woodlands History," 71–72, 110–11. For Porter's account of how he developed the planting machine, see Earl Porter, "Plant More Trees," *The Unit* (January 16, 1952): 26–33.

86. *Centennial Report: The Financial Story of Our First Hundred Years, 1851–1951, Illinois Central Railroad* (Chicago: Illinois Central Railroad, 1951), 7–8; "The Illinois Central Railroad in Mississippi: A Presentation to the Mississippi Agricultural and Industrial Board at Jackson on Tuesday, April 21, 1953," MFA Records.

87. Art Nelson, "Tree Planter Boosts Mississippi Forestry," *Tree Talk* 15 (fall 1993): 28–29; Arthur W. Nelson Jr., "South's Third Forest"; William W. May to A. W. Nelson Jr., July 7, 1975, MFA Records. IP claimed that its planter could plant eight to ten acres daily at the rate of five to six hundred seedlings per acre. In contrast, said IP, a two-man crew could plant approximately one thousand to fifteen hundred trees in a hard day ("Woodlands History," 110–11). See also Roy V. Scott, "American Railroads," 77–78. Scott says that the Illinois Central established a forestry department in 1945 and by 1954 employed four foresters and claimed to have the country's largest railroad forestry department. The importance the Illinois Central placed on forestry was reflected in its publication in 1950 of Myers, *Opportunities Unlimited.* While Nelson and others say that the Illinois tree planter sold for two hundred dollars, Myers says it was three hundred dollars. He also reports that by 1950 a total of fourteen railroads had forestry programs (*Opportunities Unlimited,* 51, 69–70). For Guthrie's account of the creation of the Illinois Central tree-planting machine and the railroad's planting campaign, see Guthrie, interview, 10–15. Guthrie was nicknamed "Johnny Pinetree" by a New Orleans newspaper ("Meet Johnny Pinetree," *Times-Picayune New Orleans States Magazine,* September 18, 1949; see also John G. Guthrie, "Illinois Central Promotes Mississippi Re-Forestation," *Railroad Journal* 14 [September 1949]: 48–84). For the early forestry efforts of railroads in the Midwest and prairie states, see Sherry H. Olson, "Commerce and Conservation: The Railroad Experience," *Forest History* 9 (January 1966): 4–5, 9–13.

88. "History of Forestry in Mississippi," 11; W. R. Hine to Mrs. G. H. Reeves, August 1, 1941, MFA Records, box 50; Barber, *Impacts,* 56–58.

89. Gragg, interview; John W. Johnson, "Growing Pine: Methods and Techniques for the Seventies," in *Forest Farmer Manual* (Atlanta: Forest Farmers Cooperative Association, 1971), 52. Because of the differences in scope of operations and other factors, it is difficult to develop accurate estimates of the average or normal costs of various forestry activities. Nonetheless, researchers occasionally have attempted to establish these figures. See, for example, James G. Yoho and Robert B. Fish, "A Survey for the South: What It Costs to Practice Forestry," *Forest Farmer* (November 1961): 6–8, 19; Thomas J. Straka and William F. Watson, "Costs of Forestry Practices," in *Forest Farmer Manual,* 25th ed. (Atlanta: Forest Farmers Cooperative Association, 1985); Seymour I. Somberg, Larry D. Eads, and James G. Yoho, "What It Costs to Practice Forestry in the South," *Forest Farmer* (September 1963): 6–8, 15–17; and Albert C. Worrell, "What Does It Cost to Practice Forestry in the South?" *Journal of Forestry* 51 (May 1953): 5, 17.

90. Barber, "Forestry," 508. As in so many other areas of forest practice, heated disagreements arose among professionals about the efficacy of the various methods of regeneration. For example, Philip C. Wakeley of the Forest Service argued in 1954, "Planting the southern pines offers the only sure way of restoring to timber production, within the next 50 years, a huge area of forest land vital to the southern and national economy. . . . From present knowledge . . . direct seeding of southern pines can be recommended only as a supplement to, not as a substitute for, the planting of nursery stock" (*Planting the Southern Pines,* Agriculture Monograph 18 [New Orleans: U.S. Department of Agriculture, Forest Service, 1954], 1), 16–17. Ironically, at about the same time that Wakeley was writing, an effective bird repellent for coating seed was developed (in 1955), and the popularity of direct seeding soared. As W. F. Mann Jr. of the Southern Forest Experiment Station reported in 1965, "The widespread and diverse application of direct seeding has exceeded all early expectations. . . . Many sites that are virtually impossible to plant are now being regenerated economically by seeding. There is also a growing trend for direct seeding to supplant seed trees for restocking following harvest cutting. . . . Some companies have switched completely from planting to seeding; others are using both methods to maximum advantage" ("Direct Seeding the Southern Pines: Development and Application," in *Proceedings of the Direct Seeding Workshops, Alexandria, La., October 5–6, 1965* [n.p.: U.S. Forest Service, 1965], 2). By 1980 Mississippi state forester Allen was actively promoting direct seeding, but "only where the guidelines indicate that direct seeding can be successful." Allen instructed his district foresters and nurserymen, "Where conditions indicate failure, back away and plant seedlings. . . . We have enough areas which need reforesting that both methods must be used, but I encourage you to direct seed on the good direct seeding sites" (Dick Allen, state forester, to all district foresters and nurserymen, January 9, 1980, MFC Files). Natural regeneration also had its adherents. In 1974 Hamlin L. Williston and William E. Balmer of the U.S. Forest Service reported that because of costs, owner objectives, and other considerations, "thousands of forest landowners of the South are deciding 'to dance with who brung 'em.' Their forests were reforested naturally to begin with, and they'll stick with that method of regeneration. This is the viable alternative." They then went on to discuss methods for making natural regeneration most effective ("Managing for Natural Regeneration," *USDA Forest Service Forest Management Bulletin* [September 1974]). In 1979 a Forest Service task force recommended a plan for reforestation of privately owned nonindustrial pinelands in the South: "Greater reliance must be placed on natural regeneration" (Hamlin L. Williston, "The South's Pine Reforestation Problem," *Journal of Forestry* 77 [April 1979]: 234–36). For discussions of the various approaches to regeneration, see Harold J. Doerr and William F. Mann Jr., *Direct- Seeding Pines in the South,* Agriculture Handbook 391 (n.p.: U.S. Department of Agriculture, Forest Service, 1971); Ed Kerr, "Can Direct Seeding Bridge the South's Generation Gap?" *Journal of Forestry* 70 (November 1975): 720–21; W. F. Mann Jr. and H. D. Burkhalter, "The South's Largest Successful Direct-Seeding," *Journal of Forestry* 59 (February 1961): 83–100; W. F. Mann Jr., T. E. Campbell, and T. W. Chappell, "Status of Aerial Row Seeding," *Forest Farmer* (November–December 1974): 12–13, 38–40; William F. Mann Jr., "At Last— Longleaf Pine Can Be Planted Successfully," *Forest Farmer* (March 1996–97): 18–19; J. W. Johnson, "Direct Seeding of Southern Pines," APA Technical Paper 58-P36, presented at meeting of American Pulpwood Association Southeastern Technical Committee, Charleston, S.C., April 30–May 1, 1958; William F. Mann Jr., "Direct-Seeding the Southern Pine," IP Files. In November 1957 Darwin E. Fender, technical supervisor of IP's Woodlands Department, Gulf Region, described Mann's work as "the best summary of the subject available." Fender provided copies for all area forest superintendents for distribution to each of their district and unit foresters and noted, "Our work this winter may result in some changes in Mr. Mann's recommendations but this is a relatively new field and much progress is expected in the next few years. . . . This subject . . . may well prove to be the answer to many of our dreams" (Darwin E. Fender to area forest superintendents, November 22, 1957, IP Files) Other literature dealing with regeneration includes W. F. Mann Jr., "Industry Tests Loblolly Direct Seeding," *Forests and People* 9 (1st quarter 1959): 22–23, 30, 32; William F. Mann Jr., "Direct Seeding Research with Longleaf, Loblolly, and Slash Pines," in *Recent Developments in Planting and Direct Seeding in the Southern Pine Region: Proceedings of the Third Annual Forestry Symposium, School of Forestry, Louisiana State University, April 8–9, 1954* (Baton Rouge: School of Forestry, Louisiana State University, 1954); Clark W. Lantz, "Direct Seeding, a Reforestation Alternative," *Forest Farmer* (October 1984): 12–14; Richard E. Lohrey and Earle P. Jones Jr., "Natural Regeneration and Direct Seeding," in *Proceedings of Symposium: The Managed Slash Pine Ecosystem, June 9–11, 1981* (Gainesville: School of Forest Resources and Conservation, University of Florida, 1981); William D. Boyer, "Regenerating the Natural Longleaf Pine Forest," *Journal of Forestry* 77 (September 1979): 572–75; Boone Y. Richardson, "Machines for Seeding Southern Pine," paper presented at the sixtieth annual meeting, American Society of Agricultural Engineers, Saskatoon, Saskatchewan, June 27–30, 1967. Sharon G. Haines, forest soils section leader at IP's Southlands Experiment

Forest, argued in a 1974 paper that in making regeneration decisions, "The soil's potential for management will largely define the biological options available. . . . The regeneration option ultimately selected is more likely to be determined by management objective and availability of capital than by any biological consideration" ("Soil-Site Considerations for Forest Regeneration," in *Cost Effective Regeneration Practices: Proceedings of the Second Annual Forestry Forum, Clemson University, March 16, 1982* (Greenville, S.C.: Clemson University, 1982). Other literature on regeneration includes O. O. Wells, "Geographic Seed Source Affects Performance of Planted Shortleaf Pine," in *Proceedings, Symposium for the Management of Pines of the Interior South, Knoxville, Tenn., November 7–8, 1978,* Technical Publication SA-TP2 (n.p.: U.S. Department of Agriculture, Forest Service, 1979); W. F. Mann Jr., "The Planting Job: Another Look at the South's Pine Regeneration Problem," *Forest Farmer* (November 1970): 8–9, 39–42; William F. Mann Jr., "Ten Years' Experience with Direct-Seeding in the South," *Journal of Forestry* 66 (November 1968): 828–33; Bruce Zobel, "Forest Renewal on Industrial Timberlands," *Journal of Forestry* 72 (November 1974): 681–85; George Anderson, "Economics of Site Preparation and Land Regeneration in the South: Example of an Industry Concept," *Journal of Forestry* 56 (October 1958): 754–56; Susan Branham, "Seeding the South: A Technological Revolution Comes of Age," *Forests and People* (3d quarter 1987): 17–18, 26–27; Jacqueline Haymond, "Natural Regeneration Methods for Southern Pines," *Forest Farmer* (October 1983): 9–11; Michael A. Webb, "Alternative Methods of Forest Regeneration," *Forest Farmer* (May 1989): 12–13; James P. Barnett, T. E. Campbell, and Phillip M. Dougherty, "Seedling Establishment—Artificial Methods," in *Proceedings,* ed. Karr, Baker, and Monaghan; L. Keville Larson, "Why Management of a Natural Stand May Be the Best Option for You," *Forest Farmer* (May 1986): 8–9; Richard W. Guldin, "Site Characteristics and Preparation Practices Influence Costs of Hand-Planting Southern Pine," *Journal of Forestry* 82 (February 1984): 97–98; and W. F. Mann Jr., T. E. Campbell, and T. W. Chappell, "Status of Aerial Row Seeding," *Forest Farmer* (November–December 1974): 12–13, 39–40. The last article describes a study and experiment undertaken on IP lands. See also Donald W. Smith, "What Industry Is Doing to Encourage Tree Planting in the South," *Forest Farmer* (November–December 1972): 18–19.

91. "A Report of the Activities of the Woodlands Department, Year 1946, Southern Kraft Division of International Paper Company," 35; and "A Report of the Activities of the Woodlands Department, Year 1948, Southern Kraft Division of International Paper Company," both in IP Files. The shortage of seedlings was a problem for all forest-products companies interested in

regeneration. For example, in 1949 the company forester of the L. N. Dantzler Lumber Company complained to the state forester about "the apparent inability of the State Nursery to supply seedlings to people over the state who wish to plant them. . . . I . . . do not know what steps can be taken to increase the production of seedlings but something has got to be done" (P. N. Howell to Frank B. Pittman, December 31, 1949, Dantzler Records).

92. International Paper Company, Annual Report, 1955, 15; International Paper Company, Annual Report, 1956, 14; and "The Story of International Paper Company," 4–8, all in IP Files. By the mid-1950s there was feverish activity in the field of forest genetics in the South. See Philip C. Wakeley, "Forest Tree-Improvement Work in the South," *Southern Lumberman* (December 15, 1957): 126–29. For an overview of the continuing efforts in forest genetics, see Roy W. Stonecypher, "Recurrent Selection in Forest Tree Breeding," in *Proceedings of the Tenth Southern Conference on Forest Tree Improvement, Houston, Tex., June 17–19, 1969* (n.p., n.d.); E. C. Franklin, "Inbreeding as a Means of Genetic Improvement of Loblolly Pine," in *Proceedings of the Tenth Southern Conference on Forest Tree Improvement*; Roy W. Stonecypher, "Impact of Tree Improvement on Management," *Proceedings, Symposium on Management of Young Pines, 1974;* Kirk Mlinek, "The Push for Genetically Improved Pines: Weyerhaeuser's Program Exemplifies Private Research and Development," *Forest Farmer* (June 1985): 14–15; Calvin F. Bey, Daniel B. Houston, and Ronald J. Dinus, "Tree Genetics and Improvement, Part 1: The New Genetics," *Journal of Forestry* 84 (January 1986): 34–42; Calvin F. Bey, Daniel B. Houston, and Ronald J. Dinus, "Tree Genetics and Improvement, Part 2: The Business of Tree Improvement," *Journal of Forestry* 84 (February 1986): 45–56; Calvin F. Bey, Daniel B. Houston, and Ronald J. Dinus, "Tree Genetics and Improvement, Part 3: Seed Orchards," *Journal of Forestry* 84 (March 1986): 27–37; *Cooperative Forest Genetics Research Program, Twenty-Ninth Progress Report, April 1987, Department of Forestry . . . University of Florida* (Gainesville: University of Florida, 1987); and Keith W. Dorman, *The Genetics and Breeding of Southern Pine,* Agriculture Handbook 471 (Washington, D.C.: U.S. Department of Agriculture, Forest Service, 1976). Stonecypher was a senior research forester at IP's Southlands Experiment Forest at Bainbridge, Georgia.

93. "The Managed Forest," special supplement to Crown Zellerbach's 1973 annual report, FHS. See also Paul Friggens, "The Story behind the South's Third Forest," *American Forests* (October 1971): 33–34.

94. Nelson, interview. Timber-stand improvement was, of course, a continuing concern in the forest-products industry. The 1969 *South's Third Forest* report is-

sued by the Southern Forest Resource Analysis Committee estimated that 45 percent of the southern commercial forest, some 90 million acres, needed some form of timber stand improvement (Charles H. Fitzgerald, Fred A. Peevy, and Darwin E. Fender, "The Southern Region," *Journal of Forestry* 71 [March 1973]: 148–53). Over the years a great deal of research occurred on various methods such as girdling, thinning, herbicidal treatment, fertilization, and different site-preparation treatments to improve timber stands and increase production. See "Poisoning versus Girdling to Release Underplanted Pines in North Mississippi," *Journal of Forestry* 52 (April 1954): 266–68; J. Melinda Slay, B. G. Lockaby, J. C. Adams, and C. G. Vidrine, "Effects of Site Preparation on Soil Physical Properties, Growth of Loblolly Pine, and Competing Vegetation," *Southern Journal of Applied Forestry* (November 1987): 83–86; and L. P. Wilhite and W. H. McKee Jr., "Site Preparation and Phosphorus Application Alter Early Growth of Loblolly Pine," *Southern Journal of Applied Forestry* (May 1985): 103–9.

95. Hughes, interview. By the late 1980s there was still no single magic formula regarding thinning. As Phillip H. Dunham of Westvaco Corporation wrote in 1986, "There are perhaps few topics in forestry that generate more discussion than the subject of pine thinning. Mentioning the words in a room full of foresters may cause debate that makes the 'less filling/tastes great' beer commercials look like a Sunday social" ("Will a Thinning Cut Pay?" *Forest Farmer* [September 1986]). For an introduction to the research and continuing debates concerning the technological, economic, and silvicultural aspects of thinning, see W. F. Mann Jr. and D. P. Feduccia, *Tree Sizes Harvested in Different Thinnings—Another Look,* Research Paper SO-131 (New Orleans: U.S. Department of Agriculture, Forest Service, Southern Forest Experiment Station, 1976); Donald P. Feduccia, "Thinning Pine Plantations," *Forest Farmer* (September 1983): 10–11; Roger W. Dennington, Robert F. Westbrook, and Paul W. Dillard, "Modern Technology Can Improve Strategy for Thinning Timber," *Forest Farmer* (September 1986): 12–13; J. Andrew Parker, "Selection Thinning Increases Slash Pine Size and Quality," *Southern Journal of Applied Forestry* (November 1979): 169–72; William F. Mann, "Thirty- Six Years of Thinning Research with Loblolly Pine," in *Management of Young Even-Aged Stands of Southern Pine: First Annual Symposium, School of Forestry, Louisiana State University, March 13–14, 1952* (Baton Rouge: School of Forestry, Louisiana State University, 1952); Herman H. Chapman, "Effects of Thinning on Yields of Forest-Grown Longleaf and Loblolly Pines at Urania, La.," *Journal of Forestry* 51 (January 1953): 16–26; Daniel J. Leduc and Boris Zeida, "Development of Loblolly Pine Stands at Various Levels

of Density and Pruning," *Arkansas Farm Research* (May–June 1987); William R. Harms and O. Gordon Langdon, "Development of Loblolly Pine in Dense Stands," *Forest Science* 22 (1976): 331–37; Frank A. Bennett, "Height Growth Patterns and Thinning of Slash Pine," *Journal of Forestry* 58 (July 1960): 561–62; William E. Balmer and Hamlin L. Williston, "The Need for Precommercial Thinning," *Forest Management Bulletin* (July 1973); John Fedkiw and James G. Yoho, "Economic Models for Thinning and Reproducing Even-Aged Stands," *Journal of Forestry* 58 (January 1960): 26–34; and J. F. Allen, "A Revolutionary(?) Thinning Method," *Timber Harvesting* (November 1980): 24–28. In the mid-1980s IP's Land and Timber Division developed and distributed to its foresters guidelines for thinning even-aged stands of loblolly and slash pine, but these guidelines offered plenty of room for altering the prescription and approach because of site characteristics or economic conditions ("Guidelines for Thinning Even-Aged Stands of Loblolly and Slash Pine," May 1984, IP Files).

96. Heyward, *History of Industrial Forestry,* 38–39; Forest Harvesting Act, chap. 240, *Laws of 1944, State of Mississippi* (Jackson: n.p., 1944), 130; Heyward, *History of Industrial Forestry,* 39, 41; Clepper, *Professional Forestry,* 249–52.

97. Barber, "Forestry," 511.

98. Richard Allen, interview. Bob Nonnemacher makes essentially the same argument (Nonnemacher, interview). In addition to changing owner objectives, continuing disagreements arose about the efficacy of various silvicultural and managerial practices. As one writer put it in 1953, "It is small wonder that opinions differ regarding most of the details of southern pine management or even that the proper silvicultural system may be in doubt. The southern pine territory is extremely large and diverse. . . . The four major species of pine . . . differ quite markedly in their growth requirements. They occur with a variety of associated conifers and hardwoods on a variety of sites. Experience in one locality may lead to somewhat different conclusions from experience in another. And no management system, even-aged or all-aged, has been so thoroughly demonstrated in southern pine that we can know from definite records that it is superior to any other" (Robert D. McCulley, "The Case for Even-Aged Management of Southern Pine," *Journal of Forestry* 51 [February 1953]: 38–90). Yale professor and forestry consultant Herman H. Chapman published one of the classic studies of southern pine management in 1942. In his lengthy work, Chapman presented a "Summary of Rules for Management" that included his prescriptions for species selection, timber-stand improvement, selective logging, fire control, controlled burning, hardwood control, thinning, planting, grazing control, and stock-

ing. Many of the particulars of Chapman's prescriptions were immediately attacked by other pine-management specialists. See Herman H. Chapman, *Management of Loblolly Pine in the Pine-Hardwood Region in Arkansas and in Louisiana West of the Mississippi River,* Yale University School of Forestry, Bulletin 49 (New Haven: Yale University, 1942); and Henry Bull and R. R. Reynolds, "Management of Loblolly Pine: Further Study Needed," *Journal of Forestry* 41 (October 1943): 722–26. For a variety of views toward and examples of different forest-management plans, see a 1952 paper by IP division forester B. A. Ryan, "A Pulpwood Company's Views of Even-Aged Management," paper presented at the First Annual Symposium, School of Forestry, Louisiana State University, Baton Rouge, March 13–14, 1952; and R. R. Reynolds, "Management of Second-Growth Shortleaf-Loblolly Pine-Hardwood Stands," *Journal of Forestry* 45 (March 1947): 181–87. Reynolds noted that while he hoped his discussion would "whet your appetite for further study of good forest management practices," his audience should remember that "we in this country are still finding our way in forestry. . . . [M]any desirable policies are still in the experimental stage or, as yet, not even thought of" (187). See also W. E. Bond, "The Case for All-Aged Management of Southern Pines," *Journal of Forestry* 51 (February 1953): 90–93; William E Balmer and Hamlin L. Williston, "Early Considerations in Pine Management," *Forest Management Bulletin* (October 1975); Stephen G. Boyce, "How to Double the Harvest of Loblolly and Slash Pine Timber," *Journal of Forestry* 73 (December 1975): 761–66; and Peter Koch, "Concept for Southern Pine Plantation Operation in the Year 2020," *Journal of Forestry* 78 (February 1980): 78–82. For a very brief overview of the evolution of industrial forestland management, see Stephen B. Jones, "Industry Embraces More Intensive Management and Good Stewardship," *Forest Farmer* (June 1984): 13–14. At the time this article was published Jones was the Woodlands Division historian for Union Camp Corporation.

99. Earl Porter, "History of Forest Fire Prevention," 619–21; Nelson, interview. Practices like those described by Nelson and the work of the IP conservation foresters were generally believed to be important in influencing the behavior of "[p]rivate nonindustrial owners [who] are the least willing of all groups of landowners to practice forestry." In turn, this segment of the ownership population was critical, for "[w]hile the individual tracts are small, in the aggregate they comprise nearly three-fourths of the South's woodlands" (Walter C. Anderson, *Factors Influencing North Carolina Landowners to Practice Forestry,* Research Paper SO-33 [n.p.: U.S. Department of Agriculture, Forest Service, 1968]). An excellent example of the early attempt to sell the tree-farm program to small landown-

ers is found in *Flintkote Forester* 1 (May 1944). The planting of pine on nonindustrial private lands in the South more than doubled during the period from the mid-1970s to the mid-1980s, and this increase was attributed to the influence of both market factors and programs of the federal government. See Jack P. Royer, "Determinants of Reforestation Behavior among Southern Landowners," *Forest Science* 33 (September 1987): 654–56.

100. Sterling and Thompson, "Summary."

101. *South's Fourth Forest: Alternatives,* 73–74; Arthur W. Nelson Jr., "South's Third Forest." See also Friggens, "Story," 32–34, 54; and Paul Friggens, "Biggest Tree-Planting Job on Earth," *Reader's Digest* (November 1971): 3–6.

102. "Tree Farm System Declaration of Principle," *Mississippi Forest Facts* 9 (November 1943): 1; International Paper Company, Woodlands Department, Annual Report, 1948, IP Files; Tree Farm Movement Gains," news release of National Lumber Manufacturers' Association, April 18, 1945, FHS; J. C. McClellan, memorandum, August 1, 1966, FHS; *Growing Trees to Meet the Nation's Needs* (Washington, D.C.: American Forest Products Industries, 1966); Myers, *Impact of Forestry Associations,* 12–13; Clepper, *Professional Forestry,* 252–53; Charles A. Gillett, "Private Forestry on the March: The Story of Tree Farms," *Journal of Forestry* 64 (September 1966): 601–3; "A Brief History of the American Tree Farm System," SPA Records; *South's Fourth Forest: Alternatives,* 74; Terry Hadaway, "Mississippi Still Tops in Tree Farm Program," *Forest Farmer* (November–December 1985): 29–31; Richard Lewis, "Tree Farming: A Voluntary Conservation Program," *Journal of Forest History* 25 (July 1981): 166–69; "Mississippi Tree Farm System Makes Substantial Progress," *Forest Facts* (January 1947); Charles E. Twining, "Weyerhaeuser and the Clemons Tree Farm: Experimenting with a Theory," in *History of Sustained-Yield Forestry: A Symposium,* ed. Harold K. Steen (Santa Cruz, Calif.: Forest History Society, 1984), 33–41; Ed Kerr, "Tree Farming Sweeps the Country," *American Forests* (May 1960): 28–30, 52–53; and Paul F. Sharp, "The Tree Farm Movement: Its Origin And Development," *Agricultural History* 23 (January 1949): 41–45. For an overview of the origins, history, and reasons for industry's support of the tree-farms program, see Richard Lewis, "Tree Farming," 166–69. The problems inherent in selling the idea of farm forestry as a viable economic activity to small farmers at the time the tree-farm movement originated are revealed in W. E. Bond and R. E. Rhodes, "Forestry as a Farm Enterprise in Washington Parish, Louisiana," Occasional Paper 100 (New Orleans: U.S. Department of Agriculture, Forest Service, Southern Forest Experiment Station, 1941). The continuing importance of timber held in

small private ownerships (defined by the U.S. Forest Service as those of less than five thousand acres) was emphasized in Leonard I. Barrett, "Special Problems of the Small Forest Owner in the United States," paper presented at the Fifth World Forestry Congress, Seattle, Washington, August 29–September 10, 1960.

103. Arthur W. Nelson Jr., "Development of Forest Practices," 36–38. The winter 1988 issue of *Tree Talk,* the official publication of the Mississippi Forestry Association, noted, "Sponsorship of the Tree Farm program is MFA's way of giving community, state and national recognition to landowners practicing good forestry" (*Tree Talk* 10 [winter 1988]: 5).

104. Helen Phillips, interview by Pam Ivins, March 26, 1991, in *Timber Industry in the Great Depression,* 237. For Tom DeWeese's recollection of Allen and the origins of the "DeWeese Tree Farm Family," see DeWeese, interview by Edgerly. In 1944 one of Mississippi's venerable companies, the L. N. Dantzler Lumber Company, joined the tree-farm movement ("L. N. Dantzler Lumber Co. Adopts Tree Farming," *Mississippi Forest Facts* 9 [October 1944]: 4).

105. Shannon, interview, 64; *Sixteenth Census of the United States: 1940; Manufactures 1939,* vol. 2, pt. 1 (Washington, D.C.: U.S. Government Printing Office, 1942), 518.

106. Phillips, interview, 238; Cicero Sellers, interview by Eddie Ivy, March 22, 1991, in *Timber Industry in the Great Depression,* 249.

107. Raymond Gressett, interview by Renee Farmer, March 5, 1991, in *Timber Industry in the Great Depression,* 128; Alfred Frazier, interview by Mandy Goldman, February 19, 1991, in *The Timber Industry in the Great Depression,* 196. It should be noted that these accounts do not describe clear-cutting, which takes everything except, in some cases, seed trees, but instead describe high grading, taking only the best timber from a tract.

108. Pope, interview, 376.

109. For U.S. Forest Service calculations of growth, drain, and timber, see William E. Duerr, *Forest Statistics for Mississippi: A Report of the Southern Forest Survey,* Forest Survey Release 59 (New Orleans: U.S. Department of Agriculture, Forest Service, Southern Forest Experiment Station, 1949); Lee M. James and Albert L. Tofte, *Mississippi's Forest Industry: A Report of the Southern Forest Survey,* Forest Survey Release 62 (New Orleans: U.S. Department of Agriculture, Forest Service, Southern Forest Experiment Station, 1949); Lee M. James and William P. Hoffman, *Mississippi Timber Stands before and after Cutting: A Report of the Southern Forest Survey,* Forest Survey Release 60 (New Orleans: U.S. Department of Agriculture, Forest Service, Southern Forest Experiment Station, 1949); and Herbert S. Sternitzke and John A. Putnam, *Forests of the Mississippi Delta,* Forest Survey Release 78 (New Or-

leans: U.S. Department of Agriculture, Forest Service, Southern Forest Experiment Station, 1956). For a criticism of James's work, see Henry Gilbert White, "Forest Ownership Research in Historical Perspective," *Journal of Forestry* 48 (April 1950): 261–63. For a good, brief overview of the methods implemented to resurrect one company's industrial forest, see *Ten Years on the Flintkote Forest: The Story of the Development of the Forest for the Period 1941–1951* (Meridian, Miss.: Flintkote Company, Forestry Department, 1952). Nelson was the chief forester of the Flintkote Forest, and additional information on its management appears in his "The Problems of a Forest Manager during the Early Stages of Placing a Property under Management," in *Management of Young Even-Aged Stands of Southern Pine.*

Chapter 8

1. *South's Fourth Forest: Alternatives,* 509–12; David A. Pease, "Forest Resource Study Reviewed: Evaluation of Services Authorized," *Forest Industries* (June 1969): 34–36; Philip R. Wheeler, "The South's Third Forest," *Journal of Forestry* 68 (March 1970): 142–46. In some longleaf pine areas, cutting in the "Second Forest," which began before World War II, continues to the present. In the mid-1980s, some forest researchers estimated that more than 90 percent of the remaining longleaf pine was natural in origin (see Landers, Van Lear, and Boyd, "Longleaf Pine Forests," 41). Zebulon W. White claimed that he and Philip Wheeler "formalized the categories First Forest, Second Forest and Third Forest to describe the succession of the southern pine through the decades" ("Loblolly Pine," 15). A 1973 follow-up report on Mississippi's third-forest effort found that to bring regeneration up to "a reasonable rate of production" would require planting and timber stand improvement work at four to five times the current rate with annual expenditures of $12 million annually. For the South generally, the report noted, "In the five years since industry . . . set itself some goals for the stewardship, the real progress has been in publicizing the problem and organizing to do something. Very little progress has been made in establishing a productive Third Forest on those millions of understocked areas." The report concluded, "After years of building our reputations for reforestation and growing more than we are cutting, it will be devastating both to the performance of our industries and to our credibility to have to admit that we are now cutting more than we are growing" ("Five Years of Efforts on the Third Forest: A Report and Recommendations for the Southern Forest Resource Council, November 1973," 13, 19, 22, in possession of author).

2. Fickle and Ellis, "POWs in the Piney Woods"; Pope, interview, 385–86.

3. James Emanuel Moak, "The Pine Lumber Industry in Mississippi: Its Changing Aspects" (Ph.D. diss., State University College of Forestry at Syracuse University, 1965), 98–112, 125–26; John W. Thompson, "Timberland Acquisition," November 3, 1947, Johns Manville Records, box 16; Lee M. James, "Timber Supplies for Industry in Mississippi," *Southern Economic Journal* 18 (July 1951): 61, 65–67. James said that Mississippi had maintained its forest industries despite the decline in forest resources by using inferior timber, shifting from sawlog to pulp production, overcutting, and utilizing timber more fully, which he argued was inherent in pulpwood as opposed to sawlog production. He said that the resource problem could be solved through better forest management and at least a temporary reduction in utilization but decried the "generally poor level of timber management in the state." For an overview of the conditions and needs of the forests and forest industries from a national perspective at the end of World War II, see *Forests and National Prosperity: A Reappraisal of the Forest Situation in the United States,* U.S. Department of Agriculture, Forest Service, Miscellaneous Publication 668 (Washington, D.C.: U.S. Government Printing Office, 1948). See also Clement Mesavage and William A. Duerr, *Timber Resources of the Lower South, 1946,* Forest Survey Release 55 (New Orleans: U.S. Department of Agriculture, Forest Service, Southern Forest Experiment Station, 1946); and Duerr, *Forest Statistics.*

4. Moak, "Pine Lumber Industry," 128–29.

5. Ibid., 122–23.

6. Ibid., 78–79, 83–85, 125.

7. Ibid., 126–27; Lloyd C. Irland, *The South's Forest Industries: A Statistical Profile* (New Orleans: Southern Forest Products Association, 1975), iii, 6, 8, 18; James E. Moak, *Forestry: Its Economic Importance to Mississippi* (Starkville: Mississippi State University Agricultural and Forestry Experiment Station, 1971), 14, 16, 18; "How Our Garden Grows," 3; "History of Forestry in Mississippi," 63.

8. "Old Industry Returns," *Forestry News* 5 (June 1968): 1; "Lumber Firm Locating in Mississippi Again," *Jackson (Mississippi) Daily News,* April 15, 1968; Edward Hines Lumber Company, Annual Reports, 1981 and 1982, FHS.

9. Carroll Brinson, *More Than a Good Businessman: The Story of Warren A. Hood* (Jackson, Miss.: Oakdale Press, 1987), 5–26.

10. Ibid., 39–61.

11. Ibid., 50–51; Edward P. Cliff to Wendell D. Lack, April 3, 1970, MFA Records, box 51; *The Story of Camille: How Mississippi Recovered from a Disaster with a Bright Look to the Future: A Report to Governor John Bell Williams by the Governor's Forest Disaster Salvage Council, July 1970,* MFA Records, box 50; Wendell D. Lack, "Response to a Historic Forest Disaster," 1970, MFC Files; Plato Touliatos and Elmer Roth, "Hurricanes and Trees: Ten Lessons from Camille," *Journal of Forestry* 69 (May 1971): 285–89.

12. "History of Forestry in Mississippi," 59–67; "Dick Allen Receives Meritorious Service Award," *Tree Talk* 2 (winter 1980): 19; Richard Allen, interview.

13. Arthur W. Nelson Jr., "South's Third Forest"; Art Nelson, "Art, How'd You Get in This Business Anyway?" 49–50.

14. "History of Forestry in Mississippi," 55; Art Nelson, "Tree Planter," 28–29. For additional information on Guthrie's life and career, see Guthrie, interview. See also John G. Guthrie to James W. Craig, May 19, 1989, MFA Records.

15. "History of Forestry in Mississippi," 24–29; James W. Craig to Jason N. Kutack, July 5, 1988, MFA Records, box 50.

16. Jonathan Daniels, *Forest Is the Future,* 8, 10.

17. *Mississippi Forests* (New Orleans: U.S. Department of Agriculture, Forest Service, Southern Forest Experiment Station, 1958), 3–4, 8–9, 11.

18. "The Georgia-Pacific Story: A Report by Blyth and Co., Inc.," 1963, 1, 15, FHS; Owen R. Cheatham and Robert B. Pamplin, *The Georgia-Pacific Story* (New York: Newcomen Society in North America, 1966), 18; Georgia-Pacific, Annual Report, 1982, FHS. For the story of the management of L. N. Dantzler's lands following World War II until their eventual sale to IP in 1966, see J. E. Bryan Jr., "Forest History," 11–36. The rebirth of the lumber industry and the dramatic rise of the pulp and paper industry were clearly among the most significant economic developments in the South from the time of the Great Depression through 1980. It is thus curious, and somewhat typical, that they receive relatively little attention in James C. Cobb's standard work on southern industrialization efforts during that period. Cobb does, however, cite some examples of paper mills as violators of state pollution laws. See Cobb, *The Selling of the South: The Southern Crusade for Industrial Development, 1936–1980* (Baton Rouge: Louisiana State University Press, 1982).

19. Jonathan Daniels, *Forest Is the Future,* 31–32; Pesch, "Example," 99–103; "Woodlands History," 97–98; "IP Natchez Mill Keeps Pace as Industrial Climate Grows," *Natchez (Mississippi) Democrat,* April 26, 1992.

20. "IP Natchez Mill," 13; "Woodlands History," 72–73, 105; Roy V. Scott, "American Railroads," 77.

21. G. H. Weaver and Steven H. Bullard, "Mississippi's Severance Tax and Forest Resource Development Program," *Journal of Forestry* 81 (October 1983): 663; "History of Forestry in Mississippi," 37, app. 8. For an-

nouncements of new forest-products facilities, see "Woodlands History," 99; and *Tree Talk* 1 (winter 1979): 17, 22; 2 (summer 1979): 20, 24–25; 2 (fall 1979): 14; 2 (spring 1980): 12; 3 (summer 1980): 20; 3 (winter 1981): 14; 4 (winter 1982): 6; 5 (fall 1983): 6–8; 10 (fall 1988): 19–20. Weyerhaeuser's growth in Mississippi was not without controversy. Critics charged that the company exercised undue influence over state and local officials in the process of deciding to build its giant facilities at Columbus and that union labor would be excluded from the construction process. For a brief discussion of these controversies as well as a thoughtful analysis of the historical significance of the Columbus complex, see Clark, *Greening*, 121–23.

22. Amigo and Neuffer, *Beyond the Adirondacks*, 142, 145, 169; St. Regis Paper Company, Annual Report, 1967, FHS.

23. Amigo and Neuffer, *Beyond the Adirondacks*, 146, 147, 167.

24. "The Yazoo–Little Tallahatchie Flood Prevention Project," *Forestry Forum* (August 1989): 20; "The Yazoo–Little Tallahatchie Flood Prevention Project," *Forestry Forum* (October 1989): 14.

25. St. Regis news releases, April 30, 1984, July 17, 31, 1984, all in FHS; *Champion Magazine* 8 (1981), 1, 3, 8, 24; Richard W. Bryan, "Giant Board Plant Uses Pine, Hardwood," *Forest Industries* (July 1970): 46.

26. R. O. Hunt, *Pulp, Paper and Pioneers: The Story of Crown Zellerbach Corporation* (New York: Newcomen Society in North America, 1961); Parker Rouse Jr., *The Timber Tycoons: The Camp Families of Virginia and Florida and Their Empire* (Richmond, Va.: William Byrd Press for the Southampton County Historical Society, 1988), unpaginated map. Union Camp recently merged with IP.

27. Straka and Hotvedt, "Timberland Ownership," 17–19; Healy, *Competition for Land*, 100–101.

28. S. G. Boyce, E. C. Burkhardt, R. C. Kellison, and D. H. Van Lear, "Silviculture: The Next Thirty Years, the Past Thirty Years, Part 3: The South," *Journal of Forestry* 84 (June 1986): 46–47.

29. "What about Mississippi's Future Timber Supply?" *Tree Talk* 2 (fall 1979): 10, 12. For a somewhat different breakdown of the figures and analysis, see "Survey Shows Reforestation Need," *Tree Talk* 1 (fall 1978): 23–24; John F. Kelly, "USFS Survey Provides a Picture of Mississippi's Changing Forests," *Tree Talk* 12 (spring 1990): 24, 26–27, 29–31.

30. Thomas L. Bailey to members of the Mississippi Legislature, n.d., in *What the Forests and Forest Industries Mean to Mississippi* (Jackson: Mississippi State Forest Service in cooperation with U.S. Forest Service, 1945), 3; Jonathan Daniels, *Forest Is the Future*, 49; Dick Allen, "Justice for Wood Burners," *Bay Springs (Mississippi) Jasper County News*, December 2, 1981.

31. Jonathan Daniels, *Forest Is the Future*, 49, 51.

32. Herman H. Chapman, "Forest Fires and Forestry in the Southern States," *American Forestry* 18 (August 1912): 510–17; Erle Kauffman, "The Southland Revisited, Part 3," *American Forests* (October 1955): 94, 112; Wakeley, "F. O. ('Red') Bateman," 94; "1946 Annual Report, Forestry," Annual Reports 1947–48, Dantzler Records; Folweiler and Brown, *Fire in the Forests*, i, 3; J. W. Thompson and C. R. McDonald, report on Johns Manville timberlands, April 15, 1957, Johns Manville Records, box 21, folder 833. See also Crow, "Use of Fire," 629–32; and Clinton B. Phillips, "Fire in Wildland Management," *Journal of Forestry* 71 (October 1973): 624.

33. William Dean and David S. Evans, *Terms of the Trade: A Handbook for the Forest Products Industry* (Eugene, Ore.: Random Lengths Publications, 1978), 15; Bryce J. Stokes, Colin Ashmore, Cynthia L. Rawlins, and Donald L. Sirois, *Glossary of Terms Used in Timber Harvesting and Forest Engineering*, General Technical Report SO-73 (New Orleans: U.S. Department of Agriculture, Forest Service, Southern Forest Experiment Station, 1989), 5; Art Nelson, "Wood Chip Production Benefits Environment: Technology Developed in the '50s," *Tree Talk* 15 (spring 1993): 25; Art Nelson, "Pages from Art Nelson's Notebook: Railroad Rack Cars," *Tree Talk* 18 (winter 1996): 16; "Woodlands History," 113–14; Ham Sanders, interview by Art Nelson, March 4, 1991, MFA Records. The chipping head rig mills small logs simultaneously into lumber and chips. It chips away the outer part of the log and saws the inner part, ordinarily into two by fours. See also Friggens, "Story," 34, 54. The *kerf* is the "width of a saw cut; this portion of a log is lost as waste when it is sawn for lumber. The size of the kerf is dependent on saw size, saw type, sharpness, and other factors" (Dean and Evans, *Terms of the Trade*, 49). Dick Allen recalled that the DeWeese Lumber Company bought the first chipping machine in Mississippi from the manufacturer in Sweden (Richard C. Allen, interview, 17, MFA Records). For an analysis of technological change in sawmills and planing mills, pulp mills and paper mills, and logging camps and contractors between 1958 and 1976, see Christopher D. Risbrudt, "Past and Future Technological Change in the U.S. Forest Industries" (Ph.D. diss., Michigan State University, 1979).

34. "Chip Mills Provide Market for Pulpwood," *Tree Talk* 13 (winter 1991): 20; "Woodlands History," 116–17.

35. *Discover Mississippi's Forests* (Starkville: Forest and Wildlife Research Center, Mississippi State University, [late 1990s]), 12–13.

36. W. Dale Greene and Frank W. Corley, "Timber Harvesting in the South: Advances in Technology," *Journal of Forestry* 94 (June 1996): 24. By the mid-

1980s at least seven harvesting systems were used in the southern pine forests, each requiring different types or combinations of equipment. See Robert A. Tufts and Donald M. Tufts, "Harvesting Loblolly Pine," in *Proceedings,* ed. Karr, Baker, and Monaghan, 250–57; and Charles E. Cline, "The Industrial Forester and the Changing Face of Timber Harvesting," *Journal of Forestry* 72 (November 1974): 692–95.

37. W. Dale Greene and Corley, "Timber Harvesting," 24–25; Billy Watson, "Next Generation Forestry: On-Site Processing and Harvesting Technology," *Tree Talk* 18 (winter 1996): 29–32. One of the more interesting machines was the Buschmaster, developed by Thomas N. Busch, chief of operations for the Woodlands Department of IP's Southern Kraft Division in the late 1950s. The Buschmaster was a multipurpose behemoth that could plow fire lanes, spray chemicals or water, pull a tree planter, grade or scrape terrain, support a fire torch, and pull itself or other equipment with a winch. Busch also developed IP's Busch combine, which could shear a tree at ground level, pull it through a delimber, and cut it into sixty-three-inch sticks in less than two minutes and then bind the sticks into cords for loading onto a trailer ("We Present: Thomas N. Busch and the Buschmaster," *Journal of Forestry* 59 [February 1961]: 126–30).

38. Jerry D. Greer, "The View from Above: An Overview of GPS and Remote Sensing Options," *Journal of Forestry* 91 (August 1993): 10–14; "Woodlands History," 118; Charles H. Lewis Jr., "Forestry Progress in Aerial Photography," *Mississippi Forest Facts* (July 1946): 4. See also Doug Luepke, "Global Positioning System Technology for Forestry—Yesterday, Today and Tomorrow," *Tree Talk* 18 (winter 1996): 25–26.

39. McKnight, "Hardwood Research," 77; J. S. McKnight, "The Southern Hardwood Forestry Group Going Strong after Ten Years," *Southern Lumberman* (December 15, 1961); Philip A. Briegleb and J. S. McKnight, "The Place of Hardwoods in Forest Management," paper presented at the annual meeting of the Southern Pulpwood Conservation Association, Atlanta, January 13, 1960, 4; *South's Fourth Forest: Alternatives,* 71. See also *Trends in Hardwood Management and Use: Articles from "The Unit"* (Atlanta: Southern Pulpwood Conservation Association, 1966, copy in SPCA Records).

40. *South's Fourth Forest: Alternatives,* 75; "Plywood Manufacturing Moves into the South—A Special Report," *Newsletter, Gulf States Section, Society of American Foresters* 5 (fall 1963): 18–20.

41. *South's Fourth Forest: Alternatives,* 33, 75. See also Art Nelson, "Naval Stores," 30; "Naval Stores: One of America's Oldest Industries," *Forest History Today* (1996): 23–27; Butler, *Treasures*; and "Museum Receives Turpentine Still," *Tree Talk* 2 (fall 1979): 18, 20.

42. McKnight, "Southern Hardwood Forestry Group"; Burkhardt, "Hardwoods," 25; Maisenhelder and McKnight, "Southern Hardwood Research."

43. Briegleb and McKnight, "Place of Hardwoods," 1.

44. Ibid., 2.

45. Barber, "Forestry," 510; Herbert S. Sternitzke, "Impact of Changing Land Use on Delta Hardwood Forests," *Journal of Forestry* 74 (January 1976): 25–27.

46. "Managed Forest."

47. International Paper Company, Annual Report, 1976, IP Files; C. Ronald Hunt, "Site Preparation for Hardwood Tree Establishment," in *Herbicides in Forestry: 1975 Proceedings of John S. Wright Forestry Conference, Purdue University, West Lafayette, Ind.* (West Lafayette, Ind.: Purdue University, 1975), n.p. IP was actively studying the establishment of hardwood plantations during this period. See R. McGarity, "Economic Evaluation of Hardwood Management Alternatives," April 19, 1978, IP Files. McGarity was affiliated with IP's Natchez Forestry Research Center. By 1984 two researchers reported, "The economics of using greater amounts of hardwoods in pulp, the roundwood of which can be delivered to the mill at about 25% less cost than pine roundwood and which gives about 5% greater pulp yield than pine from the pulp process, have caused corporate management to dictate higher uses of hardwoods. Some pulp mills have increased the mill furnish from 10% to 30% hardwoods for linerboard production within the last 18 months. Other mills are retrofitting operations to allow greater use of hardwoods." These authors also observed that the "emphasis in the southern United States within the past decade has been to shift to regeneration and management of natural hardwood stands, as opposed to establishment of hardwood plantations" (R. C. Kellison and Richard Resovsky, "Economic Opportunities in Hardwood Silviculture: Plantation versus Natural Stand Management," in *Proceedings of the 1984 Southern Forest Economics Workshop: Payoffs from New Techniques for Managing and Processing Southern Hardwoods,* ed. Richard W. Guldin [Memphis: n.p., 1984], n.p.).

48. John A. Zivnuska, "Future Wood Markets and Forest Management," *Journal of Forestry* 49 (May 1951): 326–30.

49. *What Trees Mean to the Delta* (Jackson: Mississippi Forestry and Chemurgic Association, [1950s]), copy in FHS. Sometime between August 1, 1940, and November 1941 the name of the Mississippi Forestry Association was changed to the Mississippi Forestry and Chemurgic Association. Chemurgics referred to products made through chemical processes from natural fibers, such as rayon, plastics, and synthetic rubber. This information was gathered from the masthead of *Forest Facts,* a Mississippi Forestry Association publication that

existed from March 1940 through March 1948 and became known as *Mississippi Forest Facts.* The information concerning chemurgics appears in the December 1941 issue. Copies of *Forest Facts* are in the MFA Records. In 1948 *Mississippi Forest Facts* was replaced for a time by a monthly page called "Forest Facts" in the Jackson weekly *Conservation News* ("Change of Publication Notice," *Mississippi Forest Facts* [March 1948]: 1). See also Art Nelson, "Chemurgy—What Is It?" *Tree Talk* 14 (summer 1992): 14; and Stone, "Chemurgy's First Agent."

50. For example, in a 1960 paper delivered to the Southern Pulpwood Conservation Association, Philip A. Briegleb and J. S. McKnight of the Southern Forest Experiment Station noted the increasing utilization of hardwood by pulp mills and also noted that "the hardwood crop will support much more game than the pine crop" ("Place of Hardwoods," 4). Comments on Briegleb's presentation and the developing hardwood movement appear in "The Spirit of Austin Cary Marches On," *American Forests* (February 1960): 11; and William F. Diehl Jr., "Ignoring Hardwood Value?" *Pulp and Paper* (March 1960): 112–13. McKnight and Putnam were the region's acknowledged hardwood experts, and in a paper presented two years later at Auburn University, McKnight continued to address one of the major themes in his work: "The southern forest is predominantly hardwood. Of the 193 million acres . . . pine types cover 92 million, hardwoods 101 million acres. . . . There is little doubt that hardwoods on 31 million of these acres are growing where they do not belong. Conversion to pine is the prescription for such poor hardwood sites. Left for your consideration, then, are the 70 million acres of southern forest capable of growing hardwood at an economic rate. There are four broad physiographic classes of site where effort should be concentrated in managing hardwoods: Bottom lands of major rivers . . . Swamps . . . Bottoms of creeks and small streams . . . Rich upland soils." In response to a question concerning site specificity for hardwoods and pine, McKnight replied, "Down in the hollow, we can grow a good yellow poplar. We go up on the side of the hill, say to a slope of 20% and we have good pine there, but we may have acceptable yellow poplar or white oak there also. In that so-called gray zone we can grow pine and hardwoods together and we should consider just how far up the hill we can grow good hardwoods along with good pine, and where we should cut off and grow nothing but pine. Somewhere in there, there's a positive boundary, but we'll never define it exactly. We should recognize that hardwoods will grow along with pines in certain situations. I can think of river bottoms where there are excellent pines, some of the best swamp chestnut oak . . . in the world, and cherry-bark oak and Shumard growing right along with the pine. Certainly, 'gray zone' may not be the term, but

I mean that it's an area where pine and hardwoods should be accepted as equally important in the total forest" ("Southern Forestry Includes Hardwoods," *Proceedings of the Auburn Forestry Forum* [Auburn, Ala.: Auburn University, 1963], n.p.). In his capacity as project leader of timber management research for the Southern Hardwoods Laboratory, McKnight was frequently asked for recommendations concerning the treatment of bottomlands where hardwoods or mixed stands of pine and hardwoods were growing. A review of his correspondence file indicates that while he suggested various programs of silvicultural treatment and timber-stand improvement, McKnight never recommended the conversion of bottomland hardwood stands into pine forests. See, for example, McKnight to Roy O. Martin Jr., August 31, 1967; McKnight to Ed Leigh McMillen II, July 7, 1964; McKnight to Leonard H. Thomas, July 15, 1965; McKnight to Harold Winger, April 23, 1970; and McKnight to Richard Allen, February 18, 1970, all in J. S. McKnight Correspondence File, Southern Hardwoods Laboratory, Stoneville, Miss. In 1963 A. W. Nelson Jr., general manager of the Timber Division of Champion Paper, noted, "As the paper mills began to accumulate experience with hardwoods, it was found that they imparted certain desirable traits to the product and the use of hardwoods by industry increased." Nelson also observed, "Another area in which our thinking has been clouded is the question of offsite hardwoods. It has long been recognized that hardwoods growing on pine sites have seldom resulted in a merchantable crop and that . . . they ought to be removed. . . . Some foresters let their enthusiasm get out of hand and carried these treatments on into bottom lands. . . . It has only been in recent years that we have had a clear understanding of the potential of hardwood growing on truly hardwood sites" ("Future Timber Situation for Hardwoods," paper presented before the Southwestern Technical Committee, American Pulpwood Association, New Orleans, April 8–10, 1963). As the use of hardwoods by pulp mills increased, it was accompanied by the growth of environmental concerns about the dominance of pine plantations in the South and the diminishing area occupied by the hardwood and mixed pine-hardwood forests that many believed provided better watershed protection and wildlife habitat. See Robert J. Lentz, Daniel H. Sims, and Peter J. Ince, "Are Our Traditional Attitudes Restricting Forestry Management Options?" in *Proceedings of Pine-Hardwood Mixtures: A Symposium on Management and Ecology of the Type, April 18–19, 1989, Atlanta, Georgia,* ed. Thomas A. Wasdrop, Technical Report SE-58 (Atlanta: U.S. Department of Agriculture, Forest Service, 1989), 20–24. This conference reflected the growing interest in the preservation and management of the southern hardwood forests and mixed forests. Others were concerned that with the industry's emphasis on pulpwood and species that are easier to reproduce and faster growing, the South's stately longleaf pine forests were diminishing. See Croker, "Longleaf Pine Story," 42–43. McKnight wrote prolifically on the subject of hardwood management, although many of his papers and articles essentially restate the same themes. Among his publications are J. S. McKnight and R. L. Johnson, "Hardwood Management in Southern Bottomlands," *Forest Farmer* 23 (March 1980): 31–38; G. F. Dutrow, J. S. McKnight, and S. Guttenberg, *Investment Guide for Cottonwood Planters* (New Orleans: U.S. Department of Agriculture, Forest Service, Southern Forest Experiment Station, 1970); John A. Putnam, George M. Furnival, and J. S. McKnight, *Management and Inventory of Southern Hardwoods,* Agriculture Handbook 181 (New Orleans: U.S. Department of Agriculture, Forest Service, 1960); J. S. McKnight, "Ecology of Four Hardwood Species," *Proceedings, Louisiana State University Seventeenth Annual Forestry Symposium* (Baton Rouge: Louisiana State University, 1968), n.p.; J. S. McKnight, *Hardwood Forests of the South* (New Orleans: U.S. Department of Agriculture, Forest Service, 1965); J. S. McKnight and R. C. Biesterfeldt, "Commercial Cottonwood Planting in the Southern United States," *Journal of Forestry* 66 (September 1968): 670–75; J. S. McKnight and J. S. McWilliams, "Improving Southern Hardwood Stands through Commercial Harvest and Cull-Tree Control," *Proceedings, Society of American Foresters* (Washington, D.C.: Society of American Foresters, 1956); J. S. McKnight, "Meeting the Demand for Southern Hardwoods," *National Hardwood Magazine* 42 (February 1968): 38–39; J. S. McKnight, "Hardwood Log Marketing Should Be Improved," *National Hardwood Magazine* 42 (March 1968): 40–41; J. S. McKnight, "Getting the Most from Southern Hardwood Stands," *National Hardwood Magazine* 42 (April 1968): 44–45; J. S. McKnight, "Establishing Good, New Stands of Southern Hardwoods," *National Hardwood Magazine* 42 (May 1968); J. S. McKnight, "Southern Hardwood Forests of the Future," *National Hardwood Magazine* 42 (June 1968): 48–49; J. S. McKnight and Robert L. Johnson, "Growing Hardwoods in Southern Lowlands," *Forest Farmer* 21 (1975): 38–47; McKnight and Putnam, "Logging Cut-Over Stands," 184–86; and J. S. McKnight and H. L. Gantz, "Heavy, Light or No Cutting?" *Forest Farmer* (June 1957): 11. McKnight's publications also include J. A. Putnam and J. S. McKnight, "Depleted Bottom-Land Hardwoods Make Quick Comeback," *Southern Lumberman* (December 15, 1949); J. S. McKnight, "Intensify Forestry in Southern Hardwoods," in *Technical Papers of the American Pulpwood Association* (n.p., 1965), 10–12; J. S. McKnight, "Upland Hardwood Situation in Area I," *The Unit* (October 1966): 9–10; J. S. McKnight, "Application of Uneven-Aged Silviculture to Southern Hardwood Forests," *Proceedings, Symposium on Hardwoods of Piedmont and Coastal Plain* (n.p.: Georgia Forest Research Council, 1966); and J. S. McKnight, "Hardwood Use and Forestry in the U.S.," *American Railway Development Association Proceedings* (1965): 46–50. This is by no means a complete listing of McKnight's publications. Other works on hardwood management include Sternitzke, "Impact," 25–27; Robert L. Johnson and Roy C. Beltz, "Hardwood Management Options Hold Promise," *Forest Farmer* (January 1985); Charles McGee, "Conflict and Progress in Hardwood Management," *Forest Farmer* (July–August 1984): 23–25; Stephen H. Spurr, "Pine Plantations versus Natural Pine-Hardwood Succession," *Forest Farmer* (November–December 1982): 6–7; R. C. Kellison, Russ Lea, and D. J. Frederick, "Effect of Silvicultural Practices on Wood Quality of Southern Hardwoods," in *Proceedings of the Technical Association of the Pulp and Paper Industry, 1982 Research and Development Division Conference, Asheville, North Carolina, August 29–September 1, 1982* ([Atlanta]: [TAPPI Press, 1982]); Richard Lee Porterfield, "Financial Returns from Managing Southern Hardwood Stands for Pulpwood," *Journal of Forestry* 70 (October 1972): 624–27; Tom Cambre and Frank Shropshire, "Hardwood Regeneration," *Forest Farmer* (April 1984): 16–17 ; R. C. Kellison, D. J. Frederick, and W. E. Gardner, *A Guide for Regenerating and Managing Natural Stands of Southern Hardwoods* (n.p.: North Carolina Agricultural Research Service, n.d.); Edgar Faust, "Improvement Cuts Can Pay Way to Good Hardwood Stands," *Forest Farmer* (September 1983): 12–13; Donald E. Beck, "Planned Hardwood Regeneration," *Forest Farmer* (October 1983): 18–19; Robert L. Johnson, "Planting Hardwoods," *Forest Farmer* (October 1983): 16–17; Robert C. Kellison, "Progress in Hardwood Tree Improvement," *Forest Farmer* (November–December 1981): 14–15, 33–35; and Robert L. Johnson, "Timing and Planning for Hardwood Regeneration in the Coastal Plain," in *Proceedings—Symposium on Southeastern Hardwoods, September 15, 1971, Dothan, Alabama* ([Atlanta]: [U.S. Department of Agriculture, Forest Service, Southeastern Area, 1971]). For a brief overview of trade associations' activities in promoting hardwoods, see George E. Kelly, "Role of the Southern Hardwood Associations," *Forest Farmer* (April 1984): 20–21.

51. Gragg, interview; "Woodlands History," 118. The emphasis on computers was simply the latest chapter in the forest-products industry's long search for new technology that would improve performance in the woods, in the office, and on the bottom line of the annual financial report. For discussions and examples of this continuing process, see "Mechanical Efficiency: Exchange of Ideas, Woods Demonstrations, Sawmill Demonstrations, Contacts with Machinery Mfgrs, New

Production Methods, News and Data Releases," Bulletin 1 (August 14, 1947), and Bulletin 2 (July 28, 1948), SPA Records, box 43B; E. R. Schindler, "How Mechanical Efficiency Is Being Increased in the Southern Pine Industry," Paper 50-S-30, American Society of Mechanical Engineers, Washington, D.C., April 12–14, 1950, SPA Records, box 41A; "Southern Pine Industry Stresses Modernization and Mechanization," *The Lumberman* (June 1950): 3–12; Matthew L. Corwin, William B. Stuart, and Robert M. Shaffer, "Common Characteristics of Six Successful Mechanized Small-Tree Harvesting Operations in the South," *Southern Journal of Applied Forestry* (December 1988): 222–26; and Ragnar W. Johansen, "Taking Increment Cores with Power Tools," *Southern Journal of Applied Forestry* (November 1987): 151–53. See also Hyler, "Log Handling" (December 15, 1956), 298, 302, 306, 310–12, 316, 318, 320, 322; John E. Hyler, "Log Handling: Historical and Present Skidding Practices," *Southern Lumberman* (January 1, 1957): 60–64; Kenneth S. Rolston, "Log Hauling in the South," *Forest Farmer* (July–August 1986), 28–30; Thomas Hansbrough, "Potential Uses of Helicopters in Forestry," *Journal of Forestry* 54 (December 1956): 817–21; Evert W. Johnson, "Using Aircraft in Checking Forest Photo-Interpretation," *Journal of Forestry* 50 (November 1952): 853–55; Ross Nelson, Robert Swift, and William Krabill, "Using Airborne Lasers to Estimate Forest Canopy and Stand Characteristics," *Journal of Forestry* 86 (October 1988): 31–38; Hugh A. Devine and Richard C. Field, "GIS Applications," *Journal of Forestry* 84 (September 1986): 35–37; William L. Consoletti, "GIS in Industrial Forest Management," *Journal of Forestry* 84 (September 1986): 37–38; Harvey Fleet, "Scanning to Digitize Mapped Data," *Journal of Forestry* 84 (September 1986): 38–39, 41; Mathew R. Schwaller and Brian T. Dealy, "Landsat and GIS," *Journal of Forestry* 84 (September 1986): 40–41; Peter Koch, "Five New Machines and Six Products Can Triple Commodity Recovery from Southern Forests," *Journal of Forestry* 76 (December 1978): 767–72; "We Present: Thomas N. Busch and the Buschmaster," 126–30; R. H. Hokans and W. B. Stuart, "Yard-to-Mill Woodflow Scheduling by Microcomputer," *Southern Journal of Applied Forestry* (February 1983): 50–53; Jerome L. Clutter and James H. Bamping, "Computer Simulation of an Industrial Forestry Enterprise," IP Files; Ed Kerr, "High-Tech Cameras, Airplanes and Computers Team Up to Produce New Management Tools," *Forest Farmer* (May 1984): 8–9; John Stevenson, "Logging in the 1990s," *Timber Harvesting* (July 1989): 14–15, 33; and J. Walter Myers Jr., ed., *Forest Farmer, Fifteenth Manual Edition: Trees in Mechanization of Forestry Operations* (Atlanta: Forest Farmers Association, 1967). For discussions of various aspects of technology transfer, the process of transferring the re-

sults of research to the people on the job in the woods and mills, see G. H. Moeller and D. T. Seal, eds., *Technology Transfer in Forestry,* Forestry Commission Bulletin 61 (London: Her Majesty's Stationery Office, 1984). There is an excellent discussion of technological change in both the woods and mills of the pulp and paper industry in Pecenka, "Financial Analysis," 64–70. For the views of different forest managers regarding financial maturity, stocking, site indexes, inventory, and common sense, see Gragg, interview; Richard Allen, interview; and Nonnemacher, interview. The authors of a 1956 *Journal of Forestry* article expressed the same view in somewhat different language: "It is sometimes observed in the case of the vertically integrated forest business that trees which are not yet financially mature have to be cut or else the firm will have to purchase raw materials in the open market at prices higher than average in order to maintain a given level of production. . . . In these emergencies current tree values are higher than anticipated tree values at some future date under stable conditions of wood supply. This effects a drop in the anticipated rate of value increment in all trees owned by such a firm and results in many trees becoming financially mature" (John Fedkiw and James G. Yoho, "Financial Maturity—What's It Good For?" *Journal of Forestry* 54 [September 1956]: 587–90). See also Sam Guttenberg and R. R. Reynolds, "Cutting Financially Mature Loblolly and Shortleaf Pine," Occasional Paper 129 (New Orleans: U.S. Department of Agriculture, Forest Service, Southern Forest Experiment Station, 1953); M. Mason Gaffney, "Concepts of Financial Maturity of Timber and Other Assets," A.E. Information Series 62 (Raleigh: Department of Agricultural Economics, North Carolina State College, 1957); and Albert C. Worrell, "Financial Maturity: A Questionable Concept in Forest Management," *Journal of Forestry* 51 (October 1953): 711–14. The importance of market factors in shaping southern pine-management decisions is reflected in Clark Row and Sam Guttenberg, "Changing Price Patterns Affect Southern Pine Lumber Industry," *Journal of Forestry* 60 (February 1962): 120–23; and Carl H. Stoltenberg, "Economic Aspects of Type Maintenance and Conversion in Loblolly Pine–Hardwood Region," *Journal of Forestry* 54 (June 1956): 371–74. In a 1961 article Joseph Zaremba argued that foresters had to become more market oriented. As he put it, "much of what they have been taught about forest management is too strongly woods-oriented and is no longer sufficient to cope with the problems which today characterize this region. The southern forest economy is now strongly market-oriented, and foresters have to learn how to think and plan in terms of market requirements" ("Softwood Lumber Markets and Southern Forestry," *Journal of Forestry* 59 [May 1961]: 360–62). For examples of continuing efforts to refine the stocking concept and the enduring disagreements in this area, see C. Allen Bickford, "Stocking, Normality, and Measurement of Stand Density," *Journal of Forestry* 55 (February 1957): 99–104; Peter F. Elliott and David P. Worley, *Forest Stocking Equations: Their Development and Application,* Research Paper RM-102 (n.p.: U.S. Department of Agriculture, Forest Service, Rocky Mountain Forest and Range Experiment Station, 1973); Julia R. Ledbetter, Thomas G. Matney, and Alfred A. Sullivan, "Tree Profile and Volume Ratio Equations for Loblolly Pine Trees on Cutover Site-Prepared Lands," *Southern Journal of Applied Forestry* (October 1986): 241–44; and Robert M. Farrar Jr., *Predicting Stand and Stock Tables from a Spacing Study in Naturally Regenerated Longleaf Pine,* Research Paper SO-219 (New Orleans: U.S. Department of Agriculture, Forest Service, Southern Forest Experiment Station, 1985).

52. Kauffman, "Southland Revisited, Part 1," 36; Robert J. Weir, "The Impact of Genetics on Forest Productivity," *Tree Talk* 18 (winter 1996): 21–22, 24; "Managed Forest"; Kenneth P. Davis, ed., *Southern Forest Industry and the Environment* (New York: American Pulpwood Association, 1972), 15–23. See also Samuel B. Land Jr., "Forest Tree Improvement: Mississippi Certifies Nation's First 'Blue Tag,'" *Journal of Forestry* 72 (June 1974): 353.

53. International Paper Company, Annual Report, 1968, IP Files; "Woodlands History," 118–21. IP's emphasis on genetic research was consistent with one of the recommendations of the Southern Forest Resource Analysis Committee in *The South's Third Forest: How It Can Meet Future Demands* (n.p.: Southern Forest Resource Analysis Committee, 1969). The committee was formed by the Forest Farmers, the Southern Pine Association, the Southern Hardwood Lumber Manufacturers' Association, and the American Plywood Association in an effort to publicize and promote increased production from southern forests. See Wheeler, "South's Third Forest," 142–46; and Philip R. Wheeler, "The South's Third Forest—An Analysis," in *Forest Farmer Manual 1971* (Atlanta: Forest Farmers Cooperative Association, 1971), 21–23; *Reforestation: Keeping Land Productive for Generations to Come* (n.p.: International Paper Company, [mid-1990s]), brochure promoting the sale of seedlings, copy in possession of author.

54. Larson, "Why Management of a Natural Stand May Be the Best Option for You," 8–9.

55. Richard Allen, interview.

56. "History of Forestry in Mississippi," 65–66; *South's Fourth Forest: Alternatives,* 123, 233, 249; Branham, "Seeding the South," 17–18, 26–27.

57. Ronald J. Slinn, "The Impact of Industry Restructuring on Fiber Procurement," *Journal of Forestry* 87 (February 1989): 17–20. It should also be noted that IP's accelerated harvesting program of the early 1980s was not an isolated phenomenon in the industry. See also Mike Major, "What's the Big Deal about Corporate Mergers?" *Journal of Forestry* 83 (July 1985): 406–10. For an overview of the forest-products industry's organizational history, see David S. Dealey, "Mergers in the Forest Products Industries," *Journal of Forestry* 56 (February 1958): 99–103. See also Kathleen K. Wiegner, "A Growing Investment?" *Forbes* (November 8, 1982): 50, 55. IP's perspective is described in Steve Massieu, "International Paper Co. Expands in Solid Wood Products Programs," *Gulf Coast Lumberman* (July 1981): 10, 15.

58. International Paper Company, Woodlands Department, Annual Report, 1948, IP Files.

59. Tyler, interview; International Paper Company, Annual Report, 1964, IP Files.

60. James L. Buckner and J. Larry Landers, *A Forester's Guide to Wildlife Management in Southern Industrial Forests,* Technical Bulletin 10 (Bainbridge, Ga.: Southlands Experiment Forest, Forest Productivity and Research, International Paper Company, 1980), 1. For a modern overview of wildlife management issues and procedures in southern forests, see James C. Dickson and Eugene Maughan, eds., *Managing Southern Forests for Wildlife and Fish: A Proceedings,* General Technical Report SO-65 (New Orleans: U.S. Department of Agriculture, Forest Service, Southern Forest Experiment Station, 1987). For the pulp and paper industry's early 1970s attitudes toward wildlife management, see Kenneth P. Davis, ed., *Southern Forest Industry,* 53–58.

61. International Paper Company, Annual Report, 1960, IP Files; Darwin E. Fender, "Non-Market Values of Industrial Timberlands," *Journal of Forestry* 72 (November 1974): 713–15.

62. Fender, "Non-Market Values," 713–15; E. A. DeGrummond to Glen Jones, July 30, 1975, MFA Records.

63. Arthur W. Nelson Jr., "South's Third Forest"; *The Voice of Forestry* (February 1978): 1; "The Nature Conservancy: Protecting Natural Diversity in Mississippi," *Tree Talk* 12 (winter 1990): 24; Richard W. Bryan, "Shrinking Timber Base Presents Major Obstacle," *Forest Industries* (May 1971): 23; "International Paper Adds Property to Natural Areas Registry," *Forestry Forum* 4 (winter 1990): 8–9, 29; "International Paper Donates 2,650 Acres of Land in Mississippi to the Conservation Fund," *Tree Talk* 21 (spring 1999): 30.

64. John Gerber and Wayne McKenzie, "Building Win-Win Relationships with Hunters," *Forest Landowner* (May–June 1997); E. A. DeGrummond to Glen Jones, July 30, 1975, MFA Records; Nelson, interview. For discussions of the problems and legal ramifications of hunters and other private recreationists on

privately owned lands, see Gary L. Strodtz and C. W. Dane, "Trespassers, Guests, and Recreationists on Industrial Forest Land," *Journal of Forestry* 66 (December 1968): 898–901; and Andrew W. Ezell and Thomas A. Monaghan, "Protecting Your Timber," *Forest Farmer* (September 1989): 6–8.

65. Walter Dennis and Timothy A. Traugott, "Voluntary Guidelines for Wildlife Management," *Tree Talk* 7 (fall 1985): 6–7, 9; Robert Waters, "Oaks, Acorns, and Wildlife," *Tree Talk* 7 (winter 1986): 6–7; Sarah Mott, "Bottomland Hardwoods—A Winter Haven for Ducks," *Tree Talk* 19 (spring 1997): 14, 18. See also Buckner and Landers, *Forester's Guide.*

66. George Hurst, "Managing Your Land for Wood and Wildlife," *Tree Talk* 11 (winter 1989): 23, 25–26; Greg K. Yarrow, "Landowner Cooperatives Provide a Way to Cope with Hunting Pressure," *Tree Talk* 11 (winter 1989): 27–29; Vernon Bevill, "Wildlife Management = People Management," *Tree Talk* 11 (winter 1989): 30.

67. *Discover Mississippi's Forests,* 12.

68. Sharon S. Young and Mustian, *Impacts,* 35. J. W. Thompson to E. A. Sterling, August 18, 1948, Johns Manville Records, box 16; John W. Thompson, "History of the Johns Manville Timberlands," 7. The sale was for forty-two thousand cords of pine pulpwood at $1.40 per cord.

69. Sharon S. Young and Mustian, *Impacts,* 36; *A Development Program for the National Forests* (Washington, D.C.: U.S. Department of Agriculture, Forest Service, 1961), 8–10.

70. Sharon S. Young and Mustian, *Impacts,* 36–38; D. S. DeBell, W. R. Harms, D. A. Marquis, and R. O. Curtis, "Trends in Stand Management Practices for U.S. Forests," paper presented at the 1983 Society of American Foresters convention, Portland, Ore.

71. Sharon S. Young and Mustian, *Impacts,* 38–39; Jay Heinrichs, "Pinchot's Heirs," *Journal of Forestry* 83 (May 1985): 277. See also William Christopher Unkel, "An Evaluation of National Forest Management Act Administrative Policies Pertaining to Wildlife" (Ph.D. diss., Colorado State University, 1983); and Dickson and Maughan, eds., *Managing Southern Forests.* The latter is a collection of papers delivered at the Wildlife and Fish Ecology Technical Session of the 1986 Society of American Foresters convention in Birmingham, Ala.

72. Arthur W. Magill, "What People See in Managed and Natural Landscapes," *Journal of Forestry* 92 (September 1994): 12; R. Burton Litton Jr., "Visual Vulnerability of Forest Landscapes," *Journal of Forestry* 72 (July 1974): 392–97; Malcolm L. Hunter Jr., "What Constitutes an Old-Growth Stand? Toward a Conceptual Definition of Old-Growth Forests," *Journal of Forestry* 87 (August 1989): 34–35.

73. Paul H. Gobster, "Aldo Leopold's Ecological Esthetic: Integrating Esthetic and Biodiversity Values," *Journal of Forestry* 93 (February 1995): 7–8.

74. Maunder and Demmon, "Interview with Reuben B. Robertson," 12; "Industry Landowner Assistance Program," report from Southern Forest Institute, Donald Smith, chief forester, March 7, 1985, IP Files; Lee M. James, Hoffman, and Payne, *Private Forest Landownership,* 3, 33, 35.

75. Healy, *Competition for Land,* 116; Albert A. Legett and Meredith O. Stark, *Steps in Timber Management* (Jackson: Mississippi Forestry Commission, 1948).

76. Dennis C. LeMaster, "Timber Supply, Nonindustrial Private Forest Land, and the Conventional View," *Journal of Forestry* 76 (June 1978): 365; *South's Fourth Forest: Alternatives,* 62, 73; Richard L. Porterfield, "A Discussion of Landowner Attitudes," in *Proceedings,* ed. Karr, Baker, and Monaghan, 267.

77. "History of Forestry in Mississippi," 32, 36.

78. "The Yazoo–Little Tallahatchie Flood Prevention Project," *Forestry Forum* (July 1989): 21–22, 28.

79. Dwight Hair, "Timber Situation in the United States—1952–2030," *Journal of Forestry* 78 (November 1980): 683; Landers, Van Lear, and Boyer, "Longleaf Pine Forests," 41–42.

80. Landers, Van Lear, and Boyer, "Longleaf Pine Forests," 41–42.

81. "History of Forestry in Mississippi," 49.

82. Weaver and Bullard, "Mississippi's Severance Tax," 663–64. Hamlin L. Williston reported in 1979 that the Mississippi program had increased the state's planting rate by twenty to thirty thousand acres per year ("The South's Pine Reforestation Problem," *Journal of Forestry* 78 [April 1979]: 235).

83. Examples of materials targeting nonindustrial private landowners include "Fitler Managed Forest," an attractively illustrated brochure, and other materials from Crown Vantage; "Progressive Forests," from Champion International Corporation, promoting its landowner-support program of the same name; "Growing the Future," "Marketplace Solutions to Environmental Problems," and other brochures from Resource Management Service, a large management company headquartered in Birmingham with offices scattered across thirteen southern states; and "The Wisest Choices Are Sometimes the Easiest: Creating a Productive Forest on Your Land Is One of Them," from Sustainable Forest Technologies, another management company with foresters in several southern states, including Mississippi. Copies in possession of author.

84. Robert F. Tarrant, Robert A. Ewing, and Donald R. Gedney, "Forest Survey and the Nonindustrial Private Ownerships," *Journal of Forestry* 76 (August

1978): 471; Richard W. Bryan, "Environmental, Forestry Objectives Must Merge," *Forest Industries* (April 1971): 32.

85. James M. Vardaman, "Attitude of Foresters toward the Small, Private Landowner: A Consulting Forester's Opinion," *Journal of Forestry* 76 (June 1978): 368–69, 387; John L. Gray, "The Nonindustrial Private Forest Ownership 'Problem': A Viewpoint," *Journal of Forestry* 76 (August 1978): 466, 503; Arthur W. Nelson Jr., "South's Third Forest." See also Healy, *Competition for Land,* 116–17; and W. H. McComb, "Mismanagement by the Small Landowner: Fact or Fiction?" *Journal of Forestry* 73 (April 1975): 224–25.

86. Williston, "South's Pine Reforestation Problem," 235–36; "National Private Forest Lands Forum: Issues, Options, and Responsibilities," October 31–November 3, 1983, St. Louis, report prepared and printed by U.S. Department of Agriculture, Forest Service, Department of State and Private Forestry, copy in possession of author; *National Forum on Nonindustrial Private Forest Lands* (Washington, D.C.: U.S. Department of Agriculture, Forest Service, Department of State and Private Forestry, 1983).

87. "History of Forestry in Mississippi," 41–42; *How to Help Landowners with Forest Regeneration* (Jackson: Mississippi Forestry Commission in cooperation with U.S. Department of Agriculture, Forest Service, Southeastern Area, 1982.)

88. Richard Allen, interview; Clifton B. Marlin, biography, 38–40, MFA Records; John W. Squires to Paul Y. Burns, May 18, 1961; Paul Y. Burns, "Supporting Statement Recommending Clifton B. Marlin for Position of Assistant Professor of Forestry," both in MFA Records; Squires, interview. See also C. B. Marlin to members, Mississippi Forestry Commission, January 20, 1960, May 29, 1961, MFA Records. The Squires interview covers his forestry career; for more information on this subject, see William Eberle, "Man with Pine Tar in His Blood," *Kiwanis Magazine* 43 (February 1958): 28–31.

89. C. B. Marlin to members, Mississippi Forestry Commission, May 29, 1961; Burns, "Supporting Statement"; "Resolution Passed by the Gulf States Section of the Society of American Foresters at the Section's Meeting in Dallas, Texas—May 31, 1968"; W. D. Hagenstein to John Bell Williams, June 5, 1968, all in MFA Records; R. Rodney Foil to W. D. Hagenstein, October 30, 1968; and "Resolution Passed by the Gulf States Section of the Society of American Foresters at the Section's Meeting in Dallas, Texas—May 31, 1968," both in SAF Records, box 274; "Forest History Project Traces Industry's Growth," 32; "Society Opposes Mississippi Appointment," *Journal of Forestry* 66 (September 1968): 735–36; "Governor Signs MFC Reorganization Bill," *Tree Talk* 3 (spring 1981): 10; resolution, Sid Moss File, MFA Records, box 52.

90. "Improving Outputs from Non Industrial Private Forests," *Journal of Forestry* 77 (December 1979): 797; *South's Fourth Forest: Alternatives,* 58–59; "History of Forestry in Mississippi," 65.

91. Frank E. Taylor Jr. and Connie G. Wilkerson, "Profile of Participants in Landowner Assistance Program, Southeastern Mississippi," *Journal of Forestry* 75 (December 1977): 778–79.

92. Tarrant, Ewing, and Gedney, "Forest Survey," 471; "History of Forestry in Mississippi," app. 4.

93. Harold Anderson, "Choctaws," *Forestry Forum* 5 (winter 1991–92): 8–9.

94. "History of Forestry in Mississippi," 24–25; "The Yazoo–Little Tallahatchie Flood Prevention Project: A History of the Forest Service's Role," *Forestry Forum* (May 1989): 17–18, 20–22, 26–28. This history was prepared by John Arrechea, Robert Baker, Lee Bardwell, Carl Hoover, Victor B. MacNaughton, Charles R. Myers, John Schombert, Charles Shade, Billy Page, and Hamlin L. Williston, who served as principal author.

95. Jonathan Daniels, *Forest Is the Future,* 62–63.

96. *The Forest Returns to the Yazoo* (Atlanta: U.S. Forest Service, 1960), 3, 5, 11; *The Yazoo–Little Tallahatchie Flood Prevention Project: A History of the Forest Service's Role,* Forestry Report R8-FR 8 (Atlanta: U.S. Department of Agriculture, Forest Service, Southern Region, 1988), 13–14; "The Yazoo–Little Tallahatchie Flood Prevention Project," *Forestry Forum* (July 1989): 8. The latter two publications are identical. The report was published in parts in *Forestry Forum* between May and October 1989. The quotations are from Andrew Taylor, "One of the Biggest Land Rehabilitation Jobs Ever Tackled," *Forestry Forum* 4 (summer 1990): 8–10. See also *The New Forest on the Yazoo* (Atlanta: U.S. Department of Agriculture, Forest Service, Southeastern Area, n.d.); and V. B. MacNaughton, "For Land's Sake!" *American Forests* (January 1960): 34–35, 46–48. For a detailed account of Williston's life, including work on the Yazoo–Little Tallahatchie project, see Hamlin L. Williston, interview by Bobbie Jean Dickinson, May 10, 1989, MFA Records. Work on the project had its lighter moments. Williston told of his "right-hand man" on the project, who was "noted for doing things his own way." As Williston recalled, "One day he took the Forest Service jeep out and in trying to cross a small stream, he got it mired down in the middle of the stream. Everybody had to turn to, to pull the jeep out of the stream. Dave King was leading the rescue operation, and Dave could be very profane. Dave said, 'Warner, I don't know how in the blank blank you could be so stupid as to try to cross that stream in a jeep.' And Warner said, 'Dave, why I have crossed that stream any number of times. I just had a little bad luck. Let me show you how I usually do it.' And he

promptly drove the jeep into the stream and got it stuck again! It took them until midnight to haul it out!"

97. "History of Forestry in Mississippi," 25.

98. Ibid.; *Forest Returns to the Yazoo,* 12–13, 35, 1; *Yazoo–Little Tallahatchie Flood Prevention Project,* 13–20, 24, 37–42, 45–49; "The Yazoo–Little Tallahatchie Flood Prevention Project," *Forestry Forum* (July 1989): 9–10, 14, 21; "The Yazoo–Little Tallahatchie Flood Prevention Project," *Forestry Forum* (September 1989): 14–16, 19–20, 25–26, 29–30, 34; "The Yazoo–Little Tallahatchie Flood Prevention Project," *Forestry Forum* (October 1989): 13. For a brief overview of the career of a forester who worked for fifteen years on the Yazoo–Little Tallahatchie project, see Victor B. MacNaughton, interview by Bobbie Jean Dickinson, March 8, 1989, MFA Records. See also MacNaughton, "Yankee Grows in Dixie," 103–4.

99. "History of Forestry in Mississippi," 25, 32–33, 35.

Chapter 9

1. Leonard J. Weber, "The Social Responsibility of Land Ownership: Ethics and Profit Gain New Definitions," *Journal of Forestry* 89 (April 1991): 12–17, 25; Carl H. Reidel, "Whose Woods These Are . . . ," *Journal of Forestry* 73 (August 1975): 474–76; Samuel P. Hays, *Explorations in Environmental History: Essays by Samuel P. Hays* (Pittsburgh: University of Pittsburgh Press, 1998), 131–55.

2. John A. Stanturf, Stephen B. Jones, and William D. Ticknor, "Managing Industrial Forestland in a Changing Society," *Journal of Forestry* 91 (November 1993): 6. See Jacqueline Vaughn Switzer, *Green Backlash: The History and Politics of Environmental Opposition in the U.S.* (Boulder, Colo.: Lynne Rienner Publishers, 1997). Switzer says that the roots of antienvironmentalism in the United States can be traced back to eighteenth-century values with regard to the rights of landownership and the proper role of government in a democratic society. She focuses on the history of political opposition to intensive regulation of landownership, management, and use, which is certainly at the heart of many Mississippi forest landowners' and the Mississippi Forestry Association's attitudes concerning federal environmental regulations. See also Alston Chase, *In a Dark Wood: The Fight over Forests and the Rising Tyranny of Ecology* (New York: Houghton Mifflin, 1995). IP alone lost a great deal of land in Mississippi through eminent domain, including twenty-five thousand acres for the Ross Barnett Reservoir ("Woodlands History," 123–24). See also George E. Kelly, "Diminishing Tim-

ber Resources," *Forest Farmer* (November 1968): 20–21, 51.

3. Samuel P. Hays, "The Environmental Movement," *Journal of Forest History* 25 (October 1981): 219; John C. Hendee and Randall C. Pitstick, "Growth and Change in U.S. Forest-Related Environmental Groups," *Journal of Forestry* 92 (June 1994): 25–27. Some observers and participants questioned whether the environmental organizations' well-publicized battles with James G. Watt helped or hurt the movement. See Barry W. Walsh, "After Watt: The Environmentalists," *Journal of Forestry* 83 (April 1985): 212–17. For a brief, readable, and very favorable treatment of the modern U.S. environmental movement, see Kirkpatrick Sale, *The Green Revolution: The American Environmental Movement, 1962–1992* (New York: Hill and Wang, 1993).

4. William C. Osborn, *The Paper Plantation: Ralph Nader's Study Group Report on the Pulp and Paper Industry in Maine* (New York: Grossman Publishers, 1974), ix–xviii, 1–4, 103–28.

5. Jack Shepherd, *The Forest Killers: The Destruction of the American Wilderness* (New York: Weybright and Talley, 1975); Michael Frome, *The Forest Service,* 2d ed. (Boulder, Colo.: Westview Press, 1984).

6. Gene A. Sirmon, "President's Address," *Tree Talk* 17 (fall 1995): 7. As recently as December 1998, the Mississippi Forestry Association newsletter reported on timber-industry concerns that there might be efforts to use the "endangered" status of the Indiana bat to "halt timber harvesting on eastern hardwood forests, similar to the spotted owl controversy in the Northwest." Those who might push such efforts were termed "extreme environmental groups" (*Voice of Forestry* [December 1998]).

7. Jeffrey K. Stine, *Mixing the Waters: Environment, Politics, and the Building of the Tennessee-Tombigbee Waterway* (Akron, Ohio: University of Akron Press, 1993), 54–57; Nash, *Wilderness and the American Mind,* 249, 273.

8. Forestry education at Mississippi State began when the first forester, George Clothier, was employed in 1905. In 1936 a Department of Forestry was established in the School of Agriculture and the Agricultural Experiment Station. However, not until 1954 was the program authorized to award a bachelor of science degree in forestry. Despite earlier efforts, the program was not accredited until 1966. Mississippi State's forestry program was again accredited for a five-year period in 1972 and for a ten-year period in 1977. Full accreditation on a ten-year cycle has been maintained since that time. The school also began to offer graduate training, culminating in the Mississippi Board of Trustees' 1979 approval of a doctoral program. In 1974 the Department of Forestry created the Forestry Advisory Com-

mittee, consisting of prominent people within the Mississippi forestry community. By the 1970s more than half of the people earning bachelor's degrees in forestry from Mississippi State went to work within the state ("Brief Historical Notation of the Development of the Forest Resource in Miss. and Its Parallel with the Development of Forestry Education at MSU," School of Forest Resources, Office of the Dean [1957–76], Special Collections, Mitchell Memorial Library, Mississippi State University, Starkville; "Self-Study Report on the School of Forest Resources, Mississippi State University Institutional Self-Study," 1970–71; "Report of the Accreditation Visitation Committee of the Society of American Foresters," 1971; "Self-Study Report on the School of Forest Resources, Mississippi State University Institutional Self-Study," 1982; "The Comprehensive Revue of Teaching, Research and Extension Programs in Forestry . . . Mississippi State University, February 12–15, 1980"; "Accreditation Report," 1977; SAF Committee on Accreditation to SAF Council, October 19, 1987; "Summary Findings and Action Regarding the Continued SAF Accreditation of Certain Curricula in the Department of Forestry, School of Forest Resources, Mississippi State University, Society of American Foresters Committee on Accreditation, October 26, 1992"; all in Records of the Presidents of the University, Special Collections, Mitchell Memorial Library, Mississippi State University, Starkville; James E. Moak, "MSU School of Forest Resources Celebrates Twenty-fifth Anniversary," *Tree Talk* 3 [summer 1980]: 10, 21–22; Warren S. Thompson, "Mississippi State University's School of Forest Resources: Its Image and Its Impact," *Tree Talk* 6 [fall 1984]: 10–11; Douglas P. Richards, "A Look at the MSU Department of Forestry," *Tree Talk* 6 [spring 1985]: 12–15). Polly Anderson of Gloster was an interesting variation at Mississippi State's forestry school. An interior decorator in New Orleans, Anderson was an avid hunter who grew up close to nature in a large landowning family. With her deep interest in wildlife and hunting, she was one of the few women to enroll in forestry at Mississippi State, and after graduation she worked for a time as executive director of the Mississippi Wildlife Federation. In a letter to the *Clarion-Ledger*'s outdoor editor opposing clear-cutting, Anderson observed, "I have found that many foresters tend to disagree with me, but then most of them are fiber oriented and I am more interested in diversification" (Anderson to Herb Sandusky, *Jackson (Mississippi) Clarion-Ledger,* October 8, 1972). See also "Female Forestry Major Also Veteran Hunter," *Starkville (Mississippi) Daily News,* March 21, 1972; and Polly Anderson Robertson, "Adjunct to Mississippi History of Forestry," n.d., MFA Records. Not until the early 1950s, at about the same time that the forestry program at Mississippi State began operating, did the

Society of American Foresters and various universities began looking seriously at conservation and nontimber forest resources in their curricular considerations. See Samuel Trask Dana and Evert W. Johnson, *Forestry Education in America: Today and Tomorrow* (Washington, D.C.: Society of American Foresters, 1963), 286–94. MSU's course on forest ecology and the global environment is science oriented and does not appear to have much of a focus on the historical and philosophical development of conservation and environmentalism. Undergraduate students in the forestry program who choose the "environmental conservation" option take one course in ecology, one on forest recreation, and one on game conservation and management, plus the forest ecology and the global environment course. Students doing graduate work in biology at Mississippi State can major in ecology. The University of Southern Mississippi has an Institute of Environmental Science in the School of Engineering Technology, but it lists no courses on its web page and appears not to focus on forests and related issues. The only course in this area appearing on the University of Mississippi web site is an elective course in environmental law offered by the law school. Some environmentalists argue that the atmosphere in the Mississippi State forestry school is symbolized by the story that as the red-cockaded woodpecker issue rose to prominence in the South, people affiliated with the forestry school in the early 1990s produced and distributed T-shirts among students attending forestry summer camp with a character called "Captain Clearcut" on the front and a picture on the back of a woodpecker in the crosshairs of a gun sight with the inscription "Kill a Pecker—Save a Forester." These critics also charge that an early dean of the school took students to area mills and asked the managers, "Had any trouble with environmentalists lately?" Environmentalists also say that in the years since the red-cockaded woodpecker was placed on the endangered-species list, the last three colonies on the Mississippi State forestlands were deliberately killed. A current school official agrees that the school's atmosphere and curriculum are conservative but says that over the past twenty to twenty-five years it has been more liberal than most people in the forest-products industries. He takes pride in the school's timber-production orientation and points out that students interested in nontimber forest values can enroll in other areas, such as the wildlife and fisheries program. One leading critic of both public and private efforts to preserve the red-cockaded woodpecker places part of the blame on university forestry departments that "are dominated by the need to train foresters to maximize profits" and where "endangered species and other forest values are glossed over and at times ridiculed." He also argues that wildlife departments typically are situated within forestry schools run by foresters and pay too little attention to endangered species when focusing on game species management. See Jerome A. Jackson, "The Red-Cockaded Woodpecker," in *Audubon Wildlife Report,* ed. R. I. Silvestro (New York: Academic Press, 1987), 486.

9. Richard W. Bryan, "Environmental, Forestry Objectives Must Merge," 32; "Nature Conservancy," 24; Gene A. Sirmon, "Mississippi Federal Timber Council Report," *Tree Talk* 21 (winter 1999): 6, 36; Mike Leahy and Warren Benedetto, "Chipping Away at Our Forests? The Threat Is Real," *Greensboro (North Carolina) News and Record,* November 2, 1997; Samuel M. Hughes, "Chipping Away at Our Forests? Stop Worrying," *Greensboro (North Carolina) News and Record.* November 2, 1997 (both available on the Internet through links from the National Audubon Society's home page); Sam Hodges, "Chipping the Best with the Rest," *Mobile Register,* n.d., article available on the Internet via a link from the *Mobile Register*'s home page; Eley C. Frazer III and Marshall Thomas, "Southern Pulpwood Market Bleak; Sawtimber Better," *F&W Forestry Letter* 60 (winter 1998–99): 1, 7; Steve Corbitt, telephone conversation with author, January 15, 1999; "MFA and Partners in Flight Migratory Bird Day," *Voice of Forestry* (June 1997); national home pages and links of the Sierra Club, the Nature Conservancy, the Wilderness Society, the National Audubon Society, and the Dogwood Alliance, January 18 and 19, 1999. The Audubon Society's home page links directly to that of the Dogwood Alliance. I spoke with several members of the environmental community during January 1999. Some were state government or public university employees and were unwilling to be identified because of fears of job-related retaliation. I have no way of knowing whether or not their stories or fears are well founded or legitimate, but my sense is that they are. It should be noted that it is not yet clear that the dusky gopher frog is a distinct species. Some say it may simply be the Gulf Coast frog, which is still found in nearby areas. Responding to the continuing debate over chip mills and the state of southern forests, in August 1999 the U.S. Forest Service began a two-year study of these issues ("No Clear-Cut Answer on Chip-Mill Impact," *Memphis Commercial Appeal,* August 28, 1999, A1, A13).

10. Both of these issues are mentioned, although without direct reference to Mississippi, in Boyce, Burkhardt, Kellison, and Van Lear, "Silviculture," 45–47; Richard W. Bryan, "Environmental, Forestry Objectives Must Merge," 33.

11. Paul R. Ehrlich, "World Population Loss: A Battle Lost," in *Politics and Environment,* ed. W. Anderson (Pacific Palisades, Calif.: Goodyear Publishing, 1970), 17; Arthur W. Nelson Jr., "South's Third Forest"; Lester Brooks, "The Environmental Movement Today: A Pio-

neer Environmentalist Assesses It and Finds It Wanting," *Champion Magazine* 2 (1979): 15–19; Richard C. Allen, "Fulfilling Our Role as Foresters," speech before Area I, Southern Forest Industries, Shreveport, Louisiana, May 23, 1974, copy in SPCA Records. Allen presented essentially the same message to the 1975 annual meeting of the Society of American Foresters in Jackson ("Fulfilling Our Role as Foresters . . . by Involvement," *Forestry News* 12 [July 1975]: 4–6). For the very traditional views of a Mississippi Forestry Commission information and education forester toward the modern environmental movement, see Harold Anderson, "Speaking Out . . . Persuaded by Fact, not Fiction," *Forestry Forum* 7 (summer 1993): 15, 19. For Pinchot's ideas concerning federal regulation or ownership of the nation's forests, see *SAF at 75* (Washington, D.C.: Society of American Foresters, 1975), 5–6.

12. Robert C. Parker, "The Forester's Role in Environmental Management," *Tree Talk* 1 (fall 1978): 26–27; Jerry Perkins, "Update on Your Association's Activities," *Tree Talk* 12 (fall 1990): 5; Tom Monaghan, "Update on Your Association's Activities," *Tree Talk* 13 (spring 1991): 3.

13. Thomas M. Pullen Jr., "An Environmentalist's View of Forestry in Mississippi," *Tree Talk* 13 (spring 1991): 19–20; R. C. Allen, "Fulfilling Our Role as Foresters." See also Richard P. Gale, "Communicating with Environmentalists: A Look at Life on the Receiving End," *Journal of Forestry* 71 (October 1973): 653–55; and Gary A. Soucie, "The Sierra Club Looks at Foresters and Our Natural Resources," paper presented at meeting of the Gulf States Section, Society of American Foresters, Dallas, Texas, May 30, 1968, SAF Records, box 274.

14. John O. Moore, "Update on Your Association's Activities," *Tree Talk* 14 (spring 1992): 3; Steve Corbitt, "MFA Reports on Legislative Activities," *Tree Talk* 15 (spring 1993): 5; "MFTC Opposes Designation of the Mississippi River Heritage Corridor," *Tree Talk* 17 (summer 1995): 7.

15. G. Stephen Parker, "Defending the Rights of Property Owners," *Tree Talk* 15 (winter 1993): 23–28.

16. Bruce Vincent, "Montana Logger Bruce Vincent: On the Threats to Rural America," *Tree Talk* 15 (winter 1993): 15, 17, 19, 20–21.

17. Larry Tyner, "President's Address," *Tree Talk* 15 (fall 1993): 5; "Legislative Report: Forestry and the 1992–1995 Legislative Term," *Tree Talk* 17 (summer 1995): 12.

18. Reed Branson, "New Wildlife Group Shuns Liberalism," *Memphis Commercial Appeal,* December 11, 1997.

19. Roderick Frazier Nash, *American Environmentalism: Readings in Conservation History,* 3d ed. (New York: McGraw-Hill, 1990), 187. For a good, brief de-

scription of the origins of the term *ecology* and the concept of the "balance of nature," see Botkin, *Discordant Harmonies,* 32–36. For a history of the development of environmental issues and legislation affecting the U.S. Forest Service and its relationship with various segments of the public, see Dennis Roth and Frank Harmon, *The Forest Service in the Environmental Era* (Washington, D.C.: U.S. Department of Agriculture, Forest Service, 1995).

20. Timothy O'Keefe, "Holistic (New) Forestry: Significant Difference or Just Another Gimmick?" *Journal of Forestry* 88 (April 1990): 24.

21. Ibid., 23; Arthur W. Nelson Jr., "South's Third Forest." For the views of a veteran Forest Service administrator who also saw little new in ecosystem management, see Karl F. Wenger, "What Is Ecosystem Management?" *Journal of Forestry* 95 (April 1997): 44. For a differing view that suggests that ecosystem management is different and that one of the differences is a new emphasis on the types of considerations and values best identified and studied by social scientists, see Stewart Allen, "A Social Scientist's View of Ecosystem Management," *Journal of Forestry* 95 (September 1997): 48. See also Samuel T. Dana, "On Environmental Redundancy," *Journal of Forestry* 72 (April 1974): 200–201.

22. *Journal of Forestry* 88 (March 1990): 8; Karl F. Wenger, "What Does Ecological Soundness Mean?" *Journal of Forestry* 92 (March 1994): 60.

23. Douglas S. Powell, William H. McWilliams, and Richard A. Birdsey, "History, Change, and the U.S. Forest Inventory," *Journal of Forestry* 92 (December 1994): 8–9; "Robertson and Smyth Discuss the New RPA," *Journal of Forestry* 89 (May 1991): 18–19.

24. William H. Banzhaf, "An Opportunity Awaits," *Journal of Forestry* 91 (October 1993): 3; Luther P. Gerlach and David N. Bengston, "If Ecosystem Management Is the Solution, What's the Problem? Eleven Challenges for Ecosystem Management," *Journal of Forestry* 92 (August 1994): 18; Brian Czech, "Ecosystem Management Is No Paradigm Shift: Let's Try Conservation," *Journal of Forestry* 93 (December 1995): 19; George R. Staebler, "Have We Milked the Sacred Cow Dry?" *Journal of Forestry* 91 (October 1993): 60; John Fedkiw, "The Forest Service's Pathway toward Ecosystem Management," *Journal of Forestry* 95 (April 1997): 32–33.. For a highly critical discussion of the "greening" of the Forest Service as social scientists, biologists, and other nonforesters became more powerful in the agency and of the agency's adoption of ecosystem management and troubled relationship with the timber industry, see Tommy Walker, *An Agency Gone Sour: A Brief History of the U.S. Forest Service and the Breakdown of Its Relationship with the North American Timber Industry* (Montgomery, Ala.: Hatton-

Brown, 1994), 33–50. The material in this book appeared originally in a four-part series in *Timber Processing* magazine (August–November 1994).

25. *Journal of Forestry* 87 (June 1989): 22–49; Alan G. McQuillan, "Is National Forest Planning Incompatible with a Land Ethic?" *Journal of Forestry* 88 (May 1990): 31–37. See also Callicott, "Brief History," 17–18.

26. Hal Salwasser, "Ecosystem Management: Can It Sustain Diversity and Productivity? *Journal of Forestry* 92 (August 1994): 7.

27. Czech, "Ecosystem Management," 17; Greg Brown and Chuck Harris, "Professional Foresters and the Land Ethic, Revisited," *Journal of Forestry* 98 (January 1998): 4. The importance and meaning of Leopold's work has been a major topic of discussion among foresters and others caught up in the debates over ecosystem management. The *Journal of Forestry* devoted its January 1998 issue to two articles presenting contrasting views of Leopold, and much of its April 1998 issue was devoted to several critiques and comments on the January articles. A standard work on Aldo Leopold is Susan L. Flader, *Thinking Like a Mountain: Aldo Leopold and the Evolution of an Ecological Attitude toward Deer, Wolves, and Forests* (Columbia: University of Missouri Press, 1974). For a brief overview of Leopold's thought and contributions, see Susan Flader, "Aldo Leopold's Legacy to Forestry," *Forest History Today* (1998): 2–5.

28. Lloyd C. Irland, "Getting from Here to There: Implementing Ecosystem Management on the Ground," *Journal of Forestry* 92 (August 1994): 12; Thomas A. More, "Forestry's Fuzzy Concepts: An Examination of Ecosystem Management," *Journal of Forestry* 94 (August 1996): 19. Culling information from a series of leading texts, Irland summarized the "essential elements" of ecosystem management as follows: (1) "A key objective is the maintenance and enhancement of biodiversity"; (2) "The essence of EM lies in its objectives and its wider spatial and time scales, not in particular management practices used to achieve those objectives. Protection and enhancement of ecosystem integrity and functions are essential"; (3) "Landscape traits are emphasized—including connectivity, avoidance of fragmentation, protection of waterways and identification and protection of critical habitat components"; (4) "EM is by definition intensive forest management. Implementing it requires more intensive planning and coordination, more spatially detailed data, and more sophisticated silvicultural prescriptions. Such actions are expected, over time, to produce a richer mix of resource benefits"; (5) "A shift is planned toward the species composition of the primeval forest"; (6) Older stands will be increasingly represented, along with development of structural traits resembling old-

growth"; (7) "Extensive units of mature forest will be minimally roaded or unroaded, and minimally affected by timber management"; (8) "It is expected to provide larger populations of scarce creatures—especially wide-ranging top carnivores, forest interior dwellers, and creatures that depend on old-growth conditions. It is also supposed to set the stage for re-introducing species that no longer inhabit these woods"; (9) "Some scientists see such practices as providing a form of insurance against the ecological effects of future global climate change" (Irland, "Getting from Here to There," 16). A simpler definition calls *ecosystem management* "a management philosophy which focuses on desired states, rather than system outputs, and which recognizes the need to protect or restore critical ecological components, functions, and structures in order to sustain resources in perpetuity" (Czech, "Ecosystem Management," 17). An early definition says that *ecosystem management* is "management of natural resources using systemwide concepts to ensure that all plants and animals in the ecosystem are maintained at viable levels in native habitats and that basic ecosystem processes (e.g. nutrient cycling) are perpetuated indefinitely." An early "streamlined" definition was, "Regulating internal ecosystem structure and function, plus inputs and outputs, to achieve socially desirable conditions" (Czech, "Ecosystem Management," 18–19). As if concerns about definitions of ecosystem management were not enough, there were also debates concerning the efficacy and ethics of certain practices, particularly ecological restoration, within the ecosystem management movement. See Alan G. McQuillan, "Defending the Ethics of Ecological Restoration," *Journal of Forestry* 96 (January 1998): 26–31.

29. Irland, "Getting from Here to There," 16; Gerlach and Bengston, "If Ecosystem Management Is the Solution, What's the Problem?" 18. Some modern scholars argue that Pinchot and Leopold were actually not that far apart. See Char Miller and V. Alaric Sample's introduction to the recent edition of Pinchot's classic, *Breaking New Ground* (Washington, D.C.: Island Press, 1998).

30. William R. Maxey, "Foresters: Another Endangered Species?" *Journal of Forestry* 94 (August 1996): 44. In contrast, some educators and practitioners advocated breaking down the educational and professional walls between foresters and other natural-resource professionals. See Hanna J. Cortner, "Forestry: What's in a Name?" *Journal of Forestry* 92 (January 1994): 59; and Winifred B. Kessler, "Change, the Essence of Life," *Journal of Forestry* 91 (May 1993): 68.

31. Andrew Colaninno, "What's the Big Deal? Putting Extinction in Perspective," *Journal of Forestry* 94 (June 1996): 60; Gene A. Sirmon, "Mississippi Federal Timber Council Report," *Tree Talk* 20 (fall 1998): 11.

32. Hanna J. Cortner, "Conservation: A Magical Word?" *Journal of Forestry* 93 (December 1995): 20. Gene Sirmon, then a staff officer with the Timber, Soil, Water, and Air Office of the U.S. Forest Service in Jackson, predicted that the most dramatic change in Mississippi's national forests resulting from the advent of ecosystem management would be a "reduction in clearcutting and the increased reliance on natural systems for regeneration," although "clearcutting and planting remain acceptable and necessary practices and will be used where circumstances warrant" ("U.S. Forest Service Establishes New Policy for Eco-System Management and Timber Harvesting," *Tree Talk* 14 [fall 1992]: 12).

33. William H. Banzhaf, "We Still Need to Harvest Trees," *Journal of Forestry* 92 (May 1994): 3; "Reaffirming Our Commitment to Private-Sector Forestry," *Journal of Forestry* 92 (May 1994): 6–8; "History of Forestry in Mississippi," 55.

34. Robert G. Lee, "The Redesigned Forest: Breaking through the Cultural Barriers," *Journal of Forestry* 88 (December 1990): 32–36; MacCleery, "When Is a Landscape Natural?" 41. Another villain in traditional foresters' eyes was Bill Devall, professor of sociology at Humboldt State University and coauthor of *Deep Ecology.* Devall was a controversial and outspoken critic of commodity forest management and environmental capitalism who regarded foresters as a special-interest group controlled by the timber industry. See Stephen B. Jones, "Views from the Extremes," *Journal of Forestry* 89 (August 1991): 72.

35. Fedkiw, "Forest Service's Pathway," 30–31; Sharon S. Young and Mustian, *Impacts,* 40; *South's Fourth Forest: Alternatives,* 68.

36. Enoch F. Bell and Robert M. Randall, "Opportunities to Increase National Forest Softwood Harvest," *Journal of Forestry* 80 (March 1982): 152–56. For a historical overview of timber sales from national forests, see Tommy Walker, "Origins of an Argument," *Forest History Today* (1995): 12–15.

37. "Timber Buyers Concerned about National Forest Sales," *Tree Talk* 11 (spring 1989): 31; Fedkiw, "Forest Service's Pathway," 31; Bolinger, "For the People and by the People," 15–16; Gene A. Sirmon, "Mississippi Federal Timber Council Report," *Tree Talk* 18 (fall 1996): 8.

38. John Fedkiw, "National Forests and the Performance of the Organic Act of 1897," *Forest History Today* (1998): 17; adapted from Fedkiw, "National Forests and the Organic Act of 1897 at 100 Years," *History Line* (spring 1997).

39. "Mississippi Federal Timber Council: New Organization Will Monitor National Forest Plans and Activ-

ity," *Tree Talk* 16 (spring 1994): 6–7; "Mississippi Federal Timber Council Supporting Forest Management Programs," *Tree Talk* 16 (fall 1994): 6.

40. "Timber Buyers Concerned," 34; "U.S. Forest Service Issues for Mississippi: An Interview with Kenneth R. Johnson," *Tree Talk* 11 (summer 1989): 7.

41. "The SAF Position on Below-Cost Timber Sales: Redefining the Costs of Forest Management," *Journal of Forestry* 85 (August 1987): 37; Luke Popovich, "How Do You Account for Deficit Sales?" *Journal of Forestry* 82 (October 1984): 594–99; Charles F. Wilkinson and H. Michael Anderson, "Below-Cost Sales: Are They Legal?" *Journal of Forestry* 85 (August 1987): 21–26; John V. Krutilla, "Below-Cost Sales: Tying Up the Loose Ends of the National Forest Management Act," *Journal of Forestry* 85 (August 1987): 27–29; "Forest Roads: High Stakes in Idaho," *Potlatch Story* 25 (June 1985): 1–5.

42. *The South's Fourth Forest: Opportunities to Increase the Resource Wealth of the South,* Miscellaneous Publication 1461 (Washington, D.C.: U.S. Department of Agriculture, Forest Service, 1988), 68; Arthur W. Nelson Jr., "Environmental Considerations, Why?" in *Proceedings,* ed. Karr, Baker, and Monaghan, 292–94; *Mississippi's Best Management Practices Handbook, 1989* (Jackson: Mississippi Forestry Commission, 1989).

43. Mark F. DeLeon, comp., *Cultural Resources Overview: National Forests in Mississippi* (Jackson, Miss.: U.S. Department of Agriculture, Forest Service, 1983), 1; *Land and Resource Management Plan,* 4-44, 4-45.

44. John C. Hendee, "Public Opinion and What Foresters Should Do about It," *Journal of Forestry* 82 (June 1984): 341–42. For a history of the development of environmental issues and legislation affecting the U.S. Forest Service and its relationship with various segments of the public, see Dennis Roth and Frank Harmon, *The Forest Service in the Environmental Era* (Washington, D.C.: U.S. Department of Agriculture, Forest Service, 1995).

45. Arthur W. Nelson Jr., "Environmental Considerations, Why?" 292; "Chain Saws Buzzing in Miss. Forest Sound Like Massacre to Ex-Urbanites," *Memphis Commercial Appeal,* March 9, 1998, A1, A4; Frederick J. Deneke and Gary A. Moll, "Are We Selling America an Edsel?" *Journal of Forestry* 80 (June 1982): 395; "History of Forestry in Mississippi," 43, app. 7; Darlene Slater, "Forest Management City Style," *Forestry Forum* (June 1987): 24–25; Joe L. McDonald, "Urban Forestry Enjoys Dramatic Gains," *Forestry Forum* 5 (winter 1991–92): 19. Later letter writers to the *Commercial Appeal* penned emotional pleas to preserve the forest and angry critiques of the Forest Service (see March 13, 1998, A7).

46. Darlene Slater, "Urban Forestry in Mississippi," *Tree Talk* 14 (summer 1992): 20–21, 24; N. Robin Morgan and Kenneth J. Johnson, *An Introductory Guide to Urban and Community Forestry Programs,* Forestry Report R8-FR 16 (Atlanta: U.S. Department of Agriculture, Forest Service, Southern Region, 1993). This item is both an informational and promotional publication.

47. William E. Shands, "Problems and Prospects at the Urban-Forest Interface," *Journal of Forestry* 89 (June 1991): 23, 25, 26; Bill Lambert, "American Dream Can Become a Nightmare," *Forestry Forum* 1 (December 1987): 12–13. See also Kent Grizzard, "Urban Expansion: The Newest Enemy of Our Forest Land," *Forestry Forum* 2 (summer 1988): 28–29.

48. Shands, "Problems and Prospects," 25, 26; Bob Griffin, "The Future of Hunting in Mississippi," *Tree Talk* 18 (winter 1996): 11–12.

49. Sharon S. Young and Mustian, *Impacts,* 44; "Chain Saws Buzzing in Miss. Forest," A1, A4.

50. Sharon S. Young and Mustian, *Impacts,* 45.

51. Ibid., 47.

52. Ibid., 48, 49–50; *Land and Resource Management Plan,* 4-25, 4-37.

53. Sirmon, "Mississippi Federal Timber Council Report," *Tree Talk* 20 (spring 1998): 6; "Chain Saws Buzzing in Miss. Forest," A1, A4; Sirmon, "Mississippi Federal Timber Council Report," *Tree Talk* 20 (winter 1998): 6.

54. Sirmon, "Mississippi Federal Timber Council Report," *Tree Talk* 20 (fall 1998): 11, 38; 21 (winter 1999): 6; 21 (summer 1999): 6.

55. Arthur W. Nelson Jr., "Environmental Considerations, Why?" 292. For another view, see Deneke and Moll, "Are We Selling America an Edsel?" 395; "History of Forestry in Mississippi," 43.

56. "Mississippi Federal Timber Council Supporting Forest Management Programs," *Tree Talk* 16 (summer 1994): 6; "Mississippi Federal Timber Council Supporting Forest Management Programs," *Tree Talk* 17 (winter 1995): 6; "Morning Edition," National Public Radio, June 23, 1998; Sirmon, "Mississippi Federal Timber Council Report," *Tree Talk* 20 (spring 1998): 6.

57. Michael C. Thompson, "National Forest Mismanagement?" *Journal of Forestry* 96 (May 1998): 56; Sirmon, "Mississippi Federal Timber Council Report," *Tree Talk* 20 (fall 1998): 11.

58. Greg Brown and Harris, "Professional Foresters," 5–9, 11.

59. "Robertson and Smyth Discuss the New RPA," 16, 17.

60. "Understanding the RPA," *Journal of Forestry* 89 (June 1991): 17; Char Miller, "A Cautionary Tale: Reflections on Reinventing the Forest Service," *Journal of Forestry* 94 (January 1996): 7–10. "Understanding

the RPA" was the second part of the published record of a conversation between Mills and the national office staff of the Society of American Foresters. The first segment was published in the May 1991 issue of the *Journal of Forestry.*

61. "History of Forestry," 51.

62. For an overview of the pulp and paper industry's wildlife-management philosophy in the early 1970s, see Kenneth P. Davis, ed., *Southern Forest Industry,* 53–58; Larry Eubanks, "How Do We Value Wildlife?" *The Margin* 6 (September–October 1990): 16. For a brief description and evaluation of the Endangered Species Act, see Cheryl Cobb, "Living with the Endangered Species Act," *Forestry Forum* 6 (summer 1992): 6–9, 19.

63. Quotations concerning the Homochitto are from Joe L. McDonald, "Making a Forest for Woodpeckers," *Forestry Forum* 5 (winter 1991–92): 16–18. Sharon S. Young and Mustian, *Impacts,* 44–45; *Land and Resource Management Plan,* 4-7, 4-8, 4-46, 4-47; "Program to Increase Population of Endangered Woodpecker Instituted," *Forestry Forum* (May 1989): 19; *South's Fourth Forest: Alternatives,* 70; "Timber Buyers Concerned," 31, 34; "Timber Purchasers Sue U.S. Forest Service in Protest of Red-Cockaded Woodpecker Policies," *Tree Talk* 12 (winter 1990): 28–29; "Mississippi Federal Timber Council Supporting Forest Management Programs," *Tree Talk* 16 (fall 1994): 6. In 1994 a red-cockaded woodpecker recovery coordinator with the U.S. Fish and Wildlife Service attempted to allay the fears of Mississippi's private landowners. He estimated that there were only about twenty-five groups of the birds living on private lands in the state and 120 groups in the state's national forests. He outlined the responsibilities of the private landowners and encouraged them to participate in the decision-making process ("Red-Cockaded Woodpeckers and Private Landowners: What Are the Responsibilities?" *Tree Talk* 16 (winter 1994): 23–24). One of the leading national experts on the red-cockaded woodpecker and an articulate critic of both private and Forest Service actions and policies to protect the birds in Mississippi is Jerome A. Jackson, professor of biological sciences at Mississippi State University. Among Jackson's publications containing his criticisms are "Red-Cockaded Woodpecker"; "Use of Seed Tree Cuts as Colony Sites by Red-Cockaded Woodpeckers," *Mississippi Kite* 12 (August 1982): 6–7; "The Evolution, Taxonomy, Distribution, Past Populations and Current Status of the Red-Cockaded Woodpecker," in *The Ecology and Management of the Red-Cockaded Woodpecker,* ed. R. L. Thompson (Tallahassee, Fla.: Bureau of Sport Fisheries and Wildlife, U.S. Department of the Interior, and Tall Timbers Research Station, 1971); "Southeastern Pine Forest Ecosystem," 119–59; "Analysis of the Distribution and Population Status of the Red-Cockaded Woodpecker," in *Proceed-*

ings of the Rare and Endangered Wildlife Symposium, ed. Ron R. Odom and Larry Landers, Technical Bulletin WL4 (Atlanta: Georgia Department of Natural Resources, Game and Fish Division, 1978); "Niche Concepts and Habitat Conservation Planning," *Endangered Species Update* 14 (1997): 48–50; "Biopolitics, Management of Federal Lands, and the Conservation of the Red-Cockaded Woodpecker," *American Birds* 40 (winter 1986): 1162–68; and (with Bette J. Schardien Jackson), "Why Do Red-Cockaded Woodpeckers Need Old Trees?" *Wildlife Society Bulletin* 14 (1986): 318–22.

64. *Land and Resource Management Plan,* 4-47–52, 4-61–62; Gene A. Sirmon, "Mississippi Federal Timber Council Report: Forest Service Issues Gopher Tortoise Environmental Assessment," *Tree Talk* 18 (winter 1996): 6–7; Gene A. Sirmon, "Mississippi Federal Timber Council Report: Louisiana Quillwort Discovered on de Soto National Forest," *Tree Talk* 19 (spring 1997): 7; Wendell Neal, "Louisiana Black Bear May Be Joining the List of Endangered Species," *Tree Talk* 12 (winter 1990): 26–27; Jimmy Bullock, "Working Together for the Resource: The Black Bear Conservation Committee," *Tree Talk* 14 (winter 1992): 4–6.

65. "International Paper Proposes a Model Plan to Protect Threatened Species in the South," *Earth Times* 5 (November 29, 1993): 18; Joe McGlincy and Sharon G. Haines, "Endangered Species Management: The Art of Intelligent Tinkering," *Journal of Forestry* 92 (May 1994): 20–21, 23; "Conservation Plan Announced by International Paper Co. and Dept. of Interior," *Tree Talk* 16 (spring 1994): 16; Joe L. McDonald, "Georgia-Pacific Launches Proactive Plan for Endangered Bird," *Forestry Forum* 7 (winter 1993): 14–15, 30; Richard W. Bryan, "Environmental, Forestry Objectives Must Merge," 33.

66. "Red-Cockaded Woodpecker Protection and Habitat Management on Private Lands: A Regional Society of American Foresters Position Statement," *Journal of Forestry* 90 (August 1992): 38–39. Environmentalists' skepticism was at least partially well founded. Among the materials I have found in researching the records of forest-products companies are a computer-produced sign for bulletin board posting that proclaimed, "I Really Hate Earth Day. Go on . . . Admit it," and a list headed "L&T ENVIRONMENTAL POLICY 1. Thou shalt not go berserk with clearcutting, neither with its size nor its shape. 2. Thou shalt not molestest endangered species. 3. Thou shalt not muddy the water, that it may long and forever be potable. 4. Thou shalt not litterest. 5. Thou shalt let the good people of this nation play and frolic on company lands. 6. Thou shalt bear false witness about clearcuts by leaving timbered aesthetic strips along the nation's highways and byways. 7. Thou shalt not use forest chemicals that turnest the flora and fauna into biological abomina-

tions. 8. Honor thy Forest Service's burn recommenda-tions, that our fires may creepest low and cool. 9. Remember Arbor Day, and venerate it. 10. In the days of darkness, when the cash flow slows to a trickle, thou shalt ignorest the other nine commandments and cut like crazy."

67. John W. Thompson to Art Nelson, February 3, 17, October 24, 1987, John W. Thompson to John G. Guthrie Sr., November 30, 1986, and other Thompson correspondence, all in John Pete Switzer File, MFA Records.

68. Stanturf, Jones, and Ticknor, "Managing Industrial Forestland," 7–9. Forest-products companies soon awakened to wildlife and endangered-species protection's emotional appeal to the public and began sophisticated campaigns to publicize efforts in these areas, including handsome brochures. See "Birds and Forests: A Look at How Birds and Forests Live and Thrive Together," a 1995 brochure issued as part of a series of learning supplements for forestry and environmental education by Georgia-Pacific. Another series from Champion International Corporation included a 1995 brochure entitled "Champion Perspectives on Endangered Species," which, while claiming that Champion supported the goals of the Endangered Species Act, said that "some extreme preservationist groups use the act in ways not originally intended. For example . . . to block activities they find undesirable, such as cutting timber." The brochure said that Champion would like to see the act "reformed" and called for comments from readers of the brochure. Copies in possession of author.

69. South's Fourth Forest: Alternatives, 51, 55–56. In 1954 the Southern Institute of Forest Genetics was established at Gulfport, Mississippi (South's Fourth Forest: Alternatives, 54).

70. William E. Shands, "RPA at the Turning Point," Journal of Forestry 84 (February 1986): 20; Powell, McWilliams, and Birdsey, "History, Change and the U.S. Forest Inventory," 6–11; "Understanding the RPA," 10–14.

71. Zhiliang Zhu and David L. Evans, "Mapping Midsouth Forest Distributions: AVHRR Satellite Data and GIS Help Meet RPA Mandate," Journal of Forestry 90 (December 1992): 27–30.

72. Peter L. Lorio, Garland N. Mason, and Gordon L. Autry, "Stand Risk Rating for the Southern Pine Beetle: Integrating Pest Management with Forest Management," Journal of Forestry 80 (April 1982): 212–14; Landers, Van Lear, and Boyer, "Longleaf Pine Forests," 42; Herbert A. Knight, "The Pine Decline," Journal of Forestry 85 (January 1987): 27.

73. Robert D. Day Jr., "Turbulent Times for 2,4,5-T," Journal of Forestry 76 (May 1978): 270, 319; South's Fourth Forest: Alternatives, 63. For the Ameri-can Pulpwood Association's thinking regarding the use of herbicides and pesticides, including 2,4,5-T, in 1972, see Kenneth P. Davis, ed., Southern Forest Industry, 45–52. While endorsing the need for chemicals, the association noted, "A research objective should be to minimize, even further, need for chemical control through the development of better alternatives" (Kenneth P. Davis, ed., Southern Forest Industry, 52).

74. Luke Popovich, "Of Mice and Men—The Troubles of 2,4,5-T," Journal of Forestry 76 (December 1978): 787–89. See also "A Discussion on Herbicides," Journal of Forestry 73 (July 1975): 410–12; Journal of Forestry 76 (December 1978): 790.

75. John D. Walstad and Frank N. Dost, "All the King's Horses and All the King's Men: The Lessons of 2,4,5-T," Journal of Forestry 84 (September 1986): 28–33; Dean H. Gjerstad, Larry R. Nelson, and Patrick J. Minogue, "Chemical Forest Vegetation Management," in Proceedings, ed. Karr, Baker, and Monaghan, 176.

76. South's Fourth Forest: Alternatives, 63.

77. "Impact of Pesticides on Rural Folks Tracked," Memphis Commercial Appeal, July 26, 1998, A-1, A-18; Pat Minogue, "How Herbicides Can Enhance Wildlife Habitat," Tree Talk 19 (summer 1997): 26–28. For examples of these publications, see "Escort Herbicide," a 1996 Dupont brochure that praises this herbicide as "A Considerate Choice for the Environment and Your Neighbors"; "A Message for Our Neighbors: Facts about Trees, Powerlines, and Tree-Growth Regulators," a 1995 DowElanco brochure that promotes an herbicide that "when applied to a tree, controls growth in the tree's crown" and meets "rigorous standards set by the Environmental Protection Agency"; "Ecological and Environmental Aspects of Monsanto Forestry Herbicides," an undated brochure that promotes Roundup and Accord herbicides and cites various studies indicating that these herbicides "have little if any impact on the ecology of the forest ecosystem"; and another lavishly illustrated Monsanto brochure, "Helping Nature Mend Itself," which tells how herbicides are being used to restore ecological balance to five habitats that have been "inadvertently disturbed by the deliberate or inadvertent introduction of aggressive plants." Copies in possession of author.

78. Dick Allen is quoted in Richard W. Bryan, "Attitudes on Resources Are Not beyond Changing," Forest Industries (April 1971): 35; Gressett, interview, 115.

79. DeWeese, interview by Ryals, 361; Ernest Land, interview by Greg Williams, March 3, 1991, in Timber Industry in the Great Depression, 443.

80. Charles A. Connaughton, "The Revolt against Clearcutting," Journal of Forestry 68 (May 1970): 264–65; Arthur W. Nelson Jr., "Environmental Considerations, Why?" 294. See also Keenan Montgomery and Clyde M. Walker, "The Clearcutting Controversy,"

Journal of Forestry 71 (January 1973): 10–13; Edward C. Crafts, "Foresters on Trial," *Journal of Forestry* 71 (January 1973): 14–17; Richard N. Conner and Curtis S. Adkisson, "Effects of Clearcutting on the Diversity of Breeding Birds," *Journal of Forestry* 73 (December 1975): 781–85; and Ralph D. Nyland, ed., *A Perspective on Clearcutting in a Changing World: Proceedings of 1972 Winter Meeting, New York Section, Society of American Foresters, February 23–25, 1972, Syracuse, New York* (Syracuse: Applied Forestry Research Institute, State University of New York, 1972), copy in SAF Records, box 48.

81. Charles W. Ralston, "Clearcutting of Public Forests in the Southern Pine Region," in *Clearcutting: A View from the Top*, ed. Eleanor C. J. Horwitz (Washington, D.C.: Acropolis Books, 1974), 79–106; *Land and Resource Management Plan*, 4-9, 4-37; "Woodlands History," 158–63. This selection is a classic example of the corporate rationale for clear-cutting. A good recent example of the environmentalists' critique of clear-cuts by a writer from Oxford, Mississippi, is Jonathan Miles, "A War of the Woods: In the Aftermath of a Clear-Cut, One Man Remembers His Forest for the Trees," *Sports Afield* 223 (March 2000): 76–79.

82. James J. Kilpatrick, "No Reason to Let National Forest Trees Grow and Rot," *Paducah (Kentucky) Sun Democrat*, October 8, 1973; "Why Ravage Our Forests to Ship Lumber Overseas?" *Paducah (Kentucky) Sun Democrat*, October 8, 1973; Benton H. Box to Edwin J. Paxton Jr., October 30, 1973; Carl Hooper, "Clear Cutting of Timber Anything but Clear Cut," *Houston Post*, August 20, 1972; *Ahoskie (North Carolina) Herald*, July 28, 1972; Donald W. Smith to Carl Hooper, August 24, 1972; Donald W. Smith to Marie Wood, August 21, 1972; all in SPCA Records. The document that triggered much of this controversy is *Report of the President's Advisory Panel on Timber and the Environment* (Washington, D.C.: U.S. Government Printing Office, 1973).

83. "Meeting of Executive Committee of the Southern Pulpwood Conservation Association with Public Forestry Officials for Purpose of Revising the Cutting Rules, April 4, 1940"; "Revised Pulpwood Cutting Rules as Proposed by the Executive Committee of the Southern Pulpwood Conservation Association, April 4, 1940," both in SPCA Records; "Even-Aged Forest Management Involving Harvesting by Clearcutting Systems," *Gulf States Section, Society of American Foresters Newsletter* 17 (4th quarter 1975): 3; Owen, "Integrating Wildlife and Loblolly Pine Management," 236–38; Stanturf, Jones, and Ticknor, "Managing Industrial Forestland," 7. For the American Pulpwood Association's 1972 position and recommendations regarding clear-cutting, see Kenneth P. Davis, ed., *Southern Forest Industry*, 9–13.

Daniel Botkin, a professor of biology and environmental studies at the University of California, Santa Barbara, argues that the propriety of clear-cutting depends on the kinds of forests desired and the site's specifics: "In some cases, clear-cutting has desirable results; in other cases, it does not" (*Discordant Harmonies*, 162–63).

84. "Understanding the RPA," 18. On another front Mills said, "We've got to get trees in the ground. We've also got to take care of them once we get them in the ground. We can't just leave them there. A lot of studies demonstrated that in the Agricultural Conservation Program, on some of the big plantations like in the Tallahatchie, we got the trees in the ground and we never touched them again, so we'd better get out there and take care of the stands" ("Understanding the RPA," 19).

85. Jack P. Royer and H. Fred Kaiser, "Reforestation Decisions on Harvested Southern Timberlands," *Journal of Forestry* 81 (October 1983): 657–59; Williston, "South's Pine Reforestation Problem," 234–36; Frank E. Taylor Jr. and Wilkerson, "Profile," 778–79; and Porterfield, "Discussion," 261–68. See also *Nonindustrial Private Forest Lands Forum: Issues, Options, and Responsibilities, October 31–November 3, 1983, St. Louis, Missouri* (Washington, D.C.: U.S. Department of Agriculture, Forest Service, Department of State and Private Forestry, 1983).

86. Thomas C. Nelson, "Fire Management Policy in the National Forests—A New Era," *Journal of Forestry* 77 (November 1979): 723–25; A. D. Folweiler, "The Place of Fire in Southern Silviculture," *Journal of Forestry* 50 (March 1952): 187–90; Croker, "Longleaf Pine Story," 40–41; Croker, *Longleaf Pine*, 16–18; Squires, interview; *South's Fourth Forest: Alternatives*, 46. See also Stephen J. Pyne, "Fire Policy and Fire Research in the U.S. Forest Service," *Journal of Forest History* (April 1981): 64–77; Crow, "Use of Fire," 629–32; and Cooper, "Prescribed Burning," 776–80. For the pulp and paper industry's early 1970s thinking on prescribed burning, see Kenneth P. Davis, ed., *Southern Forest Industry*, 29–35.

87. Von J. Johnson, "Prescribed Burning," 82–90, 91. Boyce, Burkhardt, Kellison, and Van Lear, "Silviculture," 43.

88. Boyce, Burkhardt, Kellison, and Van Lear, "Silviculture," 43; Arthur W. Nelson Jr., "Environmental Considerations, Why?" 295.

89. *Yazoo–Little Tallahatchie Flood Prevention Project*, 25.

90. Kent Grizzard, "Forestry Commission Gets Legislative Boost," *Tree Talk* 20 (summer 1998): 9. An insightful discussion of the modern issues concerning natural fires, controlled burning, and fire suppression appears in Stephen J. Pyne, "Flame and Fortune," *For-*

est History Today (1996): 8–10. Pyne, *Fire in America,* is the standard work on the subject.

91. Marion Clawson, "Will There Be Enough Timber?" *Journal of Forestry* 76 (May 1978): 274.

92. Frederick W. Cubbage, Thomas G. Harris Jr., David N. Wear, Robert C. Abt, and Gerardo Pacheco, "Timber Supply in the South: Where Is All the Wood?" *Journal of Forestry* 93 (July 1995): 16–18. To put some of their figures into perspective, the authors pointed out that a large pulp mill could use 1 million cords of wood (75 million cubic feet) per year. On the local level, a landowner and manager in Copiah County noted that a timber inventory on some two thousand acres of family forestland in 1990 reported more than five times as much sawtimber as in 1962. This finding, he said, ran contrary to the beliefs of many Mississippians, who thought there had been more timber in the earlier period (R. David Sanders, "Perception, Reality, and Mississippi's Forests in the '90s," *Tree Talk* 15 [spring 1993]: 32).

93. *South's Fourth Forest: Opportunities,* 4; "Mississippi's Fourth Forest," 16–19; Bob Daniels, "Furniture from Mississippi," *Forestry Forum* 2 (summer 1988): 20–21.

94. Hair, "Timber Situation," 683; Landers, Van Lear, and Boyer, "Longleaf Pine Forests," 41–42.

95. Knight, "The Pine Decline," 25–28; Gene W. Wood, "The Art and Science of Wildlife (Land) Management: Frustrations with Old Science Drive New Forestry," *Journal of Forestry* 88 (March 1990): 10.

96. *South's Fourth Forest: Alternatives,* 7–9.

97. Ibid., 18, 20, 24, 26; "Woodlands History," 157; Adela Backiel and Frances A. Hunt, "'Acid Rain' and Forests: An Attempt to Clear the Air," *American Forests* (February 1986): 42–48. For information on the pine bark beetle problem, see Knight, "The Pine Decline," 25–28; *Proceedings of the Policy and Program Conference on "The South's Fourth Forest: Alternatives for the Future,"* Miscellaneous Publication 1483 (Atlanta: U.S. Department of Agriculture, Forest Service, 1988); and *South's Fourth Forest: Alternatives.* There was what one publication called "an alarming increase in the incidence of SPB infestations . . . in young . . . plantations of loblolly and slash pine throughout the South" since 1984 (Ron Billings and Richard Goyer, "New Approaches to Control Southern Pine Beetle," *Forest Farmer* [July–August 1987]: 22–23). One writer was impressed by "the swiftness in which perfectly healthy 50-year-old trees went from green timber to dry and barkless snags which broke into several pieces when felled." He noted, "On a collective basis, the economic damage wrought by southern pine beetles is enormous during an outbreak. On an individual basis, an attack can mean total economic destruction to a timber grower. During the last major outbreak, which began in eastern Texas in 1983 and spread east with a vengeance, some 26 million acres of southern timberland were damaged with an estimated value loss of some $500 million" (Leon Brown, "Little Bug," 11–13). See also Susan S. Taylor, "Beetle Outbreak Declines after Causing $500M in Damage," *American Papermaker* (December 1987): 11. For information on southern pine beetle attacks and control , see Susan J. Branham, Robert C. Thatcher, Garland N. Mason, and Gerard D. Hertel, *Integrated Pest Management in the South: Highlights of a Five- Year Program,* Agriculture Information Bulletin 491 (Atlanta: U.S. Department of Agriculture, Forest Service, 1985); M. W. Brown, T. E. Nebeker, and C. R. Honea, "Thinning Increases Loblolly Pine Vigor and Resistance to Bark Beetles," *Southern Journal of Applied Forestry* (November 1987): 28–31; Harold E. Burkhart, Harry L. Haney Jr., James D. Newberry, William A. Leuschner, Caleb L. Morris, and David D. Reed, "Evaluation of Thinning for Reduction of Losses from Southern Pine Beetle Attack in Loblolly Pine Stands," *Southern Journal of Applied Forestry* (October 1986): 105–8; J. E. de Steiguer and Roy L. Hedden, "Effects of Aerial Detection Schedules on the Age of Southern Pine Beetle Infestations," *Forest Science* 34 (March 1988): 229–35; Richard A. Goyer and John P. Jones, *Insects and Diseases of Southern Forests: Thirty-Fourth Annual Forestry Symposium, 1985, Louisiana State University* (Baton Rouge: Louisiana State University, 1985); J. Robert Bridges, W. A. Nettleton, and M. D. Connor, "Southern Pine Beetle (Coleoptera: Scolytidae) Infestations without the Bluestain Fungus, *Ceratocystis minor,*" *Journal of Economic Entomology* 78 (April 1985): 325–27; Roy L. Hedden, "Evaluation of Loblolly Pine Thinning Regimes for Reduction of Losses from Southern Pine Beetle Attack," paper presented at Southern Silvicultural Research Conference, Atlanta, November 25, 1982, IP Files; and G. D. Hertel, G. N. Mason, S. C. Cade, and R. C. Kucera, "Strategies for Reducing Insect and Disease Losses," paper presented at the Symposium on the Loblolly Pine Ecosystem (West Region), Jackson, Mississippi, March 20–22, 1984, IP Files. See also Gerard D. Hertel, Susan J. Branham, and Kenneth M. Swain Sr., eds., *Technology Transfer in Integrated Forest Pest Management in the South,* General Technical Report SE-34 (Asheville, N.C.: U.S. Department of Agriculture, Forest Service, Southeastern Forest Experiment Station, 1985); R. R. Hicks Jr., J. E. Coster, and G. N. Mason, "Forest Insect Hazard Rating," *Journal of Forestry* 85 (October 1987): 20–26; J. D. Hodges, T. E. Nebeker, C. A. Blanche, R. Honea, T. H. Fisher, and T. P. Schultz, "Southern Pine Beetle-Microorganisms-Host Interactions: Influence of Compounds Produced by CERATOCYSTIS MINOR" paper presented at Fifth Biennial Southern Silvicultural Research Conference, Memphis, November 1–3, 1988, IP

Files; C. R. Honea, T. E. Nebeker, and J. D. DeAngelis, "Selection of Southern Pine Beetle Hazard Rating Systems for Mississippi," in *Proceedings of the Fourth Biennial Southern Silvicultural Research Conference, Atlanta, Georgia, November 4–6, 1986* (Asheville, N.C.: U.S. Department of Agriculture, Forest Service, Southeastern Forest Experiment Station, 1987); *Managing Southern Forests to Reduce Southern Pine Beetle Impacts: Long- and Short-Term Strategies and Research Needs* (Atlanta: U.S. Department of Agriculture, Forest Service, Southern Region, 1986); Peter L. Lorio Jr. and John D. Hughes, "Theories of Interactions among Bark Beetles, Associated Microorganisms, and Host Trees," paper presented at Southern Silvicultural Research Conference, Atlanta, November 7–8, 1984, IP Files; Peter L. Lorio Jr. and William H. Bennett, *Recurring Southern Pine Beetle Infestations Near Oakdale, Louisiana,* Research Paper SO-95 (n.p.: U.S. Department of Agriculture, Forest Service, 1974); and G. N. Mason, G. D. Hertel, and R. C. Thatcher, "Southern Pine Beetle Hazard Ratings: Uses, Implementation, and Evaluation," paper presented at Southern Silvicultural Research Conference, Atlanta, November 6–7, 1982, IP Files. See also W. D. Mawby, F. P. Hain, and C. A. Doggett, "Endemic and Epidemic Populations of Southern Pine Beetle: Implications of the Two-Phase Model for Forest Managers," *Forest Science* 35 (December 1989): 1075–87; John C. Moser and Susan J. Branham, "Bugs That Eat Bugs," *Forest Farmer* (January 1988): 17–20; J. H. Roberds, F. P. Hain, and L. B. Nunnally, "Genetic Structure of Southern Pine Beetle Populations," *Forest Science* 33 (March 1987): 52–69; Robert C. Thatcher, "Forest Pest Management in the Southern Pine Forest," in *Forest Farmer Manual, 1987* (Atlanta: Forest Farmer Cooperative Association, 1987); Robert C. Thatcher, "Identification and Control of Insect Attack," in *Forest Farmer Manual, 1983* (Atlanta: Forest Farmer Cooperative Association, 1983); Robert C. Thatcher, "Integrated Pest Management," in *Forest Farmer Manual, 1985* (Atlanta: Forest Farmer Cooperative Association, 1985); Robert C. Thatcher and Julia G. Wilson, comps., *Bibliography of Southern Pine Beetle Program Publications* (New Orleans: U.S. Department of Agriculture, Forest Service, Southern Forest Experiment Station, 1982); Robert C. Thatcher, *Bark Beetles Affecting Southern Pines: A Review of Current Knowledge,* Occasional Paper 180 (New Orleans: U.S. Department of Agriculture, Forest Service, Southern Forest Experiment Station, 1960); Hamlin L. Williston, Terrence J. Rogers, and Robert L. Anderson, *Forest Management Practices to Prevent Insect and Disease Damage to Southern Pine* (n.p.: U.S. Department of Agriculture, Forest Service, 1981); and Susan J. Branham and Robert C. Thatcher, eds., *Integrated Pest Management Research Symposium: The Proceedings* (n.p., n.d.).

98. Leland DuVall, "Rebirth of Forests Jolts the Ecologists," *Little Rock Arkansas Gazette,* May 13, 1970. For representative ideas, see Clifford B. Reeves, "Ecology Adds a New Dimension: Industry Must Act Positively on Environmental Issues before They Are Taken over by the Radical Left," *Public Relations Journal* (June 1970): 6–9; and John E. Bennett, "The New Dimensions of Propaganda," *Public Relations Quarterly* 15 (1970): 10–19. Other articles reflecting the industry view are (despite the title) Leo V. Cheeseman, "Trees Cleanse the Air, Don't Cut Trees Down," *Murray (Kentucky) Ledger and Times,* January 29, 1973; "The Hippie Enters the Forest," *National Timber Industry* (June 1969): 4; and "I Think That I Shall Never See . . . ," *Forbes* (July 15, 1974), all in SPCA Records.

99. Donald W. Smith, "How Public Attitudes Are Affecting Forest Management," paper in SPCA Records.

100. Kenneth P. Davis, ed., *Southern Forest Industry,* i, 3–6.

101. Nancy P. Arny, "Project Learning Tree: Seeing the Forest for the Trees," *Journal of Forestry* 92 (March 1994): 13.

102. Bill Colvin, "A Look at MS-PLT 1987–1998 (and Beyond)," *Tree Talk* 20 (spring 1998): 23–24; "Project Learning Tree in Mississippi," 1997, MFC Files; E. R. Coleman, interview by Brenda Kerr, February 9, 1991, in *The Timber Industry in the Great Depression,* 257, 264.

103. "'Mr. PLT' Retires," *Tree Talk* 20 (spring 1998): 23.

104. "Interview with W. Henson Moore," *Tree Talk* 18 (spring 1996): 14; John Heissenbuttel, "The Sustainable Forestry Initiative," *Tree Talk* 18 (spring 1996): 18. The forest-products industry has a long history of concern about public perception of its activities and of conducting public-relations campaigns to try to fix its image. For information concerning such efforts in 1941 and 1951, see W. B. Sayers, "To Tell the Truth: 25 Years of American Forest Products Industries, Inc.," *Journal of Forestry* 64 (October 1966): 657–63.

105. Heissenbuttel, "Sustainable Forestry Initiative," 18; Stanturf, Jones, and Ticknor, "Managing Industrial Forestland," 6.

106. "Green Guarantee: Landowners May Need 'Green Certification' to Market Timber in the Future," *Tree Talk* 16 (spring 1994): 23, 25; "Next Stop, Home Depot," *Time* (October 19, 1998): 70.

107. "Green Guarantee," 25.

108. Ibid., 25–26.

109. Stanturf, Jones, and Ticknor, "Managing Industrial Forestland," 6. See, for example, some of Dick Allen's and Art Nelson's statements cited earlier in various contexts.

110. *American Forest and Paper Association Sustainable Forestry Principles and Implementation*

Guidelines (Washington, D.C.: American Forest and Paper Association, 1995), 5–8.

111. Ibid., 9. See, for example, "Forests for the Future: Georgia-Pacific's Commitment to Sustainable Forestry" and "Where We Stand: Forest Practices, Managing Forests for the Future," attractive brochures issued by Georgia-Pacific in 1995; "Sustainable Forestry," illustrated binder cover with enclosed brochures issued by the Cooperative Extension Service, Mississippi State University, in 1997 or 1998. The sponsors listed on the binder include Georgia-Pacific Corporation, International Paper, Weyerhaeuser Company, Boise Cascade Corporation, Westvaco Corporation, Tenneco Packaging, Canal Wood Corporation of Mississippi, Crown Vantage, Stone Container Corporation, Newsprint South, Riverwood International USA, Champion International Corporation, and Alabama River Woodlands. Copies of all these materials in possession of author.

112. Gene A. Sirmon, "President's Address," *Tree Talk* 17 (summer 1995): 4; *Mississippi Forest Facts;* "MFA Board Approves Sustainable Forestry Initiative Report," *Tree Talk* 17 (summer 1995): 15–22; Dr. Laurie Grace, "Logger Training and Education in Mississippi," *Tree Talk* 18 (spring 1996): 23–24; "Sustainable Forestry in Mississippi," *Tree Talk* 20 (summer 1998): 23; undated advertising card from Starr Timber, Gulfport, Miss., copy in possession of author. Art Nelson said that pioneering foresters who restored the land "as a sustainable production unit instead of a one-time storehouse of timber" earlier in the twentieth century were the first practitioners of sustainable forestry ("Sustainable Forestry," *Tree Talk* 18 [spring 1996]: 30). Even before the Sustainable Forestry Initiative training program was promulgated,

Harvey Beach Jr. of Natchez, recipient of the American Pulpwood Association's 1994 National Outstanding Logger Award, expressed the view of enlightened Mississippi loggers: "Loggers care. We are not raping the woods" (Jacqueline Cochran, "Nation's Top Logger Defends Industry," *Forestry Forum* 8 [summer 1994]: 17). Consulting foresters and forest-management companies obviously recognized the market value of environmental issues and concerns in seeking clients. See, for example, "Marketplace Solutions to Environmental Problems," an undated, lavishly illustrated brochure from Resource Management Service, a management firm headquartered in Birmingham that had more than seventy-five foresters, certified public accountants, biometricians, and silvicultural and real estate experts in twenty-five offices in thirteen states; copies of this and other Resource Management materials in possession of author.

113. *Sustainable Forestry for Tomorrow's World: 1998 Progress Report on the American Forest and Paper Association's Sustainable Forestry Initiative (SFI) Program* (Washington, D.C.: American Forest and Paper Association, 1998), i; *Sustainable Forestry* (Washington, D.C.: American Forest and Paper Association, 1995), n.p.

114. *Mississippi Forest Facts.* Representative examples of industry brochures include IP's 1995 "Our Forests: Respect and Responsibility"; Cyanamid's 1995 "Forestry Management and Our Environment"; Weyerhaeuser's 1995 "Weyerhaeuser: An Industry Leader for Nearly a Century," which contains a section on "Weyerhaeuser and the Environment"; and many similar materials from various other companies. Copies in possession of author. See also Weber, "Social Responsibility," 12–17, 25.

Index

All figures and maps appear in *italics*; tables appear in **boldface**.

Forestry Suppliers, 200

Forests, 209; changes since 1967, 247; clearing, early methods of, 44; climax stage, 5, 9; description of, 41; and the disappearance of, 117–19; evolution of, 5; and farmers and planters, 49; in the late 1950s, 200; longleaf areas and early travelers, 56; management of, 210–11; and Native Americans, 4–5, 40; in the nineteenth century, 48, 55–56, 85; and nonindustrial landowners, 3; ownership, 86; in post-World War II, 196; problems in late 1980s, 254; reserves, 124; in the twentieth century, 3, 48, 94–95, 118, 204, 209, 210, 211–12, 256, 259; virgin, xi, 3–5, 40, 103, 122, 132, 195, 200, 233, 255, 261, 262; during white settlement, 40

Forrest County, 95, 154

Fort Adams, 36, 42

Fort Adams, Treaty of, 31

Fort Bute (Manchac), 22, 26

Fort Maurepas, 16

Fort Nogales, 27

Fort Panmure. See Fort Rosalie

Fort Rosalie (Fort Panmure), 16, 22, 42

Fort St. Peter, 16

Foster Creek Lumber Company, 154–55

Foster's Creek, 213

Fourdrinier machine, 140, 141

4–H clubs, 222

Fourth Forest, 195, 223, 253

Fowler, Samuel, 61, 62

Fox River, 16

France, 42, 86, 124, 140; and Canada, 15; forts, trading posts, and settlements in America, 16; fur trade in North America, 15; and Great Britain, 20; and Louisiana, 18, 50–51; Natchez trading post, 16; and papermaking, 140; and Spain, 20

Francisco of Chicora, 11

Frank Houston Estate, 154

Franklin County, 56, 87, 182, 196

Franklin Creek, 61

Franklin, Jerry, 233

Frazier, Alfred, 194

Freedmen, 82

French and Indian War, 20

French Forest School, 124

Friends of the Holly Springs National Forest, 241

Frome, Michael, 226

Fuel, 80; coal, 48; for steamboats and locomotives, 55, 58–59; wood, 48, 55, 59

Fungus, 138

Fur trade, 35, 51; under British in West Florida, 21; French, 42; importance of, 20

Furniture, 58, 203, 253

Future Farmers of America, 222

Fusiform rust, 247

Gainesville, Ala., 47

Gainesville, Miss., 59

Game, 37, 150; abundance of, 38; supply of, in piney woods, 57

Gamill Investment Company, 154

Gang saw, 60, 61

Gardiner, George, 84

Gardiner, Philip S., 105

Gardiner, Silas, 84

Gardiner, Stimson, 83–84

Garrison, P. M., 169

Gautier, Fernando, 61

Gaylord Container Corporation, 141, 143, 144, 146, 149, 169, 174, 179, 189, 203, 223; and fire, 176

Gender, 115

General Land Office, 182

Genetics, 211, 300, 310; improved seedlings, 138, 188

Geographic Information System (GIS), 208

George County, 95, 154, 213

Georgetown, S.C., 188

Georgia, 14, 98, 121, 127, 143, 148, 170, 185, 186, 201, 209, 218, 236, 241, 246; and land claims, 17, 26, 27, 42

Georgia Pacific Plywood and Lumber Company (Georgia–Pacific Corporation), 201, 202, 203, 205, 208, 226, 245, 251, 255

Georgia Sawmill Association, 81

Georgia, University of, 130, 199

Georgia–Pacific Corporation. See Georgia Pacific Plywood and Lumber Company

Germany, 81, 86, 106, 123, 124, 140, 166, 183, 197

Gilchrist-Fordney, 77, 88, 89, 101

Gilmore, H., 110

Girdling trees, 45–46, 46, 139, 175, 222

Glendale, Miss., 90

Glisson, Joe, 240

Global Resources, 243

Gloster Lumber Company, 154, 159

Goode, Garland, 61

Goodyear, C. A., 87

Goodyear, Frank H. and Charles W., 76, 82, 86

Goodyear of Pennsylvania, 100

Gorray, Thomas, 62

Gospel of efficiency, 124

Gould, Ark., 162

Government relations, 164, 184

Graduation Act of 1854, 82

Gragg, Fred, 124, 166, 174, 181, 184, 185, 188

Grand Gulf, Miss., 71

Grand Rapids, Mich., 84

Grasslands, 10

Graves, Henry S., 129

Gray, Simon, 54

Great Britain (England), 85, 90, 140, 141, 257; agriculture, 42; colonies, 15; fur trade in North

America, 15; lumber exported to, 52, 63; and West Florida, 21
Great Lakes, 15, 58, 73; cutover lands, 122; lumber production, 79
Great Migration, 108
Great Northern Nekoosa Corporation, 201, 226
Great Northern Railroad, 85
Great Smoky Mountains National Park, 128
Great Southern Lumber Company, 75, 76, 101, 133, 159, 185, 203; nursery, 121; reforestation, 121, *122*
Greeley, William B., 101
Green Bay, 16
Green Certification, 256–57
Green, Charles, 138
Green Swamp, 98
Greene County, 56, 57, 58, 84, 95, 153, 154
Greenpeace, 259
Greenspeak, 257
Greenville, Miss., 44, 163
Greenwood, Miss., 201
Grenada County, 201
Grenada Dam, 221
Grenada, Miss., 47, 74, 202, 203
Gressett, Raymond, 194
Grey Towers, 243
Griffin, Calvin, 86
Griffin, William, 60
Griffin, Wyatt, 86
Grindstone Ford, 30
Grist mills, 21, 52
Groundwood process, 140
Gulf and Ship Island Railroad, 74, 75, 76, 84, 90, 114, 115, 200
Gulf Coast, 51, 52, 55, 61, 63, 86, 104, 107, 108, 196, 198
Gulf Coast Lumber Company, 90
Gulf Coast Lumbermen's Association, 81
Gulf, Mobile, and Ohio Railroad, 74, 154, 158
Gulf States, 144, 223
Gulfport Branch, 200
Gulfport, Miss., 74, 86, 153, 197, 211; deep water channel, 75; pine lumber, exporter of, 81
Gulledge Lumber Company, 90
Gum, 56
Guthrie, John, 186, *187*, 200

H. Weston Lumber Company, 121, 130, 133–35, 136, 169
Hagenstein, W. D., 219
Halifax, 201
Hall and Lincoln Lumber Company, 107
Hall, James, 31–33, 58
Hall, William L., 138, 286
Hamilton, Alexander, 225

Hamilton, Hoskins, and Company, 76
Hamilton, Ohio, 203
Hammond, La., 84, 87
Hammond Lumber Company, 87
Hancock County, 56, 95, 176; early sawmills, 59; fires in, 168; wood sales (1840), 55
Hand Brothers and Prother, 61
Hand, S. B., 62
Handsboro, Miss., 108, 272
Hansen, Paul, 259
Hardboard, 137, 138
Hardtner, Henry, 132–33, 134, 136, 164, 185
Hardwoods, 56, 90–91, 175, 306–08; competing land uses, 162–63, 209–10; early lumbering, 55; growth studies, 161; markets, 208; pine, compared with, 162, 209, 210; pulp, 142, 200, 201, 208, 210; technology, 208; uses of, 162, 208, 210; and wildlife habitat, 162
Hardy Graves Lumber Company, 197
Hardy, Miss., 202
Harrison County, 56, 86, 95, 153, 213; early sawmills in, 59, 62
Harrison, Senator Pat, 151
Hartman Lumber Company, 76, 78
Hartman, Miss., 76
Harvard College, 131
Harvest rotation, 188–89, 204, 211
Hattiesburg American, 103
Hattiesburg, Miss., 75, 84, 90, 104, 117, 172; as lumbering center, 88
Hawaiian Cane Company, 138
Hays, Samuel P., 124, 225
Hazlehurst, Miss., 197
Healy, Robert G., 216
Heartwood, 239–41
Henderson, 60
Henderson and Molpus Lumber Company, 89
Henry, S. S., 61, 107
Hermanville Lumber Company, 198
Hermanville, Miss., 198
Herty, Charles Holmes, 115–16, 125, 126, 141, 164
Hester, Goodman, 62
Heyward, Frank, 127, 189
Hickman, Nollie, 61, 88, 109
Hickory, 56
High grading, 65, 165–66, 194
Hilgard, Eugene, 56
Hill, James J., 85
Hillsborough, Earl of, 42
Hillsdale, Miss., 118
Hinds County, 44, 56, 85
Hines, Edward, 88, 92, 100, 197
Hinges, 58
Hinton Brothers, 88
Hodgson, Adam, 38–39

Hogs, 14–15, 65, 122, 131, 132, 133, 134, 136, 164, 284
Hogsheads, 58
Hogue, Roy L., 159, 161
Holcombe, Marvin, 62
Holistic (new) forestry, 232
Holland, 140
Hollingsworth, Jack, 172
Holly Springs Area School Board Associations, 241
Holly Springs, Miss., 34
Holly Springs National Forest, 152, 153, 154, 155; clear-cutting in, 239, 240, 241; description of, 241; and environmentalists, 239–41; and Heartwood, 239–41; Indiana bat, 241; monoculture, 240–41; timber sales, 239; urban impact on, 239; wildlife habitat in, 240–41. *See also* Citizens for Holly Springs National Forest; Friends of the Holly Springs National Forest; Holly Springs Area School Board Associations
Holly Springs unit (national forest purchase), 153
Holman, Jack, 103
Holmes County, 47, 95
Holocene period, 5
Home Depot, 256, 257
Homochitto Fire Protection Contest, 168
Homochitto Lumber Company, 87, 90, 154–55
Homochitto National Forest, 151, 152, 154, 155, 215; pine plantations, 241
Homochitto River, 36; timber theft near, 52
Homochitto unit (national forest purchase), 151, 152, 154, 155
Hood Industries, 138, 198
Hood Manufacturing Company, 198
Hood, Warren A., 198–99
Horn Island, 22
Horses, 99, 100, 101, 110, 139
Hough, Dr. Franklin B., *Report Upon Forestry* (1878), 128
Houses: changes in construction, 196; lumber for, 58, 80
Houston Brothers, 154
Houston, Miss., 198
Howard, Stephen, 55
Howell, P. N. "Posey," 130–31, 187
Huay, Daniel, 21
Huddleston, John, 62
Hudson, Charles, 9
Huffman, Jacob R., 66
Hughes, Jeff, 103–04, 166, 167, 169, 181, 183, 189
Humphreys County, 171
Hunt, C. Ronald, 210
Hunter–Benn, 86
Hunting, 37, 150, 175, 217, 232, 239; and lease programs, 181, 212, 213–14
Hurricane Camille, 198

Hurricane Hugo, 208
Hursey, Asa, 59–60
Hurst, Ben, 111–13
Hurst, Dorsey, 111–13
Hussein, Saddam, 230
Hutchins, Thomas, 51
Hyde, La., 87

Iberville River, 24
Idaho, University of, 131
Illinois, 16, 80, 88, 90, 196, 199, 227
Illinois Central Railroad, 73, 74, 76, 84, 87, 91, 186–87; and the forestry department, 158, 200, 298; and land speculators in the South, 83; lumber traffic on, 80; southern pine, promotes, 80
Illinois Central Tree Planter, 158, 186–87, *187*, 200, 298
Improved land, mid-nineteenth century, 48
India, 121
Indian Corn (Maize), 37
Indian Creek, 223
Indiana, 80, 91, 200, 239
Indonesia, 199
Ingram-Day Lumber Company, 86, 90
Insects, 162; southern pine beetle, 182; tipmoth, 247. *See also* Forest Pest Control Act
Insulation board, 137, 197
Insulite, 138
Internal Revenue Code (Section 631), 158
Internal Revenue Service (U.S.), 226
International Harvester Company, 87
International Paper Company, 130, 141, 143, 144, 146, 147, 149, 157, 167, 176, 177, 178, 184, 186, 187, 188, 201, 202, 203, 206, 209, 210, 211, 212, 213, 214, 216, 220, 223, 226, 251; as conservation foresters, 145, 191; fire control, 174; foresters, employment of, 148; "Jackie Davis" comic books, 145, 289; Southern Kraft Division, 148, 245; wildlife management, 245
International Process Company, 141
Interstate Commerce Act, 76
Iowa, 84, 90, 196
Ireland, 106
Irland, Lloyd C., 234
Iron, 58
Isle Breton, 22
Issaquena County, 47, 95, 175
Italy, 106
Iuka, Miss., 90, 161
Izaak Walton League of America, 259
Izlar, Bob, 255

J. J. Newman Lumber Company, 76, 84, 88, 90, 111, 154
J. J. White Lumber Company, 76, 87, 90, 117

Taxation, 65, 100, 101, 102, 103, 122, 125, 129, 139, 150, 157–58, 163, 164, 184, 185, 197, 218

Taylor, Calvin, 55, 61–62

Taylor, Frank E., Jr., 200

Taylor, Frederick Winslow, 110

Taylor, L. M., 62

Technological change, 63, 65, 66–71, 308–09; aerial photography, 207; circular saws, 61; debarking and chipping machinery, 205, 230; felling machines, 206–07; hardwood processing, 208; logging, 69–71, 138–39, 206–08; naval stores, 208–09; plywood, 208; skidders, 206. *See also* Geographic Information System; Navstar global positioning system

Telephones, 169, 172

Ten Mile, Miss., 106, 118

Tennessee, 14, 43, 73, 80, 108, 222, 223, 229, 239

Tennessee River, 15, 30, 31, 35, 38, 44

Tennessee River Pulp and Paper, 223

Tennessee, University of, 199

Tennessee Valley Authority, 255; erosion, 161. *See also* J. P. Coleman State Park

Tennessee–Tombigbee Waterway, 227, 229

Tetar, 60

Texarkana, 81

Texas, 34, 38, 53, 57, 59, 63, 69, 99, 108, 117, 120, 121, 140, 141, 181, 199, 245, 250

Texas Company, 154

Texas Forest Service, 177

Thinning, 145, 146, 147, 188–89, 238, 301

Third Forest, 191, 195, 303

Thomas, G. L., 62

Thompson, John W., 196, 245–46, 290

Thompson, Michael C., 242

Thoreau, Henry David, 4

Timber: below cost sales, 237; bonds, 83, 101; consumption, 217; famine, 252; harvest revenues, 153; harvest value (1993), 259; ownership, 71, 81–83, 94, 95–96, 143; prices, 71, 83, 94, 153; sales, 155–56, 215, 236–37, 240, 242; supply, 252–54; theft, 52, 53; volume, 94–95, 165, 201, 204, 253

"Timber cruisers," 82, 85, 148; methods, 92–93

Timber Cutting Practice Act, 144, 189

Timber Resource Review, 181

Timber Resources for America's Future, 252

Timber Severance Tax Law, 157, 163

Timber Stand Improvement, 139, 175, 185, 188, 194, 238, 300–01

Time–and–motion studies, 110

Tishomingo County, 90, 169

Tobacco, 58

Tombigbee National Forest, 152, 155, 237, 238

Tombigbee (Tombeckbe, Tombigbe, Tom Bigbee, Timbigbie, Tombecbee) River, 14, 24, 28–29, 31, 33, 34, 37, 55, 90, 245; settlement and population around, 44, 47

Toulme, John, 60

Toulmin, Judge Harry, 43

Trace Unit (Tombigbee National Forest), 237

Tracewitz, O. G., 181, 184

Trade associations, 80–81, 91, 108, 156, 195, 255, 256, 257

Tree City USA, 238

Tree Farms, 157, 163, 191–93, 194, 203, 210, 251, 302–03

Tree planting machines, 158, 186–87

Tree Talk, 258

Tree-length logging, 205, 206

Tung trees and oil, 136, 286

Tunica County, 95

Tunica Indians, 18; and the British, 21

Tupelo, Miss., 227, 238

Turbines, 67

Turner, I. J., 171

Tuxechaena Creek, 62

Twenty-five percent rule, 242

Tyler, John, 167, 174, 177–78, 212

Tylertown, Miss., 75

Tyner, Larry, 231

Union Bag and Paper Corporation, 148

Union Camp Corporation, 148, 201, 203

Union, Miss., 89

Urania, La., 133, 134, 136

Urania Lumber Company, 131, 132–33, 170, 185, 199

urban-forest interface, 238–39

urbanites, 225, 227, 238–39, 241, 251

U.S. Agricultural Stabilization and Conservation Service, 223

U.S. Bureau of Corporations, 80, 91; report on lumber industry, 92–98

U.S. Bureau of Indian Affairs, 221

U.S. Bureau of Land Management, 211, 216, 233, 258

U.S. Bureau of the Census, 92; on lumber and naval stores, 55

U.S. Congress, 128, 158, 182, 220, 221, 223, 258; House of Representatives, 82; Mississippi Territory, created, 31; Senate, 85, 129, 131; Senate Finance Committee, 151

U.S. Corps of Engineers, 222

U.S. Department of Agriculture, 126, 128, 185, 221, 247. *See also* Bureau of Entomology and Plant Quarantine; Bureau of Plant Industry, Soils, and Agricultural Engineering; Cooperative State Research Service; Forestry Department; Forestry Division

U.S. Department of Commerce, 81

U.S. Department of Labor, 222

U.S. Department of the Interior, 233